I
THE ROLLING STONE
NTERVIEWS

THE

I

NTE

by THE EDITORS *of*
ROLLING STONE

ROLLING STONE

Talking with the Legends of Rock & Roll

1967 — 1980

R VIEWS

INTRODUCTION *by*
BEN FONG-TORRES

EDITED *by* PETER HERBST

ST. MARTIN'S PRESS/ROLLING STONE PRESS
NEW YORK

Donovan, Bob Dylan copyright © 1967 by Straight Arrow Publishers, Inc. B. B. King, Eric Clapton, Pete Townshend, Mick Jagger copyright © 1968 by Straight Arrow Publishers, Inc. Jim Morrison, Phil Spector, Bob Dylan copyright © 1969 by Straight Arrow Publishers, Inc. Little Richard, Van Morrison, Grace Slick and Paul Kantner, Rod Stewart copyright © 1970 by Straight Arrow Publishers, Inc. John Lennon, Keith Richards copyright © 1971 by Straight Arrow Publishers, Inc. Jerry Garcia, Paul Simon, Chuck Berry, Keith Moon copyright © 1972 by Straight Arrow Publishers, Inc. James Taylor and Carly Simon, Ray Charles, Johnny Cash, Stevie Wonder, Elton John and Bernie Taupin copyright © 1973 by Straight Arrow Publishers, Inc. Paul McCartney copyright © 1974 by Straight Arrow Publishers, Inc. Jimmy Page and Robert Plant, Neil Young copyright © 1975 by Straight Arrow Publishers, Inc. Mick Jagger, Linda Ronstadt, Bob Dylan, Paul McCartney copyright © 1979 by Straight Arrow Publishers, Inc. Joni Mitchell, James Taylor copyright © 1979 by Straight Arrow Publishers, Inc. Pete Townshend, Billy Joel copyright © 1980 by Straight Arrow Publishers, Inc.

Library of Congress Cataloging in Publication Data

Main entry under title:

The Rolling Stone interviews.

1. Rock Musicians—Interviews. I. Rolling stone.
ML394.R65   784.5′4′00922 [B]   81-8796
ISBN 0-312-68954-3   AACR2
ISBN 0-312-68955-1 (pbk.)

Design by Vincent and Martine Winter

10 9 8 7 6 5 4 3 2 1

First Edition

CONTENTS

INTRODUCTION

When Jann Wenner and founding partner Ralph J. Gleason began shaping ROLLING STONE magazine, they had a lot of great new ideas. But they copped a lot of great old ones, too.

So right away, the newspaper—which is what it was in the beginning—reminded observant readers around San Francisco of the *Sunday Ramparts,* a fortnightly paper which itself borrowed from the clean, elegant typefaces and borders of the London *Times.* The *Sunday Ramparts* lasted only nine months, dying in June 1967. Among its surviving staff members was a brash young music critic fresh out of the University of California at Berkeley, Jann Wenner. He and Gleason would have the first issue of ROLLING STONE out by November.

The first essays in ROLLING STONE, on Aretha Franklin, Cream and the San Francisco rock scene, were new in their intensity to music fans raised on teen fanzines, although serious discussions of rock & roll had been published for a year in *Crawdaddy,* a scholarly and evangelical little magazine started by Paul Williams.

And I remember when I got my first assignment for a profile of a rock star, in 1968. Wenner's instructions were clear: "Get a lot of details and color," he told me. "Make it like a *New Yorker* profile."

Wenner, of course, admits to all this. "ROLLING STONE," he says, "was deliberately and purposely an assembly of traditional elements of journalism as much as it was based on any vision or inspiration." So Wenner mixed the new and hip with the tried and true. In detailed style, he emulated the *New Yorker.* In straight reporting, the *New York Times.* And he topped off everything— pretty prose, undecorated news stories and gossip items loaded with "the folksiness of our vernacular"—with arch headlines, à la *Esquire.*

From the beginning, there was talk about a regular feature called the ROLLING STONE Interview, which would be lengthy, **1** transcribed conversations with important artists. The models were obvious: *Playboy* magazine and the *Paris Review. Playboy* set a tone, with its serious treatment of well-known personalities and artists. But more like the *Paris Review,* the ROLLING STONE Interviews would try to examine—in depth, details and the theories of the craft itself—styles of working habits and processes, as well as the "big questions."

It was a time, after all, of big questions. The music of Bob Dylan, the Beatles and the Rolling Stones had become a part of our lives in ways popular music had never been before. The music was the Word. But with the exception of the early-day Bob Dylan, who'd given several cryptic but amusingly coy interviews to writer Nat Hentoff, popular musicians had never been taken seriously.

The ROLLING STONE Interview, then, was a first. The "Q & A" format offered time and room for probing questions and for thoughtful responses about the "counterculture," drugs, music and the meaning of the lyrics that so many of us quoted or sang to each other, and dissected late into so many nights. The interviewer and subject could relax into conversation, so that we could discover personality as well as information and opinions.

It was an approach brand-new to rock & roll, challenging and liberating for subject and interviewer, and a good read for all.

We interviewed people we admired and respected, and we approached them with a genuine interest. Together, we tried for a continuing intense examination of that extended moment called "the Sixties." Notions of, say, rock & roll as an indicator of changing social behavior could be stated, and proved or pushed through the interviews. Artists could begin dialogues with each other and their audiences and critics.

Without saying so, the ROLLING STONE Interviews showed a side of rock & roll musicians that many never expected to find—the intelligent, articulate, bright side. For every artist who sits down for a session—or, as Bob Dylan characterized it, "to unload my head"—there are a dozen who'll insist to their dying riff that all they have to say is in their music. But to commit to a life in rock & roll—to open oneself up to the vagaries and hazards as well as the potential riches and other highs of the music business and lifestyle; to allow oneself to become, or to seek to be a celebrity—is to be extraordinary. It's not a matter of traveling to the beat of a different drum. It's being that different drummer.

ROLLING STONE has always sought out those drummers.

The interviews in this collection are only a portion of those conducted by ROLLING STONE through the years. And, for probably a different reason in each case, ranging from the artist's lack of availability or interest to our editorial judgment that in some cases an artist may be presented more effectively in a personality profile rather than the Q & A, we missed some important people, among them Elvis Presley, Janis Joplin, and Jimi Hendrix, all of whom were profiled and interviewed in their time, but not in the Q & A style.

In later years, especially from the mid-Seventies on, when legends were either harder to come by or had by then unloaded their head, the ROLLING STONE Interview no longer seemed unique. Rock stars were being interviewed endlessly, everywhere. Many began to time their appearances to coincide with album releases and tours. Our writers tried, usually with success, to get the new, more mikewise crop to reveal themselves in a newer (and, at the time, older) way.

You may also note that the earlier interviews are not as tightly edited as the later ones. Back in the old days, we wanted to preserve the times and people's manners, quirks, odd remarks, and the idiosyncracies of their speech. By doing so, we also captured additional aspects of personalities, so that, in part, the ROLLING STONE Interview was also a profile, in the reportorial sense.

The more recent interviews are tighter, more professional, more polished. Even so, they're all spoken with one voice and conducted by a consistent, a simple, a tried-and-true set of standards: a good reason for the interviews in the first place; a knowledgeable, interested and curious interviewer—and let it roll!

—BEN FONG-TORRES

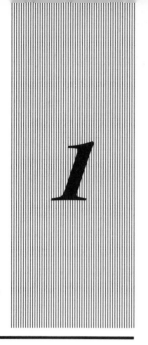

1

INTERVIEWED BY JOHN CARPENTER (1967)

The first ROLLING STONE Interview appeared in the first issue of the magazine, dated November 9, 1967, and printed late in October on a newspaper rotary press in San Francisco. On page one, which was also the "cover" for the first seven issues, a contents box declared: "DONOVAN: An incredible ROLLING STONE Interview, with this manchild of magic."

Donovan (Leitch) was the quintessential flowerchild, dressed in flowing robes, surrounded by floating lilypads and cooing folk-pop songs in a baby's breath of a voice. Listening to his music now, one can almost smell the patchouli and incense.

In an almost cosmic way he was a perfect first feature, just as John Lennon was the right cover that issue.

Donovan had scored with "Sunshine Superman" and "Mellow Yellow" in 1966, and was on tour in the fall of 1967 when the late John Carpenter, ROLLING STONE's first Los Angeles correspondent, met him at a party in Malibu. Carpenter had just moved to L.A. from San Francisco, where he'd been a partner with Chet Helms in the Family Dog rock ballroom and a manager of Grace Slick's first group, Great Society. He could relate to the twenty-one-year-old Donovan, and a few days after the party, the two taped this interview.

The article wasn't originally done for ROLLING STONE. Ralph J. Gleason knew John had the interview and acquired it for us. Yet, it well represents what the ROLLING STONE Interview was to become.

—BF-T

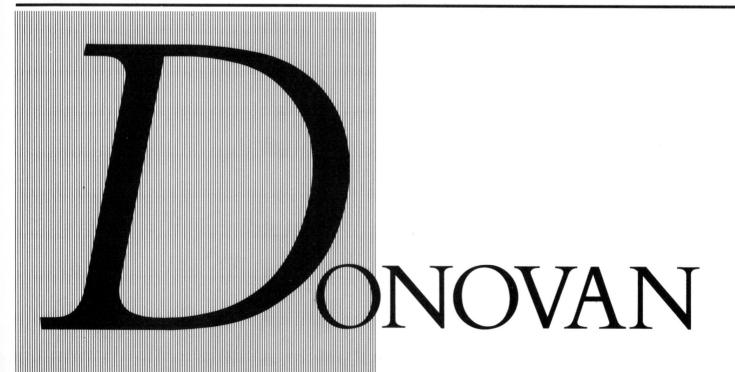

DONOVAN

5

D O YOU NOTICE ANY DIFFER-
ence in the U.S. after eighteen months?
Oh, quite a lot of difference.
Fantastic; sort of subdued. It's really
a lot much more subdued now,
after all that drumbashing and electric-guitar
twanging. Mind you, there's still a few groups
that experiment in electrical music, but at least
they're getting somewhere. But the audience
reaction is fantastic. They're at the end of one
busy thing, and now at the beginning of a soft,
quiet time. This is the change that we're in right
now. This is the one I've come to lead in
America.

*I noticed there was a nice blend at the Hollywood
Bowl of what you call soft sound, a very good use of
jazz. Is jazz coming more into your own field of
interests?*

No, I don't listen to a lot of jazz, and I don't
intend to listen to a lot of jazz. What I've heard
is like Gil Evans and just a few things. Most of
the jazz things are things I pick off of my
manager who used to be a jazz musician fifteen
years ago. I write from my point, and my point
isn't really jazz. I just call it my music, but I
suppose it's jazz-influenced.

*In the beginning of your career you were—I
wouldn't say more melodic—you were more folk-
inclined. There was less background in your records. I
heard your new record the other night. The difference in
the sound wasn't so much melodic as that, in your
approach to it, you seemed to be more interested in
communicating what you have to say.*

Yes.

*Musically, rather than "this is Donovan," it's
"Donovan does this thing." Does that come from the
freedom of acceptance?*

Yeah, like it slowly comes, and I was just
getting nearer and nearer to what a song should
be on record. It should be the artist himself. The
microphone should be in his mouth and in his
head, and it should be straight-through communication. The albums you heard—one accompanied with groups and one without—the one
without holds more importance as a communica-
tive thing. There's just me and my guitar, that's
the way the songs begin: Now there! you sound
all right. They go into their different phases of
instruments and things. But even when you use a
lot of instruments, you can still get the communication bit very fine. Every record's different.
I'm me, anyway, with the guitar, and whatever I
use is just how I feel at that time or that year or
that month, and I will go on changing and using
little different types of instruments.

You played a song Sunday that you composed the

6

*day before. Phil Ochs was out here; he said that in
London he found melody, and here he found words. Do
you find that problem? Do you find it's difficult to
write in some parts of the world and not others?*

Yes, I do. When I'm working a lot, I don't
write. I like quiet times, when I'm by myself,
but sometimes they just come squeezing out.
They come from a source so vast—so many songs
are underneath in my head—that I just pull
them down, and when I feel that they are there, I
try to put them into something and make them
and shape them into songs. But I can write
anywhere.

You can write in the back of a bus on a tour?

Oh, yeah. I don't say I write it just floating in
my head. Ideas, a week old, a month old, brand-
new, they all just come together.

*You and Bert Jansch are very good friends. "Bert's
Blues" and "House of Jansch" are the two songs that
come to mind immediately. Could you tell us a little
about Bert and yourself? How did you meet? What
influence has he had on you and vice versa?*

I met him when I started singing in pro clubs
in London. I used to get into some of the clubs.
They didn't let me sing a lot because I sounded
like a cowboy that sang cowboy songs. But Bert's
roots are in traditional music, which is great
because the traditional music of Scotland is a
migratory thing and ended up there. You know,
the Arabic influences and Turkish influences and
all the Eastern influences all the way through;
when you hear bagpipes and things, you can hear
that. But Bert is a great revolutionary writer.
He's fantastic. Having his roots in traditional
music, he had centuries of things to go on. And
as to guitar, the Edinburgh Scottish folk singers
are about the veterans of the scene. They are all
fantastic guitarists. Bert's son was playing solo
like myself, and he's got a little group with
another guy called John Ranbone who's another
one of the big guitarists, and they write together
and they have a girl singer, a bass player and a
drummer, and it's a beautiful sound.

*I hate to ask you this, but what comes first, the song
or the words?*

What comes first, the chicken or the egg?

*I was asked to ask you that. What is the influence
of the American composers, Woody Guthrie in particular, Dylan, Paul Simon—who said that you and
Jansch were the biggest influences on him—what
influence did they have on you? Was it more just
interest? I don't see any similarity between your styles.*

At the end of it all, when everyone's finished,
I'm looking and finding all the types of different
music they want to find. There's only one thing
in the end, and that's singing truth in a pleasant

way. Everyone's striving for this. The influences rebound off each other. When somebody's feeling low, they'll hear somebody else's record. When I hear Dylan's latest record, or Paul's or Bert's, I get sort of an inspiration to go on if I'm feeling dragged, or even go into new things. The influence is so healthy that people shouldn't really call it comparison. That's 'cause everybody's the same anyway. All the writers are trying for the same thing, but they just have their different technicians. They can see their different experiences. Paul is about the nearest, I suppose, in sweetness to me, although he comments a lot politically and cynically, but he's getting into a pleasant thing. We all have our different things, which is good, but the influence is very helpful.

What helps you get more ideas? When somebody's doing something that you are attempting to go into that you really don't feel like you want to, or if somebody else does it and it frees you from that kind of . . .

The subject is, as I say, one thing anyway. It's true the subject is one thing. But it's all these minstrels just writing down the happenings as they go along and the dreams of what will be. We can all see the *different* dreams we've got. I've got a very wide horizon on how things will be, and so I'm into people. So when you study the man and the woman, you can get a great sort of command of emotion with your poetry. You sort of paint for a girl—her hang-ups and her sadness and her happiness and the man. It's great, it's very, very helpful.

By opening yourself up in this way, to other people in order to give back to them, do you find at the end of, say, the Bowl appearance—I saw you come offstage and I've never seen a happier man. You were laden down with beads. You grabbed a girl who was trying to grab you and kiss you, and you grabbed her and kissed her back, and shocked her to death. Do you find that euphoria makes all of the bull that comes out of a tour—which there is a certain amount of, the people who will ask you what-you-had-for-breakfast sort of thing coming at you—does it really make it worthwhile?

Yeah. This is the first tour that ever began which I knew had a direction and which I knew how to do. All the dates we will be doing are so beautiful because the whole thing is successful inasmuch as I sang what I felt, and thousands of people returned it like a mirror. I can feel it; it's a concentration of energy, you see, and when people get butterflies before they go on, it's the fear of the concentration. But when I go on, I take it all and suck it in and breathe it all in, and when it breathes into me—this is how political leaders

were made, like Hitler and things. They get the concentrations of the mass, and therefore they can work miracles with the people. But I do it for good, which is even more potent. I suck it in, and when I pull it back out through the songs, they're even more powerful. And this is just saying that everybody is agreeing. It's just a big agreement, and when people agree there's a happier thing than when they disagree. The whole audience agrees with me and it returns, and the end of it is such a climax and crescendo, it's so beautiful. It's a peaceful thing. The softer you sing, the louder you're heard.

When you're singing what you call soft songs, you're expressing what you call "love power," or whatever you want to call it. Don't you think that's expressing a pretty potent political attitude as well, in view of what it's becoming?

Well, of course. Woody Guthrie's thing was then. His part in the tree was then, and he is so important there. And we're the next, we're up here, you know; we're the next few branches and it's just blossomed and we're getting very near the flower. The flower is very near. I can see it. "Love power," "flower power" and all that are inadequate phrases to try to say how big this movement is, because it began a long, long time ago. Such a growth, and it grows anyway. The only thing is that it gets halted with wars, and people tend to think that it's a new thing, when it's really an ancient thing. I see a flower; this is the most important thing. This civilization is going to see a civilization that was India and Egypt and was all these places, and to be in the beginning of one of them, making it, is such a gas. Nobody's aware of it, but in time . . . You see, all this civilization has to go. It will go. It will fall because it is very loosely built. There's no basis; there's no faith. There's no rock; it's not built up. It's on sand and it'll sink. But what's being built in the hearts of youth is a strong foundation for a good life.

You weren't nervous, then, in the sense most people get stage fright before the Bowl?

Yeah, well, no. San Francisco, I had just done it as another date. I felt that L.A. began me, really. A couple of years ago they gave me a great beginning, and I feel for L.A. a lot. So I wanted to give as much as I could. But when I go onstage, everything is good. I mean, you're so far away from the audience that the communication was the mike. That was my best friend onstage, 'cause I could sing as soft as I wanted and the whole audience understood. Beautiful things happened, like rain began to fall, which told me that I had to sing a song which is called "To Try for the Sun," which mentions where I used to stand in the rain with my friend, Gypsy. I felt him there—he's in England—and I felt him strong at that point, and the rain began to fall. It was a very magic thing for me, and that was a big climax in the thing. The rain began to fall very prettily. Everything was perfect. It was a fantastic concert.

I hear the word "magic" applied to you more than any other performer. Your father said a really beautiful thing at a party recently: "I knew that Donovan had magic when his mother placed him in my arms."

I don't think that I make it. I don't think it's like a reincarnation thing, but it's in the blood of my race. My race is pretty pure. It's Celtic, Scottish and the minstrelsy. The magic that you hear in tales and things was all based around the Celtic mythology of England, which is Tolkien, *The Lord of the Rings.* I just drain from that source. I just drain everything. So the magic is here. We are magic. It is magic that we're walking around. It's fantastic magic. Some people would call it miracles; I like to call it magic.

You're a rarity, and you're aware of it.

Yes, I'm very aware of this. Yes, the more aware I get, the more I can understand how big it is, how big it'll get. It'll be harder to comprehend; that's why I have to go along with it, 'cause it's so vast. To say to somebody that God is everything that lives and that ever has lived and ever will live, and you're never going to touch and see, smell and be everything that is God. Magic is very hard to comprehend. Everyone's on their own, but they're not.

I have an itinerary for you here that looks incredible.

We've never done this much work before.

You went to San Francisco at seven p.m. and came back at ten p.m., isn't that correct?

Yeah.

You just can't walk down the street.

I'd like to find the time. I wanted to go into the beatnik bit of San Francisco. I'd love to go into some of these psychedelic temples and sing softness and change the vibrations, 'cause they're very sort of metallic and gritty and hard, and they need to be a bit purer. I'd love to do that, but we haven't had the time. But I'm going back. I want to do that.

It's probably because of that methedrine problem.

Some, yes. It's so very fast that they think that if they rebel, they have to cut off and put down society. They have to cut off and enhance the society.

Was that the great success of the Bowl?

Yes.

Putting out the softness to these kids?

Yes, to everybody, not just the kids; everybody can take it. Like when George Harrison walked into the Haight-Ashbury district, you know, he just said the right things. It was beautiful. It was all there, you know, it was nice.

2

INTERVIEWED BY RALPH J. GLEASON (1967)

This one is more an historical piece than a ROLLING STONE Interview. In fact, it wasn't an interview at all but, rather, a press conference with Bob Dylan set up by Ralph J. Gleason at KQED-TV in San Francisco, where Ralph had done his *Jazz Casual* series and other music programs. Gleason kept a tape of the hour-long session from late 1965—Dylan was on his *Highway 61* tour—and suggested to Jann Wenner that ROLLING STONE transcribe and publish it.

Gleason, who introduced Dylan to the reporters, photographers, friends and hangers-on in the studio, then joined in the questioning of Dylan, and provided the informative introduction that follows. From watching a recent re-run of the conference, we'd add these notes:

Dylan, aged twenty-four, wandered into the studio behind Gleason and skipped past a TV camera on his way to the table. He wore a tight, British-style jacket, peg pants and boots. He appeared nervous at first and spoke hesitantly, often after long pauses. We caught two bits that were left off the transcript: At one point, a woman asked, "Do you sit down to write a song, or do you write it just on inspiration?" "I more or less write it on a lot of things," said Dylan, cracking up his friends, and others, in the crowd. He also got a laugh when a photographer showed him a Polaroid photo he'd just taken of him. Dylan studied the shot, then exclaimed, "Good God! I must leave right away!"

—BF-T

WHEN BOB DYLAN'S FIVE CONCERTS IN the San Francisco Bay Area were scheduled in December 1965, the idea was proposed that he hold a press conference in the studios of KQED, the educational television station.

Dylan accepted and flew out a day early to make it.

BOB

DYLAN

He arrived early for the press conference, accompanied by Robbie Robertson and several other members of his band, drank tea in the KQED office and insisted that he was ready to talk about "anything you want to talk about." His only request was that he be able to leave at three p.m. so that he could rehearse in the Berkeley Community Theater where he was to sing that night.

At the press conference there were all sorts of people. The TV news crews of all the local stations were there; so were reporters for three metropolitan dailies (their stories were subsequently compared to the broadcast of the interview by a University of California journalism department class), plus representatives of several high school papers; and personal friends of Dylan including poet Allen Ginsberg, producer Bill Graham and comedian Larry Hankin.

Thus the questions ranged from standard straight press and TV reporters' questions to teenage fan club questions, to in-group personal queries and put-ons, to questions by those who really had listened to Dylan's songs.

He sat on a raised platform, facing the cameras and the reporters and answered questions over a microphone, all the while smoking cigarettes and swinging his leg back and forth. At one point he held up a poster for a benefit that week for the San Francisco Mime Troupe (the first rock dance at the Fillmore Auditorium and one of the first public dances featuring the Jefferson Airplane). At the conclusion of the press conference, he chatted with friends for a while, jumped into a car and went back to Berkeley for the rehearsal. He cut the rehearsal off early to go to the hotel and watch the TV program which was shown that night.

I'D LIKE TO KNOW THE MEANING OF *the cover photo on your album,* Highway 61 Revisited.

What would you like to know about it?

It seems to have some philosophy in it. I'd like to know what it represents to you—you're a part of it. . . .

I haven't really looked at it that much.

I've thought about it a great deal.

It was just taken one day when I was sittin' on the steps, y'know—I don't really remember too much about it.

I thought the motorcycle was an image in your song writing. You seem to like that.

Oh, we all like motorcycles to some degree.

Do you think of yourself primarily as a singer or a poet?

Oh, I think of myself more as a song and dance man, y'know.

Why?

Oh, I don't think we have enough time to really go into that.

You were quoted as saying when you're really wasted you may enter into another field. How "wasted" is really wasted, and do you foresee it?

No, I don't foresee it, but it's more or less like a ruthless type of feeling. Very ruthless and intoxicated to some degree.

The criticism that you have received for leaving the folk field and switching to folk-rock hasn't seemed to bother you a great deal. Do you think you'll stick to folk-rock or go into more writing?

I don't play folk-rock.

What would you call your music?

I like to think of it more in terms of vision music—it's mathematical music.

Would you say that the words are more important than the music?

The words are just as important as the music. There would be no music without the words.

Which do you do first, ordinarily?

The words.

Do you think there ever will be a time when you will paint or sculpt?

Oh, yes.

Do you think there will ever be a time when you'll be hung as a thief?

You weren't supposed to say that.

Bob, you said you always do your words first and think of it as music. When you do the words, can you hear it?

Yes.

The music you want when you do your words?

Yes, oh yes.

Do you hear any music before you have words—do you have any songs that you don't have words to yet?

Ummm, sometimes, on very general instruments, not on the guitar though—maybe something like the harpsichord or the harmonica or autoharp—I might hear some kind of melody or tune which I would know the words to put to. Not with the guitar though. The guitar is too hard an instrument. I don't really hear many melodies based on the guitar.

What poets do you dig?

Rimbaud, I guess; W.C. Fields. The family, you know, the trapeze family in the circus; Smokey Robinson, Allen Ginsberg, Charlie Rich—he's a good poet.

In a lot of your songs you are hard on people—in "Like a Rolling Stone" you're hard on the girls and in "Positively 4th Street" you're hard on a friend. Do you do this because you want to change their lives, or do you want to point out to them the error of their ways?

I want to needle them.

Do you still sing your older songs?

No. No. I just saw a songbook last night; I don't really see too many of those things, but there's a lotta songs in those books I haven't even recorded, y'know. I've just written down and put little tunes to them and they published them. I haven't sung them though. A lotta the songs I just don't even know anymore, even the ones I did sing. There doesn't seem to be enough time, y'know.

Did you change your program when you went to England?

No, no, I finished it there. That was the end of my older program. I didn't change it, it was developed, and by the time we got there it was all . . . I knew what was going to happen all the time, y'know. I knew how many encores there were, y'know, which songs they were going to clap loudest and all this kind of thing.

In a concert tour like this do you do the same program night after night?

Oh, sometimes it's different. I think we'll do the same one here in this area though.

In a recent Broadside *interview, Phil Ochs said you should do films. Do you have any plans to do this?*

I do have plans to make a film but not because anybody said I should do it.

How soon will this be?

Next year probably.

Can you tell us what it will be about?

It'll just be another song.

Who are the people making films that you dig, particularly?

Truffaut. I really can't think of any more people. Italian movie directors, y'know, but not too many people in England and the United States.

You did a Chaplin bit as an exit in a concert once.

I did!!!??? That musta been an accident. Have to stay away from that kind of thing.

What do you think of people who analyze your songs?

I welcome them—with open arms.

The University of California mimeographed all the lyrics from the last album and had a symposium discussing them. Do you welcome that?

Oh, sure. I'm just kinda sad I'm not around to be a part of it.

Josh Dunson in his new book implies that you have sold out to commercial interests and the topical song movement. Do you have any comment, sir?

Well, no comments, no arguments. No, I sincerely don't feel guilty.

If you were going to sell out to a commercial interest, which one would you choose?

Ladies' garments.

Bob, have you worked with any rock 'n roll groups?

Uh, professionally?

Or just sitting in or on concert tours with them.

No, no, I don't usually play too much.

Do you listen to other people's recordings of your songs?

Sometimes. A few of them I've heard. I don't really come across it that much though.

Is it a strange experience?

No, it's like a, more or less like a heavenly kind of thing.

What do you think of Joan Baez' interpretations of your earlier songs?

I haven't heard her latest album, or her one before that. I heard one. She does 'em all right, I think.

What about Donovan's "Colors" and his things? Do you think he's a good poet?

Ehh. He's a nice guy though.

I'm shattered.

Well, you needn't be.

Are there any young folksingers you would recommend that we hear?

I'm glad you asked that. Oh, yeah, there's the Sir Douglas Quintet, I think are probably the best that are going to have a chance of reaching the commercial airways. They already have with a couple of songs.

What about Paul Butterfield?

They're good.

Mr. Dylan, you call yourself a completely disconnected person.

No, I didn't call myself that. They sort of drove those words in my mouth. I saw that paper.

How would you describe yourself? Have you analyzed . . .

I certainly haven't. No.

Mr. Dylan, I know you dislike labels and probably rightfully so, but for those of us well over thirty, could you label yourself and perhaps tell us what your role is?

Well, I'd sort of label myself as "well under thirty." And my role is to just, y'know, to just stay here as long as I can.

Phil Ochs wrote in Broadside *that you have twisted so many people's wigs that he feels it becomes increasingly dangerous for you to perform in public.*

Well, that's the way it goes, you know. I don't, I can't apologize, certainly.

Did you envision the time when you would give five concerts in one area like this within ten days?

No. This is all very new to me.

If you were draftable at present, do you know what your feelings might be?

No. I'd probably just do what had to be done.

What would that be?

Well, I don't know, I never really speak in terms of "what if," y'know, so I don't really know.

Are you going to participate in the Vietnam Day Committee demonstration in front of the Fairmont Hotel tonight?

No, I'll be busy tonight.

You planning any demonstrations?

Well, we thought—one. I don't know if it could be organized in time.

Would you describe it?

Uh—well, it was a demonstration where I make up the cards, you know; they have—uh—they have a group of protesters here—uh—perhaps carrying cards with pictures of the jack of diamonds on them and the ace of spades on them. Pictures of mules, maybe words and—oh, maybe about 25–30,000 of these things printed up and just picket, carry signs and picket in front of the post office.

What words?

Oh, words: "camera," "microphone"—"loose"—just words—names of some famous people.

Do you consider yourself a politician?

Do I consider myself a politician? Oh, I guess so. I have my own party though.

Does it have a name?

No. There's no presidents in the party—there's no presidents, or vice-presidents, or secretaries or anything like that, so it makes it kinda hard to get in.

Is there any right wing or left wing in that party?

No. It's more or less in the center—kind of on the Uppity scale.

Do you think your party could end the war with China?

Uh—I don't know. I don't know if they would have any people over there that would be in the same kind of party. Y'know? It might be kind of hard to infiltrate. I don't think my party would ever be approved by the White House or anything like that.

Is there anyone else in your party?

No. Most of us don't even know each other, y'know. It's hard to tell who's in it and who's not in it.

Would you recognize them if you see them?

Oh, you can recognize the people when you see them.

How long do you think it will be before you will finally quit?

Gee, I don't know. I could answer that, you know, but it would mean something different probably for everybody, so we want to keep away from those kinds of sayings.

What did you mean when you said . . .

I don't know, what things were we talking about?

You said, 'I- don't think things can turn out on a . . .'

No, no, no—it's not that I don't think things can turn out. I don't think anything you plan ever turns out the way you plan.

Is that your philosophy?

No, no. Doesn't mean anything.

Do you think that it's fun to put on an audience?

I don't know, I've never done it.

You wrote a song called "Mama, You Been on My Mind." Do you sing it in concerts?

No I haven't. No I haven't.

Are the concerts fun still?

Yeah. Concerts are much more fun than they used to be.

Do you consider them more important than your albums, for instance?

No. It's just a kick to do it now. The albums are the most important.

Because they reach more people?

No, because it's all concise, it's very concise, and it's easy to hear the words and everything. There's no chance of the sound interfering, whereas in a concert, we've played some concerts where sometimes they have those very bad halls. You know, microphone systems. So it's not that easy for somebody to just come and just listen to a band as if they were listening to one person, you know.

Do you consider your old songs less valid than the ones you are putting out now?

No, I just consider them something else to themselves; you know, for another time, another dimension. It would be kind of dishonest for me to sing them now, because I wouldn't really *feel* like singing them.

What is the strangest thing that ever happened to you?

You're gonna get it, man.

What is the weirdest thing that ever happened to you?

I'll talk to you about it, later. I wouldn't do that to you.

What areas in music that you haven't gotten into do you hope to get into?

Writing symphony—with different melodies and different words, different ideas—all being the same, which just roll on top of each other and underneath each other.

14

Mr. Dylan, when would you know that it was time to get out of the music field into another field?

When I get very dragged.

When you stop making money?

No. When my teeth get better—or God, when something makes a drastic—uh—when I start to itch, y'know? When something just goes to a terrifying turn and I know it's got nothing to do with anything and I know it's time to leave.

You say you would like to write symphonies. Is this in the terms that we think of symphonies?

I'm not sure. Songs are all written as part of a symphony—different melodies, different changes—with words or without them, you know, but the end result being a total . . . I mean they say that my songs are long now, y'know; well, sometime it's just gonna come up with the one that's going to be one whole album, consisting of one song. I don't know who's going to buy it. That might be the time to leave.

What's the longest song you've recorded?

I don't know. I don't really check those things, they just turn out long. I guess I've recorded one about eleven or twelve minutes long. "Ballad of Hollis Brown" was pretty long on the second record, and "With God on Our Side" was kind of long. But none of them, I don't think, are as much into anything as "Desolation Row" was, and that was long, too. Songs shouldn't seem long, y'know; it just so happens that it looks that way on paper, y'know. The length of it doesn't have anything to do with it.

Doesn't this give you a problem in issuing records?

No, they are just ready to do anything that I put down now, so they don't really care.

What happens if they have to cut a song in half like "Subterranean Homesick Blues"?

They didn't have to cut that in half.

They didn't have to, but they did.

No, they didn't.

Yeah?

No. You're talking about "Like a Rolling Stone."

Oh, yeah.

They cut it in half for the disc jockeys. Well, you see, it didn't matter for the disc jockeys if they had it cut in half because the other side was just a continuation on the other side, and if anybody was interested they could just turn it over and listen to what really happens, you know. We just made a song the other day which came out ten minutes long, and I thought of releasing it as a single, but they would have easily released it and just cut it up but it

wouldn't have worked that way, so we're not going to turn it out as a single. It's called "Freeze Out" and you'll hear it on the next album.

Of all the people who record your compositions, who do you feel does the most justice to what you're trying to say?

I think Manfred Mann. They've done the songs—they've done about three or four. Each one of them has been right in context with what the song was all about.

What's your new album about?

Oh, it's about, uh—just about all kinds of different things—rats, balloons. They're about the only things that come to my mind right now.

Mr. Dylan, how would you define folk music?

As a constitutional replay of mass production.

Would you call your songs "folk songs"?

No.

Are protest songs "folk songs"?

I guess, if they're a constitutional replay of mass production.

Do you prefer songs with a subtle or obvious message?

With a what???

A subtle or obvious message?

Uh—I don't really prefer those kinds of songs at all—"message"—you mean like—what songs with a message?

Well, like "Eve of Destruction" and things like that.

Do I prefer that to what?

I don't know, but your songs are supposed to have a subtle message.

Subtle message???

Well, they're supposed to.

Where'd you hear that?

In a movie magazine.

Oh—oh, God! Well, we won't—we don't discuss those things here.

Are your songs ever about real people?

Sure, they are, they're all about real people.

Particular ones?

Particular people? Sure, I'm sure you've seen all the people in my songs—at one time or another.

Who is Mr. Jones?

Mr. Jones, I'm not going to tell you his first name. I'd get sued.

What does he do for a living?

He's a pin boy. He also wears suspenders.

How do you explain your attraction?

Attraction to what?

Your attraction—your popularity—your mass popularity.

No, no. I really have no idea. That's the truth, I always tell the truth. That is the truth.

15

What are your own personal hopes for the future, and what do you hope to change in the world?

Oh, my hopes for the future: to be honest, you know, I don't have any hopes for the future, and I just hope to have enough boots to be able to change them. That's all, really, it doesn't boil down to anything more than that. If it did, I would certainly tell you.

What do you think of a question-and-answer session of this type (with you as the principal subject)?

Well, I think we all have different—uh—(I may have dropped an ash on myself somewhere—you'll see in a minute here)—I'm not going to say anything about it though—uh—What was the question?

What are you thinking about right now?

I'm thinking about this ash.

Right before that.

Uh—the ash is creeping up on me somewhere—I've lost—lost touch with myself, so I can't tell where exactly it is.

Was that an inadvertent evading of the question?

No, no—

What do you feel about the meaning of this kind of question-and-answer session?

I just know in my own mind that we all have a different idea of all the words we're using—uh—y'know, so I don't really have too much—I really can't take it too seriously because everything—like if I say the word "house"—like we're both going to see a different house. If I just say the word—right? So we're using all these other words like "mass production" and "movie magazine" and we all have a different idea of these words, too, so I don't even know what we're saying.

Is it pointless?

No, it's not pointless. It's—it's—you know, if you want to do it, you're there—then that's not pointless. You know, it doesn't hurt me any.

Is there anything in addition to your songs that you want to say to people?

Good luck.

You don't say that in your songs.

Oh, yes I do; every song tails off with, "Good Luck—I hope you make it."

Why couldn't you—uh—

Who are you? {Laughter} Get the camera on this person here.

What do you bother to write the poetry for if we all get different images? If we don't know what you're talking about.

Because I got nothing else to do, man.

Do you have a rhyme for "orange"?

What, I didn't hear that.

A rhyme for "orange."

A-ha . . . just a rhyme for "orange"?

Is it true you were censored for singing on the "Ed Sullivan Show"?

I'll tell you the rhyme in a minute.

Did they censor you from singing what you wanted to on the "Ed Sullivan Show"?

Yes. It was a long time ago.

What did you want to sing?

I don't know. It was some song which I wanted to sing and they said I could sing. There's more to it than just censorship there. They actually said I could sing the song, but when we went through the rehearsal of it, the guy came back afterwards and said that I'd have to change it, and he said, "Can't you sing some folk song like the Clancy Brothers do?" And I didn't know any of their songs, and so I couldn't get on the program. That's the way it came down.

Have you found that the text of the interviews with you are accurate to the original conversations?

No. That's another reason I don't really give press interviews or anything, because, you know, I mean, even if you do something—there are a lot of people here, so they know what's going on—but like if you just do it with one guy or two guys, they just take it all out of context, you know, they just take it, split it up in the middle or just take what they want to use, and they even ask you a question and you answer it and then it comes out in print that they just substitute another question for your answer. It's not really truthful, you know, to do that kind of thing, so I just don't do it. That's just a press problem there.

Do you think the entire text of your news conference today should be printed in the newspaper?

Oh, no, nothing like that, nothing like that. But this is just for the interview, you know, when they want to do interviews in places like Omaha, or in Cincinnati, man, you know. I don't do it, and then they write bad things.

Well, isn't this partly because you are often inaudible? Like, for most of this dialogue you have been inaudible, and now when you are touched personally by the misquotation, your voice rises and we can hear you.

Yeah, well, I just realized that maybe the people in the back there can't hear me, that's all.

I was just going to ask you—in your songs you sing out—

Yes, I do.

And whether . . .

You see, the songs are what I do—write the songs and sing them and perform them. That's what I do. The performing part of it could end, but like I'm going to be writing these songs and singing them and recording them, and I see no end, right now. That's what I do—uh—anything else interferes with it. I mean anything else trying to get on top of it, making something out of it which it isn't, it just brings me down, and it's not, uh—it just makes it seem all very cheap.

Well, it made me feel like you were almost kind of doing a penance of silence here . . .

No, no.

The first half.

I'm not one of those kinds of people at all.

You don't need silence?

No, no silence. It's always silent where I am.

Mr. Dylan, when you're on a concert tour, how many people travel in your party?

We travel with about twelve people now.

Does the number of people seem to go with the amount of money you're making?

Oh, yes, of course.

Is that known as Dylan's Law?

We have the band, we have five in the group. And we need other things; we have to—it's a lot of electronic equipment now, a lot of different things which have to be taken care of, so we need a lot of people. We have three road managers and things like that. We don't make any big public presentations though, like we never come into town in limousines or anything like that. We just—uh—go from place to place, you know, and do the shows. That's all.

You fly in your own plane?

Yes, yes.

Do you have to get in a certain type of mood to write your music?

Yeah, I guess so. A certain type of mood, if you want to call it that.

Do you find that you are more creative at a certain time of the day?

Yes, yes, I feel that way.

Like a night writer?

I would say night has nothing to do with it.

Have you ever sung with the Beatles?

No. Well, I think we have messed around in London, but no, I don't think anything serious.

Have you ever played a dance?

No. It's not that kind of music.

It is.

Well, what can I say? You must know more about the music than I do. How long have you been playing it?

Do you find that when you're writing, you free-associate often?

No, it's all very clear and simple to me. These songs aren't complicated to me at all. I know what they all are all about! There's nothing hard to figure out for me. I wouldn't write anything I can't really see.

I don't mean it that way. I meant when you're creating a song, are you doing it on a subliminal level?

No. That's the difference in the songs I write now. In the past year or so—in the last year and a half, maybe two, I don't know—the songs before, up till one of these records, I wrote the fourth record in Greece—there was a change there—but the records before that, I used to know what I wanted to say, before I used to write the song. All the stuff which I had written before which wasn't song was just on a piece of toilet paper. When it comes out like that it's the kind of stuff I never would sing because people would just not be ready for it. But I just went through that other thing of writing songs, and I couldn't write like it anymore. It was just too easy, and it wasn't really "right." I would start out, I would know what I wanted to say before I wrote the song and I would say it, you know, and it would never come out exactly the way I thought it would, but it came out, you know, it touched it, but now, I just write a song, like *I know* that it's just going to be all right and I don't really know exactly what it's all about, but I do know the minutes and the layers of what it's all about.

What did you think about your song, "It's Alright, Ma (I'm Only Bleeding)"? It happens to be my favorite one.

God bless you, son. I haven't heard it for a long time. I couldn't even sing it for you, probably.

How long does it take you to write a . . .

Usually not too long a time, really. I might write all night and get one song out of a lot of different things I write.

How many have you written?

Uh—I guess, well, there's one publisher that's got about a hundred. I've written about fifty others, I guess. I got about 150 songs I've written.

Have they all been published?

No, some of the scraps haven't been published. But I find I can't really sing that anyway, because I forget it, so the songs I don't publish, I usually do forget.

Have you ever taken these scraps and made them into a song?

No, I've forgotten the scraps. I have to start over all the time. I can't really keep notes or anything like that.

You can't go back to one of your earlier things and use it in your . . .

No, no. That wouldn't be right either.

17

On your songs, do you get any help from the rest of your entourage?

Robbie [Robertson], the lead guitar player, sometimes we play the guitars together—something might come up—but I know it's going to be right. I'll be just sitting around playing so I can write up some words. I don't get any ideas, though, of what I want to or what's really going to happen here.

Why do you think you're so popular?

I don't know. I'm not a reporter, I'm not a newsman or anything. I'm not even a philosopher, so I have no idea. I would think other people would know, but I don't think I know. You know, when you get too many people talking about the same thing it tends to clutter up things. Everybody asks me that, so I realize they must be talking about it, so I'd rather stay out of it and make it easier for them. Then, when they get the answer, I hope they tell me.

Has there been any more booing?

Oh, there's booing—you can't tell where the booing's going to come up. Can't tell at all. It comes up in the weirdest, strangest places, and when it comes it's quite a thing in itself. I figure there's a little "boo" in all of us.

Bob, where is Desolation Row?

Where? Oh, that's someplace in Mexico. It's across the border. It's noted for its Coke factory. Coca-Cola machines are—sells—sell a lotta Coca-Cola down there.

Where is Highway 61?

Highway 61 exists—that's out in the middle of the country. It runs down to the south, goes up north.

Mr. Dylan, you seem very reluctant to talk about the fact that you're a popular entertainer—a most popular entertainer.

Well, what do you want me to say?

Well, I don't understand why you . . .

Well, what do you want me to say? What do you want me to say, d'you want me to say—who—who—what do you want me to say about it?

You seem almost embarrassed to admit that you're popular.

Well, I'm not embarrassed, I mean, you know—well, what do you want, exactly—for me to say? You want me to jump up and say "Hallelujah!"—and crash the cameras or do something weird? Tell me, tell me. I'll go along with you; if I can't go along with you, I'll find somebody to go along with you.

I find that you really have no idea as to why you are popular, no thoughts on why you are popular.

I just haven't really struggled for that. It happened, you know? It happened like anything else happens. Just a happening. You don't try to figure out happenings. You dig happenings. So I'm not going to even talk about it.

Do you feel that part of the popularity is because of a kind of identification?

I have no idea. I don't really come too much in contact.

Does it make life more difficult?

No, it certainly doesn't.

Were you surprised the first time the boos came?

Yeah, that was at Newport. Well, I did this very crazy thing. I didn't know what was going to happen, but they certainly booed, I'll tell you that. You could hear it all over the place. I don't know who they were though, and I'm certain whoever it was did it twice as loud as they normally would. They kind of quieted down some at Forest Hills, although they did it there, too. They've done it just about all over except in Texas—they didn't boo us in Texas, or in Atlanta, or in Boston, or in Ohio. They've done it in just about—or in Minneapolis, they didn't do it there. They've done it a lot of other places. I mean, they must be pretty rich to be able to go someplace and boo. I couldn't afford it if I was in their shoes.

Other than booing, have the audiences changed much? Do they scream and get hysterical and rush onstage?

Oh, sometimes you get people rushing the stage, but you just, y'know—turn 'em off very fast. Kick 'em in the head or something like that. They get the picture.

You said that you don't know why you are so popular. That is in direct opposition to what most people who reach this level of popularity say.

Well, you see, a lot of people start out and they plan to try to be stars; I would imagine, like, however, they have to be stars. I mean I know a lot of those people, you know? And they start out and they go into show business for many, many reasons, to be seen, you know. I started out, you know, like this had nothing to do with it when I started. I started from New York City, you know, and there just wasn't any of that around. It just happened.

Don't misunderstand me, I agree with your right not to have to care; my point is that it would be somewhat disappointing for the people who think that you feel towards them the way that they feel towards you.

Oh—well, I don't want to disappoint anybody. I mean, tell me what I should say—you know, I'll certainly go along with anything, but I really don't have much of an idea.

You have a poster there.

Yeah, it's a poster somebody gave me. It looks pretty good. The Jefferson Airplane, John Handy, and Sam Thomas and the Mystery Trend and the Great Society and all playing at the Fillmore Auditorium this Friday, December 10th, and *I* would like to go if I could, but unfortunately, I won't be here, I don't think, but if I was here, I certainly would be there.

What's more important to you: the way that your music and words sound, or the content, the message?

The whole thing while it's happening. The whole total sound of the words, what's really going down is—it either happens or it doesn't happen, you know. That's what I feel is—just the thing, which is happening there at that time.

That's what we do, you know? That is the most important thing, there really isn't anything else. I don't know if I answered your question.

You mean it might happen one time, and it might not happen the next?

We've had some bad nights, but we always take good cuts for the records. The records are always made out of good cuts and in person; most of the time it does come across. Most of the time we do feel like playing. That's important, to me; the aftermath, and whatever happens before, is not really important to me; just the time on the stage and the time that we're singing the songs and performing them. Or not really performing them even, just letting them be there.

INTERVIEWED BY RALPH J. GLEASON (1968)

By the time B. B. King hit the Fillmore Auditorium in December 1967, he'd been preceded by his reputation. The late Michael Bloomfield, the highly regarded guitarist with the Paul Butterfield Blues Band, cited King as his major influence. "When I'm playing blues guitar really well," he said in his own ROLLING STONE Interview, "it's a lot like B. B. King."

King (real name: Riley B. King; his adopted name derived from "Blues Boy," as he was known in his youth in Memphis), along with Muddy Waters, was one of the most influential blues musicians working out of Chicago, shaping both the music of other bluesmen and the young, white, rock-raised players who began flourishing in the late Sixties.

Bill Graham, who'd already introduced his Fillmore rock audiences to the likes of Waters, Lightnin' Hopkins, "Big Mama" Mae Thornton, Junior Wells and the James Cotton Blues Band, had headlined King in February 1967, over Steve Miller and Moby Grape. Now, King was sharing the stage with the Byrds and Bloomfield's new band, Electric Flag, and his career had moved forever away from the "chitlin' circuit" to large clubs and auditoriums. He'd been discovered, finally, by the white audience.

During his stay in San Francisco, Ralph J. Gleason talked with the forty-two-year-old King at the studios of KQED-TV.

—BF-T

KING

THE BLUES IS THE WELLSPRING *of American popular music, the wellspring of jazz, and it's coming into a renaissance today. B. B. King, you've been playing and singing the blues all your professional life. Do you ever get tired of it?*

No. No, I don't ever get tired, Ralph. One thing that does bother me, sometimes I think that the people, maybe, are getting tired of it. I feel a little funny sometimes when I start to performing, but once they start to clap their hands or what have you, I never get tired of it.

Do you play songs that you've played over and over again over the course of years? Do you find new things to do in them? Does the music give you greater scope as time goes on?

Yes, it does in one way. Well, for instance, most times that I've recorded, we never did much rehearsing unless we were going to do certain types of tunes. With blues ballads or something like that, maybe we would do quite a bit of rehearsing because you had to have big arrangements for large orchestras. But as a whole, we go in, sit down, run it down a couple of times—in a lot of cases we cut it then. My point I'm trying to get over, you're not too familiar with it, you do it the best you can then, but over the years you find out or you say to yourself, "Why didn't I do this? Why didn't I do that?" So then you find different things that you can make it. . . . At least you think you're improving it, but the people sometimes say, "No, why don't you do it like you did five years ago?" And then the younger set they'll accept what you're doing but some of the older ones say, "No, I remember you played '3 O'Clock Blues' this way." You can't always say whether you're doing it better, but we find different ways to do it. As time changes, I believe you change a little bit with it, a lot of times not even recognizing that you are.

Do you find the blues today different than when you came up as a young player?

Oh, yes. Yes, I do in many ways. I first started out listening to people like my cousin Bukka White, Blind Lemon, people like that, Sonny Boy Williamson—all those guys was my idols then. I really dug those people just like the young kids would dig Smokey Robinson and the Miracles or the Beatles, or somebody like that. And I didn't have any feeling about what the people thought about it. In other words, I liked it and I didn't care if nobody else did like it. Then later on, after I started into trying to play myself, I found that sometimes, well, a little bit, I was almost afraid to say that I was a blues singer. Because it looked like people kind of looked down on you a lot of times when you mention the word blues. But I thank God today I can stick out my chest and say, yeah, I'm a blues singer!

The first blues that you heard, were they instrumental blues or were they vocal blues?

Ah, both, because as I mentioned, people that I idolized so much, the older blues singers, Leadbelly and all these people, Josh White, well, I don't mean Josh was that, but Leadbelly, my cousin Bukka White, all these people would sing and play. But then the people I think that influenced me most was T-Bone Walker, Lowell Fulsom, Elmo James, then there was Johnny Moore, Three Blazes, they were the people that had the bluesy feeling that made me feel so good. But then I was somewhat jazz-minded too, maybe it was a intermingling of this that created the style that I play now, because I was crazy about Charlie Christian and one of my favorites, real favorites, was Django Reinhardt and I imagine today if you listen to my playing, you'll hear a little bit of all of them. I'm telling my secret. But I think a little bit of all those people I liked, with my own ideas, created the B. B. King twinging guitar sound.

Did you hear Django and Charlie Christian when you were young or after you came off the plantation? You said you were driving a tractor during World War II?

Yes.

In the Mississippi delta. Had you heard players like that then?

I had heard Charlie Christian. I heard him with Benny Goodman. They used to have these little, I think they call them ten-cent movies. During that time we used to watch them, we got a chance to hear people. The people that I really liked then were people that seemed to have the soul that I could feel. There was a lot of big bands around during that time but Basie somehow or another always stuck to me because I liked Jimmy Rushing, see. I liked Jimmy's singing and an arrangement that they would have around Jimmy really got to me. And then I would listen to Duke Ellington. And I liked Duke because a lot of times he had people like Al Hibbler singing. And I in fact remember . . . what I'm trying to get to, Benny Goodman, during that time, would feature Charlie Christian quite a bit. And I'd get a chance to hear that and I could feel that soul down there. And I think this is one of the few things that started me listening to the guitar. Well, I take that back. I had been listening because I remember my uncle was married to a sanctified preacher's sister. And this preacher after church on a Sunday afternoon would visit his sister, which was my aunt. And he'd always lay his guitar on the bed and I'd go get it as soon as they'd turn their backs. I think this is really what started me to fooling with the guitar. Not by listening to some of the other people. But I like blues—evidently it and the spiritual music always stuck with me, I guess. My mother started me singing when I was about four or five. I used to sing with her. And I think I just had it inside.

That feeling on the guitar, that singing string, what was the phrase you used for it before?

Twing?

Twinging. This is your own contribution?

I think so. I think it is 'cause I've heard so many guys since I've started playing sound that way, and I don't remember ever hearing anybody before that. Not before that.

Do you have the feeling that your voice and the guitar are interchangeable, you sing on the guitar and you play with the voice?

I think so. You know, listening to horn players after I started trying to play, I hear a guy playing and he phrases a note, bends it like Lester Young used to do. Well, I can hear myself singing when I play. That may sound weird, but I can hear the words that I'm saying and a lot of times they don't mean as much to me as the way I say it. And I think this is the same thing I've tried to do on the guitar. It's been a sound that I've heard for years but I haven't quite got it exactly like I want it. I believe a guy should be able to phrase on a guitar almost like the singing of a violin or saxophone, really, and this, I guess, is what I've been trying to get. I can't tell anybody what I want to hear. But I hear it myself, but I can't play it. I don't know how to really get it myself.

But you'll know when you get it?

I think so, I think so.

Those tempos are so easy, and so natural. Do you have anything particular in mind when you choose tempos to do things in?

No. Well, for instance, if I'm playing a dance I'll try to play something that's not too fast for the people to dance on but just fast enough for them to move comfortably. 'Specially the younger set, because now I notice they don't dance like they did back in the late Fifties.

They sure don't.

But then boogie-woogies and things like that, if you have something where people could kind of shake about a bit, they liked that better than they did the slow, draggy thing. But today they want a medium type of tempo like, uh, well, I would say a beat on two and four where they can do like so. But if we're playing a club, especially a club where they have a lot of jazz musicians, we find that we can play something up in tempo then and they'll dig it. Well, if not like it, they'll accept it. Playing a dance you can't do it. So usually I try and play something that's comfortable for us. But with the public in mind.

Many of these young players coming along today have been really turned on by the way you play the guitar. People like Mike Bloomfield . . . do you hear yourself coming back from those bands?

He's wild. Well, yes, I believe I do. I don't want to stick my neck out there but I think so. But I'm grateful that some of them seem to like me. I'm grateful because to me, it seemed to open a few doors for us that seemed like they was never going to be opened. And we're glad when people like Mike and the rest of the fellows will take up some of the things that we do. We're very happy. Because until the days of rock & roll, a lot of times a lot of the places just wouldn't accept us. I'm not speaking racially, I'm just talking about where people as a whole just wouldn't accept us, in some of these places the door's open now for you to go into. Because of people like Mike, Elvis Presley, the Beatles, Fats Domino and people like that helped us out quite a bit.

What do you want to do with your music? And with your singing?

Play the best that I can. Reach as many people as I can, as many countries. In other words, I'd like the whole world to be able to hear B. B. King sing and play the blues.

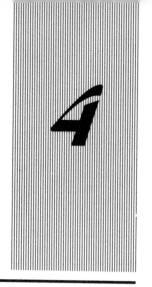

INTERVIEWED BY JANN WENNER (1968)

The ROLLING STONE Interview with Eric Clapton, which appeared in the spring of 1968, in the tenth issue of the magazine, was the second to carry Jann Wenner's byline (the first—with Michael Bloomfield—had run the previous issue). But, in fact, he'd done the interview the year before, during Cream's triumphant first tour of the United States, and before the birth of ROLLING STONE.

"I did it for Melody Maker [the London-based pop paper]," Wenner recalls. "It was done before Eric Clapton was God. It was the last of the low-key days—relaxed, old-days-type stuff."

By the time the interview appeared, Cream had broken through, and the twenty-three-year-old Clapton had become a musical legend, acclaimed as one of the greatest white blues guitar players of all time. Clapton began with the Yardbirds in the early Sixties and emerged as a major figure when he joined John Mayall, then formed Cream in 1966 with drummer Ginger Baker and bassist Jack Bruce.

But Cream wouldn't last long. In July, Clapton announced that the group was breaking up because it had "lost direction." Clapton also blamed "a change of attitudes among ourselves. You get really hung up and try to write pop songs or create a pop image," he said. "I went through that stage, and it was a shame because I was not being true to myself. I am and always will be a blues guitarist. Cream reached its peak last year in San Francisco," he said. "From that we all went on such a huge ego trip. Making it in the States was a bang in the head."

—BF-T

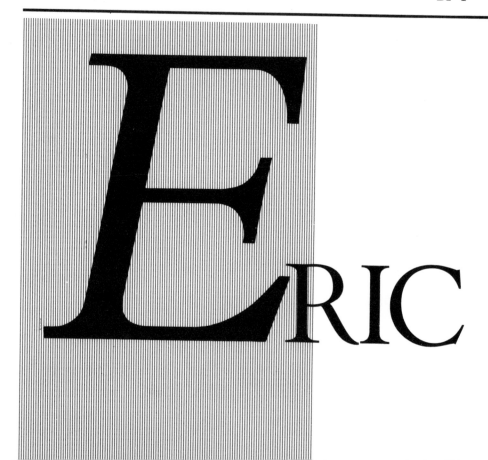

ERIC

CLAPTON

*W*HEN YOU FIRST CAME HERE *last year what did you find were people's expectations of you and the Cream?*

We seem to be a lot more popular here than I had imagined. I'd heard that we'd been heard of through the underground thing. Yet I really didn't imagine that we'd be this popular. Or that we would be accepted as readily as we were, because an American band like Butterfield can go to England now and just die at all the places. The best reception they got was at the Marquee and that wasn't as good as most English bands would have gotten. In England, they're all very uptight about it. They don't want foreigners coming in. They feel very competitive about their music scene and don't want it contaminated by Americans.

Perhaps that's due to some sort of musical inferiority complex—they know all of what they're doing is really based on the American thing.

It's a very jealous thing. They're afraid of American music being too far ahead of them. They've got this fantasy, they deny it.

Do you think that the song by Scott McKenzie, "Wear flowers in your hair," which has been Number One on the English surveys accurately reflects what's happening here?

Not in any way. It is wrapped up in fashion; it's all about fashion. Who cares what people look like?

The audience in England believes that is what it's like, flower power and flower children.

Of course; the British public have been taught that fashion is the only worthwhile thing—they'll throw away thousands of quid a year just buying clothes. That's just what they think about. I could have been taken in by the song if I hadn't come here.

How do the San Francisco and London audiences differ?

To look at? They're not very different. As far as the reception, this [San Francisco] is about the best audience. They're so obviously critical. Every little move you make and every little note you play is being noticed, being devoured, accepted or rejected. You know that whatever you do is going to be noticed and you do it right. You got to do your best 'cause they know if you're not doing your best.

Do you prefer playing in front of an audience or in an isolated situation such as a studio?

I get quite bored listening to myself play the guitar because I'm not a very good audience. If there are people there, you go further.

How much does your state of mind affect your playing?

You mean drugs?

No, not really—

Well, we did a couple of gigs in very bad places. We did them up north in England and there was one on a pier. In a ballroom on the end of a pier. It was like twenty years out of date. The whole thing was like being in another era, you know. I couldn't play there a'tall. There was nothing familiar for me to grab hold of. It was like being stuck in another time. We did another gig in a club which I used to play in with the Yardbirds. It was the same now as it was then. The same audience—which was very hysterical and neurotic. And when you get onstage and everyone's screaming and shouting—you're going mad trying to get tune. That kind of thing scares me, you know. What I actually prefer to do is concerts. I really like to play concerts, because the whole thing is more relaxed. The audience is seated, they're calmed down and then it's up to you to build it to any kind of pitch musically. It's much better to work with.

What about the groups you've seen in San Francisco?

I haven't seen any; we haven't had time.

You played with the Electric Flag, not exactly a local group but certainly some reflection of the local scene.

The Electric Flag is just the heaviest thing around. They've got a tremendous rhythm section and Barry Goldberg. And Mike Bloomfield who just lives and breathes music. He's one of those people who don't think about anything else. An incredible band.

Have you heard the Grateful Dead record? [The Grateful Dead, *their debut.*]

Yeah, it's great.

Peter Townshend said he saw the Dead at the Pop Festival and called them "one of the original ropeys."

Ropey! That means a drag. I don't think the quality of their music is as high as a lot of other good recording bands. People are more concerned with live music, maybe, than with recording. I'm not sure of that. I'm guessing. If the Grateful Dead are one of the best, they're not doing a very good job on record.

What do you think of the guitar playing? Jerry Garcia's synthesis of blues, jazz and country & western, with a little jug band thrown in?

It's very good, and very tight, but it's not really my bag.

What have you seen in San Francisco that would improve a scene like London?

As far as attitudes are concerned. There is less competition and more encouragement here from musician to musician. Music thrives wildly in England because they are jealous of someone else's success. They're jealous, so they have to do better. Here you're encouraged. Everybody digs everybody else and they don't hide it. In England they could use a little more maturity; the English music market has been bred so long on immaturity, in the press and music papers, they are concerned with nothing else but Top Forty, and music doesn't really matter. There isn't one English music newspaper that covers the whole field of music; they're all cut up in a little bunch. They could use, from San Francisco, a little more openmindedness about music, to grow up about it. Music isn't a three-year thing anymore. It's not related to "overnight successes" and things like that; it's grown out of that. The people behind it—the managers, and the people who make their bread out of it—have got to learn that and grow out of it as well. Musicians are not half-wits anymore.

What do you feel about the charts?

Personally I don't think they're amoral, you know, musically. I think they're antimusic and antiprogress. They're obsolete.

Are they really detrimental to the groups?

It brings the whole thing down to a very immature level. I mean, the chart is there to serve one purpose—to indicate to everybody what is best and what is worst. But it really doesn't go that way, because good music idiomatically is good, and bad music is bad, and it really doesn't matter what people say about it. It doesn't matter what people's tastes are. People can go out and buy a record, you know, like an Engelbert Humperdinck record, then everybody can say it's the best record available. Which is rubbish. Doesn't mean to say because it's popular it's the best music.

How much do the charts hang up the musician?

Well, you see, in principle it's still not a bad thing if it were on a small scale. If the charts weren't so overwhelming then it wouldn't be bad. It'd be like those occasional little polls they have for the best musician, and so on, and it'd be all right. But the thing is, everybody nowadays is brainwashed to accept what the charts say as right.

So there is no room for anything else. There is no room to play good music. I mean, we may be doing it now, but it's only just changing. Up until now there was no room to be able to play without making a single. You had to make a hit single to be able to go out and play somewhere. Otherwise you were just rejected. The hit single is a lever. I mean, everyone says—We'll do a commercial record for the first one. We'll get a hit and then when everyone likes us, we'll do what we want. That's what a hit single up until now has been for. You make something that's really crappy and formulated and stereotyped that will get to Number One, and then when you're there you say, look, everybody, this is what we're going to do now. I don't think that should be necessary.

What we're doing now is simply concentration on LP's. And if by accident a single should come out of an LP session, then we'll put it on the market. Whereas before, you'd have two sessions; you'd consciously go to an LP session or you'd consciously go to a single sesson. And single sessions are terrible. I can't make them at all. They're just like—you go in there and the whole big problem is whether it's commercial. That is the problem. No matter what the music is like, it's got to be commercial, it's got to have a hook line, you've got to have this and that and you just fall into a very dark hole. I can't take it a'tall.

L OCALLY YOU ARE KNOWN AS *one of the world's top blues or rock guitarists. Do you think that they've found you lived up to this?*

Everybody seemed to be pleased. I haven't met any major criticism of our group. Musically we seem to have done very well.

Where do you get your energies?

Well, it's a vicious circle thing. I mean, if I hadn't ever played an instrument, then I wouldn't ever need to play one. But now that I've been playing, I need to play. I'll make it clearer: When I come off the stage, you know, I've just expressed myself as much as I could that particular time. And I know that if I've got a gig the next day that somehow or other I've got to store up enough energy to play the next day. It's like, you know, you spend it, then you get it back again, then you spend it, then you get it back again. You've got to do this. It's like a basic reaction that goes on subconsciously the whole time. . . . I'm taking note of things, I'm expressing myself about them. It's almost forced a lot of the time when we have to work really hard.

Who do you feel are the best groups in the British scene, excluding the Beatles and Rolling Stones?

The Pink Floyd is one I like very much among live groups.

What about the Who?

I haven't seen them for a long time, but that did impress me at one time, that kind of act.

Aside from that thing.

If I can't see the Who, then I'm not really bothered, and I won't listen to them very much. They're tight and they're all very heavy, but musically I don't think they are going in a very extreme direction. They stick to their records and things like that.

What does the Pink Floyd do?

Very strange group. The nearest thing you would have to them here—well, I can't even think of a group you can relate them to. Very freaky. They're not really psychedelic. They do things like play an hour set that's just one number. They are into a lot of electronic things. They're also very funny. They're nice, they really are a very nice group. They're unambitious, and they give you a nice feeling watching them. They're not trying to put anything over.

What do you think about Jimi Hendrix?

I don't really want to be critical about it. I think Jimi can sing very well; he just puts it around that he can't sing and everyone accepts it. I think he can sing very well. I also think he's a great guitarist. I don't like to watch him too much 'cause I prefer to listen to him.

When he first came to England, you know, English people have a very big thing towards a spade. They really love that magic thing, the sexual thing. They all fall for that sort of thing. Everybody and his brother in England still sort of think that spades have big dicks. And Jimi came over and exploited that to the limit, the fucking tee. Everybody fell for it. Shit.

I fell for it. After a while I began to suspect it. Having gotten to know him, I found out that's not where he's at, not at all. The stuff he does onstage, when he does that he's testing his audience. He'll do a lot of things, like fool around with his tongue and play his guitar behind his back and rub it up and down his crotch. And he'll look at the audience, and if they're digging it, he won't like the audience. He'll keep on doing it, putting them on. Play less music. If they don't dig it, then he'll play straight 'cause he knows he has to. It's funny. I heard that here he came on and put on all that shit in his first set, and people were just dead towards it. And in his second set he just played, which is great.

He had the whole combination in England. It was just what the market wanted, a psychedelic pop star who looked freaky, and they're also still so hung up about spades, and the blues thing was there. So Jimi walked in, put on all the gear and made it straightaway. It was a perfect formula. Underneath it all, he's got an incredible musical talent. He is really one of the finest musicians around on the Western scene. If you just scrape away all the bullshit he carries around you'll find a fantastically talented guy and a beautiful guitar player for his age. I just can't take it, all the plastic things.

Who started the hair thing?

I guess Dylan started it. It's funny, 'cause it's gone into a fashionable thing in England. I did it 'cause I liked Dylan's hair. I went and had my hair curled. Then Jimi came on with curly hair, and his band did it to complete the image, and everybody else did it 'cause they dug Jimi and other people did it 'cause they dug me, I guess. It became quite a trend in England to have curly hair.

What was the first experience with music that you can remember, other than Humpty Dumpty, where you asked yourself, "What's happening on that radio?"

Chuck Berry did that. "School Day" and then "Johnny B. Goode." I got into that. I was around sixteen or seventeen, heavily when I was seventeen, by myself. I learned from records.

I guess, everybody who's played a string instrument has had an influence on me. All the Indian musicians I've heard and all the blues musicians I've heard have influenced me. There are lots of other idioms I haven't even touched on, fields of music I haven't even been near. There's also influences I've got from people who don't play string instruments. There's a blues harmonica player called Little Walter Jacobs who plays really good harmonica. He's influenced me a lot because you can transfer what he's doing to a guitar.

Any other guitarists?

At first I played exactly like Chuck Berry for six or seven months. You couldn't have told the difference when I was with the Yardbirds. Then I got into older bluesmen. Because he was so readily available I dug Big Bill Broonzy; then I heard a lot of cats I had never heard of before: Robert Johnson and Skip James and Blind Boy Fuller. I just finally got completely overwhelmed in this brand-new world. I studied it and listened to it and went right down in it and came back up in it. I was about seventeen or eighteen. When I came back up in it, I turned on to B. B. King, and it's been that way ever since. I still don't think there is a better blues guitarist in the world than B. B. King.

But is he your primary influence?

No. He covers one field, the best of one field. I am more influenced at the moment by Indian music, not structurally, but in its atmosphere and its ideals. Not the notes; I don't ever intend to start playing the sitar or playing the guitar like a sitar; I've just opened up my mind to the fact that you needn't play with arrangements and just improvise the whole time. That's where I want to be at: where I just don't ever have to play anything but improvisation.

What about the other Kings, Albert and Freddie?

Albert is great because he's still recording and going strong. Freddie, I haven't heard about in a long time.

You did one of Freddie King's numbers with John Mayall.

That was not because I dug his number so much, but because it fitted in with what I was playing. I didn't like "Hideaway" too much. I don't like his instrumentals too much actually. He never does too much when he does instrumentals. He's best when he's singing.

Who's influenced you as a person?

The first two people I think of are from the music field. That's simply because it's the world I live in. The first one is Mike Bloomfield. His way of thinking really shocked me the first time I met him and spoke to him. I never met anyone with so many strong convictions. And Dylan really turned me on. He's a really brave man—speaking out, you know. Those two are really the biggest influence 'cause they're just very believable. I believe in those two guys more than a lot of things.

Were the Yardbirds your first group?

No. I played with two amateur groups before that, in my spare time. One called "The Roosters" and one called "Casey Jones and the Engineers." I didn't stay with either of those bands for more than two weeks. It was more like jamming. Then I got offered a professional job with the Yardbirds.

From the inception of the group?

About two weeks afterwards. I was with them a year and a half. They weren't too keen to have it known that I'd left. People leaving groups in those days was dirty.

Why have they had such a long succession of guitar players?

The guitar players who play with them don't like them. I was fooled into joining the group, attracted by the pop thing, the big money, and traveling around and little chicks. It wasn't until after a year and a half that I started to take music as a serious thing. I just realized I would be

doing it for the rest of my life and I'd better be doing it right. I was playing what they wanted me to play.

After the Yardbirds?

I intended to pack up playing altogether. I was kind of screwed up about everything. Playing with a group like that puts you in a very strange frame of mind. You lose a lot of your original values. I laid up for a couple of weeks with a friend. Didn't do much, and then I got offered a job with John Mayall whom I'd always admired because of his integrity. If I was going to join anyone, it might as well be him. I played with him for about a year and a half too. Then I really got into my music and developed it more than I'd ever done before, 'cause they take it seriously. Then I just decided I wanted to go further than that band was going. They were stuck to their thing, which was playing Chicago blues. I wanted to go somewhere else and put my kind of guitar playing in a different context, in a new kind of pop music context. I thought that music was more valid than Chicago blues for me, 'cause rock & roll is more like folk music contemporary.

Would you characterize what you're doing now as more rock than blues?

Yes.

How did you get Cream together?

We knew each other from our respective bands. Jack was with Manfred Mann, and Ginger Baker was with Graham Bond.

Your first date was at the Windsor Festival, wasn't it?

Yes. We had decided we wanted to play with each other more than anyone else in the country and formed a band. Completely cooperative. We just did it. It wasn't very hard, it was easy. Putting it together was hard because we had no idea what we really wanted to play, we just knew we wanted to play together. We had no idea of what kind of material to do, and for a long time it was hard to find a real direction. We did a lot of other people's numbers. Jack couldn't get that many songs out. There are a couple of the blues and rock & roll numbers we still do, only by choice and not by force.

What does "Disraeli Gears" mean?

It's a pun; it doesn't mean anything. In England there is a big thing on racing cycling and on the back wheel, fixed to the hub you have a gear with ten gears, called a "derailer." That's the pun. We were just in a car one night kicking up puns, like Duke Elephant and Elephant Gerald, and "Disraeli Gears" just came up, and I said that would be a good name for the record.

29

Who's your producer?

Felix Pappalardi. He's been working mostly on the folk scene, people like Joan Baez and that. He was just around Atlantic City and said he wanted to do it, and we wanted him.

What kind of guitar and amplifiers do you use?

A Les Paul, a modern one. A solid one. Same pickups, more or less the same neck, just a different body than the 1958 ones. It's obviously not as good a sound as the old ones, 'cause they've got vintage, like old wine. I haven't got any old ones still intact, they've all gotten broken, warped. When a guitar is that old you've got to be careful. There's a maker, I think it's Hagstrom or someone like that, that's copying the old Les Pauls, but I wouldn't buy one.

Amps, and how do you set them?

Two 100-watt Marshalls. I set them full on everything, full treble, full bass and full presence, same with the controls on the guitar. If you've got the amp and guitar full, there is so much volume that you can get it 100 miles away and it's going to feed back—the sustaining effect—and anywhere in the vicinity it's going to feed back.

Strings?

Fender rock & roll.

What differences do you find in attitudes between the young bluesmen here—like Bloomfield or Butterfield, for instance—and in England, like John Mayall?

The blues musician is usually a fanatic; that's the common denominator among the blues musicians, they're fanatics. In England they are a lot more so 'cause they're divorced from the scene and don't really know where it's at. They don't really know what it's like to be a blues musician in America like Mike Bloomfield does. They are all romantic about it and have a lot of ideals and notions. A lot of ego gets mixed into it, and they think they're the only guys playing real music.

Would you characterize yourself as a blues musician?

No. I don't think I really represent the blues anymore. Not truly. I have more of that in me and my music than anything else, but I don't really play blues anymore.

What kind of things do you want Cream to do?

Nothing more ambitious than being as musically free as we can. You can't even guess where that will take you musically. I don't know where I'll be in the next year. I know that I have to become more free and not get tied down with labels or playing like other people or even being influenced by other people.

What's the role of a musician in England?

In the last couple of years, the role is one of more than being a musician. There is this big thing about you're going to influence the young. For some incredibly uncanny reason, a musician is more important than a politician these days. Because that is true, the role of a musician is a drag. You don't have to be that intelligent to play music; you don't have to have moral responsibility. There's no reason why they should have; they're only there to play music and people should leave them like that. Because so much responsibility is attached, it's too much, a drag, too much public opinion placed on a musician. What I'm doing now is just my way of thinking, but if it gets into a paper somewhere, people will say that what I'm saying is the way they ought to think. Which is wrong, because I'm only a musician. If they dig my music, that's great, but they don't have to know what's going on in my head.

That's because of the Beatles.

Yeah.

In London they used to say, "Clapton is God."

Wow! It's still going on! Yeah, that was going on—well, when nothing else was happening in England except me, which was a pretty weird period, you know. Like there was nothing much in the charts and I'd just left the Yardbirds and had joined John Mayall, and it was like our band, the John Mayall Band, was the only one playing like the Chicago blues. And at that time it had just begun to become fashionable—a lot of people grabbed hold of my name and started using it, you know—and people were starting to write "Clapton is God" all over the place without really knowing what they were talking about. Very funny. Very strange.

What is it like to have that?

I don't know because I don't know what the image is.

When you look into their eyes you must get some interesting feedback.

Yeah, and most of the time it's pretty disappointing. A lot of that kind of appreciation I get is usually for like what kind of shoes I'm wearing tonight. I don't think I've had that many people on the same wavelength as me—you know, appreciating me for the same reason that I appreciate me. I really can't see into their minds to see if the image is one I would like or wouldn't like. I'm basically against that, anyway. There's very funny things that would go on—like, at one gig I would wear a red military jacket, and for some reason I'd play and everyone would suddenly get knocked out. And then we'd do the next gig a couple of weeks later somewhere else, and everyone in the audience would be wearing red military jackets. And I'd have a mustache and be wearing a green suede jacket and everyone would be going—What have we done wrong? That's the kind of thing it usually amounts to.

It's not that big, you see. If I was in the position of someone like Dylan or Lennon, then I'd have to be more careful. People at most hardly ever say they like music, they hardly ever say they think I'm a good guitar player. No one has ever sort of yet committed suicide because of me, and it probably will never happen. So I mean, I'm not that much of an idol for me to think I have any responsibility, you know. So, unless anything drastic ever happens, I don't think I'll ever have to worry about that.

How do you feel about the sexual implications?

I admit, I have tried it. I've tried it like— when I was with the Yardbirds I did do it all the time. It was an obviously novel thing to try and do. You come out of school, you know, and you get into a group and you've got thousands of chicks there. I mean, you were at school and you were pimply and no one wanted to know you. And then there you are onstage with thousands of little girls screaming their heads off. Man, it's *power!* . . whew! But when you find something else that can occupy your mind a little more— like when you find that you're actually into playing the guitar, then I don't think you could do both things. I couldn't do it now mainly because I don't have the time to stop and think about it. If I was doing that, leaping around, then I'd just play chords. If I want to play and do something which is a conscious effort to do, then I can't do anything but stand still and think about what I'm doing.

Do you go through hassles at the airport when you get back to London?

No, we're not on that scene at all. We don't interest the kids under eighteen. Did you mean fans?

No. I meant being searched for drugs—due to the special notoriety musicians now have in England for being dope fiends.

Oh, yes. We get searched every time we go back to England. They never make it clear they're looking for drugs. But you can never pick the brain of a customs inspector. They might let you through sometime and might search you another time. He might let you through with a

brick of hashish sometimes. They don't make it clear what they're going to do. They're unpredictable. They might let you through with a big block of hashish and get you another time because they think you think you can get away with it all the time.

What hits you the most about San Francisco?

The first thing that hit me really hard was that the Grateful Dead were playing a lot of gigs for nothing. That very much moved me. I've never heard of anyone doing that before. That really is one of the finest steps that anyone has taken in music yet, aside from musical strides. I guess that sums it up, what I think about San Francisco, what the Grateful Dead are doing. There is this incredible thing that the musical people seem to have toward their audience; they want to give.

That ought to make an incredible headline in England.

Shit! That's the most incredible thing, man. Whenever I do any kind of interview in London, I'll say a complete paragraph, all of which will make sense as a paragraph, but someone will take three words out of it and put it on top and make it controversial. In some Irish paper I was asked if the Beatles would ever play onstage again. I went into this flowery thing about how the Beatles, if they did, would be incredible because they would put on a circus and it would be an incredible thing. I said they wouldn't just go on and only play, it would probably be very difficult for them. The paper put as a headline, "Clapton thinks the Beatles couldn't play onstage." That always happens.

Out of this, you could get the headline, "Clapton shits on London."

It's gonna happen. It's great now because musicians now are so tight among each other that they go "fuck" about if they read something that they don't think is right. Like George Harrison reads something that I say about him that he doesn't believe to be true, he doesn't believe it, 'cause I'm not going to say anything shitty behind his back. The English music papers aren't taken seriously. The drag is the kids might think it's true.

Anything else to get over?

I'd like to give everyone my love, and say hello to Auntie Flo and the kids.

5

INTERVIEWED BY JANN WENNER (1968)

For his first full-length ROLLING STONE Interview, Jann Wenner picked Pete Townshend, and for good reasons.

"The Who," he says, "were one of ROLLING STONE's original favorite bands. I saw them at their American debut at the Monterey Pop Festival in 1967, and later that year at the Cow Palace in San Francisco." The Who were still comparatively unknown in the United States, and Wenner recalls the band being "squashed in the middle of a rather dumpy concert, one of those eight-act packages that used to tour the country." After the show, he interviewed Townshend for an article in issue number four.

In the fall of 1968, the Who were back. By now they were a sensation, and this would be their second time headlining a three-night stand that year in San Francisco (first, in February, at the old Fillmore; now, in August, at the Fillmore West). This time, Townshend did the ROLLING STONE Interview.

"Peter Townshend was twenty-three years old when we sat talking at my house in San Francisco into the dawn hours," Wenner has written. "And a year or two later, Townshend told me that during our interview he articulated to himself, for the first time comprehensively, the basic plan for what became *Tommy*. And that brought back to my mind a remark he had made at the time, which I had edited out. We'd been drinking orange juice, and in the middle of a long and wandering answer he asked if I had spiked his drink. Those were the halcyon hip days in San Francisco, and when I asked him what he meant by 'spiked,' he said he felt as though he were beginning an LSD trip. I hadn't slipped him anything."

—BF-T

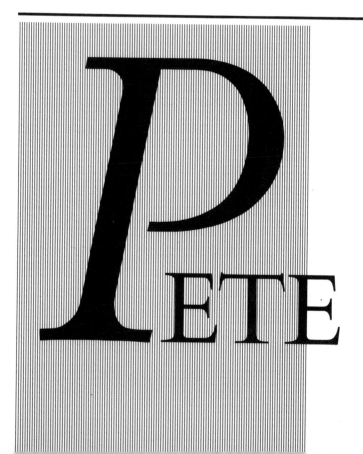

PETE

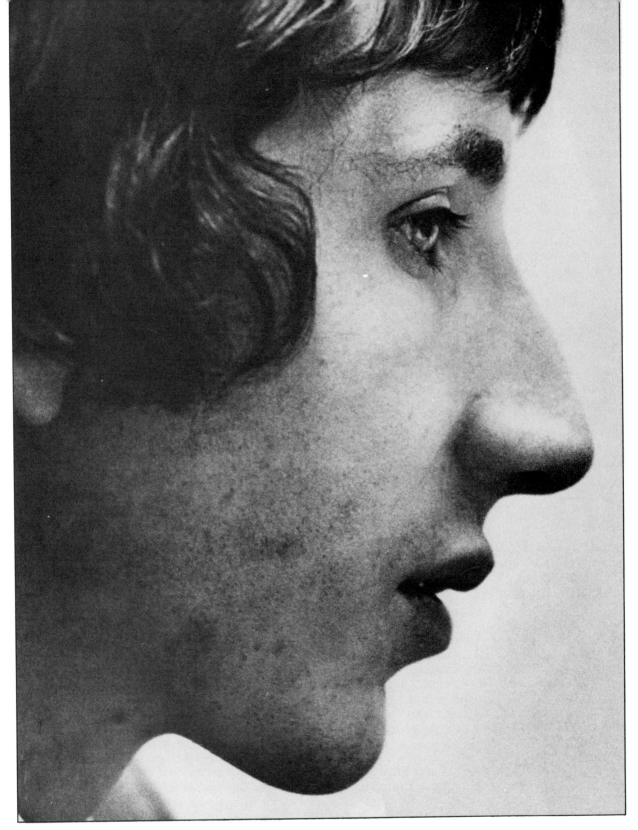

TOWNSHEND

*THE WHO {GUITARIST PETE TOWN-
shend, singer Roger Daltrey, drummer Keith Moon
and bass guitarist John Entwistle} are the most
brilliant expression of the most influential "youth
movement" ever to take Great Britain, the Mods.
Their career began in Shepherd's Bush, a lower-class
suburb of London, and took them through such places
as Brighton-by-the-Sea, scene of the great Mod-Rocker
battles of the early Sixties. Their first big recording
was "My Generation." Pete Townshend, the well-
known guitarist, is the group's main force, the author
of most of the material, the composer of most of the
music and the impetus behind the Who's stylistic
stance.*

*The Who's generation has gotten older, and the
change is seen in their records: "The Kids Are Alright"
to "Happy Jack"; and from "Happy Jack" to girls and
boys with perspiration, pimple and bad breath problems. And, as can be seen from the interview, the
changes continue.*

*This interview began at 2:00 a.m., after the Who's
second 1968 appearance at the Fillmore West in San
Francisco. Nobody quite remembers exactly under what
circumstances it was concluded.*

THE END OF YOUR ACT GOES TO
"My Generation," like you usually do,
and that's where you usually smash your
guitar. You didn't tonight—why not?

Well, there is a reason, not really
anything that's really worth talking about. But
I'll explain the pattern of thought which went
into it.

I've obviously broken a lot of guitars, and I've
brought eight or nine of that particular guitar I
was using tonight and I could very easily have
broken it and have plenty more for the future.
But I just suddenly decided before I went on that
if there was anywhere in the world I should be
able to walk off the stage without breaking a
guitar if I didn't want to, it would be the
Fillmore.

I decided in advance that I didn't want to
smash the guitar, so I didn't, not because I liked
it or because I've decided I'm going to stop doing
it or anything. I just kind of decided about the
actual situation; it forced me to see if I could
have gotten away with it in advance. And I think
that's why "My Generation" was such a down
number at the end. I didn't really want to play
it, you know, at all. I didn't even want people to
expect it to happen, because I just wasn't going
to do it.

*But Keith still dumped over his drum kit like he
usually does.*

Yeah, but it was an incredible personal thing
with me. I've often gone on the stage with a
guitar and said, "Tonight I'm not going to
smash a guitar and I don't give a shit"—you
know what the pressure is on me—whether I feel
like doing it musically or whatever, I'm just not
going to do it. And I've gone on, and *every* time
I've done it. The actual performance has always
been bigger than my own patterns of thought.

Tonight, for some reason, I went on and I
said, "I'm not going to break it," and I didn't.
And I don't know how, I don't really know why I
didn't. But I didn't, you know, and it's the first
time. I mean, I've said it millions of times
before, and nothing has happened.

*I imagine it gets to be a drag talking about why you
smash your guitar.*

No, it doesn't get to be a drag to talk about it.
Sometimes it gets a drag to do it. I can explain
it, I can justify it and I can enhance it, and I can
do a lot of things, dramatize it and literalize it.
Basically it's a gesture which happens on the spur
of the moment. I think, with guitar smashing,
just like performance itself; it's a performance,
it's an act, it's an instant and it really is
meaningless.

When did you start smashing guitars?

It happened by complete accident the first
time. We were just kicking around in a club
which we played every Tuesday, and I was
playing the guitar and it hit the ceiling. It
broke, and it kind of shocked me 'cause I wasn't
ready for it to go. I didn't particularly want it to
go, but it went.

And I was expecting an incredible thing, it
being so precious to me, and I was expecting
everybody to go, "Wow, he's broken his guitar,
he's broken his guitar," but nobody did anything, which made me kind of angry in a way
and determined to get this precious event noticed
by the audience. I proceeded to make a big thing
of breaking the guitar. I pounded all over the
stage with it, and I threw the bits on the stage,
and I picked up my spare guitar and carried on as
though I really meant to do it.

Were you happy about it?

Deep inside I was very unhappy because the
thing had got broken. It got around, and the
next week the people came, and they came up to
me and they said, "Oh, we heard all about it,
man; it's 'bout time someone gave it to a guitar,"
and all this kind of stuff. It kind of grew from
there; we'd go to another town and people would
say "Oh yeah, we heard that you smashed a

34

guitar." It built and built and built and built and built and built until one day, a very important daily newspaper came to see us and said, "Oh, we hear you're the group that smashes their guitars up. Well, we hope you're going to do it tonight because we're from the *Daily Mail.* If you do, you'll probably make the front pages."

This was only going to be like the second guitar I'd ever broken, seriously. I went to my manager, Kit Lambert, and I said, you know, "Can we afford it, can we afford it, it's for publicity." He said, "Yes, we can afford it, if we can get the *Daily Mail.*" I did it, and of course the *Daily Mail* didn't buy the photograph and didn't want to know about the story. After that I was into it up to my neck and have been doing it since.

Was it inevitable that you were going to start smashing guitars?

It was due to happen because I was getting to the point where I'd play and I'd play, and I mean, I still can't play how I'd like to play. *Then* it was worse. I couldn't play the guitar; I'd listen to great music, I'd listen to all the people I dug, time and time again. When the Who first started we were playing blues, and I dug the blues and I knew what I was supposed to be playing, but I couldn't play it. I couldn't get it out. I knew what I had to play; it was in my head. I could hear the notes in my head, but I couldn't get them out on the guitar. I knew the music, and I knew the feeling of the thing and the drive and the direction and everything.

It used to frustrate me incredibly. I used to try and make up visually for what I couldn't play as a musician. I used to get into very incredible visual things where in order just to make one chord more lethal, I'd make it a really lethal-looking thing, whereas really, it's just going to be picked normally. I'd hold my arm up in the air and bring it down so it really looked lethal, even if it didn't sound too lethal. Anyway, this got bigger and bigger and bigger and bigger until eventually I was setting myself incredible tasks.

How did this affect your guitar playing?

Instead I said, "All right, you're not capable of doing it musically, you've got to do it visually." I became a huge, visual thing. In fact, I forgot all about the guitar because my visual thing was more my music than the actual guitar. I got to jump about, and the guitar became unimportant. I banged it and I let it feed back and scraped it and rubbed it up against the microphone, did anything; it wasn't part of my act, even. It didn't deserve any credit or any respect. I used to bang it and hit it against walls and throw it on the floor at the end of the act.

And one day it broke. It just wasn't part of my thing, and ever since then I've never really regarded myself as a guitarist. When people come up to me and say like, "Who's your favorite guitarist?" I say, "I know who my favorite guitarist is, but asking me, as a guitarist, forget it because I don't make guitar-type comments. I don't talk guitar talk, I just throw the thing around." Today still, I'm learning. If I play a solo, it's a game to me because I can't play what I want to play. That's the thing: I can't get it out because I don't practice. When I should be practicing, I'm writing songs, and when I'm writing songs, I should be practicing.

You said you spend most of your time writing songs in your basement.

A lot of writing I do on tour. I do a lot on airplanes. At home, I write a lot, obviously. When I write a song, what I usually do is work the lyric out first from some basic idea that I had, and then I get an acoustic guitar and I sit by the tape recorder and I try to bang it out as it comes. Try to let the music come with the lyrics. If I dig it, I want to add things to it, like I'll add bass guitar or drums or another voice. This is really for my own amusement that I do this.

The reason "I Can See for Miles" came out good was because I sat down and *made* it good from the beginning. The fact that I did a lot of work on arrangements and stuff like that doesn't really count. I think that unless the actual song itself is good, you know, you can do all kinds of incredible things to it, but you're never gonna get it, not unless the meat and potatoes are there. Although I do fuck around in home studios and things like that, I think it's of no importance; I don't think it's really got anything to do with what makes the Who the Who.

Does what you write in your home studio ever come out on records?

Most of it gets out, but the recordings I make myself in my own studio don't. They might in the future, but they would only come out if they had the Who on them. To put out a record of me banging away on guitar or bass drums collectively and generally being a one-man band wouldn't be a very good idea. I'd like to use my studio to·record the group because interesting things·happen in small environmental sound-recording situations like Sony tape recorders, for example, which don't happen in studios. It's a well-known fact.

When you work out an arrangement and figure out the bass line and the various voices, is that just directly translated onto a record that would be released?

More or less, but then we don't really take it that grimly; I mean, what happens is I will suggest the bass riff on the demonstration record; John takes up and goes from there. But the bass (line) I would suggest on the demo, as I said earlier, would be very simple; it would be economical, tasteful and just a vehicle for the song, making the bass line, and, if I use them, the piano or drum, as simple and effective as possible in putting the song across to the group.

Instead of me hacking my songs around to billions of publishers trying to get them to dig them, what I've got to do is get the rest of the band to dig my number. If I've got a number that I dig, I know that I've got to present it to them in the best light. That's why I make my own recordings so when they first hear it, it's not me stoned out of my mind plunking away on a guitar trying to get my latest number across. It's a finished work that might take me all night to get together, but nevertheless it's gonna win them over.

I'm working on the lyrics now for the next album. When we get through that, all the lyrics cleaned out, we'll start to work through the album. We'll probably have to do it in short sections, like fifteen-minute sections. Ideally, I'd like to record one backing track for the whole album whether it lasts for two hours or two days. We sit down and we do it in one go, and then okay, we spend the next two years adding tarty voices or whatever it is that it takes to sell the record. But at least you know that what's happening in the background is real meat and immediate meat, and it's part of the present.

The whole thing about recording is that a man feels slightly cheated anyway, because he's getting a *recording* of something which has happened, so he feels like he's getting something secondhand. If he thinks he's being fucked around already, this is a whole different thing. A lot of people, I'm convinced, that buy records don't realize what happens when a group records on an eight-track machine. They don't realize that they record half of it one time, and then another eighth of it another time. They record it in eighths at different locations, and this ceases to become music to me.

What other ideas in this field do you have?

Well, the album concept in general is complex. I don't know if I can explain it in my condition, at the moment. But it's derived as a result of quite a few things. We've been talking about doing an opera, we've been talking about doing like albums, we've been talking about a whole lot of things and what has basically happened is that we've condensed all of these ideas, all this energy and all these gimmicks, and whatever we've decided on for future albums, into one juicy package. The package I hope is going to be called "Deaf, Dumb and Blind Boy." It's a story about a kid that's born deaf, dumb and blind and what happens to him throughout his life. The deaf, dumb and blind boy is played by the Who, the musical entity. He's represented musically, represented by a theme which we play, which starts off the opera itself, and then there's a song describing the deaf, dumb and blind boy. But what it's really all about is the fact that because the boy is "D, D & B," he's seeing things basically as vibrations which we translate as music. That's really what we want to do: create this feeling that when you listen to the music you can actually become aware of the boy, and aware of what he is all about, because we are creating him as we play.

Yes, it's a pretty far-out thing, actually. But it's very, very endearing to me because the thing is . . . inside; the boy sees things musically and in dreams, and nothing has got any weight at all. He is touched from the outside, and he feels his mother's touch, he feels his father's touch, but he just interprets them as music. His father gets pretty upset that his kid is deaf, dumb and blind. He wants a kid that will play football and God knows what.

One night he comes in and he's drunk, and he sits over the kid's bed and he looks at him and he starts to talk to him, and the kid just smiles up, and his father is trying to get through to him, telling him about how the other dads have a kid that they can take to football and they can teach them to play football and all this kind of crap, and he starts to say, "Can you hear me?" The kid, of course, can't hear him. He's groovin' in this musical thing, this incredible musical thing; he'll be out of his mind. Then there's his father outside, outside of his body, and this song is going to be written by John. I hope John will write this song about the father who is really uptight now.

The kid won't respond, he just smiles. The father starts to hit him, and at this moment the whole thing becomes incredibly realistic. On one side you have the dreamy music of the boy wasting through his nothing life. And on the other you have the reality of the father outside, uptight, but now you've got blows, you've got communication. The father is hitting the kid;

musically then I want the thing to break out, hand it over to Keith—"This is your scene, man, take it from here."

And the kid doesn't catch the violence. He just knows that some sensation is happening. He doesn't feel the pain, he doesn't associate it with anything. He just accepts it.

A similar situation happens later on in the opera, where the father starts to get the mother to take the kid away from home to an uncle. The uncle is a bit of a perv, you know. He plays with the kid's body while the kid is out. And at this particular time the child has heard his own name; his mother called him. And he managed to hear the word: "Tommy." He's really got this big thing about his name, whatever his name is going to be, you know, "Tommy." And he gets really hung up on his own name. He decides that this is the king and this is the goal. Tommy is the thing, man.

He's going through this, and the uncle comes in and starts to go through a scene with the kid's body, you know, and the boy experiences sexual vibrations, you know, sexual experience, and again it's just basic music; it's interpreted as music, and it is nothing more than music. It's got no association with sleaziness or with undercover or with any of the things normally associated with sex. None of the romance, none of the visual stimulus, none of the sound stimulus. Just basic touch. Its *meaningless.* Or not meaningless; you just don't react, you know. Slowly but surely the kid starts to get it together, out of this simplicity, this incredible simplicity in his mind. He starts to realize that he can see, and he can hear, and he can speak; they are there, and they are happening all the time. And that all the time he has been able to hear and see. All the time it's been there in front of him, for him to see.

This is the difficult jump. It's going to be extremely difficult, but we want to try to do it musically. At this point, the theme, which has been the boy, starts to change. You start to realize that he is coming to the point where he is going to get over the top, he's going to get over his hang-ups. You're gonna stop monkeying around with songs about people being tinkered with, and with Father's getting uptight, with Mother's getting precious and things, and you're gonna get down to the fact of what is going to happen to the kid.

The music has got to explain what happens, that the boy elevates and finds something which is incredible. To us, it's nothing to be able to see

and hear and speak, but to him, it's absolutely incredible and overwhelming; this is what we want to do musically. Lyrically, it's quite easy to do it; in fact, I've written it out several times. It makes great poetry, but so much depends on the music, so much. I'm hoping that we can do it. The lyrics are going to be okay, but every pitfall of what we're trying to say lies in the music, lies in the way we play the music, the way we interpret, the way things are going during the opera.

The main characters are going to be the boy and his musical things; he's got a mother and father and an uncle. There is a doctor involved who tries to do some psychiatric treatment on the kid which is only partly successful. The first two big events are when he hears his mother calling him and hears the word "Tommy," and he devotes a whole part of his life to this one word. The second important event is when he sees himself in a mirror, suddenly seeing himself for the first time: He takes an immediate back step, bases his whole life around his own image. The whole thing then becomes incredibly introverted. The music and the lyrics become introverted, and he starts to talk about himself, starts to talk about his beauty. Not knowing, of course, that what he saw was him but still regarding it as something which belonged to him, and of course it did all of the time anyway.

It's a very complex thing, and I don't know if I'm getting it across.

You are.

Because I don't feel at all together.

I know you don't look it, but you're coming on very together.

Good.

T*HIS THEME, NOT SO DRAMATically, seems to be repeated in so many songs that you've written and the Who have performed—a young cat, our age, becoming an outcast from a very ordinary sort of circumstance. Not a "Desolation Row" scene, but a very common set of middle-class situations. Why does this repeat itself?*

I don't know. I never really thought about that.

There's a boy with pimple problems and a chick with perspiration troubles and so on.

Most of those things just come from me. Like this idea I'm talking about right now, comes from me. These things are my ideas, it's probably why they all come out the same; they've all got the same fuckups, I'm sure.

I can't get my family together, you see. My family were musicians. They were essentially middle class, they were musicians, and I spent a lot of time with them when other kids' parents were at work, and I spent a lot of time *away* from them when other kids had parents, you know. That was the way it came together. They were always out for long periods. But they were always home for long periods, too. They were always very respectable—nobody ever stopped making me play the guitar and nobody ever stopped me smoking pot, although they advised me against it.

They didn't stop me from doing anything that I wanted to do. I had my first fuck in the drawing room of my mother's house. The whole incredible thing about my parents is that I just can't place their effect on me, and yet I know that it's there. I can't say how they affected me. When people find out that my parents are musicians, they ask how it affected me. Fucked if I know; musically, I can't place it, and I can't place it in any other way. But I don't even feel myself aware of a class structure, or an age structure, and yet I perpetually write about age structures and class structures. On the surface I feel much more concerned with racial problems and politics. Inside I'm much more into basic stuff.

You must have thought about where it comes from if it's not your parents. Was it the scene around you when you were young?

One of the things which has impressed me most in life was the Mod movement in England, which was an incredible youthful thing. It was a movement of young people, much bigger than the hippie thing, the underground and all these things. It was an army, a powerful, aggressive army of teenagers with transport. Man, with these scooters and with their own way of dressing. It was acceptable, this was important; their way of dressing was hip, it was fashionable, it was clean and it was groovy. You could be a bank clerk, man, it was acceptable. You got them on your own ground. They thought, "Well, there's a smart young lad." And also you were hip, you didn't get people uptight. That was the good thing about it. To be a mod, you had to have short hair, money enough to buy a real smart suit, good shoes, good shirts; you had to be able to dance like a madman. You had to be in possession of plenty of pills all the time and always be pilled up. You had to have a scooter covered in lamps. You had to have like an army

anourak to wear on the scooter. And that was being a mod, and that was the end of the story.

The groups that you liked when you were a mod were the Who. That's the story of why I dig the mods, man, because we were mods and that's how we happened. That's my generation, that's how the song "My Generation" happened, because of the mods. The mods could appreciate the Beatles' taste. They could appreciate their haircuts, their peculiar kinky things that they had going at the time.

What would happen is that the phenomena of the Who could invoke action. The sheer fact that four mods could actually form themselves into a group which sounded quite good, considering that most mods were lower-class garbagemen, you know, with enough money to buy himself Sunday best, you know, their people. Nowadays, okay, there are quite a few mod groups. But mods aren't the kind of people that could play the guitar, and it was just groovy for them to have a group. Our music at the time was representative of what the mods dug, and it was meaningless rubbish.

We used to play, for example, "Heat Wave," a very long version of "Smokestack Lightning," and that song we sang tonight, "Young Man Blues," fairly inconsequential kind of music which they could identify with and perhaps something where you banged your feet on the third beat or clapped your hands on the fifth beat, something so that you get the thing to go by. I mean, they used to like all kinds of things. They were mods and we're mods and we dig them. We used to make sure that if there was a riot, a mod-rocker riot, we would be playing in the area. That was a place called Brighton.

By the sea?

Yes. That's where they used to assemble. We'd always be playing there. And we got associated with the whole thing, and we got into the spirit of the whole thing. And, of course, rock & roll, the words wouldn't even be mentioned; the fact that music would have any part of the movement was terrible. The music would come from the actual drive of the youth combination itself.

You see, as individuals these people were nothing. They were the lowest, they were England's lowest common denominators. Not only were they young, they were also lower-class young. They had to submit to the middle class' way of dressing and way of speaking and way of acting in order to get the very jobs which kept them alive. They had to do everything in terms of what existed already around them. That made their way of getting something across that much more latently effective, the fact that they were hip and yet still, as far as Granddad was concerned, exactly the same. It made the whole gesture so much more vital. It was incredible. As a force, they were unbelievable. That was the Bulge, that was England's Bulge; all the war babies, all the old soldiers coming back from war and screwing until they were blue in the face—this was the result. Thousands and thousands of kids, too many kids, not enough teachers, not enough parents, not enough pills to go around. Everybody just grooving on being a mod.

How do you think that compares with what's called today the American hippie scene?

I think it compares. I think the hippie thing compares favorably, but it's a different motivation. There are beloved figures. There is pot, there is acid, there is the Maharishi, there is the Beatles, there is being anti-the-U.S.A., there are a whole lot of red herrings, which aren't what it's all about. What it is all about is *the hippies,* you know, that's what it's all about. The people, the actions, not the events, not the tripping out or the latest fad or the latest record or the latest trip or the latest thing to groove to. The thing is people.

This is what they seem to overlook. You see, this is the thing about the media barrage—you become aware only of the products around you because they're glorified, and so that when somebody gets stoned, what they do is that they don't groove to themselves, really, they just sit around and they dig everything that's around them. They perhaps dig other people. They dig the way the room looks. The way the flowers look, the way the music sounds, the way the group performs, how good the Beatles are. "How nice that is." They never say, "How fantastic am I." This is the whole thing: they're far too abject in outlook, they're far too concerned with what is feeding into them and not so much with what they are. This is the difference between the mod thing in England and the hippie thing over here. The hippies are waiting for information, because information is perpetually coming in, and they sit there and wait for it.

This is the incredible thing about the States, man. To get stoned in England is an entirely different trip. I'm not saying that you get stoned and you dig yourself or anything. What you would do is you would get stoned, perhaps you'd walk out and look at a tree or a matchstick or something and come back and have a cup of tea and then go to bed, man. But over here, you just carry on regardless. You go to Orange Julius and

you have an Orange Julius, and you watch TV and then you listen to some records, played very, very loud, and you know, it's a whole different pattern, a whole different way.

The acceptance of what one already has is the thing. Whereas the mod thing was the rejection of everything one already had. You didn't want to know about the fucking TV. "Take it away," you know. You didn't want to know about the politicians, you didn't want to know about the war. If there had been a draft, man, they would have just disappeared. If there had been a draft, there wouldn't have been mods, because something like that—the thing was that it was a sterile situation, it was perfect. It was almost too perfect.

Over here it's imperfect, it's not a sterile situation. The group themselves can't become powerful because they can be weakened at so many points. They can be weakened by their education, by their spirituality, by their intelligence, by the sheer fact that Americans are more highly educated. The average American and the average Englishman, and the Englishmen I'm talking about are people that probably left school when they were fourteen or fifteen. Some of them can't even read or write. But yet there were mods, they were like—you see something nearer, I suppose, in what it's like to be a Hell's Angel, but not as much flash, not as much gimmicking, much less part of a huge machine.

CAN YOU PIN DOWN SOME OF *the elements that make rock & roll what it is, starting with the basic elements . . . it's got the beat.*

It's a bigger thing than that. The reason it's got to have a beat is the fact that rock & roll music has got to have that bounce; it's got to have that thing to make you swing; it's got to swing in an old-fashioned sense; in other words, it's got to undulate. It's got to have a rhythm which undulates. It can't be a rhythm which you count down in a long drone like classical music. It doesn't have to be physical because when you think of a lot of Beatles music, it's very nonphysical. Like *Sgt. Pepper's* is an incredibly nonphysical album. If I hear something like the *Electric Flag* album, I jump up and dance, and I hardly get to hear the music because I'm so busy jumping up dancing.

But when I hear something like "Summertime Blues," then I do both, then I'm into rock & roll; then I'm into a way of life, into that thing about being that age and being this age and grooving to that thing that he's talking about which is, like, summertime and, like, not being able to get off work early and not being able to get out in the sunshine and not being able to borrow the car because Dad's in a foul mood. All those frustrations of summer so wonderfully and so simply, so poetically, put in this incredible package, the package being rock & roll.

There's the package, there's the vehicle. Not only is it about some incredible poignant experiences, but it's also a *gas*. The whole thing about rock & roll dynamism, in many ways, is the fact that if it does slow down, if it does start to review itself, if it takes any sort of perspective on life at all, it falls. As soon as someone makes any comment, for example, musically on something they've done before, they collapse.

You talked about maturing and settling down. How has this affected you?

It gives me a far more logical time aspect on the group. I'm not as frantically working as I used to. I always used to work with the thought in my mind that the Who were gonna last precisely another two minutes. If the tax man didn't get us, then our own personality clashes would. I never would have believed that the Who would still be together today and, of course, I'm delighted and love it. Nothing can be better really than waking up in the morning and everything is still the same as it was the day before. That's the best thing you can have in life, consistency of some kind.

It always amazes me. As an individual, it's given me an incredible freedom and all. I know that I don't have to do things like I used to. Our manager will create artificial pressures to try and get me to operate, but I know they are artificial so they don't work like they used to. "My Generation" was written under pressure; someone came to me and said, "Make a statement, make a statement, make a statement, make a statement, make a statement," and I'm going, "Oh, okay, okay, okay," and I get "My Generation" together very quickly, like in a night—it feels like that. It's a very blustering kind of blurting thing. A lot of our early records were. "I Can't Explain" was a blurter and a bluster, and "Anyway, Anyhow, Anywhere," which was our second record, was just a brag, like, you know, nothing more. "Substitute" was a takeoff on Mick Jagger or something equally banal.

The whole structure of our early songs was very, very simple. Now, with less pressure, I have to create the pressures for myself. I have to excite myself by myself. I have to say this is what we're going to do, this is what you mustn't do, this is what the Who are going to do, this is what you've got to get the Who to do, this is what you've got to ask the Who to do for you. You set yourself these pressures so that now the important thing is that the Who are the impetus behind the ideas, rather than the pressure of pop music being the impetus behind the ideas and not even the ideas. The fact was that pressure was the impetus behind the music that we used to play, whereas now our music is far more realistically geared to the time in which our audience moves.

Pop audiences and pop musicians are geared to different time structures; they lead different lives entirely. They say it's very difficult to go and see a group and feel totally in with what they're doing because they're on a different time trip. They are doing one gig out of a hundred gigs, whereas to the fan this is a very important occasion, like this is the only chance he's gonna get to see, say, the Cream and never again in his life.

For the group, it's another gig, and they're going to be on the road in another ten minutes, and the fan is going to catch a section of something which as a whole is a complicated network to them. This is important to us in our compositions. The point is not to belittle each thing. It's all very well to say, "Oh, well, it's good to have the pressure because it's the pressure that makes the music move and wild and groovy," but the music becomes thrown-out, tossed-out ideas which aren't really good. They are as much as you can give out. They are not a hundred percent.

If you slow down just a little bit and gear yourself to your audience, you can give them one hundred percent. If you do a slightly longer set on the stage, you can give all instead of having to cram a lot of unused energy into guitar smashing, for example. Unchanneled energy or misdirected energy is incredible in pop music, incredible. Like the Beatles know how to channel their fucking energy. I'm convinced that there's not a lot actually coming out, it's just that we get *all* of it. We get a hundred percent Beatles album. We don't get any halves; they know that they are in a position and they've got it together and they do.

What groups do you enjoy the most?

It's difficult to say. I always forget the groups that I really dig. I like to watch a band with a punch, with drive, who know what they're doing, with a tight sound. I used to like to watch Jimi Hendrix; sometimes he worries me now because he often gets amplifier hang-ups and stuff. I can't stand that, it kills me. I used to like to watch Cream until they got sad and fucked up. I still dig to watch a group like the Young Rascals, who just walk on with their incredibly perfect sound and their lovely organ and they're so easy, the way their numbers flow out, just to watch a group stand and go through their thing so beautifully. I dig that. I dig a guy like Otis Redding and Aretha Franklin. She's been standing still and singing the blues all night, and then when she's really into it she'll do a tiny little dance and just get her little feet going, very slightly; just a little jog, and in terms of what she's doing with her voice, it's an incredible gesture and really goes mad. I dig Mick Jagger, who I think is an incredible show, and Arthur Brown I think is an incredible show, too. What I dig in a performance, in an event, is essentially to be communicated to, to feel part of an audience. I always feel like an audience because I am an audience if I am watching anything, but I like to feel alongside the other members of things, I like to feel a part of the audience; I like to feel that I'm being effective as a member of the audience. I don't mind being asked to clap my fucking hands, let's get that straight. I like to clap my hands, and it doesn't get me uptight if someone says clap or sing or shout or scream or do what you want to do. That's exactly what I want to do, and if I feel like jumping up and down and dancing, I don't want everyone telling me that I'm bringing them down or that they can't listen to the music or something. People should be an audience, and if it's time-to-get-up-and-dance-time, everybody should do it at the same time.

This happened when Otis Redding appeared, that's what happened. When he wanted them to sit down he said, "And now we're going to play a soulful tune," and sang in a soulful way and was dead still, and when he wanted them to get up and dance he said, "Come on, clap your hands, get up and dance," and they did, man, grooved right along with him.

When you're listening to Ravi Shankar, you know what you've got to do. When you're in the Who's audience, you know—I like to know where I am. I like to go and see a group and know what my role is. I like to know whether or not I'm supposed to listen attentively, whether I'm supposed to groove, whether I'm supposed to do anything constructive, whether I'm invited up to jam or what. I like to know where I'm at. It's usually the most professional groups that give you this feeling.

Performers like Aretha Franklin, Otis Redding, Mick Jagger, Jimi Hendrix, the Who, all are tremendously physical, tremendously sensual, tremendously involved with very sexual things. Does this characterize rock & roll?

It must! It must. I mean, it does. Period. It embodies it, it's part of its life. Life revolves, if not around it, within it, if not within it, without it, but definitely along with it. Something about rock & roll has to do with sex and everything to do with sex, like becoming together and the parting and this kind of thing. The whole thing about pulling a chick and then waving goodbye. The whole process of sex is embodied in just the rock & roll rhythm—like gospel music or like native chants or something. Just banging the table is like it's the demand, and it's also the satiation as well. You bang on the table and in the same process you masturbate, you know. At the end of the show you're finished, you know, you've had it. You've come your lot, and the show's over.

"Rock me baby until my back ain't got no bone." That is the line. Man, it's such a funny line, I can never believe it. I imagine some very skinny, wizened old Negro blues singer singing that in a very frail old voice: "Rock me baby 'til my back ain't got no bone."

I forget if I read this or whether it is something Glyn Johns told me. You and the group came out of this rough, tough area, were very restless and had this thing: You were going to show everybody; you were a kid with a big nose, and you were going to make all these people love it, love your big nose.

That was probably a mixture of what Glyn told you and an article I wrote. In fact, Glyn was exactly the kind of person I wanted to show. Glyn used to be one of the people who, right when I walked in, he'd be on the stage singing. I'd walk in because I dug his group. I'd often go to see him, and he would announce through the microphone, "Look at that bloke in the audience with that huge nose" and of course the whole audience would turn around and look at me, and that would be acknowledgment from Glyn.

When I was in school the geezers that were snappy dressers and got chicks like years before I ever even thought they existed would always like to talk about my nose. This seemed to be the biggest thing in my life: my fucking nose, man. Whenever my dad got drunk, he'd come up to me and say, "Look, son, you know, looks aren't everything," and shit like this. He's getting drunk, and he's ashamed of me because I've got a huge nose, and he's trying to make me feel good. I know it's huge, and of course it became

41

incredible, and I became an enemy of society. I had to get over this thing. I've done it, and I never believe it to this day, but I do not think about my nose anymore. And if I had said this when I was a kid, if I ever said to myself, "One of these days you'll go through a whole day without once thinking that your nose is the biggest in the world, man"—you know, I'd have laughed.

It was huge. At that time, it was the reason I did everything. It's the reason I played the guitar—because of my nose. The reason I wrote songs was because of my nose, everything, so much. I eventually admitted something in an article where I summed it up far more logically in terms of what I do today. I said that what I wanted to do was distract attention from my nose to my body and make people look at my body, instead of at my face—turn my body into a machine. But by the time I was into visual things like that, anyway, I'd forgotten all about my nose and a big ego trip, and I thought, well, if I've got a big nose, it's a groove and it's the greatest thing that can happen because, I don't know, it's like a lighthouse or something. The whole trip had changed by then, anyway.

What is your life like today?

Mainly laughs, actually, mainly laughs. The Who on tour is a very difficult trip; it's a delicate one, and it could be dangerous. So it's best to keep this on the humorous side. If we take this situation seriously, we tend to feedback. Like one person gets a slight down and the rest of us get a slight down, and so we have to keep spirits up even if it's false, even if it's jokes that aren't funny, just in order to get someone to laugh. This is what it's all about to me now.

What is going to happen to rock & roll?

I'm looking to a couple of people. I've heard some of the Rolling Stones' tracks, and although I dig them I don't think they're anything more than what they are which is incredible, delicious and wonderful rock & roll and well overdue from them. The Rolling Stones should always be a nonprogressive group. I don't think that the Rolling Stones should be concerned with what they're doing in pop. That's what I dig about them.

Dylan, for example, could create a new thing. I think if he made his next record with the Big Pink, that could be interesting. That might create some new things in rock & roll. Dylan's thing about writing the lyric and then picking the guitar up and just pumping out the song as it comes out is a direct guide to what will happen in music.

People are going to want music to be more realistic, more honest and more of a gift from the *heart,* rather than a gift from the lungs, as it were. Instead of wanting to go and watch Ginger Baker run six miles before your very eyes, you'd rather dig what he's doing. I think this is what's happening.

People are always trying to find a parallel with jazz. Do you see what happened to jazz, happening here?

No. Jazz totally absolutely boiled down to a different kettle of fish. Because of the audiences. Audiences were a different breed entirely. If you're talking about the days when the people used to do the Black Bottom, then maybe you're getting nearer to what pop music is equivalent to today.

Pop is more than the Black Bottom; pop is more than short skirts. The effect pop has on society is incredible. It's a power thing. It's now in a position that if everyone that was thinking in pop music terms were to stand end to end, they'd go around the world ten times. This is what pop music is about. Pop music is basically big. It concerns far more than the twenty-year-olds. It concerns everybody now. It's lasted too long.

Jazz, in its entirety—modern jazz, progressive jazz—hasn't had the effect on the world in fucking twenty-five years that pop has had in a year today. Geniuses like Charlie Parker are completely unrecognized by the world, and yet groups like the Rolling Stones—very normal, very regular guys—are incredibly well known. This is true of everything. The whole system is a different thing entirely. The audiences then were smaller; they became snobbish, racist. They were pompous jazz audiences. They became slow to catch on to new ideas. They became prejudiced, dogmatic, everything bad. While pop music is everything good.

Pop is everything; it's all sugar and spice, it really is. Pop audiences are the cream of today's music-listening audiences. They're not the classical snobs who sit by their poxy Fisher amplifiers and listen to Leonard Bernstein conducting. Not knowing that Leonard Bernstein is completely stoned out of his crust and grooving to high heaven, thinking, "What a fine, excellent recording this is, what a fine conductor Leonard Bernstein is, really fine," and not knowing what the fucking hell is going on.

This is what the jazz listener was like. Okay, he'd have a few beers and he'd go down to the fucking Village Gate and shout out one "yeah" in a night, when he thought that someone had played something quite clever. But he didn't know what they were into. I just about know what they're into today, listening to some recordings that Charlie Parker made nearly twenty-five years ago. God knows what people thought then.

Pop's audience is right alongside; they know what's happening. Pop hasn't yet confused anybody, it really hasn't. It's kept with the people, it's kept in time with the people. It's going out now; the panic now is that the people feel it going out of step. They felt it go out of step in England and completely rebelled.

People just felt that pop was getting out of their hands; groups like the Pink Floyd were appearing, scary groups, psychedelic. So they completely freaked out. Nothing like the down-home Rolling Stones who used to have a good old-fashioned piss against a good old-fashioned garage attendant. This Pink Floyd—what were they all about? With their flashing lights and all taking trips and one of them's psycho. "What's this all about? That's not my bag."

So they all turn over to good old Engelbert Humperdinck who is a phenomenon of our age in England. Yet it's a sign of the revolt; it's a sign of the fact that the music got out of step with the people.

Why did it happen in England?

Europe is a piss place for music, and it's a complete incredible fluke that England ever got it together. England has got all the bad points of Nazi Germany, all the pompous pride of France, all the old-fashioned patriotism of the old Order of the Empire. It's got everything that's got nothing to do with music. All the European qualities which should enhance, which should come out in music, England should be able to benefit by, but it doesn't.

And just all of a sudden, bang! wack! zap-swock out of nowhere. There it is: the Beatles.

Incredible. How did they ever appear then on the poxy little shit-stained island? Out of the Germans you can accept Wagner; out of the French you can accept Debussy; and even out of the Russians you can accept Tchaikovsky. All these incredible people. Who's England got? Purcell? He's a gas, but he's one of the only guys we've got, and Benjamin Britten today who copies Purcell. There's so few people.

And all of a sudden there's the Beatles, with their little funny "we write our own songs." "Don't you have ghost writers?"

It's difficult to talk about rock & roll. It's difficult because it's essentially a category and a category which embodies something which transcends the category. The category itself becomes meaningless. The words "rock & roll" don't begin to conjure up any form of conversation in my mind because they are so puny compared to what they are applied to. But "rock & roll" is by far the better expression than "pop." It means nothing.

It's a good thing that you've got a machine, a radio that puts out good rock & roll songs, and it makes you groove through the day. That's the game, of course: When you are listening to a rock & roll song the way you listen to "Jumpin' Jack Flash," or something similar, that's the way you should really spend your whole life. That's how you should be all the time: just grooving to something simple, something basically good, something effective and something not too big. That's what life is.

Rock & roll is one of the keys, one of the many, many keys to a very complex life. Don't get fucked up with all the many keys. Groove to rock & roll, and then you'll probably find one of the best keys of all.

6

INTERVIEWED BY JONATHAN COTT (1968)

Jonathan Cott and Jann Wenner were fellow students at the University of California in Berkeley, and worked together at the short-lived *Sunday Ramparts* fortnightly. Wenner covered the pop scene and edited the arts page; Cott reviewed films.

When ROLLING STONE began, Cott was in Europe on a Fulbright fellowship and began sending reports on James Brown, Traffic, Cream and the Beatles.

In June 1968, the Stones were about to release *Beggar's Banquet,* their first album in over a year (the one previous was *Their Satanic Majesties Request*) and their most polished album up to that time. Mick Jagger himself was about to take on his first acting role, in *Performance,* with James Fox and Anita Pallenberg.

"I was a big fan of the Stones," says Cott, but he knew that Jagger rarely gave interviews, and, on top of that, Cott had never conducted an interview before. Still, the interview was set up with no difficulties, and Cott was accompanied to the session at the Stones's business offices in London by fellow writer Sue Cox, who contributed questions.

Cott found the twenty-four-year-old Jagger to be "an extremely charming guy. But when he didn't want to answer a question, he didn't answer. He knew how to handle himself."

—BF-T

MICK

JAGGER

*T*HE FIRST THING WE WOULD like to talk about are your old songs like "Poison Ivy," "Route 66" and . . .

"Poison Ivy," did we ever record that? Oh, yeah. We did two versions of that. I don't know which one you have 'cause it was never released in this country [England]. Where was it released in America?

It wasn't released in America; it was put out in England. It was a very early recording with three other things, an EP.

Right. "Bye Bye Johnny" and "Better Move On." That was the second version.

Why did you choose that type of material in the beginning?

Well, I mean, we were kids, you know, just kids. We did everything and that was a groove. You see, "Poison Ivy" was unknown in this country. It wasn't a hit here by the Coasters, and other songs like "Money" were totally unheard of.

Like "I'm a King Bee"?

Well, that was pretty unheard of in America. What I mean is, there were a lot of these hit records in the States that nobody knew about here; we did them and *after* we thought they weren't good, but at the time it was right.

But the Stones made these songs popular.

No, not really. Everybody did those kind of songs: the Beatles, the Hollies, the Searchers, everyone. I can't explain why.

Isn't it true that with songs like "Come On" and "King Bee" you really re-discovered Slim Harpo and Chuck Berry for a lot of Americans who never listened to that kind of music before?

Yeah. They never knew anything about it, and that's why we stopped doing blues. We didn't want to do blues forever, we just wanted to turn people on to other people who were very good and not carry on doing it ourselves. So you could say that we did blues to turn people on, but why they should be turned on by us is unbelievably stupid. I mean, what's the point in listening to us doing "I'm a King Bee" when you can listen to Slim Harpo doing it?

At that time did you think you were going to be a writer and get into all your own things as you have?

No, I really didn't think about it much.

Your change in style came about when you thought enough people had been turned on to blues?

I think our *change* came about the same time a lot of the beat groups *started*. When there were no hit groups and the Beatles were playing the Cavern. We were blues purists who liked ever so commercial things but never did them onstage because we were so horrible and so aware of being

blues purists, you know what I mean? You see, nobody knew each other in those days. We didn't know the Beatles and the Animals and the this and that and the other groups, yet we were all doing the same material. We used to be so surprised to hear other people do the same things we were doing. The thing is that the public didn't know about any of this music because the record companies were issuing hundreds of singles a week, so naturally most people missed a huge lot of them.

What were the first things you wrote?

The first thing was "Tell Me." Well, that wasn't the first thing we wrote, but it was one of the first things we recorded that we had written. Also, "As Tears Go By," "That Girl Belongs to Yesterday," which was a hit here by Gene Pitney. We were writing ballads, don't ask me why.

How did you come to record "I Wanna Be Your Man," the Beatles thing?

Well, we knew them by then and we were rehearsing, and Andrew [Oldham] brought Paul and John down to the rehearsal. They said they had this tune, they were really hustlers then. I mean, the way they used to hustle tunes was great: "Hey, Mick, we've got this great song" *[done with a John Lennon accent].* So they played it and we thought it sounded pretty commercial, which is what we were looking for, so we did it like Elmore James or something. I haven't heard it for ages, but it must be pretty freaky 'cause nobody really produced it. The guy who happened to be our manager at the time was a fifty-year-old northern mill owner [Eric Easton]. It was completely crackers, but it was a hit and sounded great onstage.

What happened during the time between that and "Satisfaction"?

That's a lot of time, I don't know what happened. You say, "I Wanna Be Your Man," and I'd forgotten about it. Next came "As Tears Go By." We never dreamed of doing that ourselves when we wrote it. We just gave it straight to Marianne [Faithfull]. We wrote a lot of songs for other people, most of which were very unsuccessful.

Did you write "As Tears Go By" specifically for Marianne?

Yeah, but I could never do it again. I keep trying, night after night. Then we did "Not Fade Away" and went to America, and that was really a change.

How did that affect you?

Well, we started going back to blues a bit more. I remember we went to Chess Recording

46

Studios and recorded all the old blues numbers we used to do, a lot of which have never been released.

Who was doing your production then, Andrew?

Yeah, but he didn't know anything about blues. The cat who really got it together was Ron Marlow, the engineer for Chess. He had been on all the original sessions. We did "Confessin' the Blues," "Down the Road Apiece" and "It's All Over Now." Murray the K gave us "It's All Over Now," which was great because we used to think he was a cunt, but he turned us on to something good. It was a great record by the Valentinos, but it wasn't a hit.

That was when you first ran into censorship problems with the words "half-assed games." Many of the disc jockeys in the States just cut that part out.

Did they really? I didn't know that. I really don't know what's considered rude in America 'cause it's all so different, isn't it! Here you can use Americanisms and people don't know what you're saying. Censorship is weird.

Even though you had several hits before, "Satisfaction" was really the turn-on for a vast majority of people. Was there any specific incident that brought those lyrics to you?

It was Keith, really. I mean it was his initial idea. It sounded like a folk song when we first started working on it and Keith didn't like it much, he didn't want it to be a single, he didn't think it would do very well. That's the only time we have had a disagreement.

Even when it was finished, he didn't like it?

I think Keith thought it was a bit basic. I don't think he really listened to it properly. He was too close to it and just felt it was a silly kind of riff.

Did you think "Satisfaction" would become the Number One pop song of this era as it has?

No, not at all.

Did you think about the problem of writing a song to follow it?

No, I didn't give a fuck. We knew it wouldn't be as good, but so what?

Where were you when you wrote it?

Tampa, Florida, by a swimming pool.

Did you do a lot of your writing on tour?

Oh yeah, always. It's the best place to write because you're just totally into it. You get back from a show, have something to eat, a few beers and just go to your room and write. I used to write about twelve songs in two weeks on tour. It gives you lots of ideas. At home it's very difficult because you don't want to do anything really but read and things like that.

I'd like to ask you a personal question about "Play

with Fire." There are lines about getting your kicks in Knightsbridge and Stepney, and a rich girl, and her father's away and there is a suggestion that the guy in the song is having an affair not only with the daughter but with the mother. . . .

Ah, the imagination of teenagers! Well, one always wants to have an affair with one's mother. I mean, it's a turn-on.

Oftentime when you record, you mumble your lyrics. Is this done purposely as a style?

That's when the bad lines come up. I mean, I don't think the lyrics are that important. I remember when I was very young, this is very serious, I read an article by Fats Domino which has really influenced me. He said, "You should never sing the lyrics out very clearly."

You can really hear, "I got my thrill on Blueberry Hill."

Exactly, but that's the only thing you can hear just like you hear, "I can't get no satisfaction." It's true what he said, though. I used to have great fun deciphering lyrics. I don't try to make them so obscure that nobody can understand, but on the other hand I don't try not to. I just do it as it comes.

For some reason people don't think about the fact that you and Keith are great writers and your lyrics like "Get Off of My Cloud," which are really good . . .

Oh, they're not, they're crap.

"Union Jacks and windscreens" . . . it's a nice poem.

It's nothing. Thank you for the compliment, but I don't think they are great at all. If a person is that hung up on lyrics he can go and buy the sheet music because it's all there, wrong, of course, but . . . You should see the one for "Dandelion," they made up another song!

How did you feel when you went on the Ed Sullivan Show *and had to change the lyrics from "Let's spend the night together" to "Let's spend some time together"?*

I never said "time." I really didn't. I said, mumbled, "Let's spend some mmmmm together, let's spend some mmmmm together." They would have cut it off if I had said "night."

When you first came to San Francisco in 1965, the Diggers put out a proclamation calling the Stones the embodiment of what they represented, the breaking up of old values. This came about after a series of songs like "19th Nervous Breakdown," "Mother's Little Helper," "Have You Seen Your Mother". . . .

"Have You Seen Your Mother" was like the ultimate freakout. We came to a full stop after that. I just couldn't make it with that anymore; what more could we say?

But obviously these songs bothered people because for the first time rock songs were saying things that couldn't be said before, not just on a sex level like old blues tunes.

"I'll squeeze your lemon till the juice runs down your leg." You don't get close to things like that, but what you said was strong.

I like that one very much, we used to do it. It's spending all the time in America. All these songs were written in America. It is a great place to write because all the time you are being bombarded with all of it, and you can't help but try and put it in some kind of form. I think the Mothers of Invention do it so well. It's all here as well, but not so obvious. As far as I'm concerned, those songs just reflect what's going on.

What about people who see your songs as political or sociological statements?

Well, it's interesting, but it's just the Rolling Stones sort of rambling on about what they feel.

But no other group seems to do that.

They do, lots of groups.

What other group ever wrote a song like "19th Nervous Breakdown," or "Mother's Little Helper"?

Well, Bob Dylan.

That's not really the same thing.

Dylan once said, "I could have written 'Satisfaction,' but you couldn't have written 'Tambourine Man.'"

He said that to you?

No, to Keith.

What did he mean? He wasn't putting you down, was he?

Oh yeah, of course he was. But that was just funny, it was great. That's what he's like. It's true, but I'd like to hear Bob Dylan sing "I can't get no satisfaction."

Did you like Otis Redding's version?

Yeah, I dug it but . . . not . . . well, I dug it. I think it's great 'cause it's sort of . . . no, I'm not going to say. Well, the sounds were great and he was great when he first started off singing, but then it sort of went into oooh, aaah, gotta gotta gitta which is great because that's his scene, but I like Aretha Franklin's better. I was very turned on that Otis cut it.

Your songs about girls like "Out of Time," "Please Go Home," "Gotta Get Away," "Yesterday's Papers," "Lady Jane" and many more like "Back Street Girl" seem rather bitter and mean, whereas "She Smiled Sweetly," "Ruby Tuesday," "She's A Rainbow" are all about mystical girls.

Different girls. I don't know what to say except they speak for themselves. They are all very unthought-out songs. I write them, and they are never looked at again.

But it sounds as though you mean it at the time.

Well, I do, that's the scene. Those songs reflect the day and a few stupid chicks getting on my nerves. "Lady Jane" is a complete sort of very

weird song. I don't really know what that's all about, myself. All the names are historical, but it was really unconscious that they should fit together from the same period.

'Satanic Majesties' is probably the most controversial LP you've had; people either hated it or loved it. It seems to be a personal statement rather than a collection of songs. What were your original ideas about putting it together?

None at all. Absolutely no idea behind it. No, it's wrong to say there is or was no idea at all; there was, but it was all completely external. It was done over such a long period of time that eventually it just evolved. The first thing we did was "She's a Rainbow," then "2000 Light Years from Home," then "Citadel," and it just got freakier as we went along. Then we did "Sing This Song All Together" and "On with the Show," "The Lantern" and then Bill's one "In Another Land." It took almost a whole year to make, not because it's so fantastically complex that we needed a whole year, but because we were so strung out.

That was the year in which several arrests were made.

Yeah, that took a lot of time, plus we didn't know if we had a producer or not. Sometimes Andrew would turn up, sometimes he wouldn't. We never knew if we would be in jail or what. Keith and I never sat down and played the songs to each other. We just made that album for what it is.

Were you happy when it was finished?

I was happy, yeah. I breathed a sigh of relief because we had finally finished it. It's just there to take it or leave it.

Were any of the songs written after your or Brian's arrest?

I'm very conscious of the fact that it doesn't reflect that in any of the songs. That they aren't all about policemen as they could well have been. But it is an album like *Aftermath* is an album, but *December's Children* isn't; it's just a collection of songs.

Is there any one album you consider your best?

Well, no. I like our first album very much 'cause it's all the stuff we used to do onstage. Then I like *Aftermath* 'cause I like the songs, although I don't like the way some of them were done.

What about "Between the Buttons"?

I don't like that much.

Why?

I don't know, it just isn't any good. "Back Street Girl" is about the only one I like.

Going back to "Satanic Majesties" for a minute.

I've noticed that there seems to be a constant mood of sleeping and dreaming throughout the whole thing.

I read somewhere else that it was supposed to be about traveling, which is weird too, 'cause it is when you come to look at it that way. You heard what? Dreaming and waking up? I don't know, maybe it is. That's great if you get that from it, that's fantastic.

Do you feel that 'Satanic' was your first attempt at the "Strawberry Fields" type of music?

Well, it's a very heady album, very spaced out.

What can we expect to hear in your new album, 'Beggar's Banquet'?

"Jumpin' Jack Flash" is the most basic thing we have done this time, although that may or may not be in the album. There are a couple country tunes 'cause we've always liked country music.

Have you been influenced by the Byrds and Dylan with their country albums?

Yeah, but Keith has always been country. That's what his scene was. We still think of country songs as a bit of a joke, I'm afraid. We don't really know anything about country music, really; we're just playing games. We aren't really into it enough to know. I think it's going to be a good album.

Are you interested in doing stage performances again?

I'd like to do them, but the thought of going onstage and playing "Satisfaction," "Paint It Black," "Jumpin' Jack Flash" and six others just doesn't appeal to me.

What if you could have a quiet and receptive audience?

I don't think it's going to be like that. I'd like to perform and I think the Stones would, but we're stuck because we feel it's no good having everybody sit down and be quiet. I don't want anybody to have to do anything. I think they should do whatever they like. Pop concerts are just gatherings of people who want to have a good time, and I don't think they really have a higher meaning.

People say that audiences are listening now, but to what? Like the Rolling Stones onstage just isn't the Boston Pops Symphony Orchestra. It's a load of noise. On record it can be quite musical, but when you get to the stage it's no virtuoso performance. It's a rock & roll act, a very good one, and nothing more.

It is hard to imagine you doing your sexy thing, jumping about with everyone just sitting there quietly listening.

Right. I certainly don't want to go onstage and just stand there like Scott Walker and be ever so pretentious.

I can't hardly sing, you know what I mean? I'm no Tom Jones, and I couldn't give a fuck. The whole thing is a performance of a very basic nature; it's exciting and that's what it should be. The idea of doing it all over again is a drag. I'd like very much to have someone produce a show with us. I'd like that, I'd really like to do that.

Do you ever feel guilty about getting up onstage and pointing to those little girls and singing "Everybody Needs Somebody" when you really don't want them at all?

Of course I want them.

You're getting into films now, aren't you?

Yeah, well you can do a lot with film.

What is it like to work with Jean-Luc Godard, the director?

I don't know him very well. Godard is a very nice man. I mean, I've seen all his pictures and I think they're groovy.

What is "One Plus One" about?

I have no idea, really. I know he's shooting with color film used by astronauts when re-entering the earth's atmosphere. I mean, he's completely freaky. I think the idea for the movie is great, but I don't think it will be the same when it is finished.

What is the idea Godard has told you?

Well it's his [Godard's] wife who plays the lead chick. She comes to London and gets totally destroyed with some spade cat. Gets involved with drugs or something. Anyway, while she is getting destroyed we find the Rolling Stones freaking out at the recording studio making these sounds.

Godard happened to catch us on two very good nights. He might have come every night for two weeks and just seen us looking at each other with blank faces, and it would have been the same side of the coin as the chick destroying herself and us sitting there looking bored. One night he got us going over and over this song called "Sympathy for the Devil." It started out as a folky thing like "Jigsaw Puzzle" but that didn't make it, so we kept going over it and changing it until finally it comes out as a samba. So Godard has the whole thing from beginning to end. That's something I've always wanted to do on film. It's probably very boring to most people, but when he's finished cutting it, it will be great.

When is "The Performance" due to begin?

August something.

Wasn't the script written especially for you?

Yeah, I mean it's very much me. I'm going to make it if I can, different to me. I mean, he is

49

me, the me on that album cover. He is supposed to be a great writer, like Dylan. But he's completely immersed in himself, he's a horrible person, really.

How do you feel about acting as opposed to singing onstage?

I don't know. They are both just projections of your ego, which you're not supposed to have, but you can't do without. You certainly can't act without it, that's why the Maharishi had so much trouble. This character in the film has this fantastic ego thing, which is all right 'cause I can make that. If people get the feeling that you are out there with them, and if you come on strong then you'll make it. It's just a matter of looking confident, being confident and believing the part, then it's cool.

What did you think of '2001'?

It was one of the best movies I've ever seen. It's a very commercial movie. I really got hung up on the audience more than the movie. They kept leaving at the freaky parts 'cause they just couldn't make it. I think the point of the movie is that he [Kubrick] wants to get this whole thing across to the mass audience. He's fantastically interested in doing all these games with the spaceship models and all, that's his hang-up, but it's incidental. The point is to freak everybody out, which he is very good at. But if you have already been through all that, then you can turn on to all the other levels.

If you haven't, then you get totally looned out because all the time you are being brought home by all these telephone calls and plastic shoes and you think, "Ah it's just like home really, it's all right." He lets you identify with it. I mean, the toilet thing is the greatest, it's so awful. He spent so much time doing that it's almost heartrending. It's like he's saying, "Get it across to those people, but give them a bit of relief." Then at the end it all happens. You've forgotten about the stone as soon as you enter the Space Hilton; you can think it was a bad dream, until he brings it back.

People's comments are the greatest: "You need a lot of imagination to understand the movie"; "It's a million-dollar put-on."

I heard a little girl coming out of the theater saying that the slab was just a big block of hash.

That's fantastic!

Do you find it difficult not having any privacy?

Difficult? No, it's really nice and easy. The only hang-up is the fuzz. Now, that's a drag. Once you get in trouble with the police, you're always in trouble, and that's it. Before, we were never in trouble, and they were always very nice to us. They should be looking after people and turning American tourists away from Piccadilly Circus. That's the only hang-up, but it doesn't have anything to do with being me.

Do you feel that the police made a definite effort to pick on the Stones?

Well, there always has been. Before all the hassle it was just the boring newspapers, but when the fuzz start getting into that, it can be very draggy. They have the wherewithal to do it to you if they want to. The newspapers can only scream from their drunken haunts like the Wig & Feather Club, but they can't do anything; the police can.

7

INTERVIEWED BY JERRY HOPKINS (1969)

Jim Morrison wrote poetry as well as songs; he acted as well as sang; he was wild and crazy, and intelligent and political. Putting all this together into a rock band called the Doors in 1967, he came blazing across the scene as an original; there'd be echoes of him, before and after his death (in 1971), in the work, the manners, the theatrics and the sounds of Iggy Pop, Alice Cooper, David Bowie, Bryan Ferry, Patti Smith and the Jim Carroll Band, among many.

In 1969, many young people were taken up with the politics of paranoia. One night, Jim Morrison saw a guerrilla theater performance in which a player shouted, among numerous complaints: "I'm not allowed to take my clothes off!"

The next day, on stage in Miami, Morrison was arrested and charged with exposing himself; the Doors were banned by concert promoters nearly everywhere, and Morrison became the butt of media jokes and attacks.

It was in this setting that Jerry Hopkins, ROLLING STONE's Los Angeles correspondent, met the twenty-six-year-old Morrison. "Frankly," says Hopkins, "I felt we'd portrayed Jim as a clown. He set himself up as an easy target, but I felt there was a person there of greater intelligence than was set forth in the media." Their interview, he says, "was probably the longest one he gave, and the most revealing. He seemed eager to make himself understood, and the image he projected was exactly counter to that of a clown. It was an act of public relations."

In recent years there has been something of a Doors revival. Hopkins isn't surprised. "The music holds up," he says. "There's still a lyric connection with young people today. Morrison is still a romantic figure, in the 'life-in-the-fast-lane' sense. And his performance holds up. I saw a TV clip of him recently and—Jesus!—he's terrific."

—BF-T

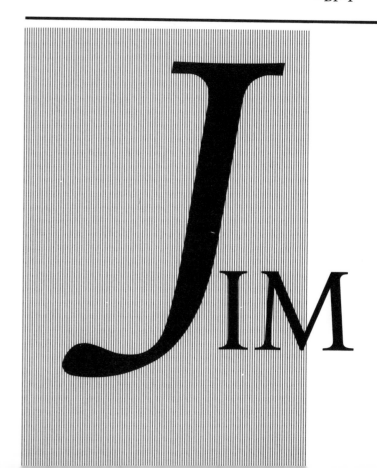

MORRISON

*THE WEEK I INTERVIEWED JIM MORRI-
son, the Doors were being banned from performing in
St. Louis and Honolulu because of exhibitionism and
drunkenness charges filed against Morrison following a
concert in Miami—yet, it was the same week that
Morrison finished writing a screenplay with poet
Michael McClure and signed a contract with Simon
and Schuster for his own first book of poetry.*

*Unlike the mythology, the music of the Doors
remains a constant—a force which has not been so
much an "influence" in rock, but a monument. "The
music is your special friend," Morrison sang in "The
Music's Over," and for millions, the music of the Doors
is just that; just as the Beatles' "Sgt. Pepper" renders
a generation weak with nostalgia, so does the Doors'
"Light My Fire." At the group's peak, in 1967–68,
there was also a strident urgency about Morrison's
music. "We want the world and we want it now."*

*Morrison was somewhat reluctant to be interviewed
by* ROLLING STONE *at first, believing the publication's coverage of the Miami concert and aftermath had
made him seem a clown. Finally he changed his mind
and in sessions that rambled over more than a week
and several neighborhood drinking spots, he proved his
manager Bill Siddons correct when Siddons said, "Jim
used to have a lot of little demons inside him . . . but I
don't think he has so many anymore." In other words,
Morrison had mellowed, matured. Still he was
playful—"This is really a strange way to make a
living, isn't it?" he said one day—but he was also
trying to get people to take him seriously. All poets
wish to be taken seriously, but many also have acted in
a style that would seem to contradict or destroy this
wish.*

*The first session we met at the Doors' office (which is
convenient to both the Elektra office and several topless
clubs) and talked in a neighborhood bar called the
Palms. The idea was to get some lunch with the beer,
but the cook was out for the day so it was just beer—
with a small group of regulars scattered along the bar
buying each other rounds and telling noisy stories in the
background, while we sat at a small table nearby.
There was no perceptible notice paid Morrison when he
entered, and the full beard he had grown since Miami
had little to do with it; he was a regular here, too.*

HOW DID YOU DECIDE YOU
were going to be a performer?
I think I had a suppressed desire
to do something like this ever since
I heard . . . y'see, the birth of rock
& roll coincided with my adolescence, my coming into awareness. It was a real turn-on, although at the time I could never allow myself to
rationally fantasize about ever doing it myself. I
guess all that time I was unconsciously ac-
cumulating inclination and listening. So when it
finally happened, my subconscious had prepared
the whole thing.

I didn't think about it. It was just there. I
never did any singing. I never even conceived it.
I thought I was going to be a writer or a
sociologist, maybe write plays. I never went to
concerts—one or two at most. I saw a few things
on TV, but I'd never been a part of it all. But I
heard in my head a whole concert situation, with
a band and singing and an audience—a large
audience. Those first five or six songs I wrote, I
was just taking notes at a fantastic rock concert
that was going on inside my head. And once I
had written the songs, I had to sing them.

When was this?
About three years ago. I wasn't in a group or
anything. I just got out of college and I went
down to the beach. I wasn't doing much of
anything. I was free for the first time. I had been
going to school, constantly, for fifteen years. It
was a beautiful hot summer, and I just started
hearing songs. I think I still have the notebook
with those songs written in it. This kind of
mythic concert that I heard . . . I'd like to try
and reproduce it sometime, either in actuality or
on record. I'd like to reproduce what I heard on
the beach that day.

Had you ever played any musical instrument?
When I was a kid I tried piano for a while, but
I didn't have the discipline to keep up with it.

How long did you take piano?
Only a few months. I think I got to about the
third-grade book.

Any desire now to play an instrument?
Not really. I play maracas. I can play a few
songs on the piano. Just my own inventions, so
it's not really music; it's noise. I can play one
song. But it's got only two changes in it, two
chords, so it's pretty basic stuff. I would really
like to be able to play guitar, but I don't have the
feeling for it. *(Pause).* You play any?

No . . .
I read a book you did—*The Hippie Papers.* It
had some nice articles in it. I've thought of
writing for the underground press, because I
don't know anywhere else you can have an idea
one day and see it in print almost immediately.
I'd like to write a column for underground
newspapers. Just reporting things I see. Not
fiction, but reporting. Just trying to get accurate
reports on things I witness—around L.A. especially. I guess I'm afraid of wasting a lot of

good ideas on journalism. If I kept them in my head long enough they might really turn into something. Although there've been some good people writing as journalists—Dickens, Dostoevski . . . and of course Mailer is a contemporary journalist.

Mailer even turned out a novel, a chapter a month under deadline for Esquire. . . .

And it's brilliant. *The American Dream.* Probably one of the best novels in the last decade.

It's interesting . . . a lot of good stuff is conceived specifically for newspapers and magazines, just as a lot of good music is conceived for records—all of which are disposable items, things which are available to just about anyone for very little money and later thrown away or traded in or gotten rid of pretty quickly. It's making several art forms very temporary. . . .

That's why poetry appeals to me so much—because it's so eternal. As long as there are people, they can remember words and combinations of words. Nothing else can survive a holocaust, but poetry and songs. No one can remember an entire novel. No one can describe a film, a piece of sculpture, a painting. But so long as there are human beings, songs and poetry can continue.

When did you start writing poetry?

Oh, I think around the fifth or sixth grade I wrote a poem called "The Pony Express." That was the first I can remember. It was one of those ballad-type poems. I never could get it together, though. I always wanted to write, but I figured it'd be no good unless somehow the hand just took the pen and started moving without me really having anything to do with it. Like, automatic writing. But it just never happened. I wrote a few poems, of course.

Like, "Horse Latitudes" I wrote when I was in high school. I kept a lot of notebooks through high school and college, and then when I left school for some dumb reason—maybe it was wise—I threw them all away. There's nothing I can think of I'd rather have in my possession right now than those two or three lost notebooks. I was thinking of being hypnotized or taking sodium pentathol to try to remember, because I wrote in those books night after night. But maybe if I'd never thrown them away, I'd never have written anything original—because they were mainly accumulations of things that I'd read or heard, like quotes from books. I think if I'd never gotten rid of them I'd never have been free.

Do you have songs you like better than others?

I tell you the truth, I don't listen to the stuff much. There are songs I enjoy doing more in person than others. I like singing blues—these free, long blues trips where there's no specific beginning or end. It just gets into a groove, and I can just keep making up things. And everybody's soloing. I like that kind of song rather than just a *song.* You know, just starting on a blues and just seeing where it takes us.

Improvisational trips . . .

Yeah. We needed another song for this album. We were racking our brains trying to think what song. We were in the studio, and so we started throwing out all these old songs. Blues trips. Rock classics. Finally we just started playing and we played for about an hour, and we went through the whole history of rock music—starting with blues, going through rock & roll, surf music, Latin, the whole thing. I call it "Rock Is Dead." I doubt if anybody'll ever hear it.

You were quoted recently as saying you thought rock was dead. Is this something you really believe?

It's like what we were talking about earlier in the movement back to the roots. The initial flash is over. The thing they call rock, what used to be called rock & roll—it got decadent. And then there was a rock revival sparked by the English. That went very far. It was articulate. Then it became self-conscious, which I think is the death of any movement. It became self-conscious, involuted and kind of incestuous. The energy is gone. There is no longer a belief.

I think that for any generation to assert itself as an aware human entity, it has to break with the past, so obviously the kids that are coming along next are not going to have much in common with what we feel. They're going to create their own unique sound. Things like wars and monetary cycles get involved, too. Rock & roll probably could be explained by . . . it was after the Korean War was ended . . . and there was a psychic purge. There seemed to be a need for an underground explosion, like an eruption. So maybe after the Vietnam War is over—it'll probably take a couple of years maybe; it's hard to say—but it's possible that the deaths will end in a couple of years, and there will again be a need for a life force to express itself, to assert itself.

Do you feel you'll be a part of it?

Yeah, but I'll probably be doing something else by then. It's hard to say. Maybe I'll be a corporation executive. . . .

Have you ever thought of yourself in that role—seriously?

I kinda like the image. Big office. Secretary . . . **55**

How do you see yourself? Poet? Rock star? What?

I don't get too much feedback except what I read. I like to read things that are written about it. That's the only time I get any kind of feedback on the whole thing. Living in L.A., it's no big deal. It's an anonymous city, and I live an anonymous life. Our group never reached the mass phenomenon stage that some did, either; there never was the mass adulation. So it never really got to me much. I guess I see myself as a conscious artist plugging away from day to day, assimilating information. I'd like to get a theater going of my own. I'm very interested in that now. Although I still enjoy singing.

A question you've been asked before, countless times: do you see yourself in a political role? I'm throwing a quote of yours back at you, in which you described the Doors as "erotic politicians."

It was just that I've been aware of the national media while growing up. They were always around the house, and so I started reading them. And so I became aware gradually, just by osmosis, of their style, their approach to reality. When I got into the music field, I was interested in securing kind of a place in that world, and so I was turning keys, and I just knew instinctively how to do it. They look for catchy phrases and quotes they can use for captions, something to base an article on to give it an immediate response. It's the kind of term that does mean something, but it's impossible to explain. If I tried to explain what it means to me, it would lose all its force as a catchword.

Deliberate media manipulation, right? Two questions come to me. Why did you pick that phrase over others? And do you think it's pretty easy to manipulate the media?

I don't know if it's easy, because it can turn on you. But, well, that was just one reporter, y'see. I was just answering his question. Since then a lot of people have picked up on it—that phrase—and have made it pretty heavy, but actually I was just . . . I knew the guy would use it, and I knew what the picture painted would be. I knew that a few key phrases is all anyone ever retains from an article. So I wanted a phrase that would stick in the mind.

I do think it's more difficult to manipulate TV and film than it is the press. The press has been easy for me in a way, because I am biased toward writing, and I understand writing and the mind of writers; we are dealing with the same medium, the printed word. So that's been fairly easy. But television and films are much more difficult, and I'm still learning. Each time I go on TV I get a little more relaxed and a little more able to communicate openly, and control it. It's an interesting process.

Does this explain your fascination with film?

I'm interested in film because to me it's the closest approximation in art that we have to the actual flow of consciousness, in both dream life and in the everyday perception of the world.

You're getting more involved in film all the time. . . .

Yeah, but there's only one we've completed—*Feast of Friends,* which was made at the end of a spiritual, cultural renaissance that's just about over now. It was like what happened at the end of the plague in Europe that decimated half the population. People danced, they wore colorful clothing. It was a kind of incredible springtime. It'll happen again, but it's over, and the film was made at the end of it.

I think of one part of the film, a performance sequence, in which you're flat on your back, still singing . . . which represents how theatrical you've gotten in your performance. How did this theatricality develop? Was it a conscious thing?

I think in a club, histrionics would be a little out of place, because the room is too small and it would be a little grotesque. In a large concert situation, I think it's just . . . necessary, because it gets to be more than just a musical event. It turns into a little bit of a spectacle. And it's different every time. I don't think any one performance is like any other. I can't answer that very well. I'm not too conscious of what's happening. I don't like to be too objective about it. I like to let each thing happen—direct it a little consciously, maybe, but just kind of follow the vibrations I get in each particular circumstance. We don't plan theatrics. We hardly ever know which set we'll play.

You mentioned that there were certain songs you liked performing over others, those which allow you some room for improvisation. I assume you mean pieces like "The End" and "The Music's Over" . . .

Once they got on record, they became very ritualized and static. Those were kind of constantly changing freeform pieces but once we put them on record, they just kind of stopped. They were kind of at the height of their effect anyway, so it didn't really matter. No . . . I mean the kind of songs where the musicians just start jamming. It starts off with a rhythm, and you don't know how it's going to be or really what it's about, until it's over. That sort I enjoy best.

When you're writing material, do you consciously differentiate between a poem, something for print . . . and a song lyric, something to be sung?

To me a song comes with the music, a sound

or rhythm first, then I make up words as fast as I can just to hold onto the feel—until actually the music and the lyric come almost simultaneously. With a poem, there's not necessarily any music. . . .

But usually a sense of rhythm, though . . .

Right. Right. A sense of rhythm and, in that sense, a kind of music. But a song is more primitive. Usually has a rhyme and a basic meter, whereas a poem can go anywhere.

Well, who provides this musical line that you hear when you're writing? The band? Or is this something you hear inside your head?

Well, most songs I've written just came. I'm not a very prolific songwriter. Most of the songs I've written I wrote in the very beginning, about three years ago. I just had a period when I wrote a lot of songs.

In the first three albums, writer credit in every song goes to the Doors, as opposed to individuals. But I understand that in the next album individual writers will be listed. Why?

In the beginning, I wrote most of the songs, the words and music. On each successive album, Robby [Krieger] contributed more songs. Until finally on this album it's almost split between us.

A lot of the songs in the beginning, me or Robby would come in with a basic idea, words and melody. But then the whole arrangement and actual generation of the piece would happen night after night, day after day, either in rehearsal or in clubs. When we became a concert group, a record group, and when we were contracted to provide so many albums a year, so many singles every six months, that natural, spontaneous, generative process wasn't given a chance to happen as it had in the beginning. We actually had to create songs in the studio. What started to happen was Robby or I would just come in with the song and the arrangement already completed in our minds, instead of working it out slowly.

Do you think your work has suffered because of this?

Yeah. If we did nothing but record, it probably would be all right. But we do other things, too, so there's not the time to let things happen as they should. Our first album, which a lot of people like, has a certain unity of mood. It has an intensity about it, because it was the first album we'd recorded. And we did it in a couple of weeks. That's all it took to get it down. It came after almost a year of almost total performance, every night. We were really fresh and intense and together.

This was at Elektra, of course. But you'd been signed to Columbia earlier. What happened there?

Well, it was just . . . in the beginning I'd written some songs and Ray [Manzarek] and his brothers had a band, Rick and the Ravens, and they had a contract with World-Pacific. They'd tried to get a couple singles out and nothing happened. Well, they still had their contract to do a few more sides and we'd gotten together by then, and so we went in and cut six sides in about three hours. At that time, Robby wasn't with the group. But John [Densmore] was the drummer. Ray was on piano, I was singing and his two brothers . . . one brother played harp, one played guitar, and there was a girl bass player—I can't remember her name.

So what we got was an acetate demo, and we had three copies pressed, right? I took them around everywhere I could possibly think of . . . going to the record companies. I hit most of them . . . just going in the door and telling the secretary what I wanted. Sometimes they'd say leave your number, and sometimes they'd let you in to talk to someone else. The reception game. At Columbia they became interested. The first person anyone meets when they come to Columbia is the head of talent research and development. Actually, the first person is his secretary. They liked it.

This was Billy James. . . .

Yeah, and a girl named Joan Wilson was his secretary. She called me a few days later and said he'd like to talk to us. We got a contract with Columbia for six months, during which they were going to produce so many sides. Having that contract was kind of an incentive for us to stay together. It turned out that no one was interested in producing us at that time, though, so we asked to get out of the contract.

Before the six months had elapsed?

Yeah. We knew we were onto something, and we didn't want to get held to some kind of contract at the last moment. By now we'd realized Columbia wasn't where it was at as far as we were concerned. It was kind of fortunate, really. We've had a good relationship with the company we're with now. They're good people to work with.

Well, how'd that come about . . . with Elektra?

Elektra at that time was very new to the rock field. . . . They had Love, and early Butterfield stuff. But Butterfield was still into blues, into the folk bag. Love was their first rock group and actually represented their first singles potential. They had been mainly an album label. After they signed Love, the president of the company heard us play at the Whisky. I think he told me once he didn't like it. The second or third night . . . he kept coming back, and finally everyone was convinced we'd be very successful. So he signed us up.

I've been told or I read somewhere that after the Columbia episode, you were somewhat reluctant to sign with anybody else.

I can't remember exactly. The people said that everyone in town was trying to sign us up, but it wasn't really true. In fact, Jac Holzman's may have been the only concrete offer we had. We may have made him come up with the best deal possible, but there *was* no question but what we weren't that much in demand.

You said the first LP went easily. . . .

Fast. We started almost immediately, and some of the songs took only a few takes. We'd do several takes just to make sure we couldn't do a better one. It's also true that on the first album they don't want to spend as much. The group doesn't either, because the groups pay for the production of an album. That's part of the advance against royalties. You don't get any royalties until you've paid the cost of the record album. So the group and the record company weren't taking a chance on the cost. So for economic reasons and just because we were ready, it went very fast.

Subsequent albums have been harder?

Harder and cost a lot more. But that's the natural thing. When we make a million dollars on each album and hit singles come from those albums, we can afford it. It's not always the best way, though.

In your early biographies, it says your parents are dead—yet your family is really very much alive. Why the early story?

I just didn't want to involve them. It's easy enough to find out personal details if you really want them. When we're born we're all foot-printed and so on. I guess I said my parents were dead as some kind of joke. I have a brother, too, but I haven't seen him in about a year. I don't see any of them. This is the most I've ever said about this.

Getting back to your film, then, there's some of the most incredible footage I've ever seen of an audience rushing a performer. What do you think in situations like that?

It's just a lot of fun [*laughter*]. It actually looks a lot more exciting than it really is. Film compresses everything. It packs a lot of energy into a small . . . anytime you put a form on reality, it's going to look more intense. Truthfully, a lot of times it was very exciting, a lot of fun. I enjoy it or I wouldn't do it.

You said the other day that you like to get people up out of their seats, but not intentionally create a chaos situation. . . .

It's never gotten out of control, actually. It's pretty playful, really. We have fun, the kids have fun, the cops have fun. It's kind of a weird triangle. We just think about going out to play good music. Sometimes I'll extend myself and work people up a little bit, but usually we're out there trying to make good music, and that's it.

What do you mean, you'll sometimes extend yourself . . . work the people up a bit?

Let's just say I was testing the bounds of reality. I was curious to see what would happen. That's all it was: just curiosity.

What did you do to test the bounds?

Just push a situation as far as it'll go.

And yet you don't feel at any time that things got out of control?

Never.

Even in your film . . . when it shows cops throwing kids back off the stage as fast as they're diving onto it? That doesn't represent some loss of control?

You have to look at it logically. If there were no cops there, would anybody try to get onstage? Because what are they going to do when they get there? When they get onstage, they're just very peaceful. They're not going to do anything. The only incentive to charge the stage is because there's a barrier. If there was no barrier, there'd be no incentive. That's the whole thing. I firmly believe that. No incentive, no charge. Action-reaction. Think of the free concerts in the parks. No action, no reaction. No stimulus, no response. It's interesting, though, because the kids get a chance to test the cops. You see cops today, walking around with their guns and uniforms, and the cop is setting himself up like the toughest man on the block, and everyone's curious about exactly what would happen if you challenged him. What's he going to do? I think it's a good thing, because it gives the kids a chance to test authority.

There are a number of cities where . . . like, you were busted for obscenity in New Haven. In Phoenix it was something else. . . .

I would say in most cases the only time we get into trouble is, like, if a person is just walking down a busy street and for no reason at all just took their clothes off and kept on walking . . . you can do anything as long as it's in tune with the forces of the universe, nature, society, whatever. If it's in tune, if it's working, you can do anything. If for some reason you're on a different track from other people you're around, it's going to jangle everybody's sensibilities. And they're either going to walk away or put you down for it. So it's just a case of getting too far out for them, or everybody's on a different trip that night and nothing comes together. As long as everything's connecting and coming together, you can get away with murder.

There is a quote attributed to you. It appears in print a lot. It goes: "I'm interested in anything about revolt, disorder, chaos . . ."

". . . especially activity that appears to have no meaning."

Right. That one. Is this another example of media manipulation? Did you make that one up for a newspaper guy?

Yes, definitely. But it's true, too. Who isn't fascinated with chaos? More than that, though, I am interested in activity that has no meaning, and all I mean by that is free activity. Play. Activity that has nothing in it except just what it is. No repercussions. No motivation. Free . . . activity. I think there should be a national carnival, much the same as Mardi Gras in Rio. There should be a week of national hilarity . . . a cessation of all work, all business, all discrimination, all authority. A week of total freedom. That'd be a start. Of course, the power structure wouldn't really alter. But someone off the streets—I don't know how they'd pick him, at random perhaps—would become president. Someone else would become vice-president. Others would be senators, congressmen, on the Supreme Court, policemen. It would just last for a week and then go back to the way it was. I think we need it. Yeah. Something like that.

This may be insulting, but I have the feeling I'm being put on. . . .

A little bit. But I don't know. People would have to be real for a week. And it might help the rest of the year. There would have to be some form or ritual to it. I think something like that is really needed.

There are a few words that recur in your dialogue. One is the word "ritual." What's that mean to you?

It's kind of like human sculpture. In a way it's like art, because it gives form to energy, and in a way it's a custom or a repetition, an habitually recurring plan or pageant that has meaning. It pervades everything. It's like a game.

Is there a ritual or a sense of game about what you and/or the Doors as a group do?

Yeah, it's a ritual in the sense that we use the same props and the same people and the same forms time after time after time. Music is definitely a ritual. But I don't think this is really clarifying ritual or adding anything to it.

Do you see yourself going more toward print?

That's my greatest hope. That's always been my dream.

Who turned you on to poetry?

I guess it was whoever taught me to speak, to talk. Really. I guess it was the first time I learned to talk. Up until the advent of language, it was touch—nonverbal communication.

What do you think of journalists?

I could be a journalist. I think the interview is the new art form. I think the self-interview is the essence of creativity. Asking yourself questions and trying to find answers. The writer is just answering a series of unuttered questions.

You've twice said you think you successfully manipulated the press. How much of this interview was manipulated?

You can't ever get around the fact that what you say could possibly turn up in print sometime, so you have that in the back of your mind. I've tried to forget it.

Is there some other area you'd like to get into?

How about . . . feel like discussing alcohol? Just a short dialogue. No long rap. Alcohol as opposed to drugs?

Okay. Part of the mythology has you playing the role of a heavy juicer.

On a very basic level, I love drinking. But I can't see drinking just milk or water or Coca-Cola. It just ruins it for me. You have to have wine or beer to complete a meal [*long pause*].

That's all you want to say? {laughter}.

Getting drunk . . . you're in complete control up to a point. It's your choice, every time you take a sip. You have a lot of small choices. It's like . . . I guess it's the difference between suicide and slow capitulation. . . .

What's that mean?

I don't know, man. Let's go next door and get a drink.

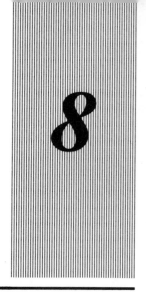

8

INTERVIEWED BY JANN WENNER (1969)

Here's one for the ages: Jann Wenner, the publishing world's boy wonder (he was twenty-one when he started ROLLING STONE), meets up with Phil Spector, pop music's boy genius (he was eighteen when he produced his first hit record).

Spector was the mastermind behind the "Wall of Sound": his hits of the early Sixties included the Ronettes' "Be My Baby" and "Walking in the Rain"; the Crystals' "Da Doo Ron Ron," "Uptown," "He's a Rebel" and "Then He Kissed Me"; Darlene Love's "Wait 'Till My Bobby Gets Home"; the Righteous Brothers' "You've Lost that Loving Feelin'"; Curtis Lee's "Pretty Little Angel Eyes"; and Bobb B. Soxx and the Blue Jeans' "Zip-a-Dee-Doo-Dah."

The drive, the pop goofiness, the sheer immensity of his sound—he made the first heavy-metal pop; something like R&B meets the Macy's Thanksgiving Day Parade—was matched only by Phil Spector's own mouth. The man—as Tom Wolfe, then millions of others, found out—could *wail*.

And now, here in 1969, at age twenty-nine, Phil Spector got himself an interesting gig: to help produce the Beatles' album, the one that would be their last: *Let It Be*. Perfect! said Wenner, hearing the news. Let it be, indeed!

—BF-T

I SAT WITH PHOTOGRAPHER BARON Wolman in a rented Mustang outside the Sunset Strip office of Phil Spector Productions for forty minutes one recent April night, listening to the car radio and waiting for the man. A black Cadillac limousine pulled up, and then away, circled the block and parked behind us. Out stepped the chauffeur, who is also one of Spector's several bodyguards. The whole Tom Wolfe legend was about to take place in front of our eyes. We

SPECTOR

changed cars and the chauffeur pulled away with us in the back seat.

Phil Spector, the first "Tycoon of Teen," was finally about to make good the promise for an interview, after two months of hassling over time and place. It was going to happen on the night of 'Mission: Impossible.' Spector, it turned out, lives only ten blocks or so from his office.

The grounds are surrounded by electric fences and gates, and after pulling into his driveway, you can see electric fencing also covering the windows and front door of his house. Once inside the doors and gates it's Phil Spectorland, with framed pictures and clippings (all the famous articles about Phil), pinball machines and jukeboxes with all his hits still on the playlist.

The house used to belong to one of the Hollywood starlets, and it's a beauty: twenty-foot gabled ceilings, sunken rooms, a grand piano, Irish wolfhounds and two borzois running around on the patio off the living room. Next to the living room is the game room, a huge pool table in the center, the walls covered with framed photos of Phil playing pool with Willie Moscone, Phil playing pool with Minnesota Fats and dozens of others.

We waited in the living room another half hour, while Phil was "getting ready." We were offered something to drink, something to eat: candy-filled dishes on the coffee table (along with the books and magazines, with bookmarks in place, which carried more of the famous articles about Phil), slices of pizza and Cokes. Baron and I sat, almost whispering, because the place seemed to have been wired for sound as well as everything else. The chauffeur-bodyguard returned to check the last-minute details, and he came in without his coat on, displaying his shoulder holster and his gun.

In walked the man: Phil Spector, short little Phil, all dressed up for the interview in outrageous yellow plastic-rimmed glasses, a tie-piece around his collar and sucking a candy cane. What a show tonight!

D O YOU SEE ANY BLACK MILI-tancy in the record business? Let's take Stax which is owned by . . .

Let's take it, man. Like, you take $4 million, and I'll take $3 million, and we all be very rich very quick. I'm rich already, what am I talking about? Go ahead, what about Stax-Volt?

Do you find any black resentment against the whites? You worked at Atlantic, another white-owned company, dealing primarily with black music. Was there any resentment from the artists?

Oh yeah, man, "We bought your home,

goddamn, and don't you forget it, boy. You livin' in the house we paid for, you drivin' a Cadillac we got, man. It's ours. You stole it from us."

You heard that from the beginning of time. All the Drifters were gettin' was $150 a week and they never got any royalties. It wasn't that Atlantic didn't pay them; it was that everybody screwed everybody in those days. I mean I was in the Teddy Bears and what did we get—one penny a record royalties!

What has disappeared completely is the black groups, other than what you have comin' out of Motown and your other few—and I don't mean Stax-Volt because I don't consider that what I'm talking about. The group on the corner has disappeared. It's turned into a white psychedelic or a guitar group, there are thousands of them. There used to be hundreds and hundreds of black groups singin' harmony and with a great lead singer and you'd go in and record them.

You used to go down to Jefferson High on Forty-Ninth and Broadway [in New York] and could get sixteen groups. Today you can't find them; they're either involved in the militant thing or they just passed, like it's not their bag anymore, or like it's just disappeared.

How has that changed the music?

It's changed the music drastically. It's given birth to English groups to come along and do it like Eric Burdon. It's also given birth for the Stones and the Beatles to come along and do it—not that they wouldn't have done it otherwise—but the first place the Beatles wanted to see when they came to America ('cause I came over on the plane with them) was the Apollo Theatre.

As bad a record as "Book of Love" by the Monotones is, you can hear a lot of "Book of Love" in the Beatles' "Why Don't We Do It in the Road." I think you hear a lot of that dumb, great-yet-nonsensical stuff that makes it—even though it's silly. It's got the same nonsense.

I believe that the English kids have soul. Really soul. When I watch Walter Cronkite or *Victory at Sea* or *You Are There*—any of those programs—I see bombs flying all over England and little kids running. Now that's probably Paul McCartney running. You know, 'cause that's where the bombs fell. They say soul comes through suffering. Slavery for the blacks. And gettin' your ass bombed off is another way of gettin' some soul legitimately. You're gonna have Dave Clark in there who don't know too much about it, and just like you're gonna have a Rosie and the Originals in America who don't know too much about it.

What do you think of groups like Sly and the Family Stone or the Chambers Brothers who have such a large, almost primarily white audience?

The Chambers Brothers have been around so long that they're just like a group I think of as "having" to have made it—a must. In other words, if they hadn't made it, it would be as much of a crime as Roy Orbison not being a star today or the Everly Brothers not making it today. It was criminal that they weren't big before.

The fact that they appear for white audiences is, I think, only because black music—if there can be such a phrase—or music as interpreted by black people—is a lot more commercial than music interpreted by white people.

The biggest English records are really when they are imitating. It's much more commercial when Eric Burdon sings a black copy. Just like Al Jolson was much more commercial when he did the blackface than he ever was when he went out and sang "My Yiddishe Momme." They love "mammy" with the blackface—Stephen Foster, I mean. Which is probably why the black people resent so much of America. We are the most commercially imitated people, we write and sing the most commercial music and yet we are the *least* talked about and the *most* oppressed.

So the black man got to figure *that* may be the reason he's passed from the musical scene to a large extent. Now when I say passed, I really mean passed. I mean it's as good as Sam Cooke being dead. You don't hear Ben E. King or any of the real soulful music anymore, and that was really commercial music, and it was good music.

I don't remember where we were. You asked me something.

The Chambers Brothers.

I don't know why they appeal to white people really. I would imagine that if you went into a black Baptist church, you'd dig it a whole lot because it's groovy music. I don't know why they are more commercial. I don't know even if they do appeal to a larger white audience than the black audience.

Being on Columbia Records has a lot to do with it. White people hear them much more. You don't see colored people going into a store sayin', "Let me have the Columbia Masterworks series number 129." Or just like you wouldn't see any of the young cats doing it. It's just not their bag.

WHAT ARTIST DO YOU REALLY *feel has not been recorded right that you'd like to record?*
Bob Dylan.
How would you record him?

I'd do a Dylan opera with him. I'd produce him. You see, he's never been produced. He's always gone into the studio on the strength of his lyrics, and they have sold enough records to cover up everything—all the honesty of his records. But he's never really made a production. He doesn't really have to.

His favorite song is "Like a Rolling Stone," and it stands to reason because that's his grooviest song, as far as songs go. It may not be his grooviest message. It may not be the greatest thing he ever wrote, but I can see why he gets the most satisfaction out of it, because rewriting "La Bamba" chord changes is always a lot of fun and anytime you can make a Number One record and rewrite those kind of changes, it is very satisfying.

I would like him to just say something that could live recording-wise forever. I would have enjoyed recording *John Wesley Harding* in its own way. He doesn't really have the time nor do any of his producers necessarily have the ambition or talent to really overrule him or debate with him. I would imagine with Albert Grossman there is a situation of business control just like it would be with Elvis Presley and Colonel Parker. Assume that there is no control, then somebody should be much more forceful. Maybe nobody has the guts, balls or the ambition to get in there, but there is no reason unless Dylan didn't want it. But there is a way he could have been made to want it.

There is no reason why Dylan can't be recorded in a very certain way and a very beautiful way where you can just sit back and say "wow" about everything—not just him and the song—just everything.

How would you have done "John Wesley Harding"?

There is a way to do it. He's so great on it and he is so honest that it's just like going into the studio with twelve of Stephen Foster's songs. There's so much you can do. There is so much you can do with Dylan; he gives you so much to work with. That's probably why he sells so many records without trying so very hard in the studio.

It's also probably why the Beatles . . . well, it's obvious that Paul McCartney and John Lennon may be the greatest rock & roll singers that we've ever had. They may be the greatest singers of the last ten years—they really may be!

63

I mean there is a reason for the Beatles other than the fact that they're like Rodgers and Hart and Hammerstein, Gershwin and all of 'em. They are *great, great* singers. They can do anything with their voices.

So to pat them on the back doesn't mean anything. It's really from the great background they had—of digging so much all their lives—that not only did they get that great gift of writing, but they have the great talent of singing; which is really where it's at. When you can get in and sing "Rocky Raccoon" that way, you know that he knows how to sing better than anybody else around, because he can switch right into "Yesterday." They've got a great gift, and for me it's much more than just sayin', "the Beatles, the Beatles, the Beatles."

I would like to record them a certain way because again, other than what they do themselves—there's nobody. I don't know how influential their producer is, and I am sure they have a great deal of respect for him and he's the fifth Beatle and all that, but I don't think he thinks the way I would think. Their ideas are so overpowering that you just sort of just go along with them and you're gonna end up with somethin' groovy. I don't think it was necessarily his idea to put "King Lear" on the end of that one record. Which did or did not have to be in the record.

I think Mick Jagger could be a lot of fun to record. It's not just the big artists; I think Janis Joplin leaves a lot to be desired recording-wise. How well she can sing when she's way up front—I don't know. How well she would sing under different circumstances—I don't know.

But the one that really would be the most satisfying probably would be Dylan because I could communicate with him and justify what he really wants to say—no matter what it is—musically, which is something that you don't see very often happening today.

Many of the artists today just sing, they don't really interpret anything. I mean the Doors don't interpret. They're not interpreters of music. They sing ideas. The Beach Boys have always sung ideas—they've never been interpreters. The Beatles interpret; "Yesterday" meant something. Whereas "Good Vibrations" was a nice idea on which everybody sort of grooved. That's what I feel is missing in the Chambers Brothers—the interpretation.

Four or five years ago . . . Sam Cooke interpreted, I have a feeling that a lot of it is the producers' fault, and a lot of it is the . . . the fact that everybody is runnin' a little too scared today. Nobody really knows, nobody really knows what Janis Joplin can do except Janis Joplin, and I don't necessarily think she puts her faith in anyone or would have anyone direct her.

What did you think of 'Beggar's Banquet'?

Well, they're just makin' hit records now. There was a time when the Stones were really writing *contributions*. See, that's a big word to me—"contributions."

What were the songs at the time?

"Satisfaction" was a contribution. They've had a few contributions. See, there's a difference: other than one or two numbers, Johnny Rivers is *not* a contribution to music, he never will be, he never can be. I don't care if all the Johnny Rivers fans say "boo." Just like Murray Roman will never be a comedian. There's just certain people that just don't have it. Moby Grape will never be a contribution. There are a lot of groups that will never be a contribution. 'Cause if you listen to just one Muddy Waters record you've heard everything Moby Grape's gonna ever do. Or if you listen to one Jimmy Reed record you've heard everything they may want to do.

The big word is "contribution," and the Stones lately have not been—although they have been writing groovy hit things—contributing anymore. You have a time when they were contributing *all* of it. Everything was contribution. They'll go down as a contribution. They'll be listed as a contributing force in music. An important influence. It's not a put-down on them, because *nobody* can keep up that pace.

If some of these groups, and some of the people in the business would dig athletics they would see more the reasons for themselves than they do now. Like Sonny Bono will never know what happened when it's all over. He'll never know why it happened because he didn't know what happened to make it happen. So he won't know what happened to make it fail. But if you go out and you want athletics and you watch a winning team lose, you watch them accept the failure. You see why they didn't win, and it makes sense. You sort of put things in perspective to yourself.

The people in today's business really don't do that. They don't know why they're making it—they just dig it, but athletes never do that. You never see athletes go crazy. They know tomorrow it's all over; one bad tackle, one bad jump and it's all over, and you're dead and nobody cares about you anymore.

In the record business they just try, try forever

and ever and ever. They don't plan nothin'. Motown, as marvelous as their recording company is . . . I mean, I've said it before: they have invented the Mustang body or the Volkswagen body and there isn't very little they can do wrong with it. They're gonna keep groovin', but I wouldn't be surprised if they release *one percent* of what they record. If they release twenty things a month, you can see how much they're recording and how much they don't release. Their studios are goin' twenty-four hours a day. Because they know that's what *their* strategy *has* to be.

The other people in the industry, like Ahmet [Ertegun] . . . I love Ahmet. When I first went to New York, he took care of me, and I love him. I mean he has no strategy. He calls up his office and says, "How many records we sell today?" I mean he can't know everything that's out there.

We had dinner with him one night and somebody said, "Ahmet, I'd really like to get the Bee Gees," and Ahmet said, "Well, man, you know, I can't, you know, do anything, man, 'cause they've got this Stigwood somebody and anyhow, man, he's a very difficult man to deal with. Anyhow, the Bee Gees ain't gonna be nothin'. Man, the Cream, you know, got two records in the top ten albums and you know that I'd never even heard of the group. But the very best group, the best that gonna be the biggest group in the world, is the Vanilla Fudge." He didn't even know, man. Because what's he care if it's Vanilla Fudge or Cream.

Like the Cream are breakin' up, and he said, "Like man, you have to do a final album for me." They said, "Why man, we hate each other," or somethin' like that. Ahmet said, "Oh, no, man, you have to do one more album for me. Jerry Wexler has cancer, and he's dyin' and he wants to hear one more album from you." So they go in, make the album and he says, "Like man, Jerry Wexler isn't dyin', he's much better, he's improved."

He's just jivin' like that 'cause it's a lot of fun and he's a *great* businessman.

Like when I met Otis Redding the first time. Otis says, "Hey Phil"—man, I loved Otis—we were just gettin' along famously talking, having dinner and he says, "How long you been knowin' Omelet?" I just sort of laughed 'cause he said "Omelet," and I know his name is Ahmet, not "Omelet." And I said, "About seven years."

And he said, "Omelet is just too much, he's too much."

I said, "Yeah, he sho' is." Afterwards, I went over to Ahmet and said, "Ahmet, how long you been knowin' Otis?"

He said, "Oh, about three years." I said, "And you mean he calls you 'Omelet'?"

So he says, "That's right, man. You know he calls the office all the time and he asks for Omelet, and they don't want to hurt his feelings by telling him my name is Ahmet."

Otis was not a dumb colored cat. You know, he was a smart cat and knew what was happening. If he ever knew that Ahmet's name was not Omelet, he would have been real upset, you know. And none of the secretaries told him 'cause they thought, "Oh, man, maybe a dumb spade." And also they loved him and didn't want to put him down, but he'd get on the phone with Jerry Wexler and he'd say, "How's Omelet doin'?" Wexler would say, "Oh, Omelet's fine, Otis, Omelet's doin' real good, Otis." The poor guy called him Omelet all his life.

[Note: Phil Walden, Otis' close friend and personal manager, says Otis knew Ahmet's real name but thought it was a laugh to call him "Omelet."]

But they love Ahmet for that, because he looks like Lenin, he has his beard and he's sophisticated and he comes on and he jives all these cats and he goes to Harlem and he cooks and he smokes the shit and everybody digs him.

Several years back we were all sitting around with some colored group, and one of them said, "Shit, man, your contract ain't worth shit." We were in a restaurant, and Ahmet looks around to make sure nobody'd hear us. The guy said, "Mercury gonna give me seven percent, you only give me five percent. That's like jive-ass." Ahmet said, "Not so loud." And he said, "Yeah, man, I can't sign your contract for five percent when I can get me seven percent over at Mercury."

And I was just sittin' back waitin' for what Ahmet was gonna say to this cat. The guy has the Mercury contract with him, and it does say seven percent. And he's got Atlantic's cockamamie contract for five percent. Now, he's got Ahmet up a wall, he's trapped, and Ahmet knows he's trapped, and we're all sittin' around, and Ahmet hit him with a line: Ahmet said, "Man, listen, man, you know what? I gonna give you fifteen percent, but I ain't gonna pay you." The guy said, "What?" Ahmet said, "That's what they gonna do. They gonna give you seven percent but they not gonna pay you, and I gonna give you five percent and pay you. Now that's a big difference isn't it?" The guy said, "That's right—never thought of it that way. That makes

65

a lot of sense. I'm gonna sign with you, Ahmet, I gonna sign with you, Ahmet."

What about Jerry Wexler?

I don't know. It's funny 'cause Jerry Wexler and I never got along, and we only really started to communicate when Lenny Bruce died, because he suddenly realized that he loved Lenny very much, and if Lenny and I were that close, it was time to break the ice between him and myself. So in the last few years we've communicated a great deal and talked. Jerry has a good time and jives a little bit, but his contribution really is the early music—all those records he did—like "A Lover's Question," "Sh-boom." That's the Jerry Wexler that for me really changed and set the standards for the recording industry.

I don't know how much he's a part of Aretha. I don't really get into it or care. I enjoyed Dusty Springfield's record, and I don't listen to music too much today 'cause I'm not inspired by a lot of it. A lot of it is a lot of crap. There is so much coming out on Atlantic, they got so many hits that I don't know what Jerry does and what he doesn't do.

I *know* that he is a *brilliant* businessman, and what he's done with Aretha is sparkling—what can you say? She was dumped from company to company, and *he* did make it happen. In many ways he's like Ahmet in another area. He just gets in that studio and if it's right . . . To sum up Jerry Wexler: As a producer he knows when something is right, and he can wrap some of these young punk producers around his little finger.

But to show you how sophisticated the kids are today, Jerry goes down South and cuts something and comes back up. Everybody listens to it. Ahmet says, "Too many highs in that record. It's shrill." Jerry says, "You're crazy, man. It's a groovy record—a smash." Ahmet says, "I don't know, man. It's awfully shrill. Somethin' the matter with the mikes down there." He says, "You're crazy, Ahmet. Man, you can go ask anybody."

And nobody knew what to say. It was like a standoff.

"What about the song?" Jerry asked. Ahmet said, "Well, the song's good, but it's just too piercing. There's something wrong with that record." So he says, "Let's go downstairs and find some kids on the street." So they go downstairs and find three long-haired kids with boots on, comin' home from school.

And Ahmet says, "Say, man, I *work* for Atlantic Records and we want you to hear a record." So the guy says, "Okay." He says,

"Man, we'll buy you some hamburgers and stuff." They say good, so they go upstairs and sit down—the kids thought we were gonna give them some joints, and we give 'em hamburgers.

They come upstairs and they go in the room and Jerry Wexler played this record for them. And these kids were sittin' there diggin' it, diggin' it, you know. And Wexler says, "What do you think of it?" One guy says, "It's a groovy song, man, and great performance." And they all said, "Yeah, man, it's a hell of a song and a great performance."

So Wexler looks at Ahmet and winks at him 'cause he knows he's won. Ahmet says, "You like the record?" And the kid says, "Yeah, but too many highs on it, it's piercing, really shrill. You gotta change the mixing—the EQ's wrong."

Jerry Wexler said, "The EQ's wrong? What you know about EQ?" Jerry got real hot. He just didn't realize that the kids today like they've all made records and they're very sophisticated and you can't jive 'em like that. And the kid said, "I don't dig the EQ on the record. Now, where's my hamburger? I gave you my opinion and I don't dig the EQ on your record." That's outta sight. I loved it.

So Wexler's a brilliant businessman; I mean he's really a groovy cat. I mean it's a great combination but if you really think of it—a Jewish cat and two Turks become the biggest R&B label—it's kinda weird. With no Mafia in there either.

What do you know about the Mafia in the record business?

I wouldn't say anything I knew anyways. I just try to hire 'em all, that's all. No, I wouldn't say a word about them. "What Mafia? What record business?" Why must we do the interview on the night of *Mission: Impossible,* man? That's a helluva good program. That's a great show, man. I don't know what day it comes on because I don't watch television that much. I'm one of those phonies that says he doesn't watch it but watches it every night—No, I really don't know.

W HAT WAS YOUR INVOLVE-ment with Lenny {Bruce}?

Other than that he recorded for me, I would say he was at the time my closest friend. He was like a teacher or a philosopher. He was like a living Socrates. Nobody will ever really know what Lenny was, and who he was, because nobody saw him in those last few years.

The people who *really* didn't see him are the people who said they did see him. I mean the Mort Sahls, Bill Cosbys, Buddy Hacketts—those are the people that really let Lenny down. They're the ones who all said, when Lenny died, that they wanted to bury him—only they wanted to bury him when he was living, not afterwards, because none of them were there.

I guess it was hard for them to look at Lenny because Lenny was obviously the very best. He was the epitome of comic brilliance, he was the greatest standup comedian of his time, he had the ingenious mind that they all wished that they had. To see the best like that would probably be too hard. They probably wouldn't have been able to stomach it.

I took Lenny to the Trip one night when it was open on Sunset, and Cosby was in there, the Smothers Brothers were in there. They all sort of tried not to say hello to Lenny and then they all sort of disappeared because not only did they steal so much from Lenny, take so much material from him, but they didn't know how to confront him. I don't think they knew what to say to Lenny or how to express themselves.

In the last year or six months Lenny had a nail tied to his foot and was going around in circles. He obviously was not guilty of anything he was charged with because the New York courts even let him go after his death. Posthumous vindication doesn't really mean anything, but he was *right* is what they meant, because the court said he was right. He just had a Kafkaesque life in that he was never allowed to do what he was charged with in front of a courtroom, and that was be obscene or not be obscene.

The film he made was him with the words and everything—'cause he never used a dirty word to use it. He would shuck with you, if he dug you he would talk like I've been talkin' to you now. I don't use a dirty word or say "fuck this" just to say it or to get you horny, I say it because I'm talkin' with you and that's it. And that's how he was with an audience.

Now, Lenny was not obscene, he was not dirty, he never posed in the nude [for an album] and he never did anything on any of his albums that should not have been heard. Yet they wouldn't touch him. We don't see anybody raising a fuss when this company comes and puts out John Lennon, you know with his schlong hanging out there and, "Hey, you know, it's a big thing," when it's really not. Now, the times may be changing, which is okay and there's nothin' wrong with John Lennon doin' whatever he wants to do.

But you have to get upset when the music industry defends that but doesn't defend it on a *general basis.*

What about John Lennon?

I haven't spoken to Lennon in some time so I don't know where he's at now. But I have a feeling that Yoko may not be the greatest influence on him. I mean, I don't know, but I have a feeling that he's a far greater talent than she is.

You know, a multimillionaire in his position just doesn't get caught in an English apartment house by the cops on a dope charge unless you're just blowing your mind or somebody is just really giving you a fucking. I mean you have dogs, you have bodyguards, you got *something* to protect you. Everybody knows the Beatles were immune. Everybody knows that George Harrison was at the Stones' party the night they got busted, and they let Harrison leave and then they went in and made the bust. I mean it was like the Queen said, "Leave them alone."

So Lennon must really have been causing a disturbance or somebody must have been setting him up to get busted, 'cause it ain't no medal of honor. Like it's no medal of honor to get the clap. Being busted for marijuana don't mean nothin'—it's just a waste of time, if anything. It wasted his time. It may have even caused . . . miscarriages.

It's almost like a weird thing to see just how bizarre he can get before he really blows it or he just teaches everybody something.

But I think without question he *is* leader of that group, and he makes the decisions. I'd like to know how the Beatles feel about him and what he's going through. I almost get the feeling that they want to help him but I don't think they really can because he's always way ahead of them.

I just hope that he doesn't hurt himself. Lenny really hurt himself. I tried to tell him, "You're going to hurt yourself, you're going to hurt yourself," and when they get going that's it, once they really get going. 'Cause Lenny would have died for any reason that day—a tooth pulled, anything. When you get going in that direction there's nothing can stop you, no amount of talk.

Lenny should have been out working at all the colleges, and influencing all the young people of the country. That's what he should have been doing, but instead he sat up in his room all night.

He wrote Supreme Court things, you know. . . . "Dear Justice Marshall: You don't seem to understand." He was brilliant; he knew

67

more than anybody, but he didn't know there was doors to go through and ladders to climb. He thought it was just one, two, three. I just hope Lennon doesn't blow it. It's his life, but he's too great a contribution.

You came over with the Beatles when they first came over to the States. What was that like?

It was a lot of fun. It was probably the only time I flew that I wasn't afraid, because I knew that they weren't goin' to get killed in a plane. That plane was really an awful trip. I mean there were twenty-eight or thirty minutes where that plane dropped thousands of feet over the ocean. It scared the shit out of me, but there were 149 people on board who were all press and Beatles' right-hand men, and left-hand men, and we just sat up there and talked about the Apollo and all that jive. Lennon was with his first wife, and he was very quiet. Paul asked a lot of questions, George was wonderful. It was a nice trip.

I'd just been in England for a couple of weeks and I went by their apartment, and they were leaving and said why don't you come back with us. It's really funny, but they were terribly frightened to get off the plane.

They were terribly frightened of America. They even said, "You go first." 'Cause the whole thing about Kennedy scared them very, very much. They really thought it would be possible for somebody to be there and want to kill them, because they were just very shocked. The assassination really dented them tremendously— their image of America. Just like it dented everybody's image of the Secret Service.

You were associated with the Stones when they first started. Was there any talk of you becoming their producer?

Um, yeah, but Andrew [Loog Oldham] was involved at that time and he was sort of . . . they told me he tried to be like me in England. And he sort of . . . I would say in all honesty that he was my publicity agent in England at that time. In other words, he called me and said he could do publicity, and I said, well, do publicity because I don't know what it involves. He sort of had a nice affection for me as a record producer, and he supposedly held me in high esteem.

The group was thinking of breaking up at the time. They were really disorganized. It wasn't so much breaking up; shit, they couldn't get . . . nobody believed in them. They were like a dirty, funky group. They were like second-class citizens, and even at my hotel they couldn't get in. They wanted 'em thrown out.

What did you do with them?

I went to see Sir Edward uh, what was his name? The owner of London Records, an old English cat. Didn't understand anything he said for half an hour. I wanted the Stones on an American label, my label, and he didn't. He offered me a percentage, anyhow, it involved things and money changed hands, and I never really was anything more than just close friends with them.

I knew there would eventually be problems between Andrew and them because . . . I don't know. I just had a feeling. Then there was another guy involved too, another Eric somebody. He was involved. I saw them in America a few times. The first time they came, they did awful; their tours were bombing. They got hung up in hotel rooms, and nobody knew what was going on.

The funniest call of all was when Mick Jagger called. Andrew used to sleep in my office in New York, when he stayed there. We used to get these phone bills to London, all kinds of nonsense. Didn't know who was doing them or who was calling. One day we got a phone call, you know, and it was Mick Jagger. I happened to pick up the phone and he said, "What you say there?" And I said, "Who's this?" He said, "This is Mick Jagger—wha' happening?" I said, "Nothing." I said, "Where are you?" He said, "In Hershey, Pennsylvania. Everything is fuckin' brown here. The phones are brown, the rooms are brown, the street is brown, every fucking thing is brown. I hate it in this fuckin' city, Hershey, Pennsylvania." He didn't know that Hershey, Pennsylvania, is where Hershey's chocolate company is located.

Did you negotiate their contract?

Well, this was an involved thing. I made a lot of bread real fast, and that's about all. But I never wanted to get anything else except to see them happen, because they were really discouraged.

I mean London Records didn't know whether to believe in them or not—their record company. It was just a thing that I felt that if another group was going to make it after the Beatles, they would make it. They were tremendously popular in London. The girls screamed for them everywhere, and yet they hadn't had a hit. I figured somethin's here, you know and they tried to get in hotels and people kept them out, and they said they were dirty and they smelled.

So I went to see Sir Edward Lewis. We talked and we worked out some kind of deal, and then they got a hit—"Not Fade Away" became a big hit in England—and then they came here and slowly they happened. But it wasn't until like a year later, when they exploded, that the contract really meant anything, as far as I was concerned. But financially, it didn't mean anything until much later on. Of course there were so many people involved in the background scene before they ever went to Allen Klein. And I don't think Allen Klein ever knew what was going on, and he's not a very good cat.

---

*W*HAT DO YOU THINK ABOUT *music now? Rock & roll music obviously has this tremendous thing with young people.*
    What tires me in this business today is that I'm tired really of hearing somebody's dreams and somebody's experiences. I would like to hear a little bit more of . . . I mean the Beatles combined it, and they do it well— their experiences, their love and their feelings. I don't know if they lived "Yesterday," but I know they wrote it.

Now I'm getting a little tired of hearing about, you know, everybody's emotional problems. I mean it's too wavy. Like watching a three- or four-hour movie. I'm getting so fed up with it. No concept of melody—just goes on and on with the lyric, and on and on with the lyric. They're making it a fad. If it had more music it would last, but it can't last this way.

I mean country & western is evidence of that, because it's lived so long by being so obvious. The old tunes have lived so long because they're obvious. I mean "All The Things You Are" and all the great songs you've heard were obvious in their way. Everybody went to a minor seventh in the bridge. I mean it was standard. You started out in a major seventh chord and you went to the minor seventh of the fourth and that was it, and you wrote a great song. So they had their formula and we have ours today, but they are ruining the formula.

They are going to really *kill* the music if they keep it up, because they're not writing songs anymore. They are only writing ideas. They don't really care about repetition. They don't care about a hook or melody. And I know the *Beatles* do. I mean "Lady Madonna" was a hit *song.* They didn't write that for an emotional experience, and you don't have to put things into those songs—they're right there—blah. That "ooh bla dee, ooh bla da . . . " I mean "life goes on." We *must* have more *songs.*

The Beatles have a fantastic feel for the market in addition to everything else.

That's commercialism; that's what is *not* existing in today's music. That's the shuck that I think is going on whereby everybody is susceptible to being fooled so much that, and they jive so much that . . . you see, these people in music don't realize that they are really forming the tastes of the young people of America. If they keep going in that direction they're going to bore themselves out of existence. It's going to get boring.

What are you gonna do with the stuff you're workin' on now? How does that differ from the last work you did with Ike and Tina Turner?

Don't know. I will go in many directions— some experimental—some not. Today "River Deep—Mountain High" could be a Number One record. I think when it came out, it was just like my farewell. I was just sayin' goodbye, and I just wanted to go crazy, you know, for a few minutes—four minutes on wax, that's all it was. I loved it, and I enjoyed making it, but I didn't really think there was anything for the public . . . nobody had really gotten into it enough yet; it really hadn't exploded the way it's exploding today with all the sounds, and they're really freaking out with the electronic stuff. Today "River Deep" would probably be a very important sales record. When I made it, it couldn't be—so, I don't know. I got what I wanted out of it.

You see, I don't have a sound, a Phil Spector sound—I have a style, and my style is just a particular way of making records—as opposed to Lou Adler or any of the other record producers who follow the artist's style. I create a style and call it a sound or a style; I call it a *style* because it's a way of doing it.

My style is that I know things about recording that other people just don't know. It's simple and clear, and it's easy for me to make hits. I think the *River Deep* LP would be a nice way to start off because it's a record that Tina deserves to be heard on—she was sensational on that record. A record that was Number One in England deserves to be Number One in America. If so many people are doing the song today, it means it's ready.

How did your association with Ike and Tina first come about?

They were introduced to me. Somebody told me to see them, and their in-person act just killed me. I mean, they were just sensational.

Have you seen it lately?

Yeah, I saw them at the Factory, of all places. They were . . . well, I always loved Tina. I never knew how great she was. She *real*-ly is as great as

69

Aretha is. I mean, in her own bag she is sensational, and Joplin and all that, but I couldn't figure how to get her on record, and then the Righteous Brothers pulled that nonsense, walked out, which cost them. MGM had to give me a ridiculous sum of money to get them. That was the stupidest . . . I mean, it was really dumb. It doesn't matter leaving me; fuck that, that don't mean nothin'. The dumb thing was to leave and suck MGM into that stupid deal, and then die as an act! I made a deal that I would not . . . we can't tell the figures of, you know, for publication, I mean, they have to give me so much money. I mean, it's ridiculous.

Why couldn't the Righteous Brothers make it without you?

I don't know if they couldn't have, but they really *should* have. I would imagine for the same reason that Mary Wells and Roy Orbison, the Everly Brothers all had only temporary success, if any, when they switched. The Righteous Brothers in particular were a strange group in that they really were nonintellectual and unable to comprehend success. They couldn't understand it and couldn't live with it and accept it for what it really was—they thought it was something that could be obtained very easily, and once it was attained, it could be *consistently* obtained.

I think managers in the tradition of Allen Klein came in and jived them—it wasn't Allen, but men like that—jived them. The boys' ability to really dissect, in a sophisticated way, what people were saying was so limited. They didn't have that ability; they could be swayed to other forms of thinking easily. I think that's what happened, and I really don't think that they had the ability to do it by themselves.

If anything, the reason they should have been successful is because they were accepted by black and white, and that's a big plus. Then they blew that because they tried, I think, to copy and emulate and use whatever it was that I did, and they didn't know how—not that they should have known how, but they shouldn't have even tried.

Really, they were not sophisticated enough to present themselves honestly. We really didn't bring them out honestly, except on the album. I mean those records were made, those songs were written, "Lovin' Feelin'" was not just a song. It was a *song* song, and you just can't go into the studio and sing "He Can Turn the Tide" and expect everybody to fall down.

I think people who don't realize their limitations can never really comprehend their ability. You have to know what you *can't* do much more than what you *can* do, because it's obvious that you know what you can do by doing it. But to fool yourself by thinking you're a tough guy and go out and just fight 'cause somebody's gonna come along who's really good.

Only an unsophisticated person would go out and start fighting everybody, and the Righteous Brothers are comparable to that because they really got fooled.

Now, I don't know what the situation was with Roy Orbison or Mary Wells. I heard there were a lot of different things, but for the Righteous Brothers I just think it was a great loss, because the two of them *weren't* exceptional talents, but they did have a musical contribution to make. I loved them, I thought they were a tremendous expression for myself. I think they resented being an expression. I think now if they had it to do again they never would have left. Two or three years later it never would have happened. In those times there was a lot of bullshit talk going around which influenced artists.

You did some of the first, I hesitate to use the phrase, "message" songs. Like "Spanish Harlem." What was the reaction of the record industry at that time to that kind of thing?

That record was a monster. The Drifters . . . well, that was to be the followup to "Save the Last Dance for Me," and then Ben E. King decided that he'd been screwed and wanted to go on his own. And then he chose that song, which drove me crazy. I said, "You can't go out with *that* song, 'cause that's gotta be done by the Drifters or it'll never get played."

I had been in New York, I was born there and had lived out here in California a great deal of the time. I went back there and I wanted to do "Spanish Harlem." It really meant exactly what it said. . . . That song had a lot of meaning to me and is still applicable today. It turned out to be a very, very valuable copyright with all kinds of records resulting from it. They've offered all kinds of money for the copyright.

I think the record industry just accepted it. I don't think they knew it was a message or it wasn't a message. I don't think they knew anything. I think it was just there, but I don't think anyone really thought it was a hit; nobody did. Nobody really understood it at first, then it started to grow on people and it made sense. I don't know. I love it and it says a lot for me. Did you know it was Lenny Bruce's favorite song?

Of the records that you've been involved with, and you've done, which do you like the most?

Well, in the beginning I made a lot of records

that I didn't put names on and nobody knows about, and it's better that way. But I did it because people in the industry somehow found out, and I needed the bread or whatever it was, and some of those records I can't give titles on, but I'm very proud of one of them. But of those that you know of, I would imagine "Be My Baby" and "Lovin' Feelin'" are the most satisfying. "River Deep" is a satisfying record.

I mean, I could tell you how "Lovin' Feelin'" was made. I could tell you I'm the greatest fuckin' record producer that ever lived and that I'll eat up all these cats in the studio if they want to put their mouths right there and their money right there.

If I say Bob Crewe is not good, it puts more pressure on me, like, to come out and really kill everybody with another "River Deep," which I really don't want to do. "He's a Rebel," it's fine; the "Da Doo Ron Ron" is fine. I'm not interested in knocking everybody's brain 'cause I'll *always* make a good record, and it'll be better than all that shit out there today.

'Cause *they* really don't know how to record. They don't know anything about depth, about sound, about technique, about slowing down. One company does know something; that's Motown. They know how to master a record. You put on a Motown record and it jumps at you. That's one thing among many they know how to do. For sure. I know how they're doing it, but it's *their* bag. But a lot of their records are not mastered for the record player, they're mastered for the radio, which is a whole different thing.

So the more things you come out and you say—the more antagonistic you are, the more hostile you are—the more is expected of you.

So when you put out something, a lot of people think . . . "Are you ashamed?" Not ashamed, but like that "Da Doo Ron Ron" thing. "Da Doo Ron Ron" was where I was at that time, just like "Yellow Submarine" was where the Beatles were; I'm glad people remember those things . . . because if people didn't know where I was, then I would be nothin'. It's like when somebody dies—all the people do is yell, "He died, he died." I yell, "He lived." A hell of a lot more important than the fact that he's dead is the fact that he lived.

What do you think of Apple?

I think it was a necessity. Why should they split their money with Capitol so much?

Aren't they still doin' it?

Yeah, but they couldn't do it alone, because the distributors would kill 'em.

Would they?

Oh, sure.

Was Philles records a . . .

A self-distributor. I distributed myself. You see, the Beatles would have made a mistake if they had left Capitol. They didn't have to. All their product was on Capitol. Capitol knows how to throw press parties, Capitol knows how to sell albums. They would have had to suddenly hire all people to do that for them. Like if Tony Bennett and Andy Williams came to A&M to negotiate a deal, in the end Jerry Moss would have had to tell 'em to stay where they are. They'd be stupid. They can't get from A&M what they can get from Columbia Records. Mathis made the biggest mistake by leaving Columbia. The Beatles wouldn't have been smart to start a new association. They would've been fighting their old Capitol product.

You would have had Capitol releasing old shit Beatle records, and the Beatles releasing new Beatle records. It would have been flooded again, it would've been that same old thing again, only this time somebody would've gotten hurt. So they got what they wanted from Capitol. They're ending up as if they owned their own company anyway. They're saving all the bookkeeping charges, saving all the personnel charges. Capitol's doin' all the work and givin' them a lot of bread. A *lot* of bread. So they're just as smart to stay in that way.

You could say that the record industry is like controlled by people who really don't care about the music.

They don't, 'cause I can make you a millionaire tomorrow! In one day I can make you a millionaire. Just make me a record, I'll send it out to every distributor and I'll bill every distributor. On paper you'll be a millionaire, 'cause I'll ship five million of your records. On paper you'll be a millionaire, and if that record don't sell you'll only be a very quick millionaire, but if I do it enough times, eventually I'm gonna get lucky and eventually you *will* be a millionaire.

That's how RCA works. You know any group that gets $100,000 from a label advance—you know that label is frightened to death. Any label that puts the Archies out is frightened. Donnie Kirshner is a friend of mine, and he wants me to say nice things about him, but . . . that's shit, the Archies; that's pure, unadulterated shit. When I see and hear stuff like that I want to throw up.

Do you think there is any way of changing the record industry?

It's not that it's so bad, it's just like it's going

71

to bore itself out. These groups are going to bore everybody to death. I mean, it's a pattern—make a Number One record, go on the *Smothers Brothers' Show;* make a Number One record, go on the *Dean Martin Show;* make a Number One record, go on *Ed Sullivan.* It's getting boring already.

I mean a few good songs are out, like I should name you a good song—a good song is "Games People Play" by Joe South. It's groovy. It's a groovy song. The best song of the year probably is "Heard It through the Grapevine" or "Abraham, Martin and John." That's probably the best lyric and message love song, ideawise, yet NARAS won't even recognize those songs. They'll give it to that guitar player Mason Williams on Warner Bros. or Paul Mariat or one of those guys.

"I heard it through the grapevine" is the most common saying; it's a great idea for a song. "For Once in My Life" is a great idea for a song; they won't even recognize this stuff. You see, I don't care about the groups. Just like who can care about the Chipmunks, let 'em make it, so what? Let the Archies make it, let the Monkees make it, so they're a lot of shit, so what? Let all these groups make it—let 'em cook, cook, cook forever.

But the people who have to *change* the industry are the people who are running the big time— the NARAS organization. Like it doesn't mean anything to me, but I've never been nominated. Now, you say it must mean something or you wouldn't say it. Well, it means something 'cause, like Dylan has never really been nominated. The Beatles have only been nominated recently, because they wrote "Yesterday," and they just couldn't stop the power of that song. Jimmy Reed and Bo Diddley and B. B. King— none of these cats have *ever* been nominated.

Excuse me, I was nominated once. I was nominated for putting thunder in "Walkin' in the Rain." That's what they nominated me for. Can you imagine that? People say I set standards in the record industry. Yet NARAS doesn't know I exist. They literally don't. The best rhythm & blues record of the year several years ago according to NARAS was Bent Fabric and "Alley Cat." I mean, can you imagine: Nancy Wilson was best R&B artist of the year! I mean, that's junk.

They're trying to change, and when we say change it, they say, "Well, why don't you come down to our meetings and help us change?" I said, "Well, if I'm gonna go to your meetings, I'd rather form my own committee and get the

dues myself. Why the fuck do I have to help you get fifty dollars a person? I'm formin' my own organization called PHIL, right? And everybody give me a hundred dollars. What do I need you for?" That's what BMI did to ASCAP—fucked them right out of all that money. Got all the young writers that way.

I mean, there *should* be a producers' society. I was gonna form one. Get every producer to join my organization—and they all would—thousand-dollar entrance fees, Felix you're vice-president, and Bob Crewe you're secretary-treasurer, and now we're powerful, we go on strike and we don't make no records, right?

"Felix goes on strike unless he gets eight percent of the Cream records." Now that's a strong idea, right? The publishers have it, the musicians have it. Fuckin' musicians walked out on the *Joey Bishop Show.* You can't put them to work. They played records in the background. So they come back, but they were on strike. Now wouldn't that be somethin'? The songwriters have it. If you're a songwriter you join a protective association. If you're a publisher, writer, you join BMI.

Producers have nothin'. They go into a record company and get fucked left and right. Make a hit . . . who made the record "Little Star"? Who knows, man? Company's out of business now . . . great record, boom, goodbye, garbage, down the drain . . . But you have an association of record producers called RPI of America, Record Producers Incorporated of America, well, you got somethin', you got a *giant* there. I was thinkin' of doin' it just for the hell of it.

If I get back in the regulars, I'm gonna do it. Engineers have it, everybody has it. We're gonna become a union; we'll join up with Hoffa and those Teamsters, get with them, and all that nonsense. Producers don't have nothin', man. I mean, it's really a shame. Where's Eric Jacobson? He's fuckin' down the tubes somewhere. He had no protection. We should have had meetings, and all the record companies should be sayin', "Oh God, the Producers of America are gettin' together again, shit, there's gonna be trouble, man, trouble." I wanted to do that long ago, but, you know, everybody thinks I'm joking around.

Everybody should be in some kind of a union, because the unions are the most powerful things. They almost put me out of business twice. I mean, they put a black mark on me for overdubbing. That's it. I couldn't make a master, I couldn't even get a dub 'cause everybody was union. There was a letter sent out to all the unions, "Don't do business with this company." That's it. I called up—nothin'. Couldn't get arrested, couldn't hire a musician 'til I paid them $50,000 and some nonsense fees that they wanted for the dead musicians' fund or the trust fund for dead musicians' wives or some shit. There is $28 million in that fund, and ain't nobody ever got none of it. Nobody knows . . . I ask all my musicians, where is all that money? They ain't never seen it.

Just like David Susskind says to me, "What's it like on Tin Pan Alley?" I said, "Where the fuck is Tin Pan Alley?" I mean, you tell me where it is, and I'll go. I mean, they jive-ass you and the people don't know. David Oppenheimer, big producer for CBS, man, he comes here and he's sittin' in my room and he says, "Are the young people really takin' over the record industry?" And he's sittin' in *my* house askin' *me* that question! He's got cameras on *me,* he's got the microphone on *me,* and he's askin' *me* if the young people are takin' over the country. Now, why ain't the camera on *him?* I mean, they don't understand. I can't change the record industry just like I can't change Jerry Rubin or I can't change Ted Kennedy; it's impossible.

I feel like an old-timer wishin' for the groovy young days, but I listen to the Beatles' album and I know they're wishin' for it too, because you can hear it. "Lady Madonna" was such a groovy old-time thing.

And Dylan is yearnin' for those days, because this was the first time he was ever able to come out and not be influenced by the people around him. They probably didn't understand a thing Dylan wrote on *John Wesley Harding,* but they probably said, "Yeah, man, yeah." He probably thought a long time before he did it. Instead of writing, "I've been sittin' in my mind, lookin' out the windows of the world"—that's what they were used to hearing—he just fucked 'em all up by writing just what he wanted to write. It must have been a big, big step for him, 'cause it's hard when your people around you are all tuned to one way of life, and then you just come and change it for them. He took a *big* risk, as an artist, by doing that. A big, big risk. He really deserves a lot more credit. He can't get anymore, I guess, but that was a big, big step for him to do that. 'Cause the people really wanted somethin' else from him.

Now, in the production world, I may be similar to what Dylan is in the popular world, but I know people expect me to come up with another "River Deep" momentous production. But that's not where it's at. It's in pleasing yourself and making the hit records. That's all that counts. That's the only reason people come to see you. That's the only reason people want to talk to you and get your opinion, 'cause you're the best; 'cause you're makin' money and you're makin' a lot of hit records. If you don't work and you got enough bread, well, then, you're cool, too.

There's no success like failure, and failure's no success at all.

I don't care if people put me down for what I say, but society sets a standard of living for you, and they create rules and record books . . . they force you to live by them. It's almost like being psychotic. It's like, if you can take a couple of pills and just cool it, that kind of life becomes a lot more exciting than going out and working and grooving. So they put you in a hospital and every day you stay in. That's why people go in the mental hospitals and very rarely get out, because they dig it. It becomes easier than to go out and face society with the cabs and the horns and the people. They make it almost impossible for you to want to get out of there.

The underground sort of does the same thing. They get your standards all twisted—like the *Los Angeles Times* ignores your standards. It's almost like the people running the underground press must be a lot of frustrated people; a lot of them who really *want* to be important, like agents want to be actors, musicians' agents want to be drummers, etc.

Are you apprehensive at all about what's going to happen and how your stuff is going to be received?

If I say yes, then I'm frightened. If I say no, that means that I'm very cocksure of myself. I'm cocksure of myself to the extent that I *know* I can make hit records. I don't worry about that. I'm apprehensive about certain people who don't have any standards but drug standards, really. If they're loaded at one time, my record will sound great; if they're not loaded, it may sound bad. I'm apprehensive about the kind of things that people expect. I mean, they don't really want hit records.

Let's face it. It's nice to see somebody on top get the shit beat out of them. That's why I stayed away for a long time, so I'll come back almost like a newcomer, because I mean, that's why everybody hates Cassius Clay; he's a very cocky son of a bitch. You want to punch him in the nose, but that's really great when you can scare the shit out of your opponents by your cockiness.

I'm apprehensive only to the extent that I don't know how to lose yet; I don't know how to say "fuck it" about my art. I get too involved.

73

See, I could just cool it, I mean, somebody's got to come in second . . . but it's guys like Bill Gavin that make me nervous. Those are the guys that get me uptight. And so I have to say, "Fuck that guy; who cares? I'll kill him, I'll stomp him." And it's true. It's just that I haven't gotten over it yet, you know.

I'm still involved with why "River Deep" wasn't a hit, and what the fuck was . . . and am I that hated? Am I too paranoid? You know, you can antagonize people if they think you're not human, if you say, "Aw, fuck, I ain't afraid." A lot of people will get very angry at that, disc jockeys in particular.

Herbie calls me in sometimes and says, "Listen to this": I mean he played me that thing, "A Taste of Honey." My engineer Larry Levine won *best* record of the year production for that record at NARAS but never won with me on *anything*—was never even nominated! The only thing we were nominated for was the thunder in "Walkin' in the Rain."

So I guess the best thing to be is not apprehensive and not give a fuck. I should be smart enough, knowing Dylan and knowing the Beatles, to know that they don't give a fuck anyway, and I don't give a fuck what they do—realistically. Because I don't sit and criticize their albums. They can't do anything wrong, and if I don't like it, so what? But who do *they* really have to impress? They have to impress all the *people*. People got to buy. So that's really where it's at.

The days of the dominating disc jockey are over. There's no more powerful disc jockey who rules anything. What does scare me a little bit is that there's not many more Tom Donahues around. That's bad. I mean, there aren't any guys with good ears that know how to play a record, and a disc jockey's not allowed to bust a record anymore. He's got to say—it's really commercial and play this one and scream—"I can dig it." The music comes on and he says, "Now here's a pimple commercial." That bothers me a little bit.

Where does the power lie?

The power lies in program directors.

Are there any groups you would consider working with today?

Yeah, a lot of groups—all black. I don't like the white groups. I think there is a great void in black music today—great void.

What is the void?

Not being heard enough. Motown should not dominate it. Stax shouldn't dominate it either.

There should be more black groups. There should be three black groups on every label around town. Hell, they've got enough of 'em and enough singers—they just don't have anybody to produce their records for them. Ben E. King should be making hits; he's a great artist.

I mean, really, Motown has got it all tied up. Stax doesn't even come near Motown. They can't get a special on television or anything. So who's dominating it?

Why do you think the Beatles' first release in this country didn't make it?

Timing. Bad timing. What else could you attribute it to but timing? It has to be timing. It has to be. I mean, I can't think of any other reason except that *we* weren't ready for *it*. They probably weren't exposed, and we weren't ready for it. I mean, there were probably many more reasons why they should have made it than why they shouldn't have. Now we can look back and say, "Yeah, we were fucked up," but we could not look back then at all. I would imagine, time and maturity. Great amount of luck involved too. Elvis Presley is another guy.

What did you think of his television show?

They ruined it; you should have seen it before they edited it. I didn't see the final version. What was originally done was sensational. How it ended up, I can't tell you. I know they cut out three scenes that were unbelievable. I mean, they cut out everything that was Elvis, *really* Elvis. They destroyed a lot of it, so I can't tell you how the final version was. But I think he's a sensation onstage.

Do you think he's gonna come back?

Yeah, he's got a hit now. I don't know what it is, but it's a hit. Oh, he should, man. He is never gonna die. Somebody ought to cut an album of him singin' the blues. You know, there's a strong belief—and judging from what I saw and heard at NBC, I believed it—that when he goes into a room with Colonel Parker, he's one way, and when he comes out, he's another way. You know, it's possible Colonel Parker hypnotizes him. That's the truth, too, and I can tell you six or seven people who believe it, too, who are *not* jive-ass people. I mean, he actually changes. He'll tell you, "Yes, yes, yes," and then he'll go in that room and when he comes out it's "No, no, no." Now, *nobody* can con you like that. I wonder about that.

What has he got that has survived the worst recording career direction in history?

He's a great singer. Gosh, he's so great. You have no idea how great he is, really, you don't.

You have absolutely no comprehension—it's absolutely impossible. I can't tell you why he's so great, but he is. He's sensational. He can do anything with his voice. Whether he will or not is something else. He and Dylan—he and Dylan I would like to record. Elvis can make some masterful records and can do anything. He can sing any way you want him to, any way you tell him. Even Dion. Look at Dion. Even Dion came back. Anybody great can come back today. That's what's so good about it.

What's the effect of drugs been upon you? Have they had an effect on your music?

I haven't made any music since that whole drug thing started.

Do you think it will?

Well, the listening audience will be affected by it. I mean, I've gotten a lot of letters and a lot of people said they've listened to "River Deep" stoned, and they had the earphones on, and they just freaked out, you know, with the sound. Well, you know nobody was stoned when they made the record, I can tell you that.

David Susskind once said that rock & roll records are out of tune. Was he stoned? Well, I've never used anybody but Barney Kessel and those kind of guys, the best musicians, they don't know *how* to play out of tune!

So you can get a tag—psychedelic or drugs. I don't know, maybe drugs will affect my music. Drugs tend to frighten me a little in an audience because it doesn't make for good hearing and concentration. Now, I'd hate like hell to have an incoherent jury listening to me when I'm tryin' to plead a case . . . just spaced out. I'd get frightened. Just like I hate to bet on a fighter or horse that's drugged. That's scary. I don't give a fuck what they do in their own time, but if a disc jockey is going to review my record, and he's stoned, well, you know, he can go either way. It depends on how good the stuff he took was, and he's gonna either love my record or hate my record. But I mean, you shouldn't be judged that way. In fact—art can't and shouldn't be judged at all! Because it's all a matter of taste.

What do you think the difference is going to be between the audience today and the audience's reaction to music today, as compared to five years ago?

I don't know. Everybody's a helluva lot hipper today, I'll tell you that. There's thirteen-year-old whores walkin' the streets now. It wouldn't have happened as much five years ago. Not thirteen-year-old drug addicts. It's a lot different today. I tell you the whole world is a dropout. I mean, everybody's a fuck-off. Everybody's miniskirted, everybody's hip, everybody reads *all* the books. How in the hell you gonna overcome all that? Sophistication, hipness, everything. They're really *very* hip today.

The music business is so different than any other business. You know, Frank Sinatra has a hit. Sister Dominique, or whatever her name is, has a hit. I can show you six groups out there today who are opposite. I mean, the Archies have a hit at the same time the Beatles do, so it really doesn't mean anything.

Now, who's buyin' the Archies' records? That's what I can't understand, and who bought all the Monkees' records—same cats who bought all the Stones' records? If they're not, then that makes the buyin' public so big . . . 'Cause the four million that bought the Monkees and the six million that bought the Beatles are different, then there's ten million kids buying records. That's a helluva lot of a better throw at the dice. I'd rather have a chance out of ten million times instead of six million times, so it probably will be easier.

Does it worry you at all, that there's been a change?

Well, anything that deteriorates music bothers me a little bit. I mean, if when Beethoven lost his hearing, if I was alive, it would have bothered me. I have to be affected by it. It bothers me that some music is very boring. I hear a lot of disc jockeys saying, "Let's throw this shit out." I hear them saying there are so many fucking groups—so boring. I hear this so much that I believe it. If it's true then yeah, it bothers me. It bothers me enough to get back in.

You're not worried that you won't be able to make the change?

If anybody's going to have to worry, *they're* going to have to worry. Not me, 'cause I'm comin' back! You know, I don't know if there has been a change, because if six million kids still buy the Monkees, then there hasn't been a change. They're the same six million that bought honky records five years ago.

The only real difference there is in the record industry is in black music. That's the big difference. But I don't consider Motown black; I consider them half and half. Black people making white music. The Monotones, the Drifters, the Shirelles, Fats . . . I mean, all those artists, not making it and around anymore. That's a big debt. But maybe it's only because nobody's doing it. We'll find out soon enough anyway.

INTERVIEWED BY JANN WENNER (1969)

From the beginning of Bob Dylan's career, he had a follower and supporter in Jann Wenner. In his days at UC Berkeley, Wenner signed his pop-scene column in the *Daily Cal* "Mr. Jones." When he started his own paper, one of the inspirations for its name was Dylan's first full-out rocker, "Like a Rolling Stone."

Soon after getting the magazine going, then,

Wenner went after Dylan for a one-on-one interview. In May of 1968, with the publication all of ten issues old, Wenner began his effort; and by June of 1969, he got the interview. Considering the subject, not bad.

When Wenner and Dylan first met, to sound out an interview, Dylan had issued his first album since his motorcycle accident of 1966, the quiet, religious ode to John Wesley Harding. Now, as they met for the interview, the twenty-eight-year-old Dylan's latest was a further drive into country music: *Nashville Skyline*.

We begin with Wenner recounting his search for Dylan.

—BF-T

THEY SAY BOB DYLAN IS THE MOST secretive and elusive person in the entire rock & roll substructure, but after doing this interview, I think it would be closer to the point to say that Dylan, like John Wesley Harding, was "never known to make a foolish move."

The preparations for the interview illustrate this well. About eighteen months ago, I first started writing Bob letters asking for an interview, suggesting the conditions and questions and reasons for it. Then, a little over a year ago, the night before I left New York, a message came from the hotel operator that a "Mr. Dillon" had called.

Two months later, I met Bob for the first time at another hotel in New York: He casually strolled in wearing a sheepskin outfit, leather boots, very well put

DYLAN

together but not too tall, y'understand. It was ten a.m., and I rolled out of bed stark naked—sleep that way, y'understand—and we talked for half an hour about doing an interview, what it was for, why it was necessary. Bob was feeling out the situation, making sure it would be cool.

That meeting was in the late fall of 1968. It took eight months—until the end of June this year—to finally get the interview. The meantime was covered with a lot of phone calls, near misses in New York City, Bob's trips to California which didn't take place and a lot of waiting and waiting for that right time when we were both ready for the show.

The interview took place on a Thursday afternoon in New York City at my hotel, right around the corner from the funeral home where Judy Garland was being inspected by ten thousand people, who formed lines around several city blocks. We were removed from all that activity, but somehow it seemed appropriate enough that Judy Garland's funeral coincided with the interview.

Bob was very cautious in everything he said and took a long time between questions to phrase exactly what he wanted to say, nothing more and sometimes a little less. When I wasn't really satisfied with his answers, I asked the questions another way, later. But Bob was hip.

Rather than edit the interview into tight chunks and long answers, I left in all the pauses, asides and laughs. So, much of the time, it's not what is said but how it is said, and I think you will dig it more just as it went down.

WHY HAVEN'T YOU WORKED *in so long?*
Well, uh . . . I do work.
I mean on the road.
On the road . . . I don't know, working on the road . . . well, Jann, I'll tell ya—I was on the road for almost five years. It wore me down, I was on drugs, a lot of things. A lot of things just to keep going, you know? And I don't want to live that way anymore. And uh . . . I'm just waiting for a better time—you know what I mean?

What would you do that would make the tour that you're thinking about doing different from the ones you did do?

Well, I'd like to slow down the pace a little. The one I did do . . . the next show's gonna be a lot different from the last show. The last show, during the first half, of which there was about an hour, I only did maybe six songs. My songs were long, *long* songs. But that's why I had to start

dealing with a lot of different methods of keeping myself awake, alert . . . because I had to remember all the words to those songs. Now I've got a whole bag of new songs. I've written 'em for the road, you know. So I'll be doing all these songs on the road. They're gonna sound a lot better than they do on record. My songs always sound a lot better in person than they do on the record.

Why?
Well, I don't know why. They just do.
On 'Nashville Skyline'—who does the arrangements? The studio musicians, or . . .

Boy, I wish you could've come along the last time we made an album. You'd probably have enjoyed it . . . 'cause you see right there, you know how it's done. We just take a song; I play it, and everyone else just sort of fills in behind it. No sooner you got that done, and at the same time you're doing that, there's someone in the control booth who's turning all those dials to where the proper sound is coming in . . . and then it's done. Just like that.

Just out of rehearsing it? It'll be a take?
Well, maybe we'll take about two times.
When are you going to do another record?
You mean when am I going to *put out* an album?
Have you done another record?
No . . . not exactly. I was going to try and have another one out by the fall.
Is it done in Nashville again?
Well, we . . . I think so . . . I mean it's . . . seems to be as good a place as any.
On 'Nashville Skyline,' do you have any song on that that you particularly dig? Above the others?

Uh . . . "Tonight I'll Be Staying Here with You." I like "Tell Me That It Isn't True," although it came out completely different than I'd written it. It came out real slow and mellow. I had it written as sort of a jerky, kind of polka-type thing. I wrote it in F. I wrote a lot of songs on this new album in F. That's what gives it kind of a new sound. They're all in F . . . not all of them, but quite a few. There's not many on that album that aren't in F. So you see, I had those chords . . . which give it a certain sound. I try to be a little different on every album.

I'm sure you read the reviews of 'Nashville Skyline.' Everybody remarks on the change of your singing style. . . .

Well, Jann, I'll tell you something. There's not too much of a change in my singing style, but I'll tell you something which is true . . . I stopped smoking. When I stopped smoking, my voice changed . . . so drastically, I couldn't believe it myself. That's true. I tell you, you stop smoking those cigarettes (*laughter*) . . . and you'll be able to sing like Caruso.

How did you make the change . . . or why did you make the change, of producers, from Tom Wilson to Bob Johnston?

Well, I can't remember, Jann. I can't remember . . . all I know is that I was out recording one day, and Tom had always been there—I had no reason to think he wasn't going to be there—and I looked up one day and Bob was there (*laughs*).

There's been some articles on Wilson, and he says that he's the one that gave you the rock & roll sound . . . and started you doing rock & roll. Is that true?

Did he say that? Well, if he said it . . . (*laughs*) more power to him (*laughs*). He did to a certain extent. That is true. He did. He had a sound in mind.

Have you ever thought of doing an album . . . a very arranged, very orchestrated album, you know, with chicks and . . . ?

Gee, I've thought of it. . . . I think about it once in a while. Yeah.

You think you might do one?

I do whatever comes naturally. I'd like to do an album like that. You mean using my own material and stuff.

Yeah, using your own material but with vocal background and . . .

I'd like to do it. Who wouldn't?

When did you make the change from John Hammond . . . or what caused the change from John Hammond?

John Hammond. He signed me in 1960. He signed me to Columbia Records. I think he produced my first album. I think he produced my second one, too.

And Tom Wilson was also working at Columbia at the time?

He was . . . you know, I don't recall how that happened . . . or why that switch took place. I remember at one time I was about to record for Don Law. You know Don Law? I was about to record for Don Law, but I never did. I met Don Law in New York, in 1962 . . . and again recently, last year when I did the *John Wesley Harding* album. I met him down in the studio. He came in . . . he's a great producer. He produced many of the earlier records for Columbia and also for labels which they had before—Okeh and stuff like that. I believe he did the Robert Johnson records.

What did you do in the year between 'Blonde on Blonde' and 'John Wesley Harding'?

Well, I was on tour part of that time . . . Australia, Sweden . . . an overseas tour. Then I came back . . . and in the spring of that year, I was scheduled to go out—it was one month off, I had a one-month vacation—I was gonna go back on the road again in July. *Blonde on Blonde* was up on the charts at this time. At that time I had a dreadful motorcycle accident . . . which put me away for a while . . . and I still didn't sense the importance of that accident till at least a year after that. I realized that it was a *real* accident. I mean, I thought that I was just gonna get up and go back to doing what I was doing before . . . but I couldn't do it anymore.

What did I do during that year? I helped work on a film . . . which was supposed to be aired on *Stage 67,* a television show which isn't on anymore . . . I don't think it was on for very long.

What change did the motorcycle accident make?

What change? Well, it . . . it limited me. It's hard to speak about the change, you know? It's not the type of change that one can put into words . . . besides the physical change. I had a busted vertebrae, neck vertebrae. And there's really not much to talk about. I don't want to talk about it.

Laying low for a year . . . you must have had time to think. That was the ABC-TV show? What happened to the tapes of that? How come that never got shown?

Well, I could make an attempt to answer that, but . . . (*laughs*) . . . I think my manager could probably answer it a lot better.

What is the nature of your acquaintance with John Lennon?

Oh, I always love to see John. Always. He's a wonderful fellow. . . . and I always like to see him.

He said that the first time that you met, in New York, after one of the concerts or something like that, it was a very uptight situation.

It probably was, yes. Like, you know how it used to be for them. They couldn't go out of their room. They used to tell me you could hardly get in to see them. There used to be people surrounding them, not only in the streets, but in the corridors in the hotel. I should say it was uptight.

How often have you seen them subsequently?

Well, I haven't seen them too much recently.

What do you think of the bed-ins for peace? Him and Yoko.

Well, you know . . . everybody's doing what they can do. I don't mind what he does, really. . . . I always like to see him.

Do you read the current critics? The music critics, so-called "rock & roll writers"?

Well, I try to keep up. I try to keep up to date. . . . I realize I don't do a very good job in keeping up to date, but I try to. I don't know half the groups that are playing around now. I don't know half of what I should.

I DON'T WANT TO GET NOSY OR GET *into your personal life . . . but there was a series recently in the 'Village Voice,' about your growing up, living and going to high school. Did you read that series?*

Yeah, I did. At least, I read some of it.

Was it accurate?

Well, it was accurate as far as this fellow who was writing it . . . this fellow . . . I wouldn't have read it if I thought . . . he was using me to write his story. So I feel a little unusual in this case, 'cause I can see through this writer's aims. But as far as liking it or disliking it, I didn't do neither of those things. I mean, it's just publicity from where I am. So if they want to spend six or seven issues writing about me (*laughs*) . . . as long as they get it right, you know, as long as they get it in there, I can't complain.

You must have some feelings about picking up a newspaper that has a hundred-thousand circulation and seeing that some guy's gone and talked to your parents and your cousins and uncles. . . .

Well, the one thing I did . . . I don't like the way this writer talked about my father who has passed away. I didn't dig him talking about my father and using his name. Now, that's the only thing about the article I didn't dig. But that boy has got some lessons to learn.

What did he say?

That don't matter, what he said. He didn't have no right to speak about my father, who has passed away. If he wants to do a story on me, that's fine. I don't care what he wants to say about me. But to, uhh . . . I got the feeling that he was taking advantage of some good people that I used to know, and he was making *fun* of a lot of things. I got the feeling he was making fun of quite a *few* things . . . this fellow, Toby. You know what I mean, Jann? Soooo . . . we'll just let that stand as it is . . . for now.

I've gone through all the collected articles that have appeared, all the early ones, and Columbia Records' biographies; that's got the story about running away from home at eleven and twelve and thirteen and a half . . . why did you put out that story?

I didn't put out *any* of those stories!

Well, it's the standard Bob Dylan biography. . . .

Well, you know how it is, Jann. . . . If you're sittin' in a room, and you have to have something done . . . I remember once, I was playing at Town Hall, and the producer of it came over with that biography . . . you know, I'm a *songwriter,* I'm not a biography writer, and I need a little help with these things.

So if I'm sitting in a room with some people, and I say, "Come on, now, I need some help; gimme a biography," so there might be three or four people there, and out of those three or four people maybe they'll come up with something, come up with a biography. So we put it down, it reads well and the producer of the concert is satisfied. In fact, he even gets a kick out of it. You dig what I mean?

But in actuality, this thing wasn't written for hundreds of thousands of people . . . it was just a little game for whoever was going in there and getting a ticket, you know, they get one of these things, too. That's just show business. So you do that, and pretty soon you've got a million people who get it on the side. You know? They start thinkin' that it's written all for them. And it's *not* written for them—it was written for someone who bought the ticket to the concert. You got all these other people taking it too seriously. Do you know what I mean? So a lot of things have been blown out of proportion.

At the time when all your records were out, and you were working and everybody was writing stories about you, you let that become your story . . . you sort of covered up your parents and your old friends . . . you sort of kept people away from them. . . .

Did I?

Well, that was the impression it gave. . . .

Jann, you know, my best friends . . . you're talking about old friends, and best friends . . . if you want to go by those standards, I haven't seen my best friends for over fifteen years. You know what I mean?

I'm not in the business of covering anything up. If I was from New Jersey, I could make an effort to show people my old neighborhood. If I was from Baltimore, same thing. Well, I'm from the Midwest. Boy, that's two different worlds.

This whole East Coast . . . there are a few *similarities* between the East Coast and the Midwest, and, of course, the people are similar, but it's a big jump. So, I came out of the Midwest, but I'm not interested in leading anybody back there. That's not my game.

Why didn't you publish 'Tarantula'?

Why? Well . . . it's a long story. It begins with when I suddenly began to sell quite a few records, and a certain amount of publicity began to be carried in all the major news magazines about this "rising young star." Well, this industry being what it is, book companies began sending me contracts *because* I was doing interviews before and after concerts, and reporters would say things like, "What else do you write?" And I would say, "Well, I don't write much of anything else." And they would say, "Oh, come on. You must write other things. Tell us something else. Do you write books?" And I'd say, "Sure, I write books."

After the publishers saw that I wrote books, they began to send me contracts . . . Doubleday, Macmillan, Hill and Range (*laughter*) . . . we took the biggest one and then owed them a book. You follow me?

But there was no book. We just took the biggest contract. Why? I don't know. Why I *did,* I don't know. Why I was *told* to do it, I don't know. Anyway, I owed them a book.

So I sat down and said, "Wow, I've done many things before, it's not so hard to write a book." So I sat down and wrote them a book in the hotel rooms and different places, plus I got a lot of other papers laying around that other people had written, so I threw it all together in a week and sent it to them.

Well, it wasn't long after that when I got it back to proofread it. I got it back and I said, "My gosh, did I write this? I'm not gonna have this out." Do you know what I mean? "I'm not gonna put this out. The folks back home just aren't going to understand this at all," I said. "Well, I have to do some corrections on this," I told them and set about correcting it. I told them I was improving it.

Boy, they were hungry for this book. They didn't care what it was. They just wanted . . . people up there were saying, "Boy, that's the second James Joyce," and, "Jack Kerouac again," and they were saying, "Homer revisited" . . . and they were all just talking through their heads.

They just wanted to sell *books,* that's all they wanted to do. It wasn't about anything . . . and I knew that—I figured they *had* to know that, they were in the business of it. I knew that, and I was just nobody. If I knew it, where were they at? They were just playing with me. My book.

So I wrote a new book. I figured I was satisfied with it, and I sent that in. Wow, they looked at that and said, "Well, that's another book." And

I said, "Well, but it's better." And they said, "Okay, we'll print this." So they printed that up and sent that back to proofread it. So I proofread it—I just looked at the first paragraph—and knew I just couldn't let that stand. So I took the whole thing with me on tour. I was going to rewrite it all. Carried a typewriter around . . . around the world. Trying to meet this deadline which they'd given me to put this book out. They just backed me into a corner. A lot of invisible people. So finally, I had a deadline on it and was working on it, before my motorcycle accident. And I was studying all kinds of different prints and how I wanted them to print the book, by this time. I also was studying a lot of other poets at this time. . . . I had books which I figured could lead me somewhere . . . and I was using a little bit from everything.

But still, it wasn't any book; it was just to satisfy the publishers who wanted to print something that we had a contract for. Follow me? So eventually, I had my motorcycle accident, and that just got me out of the whole thing, 'cause I didn't care anymore. As it stands now, Jann, I could write a book. But I'm gonna write it first and then give it to them. You know what I mean?

Do you have any particular subject in mind, or plan, for a book?

Do you?

For yours or mine?

(*Laughs*) For any of them.

What writers today do you dig? Like, who would you read if you were writing a book? Mailer?

All of them. There's something to be learned from them all.

What about the poets? You once said something about Smokey Robinson. . . .

I didn't mean Smokey Robinson, I meant Arthur Rimbaud. I don't know how I could've gotten Smokey Robinson mixed up with Arthur Rimbaud (*laughter*). But I did.

Do you see Allen Ginsberg much?

Not at all. Not at all.

Do you think he had any influence on your songwriting at all?

I think he did at a certain period. That period of . . . "Desolation Row," that kind of New York-type period, when all the songs were just "city songs." His poetry is city poetry. Sounds like the city.

Before, you were talking about touring and using drugs. During that period of songs like "Mr. Tambourine Man" and "Baby Blue," which a lot of writers have connected to the drug experience, not in the

sene of them being "psychedelic music," or drug songs, but having come out of the drug experience.

How so?

In terms of perceptions. A level of perceptions . . . awareness of the songs . . .

Awareness of the *minute*. You mean that?

An awareness of the mind.

I would say so.

Did taking drugs influence the songs?

No, not the writing of them, but it did keep me up there to pump 'em out.

Why did you leave the city and city songs for the country and country songs?

The country songs?

The songs . . . you were talking about "Highway 61" being a song of the city, and songs of New York City . . .

What was on that album?

"Highway 61"? "Desolation Row," "Queen Jane" . . .

Well, it was also what the audiences wanted to hear, too . . . don't forget that. When you play every night in front of an audience, you know what they want to hear. It's easier to write songs then. You know what I'm talking about?

Many people—writers, college students, college writers—all felt tremendously affected by your music and what you're saying in the lyrics.

Did they?

Sure. They felt it had a particular relevance to their lives. . . . I mean, you must be aware of the way that people come on to you.

Not entirely. Why don't you explain to me?

I guess if you reduce it to its simplest terms, the expectation of your audience—the portion of your audience that I'm familiar with—feels that you have the answer.

What answer?

Like from the film, 'Don't Look Back'—people asking you, "Why? What is it? Where is it?" People are tremendously hung up on what you write and what you say, tremendously hung up. Do you react to that at all? Do you feel responsible to those people?

I don't want to make anybody *worry* about it . . . but, boy, if I could ease someone's mind, I'd be the first one to do it. I want to lighten every load. Straighten out every burden. I don't want anybody to be hung up . . . (laughs) especially over *me* or anything *I* do. That's not the point at all.

Let me put it another way . . . what I'm getting at is that you're an extremely important figure in music and an extremely important figure in the experience of growing up today. Whether you put yourself in that position or not, you're in that position. And you must have thought about it . . . and I'm curious to know

82

what you think about that. . . .

What would I think about it? What can I do?

You wonder if you're really that person.

What person?

A great "youth leader" . . .

If I thought I was that person, wouldn't I be out there doing it? Wouldn't I be, if I thought I was meant to do that, wouldn't I be doing it? I don't have to hold back. This Maharishi, he thinks that—right? He's out there doing it. If I thought that, I'd be out there doing it. Don't you . . . you agree, right? So obviously, I don't think *that*.

What do you feel about unwillingly occupying that position?

I can see that position filled by someone else . . . not by . . . the position you're speaking of. . . . I play music, man. I write songs. I have a certain balance about things, and I believe there should be an order to everything. Underneath it all, I believe, also, that there are people trained for this job that you're talking about—"youth leader" type of thing, you know? I mean, there must be people *trained* to do this type of work. And I'm just one person, doing what I do. Trying to get along . . . staying out of people's hair, that's all.

You've been very reluctant to talk to reporters, the press and so on . . . why is that?

Why would you think?

Well, I know why you won't go on those things.

Well, if you know why, *you tell 'em* . . . 'cause I find it hard to talk about. People don't understand how the press works. People don't understand that the press, they just use you to sell papers. And, in a certain way, that's not *bad* . . . but when they misquote you all the time, and when they just use you to fill in some story. And when you read it after, it isn't *anything* the way you pictured it happening. Well, anyhow, it hurts. It hurts because you think you were just played for a fool. And the more hurts you get, the less you want to do it. Ain't that correct?

Were there any writers that you met that you liked? That you felt did good jobs? Wrote accurate stories . . .

On what?

On you. For instance, I remember two big pieces—one was in the 'New Yorker,' by Nat Hentoff. . . .

Yeah, I like 'em. I like that. In a way, I like 'em all, whether I feel bad about 'em or not, in a way I like 'em all. I seldom get a kick out of them, Jann, but . . . I mean, I just can't be spending my time reading what people write (laughter). I don't know anybody who can, do you?

Do you set aside a certain amount of time during the

day to . . . how much of the day do you think about songwriting and playing the guitar?

Well, I try to get it when it comes. I play the guitar wherever I find one. But I try to write the song when it comes. I try to get it all . . . 'cause if you don't get it all, you're not gonna get it. So the best kinds of songs you can write are in motel rooms and cars . . . places which are all temporary. 'Cause you're forced to do it. Rather, it lets you go into it.

You go into your kitchen and try to write a song, and you can't write a song—I know people who do this—I know some songwriters who go to work every day at eight-thirty and come home at five. And usually bring something back . . . I mean, that's legal, too. It just depends on . . . how you do it. Me, I don't have those kinds of things known to me yet, so I just get 'em when they come. And when they don't come, I don't try for it.

What do you look for when you make a record . . . I mean, what qualities do you judge it by when you hear it played back?

Ummmm . . . for the spirit. I like to hear a good lick once in a while. Maybe it's the spirit . . . don't you think so? I mean, if the spirit's not there, it don't matter how good a song it is or . . .

What was the origin of that collection of songs, of that tape?

The origin of it? What do you mean?

Where was that done?

Well, that was done out in . . . out in somebody's basement. Just a basement tape. It was just for . . .

Did you do most, did you write most of those songs, those demos, for yourself?

Right.

And then decide against them?

No, they weren't demos for myself, they were demos of the songs. I was being PUSHED again . . . into coming up with some songs. So, you know . . . you know how those things go.

Do you have any artists in mind for any of those particular songs?

No. They were just fun to do. That's all. They were a kick to do. Fact, I'd do it all again. You know . . . that's really the way to do a recording—in a peaceful, relaxed setting—in somebody's basement. With the windows open . . . and a dog lying on the floor.

What is your day-to-day life like?

Hmmmm . . . there's no way I could explain that to you, Jann. Every day is different. Depends on what I'm doing.

Do you paint a lot?

Well, I may be fiddling around with the car or I may be painting a boat, or . . . possibly washing the windows. I just do what has to be done. I play a lot of music, when there's a call in . . . I'm always trying to put shows together which never come about. I don't know what it is, but sometimes we get together and I say, "Okay, let's take six songs and do 'em up." So we do six songs, we got 'em in, let's say, forty minutes . . . we got a stopwatch timing 'em. But I mean, nothing happens to it. We could do anything with it, but I mean . . .

Boy, I hurried . . . I hurried for a long time. I'm sorry I did. All the time you're hurrying, you're not really as aware as you should be. You're trying to make things happen instead of just letting it happen. You follow me?

That's the awkwardness of this interview.

Well, I don't find anything awkward about it. I think it's going real great.

The purpose of any interview is to let the person who's being interviewed unload his head.

Well, that's what I'm doing.

And trying to draw that out is . . .

Boy, that's a good . . . that'd be a great title for a song. "Unload my head. Going down to the store . . . going down to the corner to unload my head." I'm gonna write that up when I get back (*laughter*). "Going to Tallahassee to unload my head."

You said in one of your songs on 'Highway 61' . . . "I need a dump truck, mama, to unload my head." Do you still need a dump truck or something? (laughter).

What album was that?

It was on 'Highway 61.' What I'm trying to ask is what are the changes that have gone on between the time you did 'Highway 61' and 'Nashville Skyline' or 'John Wesley Harding'?

The changes. I don't think I know exactly what you mean.

How has life changed for you? Your approach to . . . your view of what you do . . .

Not much. I'm still the same person. I'm still uhh . . . going at it in the same old way. Doing the same old thing.

Do you think you've settled down, and slowed down?

I *hope* so. I was going at a tremendous speed . . . at the time of my *Blonde on Blonde* album, I was going at a tremendous speed.

How did you make the change? The motorcycle accident?

I just took what came. That's how I made the changes. I took what came.

What do they come from?

THE ROLLING STONE INTERVIEWS

What was what coming from? Well, they come from the same sources that everybody else's do. I don't know if it comes from within oneself anymore than it comes from without oneself. Or outside of oneself. Don't you see what I mean? Maybe the inside and the outside are both the same. I don't know. But I feel it just like everyone else. What's that old line—there's a line from one of those old songs out. . . . "I can recognize it in others, I can feel it in myself." You can't say that's from the inside or the outside, it's like *both*.

Are there any albums or tracks from the albums that you think now were particularly good?

On any of my old albums? Uhh . . . As songs or as performances?

Songs.

Oh yeah, quite a few.

Which ones?

Well, if I was performing now . . . if I was making personal appearances, you would know which ones, because I would play them. You know? But I don't know which ones I'd play now. I'd have to pick and choose. Certainly couldn't play 'em all.

Thinking about the titles on 'Bringing It All Back Home.'

I like "Maggie's Farm." I always liked "Highway 61 Revisited." I always liked that song. "Mr. Tambourine Man" and "Blowin' in the Wind" and "Girl from the North Country" and "Boots of Spanish Leather" and "Times They Are a-Changin'" . . . I liked "Ramona."

Where did you write "Desolation Row"? Where were you when you wrote that?

I was in the back of a taxicab.

In New York?

Yeah.

During the period where you were recording songs with a rock & roll accompaniment, with a full-scale electric band, of those rock & roll songs that you did, which do you like?

The best rock & roll songs . . . which ones are there?

Uhh . . . "Like a Rolling Stone."

Yeah, I probably liked that the best.

And that was the Tom Wilson record . . . how come you never worked with that collection of musicians again?

Well, Michael Bloomfield, he was touring with Paul Butterfield at that time . . . and I could only get him when I could. So I wouldn't wait on Michael Bloomfield to make my records. He sure does play good, though. I missed having him there, but what could you do?

In talking about the songs as performances, *which*

of the performances *that you did, that were recorded . . .*

I like "Like a Rolling Stone" . . . I can hear it now, now that you've mentioned it. I like that sound. You mean, which recorded performances?

Yeah, I mean in your performance *of the song . . .*

Oh . . . I like some of them on the last record, but I don't know, I tend to close up in the studio. After I've . . . I could never get enough presence on me. Never really did sound like me, to me.

There's a cat named Allen Weberman who writes in the 'East Village Other.' He calls himself the world's leading Dylanologist. You know him?

No . . . oh, yes. I did. Is this the guy who tears up all my songs? Well, he oughta take a rest. He's way off. I saw something he wrote about "All Along the Watchtower," and boy, let me tell you, this boy's *off*. Not only did he create some type of fantasy—he had Allen Ginsberg in there—he couldn't even hear the words to the song right. He didn't hear the song right. Can you *believe* that? I mean, this fellow couldn't hear the words . . . or something. I bet he's a hardworking fellow, though. I bet he really does a good job if he could find something to do, but it's too bad it's just my songs, 'cause I don't really know if there's enough material in my songs to sustain someone who is really out to do a big job. You understand what I mean?

I mean, a fellow like that would be much better off writing about Tolstoy, or Dostoevski, or Freud . . . doing a really big analysis of somebody who has countless volumes of writings. But here's me, just a few records out. Somebody devoting so much time to those few records, when there's such a wealth of material that hasn't even been touched yet, or hasn't even been heard or read . . . that escapes me. Does it escape you?

I understand putting time into it, but I read this, in this *East Village Other*; I read it . . . and it was clever. And I got a kick out of reading it *(laughter)* on some level, but I didn't want to think anybody was taking it too seriously. You follow me?

He's just representative of thousands of people who do take it seriously.

Well, that's their own business. Why don't I put it that way? That's their business and his business. But . . . I'm the source of that and I don't know if it's my business or not, but I'm the source of it. You understand? So I see it a little differently than all of them do.

People in your audience, they obviously take it very seriously, and they look to you for something. . . .

Well, I wouldn't be where I am today without them. So, I owe them . . . my music, which I would be playing for them.

Does the intensity of some of the response annoy you?

No. No, I rather enjoy it.

I'm trying to get back to the thing about being a symbol of youth culture, being a spokesman for youth culture . . . what're your opinions or thoughts on that? At some point you pick up the paper or the magazine and find out that this is happening, and you know that you're considered like this. That people are watching you for that . . . and you've got to say to yourself, "Am I hung up?"

Well, not any more than anybody else is who performs in public. I mean, everyone has his following.

What do you think your following is like?

Well, I think there are all kinds . . . I imagine they're . . . you would probably know just as much about that as I would. You know, they're all kinds of people. I remember when I used to do concerts, you couldn't pin 'em down. All the road managers and the sound-equipment carriers and even the truck drivers would notice how different the audiences were, in terms of individual people. How different they . . . like sometimes I might have a concert and all the same kind of people show up. I mean, what does that mean?

Did you vote for president?

We got down to the polls too late (*laughter*).

People are always asking about what does this song mean and what does that song mean, and a lot of them seem to be based on some real person, just like any kind of fiction, you expect . . . are there any songs that you can relate to particular people, as having inspired the song?

Not now, I can't.

What do you tell somebody who says, "What is 'Leopard-Skin Pill-Box Hat' about?"

It's just about that. I think that's something I mighta taken out of the newspaper. Mighta seen a picture of one in a department-store window. There's really no more to it than that. I know it can be blown up into some kind of illusion. But in reality, it's no more than that. Just a leopard-skin pill-box. That's *all*.

_____

Hᴏw ᴅɪᴅ ʏᴏᴜ ᴄᴏᴍᴇ ɪɴ ᴄᴏɴ-tact with the Band?

Well. There used to be this young lady that worked up at Al Grossman's office—her name was Mary Martin, she's from Canada. And she was a rather persevering soul, as she hurried around the office on her job; she was a secretary; did secretarial work and knew all the bands and all the singers from Canada. She was from Canada. Anyway, I needed a group to play electric songs.

Where did you hear them play?

Oh, I never did hear them play. I think the group I wanted was Jim Burton and Joe Osborne. I wanted Jim Burton, and Joe Osborne to play bass, and Mickey Jones. I knew Mickey Jones, he was playing with Johnny Rivers. They were all in California, though. And there was some difficulty in making that group connect. One of them didn't want to fly and Mickey couldn't make it immediately, and I think Jim Burton was playing with a television group at that time.

He used to play with Ricky Nelson?

Oh, I think this was after that. He was playing with a group called the Shindogs, and they were on television. So he was doing that job. Anyway, that was the way it stood, and Mary Martin kept pushing this group who were out in New Jersey—I think they were in Elizabeth, New Jersey, or Hartford, Connecticut, or some town close to around New York. She was pushing them, and she had two of the fellows come up to the office so we could meet. And it was no more . . . no more, no less. I just asked them if they could do it, and they said they could (*laughs*). These two said they could. And that was how it started. Easy enough, you know.

How come you never made an album with them?

We tried. We cut a couple sides in the old New York Columbia studios. We cut two or three, and right after "Positively 4th Street," we cut some singles, and they didn't really get off the ground. You oughta hear 'em. You know, you could find 'em. They didn't get off the ground. They didn't even make it on the charts.

Consequently, I've not been back on the charts since the singles. I never did much care for singles, 'cause you have to pay so much attention to them. Unless you make your whole album full of singles. You have to make them separately. So I didn't really think about them too much that way.

But, playing with the Band was a natural thing. We have a real different sound. Real different. But it wasn't like anything heard. I heard one of the records recently . . . it was on a jukebox. "Please Crawl Out Your Window."

That was one of them? What were the others?

There were some more songs out of that same session . . . "Sooner or Later"—that was on *Blonde on Blonde.* That's one of my favorite songs.

What role did you play in the 'Big Pink' album, the album they made by themselves.

Well, I didn't do anything on that album. They did that with John Simon.

Did you play piano on it or anything?

No.

What kind of sound did you hear when you went in to make 'John Wesley Harding'?

I heard the sound that Gordon Lightfoot was getting, with Charlie McCoy and Kenny Buttrey. I'd used Charlie and Kenny both before, and I figured if he could get that sound, I could. But we couldn't get it (*laughs*). It was an attempt to get it, but it didn't come off. We got a different sound . . . I don't know what you'd call that . . . it's a muffled sound.

There used to be a lot of friction in the control booth on these records I used to make. I didn't know about it; I wasn't aware of them until recently. Somebody would want to put limiters on this and somebody would want to put an echo on that, someone else would have some other idea. And myself, I don't know anything about any of this. So I just have to leave it up in the air. In someone else's hands.

The friction was between the engineer and the producer. . . .

No, the managers and the advisers and the agents.

Do you usually have sessions at which all these people are there, or do you prefer to close them up?

Well, sometimes there's a whole lot of people. Sometimes you can't even move, there's so many people . . . other times, there's no one. Just the musicians.

Which is more comfortable for you?

Well, it's much more comfortable when there's . . . oh, I don't know, I could have it both ways. Depends what kind of song I'm gonna do. I might do a song where I *want* all those people around. Then I do another song and have to shut the lights off, you know?

Was "Sad Eyed Lady of the Lowlands" originally planned as a whole side?

That song is an example of a song . . . it started out as just a little thing. "Sad Eyed Lady of the Lowlands," but I got carried away somewhere along the line. I just sat down at a table and started writing. At the session itself. And I just got carried away with the whole thing. . . . I just started writing and I couldn't stop. After a period of time, I forgot what it was all about, and I started trying to get back to the beginning (*laughs*). Yeah.

'John Wesley Harding'—why did you call the album that?

Well, I called it that because I had that song, "John Wesley Harding." It didn't mean anything to me. I called it that, Jann, 'cause I had the song "John Wesley Harding," which started out to be a long ballad. I was gonna write a ballad on . . . like maybe one of those old cowboy . . . you know, a real long ballad. But in the middle of the second verse, I got tired. I had a tune, and I didn't want to waste the tune; it was a nice little melody, so I just wrote a quick third verse, and I recorded that.

Why did you choose the name of the outlaw John Wesley Harding?

Well, it fits in tempo. Fits right in tempo. Just what I had at hand.

What other titles did you have for the album?

Not for that one. That was the only title that came up for that one. But for the *Nashville Skyline* one, the title came up *John Wesley Harding, Volume II*. We were gonna do that . . . the record company wanted to call the album *Love Is All There Is*. I didn't see anything wrong with it, but it sounded a little spooky to me. . . .

What about 'Blonde on Blonde'?

Well, that title came up when . . . I don't even recall exactly how it came up, but I do know it was all in good faith. It has to do with just the word. I don't know who thought of that. I certainly didn't.

Of all the albums as albums, excluding your recent ones, which one do you think was the most successful in what it was trying to do? Which was the most fully realized, for you?

I think the second one. The second album I made.

Why?

Well, I got a chance to . . . I felt real good about doing an album with my own material. My own material, and I picked a little on it, picked the guitar, and it was a *big* Gibson—I felt real accomplished on that. "Don't Think Twice." Got a chance to do some of that. Got a chance to play in open tuning. . . . "Oxford Town," I believe that's on that album. That's open tuning. I got a chance to do talking blues. I got a chance to do ballads, like "Girl from the North Country." It's just because it had more variety. I felt good at that.

Of the electric ones, which do you prefer?

Well, soundwise, I prefer this last one. 'Cause it's got the sound. See, I'm listening for sound now.

As a collection of songs?

Songs? Well, this last album maybe means more to me, 'cause I did undertake something.

In a certain sense. And . . . there's a certain pride in that.

It was more premeditated than the others? I mean, you knew what you were gonna go after?

Right.

Where did the name 'Nashville Skyline'. . .

Well, I always like to tie the name of the album in with some song. Or if not some song, some kind of general feeling. I think that just about fit because it was less in the way, and less specific than any of the other ones on there.

Certainly couldn't call the album *Lay, Lady Lay.* I wouldn't have wanted to call it that, although that name was brought up. It didn't get my vote, but it was brought up. *Peggy Day—Lay, Peggy Day,* that was brought up. A lot of things were brought up. *Tonight I'll Be Staying Here with Peggy Day.* That's another one. Some of the names just didn't seem to fit. *Girl from the North Country.* That was another title which didn't really seem to fit. Picture me on the front holding a guitar and *Girl from the North Country* printed on top (*laughs*). *Tell Me That It Isn't Peggy Day.* I don't know who thought of that one.

What general thing was happening that made you want to start working with the Band, rather than working solo?

I only worked solo because there wasn't much going on. There wasn't. There were established people around . . . yeah, the Four Seasons . . . there were quite a few other established acts. But I worked alone because it was easier to. Plus, everyone else I knew was working alone, writing and singing. There wasn't much opportunity for groups or bands then; there wasn't. You know that.

When did you decide to get one together, like that? You played at Forest Hills, that was where you first appeared with a band. Why did you feel the time had come?

To do that? Well, because I could *pay* a backing group now. See, I didn't want to use a backing group unless I could pay them.

Do you ever get a chance to work frequently with the Band? In the country?

Work? Well, *work* is something else. Sure, we're always running over old material. We're always playing, running over old material. New material . . . and different kinds of material. Testing out this and that.

What do you see yourself as—a poet, a singer, a rock & roll star, married man . . .

All of those. I see myself as it all. Married man, poet, singer, songwriter, custodian, gatekeeper . . . all of it. I'll be it all. I feel "confined" when I have to choose one or the other. Don't you?

You're obligated to do one album a year?

Yes.

Is that all you want to do?

No, I'd like to do more. I would do dozens of them if I could be near the studio. I've been just lazy, Jann. I've been just getting by, so I haven't really thought too much about putting out anything really new and different.

You've heard the Joan Baez album of all your songs. . . .

Yeah, I did . . . I generally like everything she does.

Are there any particular artists that you like to see do your songs?

Yeah, Elvis Presley. I liked Elvis Presley. Elvis Presley recorded a song of mine. That's the one recording I treasure the most . . . it was called "Tomorrow Is a Long Time." I wrote it but never recorded it.

Which album is that on?

Kismet.

I'm not familiar with it at all.

He did it with just guitar.

10

INTERVIEWED BY DAVID DALTON (1970)

Just as Little Richard believes in God, rock & roll, and Long Tall Sally, David Dalton believes in Little Richard, "His Majesty, the King of Rock and Soul!"

Dalton, who has also written extensively about James Dean, the Rolling Stones and Charles Manson, was a long-time fan of Richard's, dating back to the Fifties and "Tutti-Frutti." Now, in 1969, the 34-year-old Richard Penniman, who'd given up pop music in 1957 to become a preacher, was back—and Dalton went and got him.

"I went as a fan," Dalton says. "That was the whole point. Back then, ROLLING STONE was sort of a cult magazine. So you didn't have to frame the interview. You could just ask the questions you wanted the answers to. The people reading were interested in the same things you were."

Dalton's goal was simple: "to meet him and interview him in detail on his past." On his own, he approached Richard at a concert, transcribed their talk and showed it to ROLLING STONE, and got the assignment. The interview, he says, "was my first encounter with big-deal R&B, where the manager asks for money to do the interview. I told him it would be good publicity, possibly a cover. Richard understood."

Little Richard's comeback, begun in 1964 and inspired by the Beatles (who in turn had been inspired by Richard), hadn't set the world on fire. Still, there was the past.

"I approached the interview with a sense of history," says Dalton. "I really felt like I was in the presence of someone who had been involved with inventing a new genre of music."

Dalton saw Richard after the interview was published, "and he told me he had gotten hundreds of copies. He had papered his living room with the ROLLING STONE cover!"

—BF-T

LITTLE

RICHARD

I DIDN'T GET TO SEE LITTLE RICHARD at the Atlantic City Pop Festival where he followed Janis Joplin and revived his own legend, but when he appeared in Central Park skating rink during the summer of 1969, he really tore it up. His effect was magnetic. You couldn't really call it a comeback because most of the kids there had never seen him when he first appeared; some weren't even born then.

But it was a revival, a spontaneous generation of the rocking pneumonia. For the first show he came out in a red velvet suit with a gold embroidered jacket, prancing up and down like an exhibitionist talking to the kids, posing to let chicks take his picture, his "wings held high," throwing kisses, camping about and right away starting to take off his clothes. "You want my vest?"—takes it off and throws it into the audience.

"All you want is my vest?" he asks incredulously, pointing to his velvet pants. The audience shrieks, and Little Richard comes back: "Shut up! I rather do it myself!"

Then the classic speech:

"Look anywhere . . . I am the only thing left. I am the beautiful Little Richard from way down in Macon, Georgia. You know Otis Redding is from there, and James Brown's from there and Wayne Cochran's from there . . . I was the best-lookin' one so I left there first. Prettiest thing in the kitchen, yes sir! I want you to know I am the bronze Liberace! Shut up, shut up!"

His thing is a contagious induced frenzy, a contagious explosion that is compelling in spite of the set responses, perhaps because of them, the infectious responses and repetitions of the gospel formula, fusing the audience into a single reverberation. All flesh shall see it together. "Let all the womenfolk say 'woooh,' an' let all the men say 'uhnnn,' come on, everybody!" Sympathetic magic. Little Richard calls it the "thang."

"I always did have that thang, I didn't know what to do with the thang. I had ma own thang I wanted the world to hear." And the Word was made flesh. "If you hear a funny tone in my voice, that's the Angletown sound."

The second show, he came out in a vest made of tiny mirrors (he'd already given the first lot of clothes away). Under the brilliant klieg lights they flashed out like rays from a disintegrator gun, doodling puddles of light on the floor and roof, splashing into the audience. But Little Richard is dazzling without his coat of light. His stage act is mesmerizing because like all great shamans, demagogues, preachers and prophets, he hits the cosmic mainline, a source of radiant energy that has the power to dissolve the ghosts of identity. Unclean spirits crying with loud voice came

out of many that were here possessed. Soul Music. Driving out the demons, letting the body speak.

Like any true shaman, all Little Richard asks for is a little respect. His Majesty the King of Rock and Soul! "I don't want you goin' out tellin' the people Little Richard is conceited. I am not conceited!" It's just that, well, the Spirit of the Lord came to Richard Penniman and entered into him.

Outside the gates a crowd of young kids has gathered to touch him, get his autograph, exchange a glance. His Majesty emerges in a long embroidered cloak, like a bishop in hip threads. He takes each of their hands gently, stretching out his arms in a ritual gesture of benediction, whispering in a soft hoarse voice, "God bless you." St. Augustine could not have done it better.

Back at the hotel, Little Richard's manager, producer and the co-author of some of Little Richard's classics, "Bumps" Blackwell, entertains us while His Majesty gets ready to receive us. "Why did it take Little Richard so long to surface after he left the ministry?" "Well, principally I'd put it down to the martyrs." The martyrs? A conspiracy of martyrs? The idea itself is as bizarre as anything out of Genet. "Bumps" explains that the martyrs are certain revival preachers who disapprove of show business, and when Little Richard started to appear at clubs and concerts in the South, they made life very hard for him by sabotaging his appearances, canceling shows and forbidding DJ's to play his records. It's enough to make you want to sing the blues.

TV static crackles and flashes like someone deep-frying electricity, the road manager wrangles on the phone, "Bumps" raps about that time in Chicago when Little Richard was coming offstage and pouring with sweat and this chick (a spade) came up and handed him her handkerchief . . . on TV it's a program about training animals for the movies . . . then the road manager: "He's been breaking box office records right across the country" . . . "And here's a little fellow I think you'll all remember" . . . "See, so he reaches out to grab it" . . . "Here's an episode where Cheetah saves Tarzan from the alligator men" . . . "This razor blade drops out . . . "

We are led into the room. Little Richard is lying out regally on the bed, resplendent in an iridescent jump suit like the shell of a cerambycidae beetle. He speaks in a confidential whisper, greeting us. He says everything very sincerely and when you ask him something that gets him going, he gathers momentum, letting out his famous phrases like little supplications that add fuel to the fire, a kind of instant revival meeting. . . . "My, my, my . . . oh, my sooooul!" And there appeared unto them cloven tongues as of fire. My power's comin', my power's comin'! Hallelujah! Little Richard Child of God!

WHAT DO YOU THINK ABOUT what James Brown is doing now— "I'm Black and I'm Proud" kind of thing?

I imagine he's doing what he feels, but I have a different feeling. My feeling is, if I die I must be truthful, to me; I figure that the nations of the world—I call it God's bouquet—I figure with my brown here—you understand what I mean—it's just like my little sister picking some roses and sunflowers and medallions and lilies is a bouquet, the nations are a bouquet—the Chinese, the Japanese, the white man, the brown man—we all belong to God; God is a God of beauty of love of peace, so I think that we are all together this bouquet. He's not a God of one race, He's a God of all races, and I don't think God intended us to have hatred against any man, because hatred is a sickness, and God wanted us to be well, we should stay well.

How did you come to write "Tutti-Frutti"?

Oh my God, my God, let me tell the good news! I was working at the Greyhound bus station in Macon, Georgia, oh my Lord, back in 1955.

How old were you then?

Oh my Lord, that's the only secret I've got. I'm only twenty-four, folks. I was washing dishes at the Greyhound bus station at the time. I couldn't talk back to my boss man. He would bring all these pots back for me to wash, and one day I said, "I've got to do something to stop this man bringing back all these pots to me to wash," and I said, "A wop bop alu bop a wop bam boom, take 'em out!" and that's what I meant at the time. And so I wrote "Good Golly, Miss Molly" in the kitchen, I wrote "Long Tall Sally" in that kitchen.

How did you get them onto record?

I met a singer, Lloyd Price, who had a big hit, "Lawdy Miss Clawdy." So he came to my hometown, I was selling drinks in a little bucket at his dance, and so he saw me and I stopped by the stage and I said, "I could do that," but they wouldn't let me, so I went back in the dressing room, they had a piano in the dressing room, so I played "Tutti-Frutti" on the piano for Lloyd. Lloyd said, "Man, say I believe that could be a hit. I want you to send a tape to Specialty Records." So I sent a tape to Specialty and they waited one year before they wrote me back. So I forgot about it, I just kept washing dishes. So I recorded "Tutti-Frutti" and it was an instant hit.

What was your reaction?

I didn't know I had sold a million; I was sittin' in Macon broke with no money, hungry. And the record company said, "You know you're the hottest thing in the country." I said, "Me? Me?" I had never been on a airplane before so they said, "We're sending you a ticket, you're coming to Hollywood." So I went to Hollywood and "Tutti-Frutti" was Number One, and so immediately they released "Long Tall Sally" and "Slippin' and Slidin'," which I wrote, and so that's when everything began happening.

What inspired you to write "Tutti-Frutti"? Where did the style come from?

Well, you know I used to play piano for the church. You know that spiritual, "Give Me That Old Time Religion," most churches just say [sings], "Give me that old time religion" but I did [sings], "Give me that old time, talkin' 'bout religion," you know I put that little *thing* in it you know, I always did have that *thing* but I didn't know what do do with the *thing* I had. So the style has always been with me but I had never introduced it for the people to hear. Because I would hear Fats Domino, Chuck Berry, Ruth Brown, Faye Adams, the Clovers, the Drifters, Muddy Waters, Howlin' Wolf, John Lee Hooker, Elmore James, and I admired them, but I always had my little thing I wanted to let the world hear, you know.

How did you feel when you came back into music after eight years?

I was at a loss. I thought, "Oh God, these people don't know me." I went to England and I felt good because the Beatles brought me to England, I gave them their first tour before they made a record, I carried them to Hamburg, Germany, to the Star Club, I was the star of the show, and by the way they used to order a lot of steaks and I had to pay for them because they didn't have the money. I gave Mick Jagger his first tour with the Rolling Stones. I also put another man into show business, I saw him the other day on *The Mike Douglas Show* and was very disheartened because he never mentioned my name; you know, I put James Brown in show business and he never mentioned my name. I put Joe Tex in the business, I put Jimi Hendrix in the business—he played in my band for two years before he made a record, I put Don Covay in the business, Otis Redding was in the business because of me, Billy Preston met the Beatles through me—it was in *Time* magazine last week. You know all these people, I put them in it, and they never mention what you've done, not that you want the credit, but when I hear James

Brown lyin'; giving credit to other people. I put him in the business, I'm the one who put him in, and he never mentioned my name.

One difference between the rock audiences today and in the Fifties is drugs. . . .

Well, people have been smoking grass for years, it's been growing for years. I think that when they talk about the Indians smoking the peace pipe, I believe when the Indians came over the hill that they was high. I believe that pipe the Indians were smoking was full of Acapulco Gold mixed with a little hashish. I believe it very firmly, and they had to be high the way they were runnin', they couldn't have gotten the strength no other way. So what I think about the thing today is I go with the Bible, which says let every man be persuaded by his own opinions. I don't condemn the young people for what they're doing, the same as I don't condemn the old person for taking an aspirin when he has a headache.

The same as if someone asks me, "Little Richard, have you ever seen God? How do you know there is a God?" I say, "Did you ever have a pain?" They say, "yes," and I say, "Did you see it?" I don't condemn anyone, there are a lot of drugs and things I don't know anything about it, but I don't condemn it, I want to know why, I think we should know why they're doing it, they could be disheartened, it could be the only way they know out. Who am I to say—I'm not a criteria—that this man is evil because he smokes marijuana. I smoke Kool cigarettes and I believe that marijuana is not as harmful as the Kool cigarettes. I'm not down on the man because he smokes marijuana; to me he's just as great as President Nixon or Lady Bird or Mrs. Eisenhower or Mr. Eisenhower.

What do you think about the resurgence of blues?

The reason that people like B. B. King are coming through now is, you see, a long time ago music like that was considered race music. As you know, Muddy Waters has never gotten the recognition he should've gotten, Howlin' Wolf has never gotten the recognition, the Rolling Stones used to sit and talk to me and they were saying, "These people are great, how come you never hear them?" And I think that people like Janis Joplin have made it possible for these people to come through. By them doing it, it makes kids want to see the originators.

Like, see, when Elvis came out, a lot of black groups would say, "Elvis cannot do so and so and so, shoo shoo shoo" [huffs and grumbles]. And I'd say, "Shut up, shut up." Let me tell you this—when I came out they wasn't playing no black artists on no Top 40 stations, I was the first to get played on the Top 40 stations—but it took people like Elvis and Pat Boone, Gene Vincent, to open the door for this kind of music, and I thank God for Elvis Presley. I thank the Lord for sending Elvis to open that door so I could walk down the road, you understand? And people like Janis Joplin and B. B. King, I'm glad to see what's happening to them, because they're true people, and rhythm & blues is the type of music that can't nobody teach you, you have to be dedicated. So it proves that she is dedicated. It proves that B. B. King is dedicated. A lot of the music I see today is trash, it's a lot of banging and the kids are not really doin' it, but a lot of the people are doin' it.

WHAT WAS THE FIRST LIVE *show you did after coming out of the ministry?*

London. At the Savoy Theater, which is the Beatles' theater. Fantastic. The Beatles were there, Princess Margaret, the Dave Clark Five, Tommy Jones, everybody, and we was having a ball.

Were you nervous at all?

I don't get nervous. You know, I'd be so glad when they introduced me I could hardly wait to get out there. I'd get mad because I had to come off. I just love it.

That's all I live for, to make people happy, I feel like I could just die! It's a good feeling.

If you couldn't sing or perform tomorrow, what would you do?

Just put me in my casket and let me go if I couldn't do my thing. That's my thing. Some people got two things, but I only got one and that's it.

How did you get into giving away your clothes at the end of the show?

Well, you see so many people there admiring what you have on. I would have thrown that glass shirt in the audience last night but it would've cut, so that's the reason I didn't throw it. It's real glass. It's a shirt that weighs ten pounds so if I'd have threw it in the audience the kids would've cut themselves up. So I thought about that, I said, oh God, I would have a heart attack if that ever happened, so that's the reason I didn't.

But everywhere I play I give my outfits away. I'm sure it's over a half a million dollars in clothes I've given away to my fans, but I don't care because without them, you're not a star. I threw away a mink coat on the first show last night, a beautiful mink coat. But I tell you, I don't mind doing that, because without the people you're not a star. And so why can't you give them something back what they've given you? They really bought it. It's just like someone bought you a loaf of bread, and you can't give them a slice? When you got to buy something cheap to give them, you're gonna give them some burnt bread when they've given you good bread? It's like a lady said to me, "Why don't you buy something cheap to throw away?" And I said, "No, I'm gonna give them just what I like, and if it's not something I like, I'm not gonna throw it out there, I want it to be something that I like." I had to go out and buy two pairs of shoes today because I threw my shoes in the audience.

Who was your hero when you were growing up in Macon, Georgia?

Well, I came from a family where my people didn't like rhythm & blues. Bing Crosby— "Pennies From Heaven"—Ella Fitzgerald, was all I heard. And I knew there was something that could be louder than that, but I didn't know where to find it. And I found it was me.

Don't you play the piano anymore?

The reason I don't play that one was it was out of tune, and when I played I put the band out of tune. In Vegas I played the piano on every number. I stand and play with my toes, you should see me with my toes, you've never seen toes like Little Richard's. The livin' toe, yes, Lord. Shut up.

Are you conscious of being very vocal when you perform or is it intuitive?

The beautiful thing is I just like to say it, and the way I say it they know I don't mean no harm—shut up, I'd rather do it myself. I just love to talk to the young people; I don't like to talk to all those old people. They're old and I'm young and out of place.

Do you get much chance to talk to young people?

Yes, everywhere I go I talk to the young people. In fact, in my personal help, I don't have nothing but young people. My whole staff is young. I don't want no old people; I want young ideas so if I don't think right, they can help me. All those old people thinking about engines, things that happened back in 1900. My Lord, we weren't even making records then.

What do you think is bugging young people?

Realism. They're not gonna accept no "who shot John," "who came and got Jimmy," Minnie Pearl. They're not gonna accept nothing less than realism. And they tell their mothers and fathers what they think, if they get put outdoors they're still gonna talk. And they're tired of the old people pouring their thoughts and minds on them. And this thing about a young man of eighteen going in the army but he still can't vote, if he's old enough to fight he's old enough to vote, but they don't want them to vote because they'll put a young man in office.

Rock has always been related to religion; what connection do you see in your life between them?

Between my type of music and religion? I believe my music is the healin' music. Just like Oral Roberts says he's a divine healer, I believe my music can make the blind see, the lame walk, the deaf and dumb hear and talk, because it inspires and uplifts people. I've had old women tell me I made them feel they were nineteen years old. It uplifts the soul, you see everybody's movin', they're happy, it regenerates the heart and makes the liver quiver, the bladder splatter, the knees freeze.

Is there anything you want to say to all your fans?

All right, everybody, let your hair down. If you have a wig take your wig off and get down with it. I just think that everybody needs to get down with it, today. All the real people are down with it, but it's the squares that ain't gettin' nowhere. Just get down with it. This record has a whole lot of feeling in it [Little Richard "live" album], but the new one I got coming is outtasight. I got one called "Miss Lucy." "Miss Lucy, where is your daughter?" It's outtasight. I want to tell all the kids, if they haven't seen me to get the chance to see me. When you see the name, come, because it's an experience. The Jimi Hendrix Experience, but they got to see the Little Richard Experience. The twenty-year experience and I'm still twenty-four.

I've heard you sing a couple of Hank Williams numbers at your concerts, like "Your Cheatin' Heart," "Love Sick Blues," you really add another dimension to country, not just that tiny, whiny sound you're always hearing.

Yeah, well, you see, I put a little something of myself into it, I don't just *do* the country sound, I make it mine, you understand, I sing it with an R&B rhythm and it makes it into something else.

I saw you on a talk show last week with Margaret Mead and you were saying something about . . .

About marijuana [*laughs*]. Yeah, she reminds me of my Aunt Lulu back in Macon, Georgia. She used to swing! And she used to get high! They used to slip grass in her pipe, and they would fill the pipe full of grass, put tobacco on top. She'd puff away. She didn't know what was happenin', she be just laughin'. My momma'd say, "What's wrong with Aunt Lulu?" She'd be swinging high. She would swing up, she was a little lady, she didn't have teeth; she'd swing almost over the rim. And I said to Miss Mead, "You remind me of my Aunt Lulu," and then I told her to *shut up!* [*laughs*]. That's where I got the idea for "Good Golly, Miss Molly," somethin' she used to say when she got high swinging up there. Everything I sung was really something that happened around my hometown; I was born in the slums, you see, my daddy sold whiskey, bootleg whiskey, white lightnin'!

Wasn't he a preacher too?

No, his father was a minister, and I have two uncles besides that are ministers. And my daddy, he would sell this whiskey and there used to be a man comin' around singin', beatin' a washboard, you ever seen a washboard? In those days they didn't call 'em washboards, they called them rub-boards. And the man'd come around singin':

Bam-a-lam-bam
You shall be free
In the mornin'
You shall be free

and he'd beat the thing, you know. I'd follow him around, goin' "Bam-a-lam-bam/You shall be free." Then the vegetable man would come by. He would draw the people out and he would sing [*sings in a high gospel voice*]:

Blackeyed peas
And a barrel of beans
Grocer man comin' with a cart of greens,
Honey.

and people would all come to the door, and the man would be ridin' down the street with a horse, a wagon, and singin' and everybody would come to the door, and he'd just keep singin':

Blackeyed peas
And a barrel of beans
Grocer man comin' with a cart of greens,
Honey.

It was really somethin'. Everybody be singin'. We would be washin' in the backyard, just singin', and we sound like a big choir, and we never practiced: it was a big choir like fifty voices all over the neighborhood, and that's what I came from, Otis Redding came from it and James, he came from there too.

CAN YOU TELL ME THE STORY that's behind "Long Tall Sally"?

Yeah . . . it was a lady who used to drink quite a bit, she always like pretend she had a cold when she came to our house. She would call up and she would say, "Oh, Mrs. Penniman, I got this awful cough here!" She'd put sugar in her whiskey, and they called it a toddy, so she toddied all day, and when she'd get drunk, she would get up and say, "Can't make it, this cold is killing me, Mrs. Penniman," and oh, God, I came out of all that. That was a bad vibration, but a good vibration, too, because if I hadn't been through that, I would never have become Little Richard.

What about Long Tall Sally?

I was losing that, thank you for bringing me back. Sally used to come back with all of this whiskey, and she'd get drunk, and she was tall and ugly, man, that was an ugly woman. She was so ugly that people used to turn their heads, she didn't have but two teeth and they were on each side of her tongue, and she was cockeyed.

So we used to say, "Long Tall Sally, she's built for speed," and her old man they called John. In Georgia, when you're raised around a lot of people, you call them your uncle and your aunt, so we used to call this cat Uncle John, but he was really married to Mary, which was a big, fat lady, who used to sit on the porch and eat watermelon all the time, she was a sight to see, too. We used to call her Short Fat Fanny. This cat would be out there, and they'd get to fighting on Saturday. All the black people got paid off on Friday, and you'd know when Friday came, because of whiskey and fights and joyful times, too, and she and he started a good fight.

So when he'd see her coming, he'd duck back in this little alley. I just thought of my whole experience. All my songs are really experiences, like "Miss Ann"—Ann Johnson. I'd never sung like this before, I was singing ballads, and when I started singing like this it was hard at first, boy, I used to get hoarse, because I was singing so hard, but now I've gotten used to it, but it's really given me an experience and courage to go on. Very few people get two chances, I think it's a chosen bunch that paid their dues right, and I'm glad that I'm one of the ones that was selected, and I'm grateful to everyone everywhere, all races, creeds and colors, thank you, thank you, thank you, ohh, ohh, thank you.

What was a recording session like in the Fifties?

The studio was about the size of this room,

about fifteen by ten feet, air coming from everywhere; in the wintertime we froze, if he was playing saxophone he was a froze saxophone player. And I would sit there, man, and play, and me and the band would get together and jam and pick out riffs, and I'd hum ideas to them, pick them out on the piano, and we never missed, because I always came out with something different, because I like to create like the "Freedom Blues"; it's a message I want the whole world to hear. I want the black power, the red power, the white power, the brown power, the green power to listen because this is what we need—get rid of those freedom blues. "It may seem very hard to do, just open your mind, let love come through." You hear me call, and you hear my plea, everybody, every man, I don't care where he's from, I don't care if he's rich, poor, black or white, whatever race, that man wants to be free, let him do his thing.

Where was the studio?

New Orleans. Cosimo's studio [Cosimo Matassa's J&M Studios]. I cut all of my hits there. Fats and I were using the same recording band at this time, but we got two different sounds. Bumps Blackwell produced them, he wrote some of the songs with me, not really arranged them, just copied what I was doin' on the piano, that's all the people in the band do, they copy what I'd be doin'; when you hear them, you're really hearing me, because what they've done, I've showed them. Besides, I have a thing I want to hear that makes me work—I have to hear the guitars, I must hear the guitars, and then I can get my feel. I'd rather the bass and everything is off, let me hear the guitars!

On the early things, did you start off with the piano because of the church thing?

Yeah, well, if you notice, on "Spreadin' Natta," I start off on the piano. The name of it is "Spreadin' Natta," Spreadin' Natta, a girl. Spreadin' Natta, what's the matta? A girl gave me some of the words to this song, a lady named Mabel. She wrote "Heebie Jeebies." She brought me some words and I added on to them. She had some words that I didn't like, like she brought one song called "The Wine Drinking Rooster," and I never saw a rooster drink wine, so I couldn't get the song together, because that would be a drunk rooster, and I'd hate to meet him.

What about "Ready Teddy"?

I didn't write "Ready Teddy." They brought me the words and I made up the melody, and at the time I didn't have sense enough to claim so

much money, because I really made them hits. But now I've learned; you know, you pay a whole lot of big dues, and I've paid almost two million dollars worth of dues, but I still didn't cheat nobody. I was cheated, but I didn't cheat nobody, so I let that man sleep at night at his house and let his conscience be his guide while he's resting. I didn't get the money, but I still have the freedom.

What about "Slippin' and Slidin'"?

A fellow in my band, Lee Diamond, gave me some of the words and I changed them around. Another cat put "Slippin' and Slidin'" out before I did, Eddie Bow, and it was a hit by him in New Orleans, and they put mine out the following week, and it killed him, because he didn't have the rhythm, you see, he didn't have that thing I have.

Who played in the band you and Fats used?

Lee Allen, Red Tyler, Earl Palmer. Red Tyler died the other day, and Lee Allen died the other day. Lee Allen took all the solos on tenor sax, Red Tyler played the baritone sax and Earl Palmer, he's a big drummer here in L.A., he played on all the sessions.

"Lucille, won't you do your sister's will," it was another kind of song, so I put it in this rhythm. "Lucille" reminds me of the song "Spreadin' Natta," it's got that raunchy thing. And the song just tore the country down, everywhere you turned, and all the kids loved it, because they could do the dance. But really, I didn't know what inspired me to write "Lucille," I could tell you a lie, but I gotta be truthful—I don't know what inspired me to write it, it may have been the rhythm.

IS IT TRUE THAT YOU HAD A *throne and a carpet in the fifties?*

YES, I used all that, but I got out of that, it was almost like a Pope, and if I wasn't doing it, the Pope ain't Catholic. I had the guards and everything. Pouche was one of my guards. They dressed like Queen Elizabeth's guards. And when we went to restaurants, we'd have a flag with my picture on it, and we'd spread out the carpet, and it was a big attraction, people used to come from everywhere to see it. And I had the nerve to do it. I used to sit up on that throne. I liked it, too, I used to feel so good sittin' up there, I didn't want to come down, when it was time to come down. I used to sit up there and drink a cup of coffee. I used to have a ball on the throne, I can say I *have* sat on the throne.

Why did you give up singing in the Fifties?

It was at the time they sent the satellite up, and I was in Sydney, Australia, on a tour with Eddie Cochran, Gene Vincent, and it was a fantastic, monstrous tour. And I had a dream, and I saw some terrible things in this dream. And then I was on the airplane, and I just prayed, I felt like I was holding the plane up. I just had that feeling that God was holding the plane up because I was on that plane; I just felt that so strongly. So I came out of show business and went back to school to study theology, but eventually I decided to come back in this business and teach goodness in this business, not that I'm a minister—but to teach love, because music is the universal language, and to teach love to all people, all men, all women, not separatism, but to teach that we are one, we are God's bouquet, and teach it through music, through joy, through happiness.

What did you do at the college?

Oakwood College at Huntsville, Alabama. I studied the Bible—a book called *Daniel and the Revelations, Steps to Christ, Daniel and the Prophets,* about Moses, about Pharaoh, about God's great plan for man and about how black people have ruled before—King Solomon was black. So God gives everyone a chance and the next ruler will be Him, I believe, wholeheartedly. I studied about how you can praise God through music—there are a lot of people who are devoted to music, because music can bring something to people that nothing else can. In fact, I don't like to be without music too long, I feel lost; when I get in the car, music goes everywhere—loud—I don't like it low—*loud.*

It shakes up your body, right?

One of my records is called, "You Got to Have a Beat in Your Body." It's on the new album. You got to have a beat in your body—that's the truth.

You put out some gospel records, too, right?

Yes, I put out an album of gospel songs, on Mercury. It was beautiful, with strings. Quincy Jones did all the arrangements, and he conducted.

Did you make the album while you were in the ministry?

Yes, I did. I never cut music out of my life because music is my life, my whole life. I live for it. It's beautiful how you can talk to people through music.

When you say you're the bronze Liberace, what do you mean?

It's more of a joke situation, about me being a black man and he being white, I'm the bronze. The flamboyant dress, he does it and I do it, it's just the thing. I think he's a great artist, one of the greatest.

Who designs your costumes?

I designed them myself, and a fellow named Tommy Ruth and another fellow named Melvin James make them. Melvin James lives in Detroit, and Tommy Ruth lives in Oakland, California, and has Mr. T's Boutique.

Do you think it was a mistake recording on the Okeh label?

Yes. This is the only thing that I've recorded since I got back in the business that I really enjoyed. It was my fault, though, when I went with other companies, I should have made a stipulation like I did when I went with Warner Bros. that I am my own producer and they have to record whatever I want to record, and I want it in black and white—everything you want me to have and promise me, put it in black and white. So they did, and I got my sound; it's the first time I got something nice. I would have hit before now if I'd had it. They see one thing onstage and another on the record, so you can see somebody was messing up. I have it onstage but when I get in the studio it wasn't there because they was in charge of it. All those trumpets and things were drowning me out, so you can't hear no rhythm. The worst records I ever made in my life was on Okeh, and Brunswick. Very bad promotion and very bad management.

Did you like the live album 'Little Richard's Greatest Hits'?

Somewhat, not really, though. This new one is the only thing I've done since I was back in the business that I think is really good, because it's got the thing that I like, the thing that I feel. You see, when I make records, I ain't making them for no black or white, I'm making them for everybody, and I believe that you can create a groove and a mood, you don't have to sound like Motown or you're not a star. If they turn from you tomorrow, you're just another man. A star spelled backwards means rats.

Are you going to do some more blues?

I'm gonna do some raunchy blues this time. I'm gonna get down in it, way, way down. I'm gonna do it all this time. I'm gonna put out an album singing ballads, an album singing country tunes. I'm going in all the fields, I'm gonna *sing.* This album has a country tune, "The Lovesick Blues."

Sometimes when you do a country song, you seem to make fun of it a little.

I don't make fun of it, I love country music. But when I started out, my friends downed me for listening to country music, and I used to have to hide my records, because the kids would laugh, but I like it. I really like it, and I'm glad I don't have to hide it any more. I like "Galveston" and "Wichita Lineman," whose songs have a whole lot of feeling in them. I like a lot of country phrasing, because it's soulful to me. Like when Glen Campbell says one word "Galveston"—it shakes me up. "Galveston, oh Galveston, da-da-da da-dum-dum-dum," it takes me, man, that's the whole soul of it right there, when he says that one word. It's a thing, and so I dig it. I wouldn't make fun of it because it's too pure and real, that music is as real as blues.

Most of your songs are closer to gospel than to blues; is that because blues represented the old kind of thing, was too depressing?

Yes. There are songs I've heard you probably never would have heard. I've heard people sing with no music, just walkin' the streets, you can hear them late at night, at two o'clock in the morning. You hear somebody singin', you hear the birds, and some water runnin' and you hear somebody wailin' away. They sound like they are without a friend in the world. And there is this raggedy house that you can see through the boards, and they got paper to keep the air from comin' in. Oh, God, what a day.

Can you talk about your life with the Johnsons?

My father put me outdoors when I was 13, and there was a club called the Tick Tock Club, and a white couple named Ann and Johnny ran it. So I went there and played one night, and I sang "Tutti-Frutti" and some other songs, and the people went mad. I played this song called "Guitar Rag" on the piano, and I used to have to play that four or five times a night. So they adopted me and bought me a brand-new car, and I went to school, and she was just like my mother for many years. Then Johnny passed away, and I got famous, but she wouldn't ever take any money from me; I offer her money, but she won't take it. They are millionaires themselves, but they were really sweet to me. I slept in the same bed between them and I'll never forget them. I think they had a lot to do with me loving people today; I know there is love in every race. That is very unreal in Georgia; it was real real, though, because they didn't get nothing out of it, period, and they didn't have to do it, and they did. They really put me together in a big way, and I can't forget it, it's a beautiful thing. I see her now once every year, she still lives in Georgia, and she still has her club, too. I think they had a lot to do with me being Little Richard.

Why did your father put you out?

My father didn't like loud music, so that's why he put me out, and because I dressed loud. It's just like the kids getting put out of the house today. It was one of those tight situations, but I got through it, with the help of God inspiring these people to do what they did for me, and what I believe they'll do for me today if I really needed them.

How many brothers and sisters do you have?

There are twelve. Seven boys and five girls. I'm the only one in show business, the only one that has something to say in public, period. I have two sisters that are registered nurses, and one of my brothers is a C.P.A., all of them have good positions now. I raised them, they were little bitty kids when I brought them to California. My brother Peyton, who played in the group, is in the service and will be out in another month.

What was the dream that made you leave show business to go to college?

It was about the world ending soon, and I was lost, I could see myself running in that dream, and it was very frightening to me. About how close the coming of God is, and how people are letting hate control them instead of letting love rule their lives, and how we let color differences block us from love, instead of realizing that God is a God of beauty and we are his bouquet. I think in show business there is a need for people who have love and want to spread something good to young people.

Can you describe tours of the Fifties?

The rage was just like the Beatles rage was, but the rage wasn't for just one star, it was for all the rock stars. It was a rage over Elvis, a rage over me; you would hear of riots everywhere, there were policemen outside the hotel and kids out there trying to get autographs.

What does the saxophone player think about you putting him on?

Boogie? Oh, he loves it. If I didn't do it, he'd probably cry, that's more attention than he probably gets in a year. He loves for me to tell them to give Boogie a hand. He's just like a big, fat baby; the only thing missing is the bottle. He's part of my act now, but it cracks the people up everywhere we go, they fall out over this big ole Boogie. Shut up. Mike Douglas went crazy over my "shut up," he just kept saying, "Shut up, shut up."

If you had left show business to do something other

than theology, do you think you'd have made a faster comeback?

Yes, there wouldn't have been the criticism. But show business is a timing thing, too, and I think now is the time for something like me to come out. You can feel it, it's time for something else, and it's *me.* I had to wait on my time, so I waited and I didn't stop, I passed the test 'cause I waited. Like the Bible says, "Them that wait on the Lord, He shall renew their strength."

What do you think of the Creedence Clearwater Revival's song "Travelling Band"?

That's just "Long Tall Sally." They're really rocking and it ain't bull, they're really rocking. And his voice is strong, he's got the same thing that I have, it's strong, it's there. It's strong without any doubt, it's not weak, and there's no letup, it stays forceful. Everything the cat touches is a smash; it's funky, you can't say nothing but it's funky. John Fogerty asked me if I'd do a record with him. You know, me singing along with them doing my old numbers. But I don't need it. I'm a star just with myself, it'd put me in the background, and I don't need that. If anyone is going to revive Little Richard, it's gonna be Little Richard.

Do you plan to release a single soon?

Yes, we're going to put out "Freedom Blues" with "Do Drop In" on the other side. It will be out next week.

Richard, did you ever see this button? It reads, "I'd rather do it myself."

Oh, my Lord! Ain't that somethin'? They musta got it from me, they musta heard me sayin' it. They should have one that says, "Shut up!" That's what I'm thinkin' of callin' the album—*Shut Up!* Don't you like that? Yeah, that's what I'll call it—*Shut Up! I'd Rather Do It Myself.*

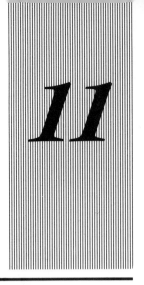

11

INTERVIEWED
BY
HAPPY
TRAUM (1970)

Van Morrison, spiritual son and soul brother of Ray Charles and Leadbelly, jazz and blues, Ireland and America, is not for sale.

That quality accounts for what the merchants would call an "erratic" career of hits—from "Gloria," with the rock band Them, in 1965, to "Wavelength" in 1978—and misses.

But the thing is, Morrison has rarely bothered

to take aim. Which may have been what attracted him to the community of Woodstock, New York, in the early seventies and which made him attractive to fellow musician Happy Traum.

"He was intensely involved in the music," says Traum, who, aside from performing, was an editor of the folk music magazine *Sing Out!*, an occasional writer for ROLLING STONE and a music teacher. "Other people around him were pushing the business, but he was wrapped up in the music. And we had a lot in common—we both were into John Lee Hooker, Leadbelly and Robert Johnson."

The two lived close to each other and would get together occasionally to play music "informally." One day in July 1970—between the twenty-five-year-old Morrison's *Moondance* album and *His Band and the Street Choir* (which would result in a rare hit single, "Domino")—Traum suggested an interview. "He immediately said OK," says Happy. "He hadn't done many and wasn't very verbal, but he was willing to talk."
—BF-T

VAN MORRISON SITS ON THE EDGE OF the bed and absently picks an old Gibson. He is moody, his eyes intense and his smile sudden; his Belfast accent is thick but musical, statements often lilting into a half question mark.

The only child of a Scottish dockworker and his Irish wife, Van left home at the age of fifteen and has

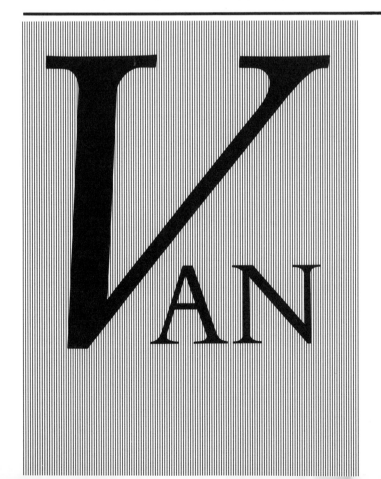

MORRISON

been on the streets or on the road ever since. He has settled in Woodstock, with his wife Janet, their young song Peter and a new baby girl, Shannon. Van is twenty-four now; he will probably be one of the most important singers of our time.

WAS THEM THE FIRST GROUP *you were in?*

Oh, no, by no means. I used to play in a group called Deanie Sands and the Javelins. This chick called Deanie Sands did half the singing and I did half the singing, and I played guitar. We did a sort of country-blues-rock. That was in Belfast.

How does someone from Belfast get into American country blues?

We get it both live and from records. Memphis Slim has been in Belfast; Jesse Fuller, Champion Jack Dupree, John Lee Hooker's been there. They've got folk clubs and rock clubs there, but it's got nothing to do with the English scene. In fact I'd go so far as to say it doesn't have much to do with the Irish scene either; it's just Belfast. It's got its own identity, it's got its own people . . . it's just a different race, a different breed of people. There's a lot of changes here, too. Like the McPeaks [a family group of traditional Irish singers] on one hand, and some others of us on the other hand, and they're open to all kinds of music, not just one thing. Maybe a third of the people that are into R&B would go to hear the McPeaks.

Jean Ritchie once told me that on her collecting trips to Ireland traditional singers would often sing turned away from a visitor, or standing behind someone, possibly because of a traditional feeling that singing is a very private experience, and in singing a song you were exposing something very private about yourself.

I used to stand on my head and sing, I remember that, but I don't remember standing behind anybody.

What kind of music did you have around the house when you were growing up?

Everything. I heard a lot of blues records; we always had that. And I heard a few street players, street singers and dancers; and my parents played music. We lived in a pretty funky neighborhood. I mean, it wasn't a white-collar district, let me put it that way. The people weren't involved in any other place but Belfast. If you lived in London, you could relate to a whole different scene, but when you lived in Belfast, you'd just relate to *that* scene. Either you'd accept that, or you'd go somewhere else.

But it's not like any other place in the world.

Like Boston and New York, they're different places on the *map*. You'd have to be there to really get an idea of what I'm talking about. If I took you to some of these places and you hung out and met the people, you'd understand. But I can't even scratch the surface now because it's so delicate.

Was Them a Belfast group?

Yes, but as soon as things started going pretty good they didn't call us an Irish group anymore; they called it a British group, and we got stuck with that. Then, after that, we became an English group! I don't know how in the world they mistook it for an English group, 'cause if they ever heard us talk they'd know it wasn't. It was an Irish group!

When was Them together?

In 1964 and 1965. Around mid-1965 we all decided to split it up. I was still under contract, as was one of the other guys, the bass player, so we decided to finish the contract out. We got a new group together, but it was just the same group. I mean, the name was "Them," but it ended up that I was making records with four session men, and they were putting "Them" on the label. Then they got me and some other people on the road, and "Them" was just a name. That's all it ever was, except for the original group that played at the Maritime in Belfast. The group that played there was Them, but after we went out of that club it just wasn't the same people.

Our main success was with a song I wrote, "Gloria." It was capitalized on a lot by other people, especially a lot of American groups, whereas I really didn't capitalize on it all that much. But that's another story.

Then we put out a record called *Them Again.* We weren't putting out records at that time to *get* anywhere; it wasn't that scene at all. I mean, it was hard enough to get us in one place together without having to think about that. We were making records where I was making maybe three songs on an album with just studio cats, and maybe the rest of the songs with two studio cats and three members of the group. It was kinda like mishmash, and it wasn't really any good. But they released it as *Them Again* because obviously the record company wanted to do its thing.

When I was with the group I was still kind of on my own. I was hung up with this stupid contract, but I was always on my own. I just played with Them because that was what was happening then, but I was still playing with my friends and pickin' my own stuff.

I did "Brown-Eyed Girl" in 1967. One of the

guys that produced some of the records for the group, Bert Berns, came over to London to meet the group. He produced one of his songs with the group, and it was a hit. He called me in Belfast from New York and said, how about getting together to do another record. I had a couple of offers, but I thought this was the best one, seeing as I wanted to come to America anyway, so I took him. The two things sort of coincided, so I came over and played him a few songs, and we made the record.

Did your success on the charts change your professional life to a large extent?

Well, it did, but it didn't really change *me*, 'cause I was still there. But I got to play in some wrong places. That's one thing, it put me in some of the worst joints I ever worked. I don't want to mention any names or offend anybody in the business, but it just put me in some awkward positions, because they were *unreal*, they were totally unreal. Like lip-synching to the record on a television show. I can't lip-synch, 'cause every-time I do a song I do it differently. I just can't sing any song the same way twice. I didn't really see how that had anything to do with me. Obviously, it was what *they* wanted, but they didn't want *me*. They had some kind of singer in mind for that, but it wasn't me. I just couldn't do that kind of thing.

Was there a lot of pressure for you to give in to that kind of thing?

Oh, sure. Bert wanted me to write a song with him that would be a hit, but I just didn't feel that kind of song. I mean, maybe that was *his* kind of song, but it wasn't *my* kind of song, so I just told him. I mean, if you want to do that kind of song, man, you should just go in and *do* it, get yourself a group and sing that song, but I've got *my* kind of song that's different. I've always been writing the kind of songs I do now, even with Them.

I'd write a song and bring it into the group, and we'd sit there and bash it around, and that's all it was—they weren't playing the *song*, they were just playing whatever it was. They'd say, "Okay. We got drums so let's put drums on it," and they weren't thinking about the song; all they were thinking about was putting *drums* on it, or putting an electric guitar on it, but it was my song, and I had to watch it go down. So there was a point where I had to say, "Wait a minute. Hold it! Stop!" Because I just couldn't see my songs go down like that all the time. It was wrong. There was much more involved in them than that.

Do your songs come easily to you, or do you really have to struggle with them?

It all depends on the song. Some of them are hard, and I really have to work on them. One song I wrote when I was living in Cambridge—I was just involved in it for two hours. It wasn't like I planned to write it—I planned to go out for the night—and I found myself *forced* to write a song. Sometimes it just flows out—it all depends what the song is—but I can't be forced to write by someone else. That's just where I'm at. I can't be forced to do anything. I just have to do it my own way.

To what extent are your songs about real people or events? Cyprus Avenue, for instance? You mention it twice on 'Astral Weeks.'

Cyprus Avenue is a pretty real place. If you're ever over in Belfast, I'll take you to see it. It's not a jive place, it's real. A lot of things I do are real. Whatever people want to confront, I can confront them with it. Of course, I don't always *want* to confront them with it; maybe I do because it just comes out. A guy in Boston one time asked me about this song, but he just asked me about two lines because he seemed to identify with these two lines. Well, at the time I wrote those two lines he was thinking about . . . well, you don't have to live *that;* I mean, if you want to live *that,* that's your business, but I'm writing a song to entertain people. If I write something, it's not necessarily how I'm going to feel in a year, or tomorrow; it's just that at the time. That's what it is. An album can last for a long time; then that's the way it is. But if I do something else, it's entertainment; that's what *that* is. People try to pick out particular things and bring them up, when they should bring everything out because it's a total thing, a flow.

There was a review in ROLLING STONE *that said, "If he had stage presence he'd be hard to take. . . ." Do you know what they meant by that?*

Why don't you come and see the show? Do *you* know what he means?

I've seen you in a lot of situations, and sometimes you are *hard to take. You told me once after you played with the Band in Boston that you didn't feel you were able to reach such a large audience. Do you prefer a small audience?*

We just did that on the spur of the moment, and we didn't have our sound thing together. I go through quite a few changes; like in a period of two weeks, three weeks, four weeks, I go through a lot of changes, and sometimes I'm not doing what I really want to do. Sometimes I'm doing something because that's what's happening at the moment, that's what's available. It's all part of it, sure, but it doesn't represent where I'm at.

You have a very intimate appeal to a lot of people. I

103

think you get inside of your listeners as very few other performers do. It's almost a private relationship between you and your audience. Do you think this can be projected to a large festival audience?

It all depends on what people want. Do they want to be touched? Do they really want to be part of that spiritual thing? If they want that, they can get it off me, but they can't get it by just calling it a festival . . . that's just not the way to get it. I do feel I can communicate to large groups of people, but they have to know what they're getting, and I have to know what I'm giving. It's quality, not quantity.

WHAT MADE YOU DECIDE TO *produce your new album, 'Moon-dance,' yourself?*

That's a good question because that was the hardest part. The rest comes naturally to me—singing it and playing it—but producing it was a whole other thing. It was the first time I had ever done it, and I had to tax my imagination for all sorts of stuff. It was a big job for me—it was fun, but it was hard work. The reason I decided to do it in the first place was just that I couldn't find anyone else to do it. I looked around and I spoke to a lot of cats, and I had some people come up here to Wood-stock, and we pushed around ideas, but no one knew what I was looking for except me, so I just did it.

Most of my own singing was done live, although sometimes we did a rhythm track and then the vocal, or sometimes the vocal and the rhythm track and then added the horns. But mostly it was live.

How were all the arrangements done? Were they head arrangements, or did somebody write out charts?

They were kind of head arrangements; four of us did them. The piano, horns and myself took care of all the arrangements. There were no charts, and a lot of it was spontaneous. But it wasn't like a jam; it was more than that. I did all the mixing myself, too . . . I was stuck with the engineer. I learned so much from doing it that I would never have known about because there's so many groovy people that are doing that. There's two engineers in particular, Elliott Scheiner and Tony May, who I worked with at A&R and who were really a bitch to work with, so I dug that. They gave me a lot of help on the technical end of things.

'Astral Weeks' was produced by someone else. Did you feel as comfortable in that situation?

No, I didn't really feel comfortable; I've got to say it, I didn't feel comfortable at all, even though it did justice to what I was trying to say. My producer, Lew [Merenstein], must have pulled himself up to scratch to do it, but I had something else in mind. I'm just glad that he was around at the time to do it. That's all, I'm just glad he was around because it could have come out entirely different. You know what the album scene is like, right? I've been very lucky, and I'm very grateful.

Is 'Astral Weeks' still selling steadily?

As a matter of fact, it is. *Astral Weeks* is the kind of album . . . you know, Joe Smith [Vice President of Warner Bros.] called me and said, "We know what's going down with this album now. We're going to be selling it for another six years." It's not a pop album; it's an album that's going to be bought over a long period of time. It's not going to be a chart thing, but it's going to sell a lot.

Did you consciously change the style on this new record, or did it just happen?

It was more or less the songs. . . . There were certain songs on this album that I had to do. I don't know if it was conscious, but everybody involved in the album, the other musicians and myself, had a certain feeling about the whole thing that went down. It was very human, and everybody enjoyed it. There was no uptightness about doing the album. I wouldn't dream of doing it any other way.

It is very different from 'Astral Weeks,' which from beginning to end is almost a continuous song. On 'Moondance,' each song is very distinctive and separate.

I'll tell you, *Astral Weeks* is not like one song at all. Believe it or not, *Astral Weeks* is a rock opera, but it was long before its time. It didn't get arranged so on the album. The way I do it personally is entirely different from the way it's done on the album. I was kind of restricted because it wasn't really understood what I really wanted on the date, so it tended to come out like it did, but it wasn't meant to be like that. I wrote it as an opera, but it didn't really surface the way it could have.

When you say it was an opera, do you mean that there was a story line that could be followed?

Oh, sure. A definite story line.

If you were to do it over again, how would you change it so that it was in some kind of context?

I would change the arrangements, because the arrangements are too samey. Guys like Richard Davis and Jay Berliner, those guys have got a distinctive style, and they're groovy for like two songs, and they can really do it, but four or five other songs should have had a change in mood. That should have happened, and it didn't. I didn't have the same mood in mind for the whole album. But that's the way I wrote it, as an opera, at the very beginning, and I've still got it like that in poetry form.

How did you happen to write a song like "Madame George"?

I don't know, I just remember writing it, that's all.

Did you have anyone in particular in mind? Did you know anyone like that?

Like what? What's Madame George look like? What are you trying to say . . . in front? So I know.

It seems to me to be the story of a drag queen.

Oh, no. Whatever gave you that impression? It all depends on what you want, that's all, how you want to go. If you see it as a male or a female or whatever, it's your trip. How do I see it? I see it as a . . . a Swiss cheese sandwich. Something like that.

I'm not the only one that's come up with that interpretation, am I?

Nobody's really hit me with that, nobody's really said that at all. Everybody gives me a quizzical look, a question-mark stare, and they think I know what they're talking about. "What about like blah blah blah . . ." and they expect me to go, "Yeah!" It's just not that simple.

Just imagine we had a sponsor, and he gave you a plane ticket and me a plane ticket, two-way tickets from Woodstock to Ireland, and we got on a plane and we went from here to Belfast, and we hung out and came back, then you would know the song. But I don't think I could tell you about the song if we didn't do that. But it's part of the opera. Like I said, Cyprus Avenue is a real place with definite people, and it's true.

Is Cyprus Avenue a street that only you've had personal experiences on, or is it a famous street, like, say, MacDougal Street, where everyone in Belfast would know that street?

It's not a famous street, but it's gonna be after this is over {laughs}. It's not a commercial street, though, far from it. It's near where I grew up.

You ask a lot of good questions that I'd never think of. I'm sick of hearing, "What's your favorite color," or, "What kind of girls do you like." There was one point where these people I was with just thought that all there was in the world was interviews like that. I did about four a day, and I just got so pissed off I was ready to . . . Like all these teeny-bopper magazines. Everyone just asked me dumb questions, and

they had dumb faces. Bang Records was a mistake for me; it was the wrong label. That just wasn't my market.

You don't seem too hassled about your situation now.

No, I'm pretty easy now.

In the song "Astral Weeks," you mention Huddie Ledbetter. Was he an influence on you?

I'd say he was *the* influence, not just any influence. I never got to hear him in person, which was a shame because he must've been something else. Did you ever hear his version of "Easy Rider"? That man was so great; it's hard to find people like that today. We've got Ray Charles, but when you look around, who else have you got? I mean, you've got a couple of people, but who else? I'd go as far as to say that that's how I got into the business, that's how I got here, with Leadbelly and Woody Guthrie and Jelly Roll Morton and Ray Charles. That's what made me start singing.

Nowadays you say, "Leadbelly," and people say, "What's this cat, crazy or something?" It's always been like that, not only over there but in America; it's like a minority thing. But the people who dig it really dig it a hundred percent, which is beautiful. As I said, the major influence was Leadbelly . . . if it wasn't for him I may never have been here, so I'm glad if I can get him into a song.

I didn't really hear a lot of things that were going down when I was over there. I heard some of them and wanted to hear more, but I couldn't because it was happening over *here,* which was a down for me. So I just grabbed as many Leadbelly and Guthrie and Hank Williams records as I could grab and tried to learn something.

It's fantastic the way those kinds of influences work. Here's a man who lived in a whole different culture, worked his balls off all his life, and now, twenty years after his death, you are a living example of his influence.

I don't think he's really dead. A lot of people's bodies die, but I don't think they die with them. I think a lot of them are still hanging around somewhere in the air. It can't be that weak because these people are so strong. You've got people like Leadbelly, like Woody, like Hooker (he's alive), you've got people of that stance who are so strong that those people can't die, they just leave something behind. I just don't believe that those people will ever die.

All those people that you've mentioned would have played exactly the same music whether there was money in it for them or not. I'd like to think that the best of today's performers would be playing the same thing, too, regardless of the money aspect.

I don't want to hype anybody. I don't want to say that this is biddy-biddy-bom-bom, because it's not. Because whenever they see it they'll know what it is in front, so I'm not going to hype anybody about what it is. I'm just going to let it flow, and whatever comes out is gonna be honest, otherwise I can't give it out. I'm not looking to give them what they've had, man, because what they've had is what they've had. I'm looking to give them what they haven't had.

You're giving them something they haven't had, but at the same time it's something that's been culled from experience of fifty and more years ago. It's all in there.

If you're talking about influences, sure, it's there. How do you learn how to speak? When you're a baby you say ma-ma and da-da; you've got to start somewhere. But I've got to the point where I don't need all those people now. I don't need somebody to go ma-ma and da-da because I've matured into my own thing. I'm very grateful that they were there, but I don't need them anymore. You find yourself.

But those people are giants, man; how can you miss them? They're just giants. It's like "How Many Roads"; there's just so many people, and when somebody's really making it, you know it. There's no doubt about it. Thank God you know it, that's all, because if you don't know it, too bad.

12

INTERVIEWED BY BEN FONG-TORRES (1970)

Of all the ROLLING STONE Interviews that I did, this was the least like an R.S.I. This one, with Grace Slick and Paul Kantner, was more like a stoned rap session, as we called them back then.

With Slick and Kantner in the fall of 1970, none of us expected anything else. The Jefferson Airplane were the one San Francisco band of the Sixties that maintained a high drugs and political profile while enjoying consistent commercial success. Grace Slick, at age thirty-one, was the Acid Queen of outrageousness, and Kantner, twenty-nine, was her calm, dry, sardonic flip side.

In 1970, Marty Balin, the group's founder, was making moves to leave the group, and Grace and Paul were assuming the stewardship of what would become the Jefferson Starship. Slick and Kantner were expecting their first child, and there was talk about the band starting their own label and breaking away from RCA. It was time for a sitdown. Airplane members were never more than a phone call away, and this interview would become one of a dozen stories I did on the Airplane and its various parts. I just called up and dropped by the Airplane House in midtown. The entire interview was done with all three of us in their bed upstairs. And, as I recall, a joint or two got to be part of the afternoon.

Grace never named her child "god"—she opted to call her daughter China; the group never split from RCA. Grace, however, split from Paul, and finally from the Starship. But the band, with Kantner its most stable force, closed out the Seventies with several hit records, and, as it coasted into the Eighties, even welcomed Grace back for some background vocals.

And they still operate out of the Airplane House.

—BF-T

GRACE SLICK &

PAUL KANTNER

GRACE SLICK AND PAUL KANTNER have unofficially assumed the leadership of that mindless, mindful San Francisco rock & roll starship, the Jefferson Airplane.

They hadn't planned on it. Members of the Airplane foresee very little of what happens to them. But Marty Balin, who put together the first Jefferson Airplane (including Kantner, Jorma Kaukonen, Skip Spence as drummer, Bob Harvey as bassist and Signe Toly Anderson as second lead vocalist behind Balin) in the summer of 1965, has stepped back behind Grace. For years and two or three albums, their soaring vocal trade-offs have been a mark of the Indian/jazz/mechanical/blues/rock sound of the group. But now Kantner is writing and singing more and more; he's been busted again and again for dope and other extralegal activities; and he's hanging out with people like the Dead's Jerry Garcia, and CSN&Y's David Crosby and the Airplane's Grace Slick, who in December will be the mother of his child, to be named god ("Just 'god,'" said Grace. "No last name, no capital G. And he can change his name when he feels like it.")

When Grace and Paul speak for the Airplane, they're representing a haphazard community of people who've set some important paces—for San Francisco, for the elite of the hip scene and for rock & roll bands everywhere. Sure, it's "gotta revolution," but it's still "Jefferson Airplane Loves You," the slogan for their first promotional button in 1966. The Airplane still plays free park concerts. They still battle their record company on behalf of the people (RCA recently re-released 'After Bathing at Baxters' with a reduction on the original $5.98 retail price, which had outraged the Airplane in early 1968) and their own aesthetics and politics.

From the very beginning, the Airplane has been short and terse, their humor simple and unanswerable—unlike their music. In the very first story of the band, in the San Francisco Chronicle, *in August 1965, the writer described Balin's new-found base, the Matrix nightclub. "One wall is a huge collage," he wrote, adding Balin's explanation: "We call it the huge collage wall." Grace, for an interview for a women's page feature, explained her housekeeping: "Yeah, we try to keep the house from falling down."*

But the anti-norm, anti-intellectual, anti-art stance isn't an obligatory posture. That's just the way they choose to live their life, in line with or despite what the media has forced upon them. And there is that aristocratic air about them as they sit in their bed in their overwrought Tiffany mansion/rehearsal place. The room is just naturally littered, just as the second-floor office is filled with whimsical art, the Jefferson Airplane's anti-idea of what's funny. (That ten-inch-square color photo of the peanut butter and jelly sandwich that surprised you when you opened up the 'Volunteers' album—that was funny, see?) And downstairs, instead of furniture, there's a pool table and a torture rack, the rack occupied by a stuffed walrus.

It all fits if you and he and she are all together in that aristocratic circle that moves between the mansion across Golden Gate Park down to the studios in the whorehouse district and out to Marin County where the Dead and Quicksilver live. One musician called it a "booster club" in ROLLING STONE. *And Kantner explained: "Well, he doesn't get off in this situation." And Garcia would add: "Of course, it's our situation."*

A couple of weeks ago—after Jimi, before Janis—Annie Leibovitz, the photographer, and I went to the Airplane mansion for the interview, waited half an hour while they were waking up and retreated briskly up the stairs as the office was invaded by a suntanned promotion team from RCA.

I REMEMBER ONCE YOU WERE TALK-*ing about why Signe Anderson left the Airplane, and you'd said it was because she was pregnant and couldn't handle all those things—touring, recording, having a baby, hanging out—all at the same time. And that's what forced her out. How does that compare with your situation now?*

Grace: Well, people all around me have been trying to force me out. . . . It's been going on for five years now. But I think there were other pressures on Signe that made her leave. In my case, there are a whole lot of different chicks around, and everybody is sort of helping each other out with various different things, and they can take the child for a while and I can theirs at the house at the beach, and we can trade off.

That kid's going to get mixed up.

Grace: Well, not really. Some of the most interesting and happiest kids I've seen have lived with a lot of different adults, because a kid can go up to one guy and wear him out. And as soon as the adult gets tired, there are five other guys, or five other chicks to go and wear out, and the kid gets to be very bright—and tolerant, you know, with that many kinds of people around.

Why did you decide to have a child?

Grace: Oh, it's just a small person, and they expand more than animals do. Some people have animals around. I like animals, but I thought I'd try a human being because they have more happening. I think it's partly an ego thing; you get an old man that you like or dig a lot of qualities about, and you have to like yourself to a certain extent, and you want to see what the combination of those two minds and bodies will turn out like—you're really curious.

Your contract with RCA is going to be up in November. Any idea who you'll go with?

Paul: Whoever gives us what we want most.

Bill Thompson mentioned the possibilty of forming a record label of your own, and just finding a distributor.

Paul: Yeah, it's not too hard, and it doesn't involve too much, other than having them print your names on the album—if we wanted to get into it on just that level. We'd just get that much more control over everything.

How much control do you have now?

Paul: Almost total.

That's from fighting over five years. . . .

Paul: It has a lot to do with the fact our contract's up and they really want us to sign again. So they'll do almost anything.

It seems that with every album you've done, there's been a clash. For the cover, for the lyrics, for whatever . . .

Grace: Well, you know, when you come in late at three o'clock in the morning, a fourteen-year-old kid knows he's going to have to say something about it. It doesn't matter that it's right or wrong, he knows that that's going to have reprisals. So we know that every time we put something out, there's going to be something, even if it isn't the stuff we assume we're going to have hassles with. We put out some word and everybody thinks, "Oh, God, we're gonna have to hassle with them on that," and they'll pick out something else. Like that cupcake thing. We were in the studio doing the musical end of it, and Thompson comes in and says, "Hey, how about everybody drawing a little something on this piece of paper, whatever you feel like," and everybody's doodling on paper. And Paul's eating a cupcake. He put, you know, one of these fluted things that are around cupcakes—he just put it down on the paper and drew around it. And passed it off and went on with what he was doing. RCA said, "You can't put it out; it looks like a psychedelic cunt."

How did RCA know what a psychedelic cunt looks like?

Grace: So it's actually just silly. You just hand it in and wait for them to worry about it, and then talk to them. And they usually manage after a while to understand some of the proportions.

Was there any problem with "Mexico" before it came out?

Grace: No, 'cause nobody's ever in the studio.

Paul: We just told them, here's a new single, and didn't get any hassle. All very simple. Of course, there was nothing dirty in it.

What about Dick Cavett? "Mexico" was banned there, too. To you, privately, did he say, "Hey, I really want you to be able to do this song?"

Paul: Oh, yeah, he held up the show for an hour and a half—it was taped late—with all the audience sitting there—'cause he was upstairs with the executives arguing with them, telling them what assholes they were for not having us play the song. So they finally still said we couldn't do it, and he came down, all pissed off. Said, "Sorry, man, I really feel like an asshole to have to tell you . . ."

And ABC had censors there waiting with scissors to cut out "motherfuckers" from "We Can Be Together." But they had fucked the sound up so much when we did it that we spent a whole night in New York blasting at them and telling them how shitty they were and they'd better fucking get the sound together or we'd blow your radio station up or something. So they spent the whole time—see, it's like taped a day in advance—and you have to get a certain amount of time filled, so if they were to snip four or six minutes, they'd have to find something else to fill. So they spent a good deal of time trying to work with that, and they didn't have time to look at it for censoring or anything.

Thompson was talking about instead of going with a particular record company, to form your own company—and it could go beyond rock & roll and records and get into the future of the media—videotape, cassettes, holograms.

Paul: I'm going to try and get my starship thing onto videotape. That's a song, side two of my album. It's about us—me and Jerry Garcia and David Crosby stealing a starship—hijacking a spaceship, going where whoever comes along wants to go.

It's my answer to the ecology problem. It's the only way it's all going to get together and work. Unless we have a war or a big disease or a famine, there's just too many people, and they're gonna have to get off the planet. This is my way of starting to get off a little earlier.

We don't have to stay anywhere; we'll land wherever we want and then take off again. The sun is only one solar system out of millions of solar systems. The orbit of Pluto is probably a speck of tiny dust in the whole universe. There's millions of other whole planetary systems. It would be interesting to just keep going till you stop, to see what stops you, until you run into

111

the side of the bowl or something and see this guy out there looking at you.

That's what old Owsley could do, is to make a machine that would go that far that fast. He'd just read some books for a couple of weeks and get it down. That's how he made acid. Just went out, got some chemistry books and decided to do it, and did it. He does it with sound systems; he's been doing the Grateful Dead sound from one aspect or another for five years. He fucks up at it a lot because he doesn't have great equipment or enough money to really get it together. I mean, if you give him $50 billion and an island and a machine shop, he'd have the starship together in less than a year.

I HEAR LITTLE RICHARD HELPED out on the new album. Delaney and Bonnie said he'd "helped" on one of their songs, but it sure sounded like one of his songs.

Paul: You'd probably say the same thing about Joey's song. It's Joey's song, but there's a Little Richard song in there, too. Joey wanted a piano part that Grace couldn't play—you know, that real heavy thing? Ta-ta-ta-ta-ta—TA-to, sixteen times. It takes a lot of muscles, man. And Joey was saying, "Gotta have that Little Richard thing." Then I said to him one night, "Why don't you call up Little Richard?" Somebody said it; I'm not sure it was me. Hey, far out. So we call, *"Thompson! Thompson!* Get ahold of Little Richard's manager for me." And they went through a whole scene of going through his manager, which was really a drag. But Joey finally did get together with him.

So how was Richard altogether? Did he dig your music? Stick around and listen to it?

Grace: He seemed interested. He had a great expression on his face, you know. There were about thirty people in this little studio; everybody'd come down to see Little Richard . . . he was good.

Did he do his act?

Paul: Not really; he was just being real warm. He sits down and says, "No, man, I don't play worth shit; I just sort of crash around here, and hey, we could do it in this other key, 'cause I like this key. Okay?" Then a little while later, "Hey, how about this tempo? I really get off on this tempo." So it got into that, so it's Little Richard's tempo and key. That's Joey's song, but it became a little bit of both, and it worked out nice. It's called "Bludgeon of a Bluecoat."

I have a song called "To Diana," the chick who got blown up in New York with the Weatherman. For the woman Diana. "Crazy Miranda" is the Women's Liberation freak.

Grace: It's more or less pathetic. The whole song is actually the second line, which is, "She believes in anything she reads." And the rest of it's more or less superfluous. There's a lot of information coming in; it's the inability to make up your mind as to what part of that information applies to you. And I think a lot of chicks who are into that are having trouble figuring it out. What they're supposed to be doing. Well, should I sit back and let it happen or go out there and grab that guy by the balls? And they sort of do a little bit of each of it and look and sound confused.

I mean, brassieres and stuff; if you don't want to wear one, just take it off. But burning it . . . I think a lot of street theater is fun, but like anything else I'd also like to see people who are good at it. It's preferable to see people who are capable of getting together more or less what they've decided to do. Like I prefer Abbie Hoffman to Richard Nixon simply because he's more entertaining, more interesting to listen to. I don't care what the two of them are talking about, they could be talking about toothpaste, and Abbie's gonna come out hands down because he's just a more entertaining guy. And if those chicks were to send out their best representatives—figure out who is good at those various things, instead of just sending out anybody and it looks dumb and makes them look stupid.

I'd like to see Bobby Seale doing his nightclub comedy relating to what's going on today.

Paul: I'd like to see Bobby Seale out.

Grace: I think that kids are the reason all that flamboyant stuff is going down, because you realize after a while that there is little to distinguish yourself from animals except entertaining other human beings. I mean, we all essentially do the things animals do—shit, fuck, sleep and eat. And art is the only thing that separates us at all. Science, art—those two things, being together or apart.

Paul: When they're together, it's called Magic.

Grace: Bucky Fuller. Bucky Mod. He's incredible. But he's trying to point out something, that people are taught that they are almost useless for a number of other things. Like I'll talk to people, say, I'll draw something. "Hey, that sure is neat." Then why don't you draw, then? "I can't draw." They've been told they can't draw. Instead of just doing it and assuming that you can do anything you've decided. And people are told—like if Paul was good at math at four or five, he's told, "You ought to be a scientist, you ought to be a scientist." And he figures, "That's what I can do. And that's all I can do." But it isn't all they can do, necessarily. They can do a whole bunch of junk. And that's what Fuller was talking about—letting people do anything they feel like—get into all of it, as much of it as you can. People being channeled is kind of sad.

It ties back to what you said about street theater. What's to stop hundreds, thousands from saying, "I want to be their representative," if they want to try?

Paul: What's to stop them is the ability to do it.

Grace: You do have to think about what you're doing. You can't just say, "Since I put a pencil to a piece of paper, it's a good drawing." So like the chicks going out and arranging little performances, like I saw a thing on television, it was just astonishingly pathetic.

There has to be a certain amount of organization to any community of people, but it should be done as locally as possible because it's very different to govern yourself, let alone anybody else. One guy telling hundreds of people what to do is really outrageously stupid if you think about it. It's hard to take all your own personal pieces that you've got and set them so that they all move smoothly. Running millions of people . . . it's silly. The communes are a fairly good idea, there would be natural leaders; you don't have to call them President-anything or Superintendent-anything; they are people who are just plain capable of organizing, guys that are good at cutting up avocados, and they more or less organize that way in a small community—you can see all the problems, everybody knows everybody else and you can more or less take care of immediate stuff that needs to be done.

But that guy doesn't even know what's going on. Ideal government would be a very boring job—it would be a matter of organizing a lot of utilities and keeping the wires together and the power plant and all that kind of stuff. It's not a matter of telling people how to live; it's a matter of making it pleasant for them to live. Government should be in the position of distributing food, stuff like that. It might be a good idea to have government totally by the people—that each person takes four or five hours of the week doing some kind of government job—in other words, along with what you do you also help maintain the government so no one person has total control—I might go down to an office for four hours and do whatever I'm capable of doing—writing out receipts for food distribution

in a certain area—but it's all actually a monstrous secretarial job, and that's all I think it should be.

And you'd be willing to give part of your time.

Grace: Sure, if you reduce government to the level of just paperwork and making sure that train gets to that city with this amount of stuff on it for that amount of people. I'd do it; that'd be fantastic. It goes at a snail's pace, but just because of fantastic ideas that people have, a small portion of it gets done.

People are calling you and the Stones the rock & roll bands most outwardly calling for violent revolution.

Paul: Violent in terms of violently upsetting what's going on, not a violence of blowing buildings up or a violent "shoot policemen" or violent running down the street with an AR-18 shooting everything you can see. But violent shit, changing one set of values to another.

Or something violent in the eyes of the establishment.

Paul: Oh, yeah, just a whole turnaround of values. That's violent to them. It's extreme.

I like, "It doesn't mean shit to a tree."

Paul: It doesn't. Don't get serious about it at all. 'Cause it's not serious.

So this whole conversation is just a gag.

Paul: There's no real importance to attach to it in the general scheme of the universe.

So what's the importance of what you do—rock & roll, live performing?

Paul: Important's a shitty word.

What's the reason for it?

Paul: Trying to make consciousness. Pointing things out. Just make people enjoy themselves. We didn't even know what we were doing when we started doing it. Looking back, all we were saying was, "Look, we're having a good time." And nothing else. Just sitting around having a good time with all this shit going on around us. Pretty soon people start filtering in, saying, "Hey, they're having a good time." David calls it "egg snatching." Kidnapping children.

It's also very safe to be in a rock & roll band if you want to smoke dope. You have a lot of shield between you and the gun folk. People get uptight at us riding a Cadillac when we're in New York, but it's the single most effective weapon against getting busted in the world. It's the one thing they recognize. We're driven through New York with police leading, in front of us.

But outside of that shield, aren't you more liable to be busted because of the things you say or promote?

Paul: No . . . it's very hard to bust people these days.

Another shield, I suppose, is to have people around

you who know what's going on in any situation and know how to handle it.

Paul: Well, it's like they know if they bust us it's going to involve a lot more shit that they're going to have to do right up front, than if they bust some kid out in the street and has no lawyer in back of him. . . . It almost feels like Al Capone or the Mafia or the Untouchables, 'cause you get down there and a lawyer will come and *{fingersnaps}* pick you out. When they busted me in Hawaii I even got another guy out of jail, a spade cat they'd busted the night before and beat fuck out of, and we just bailed him out, and they were really pissed off, 'cause it was easy to do. It was pleasant to do, just to get them uptight, 'cause they did a bad thing to him in front. It wasn't a bad thing they'd done to me—more inconvenient. Humorous inconvenience.

I WANT TO KNOW HOW YOU GOT *into rock & roll. You're doing a gig with Sha Na Na at Kent State. Were you into jukeboxes or what?*

Grace: Rock & roll, rock & roll, rock & roll. I think it was just I went down to see Jefferson Airplane because there was an article in the *Chronicle,* and there was a picture of Marty, and he looked sort of like he was Japanese or Filipino or something, with a Prince Valiant hairdo, which nobody had at the time, and underneath, it said, "He's got a rock & roll band," and it sounded very weird, and I went down to see it. And I said, "Hey, that looks great, let's do that. Those people are having fun; let's do one." So that's the Great Society thing. But that's not rock & roll, it's kind of electric, folk freak stuff.

That's a story you've given out several times, and several times you've also said you're not a singer, that you're just talking. But obviously, you're developing or sharpening some kind of technique.

Grace: Well, I don't think you can get away from yourself. I mean, you have a certain kind of nose; I mean, unless you go in for plastic surgery you got a certain kind of nose that distinguishes you and the same thing with your voice and the way you pronounce words, it's going to come out a certain way so anybody essentially that sings is going to sound the way they sound, unless you work on sounding like somebody else or changing it. So it's not a singing style; it's just the way my nose looks or the way my fingers feel.

You still learn about phrasing, learn about breath control. . . .

Grace: Hmm, yeah, more or less. It's nothing compared to people who actually study singing four or five hours a day and all kinds of tiny little things that they learn but are actually worthless when it comes to singing over 115 db, because you have to be able to hear yourself to do the correct pronunciations and all that kind of stuff. So, you develop something else and there's no name for it as yet; it's like trying to tell a classical guitarist I want you to do one of those high, whining *woooows,* and that's all you can do; you can't give him notes to have him reproduce the sound, and there's nothing you can tell Jorma except with your hands and with your mouth kind of trying to duplicate the kind of sound you heard him make that you want him to make again. And I watch Paul in the studio, and he'll go out there and he looks like an airplane going out of control, you know; he'll be directing because you can't write it down. There are too many names for whatever it is.

It seems like most of your professional life is entwined with your personal life, that it all comes out of what you need or what you want. Convenience defines your singing, or why you're a singer, why you're doing a book, why you're having a baby. Everything's a principle.

Grace: Chaotic circumstance—I was on that corner at that time. A lot of it. And it depends on what you do with the corner when it presents itself to you.

I remember a story about Sly Stone being producer of a single you were trying to record when you were with Great Society. . . .

Grace: He's incredible. God, the guy—he's amazing. He went around to each instrument and played—we watched him—from instrument to instrument, played *really* well, and sang, and produced.

How did that affect your group?

Grace: Oh, we were so . . . people had picked up their instruments two weeks before—you know, like, "why don't we start a rock & roll band? The Jefferson Airplane looks like that's pretty much fun." So there was no professional hassle at all. I think now if someone comes up to Jorma and says, "Jorma, let me show you how to play that," that's a little different, 'cause he's been playing for a long time.

Paul: But even in the beginning, who was it, Bernie Krause was hired by Matthew Katz to try and orchestrate the band while we were at the Matrix. And he had a shattering experience for himself, trying to direct Jorma . . . saying, "Guys, if you could just play, dom-da-de-da-dom . . ."

Grace: You guys were different, though; you weren't never really children, and I've told people before, like the Airplane was the top money-maker in San Francisco, and all the rest of us were on sort of the underneath level, and they were always the star billing, and all the other bands—Great Society, Big Brother, Charlatans, Marbles—we were all underneath them. And at the time you didn't have the individual dressing rooms; everyone just piled into one room, and the Airplane would come in and they wouldn't talk to anybody; they'd just come storming in with this really arrogant attitude, carrying their guitars and kicking things over and stuff like that, and we used to laugh at them—"Lookit those big shots, they think they're such hot shit," and they never really were a young group; they started out being arrogant like that and have not finished with it yet.

I wonder why. Well, I know why. Marty owned the Matrix where you started. . . .

Paul: Yeah, we had it pretty easy for a group starting out.

Pretty good timing . . .

Paul: And also not too much was happening in the city musically, and we were sort of floating. . . .

Grace: The Four Seasons used to hold auditions at the Jack Tar Hotel periodically when they had the record company, and we used to go down and look at them, and they had incredible acts going down there, and that was one of the most enjoyable occasions, watching the amateurs' thing for the Four Seasons. Great stuff.

Paul: I got into it when I saw the Byrds doing it.

What, auditioning for the Four Seasons?

Paul: No, I got into making a rock & roll band on the same level that she's saying how the Great Society started. You know, from being David's friend . . .

Grace: Well, you guys weren't my friends. They weren't anybody's friend. They were their own friends. Gosh, you guys were arrogant. Except Casady. Everybody liked Jack. But they didn't like anybody else in the band. I think it was 'cause he was kind of shy, and he was the only member of the band that wasn't a superstar at age three.

How'd you meet David Crosby?

Paul: When I was in school, he came to me and said, "Hey, have some of this. The first one's free." Then I was hooked, and I could never get away from him after that.

Grace: Yeah, he's just the old dope pusher.

Paul: I met him in L.A. Me and [David]

Freiberg and a couple of other people went down there to achieve stardom and all that, and we got together and got a little house in Venice on the beach, and we'd practice every day and night, and spend every day on the beach incredibly fucked up on grass that Crosby'd get for us.

Did you do that trip of having a guitar on your back and going from coffee club to coffee club?

Paul: Just mildly.

Grace: Marty said that's how he got you for the band. You walked into the club with your cap on and all this hair sticking out and a banjo on your back, and it sounded like the ethnic folk story of all time. "I saw him, and I knew he had to be a member of my band!"

"You play drums, kid?"

Grace: Right. "No, but I play banjo." "Learn the drums. We don't need any banjo." He still plays banjo. Got a banjo track on your album.

There's a persistent story around that Spencer Dryden never played drums before he joined the Airplane. I thought he had a jazz background.

Grace: Yeah, he's been playing for a long time. Spencer had to answer the question eight million times because the story got printed and reprinted and reprinted.

A NNIE, *DID YOU HAVE ANY questions?*

Grace: My favorite color is black.

Annie: Yeah, I wondered how you saw yourself in a photograph?

Grace: Oh, being pregnant. All I see it as is a very large stomach. . . .

Annie: Would you like to be photographed with a very large stomach?

Grace: No, for some reason I don't . . . it's not the large stomach, it's the posing that I don't like, and my old man figured that out. He tried for maybe two weeks as a young fledgling photographer to position me, and living with me he finally got real good at candid photography. Because if he ever said, "Move your arm a bit," I'd say, "What for? It's not real." The arm's there.

Boy, you'd be a good model, wouldn't you?

Grace: I hated modeling. I did it for two or three years. It's also a matter of a personality flaw, of being almost totally stubborn. I don't like to be told what to do at all. That's unfortunate because a lot of people come up with good ideas and can direct you. . . .

Do you mind being advised?

Grace: Yeah . . . I don't like it at all. And I

115

think it's wrong sometimes because I lose out in that process. I feel really restricted if someone says, "I want you to play that faster." And I think, well, I won't play it at all. Like a kid. "I don't wanna do it! I don't wanna do it!"

Are you also very insistent, then, when you direct others?

Grace: No. I don't care what they do. All I do is get someone who's a real good musician and I can trust him, and they always do come out with something good.

The phone's going to ring. *{Two seconds later, it does. It's a special, super-compact Trimline that Grace calls "the Ferrari." She answers:}* Yes? You have a very direct voice today, whoever you are, Abbie.

Paul: Where's our tickets to the show, you fucker?

Grace: When do you spreck? *{Abbie Hoffman was in town for a speech—later canceled.}* You all by yourself? Come on by. . . . Yeah, we talked to him for a couple of hours. Crosby, Paul . . . good stuff. Just a second, I'll give you the man.

{Kantner, on the phone, tells Abbie about his album and promises a tape copy.}

How was your date with Abbie at the White House?

Grace: Oh, it was funny. God . . .

Did you see Tricia?

Grace: No . . . I suppose it could've been done because the White House didn't know who we were until the reporters let them know because the reporters were taking pictures, so the guard said, "Sorry, you can't come in," and I said, "I've got an invitation." "Don't care if you've got an invitation. Guards say you're a security risk." "Hey, man, I'm a singer." "Well, sorry, you can't come in." If Abbie hadn't been there I think it would've been smoother. But I preferred that silly business. I always like that.

We got the invitation. It said, "Mr. and Mrs. Gerald Slick." And I showed it to Jerry, and he was lukewarm about going. So I called Abbie and he got this flag together and slicked his hair back—he looked like a pimp, you know. Greasy hair and this funny suit that didn't quite fit. Draped a flag that his old lady Anita had made over the fence.

They were right, though, 'cause I had acid powder in my pocket and I don't know that I would have used it, because I don't know the setup of the White House or how it would've gone down, but in case everything would've been cool, they would've had good reason to keep me out. You see, it was a tea, and what I'd envisioned in my head was White House and Finch College and all that junk, those formal teas, they have a table, 'cause you're taught that, that's one of the things a finishing school teaches you—how to serve tea. The usual setup is a long table with two silver-encrusted large teapots, and the hostess and whoever she figures is the maid of honor serves at either end, and you each get cups and stand around like at a cocktail party.

And the amount of acid that I could just have on the sweat on the end of my finger could have gone by just like that *{flick}* and nobody would've even noticed it going into a cup. And I was thinking of talking to Tricia and saying, "Thank you for a nice tea, and I think you're probably going to enjoy the rest of the afternoon considerably," dump, and she'd be thinking about that remark for a while . . . and that's the only reason I was sort of disappointed at not getting in; otherwise it was just great fun.

I see you're starting to a few gray hairs. You must be over thirty!

Grace: I wish it was all the way out to here. It's only about five inches long because I used to dye it black, and it's been there since I was about twenty-four, but I'm just starting to let it grow out, and it's five inches of gray hair and five inches of red. . . .

How's your throat now? It sounds like the nodes are something that'll keep recurring. . . .

Grace: It'll probably keep doing it. It's like some people have large calves on their legs, other people don't. A person with smaller calves is going to have more trouble pumping a bicycle. I've got a stupid throat. I enjoy singing, but it's not strong, so that's it. Fortunately, the operation is less painful than having a tooth filled.

It's like Crosby said, I don't think it'll be too much of a problem because I don't plan to be singing that long. There's nothing more ridiculous than old people on the stage. And it's getting to be so that the level ought to come way down as to who ought to be cavorting around on a stage. When I was young, around ten, and my parents' friends would come over and try to be real chummy, like be your friend or peer, and you just thought they were assholes. And people who continue to perform on stage figure everybody really thinks they're neat, and they don't. They think, "Look at that old jerk." There's a time. And also there's a matter of your head wanting to do a number and being able to handle a number of other things. You start out performing because it's fun; then you learn more things and you want to do more than go "Na-na-na-na" on a stage. The production end is interesting, writing is interesting, and you learn to coordinate all these things.

So in later years you may see your role not necessarily as an entertainer singing rock songs, but maybe as a communicator. . . .

Grace: Yeah, there's just a certain appearance and attitude with rock & roll—like the guy Alice Cooper—and stuff like that, and I enjoy that, young kids goofing around and making a lot of people uptight about it. There's no reason to be uptight, it's like that reviewer in New York who got really upset with Jagger's film *Performance,* and he just laid himself all out in this review by making these incredibly stupid statements. . . . You just make statements to amuse people, and you wear certain colors just to make people laugh, and there's no big deal about it—and he has lipstick on, all right, it's just not that big a problem. And people get excited by Alice Cooper because he's got false eyelashes on. Well, that's for your amusement, you just go, "Ho ha, look at that guy with false eyelashes on." But that's good stuff, and I think a thirty-five-year-old person still having the mentality or the desire

of a twenty-year-old is sad, actually.

I don't think so.

Grace: I don't mean to close yourself up and become conservative. I mean by that time it would seem that you would have learned enough to extend yourself further than that.

It's hard to say what will happen to this whole scene in ten years, though. Like you might grow with the audience while they grow with you, and you'll probably move to a different place and still be valuable in some kind of communications role.

Paul: We seek to eradicate that audience/performer relationship as much as possible. That's not really valid anymore, for us. Just don't like it.

Well, whatever you do, whether it's film, TV, records, you're still performing on some form of stage, and they're receiving it.

Paul: I like a live stage.

Grace: All I'm talking about is being a huge fat full person as much as you possibly can, and it doesn't necessarily mean that you have died because you're not prancing around on a stage. Prancing around on a stage is not the entire purpose of my life.

117

13

INTERVIEWED BY JOHN MORTHLAND (1970)

Rod Stewart, in the Seventies, was one of rock music's most blatant and fun-loving sex symbols, dancing in sequined tights, teasing and laughing his way through sets.

But in 1970, Stewart, 25, had other priorities. Although he'd done a couple of solo albums that got some airplay on FM stations, he saw himself as primarily a member of the Faces.

The Faces, for all their talent and beery good times onstage, spent most of their career on the verge. So did Stewart. But by mid-decade, he'd become by far the biggest Face. In 1975, the band broke up, and Stewart was free to fulfill his promise.

Staff writer John Morthland had talked briefly with Stewart early in 1970, when he was through town plugging his second solo album. By September, when they met again, the Faces were touring, and, thanks a lot to Stewart, momentum was building.

Morthland recalls doing the interview at his flat in San Francisco after a concert. "We didn't do it at the hotel," he says, "because we wanted quiet. The Faces was a particularly raucous band."

Beyond that, John's most vivid memory of their session "was that we were sitting at my kitchen table, and the tape recorder was pretty close to him. It seemed to make him uncomfortable. He would move it away. I wasn't sure the microphone was picking up, so I moved it back. And we kept pushing it back and forth across the table."

—BF-T

118

STEWART

*I*N THE SEASON OF THE SOLO STAR, the attention is focusing on people like Neil Young, Randy Newman, Elton John, Van Morrison and, yes, John Lennon, Paul McCartney, George Harrison and Ringo Starr.

And Rod Stewart, sort of. Sort of, because he's unwilling. While he has put out two superb albums of his own since leaving the Jeff Beck Group, he insists that his main gig is as vocalist with the Faces, and he wouldn't have it any other way. He resents it when they're billed as Rod Stewart and the Faces, because they're equals in their own eyes.

The night before this interview was conducted, the Faces—Stewart, guitarist Ronnie Wood, bassist Ronnie Lane, drummer Kenny Jones and keyboard player Ian MacLagan—had packed Fillmore West on a Wednesday night as the only act on the bill. They were in the middle of one of those ball-breaking six-week tours that has maybe four days off in a string of one-nighters.

In America, the Faces' chief claim to fame is "Itchycoo Park" (and maybe the round-jacketed "Ogden's Nut Gone Flake"), and they still seem to think they have to live that single down before they will get the kind of recognition they seek. They're well on their way to doing just that, and perhaps it won't be long before people quit thinking of them as the Small Faces. 'First Step,' the initial album with the new group, is certainly little indication of what they displayed at the Fillmore.

The Faces do play loud, but with care. And let's face it, friends, there are few better things in life than a rock & roll band that is loud and still musical. Wood, who was bassist with Beck when Stewart was in that group, is developing into a fine lead guitarist and plays a beautiful bottleneck. On a bad night, they're probably extra bad, just as they're extra good on a good night, because they are that kind of band, much like the early Stones.

This was a good night. On this tour, they're playing songs from 'First Step,' from Stewart's own 'Gasoline Alley,' some new ones and a few surprises like "Baby I'm Amazed" and "Love in Vain." They did a rocking two-hour set, passed out bottle after bottle of wine and were rewarded with a long encore. They loved every minute of it, as much as their audience did.

Stewart himself is a dynamic performer. He never stands still, moving about with abandon but not a trace of self-consciousness, as if being on a stage was the natural thing for him to be doing. His trademark is picking up the whole mike stand and swinging it about; in Chicago, he literally brought the house down when he put the mike stand through the low ceiling of the club. When the other Faces lean into a microphone to sing harmony, they occasionally mime his gestures,

throwing their arms out just like he does, done all in fun.

Still, they're not sure of it all. "How did we sound, really, in your honest opinion? Was it good?" Ronnie Wood asked backstage after the show, after they'd told the audience they couldn't continue because they'd exhausted their repertoire. Self-confidence—or, more accurately, lack of it—seems to be an obstacle.

The fun's just beginning when the show ends. Backstage, a photographer walks up, and the five Faces immediately wrap themselves up in each other, like the Lovin' Spoonful on the cover of the first album, all writhing and squirming and shrieking: "Take our picture! Take our picture!" The Faces are an unusually close group; they're good friends with each other offstage, and they stick together.

As the Faces leave the dressing room to head back to their hotel, they stop for a chat with some of the crowd waiting outside. A black guy walks up to Stewart and says, "Keep singing with all your heart and soul, man, 'cause you got it."

"Thanks," Stewart replies. "But, remember, the king is gone. Sam Cooke is dead."

Stewart was a gas to interview. Like the rest of the Faces, he's warm and exuberant, loves to tell a funny story and has a bit to say on most anything you'd want to ask him about. And on top of all that, he's humble.

---

*E*ARLIER THIS YEAR, YOU SAID you'd never go out as a solo performer. Do you still feel the same way, after the success of 'Gasoline Alley'?

I'll stay solo as far as records, yes; as far as live performances, no. I'm just not responsible enough to put a band together and keep it together. I have enough of a time keeping myself together, let alone a band. And if I chose a band. I'd choose the same guys I got in the band now anyway.

Have you ever performed as a solo act?

For money? No, not for money, I've done it for free, on the streets and stuff. That was in my old nomadic days, when I was about seventeen or eighteen. I'm twenty-five now. Then I was wandering around, mostly Spain and Italy, trying to get myself together. I think that's something everybody should get out of them; when my kids grow up, I'm going to say, "Out, you bastards, get out on the road and live."

I did that for two years, mostly in Spain. It was a banjo; I learned how to play banjo before guitar. I played with Wiz Jones—he's a folk legend in England. Mostly American folk music, like Jack Elliott. We weren't really aware of any English folk music then. I got sent back from Spain; we got kicked out for being vagrants. Flown back on BOAC, and I still owe BOAC the money for that flight. We'd started out in Belgium, lived in Paris, the South Bank, for about eight months, then got to Spain, Barcelona.

What'd you do then, after being kicked out and sent home?

I was in England, making picture frames. Did a bit of grave-digging—that was all right, we only had to work two days a week, and you didn't spend the whole day digging holes; we did a lot of other things there.

Were you singing professionally then?

The first band I ever sang in professionally was Jimmy Powell and His Five Dimensions. This was when I was nineteen or twenty; it was part-time, between making the picture frames, and we didn't get paid much; we used to play in the Stones' intervals in London. I used to play the harmonica; I never used to sing. They backed Chuck Berry in England after I left; by then I had joined Long John Baldry and the Steampacket with Julie Driscoll, Brian Auger and Baldry himself. We were doing our soul routine, like "Midnight Hour" and "Mr. Pitiful" and all the early Otis Redding hits.

Were Otis and Sam Cooke, whom you mentioned last night, the singers you liked the most?

I listened to everybody and probably picked up a bit from them all. Sam Cooke was the only one that really influenced me. Over a period of about two years, that's all I listened to. This was about three years ago, just before I joined Beck. I'm really open-minded, though; I'll listen to anybody. It had to do with the way I sounded; I didn't sound at all like anybody, Ray Charles or anybody, but I knew I sounded a bit like Sam Cooke, so I listened to Sam Cooke.

Where does your voice come from?

Last night it was coming from there [strokes neck] too much. I was straining it a bit. Usually it comes from way down [patting stomach]. When I first started playing the guitar, I had a sort of very bad mid-Atlantic cowboy voice, really a bad one. And it just developed from there, partly by listening to Sam Cooke.

Were you consciously trying to emulate Sam Cooke?

No, I don't think so, not really. If I'd sung one of his numbers, I might have, but I've never sung one of his numbers, probably never will. I wouldn't touch one of his numbers after he's

sung them himself. It was just the *tone* of his voice—not the phrasing or whatever—just the tone.

Well, how did you get your voice so hoarse?

Just belting my ass off for five years. But it's stronger now than it's ever been, which is weird. Like I can work hard, two hours a night, and it doesn't give out like it used to, three or four years ago.

When did it start to get that way?

I think probably after the first record I made. Let me see, what was the first record I made? I made a tape of "Good Morning, Little Schoolgirl," about four years ago, with studio men; John Paul Jones was on bass, I remember that. I was singing with Jimmy Powell's band by then, and I got called out to make one record. It was a dismal failure. It was a good record; it was like a white attempt . . . five years ago, before its time, but I thought it was good.

How do you describe your own voice; do you listen to yourself sing much?

Obviously, the only way to improve on anything is to listen to what you've already done, and probably after I did the first Beck album, which is the first album I ever did, then I had a collection of songs I could really listen to. I seemed to have improved far more over the last two years than I did the three years previous. It's pretty much down to that *Truth* album, really; I could take it home and listen to it, and I've improved since then.

How do you think you've improved?

My voice has become more sandpapery—that's an improvement in itself. And I learned a lot from Beck—how to be a lead vocalist and fit in with the guitar. I think I learned that, which now comes out so I can phrase well. I think I phrase very well.

What do you think when you hear your voice on record? It's a very distinct voice; no one else has anything like it.

Everyone tells me that; I can't believe that at all. I wouldn't call it a distinct voice. I sometimes think, oh, Christ, I sound too much like Sam Cooke, or Arthur Conley, or someone like that. What happened with *Gasoline Alley* was I picked the right songs, that suit my voice. So on that album, probably it sounds distinct.

You didn't do that on the first one, you don't think, 'The Rod Stewart Album'?

No, not really, because I was out to try to prove myself as a singer more than anything. On *Gasoline Alley,* I thought I picked the right numbers to suit the voice, and that's a start. Like

121

"It's All Over Now," which I thought was a good choice.

Let me think of someone who picks the wrong songs to fit his voice to show you what I mean. . . . David Ruffin, the old Tempts' [Temptations] singer. I'd love to produce that guy and pick the songs he should sing, because he doesn't know, you know? Tim Hardin sometimes falls down on that. He writes most of his own songs for himself, but listen to the *Tim Hardin II* album, where he does beautiful songs all the way through, and then he does something like "I'm a Smuggling Man." It spoils the album. There's an ideal example of someone picking a song they can't sing.

I'm sure if you looked into it you'd find loads of people who don't know how to pick the material for their own voice. Someone who does is Van Morrison. Not the world's best singer, but he doesn't write his songs so he can't conquer them.

How much of your songs are autobiographical?

Two songs on *Gasoline Alley* are very true: "Jo's Lament" and "Lady Day." Old loves.

What's Gasoline Alley? I get the impression that it's English slang for a working-class neighborhood, or something like that.

Oh, no, Gasoline Alley is somewhere in San Francisco, right?

Not to my knowledge.

I got the idea from a girl at the Fillmore, last time we were here. We were talking, and she said something like, "I must get home, because my mother will say, 'Where have you been, down Gasoline Alley?'" And I said, "What?"

That doesn't sound too autobiographical.

Well, in a way it is, yes; it's just a return to a place that you are very fond of, which must happen to everybody, I'm sure. Gasoline Alley is nowhere in particular to me. It was about a feeling I had when I was in Spain, and I couldn't get back to England. I wanted to get back to England, but I didn't have the money to get back. So it's a song about going home; I've experienced that. "Jo's Lament" is a song about a girl I put in a family way, and "Lady Day" is very true, about a girl I fell in love with a long time ago and she didn't want to know me.

What are you looking for when you choose songs for your own album, as opposed to a Faces album?

Two things, mainly. I look for a song that's probably been forgotten, that no one's done for a time. Something that can fit my voice so I can sing it right, and something with a particularly strong melody. Three things, actually.

Do you do much improvising of lyrics when you're singing?

Oh, yeah, but you must have the set pattern there to start with. I do it all the time; I never sing a song the same way twice in a row, or I try not to.

You seem to anticipate a song, to really anticipate going up on stage to sing. . . .

I'm afraid to get up and sing, usually. I was really afraid last night. I always find out once I get onstage that it's okay, I sorta rise to the occasion, we all do, but we're all bloody nervous before we go on. And we were last night, because this was our second tour, and this is the first time I've—I don't know; I'm trying to find the right word—"fronted" a band as such. It was a big night for me last night, it really was. I only started coming to America a year and a half ago, with Beck. I never got scared with Beck, and we played for really big audiences. Beck was the man in that band. I feel more responsible mentally with this band than I ever did with Beck. If we died a death one night, I didn't used to care: "It's not my band; it's Beck's band. Too bad." I tried, but I didn't lose sleep over it if we did bad. With this band, if we do a bad show, I lose sleep over it.

Do you see yourself as the leader of this band?

No, very far from it. I'm not the "leader." It's probably something I brought upon myself, because *Gasoline Alley* was so big, and I feel like a lot of the people are coming to hear the numbers off that album. It's weird, really, I shouldn't worry about it, but I do. And I want this band to be really successful.

Do you get the feeling people are coming to see Rod Stewart or are they coming to see the Faces?

This is one of the things that worries me; I hope they're not just coming to see me. Because we're a band, and I want people to realize it's a *band* up there. The other guys in the band are strong, too, in what they do. I wouldn't be in this band if I didn't think they were equally strong. I think if the band makes a really good album, better than *Gasoline Alley,* then people will recognize that fact. What I'm gonna try to do is really separate the two, by doing a solo album of really slow things, like a nice midnight-type album.

Will you use the Faces, like on 'Gasoline Alley'?

No, I won't use them at all—I might use Ronnie Wood a bit—but we really gotta separate the two issues. Put the band over there and my albums over here. And keep the music as far away from each other as you can. So we can make nice heavy albums with the band—not heavy, that's such a played-out word—but nice rocker-type albums, and I can do a bit of smooth stuff on the quiet.

Who will you use on your own album, then?

Oh, there's a wealth of musicians in England. I wanna make an album like "Only a Hobo" all the way through, those kind of songs. If I can sell an album like that, I'd be really happy, more pleased than with *Gasoline Alley*.

Do you prefer to sing the slower songs?

Every time, yeah.

You don't do too many slower things with the Faces.

Sure, we do enough; we do about four: "Love in Vain," "Baby I'm Amazed," "Devotion," "Country Comforts." A bit of twelve-bar blues, yeah. On records, I prefer doing slower numbers.

How come?

For a vocalist, a slower number lends itself better than anything else. In opportunities for phrasing, it's much more free. I've had my days of belting it out over 2000 watts of amplifiers, and doing the exact same on records.

The Faces play pretty loud; you have to belt to get over them.

Well, this is why I asked you when we came off last night if we played a bit too loud towards the end. I think we started off quiet, but we all got carried away and a bit frantic toward the end. Compared to the Beck group, we're really quiet. We play loud, but we try to play . . . there's a difference, let me think of someone . . . Grand Funk Railroad really do me in; they've gotta be the all-time loud white noise, haven't they?

Indisputably, but lots of people come to hear you play really loud. If there's one thing a Fillmore audience likes, it's volume.

Oh, I don't believe that; they're not dumb. They're the hardest audience I've ever gotten up and played for. I was really scared last night, believe me; nobody ever believes me when I say that. We went on in Detroit and broke Cocker's record, biggest crowd they've ever had, and I just had to get up and say, I'm shit-scared. They don't believe it! They all say, "Nyah, come on," and I was really scared!

Are you all happy with the first album?

The First Step? It did well for a first album. Everybody in the band thinks of it as a first album. It really was, for this band. Something completely new. Did you ever listen to the old Small Faces album?

Sure.

There you go, it's a completely different thing, isn't it? It wasn't a good album, it was a bloody awful album, it was a poor album. It was very tight, but we played a lot of numbers off it last night, and it was much looser. On the album, they're mechanical, you know, clinical. Now, how can music be clinical?

Do you write much?

Not a great deal, no. It takes me a long time to write a song. I write lyrics best. Woody and I—Ronnie Wood and I—have got a really good combination, because he writes beautiful melodies but can't write words. I can't write melodies at all, but I can words. He did the melody to "Gasoline Alley."

How about the songs on your first album?

That was a weird album. I was so naive when I went into the studio, yet I knew exactly what I wanted, whereas I don't really now, for a third album. I know I wanna do all slow songs, but I'm not really that sure about the idea. For the first album, I had ideas of riffs. I said, go in, mates, play a riff, make a progression and do this, and then I took the track from it and wrote the words. Which is a great way to do it, because the backing track always conjures up something for you, and you can write the words around it. I think that's the way it should be done. The Faces will go in and play something, have a jam, and then they'll give the thing to me and say, all right, put the words around it. It doesn't always work. I had a definite goal when I did my first album for a song about something definite. I had no idea what the words were going to be, but I had an idea what the song would be about. Whereas we sometimes don't with the Faces, and this is one of the things we're trying to overcome.

You mean for the next Faces album?

Yeah, most of the songs are originals.

You seem to really prefer 'Gasoline Alley' to 'The Rod Stewart Album,' though they're both very good. Any reasons besides the ones you've mentioned?

There's a lot more variation on *Gasoline Alley*, different styles of music, like the soul thing, sort of a Memphis thing: "You're My Girl." A bit of folk music, a bit of everything. I don't know if that's the hallmark of a good album, but it is for me—to put different styles of music together but still make the whole album jell. I don't think my songs are good enough on the first album. I tried out my own songwriting on my first album, and I didn't think my songs were up to much. I know my limitations now.

What are they?

Basically, I can write slow songs around the chords of G, C, D and E minor. And I twist the

123

chords around. I don't pretend to be a songwriter, really. I try really hard, but it takes me about three weeks to write a song. [*Laughs*] It does! If I'm pressurized, I can write lots of songs; people do good things under pressure.

What finally did happen with the Jeff Beck Group?

I think very much we would have stayed together had we played Woodstock, but we passed it up because we all wanted to go home. The trouble started right about when we started doing the second album, *Beck-Ola*. That was really out of the blue for me, when Beck suddenly decided he wanted to get rid of Ronnie and Mickey. He told me, and I said that was a big mistake. Really, that was the tightest rhythm section I ever heard, Mickey Waller on drums and Ronnie Wood on bass. But he wanted to get rid of them, and I couldn't change his mind.

So he sacked Ronnie and Mickey; then he got Tony Newman on drums, and we got an incredibly bad Australian bass player that rehearsed with us once, the night before we went onstage. That was in Washington D.C., and we died the all-time death. So the bass player got sent back to Australia, and Jeff called back Ronnie Wood. So by that time, Ronnie was really pissed off, as well he should have been, because he'd been sacked and it hurts the old pride. So he was looking for another band to play with, and when the Faces opportunity came up, he left. And I was really close to him, as I still am, and I didn't want to be in the band if he wasn't still around, so I split.

This was all, of course, after the Vanilla Fudge shit, where Beck and I were supposed to be forming with Timmy and Carmine. So anyway, the band broke up, Ronnie went to the Faces, Jeff didn't phone me up or anything, let me know what was going on, so I said, "Fuck it," and I split.

How did you come to join the Faces?

Ronnie Wood asked me to go down and see them rehearse, which is what I did. I wasn't too impressed at the time. I thought they were putting together some nice things but that there was no direction to what they were doing. Then Kenny asked me to join, and I took the plunge—the plunge—it was definitely a blind plunge because I didn't know what I was getting myself into. I was more impressed with them as people—I said, "What a nice bunch of guys—I'll join that band!" Literally, that's what I said, and that's exactly what I did. We're good drinking partners. [*Laughs*] We do drink a bit too much.

Really, no, we'd be the first to tell you we're not the world's greatest musicians, but as a group we've got something going for us. Last night proved that, and we really were nervous about going up there and getting the audience on our side. I think for a band together a year, we're doing really good.

You have to give and take. I don't get a great deal of pleasure from singing "Plynth," I don't like singing "Wicked Messenger." They love playing that one—they really get into it. I'm just singing the words. But I do like singing "Love in Vain" or "Devotion," which I suppose isn't a good number for them to play. That's why it's so good to be in a band with five blokes instead of alone: so much give-and-take. Whereas as a solo I'd just say, "Fuck it, play this, it's good to sing," and they'd say, "Oh, okay." I want the band to give as much to me as I can give to them. It's a psychological thing: if they feel they're a backing group, that's when trouble starts. They're not a backing group; Ronnie Wood is about the best guitar player I know.

That was a lot of the trouble with Beck; neither Ronnie or I got enough attention. It wasn't all Beck's fault, either; it was the management, the record company, too. Nobody at Epic even knew Jeff Beck; they didn't even know they had us under contract when we made our first American tour. They'd come around to see a concert once, and somebody from Epic actually came up to me and said, "Hey, Jeff, you sang great, fucking good guitar player you got in the band, too." Really! The management was the same; they fucking brainwashed Jeff into thinking nobody had come for any reason except to see him. It was true, I admit it, but he really believed it. He really lived the life of a pop star right down to the last. Shit, it seems like I'm always running Jeff down; I do feel bitter about it in so many ways, but I still admire the guy.

How do you feel bitter, and how do you admire him?

I admire him as a guitar player, which is what he does; socially, we never really got on. Like I said earlier, I probably learned more from being with Beck and in the band than I did the three years previous. I learned a lot from him; I hope he learned something from me. The Beck band was the first band I took seriously; I can't take music too seriously, but that *Truth* album was really a landmark.

Why can't you take music seriously?

It's not a question of why I can't take music seriously. I refuse to take it seriously, I don't want to take it seriously. When you come to see us, and we're up there on the stage having a ball, it's not put on, we do mean it. We mean to have a ball when we play, and we do. Like somebody said to me the other day, "Boy, I was listening to *Gasoline Alley* the other day, and I was tripping, and, boy, it was *unbelievable*." And I said, "That's funny, I made the album on a bottle of brandy."

If people are trying to find something in music that's not there . . . this happens a lot in America; they look too deep into the music. Like "Street Fighting Man"—it was like I was trying to lead the revolution over here or something because I recorded "Street Fighting Man." Really, now! That had nothing to do with it at all. I recorded it because it was a funky old number, and because somebody had to hear those incredible lyrics. So now do you see what I mean about not taking it seriously? I don't try to find anything that's not there. There's a definite lacking of fun in music at the moment. We play our best, you know, we really do, but we like a big grin on our faces when we're playing.

YOU TALKED BEFORE ABOUT A *tight "circle" of people in England who were sort of emulating the American beat scene in Greenwich Village. Could you describe that a little better?*

After Dylan brought out that first album, we had thousands of Bob Dylans running about in their Bob Dylan caps, as you probably did over here. Everybody was doing a Dylan—it was a big scene in London, Soho. This was about 1962, and it was a close circle of folkie types. Donovan was in that routine, limping about on one leg, probably no one else that you would have heard of over here. The Stones were playing down the road, just getting it together. You could either go see somebody with an acoustic guitar at a folk club, or you could go see some blues types like the Stones—it was very close.

I remember seeing the early Stones: I remember Jagger's old lady taking me over to see them—Chrissie Shrimpton, Jean Shrimpton's sister, the model. She took me over to see them, saying it was this "unbelievable" band, and there were about fifteen people there. They were incredible, and they've still got it all together. They used to have stools—they'd sit there on these stools and play, and that was their big thing.

The Stones? You mean they sat *there on stools and played their raucous electric music, the Chuck Berry and stuff?*

[Laughs] Yeah, it was really weird. Till they started getting really popular. Then they got out their first album. I was really naive then—I thought they were playing the blues. Chuck Berry's not blues.

Is this when your band was playing during their break?

No, that was later. At this time, I was doing the whole bit with the banjo and harmonica and hat, washed-out denims. It's embarrassing, really, talking about it, because it was so weird, everybody going through that whole bit.

What got you out of that bit, then, and into the next thing?

If the Stones hadn't been successful, I'd probably never have gotten the chance. They moved out of this little club to go on a tour with Bo Diddley, and that gave our little band, the Dimensions, the chance to make our first public appearance. So that's how they helped us. But they cleared the way for a lot of other bands, too, just making it possible for that kind of music to be played. If you moved out of London and gave them a bit of twelve-bar blues, they'd boo you off the stage. As they did the Stones sometimes. But thanks to the Stones, that's not true anymore.

Is that the kind of music the Five Dimensions played?

Well, we had two guys who wanted to do all the Beatles hits, there was me, and I wanted to do the blues—dee blooze—and the other guy wanted to imitate Ray Charles, so the combination never quite hit off. The guys who wanted to do the Beatle things went back to being bricklayers, I got Jimmy Powell to start playing dee blooze [laughs] because I was a blooze singer, and that's what we started doing, playing the twelve-bars, Jimmy Reed . . . we had three chords and we used all of them. Jimmy Reed I used to love.

There don't seem to be too many artists anymore that are everybody's favorites, like the Beatles or Stones used to be; tastes seem to be getting more diffuse, and one person spends a lot of time listening to a few albums in particular, and the next person is doing the same, but with different albums.

Well, the whole thing is like split up now; I learned this with Beck, actually. We had a certain audience that would come and see us, and every time we'd go to the Fillmore for a sound balance, there'd be people queuing up, and the audience was getting younger and younger every time we played there.

I think that's happening all over, now.

That's the same thing that happened to Led Zeppelin. They draw all the fourteen year-olds out now, don't they.

125

Did you notice you had a lot of screamers last night?

Oh, yeah, I didn't know *what* that was all about. I didn't know what to do about that [laughs]. We got a few in Detroit, but I didn't know fucking what was going on here. The ones in Detroit were like nice screaming, not silly screaming like those birds on the left-hand side of the stage of the Fillmore. I was afraid to go over on that side of the stage. But we had a good time; that's what counts, really.

Girl-type screams are silly. When you get a guy that screams, an appreciative-type yell, encouragement, that can kind of turn you on when you're performing. . . . I don't know quite how to describe it. But I wouldn't go anywhere near that side of the stage; I was getting like five yards from the side and walking back again. Don't know what that was about, didn't know how to cope with it. The old Small Faces probably used to get it, but this band never had. That's probably what threw the Stones off when they came here; not playing for three years, and then nobody screamed.

How is it for the Faces in England, as opposed to America?

In England now it's very different than about two and a half years ago, because England is very influenced by America now. It's just like playing in America now, in England, really. The audiences all sit down on the floor . . . the whole bit; no one dances anymore. Whereas two and a half years ago, it was completely the other way around. Yet there's still not that many American bands doing well in England. As far as albums go, they do bloody well, but when they go over for live concerts, they seem to bomb out. . . . Three Dog Night played miserable, but I dig them, did when they first started a couple years ago. The best concert I ever saw was Joplin's at Royal Albert Hall—*unbelievable,* really, I never thought I'd see an English audience like that.

Do you get the feeling rock is stagnating now?

I don't know. It's difficult for me to say, because I'm on the stage and no longer part of the regular audience. We don't go and follow a band, we don't have that thing of "Oh, I must see them, I've really got to go and see that band." I used to have that with the Stones when I was about eighteen; I used to want to go and see them everywhere. And we don't get that way anymore, unless it's something really special, because we've gotten a bit older, so it's really hard to judge. Going by our tour, I would say it's exactly the same way it was when I first came over with Beck.

It seems as if the music isn't as good, like we've hit a low point on the cycle for a while.

I think it's as good—I just think there's too much of it. There's a lot of good bands around now; the competition over here is incredible. But there's a lot of bad stuff being put out, too, under the "underground" tag. I think what it will always come down to is tunes . . . nice little tunes, lots of tunes. Free are knocking me out now, actually—what a tight band!

We have a lot more solo stars now than we do groups.

I don't think it's a trend toward solo stars; I think it's a trend toward singers. It's leading away from guitar players now. Three years ago it seemed there was only guitar players. I think the lyrics count a lot more now than they ever did. People are prepared now to like lyrics like "the red train went up the hill," or "I am a pot of bricks, mate," deep, stupid lyrics. So with the lyrics, you really have to try to hit people right between the eyes; the lyric has to do that. So there's definitely a trend toward, not necessarily solo stars, but singer-songwriters.

14

INTERVIEWED BY JANN WENNER (1971)

The first John Lennon interview was conducted in late 1970, on the occasion of his first solo album, *John Lennon/Plastic Ono Band,* with its musical exorcisms in the songs "God," "Mother" and "Working Class Hero."

"John Lennon was on the cover of the first issue of ROLLING STONE," wrote interviewer Jann Wenner in the memorial issue following Lennon's death [December 8, 1980], "and that choice explained what we hoped to stand for. In November 1968, after the *Two Virgins* album was released and banned, John sent the art to us, and it became the cover and centerspread in issue twenty-two. We were a small newspaper in San Francisco then, but John looked upon us fondly. As his leadership of the Beatles continued to deteriorate and then dissolve, he involved himself with antiwar causes, the London underground and the far-flung first cousins of such things around the world. John and Yoko married and made their marriage a crusade for peace."

In 1970, John and Yoko visited Wenner and his wife Jane in San Francisco and Los Angeles, and at year's end, Wenner and Lennon did the "Working Class Hero" interview that would later be published in book form as *Lennon Remembers.*

The interview was a thunderbolt; no Beatle had explained the group's breakup or vented his feelings about fellow members. And the thirty-year-old Lennon's scathingly honest comments drew an official close to the Beatles era of rock & roll.

"The Lennon interview," Wenner says now, "was the most important, and the peak, of the whole concept of the ROLLING STONE Interview. He went all the way with the theory of it, to the hilt." Wenner, in fact, never did another one,

JOHN

LENNON

129

except the sessions with another musician/friend, Jerry Garcia of the Grateful Dead.

—BF-T

THIS INTERVIEW TOOK PLACE IN NEW York City on December 8th, shortly after John and Yoko finished their albums in England. They came to New York to attend to the details of the release of the album, to make some films and for a private visit.

W HAT DO YOU THINK OF YOUR *album 'Plastic Ono Band'?*
I think it's the best thing I've ever done. I think it's realistic, and it's true to the me that has been developing over the years from my life. "I'm a Loser," "Help," "Strawberry Fields," they are all personal records. I always wrote about me when I could. I didn't really enjoy writing third-person songs about people who lived in concrete flats and things like that. I like first-person music. But because of my hang-ups and many other things, I would only now and then specifically write about me. Now I wrote all about me, and that's why I like it. It's me! And nobody else. That's why I like it. It's real, that's all.

I don't know about anything else, really, and the few true songs I ever wrote were like "Help" and "Strawberry Fields." I can't think of them all offhand. They were the ones I always considered my best songs. They were the ones I really wrote from experience and not projecting myself into a situation and writing a nice story about it. I always found that phony, but I'd find occasion to do it because I'd have to produce so much work, or because I'd be so hung up, I couldn't even think about myself.

On this album, there is practically no imagery at all.
Because there was none in my head. There were no hallucinations in my head.

There are no "newspaper taxis."
Actually, that's Paul's line. I was consciously writing poetry, and that's self-conscious poetry. But the poetry on this album is superior to anything I've done because it's not self-conscious, in that way. I had least trouble writing the songs of all time.

Yoko: There's no bullshit.
John: There's no bullshit.

The arrangements are also simple and very sparse.
Well, I've always liked simple rock. There's a great one in England now, "I Hear You Knocking." I liked the "Spirit in the Sky" a few

months back. I always liked simple rock and nothing else. I was influenced by acid and got psychedelic, like the whole generation, but really, I like rock & roll, and I express myself best in rock. I had a few ideas to do *this* with "Mother" and *that* with "Mother," but when you just *hear,* the piano does it *all* for you, your mind can do the rest. I think the backings on mine are as complicated as the backings on any record you've ever heard, if you've got an ear.

Anybody knows that. Any musician will tell you, just play a note on a piano, it's got harmonics in it. It got to that. What the hell, I didn't need anything else.

How did you put together that litany in "God"?
What's "litany"?

"I don't believe in magic," that series of statements.
Well, like a lot of the words; it just came out of me mouth. "God" was put together from three songs, almost. I had the idea that "God is the concept by which we measure pain," so that when you have a word like that, you just sit down and sing the first tune that comes into your head, and the tune is simple because I like that kind of music, and then I just rolled into it. It was just going on in my head and I got by the first three or four, the rest just came out. Whatever came out.

When did you know that you were going to be working towards "I don't believe in Beatles"?
I don't know when I realized that I was putting down all these things I didn't believe in. So I could have gone on, it was like a Christmas card list: where do I end? Churchill? Hoover? I thought I had to stop.

Yoko: He was going to have a do-it-yourself type of thing.

John: Yes, I was going to leave a gap and just fill in your own words: whoever you don't believe in. It had just got out of hand, and Beatles was the final thing because I no longer believe in myth, and Beatles is another myth.

I don't believe in it. The dream is over. I'm not just talking about the Beatles, I'm talking about the generation thing. It's over, and we gotta—I have to personally—get down to so-called reality.

When did you become aware that the song would be the one that is played the most?
I didn't know that. I don't know. I'll be able to tell in a week or so what's going on, because they [the radio] started off playing "Look at Me" because it was easy, and they probably thought it was the Beatles or something. So I don't know if that is the one. Well, that's the one; "God" and

130

"Working Class Hero" probably are the best whatevers—sort of ideas or feelings—on the record.

Why did you choose or refer to Zimmerman, not Dylan.

Because Dylan is bullshit. Zimmerman is his name. You see, I don't believe in Dylan, and I don't believe in Tom Jones, either, in that way. Zimmerman is his name. My name isn't John Beatle. It's John Lennon. Just like that.

Why did you tag that cut at the end with "Mummy's Dead"?

Because that's what's happened. All these songs just came out of me. I didn't sit down to write, "I'm going to write about Mother," or I didn't sit down to think, "I'm going to write about this, that or the other." They all came out, like the best work that anybody ever does. Whether it is an article or what, it's just the best ones that come out, and all these came out because I had *time*. If you are on holiday or in therapy, wherever you are, if you do spend time . . . like in India I wrote the last batch of best songs, like "I'm So Tired" and "Yer Blues." They're pretty realistic, they were about me. They always struck me as—what is the word? Funny? Ironic?—that I was writing them supposedly in the presence of a guru and meditating so many hours a day, writing "I'm So Tired" and songs of such pain as "Yer Blues" which I meant. I was right in the Maharishi's camp writing, "I wanna die . . ."

"Yer Blues," was that also deliberately meant to be a parody of the English blues scene?

Well, a bit. I'm a bit self-conscious—we all were a bit self-conscious, and the Beatles were super self-conscious people about parody of Americans which we do and have done.

I know we developed our own style, but we still in a way parodied American music . . . this is interesting: In the early days in England, all the groups were like Elvis and a backing group, and the Beatles deliberately didn't move like Elvis. That was our policy because we found it stupid and bullshit. Then Mick Jagger came out and resurrected "bullshit movement," wiggling your arse. So then people began to say the Beatles were *passé* because they don't move. But we did it as a conscious move.

When we were younger, we used to move; we used to jump around and do all the things they're doing now, like going onstage with toilet seats and shitting and pissing. That's what we were doing in Hamburg and smashing things up. It wasn't a thing that Pete Townshend worked out;

it is something that you do when you play six or seven hours. There is nothing else to do: you smash the place up, and you insult everybody. But we were groomed, and we dropped all of that and whatever it was that we started off talking about, which was what singing . . . what was it? What was the beginning of that?

Was "Yer Blues" deliberate?

Yes, there was a self-consciousness about singing blues. We were all listening to Sleepy John Estes and all that in art school, like everybody else. But to sing it was something else. I'm self-conscious about doing it.

I think Dylan does it well, you know. In case he's not sure of himself, he makes it double entendre. So therefore he is secure in his hipness. Paul was saying, "Don't call it 'Yer Blues,' just say it straight." But I was self-conscious and I went for "Yer Blues." I think all that has passed now, because all the musicians . . . we've all gotten over it. That's self-consciousness.

Yoko: You know, I think John, being John, is a bit unfair to his music in a way. I would like to just add a few things . . . like he can go on for an hour or something. One thing about Dr. Janov, say, if John fell in love, you know, he is always falling in love with all sorts of things, from the Maharishi to all what not.

{John and Yoko went through four months of intensive therapy with Dr. Arthur Janov, author of 'The Primal Scream,' in Los Angeles, June through September of this year. In October they returned to England where they made their new albums. "Having a primal," or "primaling," is an extremely intense type of re-living/acting-out experience, around which many of Janov's theories are based.}

You once said about "Cold Turkey": "That's not a song, that's a diary."

So is this, you know. I announced "Cold Turkey" at the Lyceum, saying, "I'm going to sing a song about pain." So pain and screaming was before Janov. I mean, Janov showed me more of my own pain. I went through therapy with him like I told you, and I'm probably looser all over.

Are you less paranoid now?

No. Janov showed me how to feel my own fear and pain; therefore I can handle it better than I could before, that's all. I'm the same, only there's a channel. It doesn't just remain in me, it goes round and out. I can move a little easier.

What was your experience with heroin?

It was not too much fun. I never injected it or anything. We sniffed a little when we were in real pain. We got such a hard time from everyone, and I've had so much thrown at me, and at Yoko, especially at Yoko. Like Peter Brown in our office—and you can put this in—after we come in after six months he comes down and shakes my hand and doesn't even say hello to her. That's going on all the time. And we get into so much pain that we have to do something about it. And that's what happened to us. We took "H" because of what the Beatles and others were doing to us. But we got out of it.

Yoko: You know, he really produced his own stuff. Phil Spector is, as you know, well-known about as a very skillful sort of technician with electronics and engineering.

John: But let's not take away from what he did do, which expended a lot of energy and taught me a lot, and I would use him again.

Like what?

Well, I learned a lot on this album, technically. I didn't have to learn so much before. Usually Paul and I would be listening to it, and we wouldn't have to listen to each individual sound. So there are a few things I learned this time, about bass, one track or another, where you can get more in and where I lost something on a track and some technical things that irritated me finally. But as a concept and as a whole thing, I'm pleased, yes. That's about it, really. If I get down to the nitty-gritty, it would drive me mad, but I do like it, really.

When you record, do you go for feeling or perfection of the sound?

I like both. I go for feeling. Most takes are right off, and most times I sang it and played it at the same time. I can't stand putting the backing on first, then the singing, which is what we used to do in the old days, but those days are dead, you know.

You said that this would be the first "Primal Album."

When did I say that?

In California. Have you gone off it?

I haven't gone off it, it is just that "Primal" is like another mirror, you know. But then, of course, I'm not *through* with it; it's a process that is going on. We primal almost daily. You *see*, I don't really want to get this big primal thing going because it is so embarrassing. The thing in a nutshell: Primal therapy allowed us to feel feelings continually, and those feelings usually make you cry. That's all. Because before, I wasn't feeling things, that's all. I was blocking the feelings, and when the feelings come through, you cry. It's as simple as that, really.

Do you get embarrassed sometimes when you hear the album, when you think about how personal it is?

I get embarrassed. You see, sometimes I can hear it and be embarrassed just by the performance of either the music or the statements, and sometimes I don't. I change daily, you know. Like just before it's coming out, I can't bear to hear it in the house or play it anywhere, but a few months before that, I can play it all the time. It just changes all the time.

What is your concept of pain?

I don't know what you mean, really.

On the song "God" you start by saying: "God is a concept by which we measure our pain . . ."

Well, pain is the pain we go through all the time. You're born in pain. Pain is what we are in most of the time, and I think that the bigger the pain, the more God you look for.

There is a tremendous body of philosophical literature about God as a measure of pain.

I never heard of it. You see, it was my own revelation. I don't know who wrote about it or what anybody else said. I just know that's what *I know.*

Yoko: He just felt it.

John: Yes, I just felt it. It was like I was crucified, when I felt it. So I know what they're talking about now.

What is the difference between George Martin and Phil Spector?

George Martin . . . I don't know. You see, for quite a few of our albums, like the Beatles' double albums, George Martin didn't really produce it. In the early days, I can remember what George Martin did.

What did he do in the early days?

He would translate . . . If Paul wanted to use violins he would translate it for him. Like "In My Life" there is an Elizabethan piano solo in it, so he would do things like that. We would say, "Play like Bach," or something, so he would put twelve bars in there. He helped us develop a language, to talk to musicians.

I was very, very shy, and there are many reasons why I didn't very much go for musicians. I didn't like to have to see twenty guys sitting there and try to tell them what to do. Because they're all so lousy, anyway. So apart from the early days—when I didn't have much to do with it—I did it myself.

Why did you use Phil now instead of George Martin?

Well, it's not *instead* of George Martin. That's nothing personal against George Martin. He's more Paul's style of music than mine. But I don't know, really . . . it's a drag to do both. To go in the recording studio and then you run back and say, did you get it?

Did Phil make any special contribution?

Yes, yes. Phil, I believe, is a great artist, and like all great artists he's very neurotic. But we've done quite a few tracks together, Yoko and I, and she'd be encouraging me in the other room and all that, and—at one point in the middle we were just lagging—Phil moved in and brought in a new life. We were getting heavy because we had done a few things, and the thrill of recording had worn off a little. So you can hear Spector here and there. There is no specifics, you can just hear him.

I read a little interview with you done when you went to the Rock & Roll Revival over a year ago in Toronto. You said you were throwing up before you went onstage.

Yes. I just threw up for hours until I went on. I even threw up . . . I read a review in STONE, the one about the film [*Toronto Pop,* by D. A. Pennebaker] I haven't seen yet, and they were saying I was this and that. I was throwing up nearly in the number, I could hardly sing any of them, I was full of shit.

Would you still be that nervous if you appeared in public?

Always that nervous, but what with one thing and another, it just had to come out some way. I don't think I'll do much appearing; it's not worth the strain. I don't want to perform too much for people.

WHAT DO YOU THINK OF *George's album? {'All Things Must Pass'}?*

I don't know . . . I think it's all right, you know. Personally, at home, I wouldn't play that kind of music. I don't want to hurt George's feelings; I don't know what to say about it. I think it's better than Paul's.

What did you think of Paul's {'McCartney'}?

I thought Paul's was rubbish. I think he'll make a better one, when he's frightened into it. But I thought that first one was just a lot of . . . Remember what I told you when it came out? "Light and easy," you know that crack. But then I listen to the radio and I hear George's stuff coming over, well, then, it's pretty bloody good. My personal tastes are very strange, you know.

What are your personal tastes?

Sounds like "A wop bop alu bop." I like rock & roll, man, I don't like much else.

Why rock & roll?

That's the music that inspired me to play music. There is nothing conceptually better than rock & roll. No group, be it Beatles, Dylan or Stones, have ever improved on "Whole Lot of Shakin'" for my money. Or maybe I'm like our parents: That's my period and I dig it and I'll never leave it.

What do you think of the rock & roll scene today?

I don't know what it is. You would have to name it. I don't think there's . . .

Do you get any pleasure out of the Top Ten?

No, I never listen. Only when I'm recording or about to bring something out will I listen. Just before I record, I go buy a few albums to see what people are doing. Whether they have improved any, or whether anything happened. And nothing's really happened. There's a lot of great guitarists and musicians around, but nothing's happening, you know. I don't like the Blood, Sweat and Tears shit. I think all that is bullshit. Rock & roll is going like jazz, as far as I can see, and the bullshitters are going off into that *excellentness* which I never believed in and others going off . . . I consider myself in the avant garde of rock & roll. Because I'm with Yoko and she taught me a lot and I taught her a lot, and I think on her album you can hear it, if I can get away from her album for a moment.

What do you think of Dylan's album {'New Morning'}?

I thought it wasn't much. Because I expect more—maybe I expect too much from people— but I expect more. I haven't been a Dylan follower since he stopped rocking. I liked "Rolling Stone" and a few things he did then; I like a few things he did in the early days. The rest of it is just like Lennon-McCartney or something. It's no different, it's a myth.

You don't think then it's a legitimate "New Morning"?

No, it might be a new morning for him because he stopped singing on the top of his voice. It's all right, but it's not him, it doesn't mean a fucking thing. I'd sooner have "I Hear You Knocking" by Dave Edmonds; it's the top of England now.

It's strange that George comes out with his "Hare Krishna" and you come out with the opposite, especially after that.

I can't imagine what George thinks. Well, I suppose he thinks I've lost the way or something like that. But to me, I'm home. I'll never change much from this.

Let's re-approach that: Always the Beatles were talked about—and the Beatles talked about themselves—as being four parts of the same person. What's happened to those four parts?

They remembered that they were four individuals. You see, we believed the Beatles myth, too. I don't know whether the others still believe it. We were four guys . . . I met Paul, and said, "You want to join me band?" Then George joined and then Ringo joined. We were just a band that made it very, very big, that's all. Our best work was never recorded.

Why?

Because we were performers—in spite of what Mick says about us—in Liverpool, Hamburg and other dance halls. What we generated was fanastic, when we played straight rock, and there was nobody to touch us in Britain. As soon as we made it, we made it, but the edges were knocked off.

You know, Brian put us in suits and all that, and we made it very, very big. But we sold out, you know. The music was dead before we even went on the theatre tour of Britain. We were feeling shit already, because we had to reduce an hour or two hours' playing, which we were glad about in one way, to twenty minutes, and we would go on and repeat the same twenty minutes every night.

The Beatles' music died then, as musicians. That's why we never improved as musicians; we killed ourselves then to make it. And that was the end of it. George and I are more inclined to say that; we always missed the club dates because that's when we were playing music, and then later on we became technically efficient recording artists—which was another thing—because we were competent people, and whatever media you put us in we can produce something worthwhile.

How did you choose the musicians you use on this record?

I'm a very nervous person, really, I'm not as big-headed as this tape sounds; this is me projecting through the fear, so I choose people that I know, rather than strangers.

Why do you get along with Ringo?

Because in spite of all the things, the Beatles could really play music together when they weren't uptight, and if I get a thing going, Ringo knows where to go, just like that, and he does well. We've played together so long that it fits. That's the only thing I sometimes miss—just being able to sort of blink or make a certain noise and I know they'll all know where we are going on an ad lib thing. But I don't miss it that much.

How do you rate yourself as a guitarist?

Well, it depends on what kind of guitarist. I'm okay, I'm not technically good, but I can make it fucking howl and move. I was rhythm guitarist. It's an important job. I can make a band drive.

How do you rate George?

He's pretty good. (*Laughter*). I prefer myself. I have to be honest, you know. I'm really very embarrassed about my guitar playing, in one way, because it's very poor. I can never move, but I can make a guitar speak.

You say you can make the guitar speak; what songs have you done that on?

Listen to "Why" on Yoko's album, "*I Found Out.*" I think it's nice. It drives along. Ask Eric Clapton, he thinks I can play, ask him. You see, a lot of you people want technical things; it's like wanting technical films. Most critics of rock & roll, and guitarists, are in the stage of the Fifties when they wanted a technically perfect film finished for them, and then they would feel happy.

I'm a cinema verite guitarist; I'm a musician, and you have to break down your barriers to hear what I'm playing. There's a nice little bit I played, they had it on the back of *Abbey Road*. Paul gave us each a piece; there is a little break where Paul plays, George plays and I played. And there is one bit, one of those where it stops, one of those "carry that weights" where it suddenly goes boom, boom on the drums, and then we all take it in turns to play. I'm the third one on it.

I have a definite style of playing. I've always had. But I was overshadowed. They call George the invisible singer. I'm the invisible guitarist.

You said you played slide guitar on "Get Back."

Yes, I played the solo on that. When Paul was feeling kindly, he would give me a solo! Maybe if he was feeling guilty that he had most of the "A" side or something, he would give me a solo. And I played the solo on that. I think George produced some beautiful guitar playing. But I think he's too hung up to really let go, but so is Eric, really. Maybe he's changed. They're all so hung up. We all are, that's the problem. I really like B. B. King.

Do you like Ringo's record, his country one ['Beaucoups of Blues']?

I think it's a good record. I wouldn't buy any of it, you know. I think it's a good record, and I was pleasantly surprised to hear "Beaucoups of Blues," that song you know. I thought, good. I was glad, and I didn't feel as embarrassed as I did about his first record.

It's hard when you ask me; it's like asking me what do I think of . . . ask me about other people, because it looks so awful when I say I don't like this and I don't like that. It's just that

I don't like many of the Beatles records either.

My own taste is different from that which I've played sometimes, which is called "cop out," to make money or whatever. Or because I didn't know any better.

————————————

I WOULD LIKE TO ASK A QUESTION about Paul and go through that. When we went and saw 'Let It Be' in San Francisco, what was your feeling?

I felt sad, you know. Also I felt . . . that film was set up by Paul for Paul. That is one of the main reasons the Beatles ended. I can't speak for George, but I pretty damn well know we got fed up of being sidemen for Paul.

After Brian died, that's what happened, that's what began to happen to us. The camera work was set up to show Paul and not anybody else. And that's how I felt about it. On top of that, the people that cut it did it as if Paul is God and we are just lyin' around there. And that's what I felt. And I knew there were some shots of Yoko and me that had been just chopped out of the film for no other reason than the people were oriented for Englebert Humperdinck. I felt sick.

How would you trace the breakup of the Beatles?

After Brian died, we collapsed. Paul took over and supposedly led us. But what is leading us when we went round in circles? We broke up then. That was the disintegration.

When did you first feel that the Beatles had broken up? When did that idea first hit you?

I don't remember, you know. I was in my own pain. I wasn't noticing, really. I just did it like a job. The Beatles broke up after Brian died; we made the double album, the set. It's like if you took each track off it and made it all mine and all George's. It's like I told you many times, it was just me and a backing group, Paul and a backing group, and I enjoyed it. We broke up then.

Where were you when Brian died?

We were in Wales with the Maharishi. We had just gone down after seeing his lecture the first night. We heard it then, and then we went right off into the Maharishi thing.

Where were you?

In Wales. A place called Bangor, in Wales.

Were you in a hotel or what?

We were just outside a lecture hall with Maharishi, and I don't know . . . I can't remember, it just sort of came over. Somebody came up to us . . . the press were there, because we had gone down with this strange Indian, and they said, "Brian's dead," and I was stunned, we all

were, I suppose, and the Maharishi, we went in to him. "What, he's dead," and all that, and he was sort of saying, oh, forget it, be happy, like an idiot, like parents, smile, that's what the Maharishi said. And we did.

What was your feeling when Brian died?

The feeling that anybody has when somebody close to them dies. There is a sort of little hysterical sort of hee, hee, I'm glad it's not me or something in it, the funny feeling when somebody close to you dies. I don't know whether you've had it, but I've had a lot of people die around me, and the other feeling is, "What the fuck? What can I do?"

I knew that we were in trouble then. I didn't really have any misconceptions about our ability to do anything other than play music, and I was scared. I thought, "We've fuckin' had it."

What were the events that sort of immediately happened after Brian died?

Well, we went with Maharishi. . . . I remember being in Wales, and then, I can't remember, though. I will probably have to have a bloody primal to remember this. I don't remember. It just all happened.

How did Paul react?

I don't know how the others took it, it's no good asking me . . . it's like asking me how you took it. I don't know. I'm in me own head, I can't be in anybody else's. I don't know really what George, Paul or Ringo think anymore. I know them pretty well, but I don't know anybody that well. Yoko, I know about the best. I don't know how they felt. It was my own thing. We were all just dazed.

So Brian died, and then you said what happened was that Paul started to take over.

That's right. I don't know how much of this I want to put out. Paul had an impression, he has it now like a parent, that we should be thankful for what he did for keeping the Beatles going. But when you look back upon it objectively, he kept it going for his own sake. Was it for my sake Paul struggled?

Paul made an attempt to carry on as if Brian hadn't died by saying, "Now, now, boys, we're going to make a record." Being the kind of person I am, I thought, well, we're going to make a record all right, so I'll go along, so we went and made a record. And that's when we made *Magical Mystery Tour*. That was the real . . .

Paul had a tendency to come along and say, well, he's written these ten songs, let's record now. And I said, "Well, give us a few days, and I'll knock a few off," or something like that. *Magical Mystery Tour* was something he had worked out with Mal [Evans], and he showed me what his idea was and this is how it went, it went around like this, the story and how he had it all . . . the production and everything.

Paul said, "Well, here's the segment, you write a little piece for that," and I thought, bloody hell, so I ran off and I wrote the dream sequence for the fat woman and all the thing with the spaghetti. Then George and I were sort of grumbling about the fuckin' movie, and we thought we better do it, and we had the feeling that we owed it to the public to do these things.

When did your songwriting partnership with Paul end?

That ended . . . I don't know, around 1962, or something, I don't know. If you give me the albums I can tell you exactly who wrote what, and which line. We sometimes wrote together. All our best work—apart from the early days, like "I Want to Hold Your Hand," we wrote together and things like that—we wrote apart always. The "One after 909," on the *Let It Be* LP, I wrote when I was seventeen or eighteen. We always wrote separately, but we wrote together because we enjoyed it a lot sometimes, and also because they would say, well, you're going to make an album, get together and knock off a few songs, just like a job.

Whose idea was it to go India?

I don't know . . . I don't know, probably George's, I have no idea. Yoko and I met around then. I lost me nerve because I was going to take me ex-wife *and* Yoko, but I don't know how to work it. So I didn't quite do it.

"Sexy Sadie" you wrote about the Maharishi?

That's about the Maharishi, yes. I copped out and I wouldn't write "Maharishi, what have you done, you made a fool of everyone." But now it can be told, Fab Listeners.

When did you realize he was making a fool of you?

I don't know, I just sort of *saw* him.

While in India or when you got back?

Yes, there was a big hullaballoo about him trying to rape Mia Farrow or somebody and trying to get off with a few other women and things like that. We went to see him, after we stayed up all night discussing was it true or not true. When George started thinking it might be true, I thought, well, it must be true, because if George started thinking it might be true, there must be something in it.

So we went to see Maharishi, the whole gang of us, the next day, charged down to his hut, his bungalow, his very rich-looking bungalow in the mountains, and, as usual, when the dirty work

came, I was the spokesman—whenever the dirty work came, I actually had to be leader, wherever the scene was; when it came to the nitty-gritty, I had to do the speaking—and I said, "We're leaving."

"Why?" he asked, and all that shit, and I said, "Well, if you're so *cosmic,* you'll know why." He was always intimating, and there were all these right-hand men always intimating, that he did miracles. And I said, "You know why," and he said, "I don't know why, you must tell me," and I just kept saying, "You ought to know," and he gave me a look like, "I'll kill you, you bastard," and he gave me such a look. I knew then. I had called his bluff, and I was a bit rough to him.

Yoko: You expected too much from him.

John: I always do. I always expect too much. I was always expecting my mother and never got her. That's what it is, you know, or some parent, I know that much.

You came to New York and had that press conference.

The Apple thing. That was to announce Apple.

But at the same time you disassociated yourselves from the Maharishi.

I don't remember that. You know, we all say a lot of things when we don't know what we're talking about. I'm probably doing it now, I don't know what I say. You see, everybody takes you up on the words you said, and I'm just a guy that people ask all about things, and I blab off and some of it makes sense and some of it is bullshit and some of it's lies and some of it is— God knows what I'm saying. I don't know what I said about Maharishi, all I know is what we said about Apple, which was worse.

Will you talk about Apple?

All right.

How did that start?

Clive Epstein, or some other such business freak, came up to us and said, you've got to spend so much money or the tax will take you. We were thinking of opening a chain of retail clothes shops or some balmy thing like that . . . and we were all thinking that if we are going to have to open a shop, let's open something we're interested in, and we went through all these different ideas about this, that and the other. Paul had a nice idea about opening up white houses, where we would sell white china and things like that, everything white, because you can never get anything white, you know, which was pretty groovy, and it didn't end up with

136

that, it ended up with Apple and all this junk and the Fool and all those stupid clothes and all that.

When did you decide to close that down?

I don't know. I was controlling the scene at the time, I mean, I was the one going in the office and shouting about. Paul had done it for six months, and then I walked in and changed everything. There were all the Peter Browns reporting behind my back to Paul, saying, "You know, John's doing this and John's doing that, that John, he's crazy," I was always the one that must be crazy because I wouldn't let them have status quo.

Well, Yoko and I together, we came up with the idea to give it all away and stop fuckin' about with a psychedelic clothes shop, so we gave it all away. It was a good happening.

Were you at the big giveaway?

No, we read it in the papers. That was when we started events. I learned events from Yoko. We made everything into events from then on and got rid of it.

You gave away your M.B.E.?

I'd been planning on it for over a year and a bit. I was waiting for a time to do it.

You said then that you were waiting to tag it to some event, then you realized that it was the event.

That's the truth.

You said you quit the Beatles first.

Yes.

How?

I said to Paul "I'm leaving."

I knew on the flight over to Toronto or before we went to Toronto: I told Allen [Klein] I was leaving, I told Eric Clapton and Klaus [Voormann] that I was leaving then, but that I would probably like to use them as a group. I hadn't decided how to do it—to have a permanent new group or what—then, later on, I thought, fuck, I'm not going to get stuck with another set of people, whoever they are.

I announced it to myself and the people around me on the way to Toronto a few days before. And on the plane—Klein came with me—I told Allen, "It's over." When I got back, there were a few meetings, and Allen said, well, cool it, cool it, there was a lot to do, businesswise, you know, and it would not have been suitable at the time.

Then we were discussing something in the office with Paul, and Paul said something or other about the Beatles doing something, and I kept saying, "No, no, no," to everything he said. So it came to a point where I had to say

something, of course, and Paul said, "What do you mean?"

I said, "I mean the group is over, I'm leaving."

Allen was there, and he will remember exactly and Yoko will, but this is exactly how I see it. Allen was saying, don't tell. He didn't want me to tell Paul even. So I said, "It's out," I couldn't stop it, it came out. Paul and Allen both said that they were glad that I wasn't going to announce it, that I wasn't going to make an event out of it. I don't know whether Paul said, "Don't tell anybody," but he was darned pleased that I wasn't going to. He said, "Oh, that means nothing really happened if you're not going to say anything."

So that's what happened. So, like anybody when you say divorce, their face goes all sorts of colors. It's like he knew really that this was the final thing; and six months later he comes out with whatever. I was a fool not to do it, not to do what Paul did, which was use it to sell a record.

You were really angry with Paul?

No, I wasn't angry.

Well, when he came out with this "I'm leaving."

No, I wasn't angry—shit, he's a good PR man, that's all. He's about the best in the world, probably. He really does a job. I wasn't angry. We were all hurt that he didn't tell us that was what he was going to do.

I think he claims that he didn't mean that to happen, but that's bullshit. He called me in the afternoon of that day and said, "I'm doing what you and Yoko were doing last year." I said, good, you know, because that time last year they were all looking at Yoko and me as if we were strange, trying to make our life together instead of being fab, fat myths. So he rang me up that day and said, I'm doing what you and Yoko are doing, I'm putting out an album, and I'm leaving the group, *too*, he said. I said, good. I was feeling a little strange because *he* was saying it this time, although it was a year later, and I said, "Good," because he was the one that wanted the Beatles most, and then the midnight papers came out.

How did you feel then?

I was cursing because I hadn't done it. I wanted to do it, I should have done it. Ah, damn, shit, what a fool I was. But there were many pressures at that time with the Northern Songs fight going on; it would have upset the whole thing if I would have said that.

How did you feel when you found out that Dick

James had sold his shares in your own company, Northern Songs? Did you feel betrayed?

Sure I did. He's another one of those people who think they made us. They didn't. I'd like to hear Dick James' music and I'd like to hear George Martin's music, please, just play me some. Dick James actually has said that.

What?

That he *made* us. People are under a delusion that *they* made *us*, when in fact *we* made *them*.

How did you get Allen Klein into Apple?

The same as I get anything I want. The same as you get what you want. I'm not telling you; just work at it, get on the phone, a little word here and a little word there, and do it.

What was Paul's reaction?

You see, a lot of people, like the Dick Jameses, Derek Taylors and Peter Browns, all of them, they think they're the Beatles, and Neil [Aspinal] and all of them. Well, I say, fuck 'em, you know, and after working with genius for ten, fifteen years they begin to think they're it. They're not.

Do you think you're a genius?

Yes, if there is such a thing as one, I am one.

When did you first realize that?

When I was about twelve. I used to think I must be a genius, but nobody's noticed. I used to wonder whether I'm a genius or I'm not, which is it? I used to think, well, I can't be mad because nobody's put me away; therefore, I'm a genius. A genius is a form of madness, and we're all that way, you know, and I used to be a bit coy about it, like my guitar playing.

If there is such a thing as genius—which is what . . . what the fuck is it?—I am one, and if there isn't, I don't care. I used to think it when I was a kid, writing me poetry and doing me paintings. I didn't become something when the Beatles made it, or when you heard about me, I've been like this all me life. Genius is pain, too.

How do you feel towards the Beatle people? All of them who used to—some still do—work at Apple, who've been around during those years. Neil Aspinal, Mal Evans . . .

I didn't mention Mal. I said Neil, Peter Brown and Derek. They live in a dream of Beatle past, and everything they do is oriented to that. They also have a warped view of what was happening. I suppose we all do.

They must feel now that their lives are inextricably bound up in yours.

Well, they have to grow up, then. They've only had half their life, and they've got another whole half to go and they can't go on pretending

138

to be Beatles. That's where it's at. I mean, when they read this, they'll think it's "cracked John," if it's in the article, but that's where it's at; they live in the past.

You see, I presumed that I would just be able to carry on and bring Yoko into our life, but it seemed that I had to either be married to them or Yoko, and I chose Yoko, and I was right.

What were their reactions when you first brought Yoko by?

They despised her.

From the very beginning?

Yes, they insulted her, and they still do. They don't even know I can see it, and even when it's written down, it will look like I'm just paranoiac or she's paranoiac. I know, just by the way the publicity on us was handled in Apple, all of the two years we were together, and the attitude of people to us and the bits we hear from office girls. We know, so they can go stuff themselves.

Yoko: In the beginning, we were too much in love to notice anything.

John: We were in our own dream, but they're the kind of idiots that really think that Yoko split the Beatles, or Allen. It's the same joke, really; they are that insane about Allen, too.

How would you characterize George's, Paul's and Ringo's reaction to Yoko?

It's the same. You can quote Paul, it's probably in the papers; he said it many times, at first he hated Yoko and then he got to like her. But it's too late for me. I'm for Yoko. Why should she take that kind of shit from those people? They were writing about her looking miserable in the *Let It Be* film, but you sit through sixty sessions with the most big-headed, uptight people on earth and see what it's fuckin' like and be insulted—just because you love someone—and George, shit, insulted her right to her face in the Apple office at the beginning, just being "straightforward," you know that game of "I'm going to be up front," because this is what we've heard and Dylan and a few people said she'd got a lousy name in New York, and you give off bad vibes. That's what George said to her! And we both sat through it. I didn't hit him, I don't know why.

I was always hoping that they would come around. I couldn't believe it, and they all sat there with their wives like a fucking jury and judged us, and the only thing I did was write that piece (ROLLING STONE, April 16th, 1970) about "some of our *beast* friends" in my usual way—because I was never honest enough, I always had to write in that gobbly-gook—and that's what they did to us.

Ringo was all right, so was Maureen, but the other two really gave it to us. I'll never forgive them, I don't care what fuckin' shit about Hare Krishna and God and Paul and his, "Well, I've changed me mind," I can't forgive 'em for that, really. Although I can't help still loving them either.

Yoko played me tapes I understood. I know it was very strange, and avant garde music is a very tough thing to assimilate and all that, but I've heard the Beatles play avant garde music—when nobody was looking—for years.

But the Beatles were artists, and all artists have fuckin' big egos, whether they like to admit it or not, and when a new artist came into the group, they were never allowed. Sometimes George and I would have liked to have brought somebody in like Billy Preston, that was exceptional, we might have had him in the group.

We were fed up with the same old shit, but it wasn't wanted. I would have expanded the Beatles and broken them and gotten their pants off and stopped them being God, but it didn't work, and Yoko was naive; she came in and she would expect to perform with them, with any group, like you would with any group, she was jamming, but there would be a sort of coldness about it. That's when I decided: I could no longer artistically get anything out of the Beatles, and here was someone that could turn me on to a million things.

You say that the dream is over. Part of the dream was that the Beatles were God or that the Beatles were the messengers of God, and, of course, yourself as God . . .

Yeah. Well, if there is a God, we're all it.

When did you first start getting the reactions from people who listened to the records, sort of the spiritual reaction?

There is a guy in England, William Mann, who was the first intellectual who reviewed the Beatles in the *Times* and got people talking about us in that intellectual way. He wrote about aeolian cadences and all sorts of musical terms, and he is a bullshitter. But he made us credible with intellectuals. He wrote about Paul's last album as if it were written by Beethoven or something. He's still writing the same shit. But it did us a lot of good in that way, because people in all the middle classes and intellectuals were all going, "Oooh."

When did somebody first come up to you about this thing about John Lennon as God?

About what to do and all of that? Like "You tell us, Guru"? Probably after acid. Maybe after *Rubber Soul.* I can't remember it exacty happen-

ing. We just took that position. I mean, we started putting out messages. Like "The Word Is Love" and things like that. I write messages, you know. See, when you start putting out messages, people start asking you, "What's the message?"

HOW DID YOU FIRST GET IN-*volved in LSD?*

A dentist in London laid it on George, me and wives, without telling us, at a dinner party at his house. He was a friend of George's and our dentist at the time, and he just put it in our coffee or something. He didn't know what it was; it's all the same thing with that sort of middle-class London swinger, or whatever. They had all heard about it, and they didn't know it was different from pot or pills, and they gave us it. He said, "I advise you not to leave," and we all thought he was trying to keep us for an orgy in his house, and we didn't want to know, and we went to the Ad Lib and these discotheques, and there were these incredible things going on.

It was insane, going around London. When we went to the club we thought it was on fire, and then we thought it was a premiere and it was just an ordinary light outside. We thought, "Shit, what's going on here?" We were cackling in the streets, and people were shouting, "Let's break a window," you know; it was just insane. We were just out of our heads. When we finally got on the lift [elevator], we all thought there was a fire, but there was just a little red light. We were all screaming like that, and we were all hot and hysterical, and when we all arrived on the floor, because this was a discotheque that was up a building, the lift stopped and the door opened and we were all [*John demonstrates by screaming*] . . .

I had read somebody describing the effects of opium in the old days, and I thought, "Fuck! It's happening," and then we went to the Ad Lib and all of that, and then some singer came up to me and said, "Can I sit next to you?" And I said, "Only if you don't talk," because I just couldn't think.

This seemed to go on all night. I can't remember the details. George somehow or another managed to drive us home in his Mini. We were going about ten miles an hour, but, it seemed like a thousand, and Patti was saying, let's jump out and play football. I was getting all

139

these sort of hysterical jokes coming out like speed, because I was always on that, too.

God, it was just terrifying, but it was fantastic. I did some drawings at the time, I've got them somewhere, of four faces saying, "We all agree with you!" I gave them to Ringo, the originals. I did a lot of drawing that night. And then George's house seemed to be just like a big submarine. I was driving it, they all went to bed, I was carrying on in it; it seemed to float above his wall which was eighteen foot, and I was driving it.

When you came down, what did you think?

I was pretty stoned for a month or two. The second time we had it was in L.A. We were on tour in one of those houses, Doris Day's house or wherever it was we used to stay, and the three of us took it, Ringo, George and I. Maybe Neil and a couple of the Byrds—what's his name, the one in the Stills and Nash thing, Crosby and the other guy, who used to do the lead. McGuinn. I think they came, I'm not sure, on a few trips. But there was a reporter, Don Short. We were in the garden; it was only our second one, and we still didn't know anything about doing it in a nice place and cool it. Then they saw the reporter and thought, "How do we act?" We were terrified waiting for him to go, and he wondered why we couldn't come over. Neil, who never had acid either, had taken it, and he would have to play road manager, and we said go get rid of Don Short, and he didn't know what to do.

Peter Fonda came, and that was another thing. He kept saying [*in a whisper*], "I know what it's like to be dead," and we said, "What?" and he kept saying it. We were saying, "For Christ's sake, shut up, we don't care, we don't want to know," and he kept going on about it. That's how I wrote "She Said, She Said"—"I know what's it's like to be dead." It was a sad song, an acidy song, I suppose. "When I was a little boy" . . . you see, a lot of early childhood was coming out, anyway.

So LSD started for you in 1964: How long did it go on?

It went on for years, I must have had a thousand trips.

Literally a thousand, *or a couple of hundred?*

A thousand. I used to just eat it all the time. I never took it in the studio. Once I thought I was taking some uppers, and I was not in the state of handling it. I can't remember what album it was, but I took it and I just noticed . . . I suddenly got so scared on the mike. I thought I felt ill, and I thought I was going to crack. I said, I must get some air. They all took me upstairs on the roof and George Martin was looking at me funny, and then it dawned on me I must have taken acid. I said, "Well, I can't go on, you'll have to do it and I'll just stay and watch." You know, I got very nervous just watching them all. *I was saying, "Is it all right?"* And they were saying, "Yeah." They had all been very kind, and they carried on making the record.

The other Beatles didn't get into LSD as much as you did?

George did. In L.A., the second time we took it, Paul felt very out of it because we are all a bit slightly cruel, sort of, "We're taking it, and *you're* not." But we kept *seeing him,* you know. We couldn't eat our food. I just couldn't manage it, just picking it up with our hands. There were all these people serving us in the house, and we were knocking food on the floor and all of that. It was a long time before Paul took it. Then there was the big announcement.

Right.

So, I think George was pretty heavy on it; we are probably the most cracked. Paul is a bit more stable than George and I.

And straight?

I don't know about straight. Stable. I think LSD profoundly shocked him, and Ringo. I think maybe they *regret* it.

Did you have many bad trips?

I had many. Jesus Christ, I stopped taking it because of that. I just couldn't stand it.

You got too afraid to take it?

It got like that, but then I stopped it for I don't know how long, and then I started taking it again just before I met Yoko. Derek came over and . . . you see, I got the message that I should destroy my ego, and I did, you know. I was reading that stupid book of Leary's; we were going through a whole game that everybody went through, and I destroyed myself. I was slowly putting myself together round about Maharishi time. Bit by bit over a two-year period, I had destroyed me ego.

I didn't believe I could do anything and let people make me, and let them all just do what they wanted. I just was nothing. I was shit. Then Derek tripped me out at his house after he got back from L.A. He sort of said, "You're all right," and pointed out which songs I had written. "You wrote this," and, "You said this," and, "You are intelligent, don't be frightened."

The next week I went to Derek's with Yoko and we tripped again, and she filled me completely to realize that I was me and that it's all right. That was it; I started fighting again, being a loudmouth again and saying, "I *can* do this, fuck it, this is what I want, you know. I want it and don't put me down." I did this, so that's where I am now.

At some point, right between 'Help' and 'Hard Day's Night,' you got into drugs and got into doing drug songs?

A Hard Day's Night I was on pills; that's drugs, that's bigger drugs than pot. Started on pills when I was fifteen, no, since I was seventeen, since I became a musician. The only way to survive in Hamburg, to play eight hours a night, was to take pills. The waiters gave you them— the pills and drink. I was a fucking dropped-down drunk in art school. *Help* was where we turned on to pot and we dropped drink, simple as that. I've always needed a drug to survive. The others, too, but I always had more, more pills, more of everything because I'm more crazy, probably.

There's a lot of obvious LSD things you did in the music.

Yes.

How do you think that affected your conception of the music? In general.

It was only another mirror. It wasn't a miracle. It was more of a visual thing and a therapy, looking at yourself a bit. It did all that. You know, I don't quite remember. But it didn't write the music; neither did Janov or Maharishi in the same terms. I write the music in the circumstances in which I'm in, whether it's on acid or in the water.

WHAT DID YOU THINK OF 'A Hard Day's Night'?

The story wasn't bad, but it could have been better. Another illusion was that we were just puppets and that these great people, like Brian Epstein and Dick Lester, created the situation and made this whole fuckin' thing, and *precisely* because we were what we were, realistic. We didn't want to make a fuckin' shitty pot movie; we didn't want to make a movie that was going to be bad, and we insisted on having a real writer to write it.

Brian came up with Allan Owen, from Liverpool, who had written a play for TV called "No Trams to Lime St." Lime Street is a famous street in Liverpool where the whores used to be in the old days, and Owen was famous for writing Liverpool dialogue. We auditioned people to write for us, and they came up with this guy. He

was a bit phony, like a professional Liverpool man—you know, like a professional American. He stayed with us two days and wrote the whole thing based on our characters then: me, witty; Ringo, dumb and cute; George this; and Paul that.

We were a bit infuriated by the glibness and shiftiness of the dialogue, and we were always trying to get it more realistic, but they wouldn't have it. It ended up okay, but the next one was just bullshit because it really had *nothing* to do with the Beatles. They just put us here and there. Dick Lester was good; he had ideas ahead of their times, like using Batman comic-strip lettering and balloons.

My impression of the movie was that it was you, and it wasn't anyone else.

It was a good projection of one facade of us, which was on tour, once in London and once in Dublin. It was of us in that situation together, in a hotel, having to perform before people. We were like that. The writer saw the press conference.

'Rubber Soul' was . . .

Can you tell me whether that white album with the drawing by Voormann on it, was that before *Rubber Soul* or after?

After. You really don't remember which?

No. Maybe the others do; I don't remember those kind of things because it doesn't mean anything, it's all gone.

'Rubber Soul' was the first attempt to do a serious, sophisticated, complete work, in a certain sense.

We were just getting better, technically and musically, that's all. Finally we took over the studio. In the early days, we had to take what we were given; we didn't know how you can get more bass. We were learning the technique on *Rubber Soul*. We were more precise about making the album, that's all, and we took over the cover and everything.

'Rubber Soul,' that was just a simple play on . . .

That was Paul's title; it was like "Yer Blues" I suppose, meaning English Soul, I suppose, just a pun. There is no great, mysterious meaning behind all of this; it was just four boys working out what to call a new album.

The Hunter Davies book, the "authorized biography," says . . .

It was written in [London] *Sunday Times* sort of fab form. And no home truths were written. My auntie knocked out all the truth bits from my childhood, and my mother and I allowed it, which was my cop-out, etcetera. There was nothing about orgies and the shit that happened on tour. I wanted a real book to come out, but

141

we all had wives and didn't want to hurt their feelings. End of that one. Because they still have wives.

The Beatles tours were like the Fellini film *Satyricon*. We had that image. Man, our tours were like something else; if you could get on our tours, you were in. They were Satyricon, all right.

Would you go to a town . . . hotel . . .

Wherever we went, there was always a whole scene going; we had our four separate bedrooms. We tried to keep them out of our room. Derek's and Neil's rooms were always full of junk and whores and who-the-fuck-knows-what, and policemen with it. Satyricon! We had to do something. What do you do when the pill doesn't wear off and it's time to go? I used to be up all night with Derek, whether there was anybody there or not, I could never sleep, such a heavy scene it was. They didn't call them groupies then, they called it something else, and if we couldn't get groupies, we would have whores and everything, whatever was going.

Who would arrange all that stuff?

Derek and Neil, that was their job, and Mal, but I'm not going into all that.

Like businessmen at a convention.

When we hit town, we hit it. There was no pissing about. There's photographs of me crawling about in Amsterdam on my knees coming out of whorehouses and things like that. The police escorted me to the places because they never wanted a big scandal, you see. I don't really want to talk about it because it will hurt Yoko. And it's not fair. Suffice to say that they were Satyricon on tour and that's it, because I don't want to hurt their feelings, or the other people's girls either. It's just not fair.

Yoko: I was surprised; I really didn't know things like that. I thought, well, John is an artist, and probably he had two or three affairs before getting married. That is the concept you have in the old school. New York artists' group, you know, that kind.

The generation gap.

Right, right, exactly.

Let me ask you about something else that was in the Hunter Davies book. At one point it said you and Brian Epstein went off to Spain.

Yes. We didn't have an affair, though. Fuck knows what was said. I was pretty close to Brian. If somebody is going to manage me, I want to know them inside out. He told me he was a fag.

I hate the way Allen is attacked and Brian is made out to be an angel just because he's dead. He wasn't you know, he was just a guy.

What else was left out of the Hunter Davies book?

That I don't know because I can't remember it. There is a better book on the Beatles by Michael Brown, *Love Me Do.* That was a true book. He wrote how we were, which was bastards. You can't be anything else in such a pressurized situation, and we took it out on people like Neil, Derek and Mal. That's why underneath their facade, they resent us, but they can never show it, and they won't believe it when they read it. They took a lot of shit from us because we were in such a shitty position. It was hard work, and somebody had to take it. Those things are left out by Davies, about what bastards we were. Fuckin' big bastards, that's what the Beatles were. You have to be a bastard to make it, that's a fact, and the Beatles are the biggest bastards on earth.

Yoko: How did you manage to keep that clean image? It's amazing.

John: Everybody wants the image to carry on. You want to carry on. The press around, too, because they want the free drinks and the free whores and the fun; everybody wants to keep on the bandwagon. We were the Caesars; who was going to knock us, when there were a million pounds to be made? All the handouts, the bribery, the police, all the fucking hype. Everybody wanted in, that's why some of them are still trying to cling onto this: Don't take Rome from us, not a portable Rome where we can all have our houses and our cars and our lovers and our wives and office girls and parties and drink and drugs, don't take it from us, otherwise you're mad, John, you're crazy, silly John wants to take this all away.

WHAT WAS IT LIKE IN THE *early days in London?*

When we came down, we were treated like real provincials by the Londoners. We were, in fact, provincials.

What was it like, say, running around London, in the discotheques, with the Stones and everything?

That was a great period. We were like kings of the jungle then, and we were very close to the Stones. I don't know how close the others were, but I spent a lot of time with Brian and Mick. I admire them, you know. I dug them the first time I saw them in whatever that place is they came from, Richmond. I spent a lot of time with them, and it was great. We all used to just go around London in cars and meet each other and talk about music with the Animals and Eric and all that. It was really a good time, that was the best period, famewise. We didn't get mobbed so much. It was like a men's smoking club, just a very good scene.

What was Brian Jones like?

Well, he was different over the years as he disintegrated. He ended up the kind of guy that you dread when he would come on the phone because you knew it was trouble. He was really in a lot of pain. In the early days, he was all right because he was young and confident. He was one of them guys that disintegrated in front of you. He wasn't sort of brilliant or anything, he was just a nice guy.

When he died?

By then I didn't feel anything. I just thought, another victim of the drug scene.

What do you think of the Stones today?

I think it's a lot of hype. I like "Honky Tonk Women," but I think Mick's a joke, with all that fag dancing, I always did. I enjoy it; I'll probably go and see his films and all, like everybody else, but really, I think it's a joke.

Do you see him much now?

No, I never do see him. We saw a bit of each other around when Allen was first coming in—I think Mick got jealous. I was always very respectful about Mick and the Stones, but he said a lot of sort of tarty things about the Beatles, which I am hurt by, because, you know, I can knock the Beatles, but don't let Mick Jagger knock them. I would like to just list what we did and what the Stones did two months after on every fuckin' album. Every fuckin' thing we did, Mick does exactly the same—he imitates us. And I would like one of you fuckin' underground people to point it out; you know *Satanic Majesties* is *Pepper*; "We Love You," it's the most fuckin' bullshit, that's "All You Need Is Love."

I resent the implication that the Stones are like revolutionaries and that the Beatles weren't. If the Stones were or are, the Beatles really were, too. But they are not in the same class, music-wise or powerwise, never were. I never said anything. I always admired them because I like their funky music and I like their style. I like rock & roll and the direction they took after they got over trying to imitate us, you know, but he's even going to do Apple now. He's going to do the same thing.

He's obviously so upset by how big the Beatles are compared with him; he never got over it. Now he's in his old age, and he is beginning to knock us, you know, and he keeps knocking. I resent it, because even his second fuckin' record,

we wrote it for him. Mick said, "Peace made money." We didn't make any money from Peace. You know.

Yoko: We lost money.

When 'Sgt. Pepper' came out, did you know that you had put together a great album? Did you feel that while you were making it?

Yeah, yeah, and *Rubber Soul*, too, and *Revolver*.

WHY CAN'T YOU BE ALONE *without Yoko?*

I can be, but I don't wish to be. There is no reason on earth why I should be without her. There is nothing more important than our relationship, nothing. We dig being together all the time, and both of us could survive apart, but what for? I'm not going to sacrifice love, real love, for any fuckin' whore, or any friend, or any business, because in the end you're alone at night. Neither of us want to be, and you can't fill the bed with groupies. I don't want to be a swinger. Like I said in the song, I've been through it all, and nothing works better than to have somebody you love hold you.

You say on your record that, "The freaks on the phone won't leave me alone, so don't give me that brother, brother."

Because I'm sick of all these aggressive hippies or whatever they are, the "Now Generation," being very uptight with me. Either on the street or anywhere, or on the phone, demanding my attention, as if I owed them something.

I'm not their fucking parents, that's what it is. They come to the door with a fucking peace symbol and expect to just sort of march around the house or something, like an old Beatle fan. They're under a delusion of awareness by having long hair, and that's what I'm sick of. They frighten me, a lot of uptight maniacs going around, wearing fuckin' peace symbols.

What did you think of Manson and that thing?

I don't know what I thought when it happened. A lot of the things he says are true: He is a child of the state, made by us, and he took their children in when nobody else would. Of course, he's cracked, all right.

What about "Piggies" and "Helter Skelter"?

He's balmy, like any other Beatle kind of fan who reads mysticism into it. We used to have a laugh about this, that or the other, in a light-hearted way, and some intellectual would read us, some symbolic youth generation wants to see something in it. We also took seriously some

143

parts of the role, but I don't know what "Helter Skelter" has to do with knifing somebody. I've never listened to the words properly; it was just a noise.

Everybody spoke about the backwards thing on 'Abbey Road.'

That's bullshit. I just read that one about Dylan, too. That's bullshit.

The rumor about Paul being dead?

I don't know where that started, that's balmy. You know as much about it as me.

Were any of those things really on the album that were said to be there? The clues?

No. That was bullshit; the whole thing was made up. We wouldn't do anything like that. We did put in like "tit, tit, tit" in "Girl," and many things I don't remember, like a beat missing or something that could be interpreted like that. Some people have got nothing better to do than study Bibles and make myths about it and study rocks and make stories about how people used to live. It's just something for them to do. They live vicariously.

WHAT DO YOU THINK ROCK & roll will become?

Whatever we make it. If we want to go bullshitting off into intellectualism with rock & roll, then we are going to get bullshitting rock intellectualism. If we want real rock & roll, it's up to all of us to create it and stop being hyped by the revolutionary image and long hair. We've got to get over that bit. That's what cutting hair is about. Let's own up *now* and see who's who, who is doing something about what, and who is making music and who is laying down bullshit. Rock & roll will be whatever we make it.

Why do you think it means so much to people?

Because the best stuff is primitive enough and has no bullshit. It gets through to you; it's beat, go to the jungle and they have the rhythm. It goes throughout the world and it's as simple as that, you get the rhythm going because everybody goes into it. I read that Eldridge Cleaver said that blacks gave the middle-class whites back their bodies and put their minds and bodies together. Something like that. It gets through; it got through to me, the only thing to get through to me of all the things that were happening when I was fifteen. Rock & roll then was real, everything else was unreal. The thing about rock & roll, good rock & roll—whatever good means and all that shit—is that its *real*, and realism gets

through to you despite yourself. You recognize something in it which is true, like all true art. Whatever art is, readers. Okay. If it's real, it's simple, usually, and if it's simple, it's true. Something like that.

What was it in your music that turned everyone on at first? Why was it so infectious?

We didn't sound like everybody else. We didn't sound like the black musicians because we weren't black and we were brought up on an entirely different type of music and atmosphere. So "Please, Please Me" and "From Me to You" and all of those were our version of the chair. We were building our own chairs, that's all, and they were sort of local chairs.

The first gimmick was the harmonica. There had been "Hey, Baby" with a harmonica, and there was a terrible thing called "I Remember You" in England. All of a sudden we started using it on "Love Me Do." The first set of tricks was double tracking on the second album. I would love to remix some of the early stuff because it is better than it sounds.

What do you think of those concerts like the Hollywood Bowl?

It was awful, I hated it. Some of them were good, but I didn't like Hollywood Bowl. Some of those big gigs were good, but not many of them.

In an interview with Jon Cott a year or so ago, you said something about your favorite song being "Ticket to Ride."

Yeah, I liked it because it was a slightly new sound at the time. But it's not my favorite song.

In what way was it new?

It was pretty fuckin' heavy for then. It's a heavy record, that's why I like it. I used to like guitars.

In "Glass Onion" you say, "The Walrus is Paul," yet in the new album you admit that you were the Walrus.

"I Am the Walrus" was originally the B side of "Hello Goodbye"! I was still in my love cloud with Yoko, and I thought, well, I'll just say something nice to Paul: "It's all right, you did a good job over these few years, holding us together." He was trying to organize the group, and organize the music, and be an individual and all that, so I wanted to thank him. I said, "The Walrus is Paul," for that reason. I felt, "Well, he can have it. I've got Yoko, and thank you, you can have the credit."

But now I'm sick of reading things that say Paul is the musician and George is the philosopher. I wonder where I fit in, what was my contribution? I get hurt, you know, sick of it. I'd sooner be Zappa and say, "Listen, you fuckers, *this* is what *I* did, and I don't care whether you like my attitude saying it." That's what I am, you know; I'm a fucking *artist*, and I'm not a fucking PR agent or the product of some other person's imagination. Whether you're the public or whatever, I'm standing by my work, whereas before I would not stand by it.

That's what I'm saying: *I* was the Walrus, whatever that means. We saw the movie *Alice in Wonderland* in L.A., and the Walrus is a big capitalist that ate all the fuckin' oysters. If you must know, that's what he was even though I didn't remember this when I wrote it.

What did you think of 'Abbey Road'?

I liked the "A" side, but I never liked that sort of pop opera on the other side. I think it's junk because it was just bits of songs thrown together. "Come Together" is all right, that's all I remember. That was my song. It was a competent album, like *Rubber Soul.* It was together in that way, but *Abbey Road* had no life in it.

What do you think are your best songs that you have written?

Ever? The one best song?

Have you ever thought of that?

I don't know. If somebody asked me what is my favorite song, is it "Stardust" or something, I can't answer. That kind of decision making I can't do. I always liked "Walrus," "Strawberry Fields," "Help," "In My Life," those are some favorites.

Why "Help"?

Because I meant it—it's real. The lyric is as good now as it was then. It is no different, and it makes me feel secure to know that I was that aware of myself then. It was just me singing "Help," and I meant it.

I don't like the recording that much; we did it too fast trying to be commercial. I like "I Want to Hold Your Hand." We wrote that together, it's a beautiful melody. I might do "I Want to Hold Your Hand" and "Help" again, because I like them and I can sing them. "Strawberry Fields" because it's real, real for then, and I think it's like talking, "You know, I sometimes think no . . ." It's like he talks to himself, sort of singing, which I thought was nice.

I like "Across the Universe," too. It's one of the best lyrics I've written. In fact, it could be the best. It's good poetry, or whatever you call it, without chewin' it. See, the ones I like are the ones that stand as words, without melody. They don't have to have any melody; like a poem, you can read them.

That's your ultimate criterion?

No, that's just the ones I happen to like. I like to read other people's lyrics, too.

So what happened with 'Let It Be'?

It was another one like *Magical Mystery Tour.* In a nutshell, it was time for another Beatle movie or something; Paul wanted us to go on the road or do something. He sort of set it up, and there were discussions about where to go, and all of that. I had Yoko by then, and I would just tag along. I was stoned all the time and I just didn't give a shit. Nobody did. It was just like it was in the movie; when I got to do "Across the Universe" (which I wanted to re-record because the original wasn't very good), Paul yawns and plays boogie. I merely say, "Anyone want to do a fast one?" That's how I am. Year after year, that begins to wear you down.

How long did those sessions last?

Oh, fuckin' God knows how long. Paul had this idea that he was going to rehearse us. He's looking for perfection all the time and had these ideas that we would rehearse and then make the album. We, being lazy fuckers—and we'd been playing for twenty years! We're grown men, for fuck's sake, and we're not going to sit around and rehearse. I'm not, anyway—we couldn't get into it.

We put down a few tracks, and nobody was in it at all. It was just a dreadful, dreadful feeling in Twickenham Studio, being filmed all the time, I just wanted them to go away. We'd be there at eight in the morning. You couldn't make music at eight in the morning in a strange place, with people filming you and colored lights flashing.

So how did it end?

The tape ended up like the bootleg version. We didn't want to know about it anymore, so we just left it to Glyn Johns and said, "Here, mix it." That was the first time since the first album that we didn't want to have anything to do with it. None of us could be bothered going in. Nobody called anybody about it, and the tapes were left there. Glyn Johns did it. We got an acetate in the mail, and we called each other and said, "What do you think?"

We were going to let it out in really shitty condition. I didn't care. I thought it was good to let it out and show people what had happened to us; we can't get it together; we don't play together any more; you know, leave us alone. The bootleg version is what it was like, and everyone was probably thinking they're not going to fucking work on it. There were twenty-nine hours of tape, so much that it was like a movie. Twenty takes of everything, because we were rehearsing and taking everything. Nobody could face looking at it.

When Spector came around, we said, well, if you want to work with us, go and do your audition. He worked like a pig on it. He always wanted to work with the Beatles, and he was given the shittiest load of badly recorded shit, with a lousy feeling toward it, ever. And he made something out of it. He did a great job.

When I heard it, I didn't puke; I was so relieved after six months of this black cloud hanging over me that this was going to go out.

I had thought it would be good to let the shitty version out because it would break the Beatles, break the myth. It would be just us, with no trousers on and no glossy paint over the cover and no hype: This is what we are like with our trousers off, would you please end the game now?

But that didn't happen. We ended up doing *Abbey Road* quickly and putting out something slick to preserve the myth. I am weak as well as strong, you know, and I wasn't going to fight for *Let It Be* because I really couldn't stand it.

Finally, when 'Let It Be' was going to be released, Paul wanted to bring out his album.

There were so many clashes. It did come out at the same time or something, didn't it? I think he wanted to show he was the Beatles.

Were you surprised when you heard it, at what he had done?

Very. I expected just a little more. If Paul and I are sort of disagreeing, and I feel weak, I think he must feel strong, you know, that's in an argument. Not that we've had much physical argument, you know.

What do you think Paul will think of your album?

I think it'll probably scare him into doing something decent, and then he'll scare me into doing something decent, like that.

I think he's capable of great work, and I think he will do it. I wish he wouldn't, you know. I wish nobody would, Dylan or anybody. In me heart of hearts, I wish I was the only one in the world or whatever it is. But I can't see Paul doing it twice.

W HAT WAS IT LIKE TO GO ON tour? You had cripples coming up to you.
That was our version of what was happening. People were sort of touching us as we walked past, that kind of thing. Wherever we went we were supposed to be not like normal, and we were supposed to put up with all sorts of shit from lord mayors and

146

their wives, be touched and pawed like *Hard Day's Night,* only a million more times, like at the American Embassy or the British Embassy in Washington here or wherever it was when some bloody animal cut Ringo's hair. I walked out of that, swearing at all of them. I'd forgotten but you tripped me into that one. What was the question?

The cripples.

Wherever we went on tour, in Britain and everywhere we went, there were always a few seats laid aside for cripples and people in wheelchairs. Because we were famous, we were supposed to have epileptics and whatever they are in our dressing room all the time. We were supposed to be sort of "good," and really, you wanted to be alone. You don't know what to say, because they're usually saying, "I've got your record," or they can't speak and just want to touch you. It's always the mother or the nurse pushing them on you; they themselves would just say hello and go away, but the mothers would push them at you like you were Christ or something, as if there were some aura about you which would rub off on them. It just got to be like that, and we were very sort of callous about it. It was just dreadful; you would open up every night, and instead of seeing kids there, you would just see a row full of cripples along the front. It seemed that we were just surrounded by cripples and blind people all the time, and when we would go through corridors, they would be all touching us and things like that. It was horrifying.

You must have been still fairly young and naive at that point.

Yeah, well, as naive as *In His Own Write.*

Surely that must have made you think for a second.

Well, I mean we knew what the game was.

It didn't astound you at that point that you were supposed to be able to make the lame walk and the blind see?

It was the "in" joke that we were supposed to cure them; it was the kind of thing that we would say because it was a cruel thing to say. We felt sorry for them, anybody would, but there is a kind of embarrassment when you're surrounded by blind, deaf and crippled people. There is only so much we could say, you know, with the pressure on us, to do and to perform.

The bigger we got, the more unreality we had to face; the more we were expected to do until, when you didn't sort of shake hands with a mayor's wife, she would start abusing you and screaming and saying, "How dare they?"

There is one of Derek's stories in which we were asleep after the show in the hotel somewhere in America, and the mayor's wife comes and says, "Get them up, I want to meet them." Derek said, "I'm not going to wake them." She started to scream, "You get them up or I'll tell the press." That was always that—they were always threatening that they would tell the press about us if we didn't see their bloody daughter with her braces on her teeth. It was always the police chief's daughter or the lord mayor's daughter, all the most obnoxious kids—because they had the most obnoxious parents—that we were forced to see all the time. We had these people thrust on us.

The most humiliating experiences were like sitting with the mayor of the Bahamas, when we were making *Help,* and being insulted by these fuckin' junked-up middle-class bitches and bastards who would be commenting on our work and commenting on our manners.

I was always drunk, insulting them. I couldn't take it. It would hurt me. I would go insane, swearing at them. I would do something. I couldn't take it.

All that business was awful; it was a fuckin' humiliation. One has to completely humiliate oneself to be what the Beatles were, and that's what I resent. I didn't know, I didn't foresee. It happened bit by bit, gradually, until this complete craziness is surrounding you, and you're doing exactly what you don't want to do with people you can't stand—the people you hated when you were ten. And that's what I'm saying in this album—I remember what's it all about now, you fuckers—fuck you! That's what I'm saying, you don't get me twice.

WOULD YOU TAKE IT ALL back?
What?
Being a Beatle?
If I could be a fuckin' fisherman, I would. If I had the capabilities of being something other than I am, I would. It's no fun being an artist. You know what it's like, writing, it's torture. I read about Van Gogh, Beethoven, any of the fuckers. If they had psychiatrists, we wouldn't have had Gauguin's great pictures. These bastards are just socking us to death; that's about all that we can do, is do it like circus animals.

I resent being an artist, in that respect; I resent performing for fucking idiots who don't know anything. They can't feel. I'm the one

that's feeling because I'm the one that is expressing. They live vicariously through me and other artists, and we are the ones . . . even with the boxers—when Oscar comes in the ring, they're booing the shit out of him; he only hits Clay once and they're all cheering him. I'd sooner be in the audience, really, but I'm not capable of it.

One of my big things is that I wish to be a fisherman. I know it sounds silly—and I'd sooner be rich than poor, and all the rest of that shit—but I wish the pain was ignorance or bliss or something. If you don't know, man, then there's no pain; that's how I express it.

What do you think the effect was of the Beatles on the history of Britain?

I don't know about the "history"; the people who are in control and in power, and the class system and the whole bullshit bourgeoisie is exactly the same, except there is a lot of fag middle-class kids with long, long hair walking around London in trendy clothes, and Kenneth Tynan is making a fortune out of the word "fuck." Apart from that, nothing happened. We all dressed up, the same bastards are in control, the same people are runnin' everything. It is exactly the same.

We've grown up a little, all of us, there has been a change, and we're all a bit freer and all that, but it's the same game. Shit, they're doing exactly the same thing, selling arms to South Africa, killing blacks on the street; people are living in fucking poverty, with rats crawling over them. It just makes you puke, and I woke up to *that,* too.

The dream is over. It's just the same, only I'm thirty, and a lot of people have got long hair. That's what it is, man, nothing happened except that we grew up, we did our thing—just like they were telling us. You kids—most of the so-called "now generation" are getting a job. We're a minority, you know; people like us always were, but maybe we are a slightly larger minority because of maybe something or other.

Why do you think the impact of the Beatles was so much bigger in America than it was in England?

The same reason that American stars are so much bigger in England: The grass is greener. We were really professional by the time we got to the States; we had learned the whole game. When we arrived here we knew how to handle the press; the British press were the toughest in the world, and we could handle anything. We were all right.

On the plane over, I was thinking, "Oh, we won't make it," or I said it on a film or something, but that's that side of me. We knew

147

we would wipe you out if we could just get a grip on you. We were new.

And when we got here, you were all walking around in fuckin' Bermuda shorts, with Boston crew cuts and stuff on your teeth. Now they're telling us, they're all saying, "Beatles are *passé*, and this is like that, man." The chicks looked like fuckin' 1940 horses. There was no conception of dress or any of that jazz. We just thought, "What an ugly race"; it looked just disgusting. We thought how hip we were, but, of course, we weren't. It was just the five of us, us and the Stones were really the hip ones; the rest of England were just the same as they ever were.

You tend to get nationalistic, and we would really laugh at America, except for its music. It was the black music we dug, and over here even the blacks were laughing at people like Chuck Berry and the blues singers; the blacks thought it wasn't sharp to dig the really funky music, and the whites only listened to Jan and Dean and all that. We felt that we had the message which was, "Listen to this music." It was the same in Liverpool; we felt very exclusive and underground in Liverpool, listening to Richie Barret and Barrett Strong, and all those old-time records. Nobody was listening to any of them except Eric Burdon in Newcastle and Mick Jagger in London. It was that lonely, it was fantastic. When we came over here and it was the same—nobody was listening to rock & roll or to black music in America—we felt as though we were coming to the land of its origin, but nobody wanted to know about it.

What part did you ever play in the songs that are heavily identified with Paul, like "Yesterday"?

"Yesterday" I had nothing to do with.

"Eleanor Rigby"?

"Eleanor Rigby" I wrote a good half of the lyrics or more.

When did Paul show you "Yesterday"?

I don't remember—I really don't remember, it was a long time ago. I think he was . . . I really don't remember, it just sort of appeared.

Who wrote "Nowhere Man"?

Me, me.

Did you write that about anybody in particular?

Probably about myself. I remember I was just going through this paranoia trying to write something and nothing would come out, so I just lay down and tried to not write and then this came out, the whole thing came out in one gulp.

What songs really stick in your mind as being Lennon-McCartney songs?

"I Want to Hold Your Hand," "From Me to You," "She Loves You"—I'd have to have the list, there's so many, trillions of 'em. Those are the ones. In a rock band you have to make singles; you have to keep writing them. Plenty more. We both had our fingers in each other's pies.

A song from the 'Help' album, like "You've Got to Hide Your Love Away." How did you write that? What were the circumstances? Where were you?

I was in Kenwood, and I would just be songwriting. The period would be for songwriting, and so every day I would attempt to write a song, and it's one of those that you sort of sing a bit sadly to yourself, "Here I stand, head in hand . . ."

I started thinking about my own emotions—I don't know when exactly it started, like "I'm a Loser" or "Hide Your Love Away" or those kinds of things—instead of projecting myself into a situation, I would just try to express what I felt about myself, which I'd done in me books. I think it was Dylan helped me realize that—not by any discussion or anything but just by hearing his work—I had a sort of professional songwriter's attitude to writing pop songs; he would turn out a certain style of song for a single, and we would do a certain style of thing for this and the other thing. I was already a stylized songwriter on the first album. But to express myself I would write *Spaniard in the Works* or *In His Own Write,* the personal stories which were expressive of my emotions. I'd have a separate songwriting John Lennon who wrote songs for the sort of meat market, and I didn't consider them—the lyrics or anything—to have any depth at all. They were just a joke. Then I started being me about the songs, not writing them objectively, but subjectively.

What about on 'Rubber Soul,' "Norwegian Wood"?

I was trying to write about an affair without letting me wife know I was writing about an affair, so it was very gobbledygook. I was sort of writing from my experiences, girls' flats, things like that.

Where did you write that?

I wrote it at Kenwood.

When did you decide to put a sitar on it?

I think it was at the studio. George had just got his sitar and I said, "Could you play this piece?" We went through many different sort of versions of the song; it was never right, and I was getting very angry about it, it wasn't coming out like I said. They said, "Well, just do it how you want to do it," and I said, "Well, I just want to do it like this." They let me go, and I did the guitar very loudly into the mike and sang it at the same time, and then George had the sitar and I asked him could he play the piece that I'd written, you know, dee diddley dee diddley dee, that bit, and he was not sure whether he could play it yet because he hadn't done much on the sitar but he was willing to have a go, as is his wont, and he learned the bit and dubbed it on after. I think we did it in sections.

You also have a song on that album, "In My Life." When did you write that?

I wrote that in Kenwood. I used to write upstairs where I had about ten Brunell tape recorders all linked up. I still have them. I'd mastered them over the period of a year or two—I could never make a rock & roll record, but I could make some far-out stuff on it. I wrote it upstairs; that was one where I wrote the lyrics first and then sang it. That was usually the case with things like "In My Life" and "Universe" and some of the ones that stand out a bit.

Would you just record yourself and a guitar on a tape and then bring it in to the studio?

I would do that just to get an impression of what it sounded like *sung* and to hear it back for judging it—you never know 'til you hear the song yourself. I would double track the guitar or the voice or something on the tape. I think on "Norwegian Wood" and "In My Life" Paul helped with the middle eight, to give credit where it's due.

Let me ask you about one on the double album, "Glass Onion." You set out to write a little message to the audience.

Yeah, I was having a laugh because there'd been so much gobbledygook about *Pepper,* play it backwards and you stand on your head and all that. Even now, I just saw Mel Torme on TV the other day saying that "Lucy" was written to promote drugs and so was "A Little Help from My Friends," and none of them were at all—"A Little Help from My Friends" only says get high in it; it's really about a little help from my friends, it's a sincere message. Paul had the line about "little help from my friends," I'm not sure, he had some kind of structure for it, and—we wrote it pretty well fifty-fifty, but it was based on his original idea.

"Happiness Is a Warm Gun" is a nice song.

Oh, I like that, one of my best; I had forgotten about that. Oh, I love it. I think it's a beautiful song. I like all the different things that are happening in it. Like "God," I had put together some three sections of different songs; it was meant to be—it seemed to run through all the different kinds of rock music.

It wasn't about "H" at all. "Lucy in the Sky" with diamonds which I swear to God, or swear to Mao, or to anybody you like, I had no idea spelled L.S.D.—and "Happiness"—George Martin had a book on guns which he had told me about—I can't remember—or I think he showed me a cover of a magazine that said "Happiness Is a Warm Gun." It was a gun magazine, that's it: I read it, thought it was a fantastic, insane thing to say. A warm gun means that you just shot something.

You said to me, "'Sgt. Pepper' is the one." That was the album?

Well, it was a peak. Paul and I were definitely working together, especially on "A Day in the Life," that was a real . . . The way we wrote a lot of the time: You'd write the good bit, the part that was easy, like "I read the news today" or whatever it was, then when you got stuck or whenever it got hard, instead of carrying on, you just drop it; then we would meet each other, and I would sing half, and he would be inspired to write the next bit and vice versa. He was a bit shy about it because I think he thought it's already a good song. Sometimes we wouldn't let each other interfere with a song either, because you tend to be a bit lax with someone else's stuff, you experiment a bit. So we were doing it in his room with the piano. He said, "Should we do this?" "Yeah, let's do that."

I keep saying that I always preferred the double album because *my* music is better on the double album; I don't care about the whole concept of *Pepper;* it might be better, but the music was better for me on the double album because I'm being myself on it. I think it's as simple as the new album, like "I'm So Tired" is just the guitar. I felt more at ease with that than the production. I don't like production so much. But *Pepper* was a peak, all right.

Yoko: People think that's the peak, and I'm just so amazed. . . . John's done all that Beatle stuff. But this new album of John's is a real peak; that's higher than any other thing he has done.

John: Thank you, dear.

Do you think it is?

Yeah, sure. I think it's *Sgt. Lennon.* I don't really know how it will sink in, where it will lie in the spectrum of rock & roll and the generation and all the rest of it, but I know what it is. It's something else, it's another door.

149

DO YOU THINK THE BEATLES *will record together again?*

I record with Yoko, but I'm not going to record with another ego-maniac. There is only room for one on an album nowadays. There is no point, there is just no point at all. There was a reason to do it at one time, but there is no reason to do it anymore.

I had a group, I was the singer and the leader; I met Paul, and I made a decision whether to—and he made a decision, too—have him in the group: Was it better to have a guy who was better than the people I had in, obviously, or not? To make the group stronger or to let me be stronger? That decision was to let Paul in and make the group stronger.

Well, from that, Paul introduced me to George, and Paul and I had to make the decision, or I had to make the decision, whether to let George in. I listened to George play, and I said, "Play 'Raunchy'," or whatever the old story is, and I let him in. I said, "Okay, you come in"; that was the three of us then. Then the rest of the group was thrown out gradually. It just happened like that; instead of going for the individual thing, we went for the strongest format, and for equals.

George is ten years younger than me, or some shit like that. I couldn't be bothered with him when he first came around. He used to follow me around like a bloody kid, hanging around all the time. I couldn't be bothered. He was a kid who played guitar, and he was a friend of Paul's, which made it all easier. It took me years to come around to him, to start considering him as an equal or anything.

We had all sorts of different drummers all the time, because people who owned drum kits were few and far between; it was an expensive item. They were usually idiots. Then we got Pete Best because we needed a drummer to go to Hamburg the next day. We passed the audition on our own with a stray drummer. There are other myths about Pete Best was the Beatles, and Stuart Sutcliffe's mother is writing in England that *he* was the Beatles.

Are you the Beatles?

No, I'm not the Beatles. I'm me. Paul isn't the Beatles. Brian Epstein wasn't the Beatles, neither is Dick James. The Beatles are the Beatles. Separately, they are separate. George was a separate individual singer, with his own group as well, before he came in with us, the Rebel Rousers. Nobody is the Beatles. How could they be? We all had our roles to play.

How would you assess George's talents?

I don't want to assess him. George has not done his best work yet. His talents have developed over the years, and he was working with two fucking brilliant songwriters, and he learned a lot from us. I wouldn't have minded being George, the invisible man, and learning what he learned. Maybe it was hard for him sometimes, because Paul and I are such egomaniacs, but that's the game.

I'm interested in concepts and philosophies. I am not interested in wallpaper, which most music is.

When did you realize that what you were doing transcended . . .

People like me are aware of their so-called genius at ten, eight, nine. . . . I always wondered, "Why has nobody discovered me?" In school, didn't they see that I'm cleverer than anybody in this school? That the teachers are stupid, too? That all they had was information that I didn't need?

I got fuckin' lost in being at high school. I used to say to me auntie, "You throw my fuckin' poetry out, and you'll regret it when I'm famous," and she threw the bastard stuff out. I never forgave her for not treating me like a fuckin' genius or whatever I was, when I was a child.

It was obvious to me. Why didn't they put me in art school? Why didn't they train me? Why would they keep forcing me to be a fuckin' cowboy like the rest of them? I was different, I was always different. Why didn't anybody notice me?

A couple of teachers would notice me, encourage me to be something or other, to draw or to paint—express myself. But most of the time they were trying to beat me into being a fuckin' dentist or a teacher. And then the fuckin' fans tried to beat me into being a fuckin' Beatle or an Engelbert Humperdinck, and the critics tried to beat me into being Paul McCartney.

Yoko: So you were very deprived in a way . . .

John: That's what makes me what I am. It comes out; the people I meet have to say it themselves, because we get fuckin' kicked. Nobody says it, so you scream it: Look at me, a genius, for fuck's sake! What do I have to do to prove to you son-of-a-bitches what I can do and who I am? Don't dare, don't you dare fuckin' criticize my work like that. You, who don't know anything about it.

Fuckin' bullshit!

I know what Zappa is going through, and a half. I'm just coming out of it. I just have been in school again. I've had teachers ticking me off and marking my work. If nobody can recognize what I am, then fuck 'em; it's the same for Yoko. . . .

Yoko: That's why it's an amazing thing: After somebody has done something like the Beatles, they think that he's sort of satisfied, where actually the Beatles . . .

John: The Beatles was nothing.

Yoko: It was like cutting him down to a smaller size than he is.

John: I learned lots from Paul and George, in many ways, but they learned a damned sight lot from me—they learned a fucking lot from me. It's like George Martin, or anybody: Just come back in twenty years' time and see what we're doing, and see who's doing what—don't put me—don't sort of mark my papers like I'm top of the math class or did I come in Number One in English Language, because I never did. Just assess me on what I am and what comes out of me mouth, and what me work is, don't mark me in the classrooms. It's like I've just left school again! I just graduated from the school of Show Biz, or whatever it was called.

Do you see a time when you'll retire?

No. I couldn't, you know.

Yoko: He'll probably work until he's eighty or until he dies.

John: I can't foresee it. Even when you're a cripple you carry on painting. I would paint if I couldn't move. It doesn't matter, you see, when I was saying what Yoko did with "Greenfield Morning"—took half an inch she taped and none of us knew what we were doing, and I saw her create something. I saw her start from scratch with something we would normally throw away. With the other stuff we did, we were all good in the backing and everything went according to plan, it was a good session, but with "Greenfield Morning" and "Paper Shoes" there was nothing there for her to work with. She just took nothing—the way Spector did—that's the way the genius shows through any media. You give Yoko or Spector a piece of tape, two inches of tape, they can create a symphony out of it. You don't have to be trained in rock & roll to be a singer; I didn't have to be trained to be a singer: I can sing. Singing is singing to people who enjoy what you're singing, not being able to hold notes—I don't have to be in rock & roll to create. When I'm an old man, we'll make wallpaper together, but just to have the same depth and impact. The message is the medium.

WHAT IS HOLDING PEOPLE back from understanding Yoko?

She was doing all right before she met Elvis. Howard Smith announced he was going to play her music on FM, and all these idiots rang up and said, "Don't you dare play it, she split the Beatles." She didn't split the Beatles, and even if she did, what does that have to do with it or her fucking record? She is a woman, and she's Japanese; there is racial prejudice against her, and there is female prejudice against her. It's as simple as that.

Her work is far out; Yoko's bottom thing is as important as *Sgt. Pepper*. The real hip people know about it. There are a few people that know; there is a person in Paris who knows about her; a person in Moscow knows about her; there's a person in fucking China that knows about her. But in general, she can't be accepted because she's too far out. It's hard to take. Her pain is such that she expresses herself in a way that hurts you—you cannot take it. That's why they couldn't take Van Gogh; it's too real, it hurts; that's why they kill you.

How did you meet Yoko?

I'm sure I've told you this many times. How did I meet Yoko? There was a sort of underground clique in London; John Dunbar, who was married to Marianne Faithfull, had an art gallery in London called Indica, and I'd been going to galleries a bit on my off days in between records. I'd been to see a Takis exhibition. I don't know if you know what that means; he does multiple electromagnetic sculptures, and a few exhibitions in different galleries showed these sort of unknown artists or underground artists. I got the word that this amazing woman was putting on a show next week and there was going to be something about people in bags, in black bags, and it was going to be a bit of a happening and all that. So I went down to a preview of the show. I got there the night before it opened. I went in—she didn't know who I was or anything—I was wandering around, there were a couple of artsy-type students that had been helping lying around there in the gallery, and I was looking at it and I was astounded. There was an apple on sale there for 200 quid; I thought it was fantastic—I got the humor in her work immediately. I didn't have to sort of have much knowledge about avant garde or underground art, but the humor got me straightaway. There was a fresh apple on a stand, this was before Apple—and it was 200 quid to watch the apple decompose. But there was another piece which

151

really decided me for or against the artist, a ladder which led to a painting which was hung on the ceiling. It looked like a blank canvas with a chain with a spyglass hanging on the end of it. This was near the door when you went in. I climbed the ladder; you look through the spyglass, and in tiny little letters it says "yes."

So it was positive. I felt relieved. It's a great relief when you get up the ladder and you look through the spyglass and it doesn't say "no" or "fuck you" or something; it said "yes."

I was very impressed, and John Dunbar sort of introduced us—neither of us knew who the hell we were; she didn't know who I was, she'd only heard of Ringo, I think, it means apple in Japanese. And John Dunbar had been sort of hustling her, saying, "That's a good patron, you must go and talk to him or do something," because I was looking for action. I was expecting a happening and things like that. John Dunbar insisted she say hello to the millionaire, you know what I mean. And she came up and handed me a card which said, "Breathe," on it, one of her instructions, so I just went *(pant)*. That was our meeting.

Then I went away, and the second time I met her was at a gallery opening of Claes Oldenburg in London. We were very shy; we sort of nodded at each other, and we didn't know—she was standing behind me. I sort of looked away because I'm very shy with people, especially chicks. We just sort of smiled and stood frozen together in this cocktail party thing.

The next thing was she came to me to get some backing—like all the bastard underground do—for a show she was doing. She gave me her *Grapefruit* book, and I used to read it, and sometimes I'd get very annoyed by it; it would say things like, "Paint until you drop dead" or, "Bleed," and then sometimes I'd be very enlightened by it, and I went through all the changes that people go through with her work— sometimes I'd have it by the bed and I'd open it and it would say something nice and it would be all right, and then it would say something heavy and I wouldn't like it. There was all that, and then she came to me to get some backing for a show, and it was half a wind show. I gave her the money to back it, and the show was, this was in a place called Lisson Gallery, another one of those underground places. For this whole show everything was in half: There was half a bed, half a room, half of everything, all beautifully cut in half and all painted white. And I said to her, "Why don't you sell the other half in bottles?" having caught on by then what the game was,

and she did that—this is still before we'd had any nuptials—and we still have the bottles from the show, it's my first. It was presented as "Yoko Plus Me"—that was our first public appearance. I didn't even go to see the show, I was too uptight.

When did you realize that you were in love with her?

It was beginning to happen; I would start looking at her book and that, but I wasn't quite aware what was happening to me, and then she did a thing called Dance Event where different cards kept coming through the door everyday saying, "Breathe" and "Dance" and "Watch all the lights until dawn," and they upset me or made me happy, depending on how I felt.

I'd get very upset about it being intellectual or all fucking avant garde; then I'd like it and then I wouldn't. Then I went to India with the Maharoonie, and we were corresponding. The letters were still formal, but they just had a little side to them. I nearly took her to India as I said, but I still wasn't sure for what reason, I was still sort of kidding myself, with all sort of artistic reasons, and all that.

When we got back from India we were talking to each other on the phone. I called her over; it was the middle of the night and Cyn was away, and I thought, well, now's the time if I'm gonna get to know her anymore. She came to the house and I didn't know what to do; so we went upstairs to my studio and I played her all the tapes that I'd made, all this far-out stuff, some comedy stuff and some electronic music. She was suitably impressed, and then she said, well, let's make one ourselves, so we made "Two Virgins." It was midnight when we started "Two Virgins"; it was dawn when we finished, and then we made love at dawn. It was very beautiful.

What was it like getting married? Did you enjoy it?

It was very romantic. It's all in the song, "The Ballad of John and Yoko"; if you want to know how it happened, it's in there. Gibraltar was like a little sunny dream. I couldn't find a white suit—I had sort of off-white corduroy trousers and a white jacket. Yoko had all white on.

What was your first peace event?

The first peace event was the Amsterdam Bed Peace when we got married.

What was that like—that was your first re-exposure to the public.

It was a nice high. We were on the seventh floor of the Hilton looking over Amsterdam—it was very crazy; the press came expecting to see us fuck in bed—they all heard John and Yoko were going to fuck in front of the press for peace. So when they all walked in—about fifty or sixty reporters flew over from London all sort of very edgy, and we were just sitting in pajamas saying, "Peace, Brother," and that was it. On the peace thing, there's lots of heavy discussions with intellectuals about how you should do it and how you shouldn't.

When you got done, did you feel satisfied with the Bed Peace?

They were great events when you think that the world newspaper headlines were the fact that we were a married couple in bed talking about peace. It was one of our greater episodes. It was like being on tour without moving, sort of a big promotional thing. I think we did a good job for what we were doing, which was trying to get people to own up.

What accounts for your great popularity?

Because I fuckin' did it. I copped out in that Beatle thing. I was like an artist that went off . . . Have you never heard of like Dylan Thomas and all them who never fuckin' wrote but just went up drinking and Brendan Behan and all of them, they died of drink . . . everybody that's done anything is like that. I just got meself in a party; I was an emperor, I had millions of chicks, drugs, drink, power and everybody saying how great I was. How could I get out of it? It was just like being in a fuckin' train. I couldn't get out.

I couldn't create, either. I created a little; it came out, but I was in the party and you don't get out of a thing like that. It was fantastic! I came out of the sticks; I didn't hear about anything—Van Gogh was the most far-out thing I had ever heard of. Even London was something we used to dream of, and London's nothing. I came out of the fuckin' sticks to take over the world, it seemed to me. I was enjoying it, and I was trapped in it, too. I couldn't do anything about it; I was just going along for the ride. I was hooked, just like a junkie.

What did being from Liverpool have to do with your art?

It was a port. That means it was less hick than someone in the English Midlands, like the American Midwest or whatever you call it. We were a port, the second biggest port in England, between Manchester and Liverpool. The North is where the money was made in the eighteen hundreds; that was where all the brass and the heavy people were, and that's where the despised people were.

We were the ones that were looked down upon as animals by the Southerners, the Londoners. The Northerners in the States think that people are pigs down South, and the people in New York think West Coast is hick. So we were hicksville.

We were a great amount of Irish descent and blacks and Chinamen, all sorts there. It was like San Francisco, you know. That San Francisco is something else! Why do you think Haight-Ashbury and all that happened there? It didn't happen in Los Angeles, it happened in San Francisco, where people are going. L.A. you pass through and get a hamburger.

There was nothing big in Liverpool; it wasn't American. It was going poor, a very poor city, and tough. But people have a sense of humor because they are in so much pain, so they are always cracking jokes. They are very witty, and it's an Irish place. It is where the Irish came when they ran out of potatoes, and it's where black people were left or worked as slaves or whatever.

It is cosmopolitan, and it's where the sailors would come home with the blues records from America on the ships. There is the biggest country & western following in England in Liverpool, besides London—always besides London, because there is more of it there.

I heard country & western music in Liverpool before I heard rock & roll. The people there—the Irish in Ireland are the same—they take their country & western music very seriously. There's a big, heavy following of it. There were established folk, blues and country & western clubs in Liverpool before rock & roll, and we were like the new kids coming out.

I remember the first guitar I ever saw. It belonged to a guy in a cowboy suit in a province of Liverpool, with stars, and a cowboy hat and a big dobro. They were real cowboys, and they took it seriously. There had been cowboys long before there was rock & roll.

What do you think of America?

I love it, and I hate it. America is where it's at. I should have been born in New York, I should have been born in the Village, that's where I belong. Why wasn't I born there? Paris was it in the eighteenth century, London I don't think has ever been it except literarywise when Wilde and Shaw and all of them were there. New York was it.

I regret profoundly that I was not an American and not born in Greenwich Village. That's where I should have been. It never works that way. Everybody heads toward the center; that's why I'm here now. I'm here just to breathe it. It might be dying and there might be a lot of dirt in the air that you breathe, but this is where it's

153

happening. You go to Europe to rest, like in the country. It's so overpowering, America, and I'm such a fuckin' cripple that I can't take much of it, it's too much for me.

Yoko: He's very New York, you know.

John: I'm frightened of it. People are so aggressive, I can't take all that I need to go home; I need to have a look at the grass. I'm always writing about my English garden. I need the trees and the grass; I need to go into the country because I can't stand too much people.

Right after 'Sgt. Pepper' George came to San Francisco.

George went over in the end. I was all for going and living in the Haight. In my head, I thought, "Acid is it, and let's go, I'll go there." I was going to go there, but I'm too nervous to do anything, actually. I thought, I'll go there and we'll live there and I'll make music and live like that. Of course, it didn't come true.

But it happened in San Francisco. It happened all right, didn't it? I mean, it goes down in history. I love it. It's like when Shaw was in England, and they all went to Paris; and I see all that in New York, San Francisco and London, even London. We created something there—Mick and us, we didn't know what we were doing, but we were all talking, blabbing over coffee, like they must have done in Paris, talking about paintings. . . . Me, Burdon and Brian Jones would be up night and day talking about music, playing records, and blabbing and arguing and getting drunk. It's beautiful history, and it happened in all these different places. I just miss New York. In New York they have their own cool clique. Yoko came out of that.

This is the first time I'm really seeing it, because I was always too nervous, I was always the famous Beatle. Dylan showed it to me once on sort of a guided tour around the Village, but I never got any feel of it. I just knew Dylan was New York, and I always sort of wished I'd been there for the experience Bob got from living around here.

What is the nature of your relationship with Bob?

It's sort of an acquaintance, because we were so nervous whenever we used to meet. It was always under the most nervewracking circumstances, and I know I was always uptight and I know Bobby was. We were together and we spent some time, but I would always be too paranoid or I would be too aggressive or vice versa, and we didn't really speak.

He came to my house, which was Kenwood, can you imagine it, and I didn't know where to put him in this sort of bourgeois home life I was living; I didn't know what to do and things like that. I used to go to his hotel rather, and I loved him, you know, because he wrote some beautiful stuff. I used to love that, his so-called protest things. I like the sound of him; I didn't have to listen to his words, he used to come with his acetate and say, "Listen to this, John, and did you hear the words?" I said, that doesn't matter, the sound is what counts—the overall thing. I had too many father figures and I liked words, too, so I liked a lot of the stuff he did. You don't have to hear what Bob Dylan is saying; you just have to hear the way he says it.

Do you see him as a great?

No, I see him as another poet, or as competition. You read my books that were written before I had heard of Dylan or read Dylan or anybody, it's the same. I didn't come after Elvis and Dylan; I've been around always. But if I see or meet a great artist, I love 'em. I go fanatical about them for a short period, and then I get over it. If they wear green socks I'm liable to wear green socks for a period, too.

When was the last time you saw Bob?

He came to our house with George after the Isle of Wight and when I had written "Cold Turkey."

Yoko: And his wife.

John: I was just trying to get him to record. We had just put him on piano for "Cold Turkey" 'to make a rough tape, but his wife was pregnant or something, and they left. He's calmed down a lot now.

I just remember before that we were both in shades and both on fucking junk and all these freaks around us and Ginsberg and all those people. I was anxious as shit; we were in London when he came.

You were in that movie with him that hasn't been released.

I've never seen it, but I'd love to see it. I was always so paranoid and Bob said, "I want you to be in this film." He just wanted me to be in the film.

I thought, why? What? He's going to put me down; I went all through this terrible thing.

In the film, I'm just blabbing off and commenting all the time, like you do when you're very high or stoned. I had been up all night. We were being smart alecks, it's terrible. But it was his scene; that was the problem for me. It was his movie. I was on his territory; that's why I was so nervous. I was on his session.

You're going back to London; what's a rough picture of your immediate future, say the next three months?

I'd like to just vanish a bit. It wore me out,

New York. I love it. I'm just sort of fascinated by it, like a fucking monster. Doing the films was a nice way of meeting a lot of people. I think we've both said and done enough for a few months, especially with this article. I'd like to get out of the way and wait till they all . . .

Do you have a rough picture of the next few years?

Oh, no, I couldn't think of the next few years; it's abysmal thinking of how many years there are to go, millions of them. I just play it by the week. I don't think much ahead of a week.

I have no more to ask.

Well, fancy that.

Do you have anything to add?

No, I can't think of anything positive and heartwarming to win your readers over.

Do you have a picture of "when I'm 64"?

No, no. I hope we're a nice old couple living off the coast of Ireland or something like that—looking at our scrapbook of madness.

15

INTERVIEWED BY ROBERT GREENFIELD (1971)

Thanks to Keith Richards' keen intelligence and vivid memory, this remains a classic among Rolling Stones interviews.

But reporter Robert Greenfield played no small part in the process. In 1971, an associate editor out of the ROLLING STONE London office, Greenfield would track the Stones for over a year, culminating in a book about their 1972 tour of the United States.

Greenfield met the twenty-eight-year-old guitarist Keith and actress Anita Pallenberg in the South of France. With Mick Jagger having just returned from his honeymoon with Bianca, the Stones were about to start what would become the *Exile on Main Street* album.

Greenfield noted a recording studio being built in the basement of Richards' house and recalls some early work tapes popping up in the background as he and Keith retraced the history of the band.

"Two cogent statements, both made by Keith, may be kept in mind while reading the questions and answers, which were asked and answered over a ten-day period at odd hours," says Greenfield:

"It's a pretty good house; we're doing our best to fill it with kids and rock 'n' roll."

And: "You know that thing that Blind Willie said: 'I don't like the suits and ties/ They don't seem to harmonize.'"

Greenfield began with a few additional notes on his subject and his house:

—BF-T

KEITH PLAYS IN A ROCK & ROLL BAND. Anita is a movie star queen. They reside in a large white marble house in the South of France people have described as "decadent-looking." The British admiral who built it had trees brought from all over the world, in ships of pine and cypress and palm. There is an

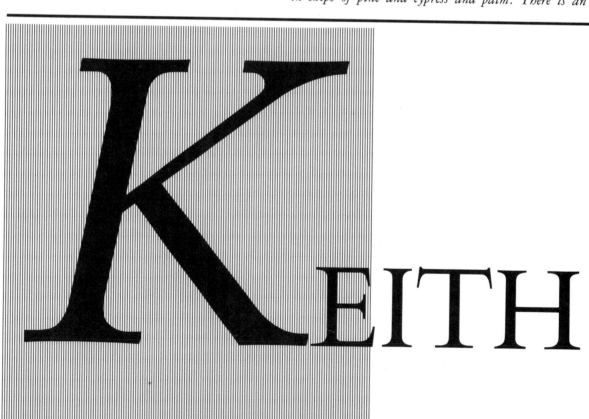

RICHARDS

exotic-colored bird in a cage in the front garden and a rabbit called Boots that lives in the back. A dog named Oakie sleeps where he wants.

Meals are the only recurring reality, and twenty-three at a table is not an unusual number. The ceilings are thirty feet from the floor, and some nights, pink lightning hangs over the bay and the nearby town of Villefranche, which waits for the fleet to come back so its hotels can turn again into whorehouses.

There is a private beach down a flight of stairs and a waterbed on the porch. Good reference points for the whole mise-en-scène are F. Scott Fitzgerald's Tender Is the Night *and the Shirelles' greatest hits.*

WHAT WERE YOU DOING *right at the beginning?*

I was hanging out at art school. Yeah. Suburban art school. I mean, in England, if you're lucky to get into art school. It's somewhere they put you if they can't put you anywhere else. If you can't saw wood straight or file metal. It's where they put me to learn graphic design because I happened to be good at drawing apples or something. Fifteen . . . I was there for three years, and meanwhile I learned how to play guitar. Lotta guitar players in art school. A lot of terrible artists, too. It's funny.

Your parents weren't musical?

Nah. My grandfather was. He used to have a dance band in the Thirties. Played the sax. Was in a country band in the late Fifties, too, playin' the U.S. bases in England. Gus Dupree . . . King of the Country Fiddle. He was a groove, y'know . . . a good musician. . . . He was never professional for more than a few years in the Thirties.

What did your father do?

He had a variety of professions. He was a baker for a while. I know he got shot up in the First World War. Gassed or something.

Were you raised middle class?

Working class. English working class . . . struggling, thinking they were middle class. Moved into a tough neighborhood when I was about ten. I used to be with Mick before that . . . we used to live close together. Then I moved to what they'd call in the States a housing project. Just been built. Thousands and thousands of houses, everyone wondering what the fuck was going on. Everyone was displaced. They were still building it, and there were gangs everywhere. Coming to Teddy Boys. Just before

rock & roll hit England. But they were all waiting for it. They were practicing.

Were you one of the boys?

Rock & roll got me into being one of the boys. Before that I just got me ass kicked all over the place. Learned how to ride a punch.

It's strange, 'cause I knew Mick when I was really young . . . five, six, seven. We used to hang out together. Then I moved and didn't see him for a long time. I once met him selling ice creams outside the public library. I bought one. He was tryin' to make extra money.

Rock & roll got to England about '53, '54, you were eleven. . . .

Yeah. Presley hit first. Actually, the music from *Blackboard Jungle,* "Rock around the Clock," hit first. Not the movie, just the music. People saying, "Ah, did ya hear that music, man?" Because in England, we had never heard anything.

Then, everybody stood up for that music. I didn't think of playing it. I just wanted to go and listen to it. It took 'em a year or so before anyone in England could make that music. The first big things that hit were skiffle—simple three-chord stuff. It wasn't really rock & roll. It was a lot more folky, a lot more strummy. Tea-chest basses. A very crude sort of rock & roll. Lonnie Donegan's the only cat to come out of skiffle.

But we were really listening to what was coming from over the Atlantic. The ones that were hitting hard were Little Richard and Presley and Jerry Lee Lewis. Chuck Berry was never really that big in England. All his big big hits made it . . . but maybe because he never came over. Maybe because the movies he made like *Go Johnny Go* never got over because of distribution problems. Fats Domino was big. Freddie Bell and the Bellboys, too; all kinds of weird people that never made it in America.

They loved the piano. Looking back on it, all the piano boys really had it together for England. More than just the cat that stood there with the guitar.

Did you start really playing in school then?

Yeah. It's funny going back that far. Things come through but . . . I'll tell you who's really good at pushing memories: Bill. He's got this little mind that remembers everything. I'm sure it's like he rolls a tape.

How things were at the start is something. It's when everybody's got short hair. And everybody thought it was long. That's the thing. I mean, we were really being put down like shit then for having long hair.

When I went to art school, people were just startin' to grow their hair and loosen up. You got in there on the favors of the headmaster. You go there and show him your shit, the stuff you've done at ordinary school, during art lessons, and he decides. You don't have to do anything apart from going to see him. He says, "You takin' anything? What are you on?" And you're about fifteen or sixteen, and you don't even know what the fuck they do in art school. You have this vague picture of naked ladies sittin' around. Drawing them . . . Well, I'll try that.

So you go there, and you get your packet of Five Weights [cigarettes] a day. Everybody's broke . . . and the best thing that's going on is in the bog [toilet] with the guitars. There's always some cat sneaked out going through his latest Woody Guthrie tune or Jack Elliott. Everybody's into that kind of music as well. So when I went to art school I was thrown into the end of it, too. Before that I was just into Little Richard. I was rockin' away, avoidin' the bicycle chains and the razors in those dance halls. The English get crazy. They're calm, but they were really violent then, those cats. Those suits cost them $150, which is a lot of money. Jackets down to here. Waistcoats. Leopardskin lapels . . . amazing. It was really, "Don't step on mah blue suede shoes."

I really, literally, got myself thrown out of school. I was livin' at home, but I had to go every day. When you think that kids, all they really want to do is learn, watch how it's done and try and figure out why and leave it at that. You're going to school to do something you wanna do, and they manage to turn the whole thing around and make you hate 'em. I don't know anyone at that school who liked it. One or two people who went to a decent school had a good teacher, someone who really knew how to teach. The nearest thing I been to it is Wormwood Scrubs [an English prison], and that's the nick. Really, it's the same feeling.

So you spent three years there, and it was coming to degree time . . .

That's when they got me. It was 1958, they chucked me out. It's amazing—Lennon, all those people, were already playing. I hadn't really thought about playing. I was still just jivin' to it. I went straight into this art school, and I heard these cats playing, heard they were layin' down some Broonzy songs. And I suddenly realized it goes back a lot further than just the two years I'd been listenin'. And I picked up the nearest guitar and started learnin' from these cats. I learned from all these amateur art school

people. One cat knew how to play "Cocaine Blues" very well, another cat knew how to play something else very well. There were a lot better guitar players at school than me.

But then I started to get into where it had come from. Broonzy first. He and Josh White were considered to be the only living black bluesmen still playing. So let's get that together, I thought, that can't be right. Then I started to discover Robert Johnson and those cats. You could never get their records, though. One heard about them. On one hand I was playing all that folk stuff on the guitar. The other half of me was listenin' to all that rock & roll, Chuck Berry, and sayin' yeah, yeah.

And one day, I met Jagger again, man. Of all places, on the fucking train. I was going to the school, and he was going up to the London School of Economics. It was about 1960. I never been able to get this one together, it's so strange. I had these two things going and not being able to plug 'em together, playing guitar like all the other cats, folk, a little blues. But you can't get the sounds from the States. Maybe once every six months someone'll come through with an album, an Arhoolie album of Fred McDowell. And you'd say: There's another cat! That's another one. Just blowin' my mind.

So I get on this train one morning, and there's Jagger and under his arm he has four or five albums. I haven't seen him since the time I bought an ice cream off him, and we haven't hung around since we were five, six, ten years. We recognized each other straight off. "Hi, man," I say. "Where ya going?" he says. And under his arm, he's got Chuck Berry and Little Walter, Muddy Waters. "You're into Chuck Berry, man, really?" That's a coincidence. He said, "Yeah, I got a few more albums. Been writin' away to this, uh, Chess Records in Chicago and got a mailing list thing and . . . got it together, you know?" Wow, man!

So I invited him up to my place for a cup of tea. He started playing me these records, and I really turned on to it. We were both still living in Dartford, on the edge of London, and I was still in art school.

There was another cat at art school named Dick Taylor, who later got the Pretty Things together. Mick found out—"Oh, you play?" he said to me. That's what amazed him. Mick had been singin' with some rock & roll bands, doin' Buddy Holly . . . Buddy Holly was in England as solid as Elvis: Everything came out was a record smash Number One. By about '58, it was either Elvis or Buddy Holly. It was split into two camps. The Elvis fans were the heavy-leather boys, and the Buddy Holly ones all somehow looked like Buddy Holly.

By that time, the initial wham had gone out of rock & roll. You were getting "By the Light of the Silvery Moon" by Little Richard and "My Blue Heaven" by Fats, "Baby Face." They'd run out of songs in a way, it seemed like. England itself was turning on to its own breed of rock & rollers. Cliff Richard at the time was a big rocker. Adam Faith. Billy Fury, who did one fantastic album that I've lost. He got it together once. One really good album. Songs he'd written, like people do now, he got some people he knew to play together and did it. His other scene was the hits, heavy moody ballads and the lead pipe down the trousers. They were all into that one.

To get back to Mick and I . . . He found out that I could play a little, and he could sing a bit. "I dig to sing," he said, and he also knew Dick Taylor from another school they'd gone to and the thing tied up, so we try and do something. We'd all go to Dick Taylor's house, in his back room; some other cats would come along and play, and we'd try to lay some of this Little Walter stuff and Chuck Berry stuff. No drummer or anything. Just two guitars and a little amplifier. Usual back room stuff. It fell into place very quickly.

Then we found Slim Harpo, we started to really find people. Mick was just singing, no harp. And suddenly in '62, just when we were getting together, we read this little thing about a rhythm & blues club starting in Ealing. Everybody must have been trying to get one together. "Let's go up to this place and find out what's happening." There was this amazing old cat playing harp . . . Cyril Davies. Where did he come from? He turned out to be a panel beater from North London. He was a great cat, Cyril. He didn't last long. I only knew him for about two years, and he died.

Alexis Korner really got this scene together. He'd been playin' in jazz clubs for ages, and he knew all the connections for gigs. So we went up there. The first or the second time Mick and I were sittin' there, Alexis Korner gets up and says, "We got a guest to play some guitar. He comes from Cheltenham. All the way up from Cheltenham just to play for ya."

Suddenly, it's *Elmore James,* this cat, man. And it's *Brian,* man, he's sittin' on this little . . . he's bent over . . . da-da-da, da-da-da . . . I said, what? What the fuck? Playing bar slide guitar.

We get into Brian after he finishes "Dust My Blues." He's really fantastic and a gas. We speak to Brian. He'd been doin' the same as we'd been doin' . . . thinkin' he was the only cat in the world who was doin' it. We started to turn Brian on to some Jimmy Reed things, Chicago blues that he hadn't heard. He was more into T-Bone Walker and jazz-blues stuff. We'd turn him on to Chuck Berry and say, "Look, it's all the same shit, man, and you can do it." But Brian was also much more together. He was in the process of getting a band together and moving up to London with one of his many women and children. God knows how many he had. He sure left his mark, that cat. I know of five kids, at least. All by different chicks, and they all look like Brian.

He was a good guitar player then. He had the touch and was just peaking. He was already out of school; he'd been kicked out of university and had a variety of jobs. He was already into living on his own and trying to find a pad for his old lady. Whereas Mick and I were just kicking around in back rooms, still living at home.

I left art school, and I didn't even bother to get a job. We were still kids. Mick was still serious; he thought he was, everyone told him he ought to be serious about a career in economics. He was very much into it.

But Brian, he was already working at it. We said, "We're just amateurs, man, but we dig to play." He invited me up to listen to what he was getting together in some pub in London. It's then it starts getting into back rooms of pubs in Soho and places. That's where I met Stew [Ian Stewart]. He was with Brian. They'd just met. He used to play boogie-woogie piano in jazz clubs, apart from his regular job. He blew my head off, too, when he started to play. I never heard a white piano like that before. Real Albert Ammons stuff. This is all '62.

A lot of these old cats had been playin' blues in those clubs for ages, or thought they were playin' blues. Just because they'd met Big Bill Broonzy at a party or played with him once, they thought they were the king's asshole.

Music was their love. They all wanted to be professional, but in those days a recording contract was a voice from heaven. It was that rare. Not like now when you get a band together and hustle an advance. It was a closed shop.

Were you and Mick and Brian very strange for them?

That's right. They couldn't figure us out. Especially when I tried to lay Chuck Berry shit on them. "What are ya hangin' with them rock

& rollers for?" they'd ask. Brian kicked a lot of them out, and I really dug it. He turned around and said, "Fuck off, you bastards, you're a load of shit and I'm going to get it together with these cats." This cat Dick Taylor shifted to bass by then. We were really looking for drums. Stew drifted with us for some reason. I sort of put him with those other cats because he had a job. But he said no, too. "I'll stick around and see what happens with you."

Were you playing electric then?

Yeah. With homemade amps, old wireless sets. It took a while longer to get the electric bit together. At the time we thought, "Oh, it just makes it louder," but it ain't quite as simple at that.

Brian was the one who kept us all together then. Mick was still going to school. I'd dropped out. So we decided we got to live in London to get it together. Time to break loose. So everybody left home, upped and got this pad in London. Chelsea.

Different Chelsea than now?

Edith Grove. World's End. That place . . . every room got condemned slowly. It was like we slowly moved till we were all in the end room. Every room was shut up and stunk to hell, man. Terrible. Brian's only possession was a radio-record player. That, and a few beds and a little gas fire. We kept on playin', playin', playin'.

Brian kicked his job. He was in a department store. He got into a very heavy scene for nickin' some bread and just managed to work his way out of it. So he thought, "Fuck it. If I work anymore I'm gonna get in real trouble." Get into jail or something.

He only nicked two pound . . . but he quit his job, and his old lady had gone back to Cheltenham so he was on the loose again.

Are you gigging?

We didn't dare, man, we didn't dare. We were rehearsin' drummers. Mick Avery came by, the drummer of the Kinks. He was terrible, then. Couldn't find that off beat. Couldn't pick up on that Jimmy Reed stuff.

Is everybody still straight?

It was very hard to find anything. No one could afford to buy anything anyway. A little bit of grass might turn up occasionally but . . . everybody'd dig it . . . everybody's turn-on was just playing.

Mick was the only one who was still hovering because he was more heavily committed to the London School of Economics, and he was being supported by a government grant and his parents and all that. So he had a heavier scene to break

away from than me because they were very pleased to kick me out anyway. And Brian, too, they were glad to kick out. From university for making some chick pregnant or something.

Brian and I were the sort of people they were glad to kick out. They'd say, "You're nothing but bums, you're gonna end up on skid row," and that sort of thing. Brian and me'd be home in this pad all day tryin' to make one foray a day to either pick up some beer bottles from a party and sell 'em back for thruppence deposit or raid the local supermarket. Try and get some potatoes or some eggs or something.

I went out one morning and came back in the evening, and Brian was *blowing harp,* man. He's got it together. He's standin' at the top of the stairs sayin', "Listen to this." *Whooooow. Whooow.* All these blues notes comin' out. "I've learned how to do it. I've figured it out." One day.

He dropped the guitar. He still dug to play it and was still into it and played very well, but the harp became his thing. He'd walk around all the time playing his harp.

Is there anything going in London in terms of music then?

Alexis had that club together, and we'd go down once a week to see what they were doing, and they wanted to know what we were doing. "It's coming," we'd tell 'em. "We'll be gigging soon." We didn't know where the fuck do ya start? Where do ya go to play?

But you were living together, unlike Cyril Davies or the older blues musicians, because you were young and broke. . . .

Yeah. Just Mick and myself and Brian. We knew Charlie. He was a friend. He was gigging at the time, playing with Alexis. He was Korner's drummer. We couldn't afford him.

One day we picked up a drummer called Tony Chapman who was our first regular drummer. Terrible. One of the worst . . . cat would start a number and end up either four times as fast as he started it or three times as slow. But never stay the same.

We did say, "Hey, Tony, d'y'know any bass players?" He said, "I do know one." "Tell him come to next rehearsal." So we all turned up and in walks . . . Bill Wyman, ladies and gentleman. Huge speaker he's got, and a spare Vox 830 amp which is the biggest amp we've ever seen in our lives. And that's spare. He says, "You can put one of your guitars through there." Whew. Put us up quite a few volts.

He had the bass together already. He'd been playin' in rock bands for three or four years. He's older than us. He knows how to play. But he doesn't want to play with these shitty rock bands anymore because they're all terrible. They're all doing that Shadows trip, all those instrumental numbers, Duane Eddy, "Rebel Rouser." There was no one who could sing very good.

Also, they don't know what to play anymore. At that point, nobody wants to hear Buddy Holly anymore. He's an old scene already to the rock & roll hip circuit. It's that very light pop thing they're all into . . . Bobby Vee was a big scene then. You wouldn't dream of going to play in a ballroom. They'd just hurl bricks at you. Still have to stick to this little circuit of clubs, back rooms for one night, a shilling for everyone to get in. For people who didn't want to go to ballrooms.

Most of these clubs at the time are filled with Dixieland bands, traditional jazz bands. An alternative to all that Bobby Vee stuff. There was a big boom in that: the stomp, stompin' about, weird dance, just really tryin' to break the ceiling to a two-beat. That was the big scene. They had all the clubs under control. That's where Alexis made the breakthrough. He managed to open it up at the Ealing Club. Then he moved on to the Marquee, and R&B started to become the thing. And all these traddies, as they were called, started getting worried. So they started this very bitter opposition.

Which is one reason I swung my guitar at Harold Pendleton's head at the Marquee thing, because he was the kingpin behind all that. He owned all these trad clubs and he got a cut from these trad bands, he couldn't bear to see them die. He couldn't afford it.

But Alexis was packin' 'em in, man. Jus' playing blues. Very similar to Chicago stuff. Heavy atmosphere. Workers and art students, kids who couldn't make the ballrooms with supposedly long hair, then, forget it, you couldn't go into those places. You gravitated to places where you wouldn't get hassled. The Marquee's a West End club, where we stood in for Alexis a couple of times.

With Charlie drumming?

No. Our first gig was down at the Ealing Club, a stand-in gig. That's the band without Charlie as drummer. We played everything. Muddy Waters. A lot of Jimmy Reed.

Still living in Chelsea?

Yeah. We had the middle floor. The top floor was sort of two schoolteachers tryin' to keep a straight life. God knows how they managed it. Two guys trainin' to be schoolteachers, they used to throw these bottle parties. All these weirdos, we used to think they were weirdos, they were as straight as . . . havin' their little parties up there, all dancing around to Duke Ellington. Then when they'd all zonked out, we'd go up there and nick all the bottles. Get a big bag, Brian and I, get all the beer bottles, and the next day we'd take 'em to the pub to get the money on 'em.

Downstairs was livin' four old whores from Liverpool. Isn't that a coincidence? "'Allo dahlin', 'ow are ya? All right?" Real old boots, they were. I don't know how they made their bread, working. . . . They used to sort of nurse people and keep us together when we really got out of it.

The cat that supported Brian, this is a long story. He came from Brian's hometown. He got eighty quid a year for being in the Territorial Army in England, which is where you go for two weeks on a camp with the rest of these guys. Sort of a civil defense thing. They all live in tents and get soakin' wet and get a cold, and at the end they learn how to shoot a rifle and they get eighty quid cash, depending on what rank you've managed to wangle yourself.

This cat arrived in London with his eighty quid, fresh out of the hills, from his tent. And he wants to have a good time with Brian. And Brian took him for every penny, man. Got a new guitar. The whole lot.

This weird thing with this cat. He was one of those weird people who would do anything you say. Things like, Brian would say, "Give me your overcoat." Freezing cold, it's the worst winter and he gave Brian this Army overcoat. "Give Keith the sweater." So I put the sweater on.

"Now, you walk twenty yards behind us, man." And off we'd walk to the local hamburger place. "Ah, stay there. No, you can't come in. Give us two quid." Used to treat him like really weird. This cat would stand outside the hamburger joint freezing cold, giving Brian the money to pay for our hamburgers. Never saw him again after that. No, no, it ended up with us tryin' to electrocute him. It ended up with us gettin' out of our heads one night. That was the night he disappeared. It was snowing outside. We came back to our pad, and he was in Brian's bed. Brian for some reason got very annoyed that he was in his bed asleep. We had all these cables lyin' around, and he pulled out this wire. "This end is plugged in, baby, and I'm comin' after ya."

This cat went screaming out of the pad and into the snow in his underpants. "They're electrocuting me, they're electrocuting me." Somebody brought him in an hour later, and he was blue. He was afraid to come in because he was so scared of Brian. The next day the cat split. Brian had a new guitar, and his amp re-fixed, a whole new set of harmonicas.

I guess the craziness comes from the chemistry of the people. The craziness sort of kept us together. When the gigs become a little more plentiful and the kids started picking up on us was when we got picked up by Giorgio Gomelsky. Before he was into producing records, he was on the jazz club scene. I don't know exactly what he did, promoting a couple of clubs a week. He cottoned onto us and sort of organized us a bit.

We still didn't have Charlie as a drummer. We were really lacking a good drummer. We were really feeling it.

All I wanted to do is keep the band together. How were we going to do it and get gigs and people to listen to us? How to get a record together? We couldn't even afford to make a dub. Anyway, we didn't have a drummer to make a dub with.

By this time we had it so together musically. We were really pleased with the way we were sounding. We were missing a drummer. We were missing good equipment. By this time the stuff we had was completely beaten to shit.

And the three of you get on? Are you the closest people for each other?

We were really a team. But there was always something between Brian, Mick and myself that didn't quite make it somewhere. Always something. I've often thought, tried to figure it out. It was in Brian, somewhere; there was something . . . he still felt alone somewhere . . . he was either completely into Mick at the expense of me, like nickin' my bread to go and have a drink. Like when I was zonked out, takin' the only pound I had in me pocket. He'd do something like that. Or he'd be completely in with me tryin' to work something against Mick. Brian was a very weird cat. He was a little insecure. He wouldn't be able to make it with two other guys at one time and really get along well.

I don't think it was a sexual thing. He was always so open with his chicks. . . . It was something else I've never been able to figure out. You can read Jung. I still can't figure it out. Maybe it was in the stars. He was a Pisces. I don't know. I'm a Sag and Mick's a Leo. Maybe those three can't ever connect completely all together at the same time for very long. There were periods when we had a ball together.

As we became more and more well known and eventually grew into that giant sort of thing, that in Brian also became blown up until it became very difficult to work with and very difficult for him to be with us. Mick and I were more and more put together because we wrote together, and Brian would become uptight about that because he couldn't write. He couldn't even ask if he could come and try to write something with us. Where earlier on Brian and I would sit for hours trying to write songs and say, "Aw, fuck it, we can't write songs."

It worked both ways. When we played, it gave Brian . . . man, when he wanted to play, he could play his ass off, that cat. To get him to do it, especially later on, was another thing. In the studio, for instance, to try and get Brian to play was such a hassle that eventually on a lot of those records that people think are the Stones, it's me overdubbing three guitars and Brian zonked out on the floor.

It became very difficult because we were working nonstop . . . I'm skipping a lot of time now . . . when we were doing those American tours in '64, '65, '66. When things were getting really difficult. Brian would go out and meet a lot of people, before we did, because Mick and I spent most of our time writing. He'd go out and get high somewhere, get smashed. We'd say, "Look, we got a session tomorrow, man, got to keep it together." He'd come, completely out of his head, and zonk out on the floor with his guitar over him. So we started overdubbing, which was a drag 'cause it meant the whole band wasn't playing.

Can you tell me about Andrew Loog Oldham?

Andrew had the opportunity. He didn't have the talent, really. He didn't have the talent for what he wanted to be. He could hustle people, and there's nothing wrong with hustling . . . it still has to be done to get through. You need someone who can talk for you. But he's got to be straight with you, too.

Was he in the business before the Stones?

Yeah, he was with the Beatles. He helped kick them off in London. Epstein hired him, and he did a very good job for them. One doesn't know how much of a job was needed, but he managed to get them a lot of space in the press when "Love Me Do" came out and was like Number Nine in the charts, and the kids were turning on to them, and it was obvious they were going to be big, big, because they were only third on the bill and yet they were tearing the house down every night. A lot of it was down to Andrew. He got them known. And he did the same gig for us. He

163

did it. Except he was more involved with us. He was working for us.

He had a genius for getting things through the media. Before people really knew what media was, to get messages through without people knowing.

Anita: But Brian, he never got on with Andrew.

Keith: Never. I've seen Brian and Andrew really pissed hanging all over each other, but really basically there was no chemistry between them. They just didn't get on. There was a time when Mick and I got on really well with Andrew. We went through the whole *Clockwork Orange* thing. We went through that whole trip together. Very sort of butch number. Ridin' around with that mad criminal chauffeur of his.

Epstein and Oldham did a thing on the media in England that's made it easier for millions of people since and for lots of musicians. It's down to people like those that you can get on a record now. They blew that scene wide open, that EMI-Decca stranglehold.

How long was Andrew involved?

From '63 to the end of '67. It still goes on, though. I got a letter the other day about some litigation, Oldham versus Eric Easton, who was our first manager proper. Oldham was only half of the team; the other was Eric Easton, who was just a bumbly old northern agent. Handled a couple of semisuccessful chick singers and could get you gigs in ballrooms in the north of England. Once it got to America, this cat Easton dissolved. He went into a puddle. He couldn't handle that scene.

Was Charlie drumming with you when Andrew first saw you work?

I'll tell you how we picked Charlie up. I told you about the people Brian was getting a band together with, and then he turned on to us and he told those other people to fuck off, etc. Our common ground with Brian back then was Elmore James and Muddy Waters. We laid Slim Harpo on him, and Fred McDowell.

Brian was from Cheltenham, a very genteel town full of old ladies, where it used to be fashionable to go and take the baths once a year at Cheltenham Spa. The water is very good because it comes out of the hills, it's spring water. It's a Regency thing, you know, Beau Brummel, around that time. Turn of the nineteenth century. Now it's a seedy sort of place full of aspirations to be an aristocratic town. It rubs off on anyone who comes from there.

The R&B thing started to blossom, and we found playing on the bill with us in a club—

there were two bands on, Charlie was in the other band. He'd left Korner and was with the same cats Brian had said fuck off to about six months before. We did our set, and Charlie was knocked out by it. "You're great, man," he says, "but you need a fucking good drummer." So we said, "Charlie, we can't afford you, man." Because Charlie had a job and just wanted to do weekend gigs. Charlie used to play anything then—he'd play pubs, anything, just to play, 'cause he loves to play with good people. But he always had to do it for economic reasons. By this time we're getting three, four gigs a week. "Well, we can't pay you as much as that band but . . ." we said. So he said okay and told the other band to fuck off. "I'm gonna play with these guys."

When we got Charlie, that really made it for us. We started getting a lot of gigs. Then we got that Richmond gig with Giorgio, and that built up to an enormous scene. In London, that was *the* place to be every Sunday night. At the Richmond Station Hotel. It's on the River Richmond, a fairly well-to-do neighborhood, but kids from all over London would come down there on a Sunday night.

There's only so far you can go on that London scene; if you stay in that club circuit eventually you get constipated. You go round and round so many times, and then suddenly, you're not the hip band anymore, someone else is. Like the High Numbers, they took over from us in a lot of clubs. The High Numbers turned out to become the Who. The Yardbirds took over from us in Richmond, and on Sunday nights we'd find we were booked into a place in Manchester.

Where are you recording now, with Giorgio?

Not with Giorgio. Eric and Andrew fucked Giorgio because he had nothing on paper with us. They screwed him to get us a recording contract. We were saying to Giorgio, "What about records?" and he didn't have it together for the record thing. Not for a long time afterwards either. He was still very much a club man. We knew that to go any further and reach out a bit, we wanted to get off the club thing and get into the ballrooms where the kids were. It turned out to be right.

It was difficult the first few months, though. We were known in the big cities, but when you get outside into the sticks, they don't know who the fuck you are, and they're still preferring the local band. That makes you play your ass off every night so that at the end of two hour-long sets, you've got 'em. You gotta do it. That's the testing ground, in those ballrooms where it's really hard to play.

Stew is driving you around now?

Yeah, there was this whole thing, because for us Stew is one of the band up until Andrew. "Well, he just doesn't look the part," Andrew said, "and six is too many for them to remember the faces in the picture." But piano is important for us. Brian at that time is the leader of the band. He pulled us all together, he's playing good guitar, but his love is the harmonica. On top of that, he's got the pop star hang-up—he wants to sing, with Mick, like "Walking the Dog."

Are you singing?

Naw, I was getting into writing then, though. Andrew was getting on to me to write because he sussed that maybe I could do it if I put my mind to it.

What are some of the first things you wrote?

They're on the first album. "Tell Me," which was pulled out as a single in America, which was a dub. Half those records were dubs on that first album, that Mick and I and Charlie and I'd put a bass on, or maybe Bill was there and he'd put a bass on. "Let's put it down while we remember it," and the next thing we know is, "Oh, look track eight is that dub we did a couple months ago." That's how little control we had; we were driving around the country every fucking night, playing a different gig, sleeping in the van, hotels if we were lucky.

A lot of it was Andrew's choice. He selected what was to be released. He was executive record producer, so-called. While we were gigging, he'd get that scene together. But remember, then it was important to put out a single every three months. You had to put out a 45, a red-hot single, every three months. An album was something like Motown—you put the hit single on the album and ten tracks of shit and then rush it out. Now, the album is the thing. Marshall has laid the figures on me, and *Sticky Fingers* album has done more than the single. They're both Number One in the charts, but the album's done more than the single.

The concept's changed so completely. Back then it was down to turning on thirteen-year-old chicks and putting out singles every three months. That was the basic force of the whole business. That was how it was done.

That's another thing. Both the Beatles and us had been through buying albums that were filled with ten tracks of rubbish. We said, "No, we want to make each track good. Work almost as hard on it as you would work on a single." So maybe we changed that concept.

That's why there became longer and longer gaps between albums coming out because we got into trying to make everything good.

The first three albums are pretty close, though.

The first one was done all in England. In a little demo studio in "Tin Pan Alley," as it used to be called. Denmark Street in Soho. It was all done on a two-track Revox that he had on the wall. We used to think, "Oh, this is a recording studio, huh? This is what they're like?" A tiny little back room. Engineers never even used to work, man. They'd flick a few switches, and that was it. The machinery was unsophisticated in those days; four track was the biggest there was.

Suddenly a whole new breed of engineers appears, like Glyn Johns, people who are willing to work with you, and not with someone from the record company. There are all those weird things which have broken up in the record industry, which haven't happened for movies yet. There are no more in-between men between you and the engineer, and you can lay it down. If you want a producer or feel you need one, which most people do, it's a close friend, someone you dig to work with, that translates for you. Eventually we found Jimmy Miller, after all those years.

Slowly and slowly, we've been finding the right people to do the right thing, like Marshall Chess, like Jo Bergman. All those people are as important as we are. Especially now that we've got Rolling Stones Records, with the Kali tongue . . . nobody's gotten into that yet, but that's Kali, the Hindu female goddess. Five arms, a row of heads around her, a saber in one hand, flames coming out the other, she stands there, with her tongue out. But that's gonna change. That symbol's not going to stay as it is. Sometimes it'll take up the whole label, maybe slowly it'll turn to a cock. I don't know yet.

You going to put two pills on the tongue?

We're going to do everything with it, slowly. Don't want to let it grow stale. It's growing change. Got to keep it growing.

What was the first time Oldham saw the band?

It was in March 1963. The next week he took us right into a big studio and we cut "Come On." We were always doing other people's material, but we thought we'd have a go at that—"Oh, it sounds catchy." And it worked out. At the time it was done just to get a record out. We never wanted to hear it. The idea was Andrew's—to get a strong single so they'd let us make an album which back then was a privilege.

Were you still a London band then?

Completely. We'd never been out of the city. I'd never been further north than the north of London.

165

Was Andrew a change in the kind of people you had to deal with?

He faced us with the real problems. That we had to find the hole to get out of the circle of London clubs and into the next circle. Lot of hustle.

Did you have an image thing already?

It's funny. He tried . . . people think Oldham made the image, but he tried to tidy us up. He fought it. There are photographs of us in suits he put us in, those dog-tooth checked suits with the black velvet collars. Everybody's got black pants, and a tie and a shirt. For a month on the first tour, we said, "All right. We'll do it. You know the game. We'll try it out." But then the Stones thing started taking over. Charlie'd leave his jacket in some dressing room, and I'd pull mine out and there'd be whiskey stains all over it or chocolate pudding. The thing just took over, and by the end of the tour we were playing in our own gear again because that's all we had left. Which was the usual reason.

You weren't the socially "smart" band yet?

No. The Beatles went through it, and they put us through it. They have to know you. They've changed a lot, too, you know. A lot of them have gone through some funny trips. Some titled gentlemen of some stature are now roaming around England like gypsies, and they've acquired this fantastic country Cockney accent. "Ai sole a fe 'orses down 'ere. Got a new caravan like, and we're thinking of tripping up to see . . ." But it's great.

It must have been amazing early on, when some young lord or some young titled lady would come to see you play?

Brian and I were really fascinated by them. They used to make us really laugh, from a real working-class thing. It was so silly to us. It happened so fast that one never had time to really get into that thing, "Wow, I'm a Rolling Stone." We were still sleeping in the back of this truck every night because of the most hard-hearted and callous roadie I've ever encountered, Stew. From one end of England to another in Stew's Volkswagen bus. With just an engine and a rear window and all the equipment, and then you fit in. The gear first, though.

But to even get out of London then was such a weird trip for Mick and me. The north. Like we went back this year right, on the English tour, and it hasn't changed a bit, man. In the Thirties, it used to look exactly the same, in the middle of the Depression. It's never ended for those people.

You're traveling alone?

Sure. Never carry chicks. Pick it up there or drop it. No room, man. Stew wouldn't allow it. Crafty Bill Wyman. For years we believed that he couldn't travel in the back of the bus or he'd spew all over us, so he was always allowed to sit in the passenger seat. Years later, we find out he never gets travel sick at all.

Is the first album out?

No, we released two singles before the album. The first single was "Come On" with Muddy Waters' "I Just Want to Make Love to You" on the other side. We were learning to record. Andrew, too. He'd never made a record in his life, and he was producing. Just to walk in and start telling people, it took guts. Andrew had his own ideas on what we were supposed to sound like. It's only been in the last few years with Jimmy that it's changed. The music went through Andrew then. He was in the booth.

Was there a period when it was all the same, just working, but you knew something was building?

It's weird. I can remember. You know it in front. Being on the road every night you can tell by the way the gigs are going, there's something enormous coming. You can feel this energy building up as you go around the country. You feel it winding tighter and tighter, until one day you get out there halfway through the first number and the whole stage is full of chicks screaming, "Nyeehhh!" There was a period of six months in England we couldn't play ballrooms anymore because we never got through more than three or four songs every night, man. Chaos. Police and too many people in the places, fainting.

We'd walk into some of those places, and it was like they had the Battle of the Crimea going on, people gasping, tits hanging out, chicks choking, nurses running around. . . .

I know it was the same for the Beatles. One had been reading about that, "Beatlemania." "Scream power" was the thing everything was judged by, as far as gigs were concerned. If Gerry and the Pacemakers were the top of the bill, incredible, man. You know that weird sound that thousands of chicks make when they're really lettin' it go. They couldn't hear the music. We couldn't hear ourselves, for years. Monitors were unheard of. It was impossible to play as a band onstage, and we forgot all about it.

Did you develop a stage act?

Not really. Mick did his thing, and I tried to keep the band together. That's always what it's been, basically. If I'm leapin' about, it's only because something's goin' drastically wrong or it's goin' drastically right.

Mick had always dug visual artists himself. He

always loved Diddley and Chuck Berry and Little Richard for the thing they laid on people onstage. He really dug James Brown the first time he saw him. All that organization . . . ten-dollar fine for the drummer if he missed the off beat.

What was Brian like onstage?

He'd worked out these movements. In those days, little chicks would all have their favorites. Yeah, when you think the *Rolling Stones* magazine, the *Beatles* magazine came out once a month. Big sort of fan thing. It was a very old thing that one had the feeling had to change. All those teenyboppers.

It might have been a great last gasp.

Yeah, I think so. Chicks, now maybe they feel more equal. I think chicks and guys have gotten more into each other, realized there's the same in each. Instead of them having to go through that completely hysterical, completely female trip to let it out that way. Probably now they just screw it out.

They used to tell us, "There's not a dry seat in the cinema." It was like that.

Were you being approached by the kids?

Yeah, I got strangled twice. That's why I never wear anything around my neck anymore. Going out of theatres was the dodgiest. One chick grabs one side of the chain and another chick grabs the other side. . . . Another time I found myself lying in the gutter with my shirt on and half a pair of pants and the car roaring away down the street. Oh, shit, man. They leap on you. "What do you want? What?"

You have to get a little crazy from that.

You get completely crazy. And the bigger it got, America and Australia and everywhere it's exactly the same number. Oh, we were so glad when that finished. We stopped. We couldn't go on anymore. And when we decided to get it together again, everybody had changed.

Was it the same kind of madness in the States before it changed?

Completely different kind of madness. Before, America was a real fantasy land. It was still Walt Disney and hamburger dates, and when you came back in 1969 it wasn't anymore. Kids were really into what was going on in their country. I remember watching Goldwater-Johnson in '64, and it was a complete little show. But by the time it came to Nixon's turn two years ago, people were concerned in a really different way.

Rock music as politics?

Who knows, man? I mean, they used to try and put it down so heavy, rock & roll. I wonder if they knew there was some rhythm in there that

was gonna shake their house down. I used to pick up those posters down South that say, "Don't let your kid buy Negro records. Savage music. It will twist their minds." Real heavy stuff against a black radio station or black records.

Was it a big thing to finally see the black lifestyle in America for the first time?

It was a real joy. It was like I imagined but even better. Always a gas to see Etta James or B. B. King work for the first time. Some of those old blues cats. Wherever I go, I still try and see whoever I can I've heard is good or is still alive. I saw Arthur Crudup and Bukka White last time. Incredible.

We all went to the Apollo Theatre the first time over. Joe Tex and Wilson Pickett and the complete James Brown Revue. Could never get over the fact that they were into that soul bag in '64. Those suits, those movements, the vocal groups. It became obvious then the spades were going to change their music. They were into that formal, professional thing, which is not half as exciting as when they just let it go. And music ties in with all the rest. Like a real rebellion against that soul thing. Like "Papa's Got a Brand New Bag." You were always told it was going to be heavy going up there, but it never was.

Actually, the first gig was in San Bernardino. It was a straight gas, man. They all knew the songs, and they were all bopping. It was like being back home. "Ah, love these American gigs" and "Route 66" mentioned San Bernardino, so everybody was into it. The next gig was Omaha with the motorcycles and 600 kids. Then you get deflated. That's what stopped us from turning into pop stars then; we were always having those continual complete somebody hittin' you in the face, "Don't forget, boy." Then we really had to work America, and it really got the band together. We'd fallen off in playing in England 'cause nobody was listening; we'd do four numbers and be gone. Don't blink, you'll miss us.

There was one ballroom number in Blackpool during Scots week when all the Scots came down and got really drunk and let it rip. A whole gang of 'em came to this ballroom, and they didn't like us and they punched their way to the front, right through the whole 7000 people, straight to the stage and started spitting at us. This guy in front spitting. His head was just football size, just right. In those days for me, I had a temper, and, "You spit on me?" and I kicked his face in. It was down to the pressure of the road, too. America to Australia to Canada to Europe, then recording.

167

You did some recording the first time over?

Yeah, at Chess: "Michigan Avenue" and "It's All Over Now" and "Confessin' the Blues." Oldham was never a blues man, which was one reason he couldn't connect with us. But a lot of things like "Spider and the Fly" were cut at the end of a session, while some guy was sweeping up. "Play with Fire" is like that, with Phil Spector on tuned-down electric guitar, me on acoustic, Jack Nitzsche on harpsichord and Mick on tambourine with echo chamber. It was about seven o'clock in the morning. Everybody fell asleep.

Did you meet Spector that first time over?

I think we met him in England before we even went to the States. We were still into the blues. Phil Spector was a big American record producer, kind of just another person that Andrew wanted you to meet. Although I really dug his sound, those records. Always wanted to know how he got such a big sound, and when I found out it was a 170-piece orchestra, okay. Jack Nitzsche was Phil's arranger and a very important part of that whole sound. It was Jack's idea of harmonies and spacing.

BRIAN HAD SOME KIND OF GEN-*ius for finding people, didn't he?*

He did. He got us together . . . Charlie, Mick and me.

He brought Nico to the Velvet Underground.

He was into Dylan, too, very early on. He was the only one of us who hung out with Dylan for a bit. A lot of people know Brian that I don't know, that I didn't know knew him, who came up and say, "Yeah, I knew Brian."

He was great. It was only when you had to work with him that he got very hung up. Anita could tell you a lot about Brian, obviously, because she was Brian's chick for a long time. Brian did have that thing for pulling people together, for meeting people, didn't he?

Anita: Mixing. Mix it. Mix it, Charlie. Fix it, Charlie.

Keith: We're just trying to figure out why Brian couldn't be with Mick and me at the same time. "Why can't Mick come in?" "No, no," he'd say . . . he was a big whisperer, too, Brian. Little giggles . . . you don't meet people like that. Since everybody got stoned, people just say what they want to say.

Brian got very fragile. As he went along, he got more and more fragile and delicate. His personality and physically. I think all that touring did a lot to break him. We worked our asses off from '63 to '66, right through those three years, nonstop. I believe we had two weeks off. That's nothing, I mean, I tell that to B. B. King, and he'll say, "I been doing it for years." But for cats like Brian . . . He was tough, but one thing and another he slowly became more fragile. When I first met Brian he was like a little Welsh bull. He was broad, and he seemed to be very tough.

For a start, people were always laying stuff on him because he was a Stone. And he'd try it. He'd take anything. Any other sort of trip, too, head trips. He never had time to work it out 'cause we were on the road all the time, always on the plane the next day. Eventually, it caught up.

Right until the last, Brian was trying to get it together. Just before he died, he was rehearsing with more people. Because it happened so quickly people think . . .

Anita: They think he was really down. But he was really up.

Keith: And they also think that he was one of the Stones when he died. But in actual fact, he'd left. We went down to see him and he said, "I can't do it again. I can't start again and go on the road again like that again." And we said, "We understand. We'll come and see you in a couple weeks and see how you feel. Meantime, how do you want to say? Do you want to say that you've left?" And he said, "Yeah, let's do it. Let's say I've left, and if I want to I can come back." "Because we've got to know. We've got to get someone to take your place because we're starting to think about getting it together for another tour. We've got itchy feet, and we've got Mick Taylor lined up." We didn't really, we didn't have Mick waiting in the wings to bring on. But we wanted to know if we should get someone else or if Brian wanted to get back into it again. "I don't think I can," he said. "I don't think I can go to America and do those one-nighters anymore. I just can't." Two weeks later, they found him in the pool, man.

In those two weeks, he'd had musicians down there every day. He was rehearsing. I'd talk to him every day, and he'd say, "It's coming along fine. Gonna get a really funky little band together and work and make a record."

Do you think his death was an accident?

Well, I don't want to say. Some very weird things happened that night, that's all I can say. It could have as well been an accident. There were people there that suddenly disappeared . . . the whole thing with Brian is . . .

Anita: They opened the inquiry again six months after his death.

Keith: But nothing happened. None of us were trying to hush it up. We wanted to know what was going on. We were at a session that night, and we weren't expecting Brian to come along. He'd officially left the band. We were doing the first gig with Mick Taylor that night. No, I wouldn't say that was true. Maybe Mick had been with us for a week or so, but it was very close to when Mick had joined. And someone called us up at midnight and said, "Brian's dead."

Well, what the fuck's going on? We had these chauffeurs working for us, and we tried to find out . . . some of them had a weird hold over Brian. There were a lot of chicks there and there was a whole thing going on, they were having a party. I don't know, man, I just don't know what happened to Brian that night.

Do you think he was murdered?

There was no one there that'd want to murder him. Somebody didn't take care of him. And they should have done because he had somebody there who was supposed to take care of him. Everyone knew what Brian was like, especially at a party. Maybe he did just go in for a swim and have an asthma attack. I'd never seen Brian have an attack. I know that he was asthmatic. I know that he was hung up with his spray, but I've never seen him have an attack.

He was really easing back from the whole drug thing. He wasn't hitting 'em like he had been; he wasn't hitting anything like he had. Maybe the combination of things. It's one of those things I just can't find out. You know, who do you ask?

Such a beautiful cat, man. He was one of those people who are so beautiful in one way, and such an asshole in another. "Brian, how could you do that to me, man?" It was like that.

How did you feel about his death?

We were completely shocked. I got straight into it and wanted to know who was there and couldn't find out. The only cat I could ask was the one I think who got rid of everybody and did the whole disappearing trick so when the cops arrived, it was just an accident. Maybe it was. Maybe the cat just wanted to get everyone out of the way so it wasn't all names involved, etc. Maybe he did the right thing, but I don't know. I don't even know who was there that night, and trying to find out is impossible.

Maybe he tried to pull one of his deep-diving stunts and was too loaded and hit his chest and

that was it. But I've seen Brian swim in terrible conditions, in the sea with breakers up to here. I've been underwater with Brian in Fiji. He was all right then. He was a goddamn good swimmer, and it's very hard to believe he could have died in a swimming pool.

But goddamnit, to find out is impossible. And especially with him not being officially one of the Stones then, none of our people were in direct contact so it was trying to find out who was around Brian at that moment, who he had there. It's the same feeling with who killed Kennedy. You can't get to the bottom of it.

Anita: He was surrounded by the wrong kind of people.

Keith: Like Jimi Hendrix. He just couldn't suss the assholes from the good people. He wouldn't kick out somebody that was a shit. He'd let them sit there, and maybe they'd be thinking how to sell off his possessions. He'd give 'em booze and he'd feed 'em, and they'd be thinking, "Oh, that's worth 250 quid and I can roll that up and take it away." I don't know.

Anita: Brian was a leader. With the Stones, he was the first one that had a car. He was the first into flash clothes. And smoke. And acid. It was back when it seemed anything was possible. Everybody was turning on to acid, young and beautiful, and then a friend of Brian's died and it affected him very much. It made it seem as if the whole thing was a lie.

Did he stop taking acid then?

Anita: No. He got further into it. And STP. DMT, which I think is the worst, no? Too chemical. The first time Brian and I took acid we thought it was like smoking a joint. We went to bed. Suddenly we looked around and all these Hieronymus Bosch things were flashing around. That was in 1965. Musically he would have got it together. I'm sure of it. He and Keith couldn't play together anymore. I don't know what causes those things, but they couldn't.

Was there a gap between Brian and the rest of the Stones because he had taken acid and they hadn't?

Anita: Yes, as far as I know, Mick took his first trip the day he got busted, in '67. Keith had started to suss, he saw us flying around all over the place. He started to live with us. Every time Brian was taking trips, he was working, making tapes. Fantastic.

He didn't dig the music the Stones were making, and he really got a block in his head that he couldn't play with them. Now, he would dig it. He never really stopped playing. It was just so different from what they were playing, he couldn't play in sessions. I'm positive he could

169

have gotten it together. Positive. He was just a musician. Pure, so pure a musician.

With Brian into acid before anyone and having been to the West Coast, was there a reluctance to play just rock & roll?

There was a point where it was difficult to do that. People would say, "What you playin' that old shit for?" Which really screwed me up 'cause that's all I can play. We just sort of laid back and listened to what they were doing in Frisco, whereas Brian was making great tapes, overdubbing. He was much more into it than we were. And we were digging what we were hearing for what it was, but the other thing in you is saying, "Yeah. But where's Chuck Berry? What's he doing?" It's got to follow through. It's got to connect.

D O YOU AND MICK STILL WRITE *now the way you used to?*

Well, I haven't seen him for a couple weeks because he went and got married, but basically, yes. We do bits that we hear, and then we throw them all together on a cassette or something, and listen to it. Mick writes more melodies now than he used to.

The first things, usually I wrote the melody and Mick wrote the words. It's not gotten like the Lennon-McCartney thing got where they wrote completely by themselves. Every song we've got has pieces of each other in it. The only thing in *Sticky Fingers* I don't have anything to do with is "Moonlight Mile," 'cause I wasn't there when they did it. It was great to hear that because I was very out of it by the end of the album, and it was like listening, really listening. It was really nice. We were all surprised at the way that album fell together. *Sticky Fingers*—it pulled itself together.

How about "Satisfaction"?

I wrote that. I woke up one night in a hotel room. Hotel rooms are great. You can do some of your best writing in hotel rooms. I woke up with a riff in my head and the basic refrain and wrote it down. The record still sounded like a dub to me. I wanted to do . . . I couldn't see getting excited about it. I'd really dug it that night in the hotel, but I'd gone past it. No, I didn't want it out, I said. I wanted to cut it again. It sounded all right, but I didn't really like that fuzz guitar. I wanted to make that thing different. But I don't think we could have done; you needed either horns or something that could really knock that riff out.

With "Satisfaction," people start to wonder what certain phrases mean like "smoke another kind of cigarette."

A lot of them are completely innocent. I don't think that one is. It might have been. I don't know if it was a sly reference to drugs or not. After a while, one realizes that whatever one writes, it goes through other people, and it's what gets to them. Like the way people used to go through Dylan songs. It don't matter. They're just words. Words is words.

After you came back to England from the first or second American tour, did you have some kind of acceptance, were you starting to get respectable?·

Still came across some opposition. It wasn't that complete acceptance that the Beatles had. Always been kicked out of our hotel for not being dressed properly or something.

"Midnight Rambler" is Mick way out on his persona, isn't it?

Usually when you write, you just kick Mick off on something and let him fly on it, just let it roll out and listen to it and start to pick up on certain words that are coming through, and it's built up on that. A lot of people still complain they can't hear the voice properly. If the words come through it's fine, if they don't, that's all right, too, because anyway they can mean a thousand different things to anybody.

But the song's almost psychotic, isn't it?

It's just something that's there, that's always been there. Some kind of chemistry. Mick and I can really get it on together. It's one way to channel it out. I'd rather play it out than shoot it out.

People come to Stones concerts to work it out.

Yeah, which in turn has been interpreted as violence or "a goddamn riot" when it's just people letting it out. Not against anybody, but with each other. That rock & roll thing, even when it was young, those songs created a domestic revolution. When the parents were out, there were all those parties. Eddie Cochran and all those people, they created some kind of thing which has followed through now and is being built on.

Like "Street Fighting Man"?

The timing of those things is funny because you're really following what's going on. That's been interpreted thousands of different ways because it really is ambiguous as a song. Trying to be revolutionary in London in Grosvenor Square. Mick went to all those demonstrations and got charged by the cops.

The basic track of that was done on a mono cassette with very distorted over-recording, on a Phillips with no limiters. Brian is playing sitar, it twangs away. He's holding notes that wouldn't come through if you had a board; you wouldn't be able to fit it in. But on a cassette if you just move the people, it does. Cut in the studio and then put on a tape. Started puttin' percussion and bass on it. That was really an electronic track, up in the realms.

Some songs, with a sixteen-track, I don't really need all that. It's nice to make it simpler sometimes. "Parachute Woman" is a cassette track.

"Salt of the Earth"?

No, that's studio. Mick's words, but I think I was there for a bit of them, too. I'd forgotten about that, actually. Nearly all Mick, that one. Funny year, '68, it's got a hole in it somewhere. Coming out of the bust and other stuff . . . I was in L.A. for a couple months.

Did you do a lot of traveling in the years when the Stones didn't work as a band?

Went to Morocco for quite a while. I drove down through Spain. It's incredible. It's like getting stoned for the first time to go through the Casbah. Mick and everybody ended up there because it was after the bust. Everybody sort of ran. Met Achmed down there; Anita had known him from before, when she went with Brian, but then in '67 he was just getting his thing together . . . he had this beautiful little shop, and he'd tell all these incredible stories, and he made this incredible stuff. I haven't been there for two or three years, and I keep meaning to go back.

It was quiet in Tangier then. Just a few American kids. Brion Gysin was there, too. That cat who wrote *The Process.* Weird. I'm expecting him down here, with Burroughs; they're talking about *Naked Lunch* and trying to get it together for a movie.

How did that picture of the band in drag come about?

There was a big rush for "Have You Seen Your Mother, Baby?" Jerry Schatzberg took the picture and Andrew ordered a truckload of costumes and Brian just laid on me this incredible stuff. He just said, "Take this." We walked down from Park Lane in that gear, and we did the pictures. It was very quiet, Saturday afternoon, all the businesses are shut but there's traffic. . . .

Wearing high heels?

Yeah, and the whole bit. Bill in a wheelchair. It took a while to get this picture, and going back, what do you do? Do you take half the stuff off and walk back . . . or do you keep it on?

Anyway, I'm thirsty, let's go and have a beer. We all zip down to this bar. Hey, what voice do you do? We sat there and had a beer and watched TV, and no one said anything. But it was just so outrageous because Bill stayed in his wheelchair and Brian was pushing him about.

Do you like that record?

I loved the track of it. I never did like the record. It was cut badly. It was mastered badly. It was mixed badly. The only reason we were so hot on it was that the track blew our heads off; everything else was rushed too quickly. Tapes were being flown . . . and lost. It needed another couple weeks. The rhythm section thing is almost lost completely.

Along with "Stupid Girl" and "Under My Thumb" and other songs of that time, there's a real down-on-chicks feeling in it.

It was all a spin-off from our environment . . . hotels, and too many dumb chicks. Not all dumb, not by any means, but that's how one got. When you're canned up—half the time it's impossible to go out, it's a real hassle to go out—it was to go through a whole sort of football match. One just didn't. You got all you needed from room service, you sent out for it. Limousines sent tearing across cities to pick up a little bag of this or that. You're getting really cut off.

Of course, there was still "Lady Jane."

Brian was getting into dulcimer then. Because he dug Richard Fariña. It has to do with what you listen to. Like I'll just listen to old blues cats for months and not want to hear anything else, and then I just want to hear what's happening and collect it all and listen to it. We were also listening to a lot of Appalachian music then, too. To me, "Lady Jane" is very Elizabethan. There are a few places in England where people still speak that way, Chaucer English.

Brian played flute on "Ruby Tuesday."

Yeah, he was a gas. He was a cat who could play any instrument. It was like, "There it is, music comes out of it, if I work at it for a bit, I can do it." It's him on marimbas on "Under My Thumb" and mellotron on quite a few things on *Satanic Majesties.* He was the strings on "Two Thousand Light Years From Home," Brian on mellotron, and the brass on "We Love You," all that Arabic riff.

How about "Goin' Home"? It was one of the earlier jams to be put on a pop album.

It was the first long rock & roll cut. It broke that two-minute barrier. We tried to make singles as long as we could do then because we just like to let things roll on. Dylan was used to

171

building a song for twenty minutes because of the folk thing he came from.

That was another thing. No one sat down to make an eleven-minute track. I mean, "Goin' Home," the song was written just the first two and a half minutes. We just happened to keep the tape rolling, me on guitar, Brian on harp, Bill and Charlie and Mick. If there's a piano, it's Stew.

Did you record during those years you didn't gig?

A lot of recording, and getting together with Jimmy Miller in '68 or late '67 when we started *Beggar's Banquet.* It's really a gas to work with Jimmy. We'd tried to do it ourselves, but it's a drag not to have someone to bounce off of. Someone who knows what you want and what he wants. I wouldn't like to produce, there's too much running up and down, too much legwork.

John Lennon said that the Stones did things two months after the Beatles. A lot of people say 'Satanic Majesties' is just 'Sgt. Pepper' upside down.

But then, I don't know. I never listened any more to the Beatles than to anyone else in those days when we were working. It's probably more down to the fact that we were going through the same things. Maybe we were doing it a little bit after them. Anyway, we were following them through so many scenes. We're only just mirrors ourselves of that whole thing. It took us much longer to get a record out for us; our stuff was always coming out later anyway.

I moved around a lot. And then Anita and I got together, and I lay back for a long time. We just decided what we wanted to do. There was a time three, four years ago, in '67, when everybody just stopped, everything just stopped dead. Everybody was tryin' to work it out, what was going to go on. So many weird things happened to so many weird people at one time. America really turned itself round, the kids . . . coming together. Pushed together so hard that they sort of dug each other.

For us, too, we had always been pushed together . . . not bein' able to get hotel rooms. Even now, it's one of the last things I say, you never pull that thing . . . that you're a Rolling Stone. I like to be anonymous, which is sort of difficult.

Do you sing for the first time alone on that album?

Please. My voice first appeared solo on the first verse of "Salt of the Earth." We did the chorus together, me and Mick. If I write a song, I usually write it all, but it's difficult. Somebody's always got their finger in there. I thought I wasn't on "Moonlight Mile," but the last riff

everybody gets into playing is a riff I'd been playing on earlier tapes before I dropped out. "Wild Horses," we wrote the chorus in the john of the Muscle Shoals recording studio 'cause it didn't finish off right.

Does it have to do with Marlon's birth?

Yeah, 'cause I knew we were going to have to go to America and start work again, to get me off me ass, and not really wanting to go away. It was a very delicate moment; the kid's only two months old, and you're goin' away. Millions of people do it all the time, but still . . .

How about earlier stuff like "Paint It Black"?

Mick wrote it. I wrote the music, he did the words. Get a single together.

What's amazing about that one for me is the sitar. Also, the fact that we cut it as a comedy track. Bill was playing an organ, doing a takeoff of our first manager who started his career in show business as an organist in a cinema pit. We'd been doing it with funky rhythms and it hadn't worked, and he started playing like this and everybody got behind it. It's a two-beat, very strange. Brian playing the sitar makes it a whole other thing.

There were some weird letters, racial letters. "Was there a comma in the title? Was it an order to the world?"

How about "Get Off of My Cloud"?

That was the followup to "Satisfaction." I never dug it as a record. The chorus was a nice idea, but we rushed it as the followup. We were in L.A., and it was time for another single. But how do you follow "Satisfaction"? Actually, what I wanted was to do it slow like a Lee Dorsey thing. We rocked it up. I thought it was one of Andrew's worse productions.

"19th Nervous Breakdown," "Have You Seen Your Mother, Baby," "Mother's Little Helper," they're all putting down another generation.

Mick's always written a lot about it. A lot of the stuff Chuck Berry and early rock writers did was putting down that other generation. That feeling then, like in '67. We used to laugh at those people, but they must have gotten the message right away because they tried to put rock & roll down, trying to get it off the radio, off records. Obviously, they saw some destruction stemming from . . . they felt it right away.

The mayor of Denver once sent us a letter asking us to come in quietly, do the show as quietly as possible and split the same night, if possible. "Thank you very much, we'll be very pleased to see you in the near future." I've got that letter with the seal of Denver on it. That's what the mayors wanted to do with us. They might entertain the Beatles, but they wanted to kick us out of town.

P ART OF THE STONES IMAGE IS sex trips.

Yeah, on our first expedition to the United States we noticed a distinct lack of crumpet, as we put it in those days. It was very difficult, man. For cats who had done Europe and England, scoring chicks right, left and center, to come to a country where apparently no one believed in it. We really got down to the lowest and worked our way up again. Because it was difficult.

In New York or L.A., you can always find something in a city that big if that's what you want. But when you're in Omaha in 1964 and you suddenly feel horny, you might as well forget it.

Did you have guys trying to hustle you?

Yeah, in America we went through a lot of that. In France and England, too, not groupies as such, they have some concrete reason for being around. They work for a radio station, they contribute to some obscure magazine.

Unlike the Beatles, the Stones—and Mick in particular—have always had the unisexual thing going.

Oh, you should have seen Mick really . . . I'll put it like this; there was a period when Mick was extremely camp. When Mick went through his camp period, in 1964, Brian and I immediately went enormously butch and sort of laughin' at him. That terrible thing . . . that switching-around confusion of roles that still goes on.

Tell us how you got your ear pierced.

Well, the cat who was doing it—a jeweler or he studied it—was on about fifteen Mandrax. Very stoned. Doing it the good old-fashioned way. None of your anesthetics and machinery. With a sewing needle and ice. Me next. Rubs the ice on, and he's dodging back and forth. God knows how he managed to do it. And he just made it. It's right at the lobe.

I've always wanted a pierced ear. I made me first bottleneck and had me ear pierced the same night, with about fifteen of the Living Theatre and I was about the fourth ear. He did Anita's, too, at a special angle. By then he had another ten Mandrax and was completely out of it. Try it from the front. No, let's go at it from the back.

But a lot of people got their ear pierced that night; it was around the time of the Hyde Park concert.

That was June 1969. You hadn't worked for two years, but had you become better musicians?

No, you always get worse laying off, in one way. You get rusty. Which you can put right if you start playing together. None of us were worried about it. I learned a lot, though. I played a lot of acoustic guitar. I did a lot of writing; I didn't use to, but I dug to do it. I was writing in a different way, not for a hit single or to keep that riff going.

Everybody let their hair grow.

The thing is, we were already getting so hassled with our hair like it was. You really weren't safe in some places. I've chopped it off now for the sun. It's usually long in the winter. You couldn't go into Omaha; you'd get the shit beat out of you.

We did a lot of things in those years, traveled, I hung around a lot with the Living Theatre when they were in Rome and London. They were still working onstage doing things which made the audience no longer an audience, which got them involved.

The whole Satan trip really comes out after 'Beggar's Banquet.'

I think there's always been an acceptance. . . . I mean, Kenneth Anger told me I was his right-hand man. It's just what you feel. Whether you've gotten that good and evil thing together. Left-hand path, right-hand path, how far do you want to go down?

How far?

Once you start, there's no going back. Where they lead to is another thing.

The same place?

Yeah. So what the fuck? It's something everybody ought to explore. There are possibilities there. A lot of people have played on it, and it's inside everybody. I mean, Doctor John's whole trip is based on it.

Why do people practice voodoo? All these things bunged under the name of superstition and old wives' tales. I'm no expert in it. I would never pretend to be; I just try to bring it into the open a little. There's only so much you can bring into the open.

There's got to be people around who know it all, man. Nobody ever really finds out what's important with the kinds of government you've got now. Fifty years after, they tell you what really went on. They'll let you know what happened to Kennedy in a few years' time. It's no

173

mystery. An enormous fuckup in the organization, a cog went wrong, and they'll say who did it. But by then it won't matter; they'll all be dead and gone and, "Now it's different, and in this more enlightened age . . ."

"I shouted out who killed the Kennedys." Does that thing hold for Mick, too, or is it more a show business thing?

Mick and I basically have been through the same things. A lot of it comes anyway from association and press and media people laying it on people. Before, when we were just innocent kids out for a good time, they're saying, "They're evil, they're evil." Oh, I'm evil, really? So that makes you start thinking about evil.

What is evil? Half of it, I don't know how much people think of Mick as the devil or as just a good rock performer or what? There are black magicians who think we are acting as unknown agents of Lucifer and others who think we are Lucifer. Everybody's Lucifer.

Does that produce things like Altamont?

I particularly didn't like the atmosphere there by the time we went on. After a day of letting some uniforms loose, what can you expect? Who do you want to lay it on? Do you want to just blame someone, or do you want to learn from it? I don't really think anyone is to blame, in laying it on the Angels.

If you put that kind of people in that kind of position . . . but I didn't know what kind of people they were. I'd heard about the Angels, but I haven't lived in California and San José, I have no contact with those people. I don't know how uncontrolled they are, how basic their drives are.

But when the Dead told us, "It's cool. We've used them for the last two or three years, Kesey cooled them out," I was skeptical about it, but I said, "I'll take your word for it. I've taken everybody's word for it up till now that they know what they're doing when they put on a show." You have to accept that for a start, that it's gonna be together when you get there, or else you never get to any gigs.

Who put the Angels in that position? Specifically.

Specifically? . . . We asked the Dead basically if they would help us get a free concert together. First we had this idea we want to do a free concert, and we want to do it in Frisco because that's where they do a lot of free concerts. Who do you ask and who's done more free concerts than anybody—the Grateful Dead. It's very nice, man; we hung around, talked about lots of things, played a bit. They said this is how they

done it and this is a big one and they think they can get it together.

It comes down to how many people can you put together? In India they're used to that many people turning up for a religious occasion. But this was not a religious occasion, and also it was in the middle of the fucking desert, in California with freeways. We were so hassled. We were in Muscle Shoals, trying to make a record. Meanwhile they're going through all these hassles with people saying, yeah, you can set up a stage and put up all your equipment and then saying, "Fuck off."

We're still in Alabama, into making records. And so we have to take people at their word. We have to trust them. And they could do it, and they did. But it wasn't their fault they didn't have enough time to think about the parking or how people are going to get there or the johns or the . . . they thought of them to a certain extent, but nobody knew exactly how many people were coming anyway. Then you get there and what a fucking place, man. Well, let's just make the best of it.

I went out there the night before Mick. Mick went back. I stayed there. I just hung around, met a few nice people. It was really beautiful. That night before, everywhere I went was a gas. People were sitting around their fires, really cool, getting high, and I ended up in a trailer and woke up when it was about a 110 degrees inside.

Were you there when Mick got hit?

I was there the whole fucking day in that trailer. Also, it's the last gig. Do this and we go home. So everybody is in sort of that final mad rush. We'd done this incredible flight from New York to West Palm Beach and sat on the tarmac in the plane for nine hours at LaGuardia, in New York, while they got it ready. We got to the gig eight hours behind schedule, after a helicopter flight. We got on at four o'clock in the morning. Below zero. And that was the last gig of the tour proper.

Those kids waited all night to see you.

They were great. Such a sight. That place wasn't much better than Altamont. Everyone was frozen stiff. We got it on for a bit, but everybody dug it. It was a gas. By the time we finished and got back to the hotel on the beach, dawn was coming up, the sun was warm and we went to Muscle Shoals.

When did you first feel things might turn out badly?

The Airplane's gig. When I heard what they done to Marty Balin, they're gettin' out of hand.

It's just gonna get worse, I thought; obviously, it's not going to get better. Nothing's gonna cool them out once they start. What a bummer. What can you do? Just sit tight.

Did you consider not going on?

Can you think what that would have caused on top of getting all the people to the place? Talk about one cat getting killed . . . on top of that, everybody was very sensitive. America suddenly seems to have developed this hypersensitivity to life and death that I'd never seen them concerned with before. I never saw them concerned when a cop got crushed at Long Beach.

I don't care who it is. Some Angel or whatever . . . the underground suddenly leaps up in a horrified shriek when some spade hippie gets done, which is a terrible thing, but they never got uptight if some cop got done. Some cop, he's probably on extra duty, and he gets crushed at a pop concert. That one really brought me down. I could never believe it ended up in the fifteenth page of the *Herald Tribune* or whatever it was called. That sort of thing makes you want to stop. I don't demand sacrifices at this stage of the game.

What information were you getting at Altamont as to what was going on?

Ah, it's obvious, man. Maybe they'll do me the next time I go there, but they were out of control, man. The Angels shouldn't have been asked to do the job. I didn't know if the Angels were still like Marlon Brando had depicted fifteen years before, or whether they'd grown up a little, or if they're still into that "don't touch my chromework" bit. All right. Someone else should have known that. If they didn't, then the Angels kept it very well hidden for a long time.

The people look very, very stoned in 'Gimme Shelter.'

People were just asking for it. All those nude fat people, just asking for it. They had those victims' faces. That guy was pathetic. Most of this I've seen from the movie. Same as anyone else. Most of the people who've seen what went down at Altamont have caught it from the movie. When I was there, I just heard a bit; I never actually saw anything flying till we went on.

What did you see when you went on?

The usual sort of chaotic scene.

Did you wait purposely until it was dark to go on to heighten the effect?

Oh, man, I'd been there twenty-four hours, I couldn't wait to get out of that place. It was fuckups, the beatups, the chaos, our people telling us not to go on yet, let the people cool

down a bit. Those campfire sessions, they always go on longer than expected anyway.

What happens when you come out onstage?

Perfectly normal. Go into "Jumpin' Jack Flash." It felt great and sounded great. I'm not used to bein' upstaged by Hell's Angels—goddamnit, man, somebody's motorbike. I can't believe it. For a stunt. What is the bike doin' there anyway, in the fourth row of the fucking . . . it would have looked better up onstage, and it would have been safer, too.

So the cat left his bike there and it got knocked over, so that was the first one. "Oh, dear, a bike's got knocked over." Yes, I perfectly understand that your bike's got knocked over, can we carry on with the concert? But they're not like that. They have a whole thing going with their bikes, as we all know now. It's like Sonny Barger. "If you've spent $1700 . . ."

Well, if that's what you want to get together, that's fine, but I really don't think if you leave it in front of half a million people, you can't expect it not to get knocked over.

What if someone tried to do your guitar? They'd get punched out very quickly, wouldn't they?

I don't kill him, man. And I don't get 500 buddies of mine to come down and put their boot in, too. I don't have it organized to that extent. If someone tries to do my guitar, and I don't want it to be done, it's between him and me. I don't call in Bill Wyman to come in and do him over for me, with one of his vicious ankle-twisters or Chinese burns.

I didn't see any killings. If I see any killing going on, I shout, "Murder." You dig, when you're onstage you can't see much, like just the first four rows. It's blinding, like a pool of light in complete darkness, unless someone out there lights up a cigarette. All you see is lights out there. If someone strikes one or shines one. Since all this went on ten or fifteen rows back, the only time we were aware of trouble was when suddenly a hundred cats would leap in front of us and everybody would start yelling.

But you stopped playing right after the stabbing, and Sam Cutler went to the mike for a doctor.

Someone asked for a doctor, yeah. Half of our concerts in our whole career have been stopped for doctors and stretchers. How much responsibility for the gig are you going to lay on the cat who's playing and how much on the cat that organized it? Rolling Stones' name is linked with Altamont. It wasn't our production particularly. Our people were involved, but they were relying on local knowledge.

There were all these rumors flashing around. "There's a bomb gone off and twenty people have been blown to bits, man." You say, "I think you got it wrong, man, I'm sure you got it wrong." 'Cause you've been hearing crazy rumors all day, that you're dead, as ridiculous as that. By the time you're in California and you've gone through a whole tour and you've heard all those rumors that seem to go around and around and around . . . you don't believe anything. I don't believe anything at the end of an American tour ever.

Mick seemed to know something was going on; he tried to cool it out.

The same as Grace Slick tried earlier. "Be cool, be cool." For all the control one can have over an audience, it doesn't mean you can control the murderers. That's a different thing, man; you can't make someone's knife disappear by just looking at him. Somehow in America in '69—I don't know about now, and I never got it before—one got the feeling they really wanted to suck you out.

Like at the Rainbow Room press conference. So ridiculous, cats asking what to do about the Vietnam War. "Why are you asking me? You've got your people to get that one together." And they're asking you about everything, about your third eye . . . it's very nice. But you can't be God. You can't ever pretend to play at being God. . . . Altamont, it could only happen to the Stones, man. Let's face it. It wouldn't happen to the Bee Gees, and it wouldn't happen to Crosby, Stills and Nash.

Except that they were there, and it didn't make a difference.

Were they? I heard they were in some airport and didn't come, all those rumors. The wisest people I saw were Jerry Garcia and Phil Lesh in that movie: "Those Angels beatin' the shit out of people? I ain't goin' in there." I don't blame the Dead for not working. I just wish they . . . ah, it's too late. Maybe what saves the whole thing is making a movie about it and showing what went down and maybe a little less belief in uniforms.

WHAT WERE THE CONCERTS *on the tour like before Altamont?*
I remember enjoying them. There's always a bummer. It was probably West Palm Beach. You could enjoy the people for hanging around that long, but it was too fucking cold to play properly and we tried to do the whole show . . . too fucking cold. A bummer. After Madison Square Garden, came out of three shows there to freeze your balls off in a Florida swamp. We always get 'em.

It was the first time you saw that America.

It was the first time we played it. Mick and I had been to L.A. in '68, the Strip every night; I dug what was going on there. Brian and I popped over a few times in '67 incognito. Went over in December '66 with Brian. Down in Watts a lot. Very stoned. We got so out of it we wanted to go back and do some more. Without having to play a gig every night. It was the only place we knew where to score, man.

And then Mick and I went in '68 to mix down *Beggar's Banquet* with Jimmy and stayed for two months. Hung out with Taj and the Burritos. Went to the Palomino a lot.

I think England has such a high standard in heavy drugs. Well, the system for junkies was beautiful. It's fucked up now because it's a halfway thing. They really had it under control. It depends how you want to see junk.

You get young kids as junkies in the cities.

You know what it does. It's on the wrong end. They should turn on to it when they're sixty. All these old ladies down here, learn a lesson from these old chicks. For a start, look at its effect on a nine-year-old. Say he kicks when he's fifteen. More than likely he'll only be ten or eleven when he's fifteen. His voice will break suddenly. Puberty is delayed.

But these old ladies, they leave it alone, then start hitting morphine and horse and they don't feel things like lumbago and arthritis and the plague or old age and things like that. They live to ninety, a hundred and five. It's a particular Europe trip. Old rich people.

If you're going to get into junk, it stands to reason you should . . . for a start, in guys particularly, it takes the place of everything. You don't need a chick, you don't need music, you don't need nothing. It doesn't get you anywhere. It's not called "junk" for nothing. Why did Burroughs kick it, after twenty-five years? He's thankful he kicked it, believe me.

How about for making music?

People have offered me a lot of things over the years, mainly to keep going. . . . "Work, ya bastard. Take one of these." I've tried a lot of shit. I don't even know what it is. I personally think . . . it depends if you're ready. Same with alcohol. You should find out what it does. If you don't know what it does and you're just putting it in, for the sake of it, you're a dummy.

What it does depends on what form you take it in. Some people snort, some people shoot it. You tell me what it does. The Peruvians chew it. You can buy it in any grocery store and you eat it with a hunk of limestone and it just freezes you . . . at 11,000 feet it's hard to breathe anyway. Those cats have forty-seven percent more red corpuscles than us lowlanders. Huge lungs, and they're chewing it all the time.

People also say the drunker you are, the better you play.

All those things are true. You go out every time roaring drunk, after five years you're a fucking wreck. And you still might think it's a gas, but you're making it for yourself, which is cool, but people are coming and paying and you're not turning them on, you're only turning yourself on. And you don't know.

What works for you?

It used to be booze. It used to be . . . I try not to get behind anything for too long anymore because . . . I've been hung up on things. I've got to travel on, I've got to be onstage, I don't want to be hung up carrying all those things with me. When I go through, I go through clean. I'm a clean man.

You, though, are in a unique position. People listen when you sing, and 'Sticky Fingers' is a heavy drug album, one way or another.

I don't think *Sticky Fingers* is a heavy drug album any more than the world is a heavy world. In 1964, I didn't used to run into cats in America who'd come up to me and say, "Do you want some skag? Do you want some coke? Do you want some acid? Do you want some peyote?" And then go through all those initials and names. Now you have trouble avoiding them.

People who think you're ready to finance every drug-smuggling expedition in the world. "Hey, listen, I'm not interested. You got the wrong idea." The cats that are into it are into it because they're good at . . . they've taken their chances at it. They're not doing it for nothing, it's either they're getting their rocks off or they're into it for bread. A lot of cats get their kicks going through customs. So what, man?

I mean, people, you can't take a fucking record like other people take a bible. It's only a fucking record, man. Goddamn it, you know, you might love it one day, you might hate it the next. Or you might love it forever, but it doesn't mean to say that whatever it says in there you've got to go out and do, you've got to go out and say.

On the face of that, what kind of music are you writing?

I'll just keep on rocking and hope for the best. That's really what in all honesty it comes down to. I mean, why do people want to be entertainers or want to listen to music or come and watch people make music? Is it just a distraction or is it a vision or God knows what? It's everything to all kinds of people. You know, it's all different things.

Okay, but the music's changing. "Can't You Hear Me Knockin'" changed because of Bobby Keys and Jim Price. "Moonlight Mile" is a change.*

Yeah, it's a gas to play. It's a gas not to be so insulated and play with some more people, especially people like Bobby, man, who sort of on top of being born at the same time of day and the same everything as me has been playing on the road, man, since '56–'57.

He was on Buddy Holly's first record. I mean, he's a fantastic cat to know, for somebody who's into playing rock & roll, because it's been an unending chain for him. The first few years that he was playing around, I was just the same as anyone, I was just listening to it and digging it and wondering where it came from. And he was there, man. Bobby's like one of those things that goes all the way through that whole thing, sails right through it.

How long has it been since 'Sticky Fingers' was finished? How long since the band recorded?

We finished—when were the last sessions, man? Was I even there for the last session of *Sticky Fingers?* When did they finish it? February, January, March? It was all finished, complete by the time we came here.

And it took over a year, did it?

Well, I mean, stretched out, the songs, one could say it stretched over two years, you know, because "Sister Morphine" comes from '68, although we cut it in early '69.

But Stones albums usually take a long time, don't they?

Which really pisses me off. Because everybody's laid back a little more and everybody has other things, they do other things now, whereas when it was just a matter of being on the road and recording, that's all you did, you know, and that was it. And obviously, you could do things much quicker that way.

But I mean, if we carried on doing it like that, we'd probably be doing it from wheelchairs already. Because you can't carry on at that pace forever.

Do you reckon you could be doing more work than you are? More recording, laying down more tracks? You, personally?

Yeah, but you know, but you can't have

weddings of the year and solo albums and you know, I mean, it's great fun.

You going to do a solo album?

No, I'm not going to do one. All I'm going to do is see if I've got enough things left over from the Stones things that they don't like that I do, that I might want to put out at some time, but I'm not going to go and make an album.

I've never had an urge to be a solo. Maybe I can get together one song, two songs a year, that I really feel that I want to sing. And so I do it, and I put it on the Stones album. Because it's cool. If I feel, if I become more productive, I'll just collect things. I'll just wait until I've got enough things.

Shit, man, I was just a hired guitar player when I started. Things grew out of that, and I learned how to write songs just by sitting down and doing it. For me it seems inconceivable that any guitar player can't sit down and write songs. I don't see how a cat can play a guitar, really, and not be able to lay something down of his own in some way.

But that's the way I feel because I happen to be able to do it. For some guitar players it's inconceivable that nobody can play the guitar, you know, that anybody can't just pick it up just like that.

I mean, I've desperately tried to remain anonymous. The state the world is in today, it's much more of an advantage to remain anonymous than it is to be identifiable or recognized.

As a musician?

Fucking Chuck Berry wrote "Let It Rock" under E. Anderson, man, and it's one of the best things he ever did. He's got some tax-publishing hassle, he puts it out under some middle name: Charles A. Berry, Edward Anderson, or whatever. He should have got recognition for it, and as far as I'm concerned he should definitely be recognized as the writer for "Let It Rock." Would the U.S. Internal Revenue kindly bear it in mind?

How do you feel about the music business?

How can you check up on the fucking record company when to get it together in the first place you have to be out on that stage every fucking night, you have to get out there every night in front of the people, saying here I am and this is what I do. You can't keep a check on it. Someone else is handling all that bread.

We found out, and it wasn't years till we did, that all the bread we made for Decca was going into making little black boxes that go into American Air Force bombers to bomb fucking North Vietnam. They took the bread we made for them and put it into the radar section of their business. When we found that out, it blew our minds. That was it. Goddamn, you find out you've helped to kill God knows how many thousands of people without even knowing it.

I'd rather the Mafia than Decca.

Gram Parsons told me a great story about the Mafia. What they're really into now is growing tomatoes. Tomatoes is the only business in America that you can still get cash on the nail, so that if you drive up with a truckload of tomatoes, you get money right off. So they have the whole tomato business sewn up.

Gram had an uncle who was growing a thousand acres of tomatoes, and one day some guys came down in a limousine and got very heavy with him and said, "Why don't you switch to citrus fruits and leave the tomatoes to us?"

Anita: Leave the tomatoes to us.

Keith: It gets so weird, one has to think about everything. I mean, they're running it. They're running America.

Anita: That's why in an interview with the *Daily Mirror* Keith said he was ready to grow tomatoes.

Keith: A subliminal message to the Mafia. "Come see me, I'm ready to grow tomatoes."

What is the conjunction of show business and crime?

A lot of money in entertainment. The criminal element is there for the bread. And where there's crime, there's cops. They're both in the same business, right? Who else deals with crime but criminals and cops? They're the only two that are hung up on it.

Anita: And Italians.

Keith: Anita's seen it all, from another viewpoint. I mean, I'm always in the middle. I've heard incredible Rolling Stones stories I know nothing about. I don't know if I was asleep in my room or . . . why did I miss out on that one?

16

INTERVIEWED BY JANN WENNER AND CHARLES REICH (1972)

Jerry Garcia, the highly acclaimed and highly articulate lead guitarist, singer, songwriter and spokesman with the Grateful Dead, had long been a candidate for a ROLLING STONE Interview, but . . . well, here's how editor Wenner told it, in the fall of '71:

"'The Interview with Garcia' was always one of those things we put off into some indefinite future because Jerry was always around," he wrote. "What finally brought it on was a meeting with Charles Reich, the law professor from Yale who wrote *The Greening of America*. It turned out he was a Dead freak, and he hit me with the question: How come you haven't done an interview with Garcia yet? I hadn't really listened to a Grateful Dead album since their first one and had only recently heard "Casey Jones."

"The truth of the matter is that I was an original Grateful Dead freak. The first time I saw them was in San José, California, after a Stones concert, when I wandered into a Kesey scene that turned out to be their first Acid Test. I distinctly remember walking up to someone who turned out to be Phil Lesh and asking who they were. He said, 'We're the Grateful Dead.' The impact, in my state of mind at that point, was severe. Anyway, it took this professor from Yale to turn me on to the Dead again."

Reich suggested that he and Jann interview the twenty-nine-year-old Garcia together. "I thought his enthusiasm a little . . . *naive,*" said Wenner, "but what the hell . . . Reich was obviously very up on them, and I knew their past history. It would be a good combination. And God knows, Charles 'Consciousness Three' Reich meets Jerry 'Captain Trips' Garcia could turn into something of its own."

In his own original introduction, Wenner picks up the action.

—BF-T

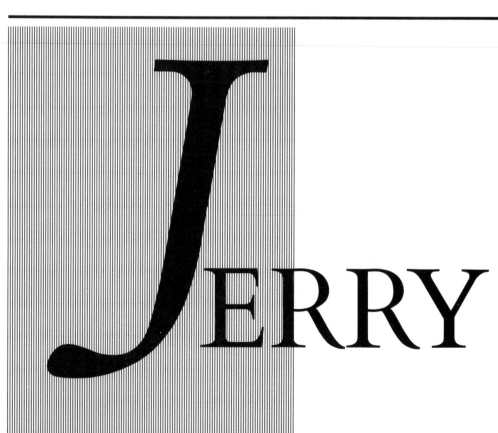

GARCIA

I CALLED UP GARCIA LAST SPRING and told him what the shot was: Reich would be on the Coast some time in early summer. Open and always amiable, he agreed. In July, Reich was at the office raring to go and to settle who was going to make sure the tape recorder was operating correctly (me).

Jerry Garcia lives near the Tamalpais Mountains (a range with magical significance in Northern California Indian lore) overlooking the Pacific Ocean, in a casual 1950 suburban house with his old lady, Mountain Girl, (once of the Merry Pranksters and a close friend of Kesey's in those days) and their little girl. The house is surrounded by eucalyptus trees, huge shrubs and six-foot rose bushes (beyond which is a magnificent view of the Pacific and the Far East, as far as the imagination can take you).

On the front lawn, which looks onto that magnificent view, Charles Reich, myself and Garcia sat on a sunny afternoon and turned the tape recorder on. Five hours later, I packed up the machine and headed back to the city, not entirely sure I could drive too well and not entirely sure at all what had just gone down. Reich was wandering around somewhere in back of the house, remarking on the vibrancy of the trees (never found out exactly when and how he left that day), and Jerry had to be somewhere at 7 for a gig.

A few days later, Reich called; there was a recording session he wanted to go to and he wanted to see Jerry again . . . Sure, sure, what the fuck, I didn't know what my old acquaintance Garcia thought of me at all at that point, so might as well let it roll.

I received the transcriptions of the tapes about three weeks later. What had happened was one interview that I did with Jerry, based on an old familiarity, best described as the good old Grateful Dead trip; and there was a whole other interview that Reich was trying to do: Garcia as spokesman, teacher, philosopher. If I played participant and historian, Reich was the true fan and amazed adult. To be honest, there came a point in that afternoon where I sank into my chair with my hands over my face, wanting out of the whole proposition. Reich was asking questions I thought either achingly obvious or obviously unanswerable.

Reich went back a few weeks later and did another two hours on tape.

In the fall, I returned also to talk to Jerry for another four hours, to complete the interview. Charles Reich put it all into a rough chronological order, and then I edited it for publication. Reich is identified as the interviewer in several passages where I felt it important to indicate the dialogue between the professor and the professional. The rest is, at long last, "The Interview with Garcia."

182

YOU'LL BE IN OUR 100TH ISSUE.
Far out. We were in the first one, too, "Grateful Dead Busted."
I wrote that story.
I loved it. It's got some stunning pictures.
In one picture you can see Phil in dark glasses, holding a gun.
And there's a picture of Bobby handcuffed to Florence, coming down the stairs with a victorious grin. It was incredible.

Reich: Start us at the beginning.
Which beginning?
Your beginning—the day you were born.
My father was a musician. He played in jazz bands in the places that I play in San Francisco, the same ballrooms. I never knew too much about my father; he died when I was young. He played clarinet, saxophone, reeds, woodwinds. He was an immigrant, with his whole family, moved out in the Twenties or the Teens from Spain.

My mother was born in San Francisco. Her mother is a Swedish lady and father is Irish, gold rush days people, who came to San Francisco then. My mother met my father somewhere back then in the Thirties, something like that; he a musician, she a nurse.

Then the Depression came along, and my father couldn't get work as a musician. I understand there was some hassle: He was blackballed by the union or something 'cause he was working two jobs or something like that, some musician's union trip, so he wasn't able to remain a professional musician, and he became a bartender, bought a bar, a little bar like a lot of guys do. He died when I was real young, and my mother took over that business.

All through this time there was always instruments around the house because of my father, and my mother played piano a little and I had lots and lots of abortive piano lessons, you know. . . . I can't read, I couldn't learn how to read music, but I could play by ear. My family was a singing family, on the Spanish side, every time there was a party everybody sang. My brother and my cousin and I when we were pretty young did a lot of street corner harmonizing . . . rock & roll . . . good old rhythm & blues, that kind of stuff, pop songs, all that. It was radio days, *Lucky Lager Dance Time* and all that.

And then, my mother remarried when I was about ten or eleven or so, and she decided to get the kids out of the city, that thing, go down to the Peninsula, and we moved down to Menlo Park for about three years and I went to school down there.

Somewhere before that, when I was in the third grade in San Francisco, I had a lady teacher who was a bohemian, you know, she was colorful and pretty and energetic and vivacious and she wasn't like one of those dust-covered crones that characterize old-time public school people; she was really lively. She had everybody in the class, all the kids in this sort of homogeneous school, making things out of ceramics and papier-mâché. It was an art thing and that was more or less my guiding interest from that time on. I was going to be a painter and I really was taken with it. I got into art history and all of it. It was finally something for me to do.

When we went down to the Peninsula, I fell in with a teacher who turned me on to the intellectual world. He said, "Here, read this." It was *1984* when I was eleven or twelve. And all of a sudden it was a whole new—that was like when I was turning on, so to speak, or became aware of a whole other world that was other than the thing you got in school, that you got in the movies and all that; something very different. And so right away I was really a long way from school at that point . . . there was two or three of us that got into that because of this teacher, who ultimately got fired that same year because of being too controversial—got the kids stirred up and all that—all the classic things.

We moved back to the city when I was about thirteen or so and I started going to Denman, a good old San Francisco rowdy roughneck school. I became a hoodlum, survival thing; you had to be a hoodlum, otherwise you walk down the street and somebody beat you up. I had my friends, and we were hoodlums and we went out on the weekends and did a lot of drinkin' and all that, and meanwhile I was still reading and buying books and going to San Francisco Art Institute on the weekends and just sort of leading this whole secret life.

I was fifteen when I got turned on to marijuana. Finally there was marijuana: Wow! Marijuana! Me and a friend of mine went up into the hills with two joints, the San Francisco foothills, and smoked these joints and just got so high and laughed and roared and went skipping down the streets doing funny things and just having a helluva time. It was great, it was just what I wanted, it was the perfect, it was—and that wine thing was so awful and this marijuana was so perfect.

So what's happening to music all this time?

Nothing much, I'm goofing around, I'm trying to play rock & roll piano and stuff like that, but I'm not settled in with my mother particularly, I'm sort of living with my grandmother and I don't really have any instruments. I want really badly a guitar during this time, about three years, I want a guitar so bad it hurts. I go down to the pawnshops on Market Street and Third Street and wander around the record stores, the music stores and look at the electric guitars, and my mouth's watering. God, I want that so bad! And on my fifteenth birthday my mother gave me an accordion. I looked at this accordion and I said, "God, I don't want this accordion. I want an electric guitar."

So we took it down to a pawnshop and I got this little Danelectro, an electric guitar with a tiny little amplifier, and man, I was just in heaven. Everything! I stopped everything I was doing at the time. I tuned it to an open tuning that sort of sounded right to me, and I started picking at it and playing at it. I spent about six or eight months on it, just working things out. It was unknown at the time, there were no guitar players around. And I was getting pretty good, and finally I ran into somebody at school that played guitar.

Reich: Can I ask for the date?

August 1st—let's see, I was born in '42— Christ, man, arithmetic, school, I was fifteen— '57. Yeah, '57, there you go, it was a good year, Chuck Berry, all that stuff.

I wanted to get an historic date like that.

Yeah, well, that's what it was, August 1st, 1957, I got my first guitar. And that was it. Somebody showed me some chords on the guitar, and that was the end of everything that I'd been doing until that time. We moved out of town up to Cazadero, which is up by the Russian River, and I went to a high school for about a year, did really badly, finally quit and joined the Army. I decided I was going to get away from everything. Yeah, seventeen. I joined the Army, smuggled my guitar in.

Reich: In joining the Army, it was probably the time to leave home.

Well, it was the time to leave it all. I wanted to just be some place completely different. Home wasn't working out really for me and school was ridiculous and, I just wasn't working out. I had to do something. At that time the only really available alternative was to join the Army, so I did that.

Do you have any brothers and sisters?

I have an older brother. Circumstances made me a different guy from my brother, made it always—it was difficult for me to communicate with my brother. He was in the Marines for four years. All that's evened out now since he's gone kind of through a straight trip and . . . sort of fell out the other side of it, and now he's a head, and living in the new world, so to speak, so now we can communicate whereas it used to be that we couldn't.

I lasted nine months in the Army. I was at Fort Ord for basic training and then they transferred me to the Presidio in San Francisco, Fort Winfield Scott, a beautiful, lovely spot in San Francisco, overlooking the water and the Golden Gate Bridge and all that, and these neat old barracks and almost nothing to do. It started me into the acoustic guitar; up until that time I had been mostly into electric guitar, rock & roll and stuff.

I was stuck because I just didn't know anybody that played guitar, and that was probably the greatest hindrance of all to learning the guitar. I just didn't know anybody. I used to do things like look at pictures of guitar players and look at their hands and try to make the chords they were doing, anything, any little thing. I couldn't take lessons—I knew I couldn't take lessons for the piano—so I had to learn it by myself and I just worked with my ear.

When I got out of the Army, I went down to Palo Alto and rejoined some of my old friends down there who were kind of living off the fat of the land, so to speak, a sort of hand-to-mouth existence. Some were living off their parents; most of 'em, most people were living off people who were living off *their* parents.

Reich: This was the beginning of the dropout world?

Yeah, yeah, well, we were—well like that's the period of time I met [Robert] Hunter. Immediately after I got out of the Army. Hunter, who is like a really good friend of mine all this time, he'd just gotten out of the Army—he had an old car and I had an old car when I got out of the Army, and we were in East Palo Alto sort of coincidentally. There was a coffeehouse, 'cause of Stanford, university town and all that, and we were hanging out at the coffeehouse and ran into each other.

We had our two cars in an empty lot in East Palo Alto where they were both broken. Neither of them ran anymore but we were living in them. Hunter had these big tins of crushed pineapple that he'd gotten from the Army, like five or six big tins, and I had this glove compartment full of plastic spoons, and we had this little cooperative scene eating this crushed pineapple day after day and sleeping in the cars and walking around.

He played a little guitar, we started singin' and playin' together just for something to do. And then we played our first professional gig. We got five bucks apiece.

What did you and Hunter used to play?

Oh, folk songs, dippy folk songs. It was before I got into a purist trip and all that.

Who are some of the people you met on the coffeehouse circuit?

I didn't get into playing the coffeehouses until a little bit later than that, really playing coffeehouses—most of that time before that I was learning to play well enough to play anywhere—'61 or '62, I started playing coffeehouses and the guys who were playing around then up in San Francisco at the Fox and Hounds, Nick Gravenites was around then, Nick the Greek they called him; Pete Stampfel from the Holy Modal Rounders, he was playing around there then. A real nice San Francisco guitar player named Tom Hobson that nobody knows about, he was one of those guys that was sort of lost in the folk shuffle, but he's still around and he's still great.

Let's see . . . in Berkeley there was Jorma [Kaukonen] playing coffeehouses about the same time that I was, and Janis [Joplin], in fact, Jorma and Janis and I met at the same time. They played at the place in Palo Alto I played at a lot called the Tangent. They came in one night and I just flipped out. Janis was fantastic; she sounded like old Bessie Smith records, and she was really good. And Paul Kantner was playing around; David Freiberg was playing around, David and Nikelah they called themselves, him and his chick played left-handed guitar, they did these rowdy Israeli folk songs. Michael Cunney was around then too. He's a guy that's kind of like Pete Seeger's junior version, he's very good, he still plays around, banjo and some. Let's see . . . a lot of the people that are around now, that are still doing stuff now.

Did you begin hanging out with Jorma and Janis?

Well, I wasn't really hanging out with them but our paths would be crossing, playing at the same place the same night, and pretty soon after two or three years of running into them you're friends. You never planned it or anything like that, it's just what's happening.

Were you making enough money to support yourself?

Nah . . . I was either not making money and mostly living off my wits, which was pretty easy to do in Palo Alto—things are very well fed—or else I was teaching guitar lessons in record stores.

Hunter and I were still more or less together; at this time we're mostly living at this place called the Chateau in Palo Alto, and me and Hunter and Phil is there a lot, Phil Lesh and Pigpen and all these . . . my fellow freaks.

Where did they turn up?

The old Palo Alto Peace Center was a great place for social trips. The Peace Center was the place where the sons and daughters of the Stanford professors would hang out and discuss things. And we, the opportunist wolf pack, the beatnik hordes, you know, would be there preying on their young minds and their refrigerators. And there would be all of these various people turning up in these scenes, and it just got to be very good, really high.

How did they come along?

Phil was from Berkeley and he had spent . . . his reason for being anywhere on the Peninsula was that he had done some time at San Mateo Junior College playing in their jazz band. Now, Phil, who I met down there at the Peace Center, was at that time composing twelve-tone and serial things. He'd also been a jazz trumpet player. We were in two totally different worlds, musically. But somehow he was working at KPFA as an engineer, and I was up there at a folk music thing or something like that, and Burt Corena who ran the folk music show there wanted me to do a show for KPFA as a folk singer, so Phil and I got together at a party. He put together a tape of me playing in the kitchen and it sounded pretty good to us. He took it up there and played it for them; they dug it, so I went up to the studio and he engineered my little performance.

Whose idea was it to have a band?

See, what happened was, I got into old-time country music, old-time string band music, and in order to play string band music you have to have a band, you can't play it by yourself. So I would be out recruiting musicians. One of the musicians I used to play with in those days was Dave Nelson, who plays guitar for the New Riders, so that's another germ, and me and Nelson were playing old-time music and we got into bluegrass music, playing around at coffeehouses. And Bobby Weir was really a young kid at that time, learning how to play the guitar, and he used to hang around in the music store and he used to hang around at the coffeehouse.

Bob came from Atherton—he's from that really upper-class trip, his folks are really wealthy and all that; he was like the Atherton kid who was just too weird for anybody. He didn't make it in school and people were beatin' up on

him and he was getting kicked out of schools all over the place. His trip was he wanted to learn to play the guitar and have a good old time, and so he'd hang around the music store. . . . I met him when I was working at a music store—he was one of the kingpin pickers—on the town—I always played at the coffeehouse and Weir would come and hear me play, and so it was that kind of thing.

At that time he was like fifteen or something, really young. He's the kid guitar player. And the band thing kept happening various ways. Bluegrass bands are hard to put together because you have to have good bluegrass musicians to play, and in Palo Alto there wasn't really very many of them—not enough to keep a band going all the time.

Now Bill Kreutzmann was working at the music store at the same time I was. My first encounter with Kreutzmann was when I bought a banjo from him way back in '61 or '62. He was just a kid then playing rock & roll. He was in high school. I may have even played a gig with him once when I was playing electric bass in a rock & roll band on weekends.

Since I always liked playing whether it was bluegrass music or not, I decided to put together a jug band, because you could have a jug band with guys that could hardly play at all or play very well or anything like that. So we put together the jug band, and Weir finally had his chance to play because Weir had this uncanny ability to really play the jug and play it really well, and he was the only guy around and so he of course was the natural candidate. And Pigpen, who was mostly into playin' Lightnin' Hopkins stuff and harmonica . . .

Where'd he come from?

He was another one of the kids from around there, he was like the Elvis Presley soul and hoodlum kid. His father was a disc jockey . . . he heard the blues, he wanted to play the blues and I was like the guitar player in town who could play the blues, so he used to hang around, that's how I got to know him. He took up harmonica and got pretty good at it for those days when nobody could play any of that stuff.

So we had the jug band with Pigpen and Weir and Bob Matthews who's the head guy at Alembic Studios now, and Marmaduke [of New Riders] even played with the jug band for a while, I believe.

The jug band we're talking about is pretty recent, that's like '63 . . . '63 or '64 . . . Phil's back from '61 or '60.

And you ran around and played the . . .

185

Played anyplace that would hire a jug band, which was almost no place, and that's the whole reason we finally got into electric stuff.

Whose idea was that?

Well, Pigpen, as a matter of fact, it was Pigpen's idea. He'd been pestering me for a while, he wanted me to start up an electric blues band. That was his trip . . . because in the jug band scene we used to do blues numbers like Jimmy Reed tunes and even played a couple of rock & roll tunes, and it was just the next step.

And the Beatles . . . and all of a sudden there were the Beatles, and that, wow, the Beatles, you know. *Hard Day's Night,* the movie and everything. Hey, great, that really looks like fun.

So Pig fronts the blues band . . .

Yeah, well . . . theoretically it's a blues band, but the minute we get electric instruments it's a rock & roll band. Because, wow, playin' rock & roll, it's fun. Pigpen, because he could play some blues piano and stuff like that, we put him on organ immediately, and the harmonica was a natural and he was doin' most of the lead vocals at the time. We had a really rough sound, and the bass player was the guy who owned this music store that I had been workin' in, which was convenient because he gave us all the equipment; we didn't have to go out and hassle to raise money to buy equipment.

But then, we were playing at this pizza parlor, this is like our first gig, we were the Warlocks, with the music store owner playing bass and Bobby and me and Pigpen . . . and Bill. And so we went . . . and played. We played three gigs at that pizza parlor.

What was your repertoire?

We did . . . we stole a lot of . . . well, at that time, the Kinks, and the Rolling Stones' "King Bee," "Red Rooster," "Walking the Dog" and all that shit, we were just doing hard simple rock & roll stuff . . . old Chuck Berry stuff,, "Promised Land," "Johnny B. Goode," a couple of songs that I sort of adapted from jug band material. "Stealin'" was one of those and that tune called "Don't Ease Me In" . . . it was our first single, an old ragtime pop Texas song . . . I don't remember a lot of the other stuff.

That first gig . . .

That first night at the pizza place nobody was there. The next week, when we played there again it was on a Wednesday night, there was a lot of kids there and then the third night there was 3–400 people . . . all up from the high schools, and in there, man, in there was this rock & roll band . . . we were playing, people were freaking out.

Phil came down from San Francisco with some friends because they heard we had a rock & roll band and he wanted to hear what our rock & roll band was like, and it was a flash to see Phil because he had a Beatles haircut, and he'd been working for the post office and livin' in the Haight-Ashbury. He wasn't playin' any music, though, and he wasn't writing or composing or anything, and I said, "Hey, listen, man, why don't you play bass with us because I know how musical you are, I know you've got absolute pitch and it wouldn't take you too long and I could show you some stuff to get you started." He said, "Yeah, well, that'd be far out." So we got him an old guitar to practice on and borrowed a bass for him, and about two weeks later we rehearsed for a week, and we went out and started playing together.

We never *decided* to be the Grateful Dead. What happened was the Grateful Dead came up as a suggestion because we were at Phil's house one day; he had a big Oxford Dictionary, I opened it up and the first thing I saw was "The Grateful Dead." It said that on the page and it was so astonishing. It was truly weird, a truly weird moment.

I didn't like it really, I just found it to be really powerful. Weir didn't like it, Kreutzmann didn't like it and nobody really wanted to hear about it. But then people started calling us that and it just started, it just got out, Grateful Dead, Grateful Dead. . . .

We sort of became the Grateful Dead because we heard there was another band called Warlocks. We had about two or three months of no name and we were trying things out, different names, and nothing quite fit.

Like what?

Oh, the Emergency Crew, uh . . . the Mythical Ethical Icicle Tricycle . . . ha, ha . . . we had a million funny names, man, really, millions of 'em, huge sheets of 'em.

What were the others?

Oh, God, man, I can't remember, really, you don't want to hear 'em, they're all really bad.

Reich: I'd like to know about your life outside of playing. What kind of scene was that?

Well, I got married back there somewhere, and it was one of those things where she got into trouble, you know, in the classic way. "I want to have the baby," "Well, okay, let's get married." We got married, and the parents thing and all that, and it was like I was tryin' to be straight, kinda. I was working in the music store, you know, in earnest now, and our baby was born and it was okay and all that, but it wasn't really workin'. I was really playin' music, I was playin' music during the day at the music store practicing, and at nights I would go out and gig.

Reich: Were you interested in anything besides music?

Yeah, I was interested in everything besides music.

Reich: I want to hear about that, too.

Well, name something. I mean, I've never had any hobbies but music; I was never doin' anything, but anything that came up would interest me.

Reich: Well . . .

Drugs, of course.

Reich: Okay, let's talk for a minute about that, how they came in at that time . . . it was an old story.

I'd been getting high for a long time, but marijuana turned up in the folk music world and there was speed. The thing about speed in those days was that you stayed up and raved all night, or played. *The Doors of Perception* and stuff like that, we were talking about. And there was mescaline; we could not find mescaline, but we could find peyote. That was the only psychedelic around at that time.

Reich: Religion?

Religion, yeah, Martin Buber and that whole existential thing was just leaving at that time. . . .

Reich: Poetry, literature, stuff like that?

All that, all of that, and on all levels. That was like a continuing thing, but then along came LSD, and that was the end of that whole world. The whole world just went kablooey.

Reich: What's the date of that?

Let's see, LSD came around to our scene I guess around . . . it all was sort of happening at the same time, around '64, I guess. We started hearing about it in '63 and started getting it about in '64.

When we were living at the Chateau, even earlier, like '61, '62, I guess, or '63, the government was running a series of drug tests over at Stanford, and Hunter was one of the participants in these. They gave him mescaline and psilocybin and LSD and a whole bunch of others and put him in a little white room and watched him. And there were other people on the scene that were into that. Kesey. And as soon as those people had had those drugs they were immediately trying to get them, trying to find

some way to cop 'em or anything, but there was no illicit drug market at that time like there is now.

Reich: Two questions together; how did it change your life and how did it change your music?

Well, it just changed everything, you know, it was just—ah, first of all, for me personally, it freed me, you know; the effect was that it freed me because I suddenly realized that my little attempt at having a straight life and doing that was really a fiction and just wasn't going to work out. Luckily I wasn't far enough into it for it to be shattering or anything; it was like a realization that just made me feel immensely relieved, I just felt good and it was the same with my wife—at that time it sort of freed us to be able to go ahead and live our lives rather than having to live out an unfortunate social circumstance, which is what the whole thing is about.

Reich: In what sense did it free you?

In making it all right to have or not have. That is, I think the first lesson that LSD taught me in sort of a graphic way was . . . just . . . it's okay to have something and it's also okay to *not* have it.

Reich: I don't understand yet.

That's it, there isn't anything to understand.

Reich: No, it's just a question of saying it another way.

Well, let's see, let me think about it.

Accepting things the way they are.

Yeah, right.

When was the first time you played music on LSD?

Uh, when we were, let's see . . . we . . . oh, we were the Warlocks and we were playing in a bar in Belmont, we were playing this straight bar and we would do five sets a night, forty-five on and fifteen off, and we'd be sneaking out in the cars smoking joints between each set and so forth. One of those days we took it. We got high and goofed around in the mountains and ran around and did all kinds of stuff, and I remembered we had to work that night. We went to the gig and we were all a little high and it was all a little strange. It was so weird playing in a bar being high on acid, it was just too weird, it was not appropriate, definitely wasn't appropriate.

The first time that music and LSD interacted in a way that really came to life for us as a band was one day when we went out and got extremely high on some of that early dynamite LSD, and we went that night to the Lovin' Spoonful . . . remember that thing, the Lovin' Spoonful whatever, the Charlatans and whoever else down at the Family Dog, Longshoreman's Hall, it was one of the first ones, and we went there and we were stoned on acid watching these bands play.

That day—the Grateful Dead guys—our scene—we went out, took acid and came up to Marin County and hung out somewhere around Fairfax or Lagunitas or one of those places up in the woods and just went crazy. We ended up going into that rock & roll dance and it was just really fine to see that whole scene—where there was just nobody there but heads and this strange rock & roll music playing in this weird building. It was just what we wanted to see.

Just Goodwill junk—old clothes. I had some striped shirts—I think that was the hippest thing I owned. We had some Acid Test pants that were painted Day-Glo—but you couldn't call it hippie stuff. There never was any hippie stuff really.

It was just truly fantastic. We began to see that vision of a truly fantastic thing. It became clear to us that working in bars was not going to be right for us to be able to expand into this new idea. And about that time the Acid Test was just starting to happen.

How did the music change? You're still playing country music and you're playing blues and . . .

Well, we got more into wanting to go . . . to take it farther. In the nightclubs, in bars, mostly what they want to hear is short, fast stuff, uhm . . . and we were always trying to play a little, stretch out a little. . . .

Mountain Girl: More . . . loud.

Jerry: So our trip with the Acid Test was to be able to play long and loud. Man, we can play long and loud, as long and loud as we wanted, and nobody would stop us.

Mountain Girl: Oh, God . . .

Reich: So like would you take something you'd played before and just make it longer and longer and louder and louder? And you were improvising?

Of course, we were improvising cosmically, too. Because being high, each note, you know, is like a whole universe. And each silence. And the quality of the sound and the degree of emotional . . . when you're playing and you're high on acid in these scenes it is like the most important thing in the world. It's truly, phew, cosmic. . . .

Our consciousness concerning music is opening up more, so the music is becoming . . . is having more facets than it seemed to, having more dimensions . . . and we've also seen the effect of all of a sudden we find a certain kind of feeling or a certain kind of rhythm and the whole place is like a sea and it goes boom . . . boom . . . boom, it's like magic and it's like that something you discover on LSD and you discover

that another kind of sound will like create a whole other, you know . . .

We're just playing what's there, is finally what it comes down to, because we're not in a position to be deciding.

When did you meet Kesey, and how?

The Chateau, where we were all livin' several years earlier, was situated physically about two or three blocks from Kesey's place, and there were people from Kesey's that were over at our scene and so on. We didn't hang out down there too much because at the time it was a college trip, you know, they were college people kind of, and it was, it made us self-conscious to be there, we were so, you know . . . undesirable, they didn't really want us, nobody really wanted us hangin' out.

When I first got into that scene, they reminded me of college people. They were all bright and clean and their whole scene was bright and clean. They were colorful, snappy and quick—college stuff.

But then, years later, here we are a rock & roll band. They were hearin' about us up at Kesey's place from our friends who are stayin' up there and gettin' high and comin' down and gettin' high with us.

There was this interaction goin' on. Just like there was interaction between our scene down on the Peninsula and the San Francisco scene . . . the San Francisco scene, all these little networks of one or two guys that go back and forth; sometimes it's dealers, sometimes it's musicians, you know, that was like the old line of communication.

So, it became obvious since you guys are a band and we're right up here in La Honda, and we're having these parties, we want to move the parties out into the world a little bit and just see what happens. So they had this first one down in San José, we took our stuff down there and . . .

Had you met Kesey?

No, I had never met Kesey. It was Page, John Page Browning, he was sort of the messenger. I don't think there was any . . . ever any real decision, just sort of a loose thing.

It was in a house . . . right, after the Stones concert, the same night, the same night. We went there and played but—you know, shit, our equipment filled the room, damn near, and we were like really loud and people were just, ah . . . there were guys freakin' out and stuff and there were hundreds and hundreds of people all around, in this residential neighborhood, swarming out of this guy's house.

We just decided to keep on doing it, that was

the gist of it. We had all these people at this house that wasn't adequate, but the idea was then to move it to a different location, and then the idea was to move it to a different location *each week.*

They had film and endless kind of weird tape recorder hookups and mystery speaker trips and all . . . just all sorts of really strange . . . it always seemed as though the equipment was able to respond in its own way. I mean it . . . there were always magical things happening. Voices coming out of things that weren't plugged in and, God . . . it was just totally mind-boggling to wander around this maze of wires and stuff like that. Sometimes they were like writhing and squirming. Truly amazing.

That was the Acid Test, and the Acid Test was the prototype for our whole basic trip. But nothing has ever come up to the level of the way the Acid Test was. It's just never been equaled, really, or the basic hit of it never developed out. What happened was light shows and rock & roll came out of it, and that's like the thing that we've seen go out.

Where was the second Acid Test?

The second Acid Test, was that at Muir Beach? Or was it at the Big Beat?

Mountain Girl: It was at the Big Beat, I think.

Jerry: It was at the Big Beat, a plushy little nightclub in Palo Alto. That was a real nice one. There was the stage with the Grateful Dead setup on it over here. . . . The Dead's onstage, and on the other side there's a kind of a long sort of a runway affair. It's sort of an L-shaped room, and on the point of the L is the Grateful Dead, and down here is where the Pranksters have their setup, which is like . . . it kinda looked like a cockpit, there was like these tables up on this runner with tape. . . .

Mountain Girl: . . . that weird table organ.

Jerry: Yeah, yeah, the Day-Glo organ and all these weird tape recorders and stuff and microphones and Babbs, who had on one of his quasi-uniforms.

Mountain Girl: That was the first week of the Pranksters shirts.

Jerry: The Pranksters shirts were quasi-uniforms, almost like uniforms but not quite, and Babbs looked kind of like a superhero.

Mountain Girl: Except they were bright green and orange and white stripes and shit like that, so they were pretty loud.

Jerry: Yeah, they were real bright, everything was getting real bright; that was what we were all starting to flash on then.

Mountain Girl: Oh, there was the two straight ladies who owned the place or something.

Jerry: Oh, right, right. They were hanging around behind the bar the whole time . . .

Mountain Girl: . . . worrying what was going on.

Jerry: Middle-aged ladies.

Mountain Girl: We had rented this place from them for fifty or a hundred dollars or something like that. They were just freaking out. Nobody could believe that Page had gotten this place—when we actually did come we were sort of surprised about it—because nobody ever took Page seriously; it was the first real thing he ever did . . . oh, man, we just got in there and set up our shit and everybody shows up and . . .

Who came?

Well, all the other psychedelic scenes at that time: There was Dick Alpert and his scene, Leary and that; Leary wasn't there, Dick Alpert may have been to that one; and there was the Berkeley psychedelic scene which was pretty well developed by that time because of the Cabale coffeehouse in the old days, the mescaline scene and all that.

Mountain Girl: A lot of drifter Palo Alto types . . . and speed freaks, lots of speed freaks.

Jerry: And weirdos. There was always weirdos at the Acid Test. There were always a lot of people that didn't know from LSD; they were like bums and hobos and strange truck driver types and shit like that who would always somehow turn up there and find themselves in this weird other world.

Mountain Girl: Oh, and Neal Cassady and Ann Murphy were there.

Jerry: Neal was really good. There was a strobe light in between our two setups. Just one small strobe light hanging out, but it was real bright, enough to flash the whole place because it was a fairly small room. We'd play stuff and the Pranksters would be doin' stuff and there was this incredible cross interference and weirdness. Stewart Brand was there with his Indian stuff.

Mountain Girl: He had this little slide show and recorded music, taped music, and he'd just show all these beautiful slides of Indian trips and Indian homes.

Jerry: All kinds of Indian trips, things like neon arrowhead signs and highways, long expanses of highways that were really lovely images, each one a jam.

Reich: How did you get into the idea . . . playing and having this visual thing?

It was just the idea of everybody having their various stuff and doing it all at once.

189

REICH: TELL US ABOUT THE *Haight-Ashbury. Where did you live and who did you live with and what was the scene like?*

We came back from L.A. and moved into Danny Rifkin's house on Seven Ten Ashbury. Actually we hung out there for about a week, we didn't actually move in because we were looking for a place in the country.

We ended up with a ranch—Rancho Olompalli—which is the site of the only Indian battle ever fought in California. It's up in Novato. It was a great place. It had a swimming pool and barns and that sort of thing.

Who lived at Seven Ten Ashbury?

A whole bunch of people. We had just one room there, and we were kinda in and out. We were mostly just catching as catch can. We were all on our own, going around staying at different places and hanging out with people.

Then we got another place out in Marin. Camp Lagunitas it was called, it used to be a summer camp. We had our office in San Francisco at Ashbury because there was only one room there that was legitimately ours. Our business was done in the city, and we were living out at Camp Lagunitas. Finally, we messed that up and got kicked out and we ended up back in San Francisco at Seven Ten. By this time most of the other boarders had moved out so we got the house, and a whole lot of us moved in. Not everybody lived there. Bobby and I and Pigpen of the band lived there, and Danny and Rock, who were our managers at the time, Tangerine, who was Rock's old lady and a really good chick, and just various other assorted people hanging out at various times.

Reich: Was it like a commune?

Well, our whole scene had been completely co-operative and entirely shared. We never structured our situation where anybody was getting any money. What we were doing was buying food, paying rent, stuff like that. That was our basic scene, and that's basically how we still operate.

Reich: How many people came drifting in off the streets?

Our place got to be a center of energy, and people were in there organizing stuff. The Diggers would hang out there. The people that were trying to start various spiritual movements would be in and out; our friends trying to get various benefits on for various trips would be in and out. There would be a lot of motion, a lot of energy exchanged, and it was all real high in those days because at that time the Haight-Ashbury was a community. We had the Psychedelic Shop—the very first one—down in the Haight-Ashbury, and that was news, and other people were starting to open stores and starting to get underway. They were looking real good. It was just about that same time that people started to come to town to find out about the hippie scene, and that's about what the hippie scene was—it was just the very small neighborhood affair when we were all working for each other's benefit.

Most of the people of the Haight-Ashbury scene were people who had been at San Francisco State and gotten into drugs and acid and stuff like that and were living out there experimenting with all the new things that they'd discovered. It was a very high, healthy kind of thing—there were no hard drugs, only pot and LSD.

Reich: No rip-offs? No paranoia?

No rip-offs—none of that kind of stuff. No shootings, no bombings, no explosions.

Mountain Girl: No hassles with spades.

*Jerry: None of that kind of stuff. Nothing that we weren't working on or handling or taking care of pretty good.

Then when the big media flash came out—when the *Time* magazine guys came out and interviewed everybody and took photographs and made it news, the feedback from that killed the whole scene. It was ridiculous. We could no longer support the tiny trickle that was really supporting everybody. The whole theory in hip economics is essentially that you can have a small amount of money and move it around very fast and it would work out, but when you have thousands and thousands of people, it's just too unwieldy. And all the attempts at free food and all that, certain people had to work too hard to justify it.

At the early stages we were operating completely purely without anybody looking on, without anybody looking through the big window. We were going along really well. And then the crowds came in. All the people who were looking for something.

Mountain Girl: The Hollywood people came.

But it wasn't the "media" which killed the Haight.

No. Do you want me to tell you the incident where I thought it started to get weird? I was walking down Haight Street, and all of a sudden in a window was a little notice. It said "Communications Company"—and it was that guy, what's his name—*Chester Anderson?* And it was this horrible bummer of a depressing story about some thirteen-year-old meth freak getting raped by nine spades and smackheads . . . it was just a *bummer*. Bad news. This guy took it upon himself to print up bad news and put it up.

Then he started putting out the whole "Free the Street" trip, and he just brought in all this political heavy-handed East Coast hard-edge shit and painted it on Haight Street, where none of it was . . . it wasn't happening like that. It was still groovy. And *that* was the point where I thought, this scene cannot survive with that idea in there. It just goes all wrong.

I was working at 'Ramparts' at the time, and I remember when Chester Anderson first came around the office and got them started on doing the first "hippie" article.

He was the guy who did it. He was representative of the thinking which was not inimicable to that scene of the people who had *already* gone to school and heard speeches and heard all that shit. The peace movements and all that.

Everybody had already been through being disillusioned. It represented a step backward. I thought, "Aw, man, not this shit again." I thought we had already gone through it and now we're into the psychedelic era. There was a whole new consciousness starting to happen and it was really working nice, but then the flood came and that was it.

The "flower power" thing had its own inherent weaknesses.

Right, the inability of not being able to say, "Get out, go away." That tells us something about what innocence is. It's that which allows itself to become no longer innocent. There's some lesson in there. There was a thing about freedom which was very much in question all through that, with the Diggers and Free and all that. Emmett [Grogan] said a thing to me once which I thought was far out, and I think it still applies. He was talking about being in his house and having somebody walk in, and the guy's rap was "Aren't I free to walk in?" And Grogan was on the trip of "Well, if there's freedom, then I'm free to kill you for entering my house. I'm free to do whatever I think I need to do."

What happened to move you out of that scene, and then where did you go?

We didn't really move out of it—we didn't get up and leave. We hung around for a long time. We lived on Ashbury for a couple of years, anyway. Various of us were living in other parts of the Haight-Ashbury—up on the hill. Our scene has always been too big to be central, and we've never really been able to get a really big

place where everybody could stay together.

It just hadn't been working. We ultimately got busted in the Haight-Ashbury and that was a good reason for everybody to leave. That was the point at which we all started to leave. We just started to find new places to be. I was the first one to move out to Marin County—to Larkspur. Then everybody else came out.

Reich: You have a reputation that during the Haight-Ashbury time and later, that you were the sort of spiritual adviser to the whole rock scene.

That's a crock of shit, quite frankly.

Jefferson Airplane says that on their first or second album.

I know. That's because at that time, they were making their second record and they were concerned about it—they didn't want it to be like their first record. And RCA had given them the producer, and he was like this straight producer who used to produce André Kostelanetz or somebody like that, and he didn't really know what they wanted to do, how they wanted to sound or how they wanted their thing to be. The Airplane thought it would be helpful to have somebody there who could communicate to their producer who they could communicate to, and since they all knew me and I understood their music and understood what they were doing pretty much at the time, it would be far out. I went down there and hung out and was a sort of go-between, between them and their producer and helped out with some arrangements and stuff like that—I just hung out.

Reich: But that's a big difference from being the "guru" of the whole scene?

Here's the thing—I would like to preface this whole interview by saying I'm one of those guys who's a compulsive question answerer. But that doesn't necessarily mean I'm right or anything. That's just one of the things I can do. It's kinda like having a trick memory. I can answer any question. I'm just the guy who found myself in the place of doing the talking every time there was an interview with the Grateful Dead.

How about among the musicians themselves?

I've played with nearly all the musicians around and we all get along okay. But the whole music scene is very groovy. Here there's very little competition, very few ego games. Everybody knows what it takes to make music pretty good around here. It's that thing of being high and playing. I think it's the scene this area has that makes it attractive for musicians, and that's why a lot of them moved here. That freedom, that lack of competition, the fact that you aren't always having to battle and you can really get into what playing music is all about. But as for coming to me for advice and shit like that, that's ridiculous. That's like "Captain Trips." That's bullshit.

REICH: NOW, CAN I ACT LIKE A *professor and ask you a long thing? People that write about rock say that it started as a rebellion, that it spoke to these needs in people to express their feelings. Tin Pan Alley was music that didn't tell the truth and rock did. The question is, do you think that rock began with that kind of revolt and has it changed?*

I don't know. I don't go for any of that stuff. If I were going to write about rock & roll music, I wouldn't write about it from that sociological standpoint and so forth because all that stuff really had to do with who you were. If you were wearing a black leather jacket and swinging a chain in the Fifties and listening to rock & roll, yeah, it was the music of rebellion. But if you were a musicologist following what music does, or a musician, it was something wholly different. It depends on who you were or who you are when they hit you.

Reich: What I'm trying to get at is your idea of what rock meant.

It was music I loved. That's what it meant; I mean it didn't mean anything—it meant have a good time, it meant rock & roll. Whatever—I like the music, that was the thing. It was the background music for the events of my life. My theme music. Them rock & roll songs—that's what was happening.

The people that are writing about rock & roll are doing it as writers, and they've got to create a situation to write about. Because if you don't create something to write about, you're left with no excuse for writing. That's not true of all writers. There are some writers that write for the flash and writers that write about the flash, too. And it's easier for me to read the flash than it is for me to read about the sociology. I think you could make a better movie. *Rock around the Clock* I think was a good movie about the source of what rock & roll was and *Rock around the Clock* was the background music for 1958 and that was right on.

Reich: Well, if knife fights and stuff like that was the background for the Fifties, what's the scene from which your music comes now?

It's everything that I've ever experienced. It's everything that we—the Grateful Dead—have ever experienced as a group. It's a combination of every crowd we've ever seen, of every time we've ever played.

How did you avoid the music business taking over your lives? Because nobody wanted it?

Yeah . . . that's a good part of it. And with us, we've never really been successful in the music business; we've never had a superbig hit album or a hit single or anything like that. Grateful Dead freaks are our audience, you know. . . . We're not mass market or anything like that, which I think is supergreat. I think that we've been really lucky because we haven't had to put up with all the celebrity stuff, or star stuff. At the same time, it's been somewhat of a struggle to survive, but we're doing good, we're doing okay . . . so it worked out okay.

Do you think you could cope with a Crosby, Stills, Nash & Young type of success?

I might be able to cope with it, but I don't think that I could be really that comfortable with it, you know, because I . . . the place where I get strung out is . . . is . . . I'd like to be fair, you know, I want to be fair, so I don't like to pull the thing of having somebody at the door that says, "No, fuck you, you can't see Garcia, you know, you're not going in no matter what, no matter how good your rap is."

Our backstage scene and all that is real open; we try to let as much stuff possible come by, and I just've gotten into the thing of being able to move around pretty fast so I don't have to get hung up into anything, but I like to let it flow rather than stop it. I think that if there's more pressure along that line—it's getting now to where maybe 50 or 100 or 200 people backstage is getting kinda outrageous and if we were like superpopular it would be that many more, and that (I'm thinking in purely physical terms) would start to get to be a problem . . . somewhere in there, if we get much more famous.

That's why I feel pretty good about finishing up our Warner Bros. thing, stopping being part of that mainstream and just kinda fallin' back so that we can continue to relate to our audience in a groovy intelligent way without having to be part of a thing that . . . really, that other world of the higher-up celebrity thing really doesn't seem to want us too badly, so, you know, we're able to avoid it. We're really not that good, I mean star kinda good, or big-selling records good.

Do you think it'll go on for a long time . . . the band?

Uh, I don't see why not. Barring everybody dying or complete disinterest or something like that. As long as it's groovy and the music is happening . . . I don't see why it shouldn't just keep on going. We don't have any *real* plans, but we're committed to this thing . . . we're following it, we're not directing it. It's kinda like saying, "Okay, now I want to be here, now I want to go there," in a way. Nobody's making any real central decisions or anything. Everything's just kinda hashed out. It stumbles. It stumbles, then it creeps, then it flies with one wing and bumps into trees, and shit, you know. We're committed to it by now, after six years. What the fuck? It's still groovy for us. It's kinda like why break up the thing when it's working, when it seems to be working good and everybody's getting off.

What happened to Mickey {Hart}?

Mickey is still working on his record. He's still got his barn and all that. He's in a good place. I saw him last night, he was at the Crosby and Nash's concert, Mickey is a very even dude. He's pretty together in his own way. He likes to walk on the edge of the cliff. But he stays cool behind it, he's able to do it. I like him.

What's the scene with Pigpen now?

He's pretty sick. But he's living. He was really, really *extremely* sick. I don't really know *how* sick, because I never hung out at the hospital that much, although I did give him a pint of blood. We all did. He was really fucked up; his liver was full of holes and then he had some kind of perforated ulcer . . . just all kinds of bum trips from juicing all these years. And he's a young dude, man, he's only twenty-six. I think he might even be younger than that.

From juicing! It's incredible, but he survived it, and he isn't dead. He survived it, and now he's got the option of being a juicer or not being a juicer. To be a juicer means to die, so now he's being able to choose whether to live or die. And if I know Pigpen, he'll choose to live. That's pretty much where he's at. For the time being he's too sick, too weak to go on the road, and I wouldn't want to expose him to that world. I don't think it's good for him at this point. It would be groovy if he could take as long as it takes to get him to feelin' right, and then to work on his solo album and get himself together in terms of becoming . . . it's sorta like stepping out of the blues story, 'cause Pigpen is a sort of guy who's like been a victim of the whole blues

trip. It's like Janis exactly, in which you must die. That's what the script says. So Pigpen went up to the line, and he's seen it now, so the question is how he's going to choose.

Reich: You feel like it's on the prow of a ship up here, that's a very good way to think of it because you can see the captain's stands.

Right, it's kinda like a retired admiral's place, little brass telescope, cranky parrot.

Reich: That's fine, captain's cabin, that's what I've been thinking of you as, see . . .

I know, that's an attractive image and sometimes it seems like it, but I always thought that Kesey was. But he ain't either. Nobody is, man, there isn't anybody, it's just a convenient, it's just a place you can be. . . . It's just a way to express yourself. . . .

The way it works is it doesn't depend on a leader, and I'm not the leader of the Grateful Dead or anything like that; there isn't any fuckin' leader. I mean, because I can bullshit you guys real easy, but I can't bullshit Phil and Pigpen and them guys watchin' me go through my changes all these years, and we've had so many weird times together. But it's that kind of thing—I know in front that the leader thing don't work, because you don't need it. Maybe it used to, but I don't think you need it anymore because everybody is the leader when it's the time for them to be the leader, you know what I mean, it all of a sudden, you're the guy that knows in that situation . . .

That's right.

You know, I think the Grateful Dead, the Grateful Dead is like one dumb guy, instead of five, you know . . . dumb guys, it's like one dumb guy, and it seems like everything that we learn comes in the form of these big dumb, you know, take this, you know, the manager, kreccccchhh, and we get hit over the head, oh yeah, manager, manager, yeah, it takes like a big one for us to notice it, man. That's kind of the way I see it.

. . . persevering . . .

Yeah, that's all we can do . . . I can't do anything else hahahaha, and the Grateful Dead is still a good trip through all of it, through all of it it's been a good trip and I've dug every minute of it, man, it's just like I really love it, it's really a good trip, and that's the payoff, ultimately, you know, and that's the reason why we're all doing it, really, that's the one thing that still makes it. And you know, now actually for us everything is making it, everything is . . . it's just going real

THE ROLLING STONE INTERVIEWS

good, it's going good enough where we can actually decide what the hell we want to do, which is—aw, fuck, what's that?

WHAT'S THE CREATIVE PART *of making your music—do you make it as you go along on the road or do you make it when you're settled back in San Francisco or do you make it all the time?*

I'd say we make it all the time. Because we've all pretty much decided after a long time that we're in fact musicians and . . . it's just something you do, it's in your head, musical pieces and records and all that. As a band, for the last two years, our music has been evolving as we play it. We haven't been rehearsing because we haven't had a place to rehearse—like that's a whole other school of problems, rock & roll rehearsal spots.

Reich: How does a song come into being, and how does it grow from its beginnings into what you might hear eventually on the record?

They're all different. Sometimes I'll start out with a set of chord changes that're just attractive to my ear. And then I'll hear a sketch of a melody over it. Then I'll just sort of let that be around my head, for however long it is there, for three or four weeks. I won't . . . I never try to work on stuff, you know, like sit down and labor it. But pretty soon there'll be more adjoining pieces to any one phrase, a melodic phrase, say. Then I hum it to myself for a long time and kind of play it on the guitar for everybody who's around, and then I'll get together with Hunter who writes our lyrics and we'll go through what he's got. If he's got lyrics already written that he likes I'll see if anything fits, or else we'll start working on something from scratch. But the whole thing is completely organic—there isn't . . . I don't have any scheme . . .

Reich: It comes from somewhere outside.

For sure. And what happens is that you're lucky enough to remember a little of it as it's going by. And then what it turns into after it's become a song in your head is it turns into a piece of material for the band—everybody plays an equal role in that part of it—and that's the way it finally evolves as a song on a record or something like that. If it's one of my songs, it's never what I originally heard, it's always something that includes more than I might have conceived myself.

Reich: And the words probably came by, too, is that right?

Well, that's the way Hunter writes—he writes his words pretty much the same way. Things come to him, you know. An idea comes by, or a picture, an image, sort of floats by, it's all in the air kind of. It's a matter of being able to tune into it.

Who wrote "Casey Jones"?

Me and Hunter. He wrote the words, I wrote the music.

Did you start off to write the same thing or did you have the melody first and then the words?

No, he had the words, and the words were just so exquisite, they were just so perfect that I just sat down with the words, picked up a guitar and played the song . . . it just came out.

In one sitting?

Yeah, it just came out . . . it just triggered. Play it, here it is.

Do you alter the words when you write with Hunter?

Many times, yeah . . . sometimes I use pieces of three or four of his different songs and put them together. I also adjust the phrasing. I sort of edit . . . to make tht things more *singable* usually. But he's gotten to be really a craftsman at it lately. In the last year or so, he's gotten to really understand what it is to sing words, and just the technique, that vowels sing a certain way and consonants sing a certain way and what you have to do. Certain things you can sing real gracefully and other things you can't sing to save your soul.

"Truckin'" seems to be the story of the Dead.

When Hunter first started writing words for us . . . originally he was on his own trip and he was a poet. He was into the magical thing of words, definitely far out, definitely amazing. The early stuff he wrote that we tried to set to music was stiff because it wasn't really meant to be sung. After he got further and further into it, his craft improved, and then he started going out on the road with us, coming out to see what life was like, to be able to have more of that viewpoint in the music, for the words to be more Grateful Dead words. "Truckin'" is the result of that sort of thing. "Truckin'" is a song that we assembled, it didn't . . . it wasn't natural and it didn't flow and it wasn't easy and we really labored over the bastard . . . all of us together.

Reich: It comes out of somewhere in the past, doesn't it?

It comes out of nothing specific but it's really a lot of like the way it is, just a lot like the way it is, the pace of it and the flow of it and the kinda like fast thoughts that you have as things are happening around you; the ideas in it are right-on in that sense. I like "Truckin'" a lot, "Truckin'"'s one of my favorites.

In "New Speedway Boogie" you say "one way or another, this darkness has got to end." Have you seen that way yet?

Ummmm. . . . Ahhh. . . . I think that that song's an overreaction, myself. I think that it's a little bit dire. Really, the thing that I've been seeing since Altamont is that periodically you have darkness and periodically you have light, like the way the universe is in the yin/yang symbol. There's darkness and light, and it's the interplay that represents the game that we're allowed to play on this planet. Just the fact that there are two opposing elements in the universe is the grace of that cosmic game that we're allowed to dick around here, you know, on the planet.

What if somebody came up to you and asked you, "What's psychedelic music?"

Ohhhhhhh, goddamn . . . Phil defined it pretty good once. He said ummmmm . . . Oh, somebody asked him once what acid rock was— which is psychedelic music. Okay, whatever, we'll use those two as an equation—and he said, "Acid rock is music you listen to when you're high on acid." Psychedelic music is music you listen to when you're psychedelic. I think that's what its real definition should be because subjectively I don't think that there really is any *psychedelic music,* unless except in the classical sense of music which is designed to expand consciousness. If you use that as a definition of psychedelic music, then I would say that Indian music was definitely that, and that certain kinds of Tibetan music are, too.

If you wanted to play all the instruments on your own record, you would lose the whole group feel, wouldn't you?

Yes, of course, except that that's the challenge. If it were possible for me to make a record where I could play by myself and sound like the whole group, I would consider it to be a successful record. In the context of this kind of experiment and in the nature of the kind of material I'm doing on my solo album, it'll be that kind of an experiment. I'll be able to make myself sound like a band. The reason, musically, I know I can do it is because it's all coming from my head, it's going to at least agree. But then you get this unified, too-much-agreement sort of

sound, and you don't have that excitement of interchange.

Does the group have a producer?

No, we are our own producer. A producer is just one of those recording studios. . . . The function that a producer sometimes fills is that he's the guy who sits in the recording studio while the band plays and tells them whether they're playing well or not, what's wrong with what they're playing, whether they're out of tune, in tune, whether it needs to be a little faster and so on. He's an ear. He translates the band's wishes to the engineer. That's essentially what the producer does.

Reich: How has your music changed from one record to another?

The first one was called *The Grateful Dead.* At that time we had no real *record* consciousness. We were just going to go down to L.A. and make a record. We were completely naive about it. We had a producer whom we had chosen—Dave Hassinger—and we were impressed by him because he'd been the engineer on a couple of Rolling Stones records that we liked the sound of; that was as much as we were into record-making.

So we went down there and, what was it we had . . . Dexamyl? Some sort of diet-watcher's speed, and pot and stuff like that. So in three nights we played some hyperactive music. That's what's embarrassing about that record now; the tempo was way too fast. We were all so speedy at the time. It has its sort of crude energy, but obviously it's difficult for me to listen to it; I can't enjoy it really. I just plain cannot enjoy it just because even as soon as we'd finished it there were things that we could hear . . .

Mountain Girl: Man, it's so fast, it's just blinding!

What music was it?

Just simply what we were doing onstage. Basically that. Just rock & roll. Plus we wanted to have one extended cut on it. But in reality, the way we played was not really too much the way that record was. Usually we played tunes that lasted a long time because we like to play a lot. And when you're playing for people who are dancing and getting high, you can dance easy to a half-hour tune and you can even wonder why it ended so soon. So for us the whole time thing was weird 'cause we went down there and turned out songs real fast—less than three minutes, which is real short.

It was weird and we realized it. The first record was like a regular company record done in three nights, mixed in one day—it was done on three track, I believe—it wasn't even four track, Studio A in L.A., an imposing place—and we really didn't much care about it while we were doing it. So we weren't surprised when it didn't quite sound like we wanted it to.

It's hard for me to go back to the past in terms of the music because for me it's a continuum and to stop it at one of those points it's got . . . to me it always looks underdeveloped and not quite working. Which in fact it was.

What kind of places were you playing at then?

We were playing all the places that were trying to become the Fillmore or trying to become the Avalon, as well as the Fillmore and the Avalon. And there were places down in L.A. that were trying to get started and places in San Diego, but all the rest of that stuff is stuff that's everywhere.

This is '66 by now, something like that.

Yeah, '66, right.

Then on the second record, we went the whole other way. We decided we'd spend time on our record. We're going to work on it, we're going to make sure it sounds good, we're really going to get into recording and go on some trips with it. So our second record turned out to be a monumental project. We started out by recording for a couple of weeks, experimentally, in L.A. where we accomplished absolutely nothing. Then we went to New York to try some studios there, and we got our producer so excited that he quit. We got him uptight—because we were being so weird and he was only human after all and didn't really have to go through all that, so he decided not to go through it and we decided, "Well, we can do it ourselves." So we just worked and worked and worked—mostly Phil and I—for months, maybe as long as six months—at least six months. It was an eight-track recording, and we worked a lot in San Francisco. We assembled live tapes, and we went through the most complex operations that you can go through in a recording studio.

Did Phil use his background or did you just learn it from scratch?

Phil used what he knew, and I was learning from scratch. I had had some experience after working with the Jefferson Airplane, pretty nominal, but at least I had some idea. And we had an engineer, Dan Healy, who is like a real good fast-on-his-feet, able-to-come-up-with-crazy-things engineer. And we worked and we assembled an enormous amount of stuff, and since it was all multitrack, it all just piled up.

196 With *Anthem of the Sun,* after an enormously

complex period of time, we actually assembled the material that was on the master tape. Then we went through the mixing thing, which really became a performance, so *Anthem of the Sun* is really the performance of an eight-track tape; Phil and I performed it and it would be like four hands, and sometimes Healy would have a hand in. We'd be there hovering around the boards in these various places at Criteria Studio, Miami, and in New York. We selected, from various performances we did, the performance which seemed the most spaced, and we did that all the way through. So that's a spaced record if there is one.

How was the music different from the first record?

We were thinking more in terms of a whole record, and we were also interested in doing something that was far out. For our own amusement—that thing of being able to do a record and really go away with it—really lose yourself.

What do you think of that second record, 'Anthem of the Sun'?

There's parts of it that sound dated, but parts of it are far out, even too far out. I feel that that's one of those things . . . see, it's hard for me to be able to listen to any of that stuff objectively, 'cause I tend to hear a thing like *Anthem of the Sun* matching it up against what it was that we thought we were gonna do, intellectually speaking. So I have to think of it in terms of something we were trying to do but didn't succeed in doing. I listen to what's *wrong* with it. I tend to listen to it in the inverse way; but on the other hand, if I have the right kind of head, and I'm not on an ego involvement trip with it . . .

Did the next record mark any kind of change?

No. The next record was really a continuation of the *Anthem of the Sun* trip—called *Aoxomoxoa*—a continuation in the style of having a complex record. When we started, *Aoxomoxoa* was an eight-track record, and then all of a sudden there was a sixteen-track recorder in the studio, so we abandoned our entire eight-track version and went to sixteen-track to start all over again. Now at the time we were sipping STP during our session, which made it a little weird—in fact, very weird. We spent too much money and too much time on that record; we were trying to accomplish too much and I was being really stupid about a lot of it, because it was material, some new tunes that I had written, that I hadn't really bothered to teach anyone in the band and I was trying to record them from the ground up, and everybody was coming in and doing over dubs. It was weird—we went about it in a very fragmentary way. We didn't go about it as a group at all.

Some of the music is pretty strange.

Now, I like that record personally, just for its weirdness, really. There are certain feelings and a certain kind of looseness that I kinda dig; but it's been our most unsuccessful record. It was when Hunter and I were both being more or less obscure, and there are lots of levels on the verbal plane in terms of the lyrics being very far out. Too far out, really, for most people.

That was one of my pet records 'cause it was the first stuff that I thought was starting to sound like how I wanted to hear songs sound. And the studio stuff was successful. I'm really happy with the remix . . . I hope you get a chance to hear 'em. All the new mixes that are coming out will say on them, "Remixed."

The next one is 'Live/Dead.'

It's good. It has "Dark Star" on it, a real good version of it. We'd only recorded a *few* gigs to get that album. We were after a certain sequence to the music. In the sense of it being a serious, long composition, musically, and then a recording of it, it's *our* music at one of its really good moments.

Live/Dead was actually recorded about the same time we were working on *Aoxomoxoa*. If you take *Live/Dead* and *Aoxomoxoa* together, you have a picture of what we were doing at that time. We were playing *Live/Dead* and we were recording *Aoxomoxoa*. When *Live/Dead* came out, it was about a year out of date.

After *Aoxomoxoa* we hadn't made a studio record for almost a year since *Live/Dead* came out in its place. We were anxious to go to the studio, but we didn't want to incur an enormous debt making the record like we had been. When you make a record, you pay for the studio time out of your own royalties. That costs plenty. *Live/Dead* was not too expensive since it was recorded live. It ended up paying for the time on *Aoxomoxoa*, which was eight months or some really ridiculous amount of time. A hundred grand or even more than that—it was real expensive. And we ended up at our worst, in debt to Warner Bros. for around $180,000.

So, when record time came around and we were getting new material together, we thought, "Let's try to make it cheap this time." So we rehearsed for a month or so before we went in to make *Workingman's Dead*. We rehearsed and we were pretty far into the material, and then we got busted in New Orleans. After we got busted, we went home to make our record. And while we were making our record, we had a big, bad scene with our manager. Actually, making the record was the only cool thing happening—everything else was just sheer weirdness.

How had your music changed?

We were into a much more relaxed thing about that time. And we were also out of our pretentious thing. We weren't feeling so much like an experimental music group but were feeling more like a good old band.

Does "Casey Jones" grate on you when you hear it sometimes?

Sometimes, but that's what it's supposed to do *(laughs)*.

It's such a sing-songy thing. . . .

Right. And it's got a split-second little delay which sounds very mechanical, like a typewriter almost, on the vocal, which is like a little bit jangly, and the whole thing is, well . . . I always thought it's a pretty good musical picture of what cocaine is like. A little bit evil. And hard-edged. And also that sing-songy thing, because that's what it *is,* a sing-songy thing, a little melody that gets in your head.

What songs on 'Workingman's Dead' do you particularly like?

I liked *all* those tunes. I loved them all, *(laughs)* to give you the absolute and unashamed truth. I felt that they were *all* good songs. They were successful in the sense you could sing 'em, and get off and enjoy singing 'em. "Uncle John's Band" was a *major* effort, as a musical piece. It's one we worked on for a really long time, to get it working right. "Cumberland Blues" was also difficult in that sense. The song that I think failed on that record is "High Time." It's a beautiful song, but I was just not able to sing it worth a shit. And I really can't do justice to that kind of song now. . . . I'm not that good of a singer. But I wish someone who could really sing would do one of those songs sometime. I would *love* to hear some good singers do that stuff. I mean, it would just tickle me. There are some people doing "Friend of the Devil," I understand. But other than that, we haven't heard of any people doing our songs at all.

What stands out in your mind about 'American Beauty'? Each song sounds closer to the others.

There isn't too much difference. And that's . . . well, I tried to block that whole trip out. You see, my mother died while we were making that record. And Phil's father died. It was raining down hard on us while that record was going on. They're good tunes, though. Every one of 'em's a gem, I modestly admit.

They had one of the few things Pigpen sings by himself.

197

One of his own tunes. He's come up with a lot of them lately.

What side of you does 'American Beauty' represent?

Well, let's call *Workingman's Dead* a song record, a singing record because the emphasis is on the vocals and on the songs. And *American Beauty* is another record in that trend where the emphasis is on the vocals and the songs. And that's basically what we're doing, the music being more or less incidental—not incidental—but structural rather than the end product.

The records are not total indicators, they're just products. Out of the enormous amount of output that we create in the course of a year, they're that little piece that goes out to where everybody can get it.

The new album, the live double set, is like listening to the old Grateful Dead

It's *us*, man. It's the prototype Grateful Dead. Basic unit. Each one of those tracks is the total picture, a good example of what the Grateful Dead really is, *musically*. Rather than "*this* record has sort of a country, light acoustics sound," and so on—like for a year we were a light acoustics band, in somebody's head. The new album is enough of an overview so people can see we're like a regular shoot-em-up saloon band. That's more what we are like. The tracks all illustrate that nicely. They're hot.

What places did you use most in that record?

The one we used most of was Fillmore East. And the one we used least was Winterland. At Winterland we used one track, "Johnny B. Goode."

Reich: Why are you doing an album by yourself?

I'm doing it to be completely self-indulgent—musically. I'm just going on a trip. I have a curiosity to see what I can do and I've a desire to get into sixteen-track and go on trips which are too weird for me to want to put anybody else I know through. And also to pay for this house!

Are you doing it with anybody?

I'll probably end up doing it with a lot of people. So far I'm only working with Bill Kreutzmann because I can't play drums. But everything else I'm going to try to play myself. Just for my own edification. What I'm going to do is what I would do if I had a sixteen-track at home, I'm just going to goof around with it. And I don't want anyone to think that it's me being serious or anything like that—it's really me goofing around. I'm not trying to have my own career or anything like that. There's a lot of stuff that I feel like doing and the Grateful Dead, just by fact that it's now a production for us to go out and play, we can't get as loose as we had been

able to, so I'm not able to stay as busy as I was. It's just a way to keep my hand in, so to speak, without having to turn on a whole big scene. In the world that I live in there's the Grateful Dead, which is one unit which I'm a part of, and then there's just me. And the me that's just me, I have to keep my end up in order to be able to take care of my part of the Grateful Dead. So rather than sit home and practice—scales and stuff—which I do when I'm together enough to do it—I go out and play because playing music is more enjoyable to me than sitting home and playing scales.

Y OU GOT INTO MONEY, YOU GOT *into business, you got into management duties and you got into records, and somehow you stayed yourselves.*

Well, we didn't really get into any of those things is the reason. See, our managers were Rock Scully and Danny Rifkin, who were really our friends, and they were a couple of heads, old-time organizers from the early Family Dog days, and they agreed to sort of manage us. Which they did as well as they could. They investigated the music business and learned as much about it as they possibly could, but really they weren't too experienced at it and we weren't very experienced at it, and so what we really managed to do in that whole world was get ourselves incredibly in debt, just amazingly in debt in just about two years.

Mountain Girl: They never wrote anything down or anything like that.

Jerry: And we never cared. I mean it was just a . . . it was a . . . we were mostly interested in just keeping going.

Didn't anybody in the band think, "Hmm, we're getting more and more in debt and . . ."

Well, no, because we didn't know about it. But nobody knew about it. Rock didn't know, Danny didn't know about it. Really. We didn't know about it until we tried to get ourselves completely organized.

Reich: Is this a different story than the other stories?

It's similar, it's different but similar; every band has gone through trips kinda like it.

Reich: So the real story is you just didn't . . .

We didn't give a shit.

We were just happy freaks, man; we didn't know anything about money, or bills, or anything of the rest of that stuff. It wasn't bad, though. Don't get the idea it was bad because it just wasn't real, and because it wasn't real was the reason that it got so outrageously out of hand. And it wasn't until somebody started saying, hey, listen, you guys are really in big trouble.

Who started saying that?

Lenny, who is Mickey's father. Now Lenny comes into the picture. And we had our office re-organized.

How did you finally get the financial act together?

All of a sudden there was a concern there that was fictionalized in our minds by somebody else. It's entirely possible that we could have fixed it without ever knowing about it. But we were made conscious of it and we became paranoid: "You guys are really in big trouble; you're out of money and there's no money coming in and you're going broke, and I think these guys have been ripping you off," and all. That is really a poisonous kind of thinking and we went for it, foolishly we went for it and said, Okay, you be our manager. So Lenny Hart said, "Okay, boys, I'll take care of you," and we thought, "Ah, at least here's a manager that we don't have to worry about, he's an old businessman and he's Mickey's father, well, we can trust him, of course, we can trust him, you know, he's his father."

But along the way all the people who were our friends and people that we trusted to work for us began to leave. He was putting them uptight . . . it was really a classical manipulation trip and really creepy. Looking back on it, at the time we were just really not sure of what was happening and we were testing Lenny a lot, too; we were putting him on the line a lot, like, "We don't want to do these kind of gigs; we don't want to do that, or we don't want you to go out and talk to people, we want to talk to 'em ourselves, you just stay in the background as much as possible."

I'd been concerned about our management scene because I knew that Lenny didn't understand us and we didn't understand him and it really wasn't working out, but we had no way to replace him. But these old friends of mine, the Parkers, who had been having straight gigs for a long time, had just gotten back from a vacation. They had nothing to do and they were kinda looking for work, and I said, "Wow, here's some people that can maybe help us out." At the same time—this was after Altamont—Sam Cutler had come back to the United States after having gone through that Altamont scene and he was looking for something to do—he came and hung out at my house for a while. I thought because of his experience in the music business that maybe he could sort of look into our scene and see if maybe he could suggest some stuff.

Sam started looking into it and they discovered that Lenny had really been taking a lot of money and that the books were really weird and there were odd bank accounts and it came down to a real heavy scene. We were recording *Workingman's Dead* when we actually fired Lenny; we'd just been busted in New Orleans and things were really looking heavy, this New Orleans threat hanging over our heads and Lenny was our only contact with the New Orleans District Attorney. What happened, what finally sprung it, was Ramrod, who's our head equipment guy, who's been with us a long time, said, "Either you gotta get rid of that Lenny guy or I'm quitting." And that flashed us: "Wow, we can't work without Ramrod, we've gotta get rid of Lenny."

What did Mickey say about all this?

Well, Mickey was dismayed. He'd never expected anything like that, of course. He knew his father had been into shady trips before but he thought he was reformed, just like we all did. He was really shocked, and he was right with us about our decision to get rid of Lenny. In fact, he was really good about working it out just 'cause it was so tacky.

As soon as we started to get closer and closer to finding out more and more of the truth and trying to get bills and old things from Lenny, he just disappeared. A great deal has been lost and is missing and has never been filed or put anywhere . . . a lot of it . . . there's really no way of estimating how much money we've lost, as a result of that. There isn't . . . there's only sort of rough estimates. That was the weirdest ever; God, that was incredible.

Have you ever gotten straightened out financially?

We *just* got straightened out financially.

What makes you think it's going to last?

Nothing. It won't . . . it can't last, you know; it's just that now at least we can decide to fuck up, we're at least free to decide to fuck up rather than bumping into it all the time.

The last time we talked about what you might do as a business by starting a true, small record company. Is that any more real now?

It's as real as it was then; that is to say, it still depends on whether or not . . . what it depends on is us getting out of our present contract, or it expiring. . . . Then we're in a position where we can start to think about that. We've been planning to do it seriously and really, but it's still a question of how best to . . . it's still an idea. See, Grunt Records is still RCA. There's no question about it. It's not *truly* independent.

199

And our fantasy is to be *completely* independent, if we can do it.

At this point it's open-ended. Obviously we want to be able to employ the people who are our friends. Who are talented and all that, and who are interested in what we're trying to do. That whole "Deadheads Unite" message [on the latest LP] was on that level. That's our story, like the basic groundwork, what we were gonna use.

Well, it's not a dislike for Warner Bros. but an antipathy towards the current form of record company systems.

Right. I don't think that they're that bad; I just think that they're incompetent. That's probably the worst thing about them. I don't object to the idea of record companies at all; in fact, record companies are *good*.

But we're already getting reports . . . this is the kind of thing that really fries me . . . we're getting reports that our new album has a slight skip on every record. Goddamn, it makes me want to scream. We go to every length we can to insure quality all along the line, on our end of it. We even suggest a place to Warner Bros. where they can have 'em pressed, where they can receive the attention that we want to give them.

I'm gonna do it with my own record, my solo record. Insist that they be pressed at a place that uses quality vinyl and allow the proper drying time and all the rest of that. Think of the billions of records that a big pressing plant has to rush through. Then when you hear that your record has a side that nobody can play, especially a double record, which is expensive, it just burns me. I feel that we have a responsibility to the people who put out their money for our record, because they are the people who are allowing us to continue what we're doing.

HOW DO YOU SURVIVE IN NEW *York, when you go on tour?*
For me, it's lock yourself in the hotel room more or less, turn on the TV, stay real high and hang out with your friends. That's one of the things about traveling with a band, like the Grateful Dead scene, a big family, and all that. You have an insular situation that reinforces what you believe to be true, although in New York it looks as though it maybe isn't.

I like to remain open to some extent, just in case there's anything to see. I don't like to turn people off, yet there are people calling up and they want to talk to me and stuff like that. It's only because of being a rock & roll star and all that which makes it very weird for me there. I think it would be groovy to go there and be anonymous, walk around and see what the street scene is like, but I've never been really able to do that.

What good things have you seen in New York—that you left yourself open for?

Well—it's mostly people. There are like good people in New York that are kind of bravely in the middle of it there, fighting the good battle. And . . . it's like year after year you go there, you see these same few people that are hassling it out in New York and you see New York just staying the same and . . . God, it's weird.

Do you find traveling on the road exhausting?

Yeah, yeah. The regular tour is exhausting, especially for us because we do a long show. We try and pace it so that we don't play every night, but it hardly ever works out that way. The alternatives are that you can either go out on the road and play as often as you possibly can and get it over with as quickly as possible and come back—that's like one school of thought that you can space it out and pace yourself while you're out on the road, but it means that you'll have to live out there for a while. We've tried a lot of different ways. This last tour [Spring 1971] was around the East Coast and it was shorter distances, 300–400 miles and that sort of thing, and we did a lot of traveling by bus, and that was really fun, we were just able to hang together all the time, we didn't have to go through a lot of airports and that. And we got to see some of the countryside. It was a little more like traveling and less like matter transmission.

But you play all night, that's what . . .

That's what makes it hard, that's what makes it really difficult. What we're doing now is working generally two or three nights in a town, in one spot, so that we have the advantage of being able to get into the room that we're playing so that it starts to sound good by about the second night and so that we don't have that oversold house and an uptight crowd that can't get in.

But really, it's getting trickier and trickier to do it, it's getting harder and harder. In Boston we played for two nights, and even so there were still about three or four thousand people outside each night that weren't able to get in because the place was sold out, and the police Maced them and did all that, it was . . . I mean, you wonder, you begin to wonder why you're doing it if what you're doing is leading people into a trap.

How many people go on the road?

This next time there's gonna be twenty-two going out; there's us and the New Riders, and our combined equipment guys, who are Jackson, Ramrod, our guys; and Sparky, who's one of the P.A. guys; and then there's this guy Gary, who's one of the New Riders' guys; and John Hagen, who's also one of the New Riders' guys. So there's those five guys, then there's Matthews, going out to mix, and then there's both bands, so that's twenty-two. Then there's Rock, he's going along, and Hunter's going along to do the radio stuff; it's great to have Hunter on the road, he's got like the *perfect* viewpoint, to be able to keep you from getting *too* crazy out there. The *more* of us there are, the cooler we stay, you know what I mean? If we go out there in a small group, we feel intimidated and get weird fast. If we go out there with a lot of us, it's much cooler. Going through airports and shit like that is much easier when there's twenty people straggling through. Fuck, they don't even want to mess with you. They don't want to know who you are or *nothing (laughs).* Get 'em outta here! Get 'em outta here! At any rate, *that's* the show.

WHAT HAPPENED AT ALTA-*mont? Did you see what was coming?*
No. God, no. It was completely unexpected. And that was the hard part—that was the hard lesson there—that you can have good people and good energy and work on a project and really want it to happen right and still have it all weird. It's the thing of knowing less than you should have. Youthful folly.

Reich: But the things you didn't know about had nothing to do with music; they had to do with logistics and they had to do with things commercial and economic. . . .

Yeah, but it was the music that generated it. I think that the music knew, it was known in the music. I realized when the Rolling Stones were playing at the crowd and the fighting was going on and the Rolling Stones were playing "Sympathy for the Devil," then I knew that I should have known. You know, you can't put that out without it turning up on you somewhere.

I remember seeing that scene down at the Heliport, waiting to fly over to Altamont.

Going over to the big rock festival.

Mountain Girl: And that girl trying to get on the helicopter, oh, man, was she weird.

And there were the Stones, walking around, and the Dead.

Totally weird.

I saw you talk to Mick for a second or two.

Mountain Girl: What did he ask? "What time is the helicopter coming?" he said. And his little entourage caught up with him and forced him away so he had to keep walking real fast to keep ahead of them.

When you look back on it, do you see anything in those moments leading up to it?

No, not really. I was completely unsuspecting. There was one thing beforehand that we all should have spotted. [Emmett] Grogan wrote up on the blackboard up at the Grateful Dead office, just as the site had been changed from whatever the first one was, he wrote a little slogan up on the blackboard which said something like "Charlie Manson Memorial Hippie Love Death Cult Festival." Something along those lines, something really funny, but ominous. And there had been—the street, certain people—certain elements of the street had been saying . . . it was a very weird time on the street in San Francisco at that time, if you recall. There was a lot of divisive hassling among all the various revolutionary scenes; the Red Guard was on one trip and Chicanos on some other trip and people were carrying guns and stuff, there was a lot of that kind of talk.

Originally the idea was that the Stones' thing was going to be a chance for all these various community elements to participate in a sort of a party for the Rolling Stones. That was the original concept, but then we couldn't have it in Golden Gate Park, so that really was the end of the plan as it was supposed to have happened. That eliminated the possibility for any community scene in San Francisco because of the transportation problem—how many Chicanos, Chinese or blacks or anything like that are going to be able to get a bus out to wherever the fuck? That was really the end of the original plan. And then we began operating on just sheer kinetic energy. . . . Rolling Stones was in the air, Rolling Stones, Rolling Stones, and thus it was just being swept along; but everybody was feeling—and it was all good people—everybody was feeling very good about it. Chet Helms was there doing stuff, and Emmett and Chip Monck and all these solid, together, hard-working people, but somehow the sense of it escaped everybody.

Whose idea was it to have the Stones to do the thing in the first place?

Rock and Sam originally conceived the idea, although it was, again, it was the music, it was an idea that was in the air. It was like San

Francisco had free stuff; the Rolling Stones hadn't been touring, they were suddenly going to be in the United States, somebody Rock used to know, Sam, and it just seemed as though it was an obvious step—and could have been under the right circumstances, I'm convinced—but it wasn't meant to be that.

Why do you think so?

I've thought about it a lot. A friend of mine, Steve Gaskin, capsulized it better than I ever could about, "Why did it happen?" Just period, "Why did it happen?" He said, and this has been quoted somewhere else, "Altamont was the little bit of sadism in your sex life, that the Rolling Stones put out in their music, coming back. It was the karma of putting that out for all those years, it was that little bit of red and black." Just there. The Hell's Angels, it's that same image.

Do you accept the necessity of having that in life, that little bit of evil?

Well, it's there, whether you accept it or not. It just has to do with how you conceive your own destiny or your own journeys through life. I just think that it's there, I'm not into judging it, really, it's not my game particularly—but I do know it's there.

People used Altamont as an attack point on rock & roll, to prove by it that rock & roll was no good.

That discussion is all gone now. I think that it's run its course and it's all over. There's too much other shit that's happening that's too important. We've seen a change of consciousness in the last year and a half traveling around the East Coast and places like that. People are really thinking differently. At last. I think that the whole negative thing is done what it's gonna do, it's killed a lot of people and left a lot of them . . . it always does. All we can hope is that the next cycle will be faster. We'll be able to say, "Ah, here it is. Zip! Here's your hat, what's your hurry?" That kind of thing. Get it out, quick. Run it through, run it through *fast.*

W HAT HAPPENED TO JANIS?
I think it was a mistake; I think it was an accident, like driving your car off the road. I don't think that there was any *why* to it, really. She probably hadn't had smack for a while or something like that . . . she probably had a few drinks or something after a gig, coming back to the hotel, take a hit and on out, go to sleep for the night, and it was probably more than she expected, and she just died. That's how easy it can happen; it can happen to anybody if you don't know what you're getting, and that's the way it is when you're having to deal with things that are illegal.

I think that it's the law that killed Janis, if anything killed her, because she couldn't go and get exactly the right hit for herself of exactly the proper purity in a drugstore and do herself up; she wouldn't be dead now. That's the thing that I think did it. In my opinion, Janis handled it pretty good, and she got a lot of weirdness, but she was more on top of it than a lot of people I've seen. I don't think that fame killed her, I don't think that being a celebrity killed her. She just accidentally, like cutting yourself with a razor or something, just accidentally died.

Reich: And Jim Morrison?

It's just—everybody dies. He was a musician, and that's the only reason people are talking about him dying. If Jim Morrison had been anybody else, nobody would be talking about Jim Morrison dying. And that's the same with every other musician. Statistically people die, and that's all. Every profession—people die in it.

What music do you listen to now?

I listen to all kinds of stuff, just all kinds of stuff.

Do you listen to the Band's records?

Some of them I do. At first I just wanta say, "Wow, they're getting into this repetitive bag," each time I hear the record for the first time. Then after a few weeks it starts creeping into the back of my mind and I start thinking, "Wow, what was that tune?" And I go and find the record and put it on . . . it's like scratching an itch. Some of them I really dig, others I probably will, and then other ones I think are halfway efforts; it's just like anybody. I dig their music more or less consistently, so I don't really know whether the record's good or not.

Which tunes on the new one do you like?

I love "Life Is a Carnival" . . . that's beautiful. Shit, that's great. All the stuff in there, all those great parts. The Dylan song is great, too. I love that song. I'll probably sing that with the barroom band. I like to do those kinda tunes. They're good songs, and good songs are fun to sing.

You like Robbie Robertson?

Yeah, yeah, he's one of the few guys I've ever liked. I went and visited with him one day, when we were on the East Coast. And I really dug being able to sit down and talk to him. It was just like that kinda stuff you do where you've never met anybody before, but you know what they do, and you respect them. We were both kinda there cause we'd been on that tour—we'd met before, actually—on that tour with Janis, that Canada thing. We got off on their music, of course, and they dug our music, 'cause really, they're kinda similar. We just have slightly different viewpoints of an almost similar trip.

When I got together with him, we were talking on pretty groovy grounds, in terms of mutual respect and understanding. It was good. We talked about guitars, and pianos, and music . . . and I went over and dug his studio. Just a friendly scene. It's one of those things that sometime in the future, I'd love to be able to spend some time and actually work with those guys, actually play music together with them, under some circumstances or another.

How would you describe his guitar playing?

He's one of those guys who descended from Roy Buchanan and those Fifties Fenderpickers. I can hear where he's picked up a lotta his stuff. His approach to it is more or less orchestral. The kinda stuff he plays and the music is like punctuation, and structural. He's an extremely subtle and refined guitar player, that's the way I think of him. I really admire him.

How would you describe your own guitar playing?

I don't know . . . I would describe my own guitar playing as descended from barroom rock & roll, country guitar. Just 'cause that's where all my stuff comes from. It's like that blues instrumental stuff that was happening in the late Fifties and early Sixties, like Freddie King.

But your guitar playing also has to do with the harmonic and the structural role. . . .

Right, and that has to do with the way I see myself in relation to the band that I'm playing in. . . . It must be like much the same way Robbie Robertson sees himself, in the sense that you write songs and you tend to think a certain way, about how the music is supposed to work, what kind of background you're lining up. It depends on whether you're approaching it on the level of a texture or whatever. I tend to think of it in terms of punctuation and stuff. Same thing.

When I get ready to go on the road, I make up cassettes of all my favorite music. Country & western stuff. Just whatever. Ali Akbar Khan; Crosby, Stills and Nash.

When did you decide to stop doing the blues stuff, the harder rock & roll thing, and go into the stressed harmonies?

That was really the result of hanging out with Crosby and those guys . . . just because they could sit down in any situation and pick up an acoustic guitar and it's instant music, these beautiful vocal harmonies.

I think that nothing really communicates like the human voice. It is really the ultimate instrument. I used to think of myself as a guitar player, but hearing singing, and seeing it up close, has kinda made me want to sing a lot; it just makes me want to do it, I don't really know what it is . . . and it's real satisfying to sing. I've always gotten off on a good singer, and that's what I'm basin' it on.

That's part of where our music wants to go, but it's record companies and the music business structure that's making it that difficult. It should be possible for everybody to do everything, especially in music, where music can only get better when people get together in different combinations. But record companies wanta be exclusive. They're getting looser and looser, and hopefully the thing could get loose enough where everybody could do whatever they want. That would be ideal.

What guitarists have you learned the most from?

I think Freddie King is the guy that I learned the most volume of stuff from. When I started playing electric guitar the second time, with the Warlocks, it was a Freddie King album that I got almost all my ideas off of, his phrasing, really. That first one, *Here's Freddie King,* later it came out as *Freddie King Plays Surfin' Music* or something like that, it has "San-Ho-Zay" on it and "Sensation" and all those instrumentals.

R EICH: I HAVE A QUESTION *right off one of the evening talk shows, and that is, "Dr. Garcia, how do you stay so high?"*

I smoke a lot of dope.

Reich: Do you think that's . . .

Would you like some?

Reich: Do you think that that's it?

Well, in reality I don't really stay that high, although I get high a lot, smoking a lot of pot, is what I'm trying to say. That's what it comes down to, but that doesn't necessarily mean that I'm high. A certain amount of seeming to be high has to do with my being more or less well rehearsed in the role of Jerry Garcia, 'cause it's kinda been laid on me. In reality, I'm like lots more worthless than any of that would make it appear.

Reich: Among the different things the kids say about you, one is "Mr. Good Vibes."

Yeah, but that always is part-true bullshit, because my old lady can tell you about how often I'm on a bummer. Really, I'm just like everybody else and it's just that I really love those times when I'm high, so my trip has always been to make them count as much as possible.

Reich: What I'm trying to get at is that you believe in being high, and many other people not only don't believe in it but think it's dangerous and hateful.

Well, you know, I . . . everybody's . . . one man's poison is another man's dope.

Reich: For instance, I believe in being high but not as much as you believe in it. In other words, I have more reservations about it than you do—or less experience with it, how about that?

That's it right there. I don't have that many illusions about it because I was never around in that world where you had to read about it. For me, it came in the form of dope. You got a joint, you didn't get a lecture; and you got a cap, you didn't get a treatise or any of that shit. You just got high; you took the thing and found out what happened to you; that's the only evidence there is. Being programmed by dope talk or any of that stuff is like somebody trying to tell you what it's like to fuck if you've never fucked anybody.

You can't know it that way, that's all, and also it'll put weird ideas in your head, misinformation and shit. Misinformation is the root of all . . . uh . . . ah . . . er . . . ah . . . ignorance—nah, that's not it—ineffectuality . . . nah, fuck it, well, nice try, maybe next time.

Really, I don't think that. I think that the whole discussion about drugs, whether to take them or not, is like . . . well, I don't think that there's a *side* on that. I know a lot of people who I respect super-highly that don't take anything, and, of course, I know people that get really high and I respect them as highly, too; and I know far-out junkies. There are people doing everything, and I just don't think that *anything's* it.

Reich: How do you manage to be so optimistic?

Music is a thing that has optimism built into it. Optimism is another way of saying "space." Music has infinite space. You can go as far into music as you can fill millions of lifetimes. Music is an infinite cylinder, it's open-ended, it's space. The *form* of music has infinite space as a part of it, and that, in itself, means that its momentum is essentially in that open place.

Reich: You said you would only play on optimistic days or I said I would only write on optimistic days.

That might be optimum, but my experience has been that a lot of times we've played sets that we didn't like or that I didn't like, or I didn't like what I was doing, but it got on and it sounded good on tape and the audience got on. There's lots of degrees. I don't like to try to paint

everything in those real, specific cartoony figures because there's degrees all over the place. For example, if I'm super-, superdepressed, I sometimes play the highest music I play.

Reich: How do you do it?

Because music can contain all of it. It can contain your bummers, it can contain your depressions, it can contain the black despair, man, it can contain the whole spectrum. The blues is a perfect example. The blues is that very effect, operating in a very sublime way. You hardly ever hear anybody say they're depressed because they've heard a lot of music. That's a pretty good example, right there. Even the worst music—the poorest, baddest, most ill-thought-of music on earth—doesn't hurt anybody.

Reich: I know some people that are angry at Lennon's album with the screaming and crying, they call it self-pity. Does that bother you?

No. I love the album myself.

Reich: I love it, too. It's very different from the kind of music the Dead plays.

That's true, but we haven't been exposed to the really extreme pressure that John Lennon has.

Reich: I read a book on rock & roll recently that said the real medium of rock & roll is records and that concerts are only repeats of records. I guess the Grateful Dead represents the opposite of that idea.

Right. Our records are definitely not it or ever have been. The things we do depend so much upon the situation we're in and upon a sort of a magic thing. We aren't in such total control of our scene that we can say, "Tonight's the night, it's going to be magic tonight." We can only say we're going to try it tonight. And whether it's magic or not is something we can't predict and nobody else can predict; and even when it's over and done with, it's one of those things where nobody's really sure. It's subtle and it's elusive, but it's real.

Reich: And the magic comes not just from you but from the whole thing.

The whole thing. The unfortunate thing about the concert situation for us is the stage; and the audience has either a dance floor where they all sit down or seats where they all stand up. It's too inflexible to allow something new to emerge. It's a box that we've been operating in; and we've been operating in it as a survival mechanism, yet hoping to get off when we can. But basically it's not set up to let us get off, and it's not set up for the audience to get off either. The reason is that anarchy and chaos are things that scare everybody, or scare a lot of the people—except for the people that get into it.

Why doesn't it scare you?

Because I've had enough experience with it to where I like it. It's where new stuff happens. I have never understood exactly why people get scared, but they do get scared for reasons, like to protect oneself, to protect one's own personal visions of oneself. They're all paranoid reasons. That's the thing you stimulate if you fight it. It's like any high-energy experience; if you fight it, it hurts; if you go with it, it's like surfing, it's like catching a big wave.

Reich: Do you think they don't believe in magic?

I think that our audience definitely does. Or, rather than dwell on the idea of magic, they know that there's a certain phenomenon that *can* happen, and if they come to see us enough, they've observed it, they've seen it, they've been part of it. And that's the payoff. That's the reason to keep on doing it. We know that it can happen, and the problem has been in trying to figure out how can we make that happen and at the same time keep our whole scene together on a survival level. And that's essentially what we're doing.

Reich: Why is it important to get high? Why is it important to stay high? What good does it do anybody—the world, the community or people themselves?

To get really high is to forget yourself. And to forget yourself is to see everything else. And to see everything else is to become an understanding molecule in evolution, a conscious tool of the universe. And I think every human being should be a conscious tool of the universe. That's why I think it's important to get high.

Reich: Getting zonked out or unconscious is a whole different thing.

I'm not talking about unconsciousness or zonked out, I'm talking about being fully conscious. Also I'm not talking about the Grateful Dead as being an end in itself. I don't think of that highness as being an end in itself. I think of the Grateful Dead as being a crossroads or a pointer sign, and what we're pointing to is that there's a lot of universe available, that there's a whole lot of experience available over here. We're kinda like a signpost, and we're *also* pointing to danger, to difficulty, we're pointing to bummers. We're pointing to whatever there is, when we're on—when it's really happening.

You're a signpost to new space?

Yes. That's the place where we should be—that's the function we should be filling in society. And in our own little society, that's the function we do fill. But in the popular world—the media world and so forth—we're just a rock & roll band.

We play rock & roll music and it's part of our form—our vehicle, so to speak—but it's not who we are totally. Like Moondog in New York City who walks around, he's a signpost to otherness. He's a signpost to something that isn't concrete. It's that same thing.

Where did you get the idea about pointing to some new place?

We never formulated it, it just was what was happening. We were doing the Acid Test, which was our first exposure to formlessness. Formlessness and chaos lead to new forms. And new order. Closer to, probably, what the real order is. When you break down the old orders and the old forms and leave them broken and shattered, you suddenly find yourself a new space with new form and new order which are more like the way it is. More like the flow.

And we just *found* ourselves in that place. We never decided on it, we never thought it out. None of it. This is a thing that we've observed in the scientific method. We've watched what happens.

What we're really dedicated to is not so much *telling* people, but to *doing* that thing and getting high. That's the thing; that's the payoff, and that's the whole reason for doing it, right there.

Reich: Does the new culture scene seem to be falling to pieces?

It does *seem* to be doing that, but it always seems to be doing that. It depends on what level you're looking at it. If you're looking at it on the level of what you *hear* about it, yeah, it's going to pieces. If you look at it on the level of the guys you know and what they're doin', I think that things are going pretty good. Everybody I know is doing stuff and nobody I know is on a particularly declining trip.

Reich: That's what I see; individual people are doing fine. Then why are we being told that it's all dying and falling apart?

I think that the people that are interested in it not dying and falling apart are probably a lot closer than we think they are. I think that's probably it. There's *always* somebody that has to say that it's *not* happening; and the people who are into saying that it's not happening are the people that aren't into stuff.

Reich: You refuse to say that the rock music world is going through some terrible times and seems to be dying.

I think the whole world is going through a terrible thing.

What about the new culture?

I don't see the rock & roll scene as being the new culture. I think the rock & roll scene is just the rock & roll scene. Basically it's a professional trip. It's business and stuff like that and that the music and musicians are still a whole other world really, and I don't think that what the musicians are up to and what their heads are like is ever really filtered out into that world. The "rock scene" is a fabrication of media. Anytime you have people doing the same thing, you have shoptalk, you have a shop scene, you have a professional scene. Because music is a high-energy trip and it's important nowadays, it's this thing called the rock scene. But I know an artists' scene that's at least as clannish as the rock scene—the comic book artists' scene. It's all kinds of scenes that are all doing stuff, and accomplishing stuff and creating stuff and defining culture and doing all those things that everybody says they're doing. They really are doing it, but I think that what is really new and what is happening now in the postrevolutionary thing is not being focused upon. I think that it's good that it's not, because it might have a chance to develop into something that really works before the focus lays in on it.

I think that what's happening is an almost infinite number of possibilities of ways to live your life are being thought out. Ultimately people are going to be able to choose any possibility and find a scene that does it.

Reich: How are you going to communicate between one kind of scene to another?

Just by hanging out.

Reich: The music scene comes to me through records. And it isn't that hard to translate. Some people think it is.

No. I think everybody sees. Now everybody in America has had so much of the same kind of influence; communication is supereasy, and images and stuff are available to everybody; and it's possible to really lay stuff out and have people know what it is. The problem with artists communicating is that the old avant-garde art world is doing what it was doing twenty years ago—it's dying and it's pretty much dead now. The new stuff, which has real energy, real vitality and really talks to people on the level of what's going on in their lives, on the level of what their personal images are and so forth, works. It's like new definitions of what has been lost in our culture in terms of where art fits in or where culture fits into people—whatever those weird terms are.

Reich: Well, it's all in the way we tell each other

about what we've found out. This leads me to our ending, something that we agree about although we come from very different worlds. We both think that everybody really knows the truth underneath all their appearances. Could you just say what you think that means, and then I'll say what I think it means.

What the truth is?

Reich: Well, when we both say that everybody knows something that most people aren't letting on to.

I don't know what it means. There is some basic premise there are some basic forces that are occurring in the universe that—in inhabiting this universe—you can't escape knowing what they are. I think of it as a universal—a cosmic conspiracy. Or, the information we're plugged into is the universe itself, and everybody knows that on a cellular level. It's built in. Just superficial stuff like what happened to you in your lifetime is nothing compared to the container which holds all your information. And there's a similarity in all our containers. We are all one organism, we are all the universe, we are all doing the same thing. That's the sort of thing that everybody knows, and I think that it's only weird little differences that are making it difficult. And there's been a trend among humans to try to stop everything, that we're going to stop the force called change in the universe and we're going to stay here. But it just doesn't happen. The thing that everyone should know is that *change* is the thing that's happening, all the time, and that it's okay to change your clothes, it's okay to change your face, it's okay to change anything. You *can* change. And you can create change. And you can do it knowing that it's what you're supposed to do.

Reich: You and I and all the others in this thing have almost a conspiracy going among us.

There's no losing. I think the way you can have a conspiracy is to have trust. A certain kind of trust. For example, the way the old power dynasties were built was somebody would marry somebody's sister and stuff like that and it would be blood trust, which is the old way of thinking it. But now it's like a new family trust—global village trust. The thing is that we're all earthlings. And in the face of the enormity of the *cosmos*, it's best for us to stick together as earthlings. The earthling consciousness is the one that's really trying to happen at this juncture and so far it's only a tiny little glint, but it's already over. The change has already happened, and it's a matter of swirling out.

It has already happened. We're living after the fact. It's a postrevolutionary age. The change is over. The rest of it is a cleanup action. Unfortunately it's very slow. Amazingly slow and amazingly difficult.

Reich: But everybody knows it now?

Well, if they don't, they will.

Reich: So the thing is to keep on . . .

Keep it on, keep it on. Just keep on keeping on, folks.

17

INTERVIEWED BY JON LANDAU (1972)

Paul Simon, one of the finest songwriters of our time, got a Number One record his first time out with singing partner Art Garfunkel. "Sounds of Silence" was followed by "Homeward Bound"; "I Am a Rock"; the *Bookends* album; another Number One, "Mrs. Robinson" (thanks to the movie, *The Graduate);* the watershed *Bridge Over Troubled Water;* and a third Number One single, the title song.

And then Simon dissolved the partnership and started all over again. He was thirty-one and just launching his solo career with his "first" album when this interview was done by associate editor and record reviewer Jon Landau in the spring of 1972. Their three days together produced thirteen hours of tape, as Landau recalls, "for some poor soul to transcribe."

Simon's second album was *There Goes Rhymin' Simon* (which produced the gospel-powered hit, "Loves Me Like a Rock"), and while he's been something short of prolific, he's made each effort worth waiting for. In 1980, he made his acting debut in a film he wrote, *One Trick Pony.* He is no longer married to Peggy, mentioned in the interview, but his relationship with his family is reflected in both the movie and his 1975 album, *Still Crazy After All These Years.*

As for Landau, the former "dean of rock critics" went into producing records, doing well with Livingston Taylor and Jackson Browne, and doing spectacularly well with Bruce Springsteen.
—B F-T

PAUL SIMON DIVIDES HIS TIME BE-tween a farm in Pennsylvania and a triplex, once owned by guitarist André Segovia, in New York's Upper East Side, where the interview was taped. Peggy, Paul's wife, was present only briefly. She and Paul are expecting their first child in September.

Paul had just completed production on the first

PAUL

SIMON

album of his friends Los Incas, whom he used for the background track on "El Condor Pasa." In September and October he plans to produce his second solo album and in November will embark on a national tour.

We had not met before and so found ourselves getting to know each other while doing the job. I found him open on virtually every subject, but always deliberate and intent on saying exactly what he meant. His voice and pace would become more measured when the subject became more important. I realized he really did approach this interview the same way he approaches writing, recording, performing—as a perfectionist.

WAS THERE A SPECIFIC CONfrontation or meeting or decision that finalized the breakup of Simon and Garfunkel?

No, I don't think there was. During the making of *Bridge over Troubled Water* there were a lot of times when it just wasn't fun to work together. It was very hard work, and it was complex. I think Artie said that he felt that he didn't want to record, and I know I said I felt that if I had to go through these kinds of personality abrasions, I didn't want to continue to do it. Then when the album was finished, Artie was going to do *Carnal Knowledge,* and I went to do an album by myself. We didn't say, "That's the end." We didn't know if it was the end or not. But it became apparent by the time the movie was out and by the time my album was out that it was over.

What were the immediate feelings brought on after the split?

Having a track record to live up to and the history of successes had become a hindrance. It becomes harder to break out of what people expect you to do. From that point of view, I'm delighted that I didn't have to write a Simon and Garfunkel followup to "Bridge over Troubled Water," which I think would have been an inevitable letdown for people. It would have been hard on me, hard on both of us. But more hard on the writer, because he takes the responsibility. If an album stiffs, I think to myself it stiffed because I didn't come up with the big songs.

So dissolving Simon and Garfunkel was a way of unburdening yourself of a lot of pressure.

Yes. And it left me free to do what I want. I wanted to sing other types of songs that Simon and Garfunkel wouldn't do. "Mother and Child Reunion," for example, is not a song that you would have normally thought that Simon and

Garfunkel would have done. It's possible that they might have. But it wouldn't have been the same, and I don't know whether I would have been so inclined in that direction. So for me it was a chance to back out and gamble a little bit; it's been so long since it was a gamble.

When Simon and Garfunkel were most active doing concerts—around '68—what was the day-to-day relationship like between the two of you? How did you function on the road?

Things were pretty pleasant from the point of view of us getting along. It was hard and boring to travel so much. But at the end, during the concerts in 1970, I would go with Peggy, and everyone would bring whomever they wanted, and it was more like festivals because we didn't go out too much, and when we did go out, we went to places we wanted to play, Paris or London. . . .

Anything on the road contribute to the breakup?

I don't think the road had much to do in exacerbating our relationship because, first of all, we weren't on the road that much in the end. The breakup had to do with a natural drifting apart as we got older and the separate lives that were more individual. We weren't so consumed with recording and performing. We had other activities. I had different people and different interests, and Artie's interest in film led him to other people. His acting took him away, and that led him into other areas. The only strain was to maintain a partnership.

Because it was unnatural?

You gotta work at a partnership. You have to work at it, you got to . . .

But at this point it was not a natural one.

At this point there was no great pressure to stay together, other than money, which exerted really very little influence upon us. We certainly weren't going to stay together to make a lot of money. We didn't need the money. And musically, it was not a creative team, too much, because Artie is a singer, and I'm a writer and player and a singer. We didn't work together on a creative level and prepare the songs. I did that. When we came into the studio I became more and more me, making the tracks and choosing the musicians, partly because a great deal of the time during *Bridge,* Artie wasn't there. I was doing things myself with Roy Halee, our engineer and co-producer. We were planning tracks out, and, to a great degree, that responsibility fell to me.

Artie and I shared responsibility but not creativity. For example, we always said Artie does the arranging. Anybody who knows anything would know that that was a fabrication—how can one guy write the songs and the other guy do the arranging? How does that happen? If a guy writes the song, he obviously has a concept. But when it came to making decisions it had always been Roy, Artie and me. And this later became difficult for me.

I viewed Simon and Garfunkel as basically a three-way partnership. Each person had a relatively equal say. So, in other words, if Roy and Artie said, "Let's do a long ending on 'The Boxer,'" I said, "Two out of three," and did it their way. I didn't say, "Hey, this is my song, I don't want it to be like that." Never did it occur to me to say that. "Fine," I'd say.

It wasn't until my own album that I ever started to think to myself, "What do I really like?" Roy would say, "That's a great vocal, listen to that." And I would listen, and I wouldn't think it was great, but he said it was great, so I believed it was great. I just suspended my judgment. I let him do it. On my own album I learned every aspect of it has to be your own judgment. You have to say, "Now, wait a minute, is that the right tempo? Is that the right take?" It's your decision. Nobody else can do it.

You said that more and more on 'Bridge' you were exercising the judgment and making the plans. Is it that Artie wasn't that interested?

It's hard to say, but I guess that's true—no, I can't say that. He had other interests that were very strong. But he certainly was interested in making the record. From the point of view of creativity, I didn't have any other interests than the music; I had no other distractions. On several tracks on *Bridge* there's no Artie on it at all. "The Only Living Boy in New York," he sang a little on the background. "Baby Driver," he wasn't there. He was doing *Catch-22* in Mexico at that time. It's a Simon and Garfunkel record, but not really. And it became easier to work by separating. On *Bridge over Troubled Water* there are many songs where you don't hear Simon and Garfunkel singing together. Because of that the separation became easier.

What was his reaction when he'd come back and you'd show him all this stuff?

"Bridge over Troubled Water" was written while he was away. He'd come back and I'd say, "Here's a song I just wrote, 'Bridge over Troubled Water.' I think you should sing it."

It seems as if his absences would tend to make you more resentful if he were to reject any of your ideas. Did they?

That's true. If I'd say, "We'll do this with a gospel piano, and it's written in your key, so you

have the song," it was his right in the partnership to say, "I don't want to do that song," as he said with "Bridge over Troubled Water."

He didn't want to do it altogether, or he didn't want to sing it himself?

He didn't want to sing it himself. He couldn't hear it for himself. He felt I should have done it. And many times I think I'm sorry I didn't do it. Many times on a stage, though, when I'd be sitting off to the side and Larry Knechtel would be playing the piano and Artie would be singing "Bridge," people would stomp and cheer when it was over, and I would think, "That's my song, man. Thank you very much. I wrote that song." I must say this: in the earlier days when things were smoother I never would have thought that, but towards the end when things were strained I did. It's not a very generous thing to think, but I did think that.

Do you mark the strain from 'Catch-22' or does it go back before that?

I think it started before that.

When did you become aware of it?

There was always some kind of strain, but it was workable. The bigger you get, the more of a strain it is, because in your everyday life, you're less used to compromising. As you get bigger, you have your own way. But in a partnership you always have to compromise. So all day long I might be out telling this lawyer to do that or this architect to build a house in a certain way, and you expect everything. You're the boss. When you get into a partnership, you're not the boss. There's no boss. That makes it hard.

There's eleven songs on *Bridge over Troubled Water*, but there were supposed to be twelve. I had written a song called "Cuba Sí, Nixon No." And Artie didn't want to do it. We even cut the track for it. Artie wouldn't sing on it. And Artie wanted to do a Bach chorale thing, which I didn't want to do. We were fightin' over which was gonna be the twelfth song, and then I said, "Fuck it, put it out with eleven songs, if that's the way it is." We were at the end of our energies over that.

We had just finished working on this television special, which really wiped us out because of all the fighting that went on, not amongst ourselves but with the Bell Telephone people. We were very tired. It was all happening in the fall. We did a tour in October. We filmed the television special from September until October. We then had to postpone working on the album until the TV special and the tour were over. And then we went into December, and we had to stop for Christmas, and we didn't finish the album

211

until like the first week in January. We were really exhausted, and we fought over that. Well, at that point I just wanted out; I just wanted to take a vacation. So did he, I guess. So we stopped at eleven songs.

The obvious question is why didn't it split up earlier?

That is a really good question. The answer has to go back to me. I always looked for partnership because I probably felt I couldn't do it myself. I would have been afraid or embarrassed. So I looked to work with a bunch of people. "We'll all do this. Actually, I'll do it all, but we'll all take the credit or take the blame." Peggy brought me out of that and made me feel like I should do it myself and take the responsibility. If it's good, it's yours, and if it's bad, it's yours, too. Go out and do your thing and say, "This is my thing."

One of the things that upset me was some of the criticism leveled at Simon and Garfunkel. I always took exception to it, but actually I agree with a lot of it, but I didn't feel it was me. Like that it was very sweet. I didn't particularly like sweet soft music. I did like sweet soft music, but not exclusively.

You thought Artie was contributing a lot to that?

That is Artie's taste. Artie's taste is much more to the sweet, and so is Roy's. Sweet and big and lush. More than me. There's nothing wrong with that; there's a place for lushness. It's not generally the way I go. This is what I've said on the new album to Roy. I want the tempo to be right; I want it to be a good tempo. I want to get like the basic rhythm section and one coloring instrument, maybe, like in "Duncan," the flutes and "Peace Like the River." That has its own coloring. . . .

───────────

S IMON AND GARFUNKEL WERE *known for their fastidiousness in recording. You seem to be looser on your own.*

It was all three of us, but particularly Artie and Roy. Many times I had arguments where I wanted to leave in something that was poorly recorded because it had the right feel, and they would always end up doing it again. They'd say, "It's bad, I didn't like it, I didn't mike it right, it was the first take and I didn't really get the balance," and I'd say, "I don't care, leave it. Leave it." That was the three-way partnership coming back to haunt me. Everybody has a voice, and everybody's voice is equal.

Was 'Bridge' your best album?

Yes. *Bridge* has better songs. And it has better singing. It is freer, in its own way. "Cecelia," for example, was made in a living room on a Sony. We were all pounding away and playing things. That was all it was. *Tick a tong tick a tick a tong tuck a tuck a toong tuck a* . . . on a Sony, and I said, "That's a great rhythm set, I love it." Every day I'd come back from the studio, working on whatever we were working on, and I'd play this pounding thing. So then I said, "Let's make a record out of that." So we copied it over and extended it double the amount, so now we have three minutes of track, and the track is great. So now I pick up the guitar and I start to go, "Well, this will be like the guitar part"—*dung chicka dung chicka dung,* and lyrics were virtually the first lines I said: "You're breakin' my heart, I'm down on my knees." They're not lines at all, but it was right for that song, and I like that. It was like a little piece of magical fluff, but it works.

"El Condor Pasa" I like. That track was originally a record. The track is originally a recording on Phillips, a Los Incas record that I love. I said, "I love this melody. I'm going to write lyrics to it. I just love it, and we'll just sing it right over the track."

That's what it is, and that works pretty different. "Bridge" is a very strong melodic song.

How was 'Bridge over Troubled Water' recorded?

We were in California. We were all renting this house. Me and Artie and Peggy were living in this house with a bunch of other people throughout the summer. It was a house on Blue Jay Way, the one George Harrison wrote "Blue Jay Way" about. We had this Sony machine and Artie had the piano, and I'd finished working on a song, and we went into the studio. I had it written on guitar, so we had to transpose the song. I had it written in the key of G, and I think Artie sang it in E. E flat. We were with Larry Knechtel, and I said, "Here's a song; it's in G, but I want it in E flat. I want it to have a gospel piano." So, first we had to transpose the chords, and there was an arranger who used to do some work with me, Jimmie Haskell, who, as a favor, he said, "I'll write the chords; you call off the chord in G, and I'll write it in E flat." And he did that. That was the extent of what he did. He later won a Grammy for that. We'd put his name down as one of the arrangers.

Then it took us about four days to get the piano part. Each night we'd work on the piano part until Larry really honed it into a good part.

Now, the song was originally two verses, and in the studio, as Larry was playing it, we decided—I believe it was Artie's idea, I can't remember, but I think it was Artie's idea to add another verse, because Larry was sort of elongating the piano part, so I said, "Play the piano part for a third verse again, even though I don't have it, and I'll write it," which I eventually did after the fact. I always felt that you could clearly see that it was written afterwards. It just doesn't sound like the first two verses.

Then the piano part was finished. Then we added bass—two basses, one way up high, the high bass notes. Joe Osborn did that. Then we added vibes in the second verse just to make the thing ring a bit. Then we put the drum on, and we recorded the drum in an echo chamber, and we did it with a tape-reverb that made the drum part sound different from what it actually was, because of that afterbeat effect. Then we gave it out to have a string part written. This was all in L.A. And then we came back to New York and did the vocals. Artie spent several days on the vocals.

Punching in a lot {recording in small segments to achieve greater control and accuracy}.

Yes. I'd say altogether that song took somewhere around ten days to two weeks to record, and then it had to be mixed.

"Bridge" was gospel, "El Condor" was South American, "Mother and Child" was reggae—you seem to be incredibly eclectic.

I like the other kinds of music. The amazing thing is that this country is so provincial. Americans know American music. You go to France: They know a lot of kinds of music. You go to Japan, and they know a lot of indigenous popular music. But Americans never get into the South American music; I fell into Los Incas, I loved it. It's got nothing to do with our music, but I liked it anyway. The Jamaican thing, there's nobody getting into a Jamaican thing. Jamaicans have a lot of good music, an awful lot.

That one you really pulled off—"Mother and Child Reunion."

I got that by making a mistake. Because "Why Don't You Write Me?" was supposed to sound like that, but it came out a bad imitation. So I said, "I'm not going to get it out of the regular guys. I gotta get it out of the guys who know it." And I gotta go down there willing to change for them. I started to play with them. I started to show them the song and play, and we started to work it out, and they were playing, and I would play, but I couldn't play with it. Couldn't fit.

So I sat down and said, "You play it. Play what you want." That's the key thing. Let them play whatever they want, and then you change. You go their way. That's how you get that.

You didn't have the words to that song written when you recorded the track?

I didn't. Know where the words came from on that? You never would have guessed. I was eating in a Chinese restaurant downtown. There was a dish called "Mother and Child Reunion." It's chicken and eggs. And I said, "Oh, I love that title. I gotta use that one."

I read a lot into that one.

Well, that's all right. What you read in was damn accurate, because what happened was this: Last summer we had a dog that was run over and killed, and we loved this dog. It was the first death I had ever experienced personally. Nobody in my family died that I felt that. But I felt this loss—one minute there, next minute gone, and then my first thought was, "Oh, man, what if that was Peggy? What if somebody like that died? Death, what is it, I can't get it." And there were lyrics straight out forward like that. "I can't for the life of me remember a sadder day. I just can't believe it's so." Those are the lyrics. The chorus for "Mother and Child Reunion"—well, that's out of the title. Somehow there was a connection between this death and Peggy, and it was like heaven, I don't know what the connection was. Some emotional connection. It didn't matter to me what it was. I just knew it was there.

I still don't see why you would do the track before you had written the words. Why did you do that?

I had no words. The words I had I never intended to use. But sometimes you get a very good record that way because you fit the words right to the track. You play with the feel of the track and the words.

The humor on 'Paul Simon' is elusive.

Yes. For example, at the beginning at "Papa Hobo," it opens light because it's stylized. It's an obviously constructed line. It's not a cry of anguish. It's too thought out. It's carbon monoxide and the old Detroit perfume. It's satirical. The "basketball town" line. It's got a little bit of bitterness, but it's also, it's in it's own way, an element of humor and a putdown of a place, a basketball town. It reminds me of a Midwest thing. The "Gatorade" line . . .

I hate that word "Gatorade". . . .

That's why I use it. That word doesn't belong in a song. It comes out, and there it is. It's the whole thing. It's where that guy came from.

You have said that "Run Your Body Down" had a

213

comic intent. *But the title line is a very real thing to many people.*

It is true. I don't mean it to be any less serious by the fact that I feel that there's humor in it. I think that that's a delicate combination. If you can get humor and seriousness at the same time, you've created a special little thing, and that's what I'm looking for, because if you get pompous, you lose everything. If I should write a preachy song about "for God's sake, take care of your health" it would sound like a Nichols and May bit: "My God, your mother and I are sick with worry." You can't do it in a song. Even "Me and Julio," it's pure confection.

What is it that the mama saw? The whole world wants to know.

I have no idea what it is.

Four people said that was the first thing I would ask you.

Something sexual is what I imagine, but when I say "something," I never bothered to figure out what it was. Didn't make any difference to me. First of all, I think it's funny to sing—"Me and Julio." It's very funny to me. And when I started to sing "Me and Julio," I started to laugh, and that's when I decided to make the song called "Me and Julio"; otherwise I wouldn't have made it that. I like the line about the radical priest. I think that's funny to have in a song. "Peace Like a River" is a serious song. It's a serious song, although it's not as down as you think. The last verse is sort of nothing; it sort of puts the thing back up in the air, which is where it should be. You end up, you think about these things that are something to do with a riot, or something in my mind in the city.

W HAT WAS SIMON AND GAR-*funkel's vocal style?*

S&G's vocal sound was very often closely worked-out harmony, doubled, using four voices, but doubled right on, so that a lot of times you couldn't tell it was four voices.

Not four-part harmony?

No. Four voices. "The Boxer" is four voices.

You're each singing your part twice—doubled back?

Singing it twice. "Mrs. Robinson" was four voices.

Harmonically, was there a lot of progression?

There wasn't a lot of harmony on it. The thing that I learned at the end of S&G was to let Artie do his thing, and let me do my thing, and come together for a thing. All of the other albums up until then, they're almost all harmony on every song. How much can you do with two voices? You can sing thirds or you can sing fifths or you can do a background harmony. Something like "The Only Living Boy in New York," where we create that big voice, all those voices in the background. That's my favorite one on that whole album, actually. The first time those background voices come in.

You recorded the album 'Sounds of Silence' in New York, Los Angeles and where else?

We tried a few cuts in Nashville. We did "Flowers Never Bend with the Rainfall." Was that on that album? [It was on *Parsley, Sage, Rosemary and Thyme.*] We tried to cut "I Am a Rock" in Nashville, and it didn't work. At that time, we had an asset that we didn't know about, which was our engineer in New York—Roy Halee.

We really didn't know Roy too well. We did "Wednesday Morning" with him, but we didn't have any sort of relationship with him. He was a young engineer at Columbia who was coming up and nice to get along with, but we didn't pay much attention to him; we looked to the producer for direction. It took a while to realize that the people who were getting what we wanted was the three of us, Arthur and me and Roy. So at that time Roy was the engineer, and he was making things good, but we weren't saying, "This is the engineer who's really doing a good job."

'Sounds of Silence' is a morbid album. It has suicides and . . .

That's right. I tend to think of that period as a very late adolescence. Those kind of things have a big impact on an adolescent mind, suicides and people who are very sad or very lonely. You tend to dramatize those things.

It depends on the song. "A Most Peculiar Man," which dealt with a suicide—that was written in England because I saw a newspaper article about a guy who committed suicide. In those days it was easier to write because I wasn't known, and it didn't matter if I wrote a bad song. I'd write a song in a night and play it around in the clubs, and people were very open then. No attention and so, no criticism.

Now I have stndards. Then I didn't have standards. I was a beginning writer then, so I wrote anything I saw. Now I sift. Now I say, "Well, that's not really a subject that I want to write a song about."

How was 'Parsley, Sage, Rosemary and Thyme'

approached differently from 'Sounds of Silence'?

Time. A lot more time. Also there was "The Dangling Conversation," which was with strings.

Whose idea was the strings?

I don't even remember now. All of us, probably. See, "The Sound of Silence" was our first single, our second was "Homeward Bound" and our third was "I Am a Rock." They were all three of them pretty good-sized hits. "The Sound of Silence" was a big hit. Our fourth record was "The Dangling Conversation," and it was not a big hit. Neither in sales, nor did it go into the Top Ten.

It must have been disappointing to you then. . . .

It was amazingly disappointing. Absolutely amazing. Between the ages of fifteen and twenty-two, I had made only one very minor hit at the age of fifteen and then flops. So I expected everything to be a flop. I was utterly amazed that "The Sound of Silence" was a big hit. More amazed that "Homeward Bound" was a big hit. By the time "I Am a Rock" was a big hit, I started to think, "Now I'm making hits," so now I got amazed when "The Dangling Conversation" wasn't a big hit. Why it wasn't a big hit is hard to know. It probably wasn't as good a song. It was too heavy.

But anyway, this album starts to be more elaborate as far as time; I remember we spent about at least four months on it. Three or four months, and I remember then, that was the first time people started to say, "Boy, you really take a lot of time to make records." Columbia, they'd said that.

What was Johnston's reaction to your taking so much time?

Fine, he didn't object. The whole time thing is a record company problem. They want you to put out records rapidly so that they can sell them. That's all they're concerned with—sales. Also, time costs a lot of money. *Parsley, Sage* started to get into the category of what albums cost today. Albums are $30,000 and upwards today, $30,000 for a medium-sized rock album. I'd say it costs between $50,000 and maybe up to $150,000.

What's the most you've spent?

I don't know. I never look at the bills. But I would say it's between $50,000 and $100,000.

These were being done on eight-track?

Sounds of Silence was done on four-track, but then we started on eight.

Did you overdub the voice back then?

We almost always overdubbed the voice, because I was playing acoustic guitar and it was hard to get decent separation between my voice and the guitar.

So from the beginning you were making a more conscious use of the studio.

Both of us had a significant amount of studio time prior to our Columbia recording days. I did a lot of demos.

Do you mean demos of your own songs?

No. Other people's songs. I was a kid of seventeen or eighteen years old who could come in and learn a song and sing it in various styles. So a publisher would get a song and they'd say, "This song would be great for Dion." So we'd get somebody in, and I would be Dion, and then I'd sing all the background, "ooh ooh wah ooh." I'd do all those things and then sing the lead and for that get paid fifteen dollars a song. I did that when I was in school, and that's how I learned a lot about the studio. I learned about overdubbing. I learned about mikes. I learned how to sing on a mike.

At the beginning, you didn't have that much sense of how much you could actually control your own thing. You would just skip the mix, wouldn't you?

We didn't show up for the mix on *Sounds of Silence*.

Did you on 'Parsley, Sage'?

Parsley, Sage, we mixed it. It was the first eight-track session we did at Columbia. We were the first people to get them to do eight-track, and we were the first people to get them to go to sixteen-track.

"Get them to"—what do you mean? You did these albums at Columbia recording studios . . .

Yes.

. . . and you pressured them to get sixteen.

Right. The first thing we did in sixteen-track was "The Boxer." It wasn't a sixteen-track machine; it was two eight-track machines synchronized, and it was a bitch to get them to work together. In other words, you had to press the button at the same time to record that way. It was hard. Halee rigged it out. It was hard.

When you come to 'Bookends,' you're making full use of the studio.

That album had the most use of the studio, I'd say, of all the Simon and Garfunkel records.

Where do you rate it among all the albums that Simon and Garfunkel did?

Right below *Bridge*. I rate each album as better than the last one. That's how I see it. In *Bookends*, we started taking much more time with the singing. I remember, in *Bookends*, we were into punching in.

You weren't in 'Parsley, Sage'?

Well, we might have repaired a line or something like that, but the concept in *Parsley, Sage* wasn't to get each line perfect, and it was in *Bookends.*

Sometimes that turns into a compulsive thing.

To a degree, that would happen to Simon and Garfunkel. They'd get too perfect, which could be disturbing. A part of Roy and Artie's thing more than mine. Because I always liked more sloppiness than they did. They got to the point where it had to be just right. Sometimes it worked. Like, "Mrs. Robinson" was punched in a lot, and it worked really good. *Bookends* was recorded sort of half and half. *Bookends* is really the one side.

And the other was made up of the most recent singles.

With the exception of "Mrs. Robinson," which was recorded at the same time as the songs on the *Bookends* side. Those other songs were for me, the dry patch of Simon and Garfunkel, which was from "The Dangling Conversation." I think the next was "Hazy Shade of Winter," "At the Zoo" and "Fakin' It"—those four. . . . They didn't mean a lot. They weren't well recorded. They just didn't have it. Then, *The Graduate* happened as we were working on *Bookends.*

'Bookends,' is really different from 'Parsley, Sage.' It's a new thing musically and lyrically. There are fewer of those vignette type of songs—like "Richard Cory" and "Poem on an Underground Wall."

Those songs that you mentioned were both written in England. Those English songs tend to sound like they have a connection. "Kathy's Song," "April Comes She Will," "Richard Cory," "Homeward Bound," "Poem on an Underground Wall," "A Most Peculiar Man" were all written in England. They all have that other feeling to me.

THE EARLY ALBUMS USED TO be explicitly about alienation—Artie used to say so in all the interviews—that was really a late Fifties, early Sixties thing. . . .

"The Sound of Silence" was written about a year before it was recorded on *Wednesday Morning.* So that puts "The Sound of Silence" in '62, '63, I guess—two years before it came out as a hit single. So, it's written about a feeling I had then. And it took me a couple of months then to write it. So, a lot of these songs are written in the past, and they come out as if this is what we're up to. Then, a kid comes back from England

with a big hit record, and everybody says, "You seem to write a lot about alienation." "Right," I said. "Right, I do." "Alienation seems to be your big theme." "That's my theme," I said. And I proceeded to write more about alienation. Actually, Dylan was writing protest, and whatever it was, everybody had a tag. They put a tag on the alienation. And it was a self-fulfilling prophecy, so I wrote alienation songs. Of course, we all had a feeling of alienation. . . .

But protest was actually an attempt to deny alienation, because protest generally reflected an active commitment, an active involvement.

Well, I don't think so. Actually, protest songs were saying, "I'm not part of you." If the world was full of me, the answer wouldn't be blowin' in the wind, you know.

Did you dislike protest music?

No, I didn't dislike it. I liked it, like everybody liked it. I thought that second Dylan album, *Freewheelin' Bob Dylan,* was fantastic. It was very moving. Very exciting. There was a lot of bad protest because protest became a thing. What was that song?

"Eve of Destruction"?

Awful. And you knew that it was already ruined when that happened.

You mentioned before, referring to the second side of 'Bookends,' that the lean period for Simon and Garfunkel was . . .

"The Dangling Conversation," "Hazy Shade of Winter," "At the Zoo" and "Fakin' It."

You didn't like any of those?

"Fakin' It" was interesting. Autobiographically, it was interesting. But we never really got it on on the records.

I'm surprised, because I like "Fakin' It" so much.

That's because you are thinking of "Fakin' It" on the album. And "Fakin' It" on the album is vastly improved over "Fakin' It" as a single. For one thing, I think it's speeded up. For two, it was re-mixed and greatly improved in stereo. It was a jumble; it was a record that was jumbled, sloppy. When you hear the original mono, it's slower and it's sloppier. It was improved on the LP, but by then it was already poisoned in my mind.

What was that business about the tailor during the interlude—and was the "Leitch" you mentioned a reference to Donovan?

During some hashish reverie I was thinking to myself, "I'm really in a weird position. I earn my living by writing songs and singing songs. It's only today that this could happen. If I were born a hundred years ago I wouldn't even be in this country. I'd probably be in Vienna or wherever my ancestors came from—Hungary—and I wouldn't be a guitarist-songwriter. There were none. So what would I be?

"First of all," I said, "I surely was a sailor." Then I said, "Nah, I wouldn't have been a sailor. Well, what would a Jewish guy be? A tailor." That's what it was. I would have been a tailor. And then I started to see myself as like, a perfect little tailor.

Then, once, talking to my father about my grandfather, whom I never knew—he died when my father was young—I found out that his name was Paul Simon, and I found out that he was a tailor in Vienna. It wiped me out that that happened. It's amazing, isn't it? He was a tailor that came from Vienna.

As for Leitch, the girl who said that on the record, her name was Beverly Martyn—did you ever hear of John and Beverly Martyn? She wasn't married to John Martyn at that time, but I knew her from way back in English scufflin' days, and we brought her over to sing at the Monterey Pop Festival. I thought she was a really talented singer. She was sort of livin' around with us. It was during the psychedelic days. Records faded in and out; things became other things. And she was friendly with Donovan. So, we decided to make up this little vignette about the shop—we wanted to come up with a name. She said, well, let's put in Donovan's name.

I really liked the chorus . . . I thought it was an important piece of confessional work. . . . When you mentioned before, your hashish reverie, was this a big dope time for you?

Yes. This was 1967, you know. The summer of flowers.

Had you been into dope all along?

Yeah.

Starting in England?

When you say dope, dope then was not what dope is today. Dope then meant you smoke grass or you smoke hash. In England everybody smoked hash—nobody smoked grass. Or you maybe took some pills. Took some ups or downs.

You took pills back then?

Yeah, I took pills.

A lot?

No.

What kind of effect was dope having on your life at that point?

Negative. A negative effect at that point.

How?

It made me retreat more into myself. It brought out fears that I had, and I don't think it helped me in my writing, although I was convinced I couldn't write without it. I had to be

high to write. It didn't matter because I was high every day, anyway. But I think a lot of the pain that comes out in some of the songs is due to the exaggeration of being high.

How about acid?

I tried acid a few times, and I didn't like it. I had a very whopping acid trip once. Owsley gave me some acid, and I took it by myself, in typical fashion, late at night. I said, "Well, I'll try this now." I dropped it about three in the morning, and I continued right on through until about nine the next night. It was some good and a lot of bad. I had a stretch of about four or five hours that was very paranoid. Then I came out of it, and it was good. I had some good times. I remember during the bad part thinking that it was vanity that made me take it. I took it because I thought I was going to get some big chunk of information for free. I was going to learn something about myself chemically, rather than learning something through my life. I said, "Look what I've done, I've fucked my brains up here."

So you stopped?

No, after that, I went right back and did it again, sort of the falling-off-a-horse theory. I wasn't going to let any acid trip throw me just because it was bad.

It seems almost competitive behavior. . . .

I don't know what it was. I would say it was stupid. I would say it was stupid behavior on my part.

And I didn't get anything from it.

You mean ultimately . . .

Absolutely not. I think it was like taking a beating. I think I came out of it about six months later. Somewhere around six months later, I said, "Oh, I think I feel about normal now." I wasn't aware of it, but I think that's what it was like. It was exhausting for nothing. For vanity, that's what. That I thought I was going to learn something, that I didn't learn.

So you don't have any involvement in drugs now?

Nothing. Zero. I don't smoke. I don't pill. I don't anything. I stopped a couple of years ago.

What specifically, if anything, caused you to stop flat like that?

For one thing, it was very unsatisfying, for me at the end, although I started out loving it. But at the end, it was bad. I couldn't write. It made me depressed. It made me antisocial. It brought out nastiness in me. When I'd deal with people while I was high, I'd listen to them and think "Boy, he's really stupid. That guy's really phony. Phony smile, phony everything." And I couldn't stand it. I didn't want to be around. And the

217

same thing with me. I'd say, "Oh, boy, you really are ridiculous. Absolutely ridiculous . . ." Then I started analysis, and the day I started analysis I stopped doing any dope. The night before, I smoked all my remaining dope, and I started on a Monday.

The doctor said, "I can't analyze you if you are high." I think he said that because he knew I wanted to stop.

That's over three years ago. Three and a half years ago. And a year later I stopped smoking cigarettes, too.

You associate the two things?

I associate them because of singing. Because when you smoke, you can't sing good. When you were high, you couldn't sing good, your throat got tight. It was a big improvement in my voice. My range went up; my ability to sing and phrase, everything got better.

Somebody told me the same thing about Mick Jagger.

I believe it. I know Dylan stopped smoking. I know McCartney stopped smoking. You can hear it in the voice. It's bad for you.

WHAT DO YOU THINK ABOUT *women's liberation?*

I'm for the feminist movement. I support it. I believe that women are a group that is discriminated against.

When did you come to that belief?

Over the last year or so. Mostly through my wife. I believe that the sex roles that we culturally assume are restricting to both males and females. They're more than restricting, they're damaging to both males and females, and it's good to be aware of what roles you're just assuming without ever thinking about it. That's what the women's liberation movement has made me aware of. I take certain things for granted, forms of behavior, just because it's culturally taught that way. Like cooking meals. Well, I can cook a little more than I used to be able to. I couldn't do anything. To do that, to participate in chores for the household, you become aware that that's no great job. That's not a job that anyone wants.

Now we're gonna have a child, and the question is, in raising the child, who'll do what? What will be the function? When you have a child, that's the main part of your life. It requires constant attention. Who'll do that constant

attention? We're gonna split it. All these things I was never aware of—I started reading and talking about it.

To approach the subject from the other end, what was the Simon and Garfunkel groupie scene like?

Simon and Garfunkel had a peculiar type of groupie. We had the poetic groupies. The girls that followed us around weren't necessarily looking to sleep with us as much as they were looking to read their poetry or discuss literature or play their own songs.

How did you feel about that?

I think that maybe that was the best thing for me, because to a great degree it embarrassed me to pick up somebody on the road because it was so obvious that you weren't interested in them. I felt it was insulting.

Ultimately, how did you cope with the situation?

Ultimately, I wound up going back to the room and smoking a joint and going to sleep by myself. Most of the time, sometimes not.

But toward the end I always avoided any contact with people after the show. I never encouraged it. There were always exceptions, but in general, compared to what I've read about most rock groups or pop groups, for me (I can't speak for Artie), I wasn't into picking up girls on the road. Couldn't do it. Too embarrassing to me. I wasn't interested in their poetry, either.

What was "Armistice Day" saying to you about politics?

Well, "Armistice Day," which I consider to be the weakest song on the album, is an old song, written in 1968—the first part of it was. That song mainly meant, let's have a truce. I chose the title "Armistice Day" because it's not even called Armistice Day anymore, it's called Veteran's Day. Armistice Day is like an old name, and I didn't really mean it to be specifically about the war. I just meant that I'm worn out from all this fighting, from all the abuse that people are giving each other and creating for each other. And I like the opening line on "Armistice Day"—"Armistice Day, the Philharmonic will play"—from strictly a songwriter's point of view, like rhyme and the way it sings.

What effect does financial success in general have upon the way you see things?

It's hard to know. On a personal level, questions of the economy, unemployment, things like that, they're not personal for me, so it becomes an abstract issue. Do I wish that in general the lot of poor people would be much improved? Yes, I do. That's an abstraction.

So from that degree, it has something to do

with it. That's really a good question. The whole question of money is because it's very confusing. I really haven't put that issue into perspective. You can't go your whole life and have, for me, an average amount of money. I came from a middle-class family; we weren't poor, but I would have always had to keep working. I rode the subway to work; I took a bus.

How do you feel about the rock liberation front, that kind of thing? Their notion, put in its most extreme form, is that rock musicians have an obligation to be actively bound and committed to radical movements, that they have some sort of political obligation, that there's something wrong with the notion, "I earn a living, I write songs, I get paid for them; whatever else I do is my business."

I think they are very illogical. I don't agree with that at all. First of all, I think if a musician is serious about his music, his obligation should be to become as fine a musician as he could. This country has a tremendous lack of people who are good in what they do, including musicians. This country places a tremendous priority on being successful, being famous or infamous, but it doesn't give you a great reward for being good.

So, for a musician to be involved in politics (and, of course, it's up to the musician), I don't see that one should be involved in radical politics any more than conservative politics, if that's their inclination. I don't see what one thing has to do with another. The fact of the matter is that popular music is one of the industries of this country. It's all completely tied up with capitalism. It's stupid to separate it. That's an illusory separation.

If one has strong political beliefs, one should do whatever they think is right about them.

So you don't recognize any specific obligations inherent in your particular situation?

Not because I'm a musician, no. Certainly not. Why should a musician have any more obligation than anybody else? I don't know what radical politics necessarily is. A million things come under the term radical.

What's your reaction to the kind of involvement that John Lennon has shown?

I have reactions to it. First reaction, he strikes me as being very interested in being seen or heard. Then I have to think, "What is he doing? What is the purpose of it? Is his purpose to get publicity for himself? Is his purpose to advance a certain political thought?" I don't know what his motivations are. Many things he's done, I think, have been pointless. Some have been in bad taste. Others have been courageous. I think he's gener-

ally a well-intentioned guy. I don't know, it's not my style.

What do you think of a record like "Power to the People"?

It's a poor record, a condescending record. Like all of these cliché phrases. They're dangerous. What does that mean—"Power to the People"? And who is he saying it to? Is he saying it to people who have any idea what it means? Isn't it really a manipulative phrase? It's not that I'm not interested in what Lennon has to say. I am. He usually has my ear. When he makes a record or makes a statement, I'll read it or listen to it. I am a potential audience for him. But I find that he seldom says anything that's interesting or innovative to me, and yet I listen, based on a long-standing respect. Based on his musicianship, based on the fact that he was involved in some great music over the years, and so I keep listening to stuff that's no longer great.

Expecting something?

Yes. Out of respect for what he once did, out of respect for what once moved me. Now how long will that keep up, I don't know. I find I'm less and less inclined to hear what he has to say.

Y OU'RE INVOLVED IN STUDYING *classical music now. Your work has always included different ways, different elements from different kinds of music. Where do you think rock fits as music?*

Well, rock is the staple. Rock is the main part of the meal for me. It's the music that I not only grew up in but I participated in, so I like rock, and I like rock & roll. I like a lot of different kinds of music. I think that there have been very talented people come up in the last decade, people who have done really good work, and there have been great performers. I think Aretha is a really fine performer. I think Otis Redding was really great. Sam Cooke was great. The Beatles were great. Dylan was great, I gotta say he was great. I don't feel that at the moment, but I feel that he was great. Although now we're into another category because I wanted to save that. I think he'll come in more as a writer; those other people are performers. Except the Beatles are both.

This is what will survive . . .

If you go for what has a chance of surviving, then you have to go for songs. You can go for artists, but to what degree has Bessie Smith survived today, by her recordings?

219

I think to a great degree.

I think not a great degree. I think Grand Funk Railroad is much more well known today by most people than Bessie Smith, and yet, I'll tell you this, a lot more people know "St. Louis Blues" than know Bessie Smith. In other words, her work is preserved on records, and that record remains a part of history. A song is capable of having several life spans.

What songs for the Sixties do you think will have additional life spans?

It's hard to remember. There's so many, so many.

Start off with the Beatles.

I would pick "Yesterday." I would pick "Strawberry Fields"—although there is your example of a total record. A very important record to me; I like it a lot. You can't even sing the song. It's really hard to sing the song.

Yes, but many of their songs have dated.

It may take a song, instead of being dated after three years, maybe some songs won't be dated for five years. Eventually all records are dated, but the song comes back. "Eleanor Rigby" was a really fine song. There's no way of picking out the best songs. There's the whole group of Smokey Robinson songs that mean something. There's a couple old Steve Cropper tunes that mean something. I think there are some of my songs that are, that will last.

Which ones?

Judging from the amount of recordings and the amount of airplay and the amount of that kind of measuring device, the most popular songs of mine are "Sound of Silence," "Mrs. Robinson," "Bridge over Troubled Water," "Feelin' Groovy" and a song that's not mine but is associated with us, "Scarborough Fair." That song's alive still. You hear it still, and those songs are, if not quite standards, almost standards. In other words, when I say standards, I think they'll live at least ten years. Now, "The Sound of Silence" has already lived about six years, and it's still played, and it's alive.

It's primarily played in your version.

No, I think it's played all over the place. There must be 100 recordings of it.

To talk more about songwriting for a bit, you started talking about the Beatles before. How about Dylan?

Well, you can go back and pick out five or six very important Dylan songs. I'm aware of that, because he became popular a year or so before we did. Many of his still make it for me, whereas only a few of mine make it for me. I like his earlier stuff. His early songs were very rich, simple but very rich, with strong melodies. "Blowin' in the Wind" has a really strong melody. He so enlarged himself through the folk background that he incorporated it for a while. He defined the genre for a while. That's quite an accomplishment.

But no longer. Not to me. Maybe for some people he still makes it. When *Nashville Skyline* came out, a lot of groups started to play country music, but it didn't move me. The rock-country sound has the same limitation as country music. There were some great songs, but you were working within a very limited musical scope. And you get the picture after a while. And that's what happened with country rock; after a while it's boring.

But country music continues. Genuine country music continues to have appeal to those people who naturally tend to like it.

It does. It doesn't have nearly the life of the other inherited American, indigenous American music, blues.

It is striking because your music has been completely devoid of the musical characteristics of blues. You've never recorded blues.

I've never recorded a blues, but it's impossible to be devoid of the character of the influence of black music. Impossible. I don't sing like a black. I don't sing like a country musician either. I sing like a white kid from the city.

It seems that especially the rock bands have failed to produce many singers of distinction.

I'll tell you one of the reasons is that you find it almost impossible to dissociate white singers from their songs. James Taylor, who has a pretty pleasant voice and sings pretty good sometimes, I'm not saying he's a great singer, but I'm saying he sings pretty good. I think of him as the package.

Did you used to take an active interest in your business affairs? Did you always try at the same time to stay informed about it?

I always did. I always published my own songs right from the beginning.

Columbia never owned part of your publishing?

Nobody ever owned part of my publishing. That's a result of having been exposed to the business since I was about fifteen. By the time it came around to do this, I knew that you can keep your own publishing. A lot of people simply don't know that. There's only a handful of writers who really own their own publishing.

You mentioned before when you were recording at a studio you never liked to look at the bills.

I never did look at them. I did not want to be inhibited. A lot of times I don't do anything but sit in a studio for an hour or so, just talk. I like the studio to become a home, to be comfortable, and then I think, "I'm talking to this guy, and if I talk to this guy for two hours that costs $300." Or, "If we don't get a track down, it's like $1500 a day here." That's no good. Studio costs are ridiculous.

Do you pay for your own studio time?

I pay for part of my studio time.

You seem to have had a good relation with your own record company.

I have had, for the most part. I had some problems, but for the most part they're pretty nice to me here. Why shouldn't they, right?

S&G must be a hard thing to let go of.

I don't find it hard. I find it a relief. It took me to a nice place. I can't say it took me where I wanted to go because I had no idea where I wanted to go, but I found myself at the point of leaving S&G in a very nice place. I've done a lot of satisfying work; we were ready to move out, and I could go and do what I wanted without being tense about succeeding or not succeeding. I'd already been successful. I mean, I knew I never could top the success of "Bridge." I'm not going to sell more than eight million records, so it's kind of a nice place to be. So you start again, but actually you have nothing to lose. I'm also older than I was, so I don't have that drive; I already had a few years of being successful.

Two people can go so far, and then they're locked to each other. There are just so many combinations of two. So that was over. As it should have been. It lasted a long long time. I've known Artie since I was twelve years old, and we were friends all that time.

I'm thirty now, so that's a long time for that partnership. It's over. We grew up. From the musical point of view, in the time that he was off in the movies, Artie didn't do anything musically. I was doing things musically, but to Artie it would have to go back to the old practicing a song, have to learn the harmony.

I wouldn't say that my ideas were bigger than S&G, but I would say that my ideas were different than S&G, and I didn't want to go in that direction of a duo. I always felt restricted as a singer, partly because there always had to be harmony, and it had to be sung in the same phrasing, and then you had to double it. You couldn't get free and loose with your singing, and in this album, I am pretty free.

What was the record company's attitude toward the split?

Oh, tremendously discouraging. They didn't want that split at all. They still don't want it.

The first form it took was self-delusion: "Paul has to get this out of his system." Then they would ask, "When do you think you'll do the next S&G album?" Which would bring me down. I'd be working on this album. It was important to me. And they would want to know when I was going to put aside this little . . . toy.

How about Clive Davis?.

He didn't encourage me at all to do this. It became obvious that I was going to do it, and it was stupid to get in the way, but nobody encouraged me to do it. Sort of a predictably conservative attitude. I was dragged. I shouldn't have been, but I was. Everybody said, "What the hell's wrong? Why don't they stay together?" And everybody said, "Gee, I always liked S&G; boy, that's too bad." It was too bad, but that was it. It was over. For the sake of me personally, it was great that I was doing this by myself, but for the sake of the world, it wasn't great. Nobody said, "Oh, boy, can't wait to hear it."

George Harrison said to me, "I'm really curious to hear your album because now you hear sort of what we are like individually, since the group broke up, and I know what you were like together, and I'd like to hear what you're like individually." And all the while in my head I thought, this breakup is not really comparable to that Beatles breakup because there was a tremendous interaction in that group that came from the sound, and I said to myself, "I write better songs now than I used to write years ago, so I'm going to make a better album, but nobody knows that. They won't know it till it comes out." That was my fantasy.

In fact, many critics said that. But the public didn't in terms of buying the record, and that's unsettling. I'm getting used to it now. I'm getting used to the fact. At first I said, "Look, when it breaks up you're going to have to start all over again. It may take you a couple of albums before people will even listen." But actually, emotionally I was ready to be welcomed into the public's arms, as I had been in the past. And not that I'm not now, because it's a successful album; this just goes to show you my perspective.

You sold 700,000, right?

About 850,000.

That's more records than any single Rolling Stones album except for 'Sticky Fingers.'

Yeah, but permit me my arrogance. I never compare myself with the Rolling Stones. I never considered that the Rolling Stones were at the same level. I always was well aware of the fact that S&G was a much bigger phenomenon in

221

general, to the general public, than the Rolling Stones. The Rolling Stones might be bigger with a certain segment, but the general public S&G really penetrated really got down to many many levels of people—older people and really young kids. That was really gratifying.

'Wednesday Morning' ended up being a good-sized selling album.

Wednesday Morning sold somewhere around 500,000–600,000. No other album that we made has sold less than two million. *Parsley, Sage* is around three million, and *Bridge,* of course, is bigger. They all sold.

When people who are forty years old buy your albums and they like your music, I liked that. That turns me on that they did that. That's very fine to me. That's what it's about—that's music. I don't say, "Don't you listen to this music, you, this isn't for you." I want everybody to listen to

it. I hope everybody likes it. That's where S&G had got me. And I wanted to be the same thing. Now I'm at the start and building slowly, and maybe I'll never get there.

Clive once said to me, "S&G is a household word. No matter, however successful you'll be, you'll never be as successful as S&G."

So I said, "Yeah, like Dean Martin and Jerry Lewis. Don't tell me that. Don't tell me that statement, that I'll never be bigger than. How do you know what I'll do? I don't even know what I'm gonna do in the next decade of my life. It could be maybe my greatest time of work. Maybe I'm finished. Maybe I'm not gonna do my thing until I'm fifty. People will say then, funny thing was, in his youth he sang with a group. He sang popular songs in the Sixties. Fans of "rock & roll," in quotes, may remember the duo Simon & Garfunkel. That's how I figure it.

INTERVIEWED BY PATRICK WILLIAM SALVO (1972)

Chuck Berry, whose hits included "Maybellene"—his first, in 1955—"Johnny B. Goode," "Memphis" and "Sweet Little Sixteen," created a body of highly American imagery from which rock & roll continues to feed.

This interview, conducted in 1972, found him in the midst of a career revival. At the age of forty-six, he was riding a naughty little song called "My Ding-a-Ling" up the charts.

We received the interview from freelancer Patrick Salvo, who told us: "The interview began in a New York hotel in early May, jumped across country in June to Las Vegas and ended in July at Wentzville, Missouri, site of Berry's ninety-eight-acre estate and entertainment center, "Berry Park." The sessions took place before and after gigs, in dressing rooms, over a Chinese dinner, in the back of a rented Cadillac, in gambling casinos, over a chessboard and on the telephone. Some sessions lasted three hours, others three seconds."

Berry, Salvo noted, had done few interviews, "and some of that old reluctance to reveal himself remains, and some of his answers are tinged with evasiveness." Especially when the talk turned to his trials in 1960 and 1961 for an alleged violation of the Mann Act, a case involving a fourteen-year-old Indian girl. Berry said he was acquitted; but, according to a St. Louis newspaper account, he was convicted and sentenced to three years. Whatever, no Chuck Berry records were issued between 1961 and 1963; his career resumed with the hit, "Nadine," put out in March 1964.

—BF-T

FOUR SPOTLIGHTS FOLLOWED THE FIGure of Chuck Berry on the Cow Palace stage as he neared the show's climax. In the cold half-light over by Box 44, this young voice was crying out repeatedly

224

CHUCK

BERRY

some unintelligible phrase. An instant before Berry hit the opening notes of "Reelin' and Rockin'," the dazed face of a kid about three peered over the wall of Box 44; the words of the screeching voice became clear. The boy was yelling: "Play 'Ding-a-Ling'! Play 'Ding-a-Ling'! Play 'Ding-a-Ling'!"

Berry led the audience in a ceremony. The spots went down, and he asked the 2500 or so gathered to light matches or lighters on signal and chant with him some praises of rock & roll. Then he taught the boys in the crowd their line in "My Ding-a-Ling," and he told the girls: "The boys have their part ready . . ." The girls at the foot of the stage were enthusiastic, and Berry taught them their line, finally telling the boys: "The girls have the longest passage—and they're ready, too."

Then, with a raunchy fervor reminiscent of the old Rusty Warren school of music, Chuck Berry, 46, sang "My Ding-a-Ling," his Number One single.

—*San Francisco*
October 1972

"'Ding-a-Ling' is something I'm sure he wrote twenty years ago . . . as I remember both Mr. Greene {Irving B. Greene, Mercury Records president} and myself threw that thing out. . . ."

—*Johnny Sippel,*
former Mercury product manager

"My Ding-a-Ling," off 'The London Chuck Berry Sessions' album, has sold close to two million copies. Berry has had some thirty-odd singles and twenty albums in his recording career, but none of the songs was as big a seller as "My Ding-a-Ling." It has earned him his first gold record, seventeen years after the release of his first single, "Maybellene," the classic which Berry followed with "Roll Over Beethoven" (later recorded by the Beatles); "School Days"; "Rock and Roll Music"; "Sweet Little Sixteen"; "Johnny B. Goode"; "Carol"; "Sweet Little Rock and Roller"; "Memphis"; "Almost Grown"; "Little Queenie"; "Back in the U.S.A."; "Nadine"; "No Particular Place To Go"; "You Never Can Tell"; and others.

Berry has recorded for Chess for all but three years. In 1966 he went to Mercury for an estimated $150,000. The association lasted until 1969, when he returned to Chess.

In the late Sixties, Berry began to build up Berry Park. The place is off something called Highway Z, about forty miles from St. Louis, and is enclosed with an electric fence. On the grounds there is a discotheque, a guitar-shaped swimming pool, a guest lodge, an outdoor bandstand and Berry's two-story, sixteen-room chalet. A rock & roll festival was held there a couple of years ago.

Berry's name is listed six times in the Wentzville telephone directory. "Quite rightly so," said the sandy-

haired attendant at the Sinclair service station. "Yes, sir, that Berry drives his Caddy through town 'bout once a week, then turns around and heads back to 'is farm; thinks he owns the place."

WHAT MODEL WAS THE FIRST *car you ever had?*
A '34 Ford—sorry, A '33 Ford. It cost thirty-four dollars. Man, it took me three months to pay for it, and I had to have some older friend sign for it 'cause I was only seventeen. You know, I even got the receipt slip for that car and the next one, too. I don't know what happened by the wayside, but I got kind of used to gettin' cars after I got the second one. The next one was a '34, incidentally, for real.

Did you get a lot of your song ideas while you were riding around in your automobile? Many of your songs seem to be about "motivating" and things like that.

Yeah, sure, and I dug cars, I ain't gonna tell you I didn't.

Did you work on them, customize them?

Yeah, I had to put doors on the '34, but we used to run through them so fast it wouldn't matter.

What was the first thing you did when you hit Chicago?

Well, it was three trips. Once, I went up there just like that, you know, hoboing.

Sort of freewheelin'?

Now that you mention it, that '39 Olds did have freewheel drive. Yeah, I hit San Francisco, New York, Chicago—the coast-to-coast trip.

Is that when you first met Muddy Waters?

I met him about a year prior to that. I knew him about a year personally before then, but, actually, he was playing at the Chicago Palladium when I walked in. You know, I was just like a fan to him. I just stood by the bandstand and watched him blow, and then when he went on intermission I talked to him a little bit about it. I asked him, "Could I blow one?" And he said, "Comme ci, comme ça, yeah." So I got up and blew one and he said, "You play pretty nice, you ought to see Leonard Chess about it." So the next morning, I went to see Chess to talk to him. He said to bring some stuff up, you know, and I had a little tape recorder. So then I went back to what I was doing at this little club in East St. Louis, the Cosmopolitan Club.

When you were playing at the Cosmopolitan Club in St. Louis, wasn't Ike Turner around?

Actually, he was down the street. Around 1953–54 we were rivals.

Who else was kicking around St. Louis at that time?

Little Milton and Albert King, but they was, excuse me, "little shit" compared to Ike and I. We was the biggest shit around at the time.

Why was Ike so much better than the rest?

Because he was from out of town and that wasn't fair. He came out of Mississippi, see, Clarksdale, playing blues, and he obviously had his stuff formulated, plus he sang a lot different than he sings now.

Was there much stealing of riffs and lyrics between the artists in the small clubs in St. Louis and Chicago? Like if someone came to see you play, would he be doing your stuff the following week?

Well, gee, I didn't have nothing they could steal. I don't think I had anything that could be recognized then, but, you know, a couple of numbers.

How about your style?

See, again, I say my style is Carl Hoagan, Charlie Christian, T-Bone Walker, and all mixed in with whatever comes through, you know. I don't recognize my style, because whenever I play something it refers me to Glen Gray and Benny Goodman, this is his riff and stuff like that. It's all mixed together, and really all I want to do is like *chop, chop chop*. Like John Lennon says, "Anything that's *chonka, chonka, chonka, chonk* is Chuck Berry."

How did you meet Johnnie Johnson, your old piano player?

He sort of gave me a call when I was in St. Louis. He had his trio and we made it a foursome. We had a tenor player and Ebby Hardy on drums and he gave me a call—he just looked me up.

At that point, could a man really make a living playing the blues? Didn't you need to have another thing going for you?

Well, I made fourteen dollars a night. You know, that was a local gig. Other cats was making five dollars a night, man, working scab. I'm proud to say we was making scale.

Were you styling hair on the side? Didn't you go to school to become a hairstylist?

Well, I went to Simmons Grammar School and at Sumner High School I majored in music, and after that I went for hairstyling at the Poro School of Beauty Culture. My two sisters and I studied to be cosmetologists and we're all hairstylists. But that was before then, actually, because I was almost playing regular. That was almost right after school, you know, and it

wasn't a year after that that we did "Maybellene," a professional recording in a professional studio.

Was that on your second trip to Chicago?

No, actually, it was on the third. You see, when I arrived back in St. Louis after my first meeting with Leonard, I said to the boys, "Well, let's make a thing," you know, just like somebody would have a demo tape nowadays. The tape machine came in boxes, like two shoe boxes, you know, a recorder. We set a mike up just like it is here with your recorder, and the band was in the corner of the living room and we played this thing. We recorded four numbers, "Maybellene," "Wee Wee Hours," "Roll Over Beethoven" and "Too Much Monkey Business." I took them back to Chicago on my second trip, and Leonard Chess played them and he said, "It sounds fairly nice," and to bring the band up and he'd record them on his big equipment.

So, two weeks later I was up there again with it, Johnnie Johnson in piano and Ebby Hardy on drums. I think we did it on May 21st, 1955, and he had it on disc and it hit the market in late July. The first of August this cat Jack Cook from the Gale Agency came down from New York and said, "You got a hit, sign here." And eight days later I played my first professional date at Gleason's in Cleveland. Then we went to Youngstown and on to the Paramount in New York that Labor Day weekend, where I first performed my duckwalk for the public.

What association did Alan Freed have with "Maybellene" and that whole era?

I suppose I can say it right quick—he grabbed a third of the writing of "Maybellene" in lieu of my rookiness.

He doesn't have a third of it anymore, does he?

Actually, it was two of them, Russ Fratto, another DJ, was in on it, too, and Freed. I got it back from Fratto, but I didn't get it from Freed. It went to his estate and it involved a lot of legal processes. What's her name, Inez or Ida or somebody was made administress of his estate, and they sure do still get a third.

Did Alan Freed actually co-author the tune with you?

No, that was a very strange thing. He got that money solely for doing us some favors in those days. He actually didn't sit down with me at all and write anything.

You had a close relationship with Freed—what about Dick Clark? I always think of Dick Clark when I think of Chuck Berry.

I had a fight with him around '55, '56. I was on his show and he wanted me to word the

227

music, mouth the song—lip-synch it, and I refused to do that. I said, "Chuck Berry is not gonna open his mouth and have nothing come out." So, Leonard Chess came over to me and we had a little talk. So, I figured if anyone is gonna tell me what to do right, Leonard would tell me to do it. And Leonard says, there are some things you gotta do in this business that you don't want to do. So, we made friends, because Dick Clark was held in esteem in those days and he had a lot of power and, of course, he also had a lot of money.

When the huge payola scandal hit, did you think that was the end of rock & roll?

At that time, I didn't know what payola was until all the news came out about it. Then I found out what it was, but I had no control over it.

Can you elaborate?

Well, as I understand from hearsay, payola was if you knew a disc jockey and he took some money for playing a record, then he played it. It takes a lot of bread 'cause there are a lot of disc jockeys. And I guess I've paid in return because I just got back about twelve grand on back monies, and lately I'm discovering back monies from bygone days—recordings and so forth. I guess I paid. Also, the way a contract was written up, you see, I immediately alleviated ten percent for publicity, and this money can go any way the record company distributes it. Of course, I'm talking about the old Chess now, you know.

After "Wee Wee Hours," the flip side of "Maybellene," which was pure blues, you released "Thirty Days," "No Money Down," "Roll Over Beethoven" and "Too Much Monkey Business." Why did Leonard Chess want you to stay away from the blues slant and stay with the heavy rock, or whatever it was called then?

You know, "Wee Wee Hours" and there's more, like "Have Mercy Judge" and "It Hurts Me Too," to me these are blues. Whereas you're right, there's nothing bluesy about "Too Much Monkey Business" and the rest, I don't think, except maybe the phrasings. Let me put it to you this way. You see, Nat Cole had a bluesy voice when he did "That Ain't Right," yet still his voice was cultured. So far as bluesy and spiritually, Sinatra's got a bluesy voice on "Only the Lonely" and there ain't nothing blue in that song.

In the Forties and early Fifties, black singers, including yourself, tended to sing in variations of the bluesy white crooning styles. Did you ever have a hankering to do a whole album of just pure blues ballads? I read that you wanted to record blues under a different name.

No. Well, I could if I wanted to, but I never thought about it. You see, when I started out I was singing everything—blues, jazz, love ballads and, well, I still try to sing as much smooth ballads as I can. I sing a love song a night. I just wish I had the voice for it; rather, I wish I had a voice for singing other music like ballads, 'cause I would sure lay it on you. 'Cause, I really don't have a voice for the songs I want to sing—love songs.

You seem to be such a deliberate man, it's funny that most of your music is so high-energy and you're so cooled out. Why did you choose such a high-energy approach in your songs?

No, I didn't actually choose. You see, when I was singing at these barbecue parties and things in backyards and evenings in the living room, I was singing nothing but Nat and Eckstine and a little bit of Muddy, too, every once in a while. But, it seems as though Charles Brown's numbers—those songs are the ones still today that move my heart. They really get to me and that goes on and on. I'm such a fan of these people, but like I can't sing them, not like they sing them. You ask why did I choose that road. It chose me, and I have no preference to what I sing—it's what they want. But like on most of my albums there is one bluesy ballad that pops up just for flavor. See, one thing, I think that blues has to be done from being blue, or at least down a little bit.

But what happens when you walk onstage and you don't feel in that particular down mood?

All right, that's just how it sounds, you know. 'Cause even in the delivery itself of the blues, I may play some little freaky flippant riffs, you know, but that's not blues. Blues drives, and the music tells what you're saying, too. But let's face it, in show business you can fake it and get it over. If somebody keeps hollering, "Blues, blues, blues," you got to do it. I just seldom feel it. Now sometimes, yeah, I do feel it and I sing three or four blues tunes. Oh yeah, and I ride right on Muddy, too, 'cause I can feel Muddy's music. But really and truthfully, blues is not my bag. I don't know what is, but I know it isn't blues.

I imagine you are aware that a lot of very young listeners only know you from association with groups like the Stones and Beatles. What's more, half of them don't even own a Chuck Berry record by Chuck Berry.

Sure, sometimes they hear a record by me and they go, "Wow, that dude is doing a Rolling Stones record." Yeah, yeah, I even say that, too.

I know that. Like I used to announce onstage that I was gonna do one of Johnny Rivers' numbers and then go into "Memphis" for a laugh. "Around and Around" was another.

Is it still a laughing matter?

We'll see. The proof of that will come when they find out. Of course, everybody likes to sell records, but see, in the last eight years, most of my heart has been in live performing. I know I couldn't get around to all the people, no, never, no one could. So, I make records. But, the whole thrill of this music business is my forty-five minutes or hour or eighty minutes or whatever that I have onstage. The rest of it is almost like a ritual. But, every show is different because I guess it's new or it's the last one that's happened. All the rest of the stuff, man, it's just hash warmed over—the planes, the dressing rooms and everything else.

Since you had no real managers, did the Chess brothers work out any long-term strategies on how your career would be managed?

First let me say that any man who can't take care of his own money deserves what he gets. In fact, a man should be able to take care of most of his business by himself. Now, I did have a manager once for about a month and he didn't work out too well. So, I dropped him immediately and since, except for just that little time, I have been in total control of my financial matters. Now, when you talk about strategies, you're talking about contracts, money. There was plenty of strategies there. Yeah, we had an awful long strategy over the contract that I signed. We came to a great financial agreement. I can't elaborate on the sums, but no stipulations or strategies were discussed in that we didn't plan out my career.

Did they coach you musically or help in the production end?

No, nothing like that. No strategies in that way. As far as producing, let me tell you for the last time that since the very start, when I first signed with Chess, I have been in total creative control. All the way up through Mercury and then when I signed back with Chess until just recently when I went with Esmond Edwards, I have been in ultimate total creative control. With them just like with any other company, even when I went to Mercury, I would just do the tape and I would hand over to them the final tape. I would do everything myself but press the records and distribute them. If I could, I would probably do that myself, too.

What is your philosophy about working with other people?

Everything you do is right, as long as you don't infringe on someone else. That's wrong. And the key word is infringe. Now like at my place, Berry Park, for instance. Now there's nine people there and like everyone owns that park when they come there. And like one thing, when you personally come there, all your expenses are diminished. There's lots of food there and there's room and board, and I'm worth three-quarters of a million dollars and that buys lots of groceries. So, if there's nine different people, then there are nine different worlds there and as long as you don't step on anybody else's fingers, it's cool, and then everything is right and there's nothing wrong. In life you can help yourself or hurt yourself but even if you choose not to help yourself, it's not wrong as long as you don't infringe on anyone else. Now, if you're the only one there at the park, then you can do no wrong.

What do your parents reckon on you now?

That's a good question. Well, my father, like on my album, I mention him in "Ding-a-Ling" when I'm talking to the audience. "My father is a Baptist minister and he told us there ain't nothing wrong with sex, there's nothing wrong with sex. He told us, 'Son, it's just the way you handle it.'" I wonder what he thinks about that. Well, he's not exactly a Baptist minister, he's assistant to the deacon or something, but I'm sure that, well, my libido is very strong. I rise in that direction and I'm sure it's inherited. I never knew his personal matters. But for the last ten years on Tuesday nights he's been going to choir practice, and for the last five Mom's not been going, and now I heard, he's gotten a new riding passenger and she's a female lady. So I don't know. Maybe he's not particularly into it anymore. But, I do know one thing, he has had a really successful and large history.

What exactly does Berry Park mean to you?

See, this too stems back to something my father told me when I was very young. I wish these young people would know this at twenty years old, because it's such an easy thing to know. Well, I shouldn't say that. See, I'm speaking from my own experience, so maybe it's not such an easy thing to know. That is, the first thing a man must do is to own a piece of land. When you're young you should have your own place, your digs, your pad, call it what you want, on a plot of land. You know, your domain. Now, you could either rent it or you could own it. Owning it is the best thing. When you go into a store and you buy something it's chattel, but when you own a piece of land that's real. And that's where the word "real estate" originated.

And that's why I own this land in St. Louis— actually it's in Wentzville, Missouri—which is Berry Park, and I also own real estate. I have several buildings with a company called The Investment Company. Owning real estate is like getting right next to the soil, like getting next to the land. And there are additional benefits. Now I know that I'm protected. If I go, if I ramble about, like if I go to Las Vegas or if I go to London or Switzerland, I know that back in St. Louis the United States Federal Government is watching my land and it's protected by the United States Government. And I know when I get back there, it'll still be mine. Now that's what I call groovy. To own a piece of land is like getting the closest to God, I'd say.

How long have you had the park?

The music is actually supporting the park, but I've had the land over ten years and little by little I've been building it up. Right now, we have about nine different people living at Berry Park. That means we have nine different worlds. Like we got one girl from Italy, we got one fellow from here, one person from there. Like all the bikers from the area come. They make it once a year now. In the beginning they were afraid, now they pick their date. They come there and they camp out in the grounds and they get these fires going, man, these large fires all the way out there. You can see them from the house and you can smell it from the house, too. I jive around there a lot. And I practice, jiving and running around with my guitar. I find that playing now, I enjoy it much more, much, much more now because of the environment I'm in. Now this guy came from one of the magazines once and he said these bad things about the park. He said that he couldn't get past the gate. Now, I don't like when they write things like that about me 'cause it's not true. When you come here, you know, it's your place, people from far and wide come here and are always welcome.

You live right there, at the park?

I actually live in the city, about thirty-eight miles from the park, and I spend much of my nights there.

What do you do there at nights?

Do like we're doing now. Listening to the birds, playing a game of chess, eating a piece of chocolate cake. Rapping. You know, normal things. Ah, yes, also watching the sunset, because sundown is the nicest time of the day since you usually don't have any idea of what the night is going to bring.

Do you have a rigid physical fitness program you adhere to at the park?

Not particularly; I work out a great deal at Berry Park. I tinker around. I mow the lawn, I cut the grass and do some carpentry. I make some frames with nails and wood for my pictures. You know, my father as well as my three brothers are carpenters, and Berry Park couldn't really have come together without my brothers.

Didn't you originally want to do the London sessions with the Rolling Stones? I also read once where you said you didn't need any of those young English kids on your sessions to help you sell records.

You're talking about two different things now. I think you are talking about going to London to do the sides instead of just putting out a live album from the Coventry Festival, because we really didn't have enough adequate or audible material from Coventry for an album. So that's why on the spur of the moment we got the London thing together; it didn't have anything to do with the Stones at all.

How well do you keep up with the current trends? Like for instance Marc Bolan of T. Rex borrowing some of your "Little Queenie" riffs in "Bang a Gong"?

Oh, that's the fuck song, isn't it? Well, this I didn't know about until somebody hipped me onto it. I'm usually unaware, just like with John Lennon's song, "Come Together."

Now, I'm not being funny at all, man, because, you see, I perform, one, which takes some time. Then I got to write to keep performing in the same pattern I have been, like writing my material, and you know that alone is a capacity. It takes up time. I have the park which I care about and then I have the real estate business that I care about. Then I got some folks back home that care about me much and in turn I have to care about them. That's the reason why that today unless I'm riding along and listening to the radio, you know, and then you hear and then you don't hear 'cause you're constantly thinking about where you're going and what you're going to do there. You know if it's a venue or something. So I'm really overcapacitated. And that's the reason I say, you talk about the top group, never heard of 'em, you know. This don't seem possible that Chuck Berry never heard of the Beatles. But later on, like nine months later or so and I find out, they were the top group. It won't be a year, but if they get heavy, you know, and they're using some of my stuff, I generally find out.

What of the current rock scene? Do you think it's just a rehash of what went before or is it moving in new directions?

I think it's all new and it's all different.

Many people considered Jimi Hendrix a modern-day

psychedelic Chuck Berry; what did you reckon on the man?

Well, he was like me in that he was different for his time, just like I was different for my time. Yeah, I dug him.

Do you get a chance to listen to all of your cover versions? Are there any that stick out in your mind?

Well, no, not particularly. It's flattering that they do it. The fact that anyone would do it at all, badly or better, comes to me as appreciation and gratification. I'm complimented regardless of its mechanics.

Would you consider the Stones Chuck Berry's finest interpreters? What about Mick Jagger's voice and Keith Richards's guitar work on your stuff?

Well, like I said, I never bear witness upon other men. When these people philosophize about the music and they say, this record is better than that record and this and that, a lot of people put their faith in that. Now, if I say this or that and in five weeks if I turn out to be wrong and a lot of people buy the record because of what I say, I'm the only one to blame. So, I don't do that or give musical opinions. As far as saying that Mick is good or the Stones are good, I don't say that one is better than the other. I just say they're all great.

How about the time Keith Richards jumped onstage at the Palladium in L.A. to jam with you? Did you know it was him?

See, nobody even mentioned this until after I got offstage. I never knew who he was till after the show.

Hadn't you met him before?

Yeah, I mean, jeez. I didn't see him since last year and he was much heavier, plus that he had that shady cap on all the way down over his eyes. But, you should have heard me after the gig, after the session was over [calls out], "Keith, Keith," I'm looking for him, to make amends, for gee, I love the cat.

Then why did you kick him off the stage?

I couldn't be heard. It was my set and, you know, I did want to be heard. You know, how do you say it? I got onstage and started playing and the backing was too loud. So, at the end of the first number I said, "Slow down, it's too loud." But there was no decrease in the volume, in fact the guitar and the piano [Dr. John] seemed to even get louder on the second number. I said if you're gonna play, play with me, not against me. So I just had to finish it after that number. The reason why they actually left was because of what it turned out to be. I surely would have wanted them to play with me, but not just then, you know. I would have suffered

on through whatever. When I got offstage my secretary said, "That was Keith Richards on guitar," and I said, "You gotta be kidding." If I'd known it then, I'd have taken a different approach, 'cause I love 'em. I guess it was just a bad night; they must have been high or something.

Let's talk a little about the early days. What kind of music was around when you were growing up?

Mostly hillbilly, jazz, ballads. I remember Nat Cole.

Were you a record collector of sorts? Did you ever go and listen to these people perform?

Not particularly. I had my favorites, but I did see Nat once in my life and also Duke Ellington.

You started piano at seven or eight and then picked up guitar at . . .

Thirteen. The guitar idea all came to me in high school. Everybody was singing things like [sings], "I think that I shall never see a poem as lovely as a tree," a kind of school song. I came up and did [sings], "Baby here I stand before you with my heart in my hand," you know, "Confessin' the Blues," which was almost like a gut-bucket thing. I was playing in school and the audience kind of grooved on it, and I only had one guitar player because the school band couldn't play it. The school band didn't play that stuff, you know, and it was so groovy with that guitarist and everything that I guess my stage fright just left forever then. Because from then on, walking onstage is like, "What time do I go on, how many songs" and so on. That's the only change I go through. Anyway, that cat, the way he played gassed me and he wasn't singing and so there again, it's all "mathematics." If I could play and sing, well, you know, then he wouldn't have to play and I could do it all by myself at home. So I started picking and plunking. He was nice enough to show me some stuff. After you play one thing, you really like an instrument, it just snowballs and I kept adding to it. And like I added something last night, four bars, and I just want to say, if it isn't mine, it came unconsciously, in a dream.

What do you think of cats like Bill Haley and Gene Vincent who broke out just the year before you? Was there much competition?

Bill Haley—I played with him many a time. We once did forty-five dates in forty-five days together. Gene Vincent as well. In fact, Bill Haley is in the movie we did, I think they shot him in Detroit. See, I remember Haley from the old schooldays at those school hops when I was receiving three or four hundred dollars. I would do a gig here and there and in between, you

231

know, and those were the days when you talk about Bill Haley and that.

In the mid-Fifties, you were virtually the musical spokesman for white middle-class America. How do you think you were able to understand all that coming from a class and culture that was alien to theirs?

Sometimes I feel that I have this power that I could put my finger on things and bring them out, like age. Right away I guessed your age and your friend's age. Now, if I had this power a few years ago, I might not have gotten into all that trouble about age. You see, the songs were like a mixture of things, things that I did and saw. Everything I wrote about wasn't about me, but about the people listening to them. Like, I didn't write "School Day" in a classroom. I wrote that in the Street Hotel, one of the big, black, low-priced hotels in St. Louis.

Do you think that the rhythms and the same sexual innuendos you were playing back in '55 are still turning them on now?

Sure, human nature is still human nature. It's still gonna be the same. Like people got off to "Silent Night" in the old days and they're still digging it this year. Time is not an element, frankly. Like, in songs like "Sweet Little Sixteen," I change the things. I used to say: "She's wearing tight dresses and lipstick," and now I'm saying "mini-skirts and hot pants." In "Too Much Monkey Business," I change the places from Okinawa to Vietnam. It's just a matter of what's contemporary and what isn't.

In such tunes as "Sweet Little Sixteen," "Rock and Roll Music" and "Johnny B. Goode," I detect some Latin-style variations and rhythms.

Well, you're right on the ball. I don't know, you detect all these little things. About that time, the mambo-calypso thing was going around, even Nat jumped in with a calypso song and made Number One. I sort of just touched around and put a little Latin bit into it for some flavor. I even cut a couple of other things like that, "Havana Moon," "La Juanda (Espanol)," and I also cut some things with some Spanish lyrics and French lyrics.

In "Johnny B. Goode," a local country boy makes it in the big city. Was that meant to be autobiographical?

More or less it is. You see, the original words for that was, of course, "that little colored boy could play," and then I changed it to "country boy," of course, or else it wouldn't get on the radio. Now, if it was a country-western type of singer, he definitely would have put in "country boy" right away, some proper names too, but you see I couldn't.

"Johnny B. Goode," "Bye, Bye Johnny" and "Let It Rock" seem like a musical trilogy.

Well, I'll tell you, the Johnny in "Johnny B. Goode" and "Bye, Bye Johnny" were the same. Now, the Johnny in "Tulane" who opened this business with his girlfriend selling weed under the counter in his novelty shop, that was just another Johnny, 'cause that's the name one uses, you know. Now, "Let It Rock" has no Johnny in it, but maybe it just sounds like it should.

Wouldn't you say that "Sweet Little Sixteen" was the original groupies' lament?

Yeah, I used plenty of names of cities in that one. Another song like that was "Route 66," with all the names. I was nurtured on that song. Yeah, sure, probably even Frank had groupies back then.

What was "Jo-Jo Gunne" all about?

Well, you know, that was a novel animal song. Now, in between I put a little of these innuendos like the Gillette razor blade, Friday-night-fight theme song, when they were having the fight. It was more or less about animals and craziness.

What about "Anthony Boy"?

Well, I wrote that in Massachusetts and it was dedicated to the people there. There was a total Italian ethnic faction of people there and it is about the Italian stud, the good-looking Italian boy who makes it with all the girls in school.

"Almost Grown"?

Well, it was about kids who want to be a little older than they are and . . . I always get kicked in the shins by my girlfriend over here for that one.

What's the story on "Memphis"?

I played all the instruments on that and we did it in the office with my secretary, this Jewish girl, Fran, playing drums. Yeah, and she also played drums on a whole album later.

How did "Ding-a-Ling" come about?

Foolishness again. You know, I am sex-oriented. Well, it's true, so there it is. But I mean, it isn't anything special. I mean, who cares about my sex, anyhow?

Did you ever hear a version of "Ding-a-Ling" titled "Toy Bells" by the Bees in 1953?

Might have heard it. Well, let's say I might have listened to it. You know, when you're riding along you hear these songs that you don't really hear.

WHAT DID YOU THINK OF *Elvis Presley, when you first heard him?*

I didn't think he was as good as the Everly Brothers the first time I ever laid eyes on him. Of course, that's kind of freaky too, because I didn't think the Beatles were as good as the Everly Brothers either; you know, I kind of like two-part harmony.

When you were both vying for the top spot, was Presley the enemy?

No, now you see there again, it's into this jealous thing. No, as a matter of fact, I liked what he was doing commercially. I was trying to see in what aspect did it reach the public. Because my view is not generally like the general public or the gross public view, and whatever he was doing, if I didn't have that, it may be well and good to add it into my thing. But, as far as success and all that, I was never jealous of him.

Didn't it ever occur to you that the color of his skin probably had a lot to do with his instant success?

Now that you mention it, actually, it did occur to me. I mean, I'm saying it like it is. It's obvious that his road was free and mine had to be paved.

Exactly what kind of detours did you come across because of that?

Well, Presley didn't ensue any of that. But no, seriously, well, jeez, lots of occurrences came up. Some people call them hassles or detours. I call them experiences. For instance, like eating in the back of the bus. Sure, I ate hot meals in the back, why not? Some of my brethren that were with me, you know, would sit in the car and wonder why I would go to the back. And here I am, and the Spaniels have got claustrophobia, hypervirginity and all that and I think I'm pretty healthy, because I ate that good back-door food, and the food at least was hot. I really didn't care which window it came out of, I just wanted some of that hot food and that was the only place to get it, in the back windows. So, as a matter of fact, a lot of times I dug it, 'cause then I not only got to eat the food, but also to see how they lived, because they were probably just like anybody else, and you know that "wisdom" is the best thing you can have in the world.

Was there any one real uncomfortable experience that popped up?

Many, many, many like [knocks three times on table], "Let me see your driver's license, boy." That's a familiar one, the knock of the law. You know, when you got company in the back seat, especially forbidden company, you know, that's a hell of an experience. Like, one time I just got an ice cream cone in something, Arkansas, in one of those gravel drive-ins where you park, and I pulled away and my wheel rubbed a little bit on the gravel. And wow, again, "Let's see your driver's license, boy." "Did I do something wrong?" "You're damn right you did, boy. They don't let you in here and that will be twenty-two dollars for reckless driving." And I was going but thirty miles an hour before he stopped me again half an hour later.

Have you ever had any trouble with parents who accuse you of corrupting their children?

Not really, why, did you?

Well, did you ever get run out of town or arrested or anything like that by some crazy momma?

Now, I been run out of town, and I've been arrested and I've been anything like that, but mostly by crazy police.

I was wondering about your run-in with the establishment and the incidents that occurred afterwards?

Well, which time? I've had many run-ins with the establishment, now which run-in and what establishment are you talking about?

The U.S. Government.

You're now talking about that Indian girl, right? Well, this is a topic you're not going to get much out of me, I have to admit.

Why are you so secretive about it? Aren't you going to divulge that information, anyway? Had it been a WASP landowner wearing your shoes back in 1961, don't you think he would have gone free?

Well, this was a strange thing. Very strange thing; you see, I am naturally a good person. I had brought this girl to my club from Mexico. You see, I had this club in St. Louis, Chuck Berry's Bandstand, in which I actually took the name in dedication of Dick Clark's show *American Bandstand.*

What year was that around?

Around '59. It was '59, the late part of '58 and '59.

How long did you manage it?

A year and a half. You see, we had all sorts of people working there. Some girls, some other people, all weird; we had an Italian girl there, we had a Jewish girl there and so on. So we dressed this Indian girl up in some feathers and got her some boxes of cigarettes and we wanted to have her walk around the club selling cigarettes. I wanted to be as far out, for the time, as I could and I was. Things were pretty good. Like across the street from the club there was another club where the blacks weren't allowed at all. It was really a strange scene. They sort of wanted to get rid of me there. They wanted to take care of me,

233

'cause I was taking a lot of their business.

And there was a hotel across the street. A black hotel. And she was there occasionally and she started to—well, for one thing, I really didn't know her right age. I met this black girl in El Paso or somewhere in Texas on my way up to St. Louis and she said that this Indian girl was twenty-two. The black girl was twenty-three and she said that this Indian was twenty-two and I totally believed her. You see, I didn't have that insight like I have now to predict ages. So, I brought the Indian girl to St. Louis and I gave her the job, and after a while she would go around to the hotel to make some extra money. I never knew she was no prostitute, but she was a prostitute. And in a little while, she had a run-in with one of the people there. He slapped her around so that the police were called in on the matter and it all came back. Who are you, where are you from, what's this, what's that, who brought you here? And boom, I was in court not knowing what age she was or that she was a prostitute. Then everything came to the surface. They brought up all past charges. They didn't want my club; they wanted to get rid of me. If I remember, my club had to close down.

Could nothing have been done by Chess at the time concerning the courts? Couldn't you grease someone's palm?

No. At that point they really wanted me. I paid $22,000 and it only cost me two or three thousand for my lawyer. He didn't even have an office. That's how bad things were. But nothing really came of it. You see, there was two or three different trials, and one was thrown out of the courts because the judge was fairly biased and finally I was acquitted, you see. That's the misconceptions that people have, that Chuck Berry went to jail. They're just totally wrong, totally wrong. It might have said something in the large papers in the bigger city headlines and things. But, you take a look at any of the local papers and you will see that I was acquitted. I never went to jail.

Are any of your songs about the incident?

Well, I don't see that. I was never to jail.

How about "Have Mercy Judge," especially the parts about "traffic of the forbidden" and "almost finished doing my parole"?

Oh, now I understand, I see where they could think that.

Well, a lot of people think that those songs refer to your jail sentence. There's even stories that you first heard the Beach Boys' version of "Surfin' U.S.A." in a prison cell.

Well, I was never in jail. I was acquitted.

What personal scars did this leave with you, bitterness, resentment, revenge?

No, no, not really any of them three things. It was a learning process, a matter of trust. As far as putting it in my own book, I mention it slightly, but it's not a major thing. See, you're probably going to call this "The Chuck Berry Interview," right? If it's Chuck Berry, that means it's all music, because Chuck Berry is music. Now, the people who read your magazine want to know about that. But Charles Berry is a man who has certain things that he wants to keep to himself; and in my biography, I'm going to put down philosophies and theories about Charles Berry as well as Chuck Berry, because they overlap. But, we'll keep this one to just Chuck, but in the book it will be Charles as well.

And Edward and Anderson?

Oh yeah, and H.W. too, the father of them all. You see, the world of Charles Edward Anderson Berry and Chuck Berry are sometimes different; although they sometimes overlap. When I'm on-stage that's totally Chuck Berry. But, Charles Edward Anderson Berry is a private man, and he can't bend over backwards for another man, if it's going to hurt him. I can't let myself get hurt, because I have to be the one that has to be happy and if I have to make another man happy at my sacrifice, or if I'm going to be unhappy, I can't do it. Now, let me tell you this; at times I become very hot and cold, moody, very schizophrenic. Now, don't take it as a personal attitude towards you because it's really controlled schizophrenia, and I'm controlling it.

19

INTERVIEWED BY JERRY HOPKINS (1972)

Keith Moon died of an overdose of a prescribed sedative mixed with alcohol on September 7, 1978. He died, as ROLLING STONE said in its obituary, "before he got old." Rejecting the talk that his death was a suicide, bassist John Entwistle said: "He loved life too much." Others would say he lived it too hard. The surviving images of Keith Moon have him playing some of the fiercest drums around—and destroying every hotel room he ever inhabited.

"Keith had this *reputation*," says Jerry Hopkins. "And rather than just hearing all these outrageous stories, we decided to get them from the horse's ass, so to say."

In late 1972, when Moon, twenty-five, managed to sit long enough for this interview, the Who had released the album, *Who's Next*, which would rank as one of the band's most successful studio recordings.

Hopkins, who interviewed Jim Morrison three years earlier, says Moon and Morrison shared an affection for wild life, "but for different reasons. Morrison was testing boundaries, in a sort of artistic, intellectual way. Moon was just mooning the world, to use a bad pun. He was like a little boy who found himself with the key to the candy store and had enough money to buy himself out of trouble."

When Moon died, Hopkins thought about Morrison, and a few other rock artists. "They played Russian roulette every day of their lives," he says. "Keith could've died any number of ways. He seemed pedaled to the metal, and the consequences be damned."

As critic Greil Marcus observed: "Keith Moon was a man of terrible destructive passion. For a time he organized it all into his music. When I listen now, the records he left behind make him sound like more than the best drummer in rock & roll history, which he quite obviously was. They make him sound like the only one."

—BF-T

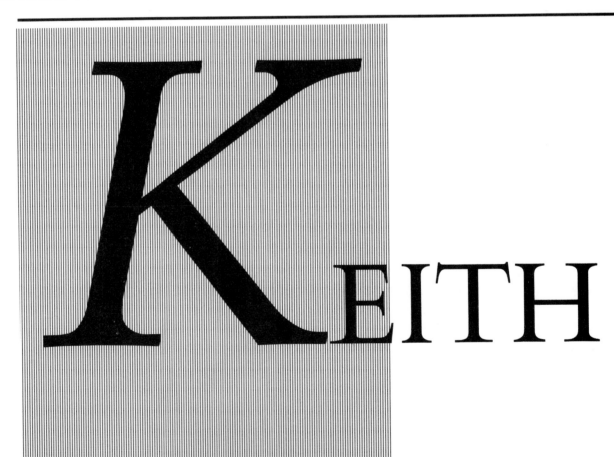

KEITH

MOON

IT IS PROBABLY FITTING THAT KEITH Moon plays the most aggressive instrument, drums, in the most explosive of groups, the Who, for Moon clearly seems more outrageous and more violent than any of his contemporaries. Behind him for a period of ten years, for more than third of his life, he has left a trail of empty Courvoisier bottles, splintered drum kits, wrecked automobiles and gutted hotel rooms, punctuating every inconceivable incident with a bark of total pleasure and amusement.

There are uncounted "Keith Moon Stories" floating around. Keith tells several here. Unfortunately, much is lost in translating Moon to print. His energetic sprints around the room, his dozen or so precise vocal impressions and dialects, the rubbery, gap-toothed face, the singing and dancing, the infectious volleys of laughter—all must be experienced.

So must his $150,000 modern house, set on the site of an ancient monastery nearly an hour from London in the green suburban stockbroker belt. The walls of the bar are painted in a Marvel Comics hero-villain motif, and the ceiling is draped like a sultan's tent. The sitting room is a huge, richly cushioned "conversation pit" with a color television and a stainless-steel fireplace that's never been used. There is almost no furniture, anywhere. But there is a stuffed albatross, a polar bear rug, several rifles, an old jukebox and a sound system that will send multidecibel music far beyond the boundaries of his seven-acre estate.

From the outside, the house looks to be a collection of square pyramids, painted a glaring white. On one side is a tree so large it had to be lowered in by two helicopters. On the other side workmen are presently excavating a swimming pool that will be lined with marble and will offer the underwater swimmer the latest recorded melodies.

When I arrived, the live-in housekeeper—Moon's mother-in-law—was in Spain on holiday. His long-haired mechanic and driver, Dougal, was working on the engine of the 1936 Chrysler, which was parked between the XKE Jaguar and the Dino Ferrari. The missus, Kim, and the child, Mandy, 6, were out. And the lord of the manor was banging away with a shotgun, firing randomly into the tall leafy reaches of a horse chestnut tree.

H*OW DID YOU BEGIN WITH THE Who?*
First they were called the Detours, then the Who, then the High Numbers, then the Who again. I joined in the second phase, when they were changing from the Detours to the Who. I was in another group on the same pub circuit called the Beachcombers.

Does that mean surfing music?

It did when I joined, yeah. AH-HAHA HAHAHA!

Ever been surfing?

Once, and I nearly fucking killed meself. We were in Hawaii, and I said I must surf. Jesus, I been buying surfing records for years, you know, I've got to try it. So I rented a board and paddled out with all these other guys. The wahines were on the beach. Woodies. Surfers' paradise, right? I took off in the distance and there's a huge wave coming. I said to one of the guys, "What do I do?" And he said {*Moon goes into a cool, anonymous American voice*}, "Well, okay, buddy, all you got to do when you see that wave there comin', she hits, boy, she hits, and you want to be traveling at relatively the same speed, so you paddle." Perfectly logical. I said, great. And then this solid wall of water came. All of a sudden this bloody thing hit me up the arse, and I move from like doing two miles an hour to two hundred! I'm hanging onto the sides of the bloody board, y'see, and I hear: "Stand up, man!" Stand up? So I stand up and I look up and there's water all around me, I'm in a great funnel, a great big sort of tube of water. And then I see the coral reef coming up. I'd only been on me feet for about two seconds, but it seemed like a fucking lifetime. Sod it! Sod it! I fell off, the wave crashed down on the reef, the board went backwards and then was thrown up in the air by the water. I surfaced, shook me 'ead and relaxed. Then I looked up and saw this bloody board coming from about sixty feet in the air straight at me 'ead. I went underwater and it went sssssshhwwwooom! I've got a bald patch ever since where it scraped me skull. AH-HA-ha-HA-HA-ha-ha-ha! Jan and Dean never told it like it really was. Certainly bloody didn't!

So the Beachcombers was a surfing band, sort of?

Sort of. It relied on vocals more than instruments. As I'm a disgusting singer . . . I mean, the boys don't let me sing. I don't blame them. I sometimes forget meself and join in, and they have to come down on me: "Moon . . . out!" I mean, I even get sent offstage during "Behind Blue Eyes" just in case I forget meself. It's the only number of the Who's that really requires precise harmony. The rest of it's all: "YEEEAAAAHHHHH-Magic-Bus!" We shout. It doesn't matter. So they send me off during "Blue Eyes" because either I'm buggering about and I put the boys off, or I try to sing and really put them off.

Anyway, I'd decided my talent as a drummer was wasted in a tight-knit harmony group like the Beachcombers, and the only band that I heard of that sounded as loud as I did was the Detours. So when I heard their drummer had left, I laid plans to insinuate meself into the group. They were playing at a pub near me, the Oldfield. I went down there, and they had a session drummer sitting in with them. I got up onstage and said, "Well, I can do better than him." They said go ahead, and I got behind this other guy's drums and I did one song—"Road Runner." I'd had several drinks to get me courage up, and when I got onstage I went arrrrggGHHHHHHH on the drums, broke the base drum pedal and two skins and got off. I figured that was it. I was scared to death.

Afterwards I was sitting at the bar, and Pete came over. He said, "You . . . come 'ere." I said, mild as you please: "Yesyes?" And Roger, who was the spokesman then, said, "What're you doing next Monday?" I said, "Nothing." I was working during the day, selling plaster. He said, "You'll have to give up work." I said, "All right, I'll pack in work." Roger said, "There's this gig on Monday. If you want to come, we'll pick you up in the van." I said, "Right." They said they'd come by at seven. And that was it. Nobody ever said, "You're in." They just said, "What're you doing Monday?"

Were you being managed by Kit Lambert and Chris Stamp at this point?

No, we were with a man who made doorknobs—young, naive lads that we were. This man's suggestions were the only ones we got, except the lewd ones from the audience. We really didn't have faith in ourselves then. Then when we settled in, the suggestions seemed ludicrous, so we decided to get rid of him, and Kit Lambert came to see us playing at the Railway 'Otel in 'Arrow. We had a meeting. We didn't like each other at first, really. Kit and Chris. They went 'round together. And they were . . . are . . . as incongruous a team as we are. You got Chris on one hand *(goes into unintelligible East London cockney)*: "Oh well, fuck it, jus, jus whack 'im in-a 'ead, 'it 'im in ee balls an' all." And Kit says *(slipping into a proper Oxonian)*: "Well, I don't agree, Chris; the thing is . . . the whole thing needs to be thought out in damned fine detail." These people were perfect for us, because there's me, bouncing about, full of pills, full of everything I could get me 'ands on . . . and there's Pete, very serious, never laughed, always cool, a grass-'ead. I was working at about ten times the speed Pete was. And Kit

and Chris were like the epitome of what we were.

When you went with them, the Mod image was . . .

. . . forced on us. It was very dishonest. The mod thing was Kit's idea. We were all sent down to a hairdresser, Robert James. Absolutely charming lad. We were then sent to Carnaby Street with more money than we'd ever seen in our lives before, like a hundred quid [$250] each. This was Swinging London. Most of our audience were mods, pill-'eads like ourselves, you see. We weren't into clothes; we were into music. Kit thought we should identify more with our audience. Coats slashed five inches at the sides. Four wasn't enough. Six was too much. Five was just right. The trousers came three inches below the hip. It was our uniform.

Your motto at the time was "maximum R&B." What did that mean?

We were playing a lot of Bo Diddley, Chuck Berry, Elmore James, B. B. King, and they are maximum R&B. You can't get any better. Most of the songs we played were their songs. Pete really got into his writing stride after "Can't Explain." Of course any song we did get 'old of, we weren't playing straight from the record. We "Who'd" it, so that what came out was the Who, not a copy.

Like "Summertime Blues."

Exactly. That's a song that's been "Who'd."

How did the stuttering effect in "My Generation" evolve?

Pete had written out the words and gave them to Roger in the studio. He'd never seen them before, he was unfamiliar with the words, so when he read them through the first time, he stuttered. Kit was producing us then, and when Roger stuttered, Kit said *(Oxonian accent)*: "We leave it in; leave in the stuttering." When we realized what'd happened, it knocked us all sideways. And it happened simply because Roger couldn't read the words.

THE FIRST AMERICAN TOUR. DO you remember it with fondness?

For me it was a tour of discovery. it was three months with 'Erman's 'Ermits. Backing up the 'Ermits was ideal. It was a position that suited us. We weren't on the line. If the place sold only a portion of what it could 'ave sold, the disaster was never blamed on us, it was blamed on 'Erman's 'Ermits. We didn't have the responsibility. We had time to discover. We found the good towns.

Which ones are they?

For the Who they're New York, *Chicago, Detroit, Los Angeles, San Francisco and Cleveland. They have the best audiences for us.

Was it on this tour you had your infamous birthday party?

Yes. That's how I lost me front tooth. In Flint, Michigan. We had a show that night. We were all around the 'Oliday Inn pool, 'Erman's 'Ermits and meself. I was twenty-one, and they started giving me presents. Somebody gave me a portable bar and somebody else the portable booze. I'd started drinking about ten o'clock in the morning, and I can't remember the show. Then the record companies 'ad booked a big room in the 'otel, one of the conference rooms, for a party. As the hours went on, it got louder and louder, and everybody started getting well out their minds, well stoned. The pool was the obvious target. Everybody started jumping in the pool with their clothes on.

The Premier Drum Company 'ad given me a 'uge birthday cake, with like five drums stacked up on top of each other. As the party degenerated into a slanging, I picked up the cake, all five tiers, and hurled it at the throng. People'd started picking up the pieces and 'urling it about. Everybody was covered with marzipan and icing sugar and fruitcake. The manager 'eard the fracas and came in. There it was, his great carpet, stained irrevocably with marzipan and fruitcake trodden in, and everybody dancing about with their trousers off. By the time the sheriff came in I was standing there in me underpants. I ran out, jumped into the first car I came to, which was a brand-new Lincoln Continental. It was parked on a slight hill, and when I took the handbrake off, it started to roll and it smashed straight through this pool surround [fence], and the whole Lincoln Continental went into the 'Oliday Inn swimming pool, with me in it. AH-HA-HA-HA-HA!

So there I was, sitting in the eight-foot-six in the driver's seat of a Lincoln Continental, underwater. And the water was pouring in—coming in through the bloody pedal 'oles in the floorboard, you know, squirting in through the windows. In a startling moment of logical I said, "Well, I can't open the doors until the pressure is the same. . . ." It's amazing 'ow I remembered those things from my physics class! I knew I'd 'ave to wait until the pressure was the same.

So I'm sitting there, thinking about me situation, as the water creeps up to me nose.

Today I can think of less outrageous ways of going than drowning in a Lincoln Continental in a 'Oliday Inn swimming pool, but at that time I 'ad no thoughts of death whatsoever. There was none of that all-me-life-passing-before-me-eyes-in-a-flash. I was busy planning. I knew if I panicked, I'd 'ave 'ad it. So when there's just enough air in the top of the car to take a gulp, I fill up me lungs, throw open the door and go rising to the top of the pool. I figured there'd be quite a crowd gathered by now. After all, I'd been down there underwater for some time. I figured they'd be so grateful I was alive, they'd overlook the Lincoln Continental. But no. There's only one person standing there and 'e's the pool cleaner, and 'e's got to have the pool cleaned in the morning, and he's furious.

So I went back to the party, streaming water, still in me underpants. The first person I see is the sheriff, and he's got 'is 'and on 'is gun. Sod this! And I ran, I started to leg it out the door, and I slipped on a piece of marzipan and fell flat on me face and knocked out me tooth. Ah-ha-ha-HA-HA-HAHAHA!

I spent the remainder of the night under the custody of the sheriff at a dentist's. The dentist couldn't give me any anesthetic because I was pissed out of me mind. So 'e 'ad to rip out what was left of the tooth and put a false one in, and the next day I spent a couple of hours in the nick [jail]. The boys 'ad chartered me a plane because they 'ad to leave on an earlier flight. The sheriff took me out in the law car, and he puts me on the plane and says {*American accent*}, "Son, don't ever dock in Flint, Michigan, again." I said, "Dear boy, I wouldn't dream of it." And I was lisping around the new tooth. AH-HAHA HAHAHA!

By now I'd learned 'ow destructive we'd all been. During the merriment someone 'ad upset all the fire extinguishers and turned them on all the cars in the car park. Six of them 'ad to 'ave new paint jobs; the paint all peeled off. We'd also destroyed a piano. Completely destroyed it. Reduced it to kindling. And don't forget the carpet. And the Lincoln Continental in the bottom of the pool. So I got a bill for $24,000. AH-HAHAHAHA! I wasn't earning 'alf that on the tour, and I'd spent everything by the time I'd got to Flint, Michigan. I was in debt up past me eyebrows before this 'appened. Luckily, 'Erman's 'Ermits and the boys split it up; about thirty of us all gave a thousand dollars each. It was like a religious ceremony as we all came up and dropped a thousand dollars into a big 'at and sent it off to the 'Oliday Inn with a small compliments card with "BALLS" written across it—and the words, "See you soon." Ah-ha-ha-HA-HA Ha-ho-HAHAHA!

You can't have destroyed as many rooms as legend has it.

You want to bet?

Have there been other times when . . .

Lots. Yes. I get bored, you see. There was a time in Saskatoon, in Canada. It was another 'Oliday Inn, and I was bored. Now, when I get bored, I rebel. I said, "FUCK IT, FUCK THE LOT OF YA!" And I took out me 'atchet and chopped the 'otel room to bits. The television. The chairs. The dresser. The cupboard doors. The bed. The lot of it. Ah-ha-ha-HAHAHAHAHAHAHAHA-HAHAHA! It happens all the time.

I've always heard it was Pete who started the destruction onstage, but you make it sound as if it might've been your idea. Was it?

The way the story goes, Pete put the neck of his guitar through a low ceiling when he jumped too 'igh, but that's not it. It 'appened when somebody got pissed off with the gig, with the way things were going. When Pete smashed his guitar it was because 'e was pissed off. When I smashed me drums, it was because I was pissed off. We were frustrated. You're working as hard as you can to get that fucking song across, to get that audience by the balls, to make it an event. When you've done all that, when you've worked your balls off and you've given the audience everything you can give, and they'd don't give anything back, that's when the fucking instruments go, because: "You fucking bastards! We've worked our fucking balls off! And you've given us nothing back!"

That's one way the instruments got smashed. Another way was if a member of the group was too fuckin' stoned to give their best. Then he was letting down the other three. In a lot of cases it was me, through drinking too much. You know, just getting out of it at the wrong time. Then Pete or Roger or John says, "You cunt! You fucking let us down! You fucking bastard, if you want to get pissed, why don't you wait until after the show!"

But every time you destroyed your drum kit, or Pete wrecked his guitar it wasn't motivated by anger . . .

Not every time. It became expected—like a song, a Number One record. Once you've done it, you're committed to it. You 'ave to play it. Because there are some people in the audience who've only come to 'ear that one song. You know they're there. You can't ignore them. So

what we do is make a spot in the act that does the job. Every part of the act works to a part of the audience, and the act as a whole must work to the entire audience.

Wasn't it pretty expensive?

It was fucking expensive. We were smashing up probably ten times if not more than we were earning. We've been going successfully for ten years, but we've only made money the last three. It took us five years to pay off three years, our most destructive period. We had to pay all that back. Musicians are renowned for not paying their bills. And we were no exception. We put it off as long as we could. But when the writs started coming in, the court orders, the injunctions, the equipment confiscations, then we 'ad to pay. And we paid for five years.

And then dropped the destructo routine?

We dropped it as a theatrical routine. We still destroy our equipment occasionally, but not on order. We'd committed one of the cardinal sins: We'd actually let the theatrics overtake the music. You can't let that 'appen. The music must be first. So we just turned around and said, "Well, this has got to fucking go, we can't have this every show. . . ." Because it was becoming too hackneyed. The spontaneity was lost.

WERE THERE EVER DISAGREE-*ments over who was the group's spokesman?*

Only in the early days. At one time Roger was the group's spokesman. Now most people say Pete is. The thing is, it doesn't matter . . . who says it. At one time we placed great importance on a spokesman and who that spokesman was. Not now. Whoever it is, 'e's just a mouthpiece for the organization, and one mouth is as good as another.

You all seem to be fairly available to the press.

We're doing fuck-all else. AH-HAHAHAHAHA-HA! Some people say I'll do anything for the press, it's true . . . that I make meself too available. I just like to 'ave fun.

For instance . . .

There was the time Keith Altham and Chris Williams, who look after our PR, phoned me up and said I 'ad to be at their office at three o'clock for an interview. Well, you know, the pubs shut at three, so I was rather delayed, because they don't turn out until ten past, and they don't turn me out until ha'-past. So it was quarter to four before I eventually started. I was back up my office at Track [Records] and finally I remembered; I'd forgotten all about it. So, uhhhh: Oh Christ, they're gonna be angry. Right opposite the office is a chemist's, so I sent Dougal, me driver, over there to pick up some rolls of bandages and plaster, and I did all me leg up, strapped me arms up and purchased a stick, a walking stick. Then I went over to the office. "Sorry I'm late, but the 'ospital delayed me."

I'd called earlier and told them I'd been run over by a bus on Oxford Street. They didn't think that unlikely. I think they've adopted the attitude that anything's likely with Moon, y'see. So I walk into the office . . . 'obble in, actually . . . and they say. "'Ow did it 'appen?" I said, "I was just crossing Oxford Street and a Number Eight from Shepherd's Bush 'it me right up the arse and sent me spinning across Oxford Circus." So Keith and Chris say they'll cancel the interview. I say no, but maybe they'd be so kind as to carry me down the four flights of steps to the street. They thought I'd come up by meself, on me walking stick, y'see.

So they carried me down the stairs and we're walking along, I'm 'obbling along the street again, and this bloody lorry comes along as I'm crossing the street and it screams to a 'alt in front of me. I say, "'Ang on, mate, I can't go fast on these legs," and Keith has a go at the lorry driver: "You 'eartless bastard, can't you see this man's injured! 'Ave you no 'eart, 'ave you no soul, you bastard! Trying to run over a cripple!"

We went on to the interview and in the middle, after about four brandies, I just ripped off all the plaster and jumped up on the seat and started dancing. Ah-HAHAHAHAH-ha-haHAHA! HAHA!

Have you ever been injured in any of your stunts? Aside from the missing front tooth?

I broke me collarbone once. That was in me own 'otel, the one I own, one Christmas. I collapsed in front of the fire at four o'clock one morning and some friends of mine decided to put me to bed, and they were in as bad a state as I was, but they were still on their feet. Just about. One of them got 'old of me 'ead, the other got 'old of me feet, and they attempted to drag me up the stairs. They got me up two flights and then promptly dropped me down, both of them, breaking me collarbone, y'see. But I didn't know this until I woke up in the morning and tried to put me fucking shirt on. I went through the fucking roof.

Now . . . I was supposed to do a television show, the *Top of the Pops* New Year's Eve special, and two days before I 'ave me arm all strapped up so I can't drum. I went to me doctor, dear Doctor Robert, and he gave me a shot on the day of the gig so I wouldn't feel anything. I put a shirt over the cast, fastened the drumstick to my wrist with sticking plaster, sat down behind the drum kit and got Mr. Vivian Stanshall to tie a rope around me wrist. We then threw the rope over the lighting pipe overhead, the one that holds the floods and all, and I kept an eye on the television monitor; every time I was on camera, I'd give the signal to Viv, and he'd give a pull on the rope, which caused me right arm to shoot up and then come crashing down on the cymbal. AH ah ah ah HAHAHAHAHAHAHAHAHAHAHAHA!

These farcical situations . . . I'm always tied up in them. They're always as if they could be a Laurel and Hardy sketch. And they always 'appen to me. AAAAHhhhhh-HAHAHA-HO-HAHA ha! I think unconsciously I want them to 'appen, and they do.

Is that the image you have of yourself?

I suppose to most people I'm probably seen as an amiable idiot . . . a genial twit. I think I must be a victim of circumstance, really. Most of it's me own doing. I'm a victim of me own practical jokes. I suppose that reflects a rather selfish attitude: I like to be the recipient of me own doings. Nine times out of ten I am. I set traps and fall into them. Oh-ha-ha-ha. HA-HA-HA-HA-HA! Of course, the biggest danger is becoming a parody.

Your wife, Kim, must be extraordinarily sympathetic and patient.

She is. She sort of takes it in 'er stride.

How did you meet her?

Eh-eh-eheeeee-eh-eh-eh. Ah-HA-HA-HA-HA-HA-HA-HA! I met her in Bournemouth when I was playing a show. She was sixteen, and she hung out at the club when we worked, the Disc. Sometime later when I went down to see her, I was on a train and Rod Stewart was on the train. This was about ten years ago. We got chatting, and we went to the bar car. It was Rod "The Mod" Stewart in those glorious days, and he'd just been working with Long John Baldry. He was playing a lot of small discotheques and pubs, doing the sort of work we were doing. I said to Rod, "Where are you going?" He said, "Bournemouth." "So'm I," I said, "I'm going down there to see my chick." He said, "So'm I." So I showed Rod a picture of Kim and he said, "Yeah . . . that's 'er." HAHAHAHAHAHAHA!

What happened?

I don't remember. We were in the bar car, and we both got paralytic. I only remember the trip back. Oh-hee-HA-HA-HAHA!

How'd your mother-in-law come to live with you?

She's me 'ousekeeper. And she's a great cook. You see, I was cradle snatching. I snatched her daughter at sixteen, right out of convent school, and she 'adn't learned 'ow to cook yet, so I said, "Get your mother up 'ere." She's been living with us for about a year now. She's not the accepted idea of a mother-in-law. At my 'ouse there's no real accepted idea of anything.

Do you have "favorite" drummers?

Not many. D. J. Fontana [Elvis' original drummer] is one. Let's see . . . the drummers I respect are Eric Delaney and Bob Henrit [from Argent] and . . . I got a 'uge list, really, and all for different reasons. Technically, Joe Morello is perfect. I don't really have a favorite drummer. I have favorite drum pieces, and that's it. I would never put on an LP of a drummer and say everything he did I love, because that's not true.

How'd you start on drums?

Jesus Christ, I think I got a free drum kit in a packet of corn flakes. Ah-Ha-HA-HA-HA-HA-ha-HA! But no . . . drum solos are fucking boring. Any kind of solo is. It detracts from the group identity.

How much of a group effort are the songs? How much do you change those demos when you record?

Not a hell of a lot. Because Pete knows. When Pete writes something, it sounds like the Who. The drum phrases are my phrases, even though it's Pete playing drums. He's playing the way I play. He's playing my flourishes. The same thing for the bass part, and the guitar, of course, is 'is own. Only the vocals change some.

Are many of the songs rejected?

No. He obviously writes a lot more . . . I mean, not every song that 'e writes is suitable for the Who. When he gets an idea 'e thinks is right for the group, 'e brings it in and we try it. It's not very often that 'e's wrong.

Do you rehearse a lot?

We've always prepared for live shows meticulously. But we rehearsed a damn sight more often several years ago than we do now. Now we've reached a peak in the band . . . well, we reached it a long time ago . . . so now Pete plays us a number or we listen to a number, and we can get it off pretty much if not the first time, the second or the third, and by the fourth or fifth it's begun to be battered into shape. In the old days, we were still getting the group together, still working out our own relationships.

The Who's never really been a "singles band." Was this by design?

Pete wrote "Can't Explain" as a single. He wrote "My Generation" as a single. But he's never really been one for writing singles. He doesn't like to sit down and write a single. He likes to write a project . . . and an LP is viewed as a project, a group project. A single is something you take off an LP. We don't go in an' do singles. The singles market really is not our market. If one of the tracks on an LP sounds like it might be a single, then it's released as such.

We had a period of singles after "My Generation"—"I'm a Boy," "Substitute," "Happy Jack." But then we went into making LPs. And once you get into making LPs, it's very difficult to go back to making singles.

Two years later, how do you look back on 'Tommy'?

With disbelief. AH-HAHAHA. I can't believe we spent six months doing it. It took six months to make. That's studio time, and that's talking about it, discussing it, arranging it, producing and writing it. Getting it all together. Recording it and then saying we could do it better and recording it again. Six months continuously in the studio.

Other than with disbelief, how do you remember it?

Well, it *is* disbelief. I just can't believe that we did that album. It was an amazing album to do. It was, at the time, very un-Who-like. A lot of the songs were sort of soft. We never played like that. And we didn't have an idea then as to how it was all going to turn out. Here we were, spending all this time on a project that none of us really knew all that much about.

Who came up with the phrase "rock opera"?

Pete. We really didn't know what else to call it. And people kept asking what we were doing.

Then came the 'Tommy' tours.

Because we'd been in the studio so long, we immediately went on an American tour. We incorporated a lot of *Tommy*. In fact, the act was mostly *Tommy*. After that, on the Opera 'Ouse tour, we played just two numbers to warm up; we'd do "Summertime Blues" and "Can't Explain" or something, and then we'd do the opera. We did about six or seven opera 'ouses. I enjoyed them. Nice sound. But it was a bit strange. It was rather like playing to an oil painting.

Did there come a time when you got tired of 'Tommy'?

Oh, yes. Very shortly after we made it. Ah-HAHAHAHAHAHAHA-HAHA! Yeah, it started becoming a bit of a bore. Everywhere we'd go we'd do our little show, and it became so we were playing it in our sleep. Toward the end we got bored. We played eighteen months nonstop. All the spontaneity was going. So somebody finally said, "All right, sod it, out with it! Who's next?" And it was. That was the next album.

The Who's always been a working band, a touring band. Do you still enjoy the road?

{*Using soft voice, as if delivering a eulogy*} I love it. It's my life. If I was to be deprived of touring . . . I love the responsibility of . . . being responsible for the enjoyment of a packed 'ouse. And knowing the four of us can go onstage and give enjoyment to that many thousand people, that's fucking something, man, that does me right in. If I'm good and the group is good, you can get 14,000 . . . 140,000!—get them on their fucking feet. Yeah. That's where it's at. That's what it's all about for me.

Can you tell me what you're worth?

I don't know. Not now. Some time ago me accountant told me I 'ad a lot of money. I said, "'Ow much?" He said, "Well, you're very well fixed." I said, "'Ow much? I mean, am I a millionaire?" "Well, technically, yes." So I said, "What should I do about it?" And he said, "Well, obviously, if you've got that much money and you've got these tax bills, it's logical to spend money so that you can claim it against the tax that's owed." "I see . . . so I should spend money?" "Well, yes, you should." So six weeks later I'd spent it all. Ah-ha-HAHAHAHAHAHA-HAHAHA! I'd bought four 'ouses, a 'otel, eight cars, a swimming pool, tennis courts, expensive wristwatches—that fall apart—a riverside bungalow just five minutes away, furnished in French renay-sance-period furniture. I'd spent it all. It was gone! AH-HAHAHAHAHA-hahahaHA-HA. HA-HA.

I get accused of being a capitalist bastard, because, you know: "How many cars you got?" "Eight." "Big 'ouse?" "Yes." Well, I love all that; I enjoy it. I have lots of friends over and we sit up, drinking and partying. I need the room to entertain. I enjoy seeing other people enjoy themselves. That's where I get my kicks. I'm kinky that way. I have the amount of cars I do because I smash them up a lot. Six are always in the garage; it's a fact. They're always saying I'm a capitalist pig. I suppose I am. But, ah . . . it ah . . . it's good for me drumming, I think. OH-HOOOOO-HAHAHA!

You really do have troubles with cars?

I came off the road in the AC Cobra at 110. We flew over a canal and sort of collapsed in a mangled heap in a field about ten foot from a reservoir. The Cobra people were very unhappy when I took the wreckage into their garage—they only made about ninety-eight of them, and they're touchy about how they're driven. HAHA HAHAHAHAHAHAHAHA! I've tried to bump-start the 1936 Chrysler several times, always with disastrous results. Once I tried to bump-start it with my X-type Jag, which is built so low to the ground, it slid under the Chrysler. Another time I tried to bump-start with the Rolls . . . forgetting there was nobody sitting in the Chrysler. I pushed it right into the fish pond on the front lawn.

When did the group swing away from drugs toward booze?

AH-HA . . . a change-of-pace question. Ah-ha-ha-ha HAHA HA! I think we just sort of grew out of drugs. The drugs aren't necessary now. They were then, as a crutch. We went through just about everything. Not Roger so much. He smoked, but that was it. The rest of us went through the same stages everybody goes through—the bloody drug corridor. You know. We were no exception. Eventually we stopped fucking about with the chemicals and started on the grape. Drinking suited the group a lot better. When we started drinking, that's when it all started getting together.

We're all pretty good drinkers. After the show there's always the celebration drink, or the non-celebration drink. Then there's always the clubs—John and I, generally, go clubbing. We just like the social side of drinking. Everybody I know is a drinker. I've met most of my best friends in pubs.

W HATEVER HAPPENED TO ALL *the Who films we've heard so much about over the years? Your publicity guy told me you've announced at least half a dozen and that he doesn't pay any attention to film talk now.*

I'd like to know meself. They've just never turned out to be Who films. We've never yet had a script that we've all liked. I think there must be a Who film. I think it'll be a gross injustice if there's not a Who film. There must be a Who film. Because there's so much Who to go 'round.

You've been in two films without the others. . . .

Yeah, one was *200 Motels* with Frank Zappa, the other was *Countdown* with Harry Nilsson, both with Ringo.

I was at the Speakeasy with Pete, and Frank 'appened to be at the next table. He overheard some of our conversation and leaned over and said

{American voice}, "How'd you guys like to be in a film?" We said {English accent}, "Okay, Frank." And he said {back to American}, "Okay, be at the Kensington Palace Hotel at seven o'clock tomorrow morning." I was the one who turned up. Pete was writing and sent his apologies, and I was given the part Mick Jagger was to play—that of a nun. Mick didn't want to do it.

Then there was a bit in one of the local papers that said Ringo was making *Countdown* with Peter Frampton and Harry Nilsson and a lot of others, so I called Ringo up and said, "Is there a part in it for me?" He said yes, and I turned up. I do some drumming.

Was that your first meeting with Nilsson?

Yes. We were supposed to be on the set at six, but it was nine before everybody was there. Then somebody brought out a bottle of brandy. Me, I think. Ah-Ha-Ha-HAHAHA! And Peter Framp-ton said no, no, too early, and some of the others said no. But 'Arry was standing there with an 'alf-pint mug. I knew at that moment it was destiny put us together. Ahhhh-HAHAHAHAHA-HAHAHA!

So we were drinking brandy at nine and, thanks to Mal Evans, white wine all the rest of the day. Then about six o'clock somebody came 'round and slipped little envelopes into our 'ands. It was a pay packet! I 'adn't 'ad a pay packet in ten years. And 'Arry'd never 'ad one. We were pretty well out of it, and we looked at each other and then tore up one-hundred and seventy pounds in one-pound notes, threw it up in the air and danced about, cackling like schoolboys. AHHHH-HAAAA-HAHAHA-AA-HAAAA-HAAA-haaa! Dancing and leaping about, clutching bottles of Blue Nun liebfraumilch in our hands, singing, "We're millionaires, aren't we?"

20

INTERVIEWED BY STUART WERBIN (1973)

In late 1972, more than two years after his first major success with the *Sweet Baby James* album, James Taylor still hadn't done a ROLLING STONE Interview. But, as staff writer Stuart Werbin reminds, we were hardly alone.

Werbin had covered a Taylor tour (for a story on opening act Carole King) a year before and knew Carly Simon's family, and after attending their wedding in their New York apartment, he scored this duet-interview.

Taylor, 24, was doing fine, with the album *Mudslide Slim and the Blue Horizon,* the hit "You've Got a Friend" and the brand-new album *One Man Dog.* Carly, 27, was on the eve of her biggest hit record, "You're So Vain."

The first session, Werbin says, was conducted "on Thanksgiving Eve, in the living room of their apartment."

A week later, Werbin and the Taylors met again. "Once we got started," Werbin says, "they took it as seriously as they would a concert or album. When the deadline that they greatly resented finally approached, they switched into high gear, and what amounted to a third session was done by phone from a Maryland Holiday Inn to my New York apartment after one of James's concerts—and ran until five in the morning."

Werbin also notes the Taylors talking about their "hypothetical children, Ben and Sarah" in the interview. "Now they do have a Ben and a Sarah. They have the kids they imagined."

—BF-T

IT BEGAN IN THE PLUSH BEDROOM OF a fashionable Riverdale home, one week before James Taylor and Carly Simon became Mr. and Ms. Simon-Taylor. Mrs. Andrea Simon was hosting a party for her son Peter whose book of photographs, 'Moving on/Holding Still,' had just been released. Up in the bathroom, Carly and Peter were diligently trying to

246

JAMES TAYLOR &

CARLY SIMON

synchronize two battery-operated cassette recorders so that a few guests could enjoy a closed-door preview of "You're So Vain," in a reasonable facsimile of stereo.

James' last tour had not been an artistic success. He had become sluggish and more distant from his audience. Rumor had it that this was due to mounting heroin addiction. His live appearances over the previous six months had been limited to stints for George McGovern.

A concert James gave the week following that party disarmed me of any vestiges of critical judgment. I was drawn smoothly into the pleasure of the music and his performance. And, to a great concert, he added his announcement that earlier in the evening he and Carly had married.

After that evening, a ROLLING STONE Interview with the Simon-Taylors seemed like a natural and well worth the delicate approach it inevitably entailed. James and Carly both had reservations about doing one, stemming from past experiences with the press. James had not done an interview for two years, and what he had done before that had been basically lip service. After Howard Hughes, one would be hard pressed to find anyone who said less to Time *and still got his picture on the cover. Carly had always been as open as possible, only to find sensationalized stories of rock & roll romances thrown back in her face.*

After speaking to Carly on the phone, I was invited over to dinner (Carly is an excellent, provocative cook; James is fair on the dishes), and in a light group-therapy session we worked out the process for the interview. James remarked that his good friend John McLaughlin had once said that he does as many interviews as he can, because they're a way to clean out the soul: "So what the hell. Let's see."

DO YOU WANT TO TALK ABOUT *why you decided to get married?*
James: That's the way we always heard it should be.

Carly: I mentioned one morning to James in London that I thought we should get married, and James was kind of hesitant in his response. He said, "Oh, well, there's really no reason to get married. We love each other, and we've been living together."

And then later on in the afternoon, James said, "You know, I've been thinking about it, and maybe we should get married." I said, "Well, what's happened between this morning and this afternoon?" He said, "This afternoon it was my idea."

When did you first meet?
Carly: It was my first opening night ever.

James: It was the fall of '71.
Carly: No, no, the first time we met was April 6th, 1971.
James: We passed once in the parking lot of my house—it's not really like a Kinney System parking lot, it holds about three cars—out in front of my mother's house were Peter Simon and Carly going to talk to my brother Livingston about a job that she and Livingston were going to do together. I passed Peter and Carly and said, "Hi," and Peter said, "Hi, this is my sister Carly," and then I left. I guess I had one album out by then.
So when was the first time you were really introduced?
Carly: When we were officially introduced, it seemed as though we'd known each other for a long time, as we knew about each other from the summer place [Martha's Vineyard, Mass.]. James came up and embraced me upon first meeting, and then we went in the bathroom and fucked.
James: Actually, we never made love until we were married [laughter]. I saw Carly on the street shortly after I met her, and I followed her, thinking she was another woman. I was thinking, "What a fine-looking woman that is." Then I discovered it was Carly. It makes you very happy when you do that. The same thing with this picture from Carly's first album. I saw it on the wall—"Hey, that's a fine-looking woman," said I, and someone said, "That's your girl." I said, "What?" They said, "It's Carly." I said, "Oh, so it is."

DO YOU EVER FEEL VENGEANCE *behind some of the songs, or some sort of emotion that you just don't want to express any other way?*
Carly: Not until "You're So Vain."
Some people think "You're So Vain" is about James.
Carly: No, it's definitely not about James, although James suspected that it might be about him because he's very vain. No, he isn't, but he had the unfortunate experience of taking a jet up to Nova Scotia after I'd written the song. He was saved by the fact that it wasn't a Lear.
James: A small twin-prop.
You've mentioned various people who downgraded your music.
Carly: Not downgraded it, but their career was always more important than mine. But the anger in that song is not necessarily about anybody who's put down my music or wanted me

248

to be subservient to them. It's at a certain type of man, very into himself, that I've been very affected by, adversely, in the past—a man who's more concerned with his image than with the relationship.

James: The fact that she and I are married means that one is more apt to work these things out rather than let them chase us away from each other. In other words, there are feelings that I have about dealing with Carly's profession and her career that I would ordinarily not talk about for fear of chasing her away or chasing myself away. That's one good reason to get married.

You both spent your childhood summers on Martha's Vineyard. How did that originate?

Carly: My parents started going there in 1934 on their honeymoon. The first summer I was there was the summer I was born and then at least once every summer. I heard a lot about James—he was referred to as Jamie Taylor.

James: I saw you on some stage there once.

When was that?

James: It was '62, '63 or '64.

Was that with Lucy {Carly's sister}?

James: Yes. They were billed as the Simon Sisters. I used to sing down there occasionally on Hootenanny nights. She was professional at this point and I wasn't, so we never sang on the same show.

Do you remember what you thought of her the first time you saw her?

James: I thought she was quite attractive, but she was, and still is, four years older than I was, so back then when she was eighteen and I was fourteen she was a bit less approachable than she was when I was twenty-four. . . .

Carly: You didn't know that I had a hankering for a fourteen-year-old man.

James: As it turns out, she actually did. But at any rate, I plan to pass her in age in about three more years. I want to send her to Alpha Centauri aboard the first ship that goes there. The law of relativity is gonna finally do it for us. When she comes back I'll be sixty and she'll be thirty.

Carly: When I get to be about forty-five, I shall freeze for five years because James will be about forty then and just wanting to get into all the young women. But I don't want to know about it.

You are both celebrities. How does that affect your marriage?

James: In the beginning of our relationship I very seldom listened to music at home, seldom played the tape recorder or the record player, and I never played my own albums. I think Carly felt I wasn't taking enough interest in her music. She might have felt that there's some competition involved. I was afraid to say anything negative about her music. Any criticism that I had, I felt would make her dislike me. So I didn't mention either side of it.

Carly, would you criticize something that James was doing if you didn't like it?

Carly: I'm very wary, especially with somebody who takes you seriously as I think James takes me. (I take him seriously.) You sometimes become overly cautious about saying something that you think might hurt, even though it could be constructive criticism. So sometimes I feel as though I'm walking on hot coals. I would be more careful about what I would say to James than I would to somebody that I knew casually. Now I think this will probably change.

It worried me terribly that James had never heard any of my songs. I took that as an indication that he wasn't interested in my music, and therefore I somehow got a lower opinion of my own music because of that.

James: I heard as few songs of yours as I'd heard of Dylan's or of Kristofferson's or Prine's or of anyone's. I just don't listen to music.

Carly: But it's a different thing with somebody that you're in love with. I'm not Dylan or Kristofferson. Up until this album, you never listened to my other albums.

James: I never listened to mine either. I don't know, honey . . .

Carly: It's a strange situation. I think it's one that has to do with fear of competition. But I definitely feel that James is involved now. It's still a precarious thing. Sometimes I feel it's a male-female thing. Because any male that I've been involved with in the past has not liked my success, has not wanted me to be successful, has felt very threatened by that fact.

James: I'm very much interested in not seeing Carly behind the kitchen stove because I see females live totally vicariously through their husbands, and it drives them crazy and it drives the husband crazy, too.

Carly, your father {the president of Simon and Schuster, a book publishing company}, comes up a lot in your works and the lyrics Jacob Brackman writes with you. Is it subconscious or accidental?

Carly: No, I don't think any lyric is by accident. The things that you dream aren't by accident either, and the things that come out, even though they might be a stream of consciousness, are there for some reason. Particularly in "Embrace Me, You Child," there is a very clear-cut picture of my father as a frightening and devilish kind of figure. That's not the way

249

that I consciously see him, but somewhere in my mind he must have seemed that way to me.

Can we take "Embrace Me, You Child" as a fairly autobiographical statement of your feelings at your father's death?

Carly: Yes. I felt abandoned, and I was angry at the thought of being abandoned by him. At the same time as I was abandoned by Daddy, I was abandoned by God, because losing my father also meant losing my faith in God who I had prayed to every night that I wouldn't lose my father. From the time that he had his first heart attack to the time that he died I used to knock on wood 500 times every night, thinking that my magic was gonna keep him away from death. I feared his death incredibly, and, in fearing his death, moved away from him, fearing that I might die.

There are religious overtones in a lot of your songs. I was somewhat surprised that you didn't get married in a church.

James: Oh, we may be religious, but that doesn't necessarily have anything to do with the church. Religion starts at home for us. The word "religion" means "relinkage." The actual word means to reassociate yourself with your roots or with whatever base, whatever you feel you came from. It can be a religious experience to look at the ocean, or it can be a religious experience for you to perform a certain kind of dance or for you to sit around a table at Thanksgiving time. That can be relinkage of a certain sort. It doesn't need to connect itself with any legal deity.

Dancing, as you said, comes up a lot on your album. "Dance" is the title of the last cut. Does this have a spiritual meaning?

James: I was thinking of two titles for the album: the first one was *Farewell to Show Biz,* which Carly and Peter Asher both didn't like. We finally settled on *One Man Dog;* I thought of calling it *Throw Yourself Away.*

I think it's religious to throw yourself away. It's interesting that a lot of religious phenomena involve really surrendering oneself, like in the film *Marjoe* where people are transported and go to pieces. And it's religious sometimes when you take acid and lose your ego and dissolve completely. I think what people are trying to get away from in their religious experiences is the isolation of the conscious mind, away from the idea proposed by Western civilization that the self is located somewhere in the cerebral cortex and that self and consciousness are tied together. Actually, one is much more comfortable locating oneself in the earth or in your body as any animal or in your body as a member of the species. At least you're immortal there.

My love for Carly is a very religious thing, to me because sometimes I just exchange with her completely, and I don't know where I end off and she begins. The idea of religion is very important to me, and I think I'm a relatively spiritual person, but every time someone starts to pin me down on it they're just barking up the wrong tree because it has nothing to do with anything specific.

Carly: I am wondering what connotation Jesus had for you.

James: Rhymes with *cheeses, Jesus, pieces,* actually, in "Fire and Rain"—"look down on me, Jesus." "Fire and Rain" has three verses. The first verse is about my reactions to the death of a friend. The second verse is about my arrival in this country with a monkey on my back, and there Jesus is an expression of my desperation in trying to get through the time when my body was aching, and the time was at hand when I had to do it. Jesus was just something that you say when you're in pain. I wasn't actually looking to the savior. Some people look at it as a confirmation of belief in Christ as the one true path and the one sole way, which I don't believe in, although he can certainly be a useful vehicle.

And the third verse of that song refers to my recuperation in Austin Riggs [a Massachusetts hospital] which lasted about five months.

Since this has come up, why don't we talk about how you first got involved with junk?

James: I got involved with junk in New York after getting out of McLean's, about halfway through the year which I spent with the Flying Machine. I got involved peripherally for a while, getting off a couple of times a week. At that point my addiction to it was more psychological than it was physical, but it's very difficult to separate the two of them. I kicked junk for about half a year and then spent that time knocking around the country. I drove across the country with a friend and then thumbed up and down the West Coast for a while, flew back to the East Coast, then spent a while in Chapel Hill, North Carolina, where I had some growths removed.

That half-year was the fall of '67 through the beginning of '68. I was clean. Then I started to take a lot of codeine. I went to Europe and started to take opium, and then I got into smack heavily for about nine months. I got into it real thick there. I came back to this country and kicked, over about a period of five months in Austin Riggs. They're not equipped to deal with junkies, and I wasn't called a junkie. I wasn't admitted or dealt with as a junkie, but that was my problem. That was the manifestation of my problem. Junk, in itself, isn't the problem with me. It's a symptom of unexpressed and inexpressible anger, in a nutshell. It's a way of retreating from the world. It's a way of finding a comfort and consistency in a chemical, and I guess I have an addictive personality.

Anyway, a year and a half ago I found myself on the road with a jones. When I got to Chicago I got in touch with a doctor who was a friend of mine. He got me off smack and onto methadone. I've been on methadone maintenance for the past year. After I got out of Austin Riggs I was clean for almost a year and a half. But by the summer of '71 I was getting high again.

Sweet Baby James was out and *Mud Slide Slim* was out. I had just kicked when I recorded *Sweet Baby James*, and I was still clean when I recorded *Mud Slide Slim*, but I was just getting back into it at that point.

You were seriously addicted during the recording of the Apple album?

James: Yeah.

How do you relate to it, Carly?

Carly: It was very harrowing for me. In the beginning of our relationship, I didn't really understand the extent to which James was addicted or needed drugs. It just kind of confused me that there was a wall up between us, and I didn't know exactly what it was because I had never been close to anybody who was really addicted to anything before. I was aware of remoteness with James, that I couldn't depend upon him.

What caused James' remoteness?

James: It was partly drug abuse, and it was partially that instead of communicating what feelings I had, I would get off on a drug instead, and my mind was occupied by the drug, the idea of getting off on a drug, the idea of keeping it from Carly. But I still needed her very much.

It seems that the times when you went to junk besides those you mentioned were at a point of reaching a new level of success. With the first album becoming more successful, the Time *magazine cover, getting close to a woman, where there seemed to be some sort of permanence—these seemed to be the times that you turned to junk.*

James: Maybe that's true. I don't know what the idea of success means to me. It carries with it an inherent quality that if I actually get what I want, I'll have to pay for it. In other words, success carries with it almost a sense of inherent and impending retribution. It's strange . . .

Are there precedents for this in your growing up?

James: Yeah. There was a period of time when my father was away. He went away for two years when he was drafted into the Navy when I was six years old. He spent two years in the Antarc-

tic, which is about the same to a six-year-old child as being on the moon. At that time I got very much into my mother, as did all of us, and I think the idea of success would be to have her love me instead of my father. That kind of an Oedipal striving carries with it the idea if you're successful you'll have your eyes pulled out. It's the kind of thing which you know you can't be successful at. And you know you mustn't be successful at it because you're not a man, you're a child.

On the other hand, being successful might have carried with it an inherent anger at my mother or father for their wanting me to perform, their wanting me to do well, and therefore if I'm successful there's an element of having done it for them and not wanting to have done it at all.

Carly, coming from a family with success as a precedent, did it give you some sort of an ambiguous view of success?

Carly: They really do parallel James'. What he just said about it was very much what happened to me. I felt as if I always had to perform in order to get any love at all. I had two older sisters who were both very talented and very beautiful and very much the apple of my father's eye, and I suppose my mother's, too.

I obviously felt that I had to be different—in a performing sense—in order to make an impression on anybody. The pressure was put on me at the age of four, to stand out in my own way, not just to be whatever I felt like being, which was, I guess, somewhere middle of the road. It had to be some kind of performance.

James: The idea of being a pop star is a very regressive thing. It's like all of a sudden anything you want to do is allowed. You become a spoiled child when you become a pop superstar. You really get spoiled something awful.

We talked earlier about James' addiction. One thing that has happened historically when one lover had an addiction, was the other lover picking it up. Were you ever tempted to try heroin or cocaine, the things that James has been doing?

Carly: Never. It had a reverse effect on me. I snorted cocaine a couple of times, but it was never as bad to me as it seemed when I saw James getting into it. Now I have a horror about cocaine. I was never tempted to try heroin or acid. I've just never been into drugs. I haven't smoked grass for the last four months. I just haven't been into ingesting anything into my system. Occasionally I smoke a cigarette.

I've felt often in our relationship that I've been addicted to James, and I have a dependency upon him that's almost like a drug I couldn't do

251

without. Maybe that's what addiction is all about.

How do you relate to the difference between your personal and more public identities at this stage of your lives?

James: It's interesting to me that no one ever recognizes me on the street. I'm very seldom recognized. Often I can walk into a bunch of kids that I know; one or two of them may own my records and have a picture of me or maybe have listened to me or been to a concert of mine. I can look at them straight in the eye, and they won't recognize me.

Carly: People don't recognize you out of context. If you were to go to a concert at the Fillmore East or something like that, everybody would recognize you, but people don't expect to see James Taylor out in Sayville.

James: Yeah, but people recognize *you.* I think it's also a matter of my face.

"Hey, Mister That's Me Up There On the Jukebox" recognizes that distinction between public and private lives. . . .

James: It's happened before where I've been in a place and they played it on the jukebox without knowing about it. That song was actually as much as anything else to Peter Asher, who bore the brunt of my discomfort about the deadline aspect of *Mud Slide Slim.* I wrote that song in the studio. The bridge, which was "Do you believe I'll go back home/Hey, mister, can't you see that I'm dry as a bone?" is about having to write a song. It's an album cut about having to make an album cut. It's kind of a rip-off, except that it's a really nice tune.

After a while, a novelist who does nothing but write novels is going to end up writing a novel about writing a novel. The first chapter will say, "I wrote these words upon my typewriter," or pretty soon "my vision is going to be turned right . . . I'm going to be looking at my feet."

How do you feel onstage?

James: My brother Livingston saw me feeling uncomfortable once onstage about the applause that I was getting, and he said, "What the fuck are you doing? These people love you. Why don't you enjoy it?" He was really angry at me on one occasion at the way I was coming on. And I read an article by Jon Landau on a concert in which he assumed that the way I had come on was on purpose, that I actually controlled that, whereas in actuality I really had no control over it at all. I'm glad when I can be happy onstage, too, but sometimes, I just don't know how to act. . . .

CARLY, LET'S TALK ABOUT THE *events leading up to your current album. What were your thoughts after finishing "Anticipation"?*

Carly: Well, after I finished it, I was tired of the whole self-pitying thing that was going on in many of my songs. I didn't like to see myself talking about disenchantment as much as I had. The whole album was about things that never quite happened, things that didn't turn out the way I wanted them to, things that were disillusioning. I wanted to wipe out all that melancholia and come up with something more positive, more interesting, subjects that hadn't been delved into.

What came out of feeling that way, which songs?

Carly: "You're So Vain," which was kind of an accusative song that came out of my wanting to write something else.

You mentioned the "contest" going on about who it's about. What would be the clearest statement you would want to make on who the song was about?

Carly: The contest is run by this man in Los Angeles named Winkler, and he had his listeners call in to cast their ballot as to who they thought the song was about. Kris Kristofferson is leading. A lot of people think it's about Mick Jagger and that I have fooled him into actually singing on it, that I pulled that ruse. And some of the people think it's about James. But I can't possibly tell who it's about because it wouldn't be fair.

James: It's none of the people who were mentioned.

James, how did you feel about the song when you first heard it?

James: Well, I thought it was a nice song. I heard it played on the piano and sung. I didn't hear the production of it.

How did Jagger get involved with it?

Carly: Last May I got this idea to do an interview with Mick Jagger. I had an idea to start a career in journalism until I found out just what it was like. I mentioned my interview idea casually to Arlyne [Rothberg], who spoke casually to Seymour Peck, who edits the *Arts and Leisure* section of the Sunday [N.Y.] *Times.* He said if Jagger was willing, it would be great. Somebody got in touch with Chris Odell, and she got in touch with Mick who really liked the idea.

So I casually went out to L.A., and I ended up hanging around there waiting for Mick for five days, waiting for him to show up. And when he finally did show, he had been on an airplane for thirteen hours and was exhausted. All we talked

252

about that night was how much we both hated airplanes, and then I had to leave for New York the next morning.

I still had ideas about doing the article when I met him again in June. Or at least I hadn't totally given up on the idea, but we became friends, and I felt it would be too difficult to write an objective piece.

Was he well acquainted with your music?

Carly: I don't think he can recite the lyrics verbatim, but he was familiar with my album covers. It was very strange, that first meeting. I expected to look so much like him because people were always commenting on the resemblance. I expected to walk into a mirror. But then I didn't think we looked anything alike.

We're the same height, but first of all he was wearing a cotton turquoise suit and very short white socks and saddle shoes, and kept apologizing for how tired he was. I couldn't imagine myself wearing that. After I saw him in June, I didn't see him again until he called up at the session when we were about to do the vocals.

How did you come up with "That's the Way I Always Heard It Should Be"?

Carly: I wrote the melody of it two years before Jacob Brackman wrote the lyrics, because I was writing a television special called *Who Killed Lake Erie?* They wanted a theme song, and that was the melody that I wrote for the theme, but they never used it. Instead, they used a song that was written by Malvina Reynolds, called "From Way Up Here." I wasn't really into writing lyrics much then. I met up with Jacob Brackman when I was teaching at Indian Hill, a camp in Stockbridge, Massachusetts.

How old were you then?

Carly: Twenty-three or twenty-four. And a couple of years later, he was writing for the *New Yorker.* Just about six months before I did my first album I just kind of felt that Jake might write some interesting songs, and so I gave him that melody and asked him to see what he could do with it.

It's such a woman's song. Did he surprise you?

Carly: No, because Jake is that sensitive to me. Every song he has written has been a song which I could identify with. He writes for me. He doesn't write with it in mind that Jack Jones will sing it, even though, in fact, Jack Jones did record "That's the Way I Always Heard It Should Be."

We kind of got married by it. We couldn't avoid it. All the radios were playing it. "Ironic twist, isn't it, that James and Carly got married."—"My father sits at night . . ."

Carly, how did you and Richard Perry get together?

Carly: Jac Holzman and Richard Perry apparently approached each other on the same day, and it was like a light bulb for both of them. Richard said, "I want you to produce Carly." And Jac said, "I want you to produce Carly." I was against the idea because while I think Richard is a fine producer, his work with Nilsson and Barbra Streisand was too slick for me, and I didn't want to have that kind of a sound.

How did you wind up feeling about Richard Perry?

Carly: Richard Perry is like a movie director. He sees himself as holding the camera, as directing the players, as calling the final shots, as doing a theme, rather than as an interpreter.

Did you feel you needed that?

Carly: I didn't feel I needed it. I felt that it was going to be very difficult to work with somebody who was trying to do the same thing I was, since I was also trying to direct all the shots. Richard has much more endurance than I have and much more perseverance, so where I would leave off, he would continue.

I think Richard was the dividing line between some of the things I did that were good and some things that I did that were very good. He pushed them over, pushed me off a diving board.

Richard's perfectionism on "You're So Vain" got the rhythm track. That was ace on that. We recorded the song three different times with three different drummers. We've got two pianos going on that track. Klaus Voormann was very instrumental on the sound of that track; just that opening bass sets the mood of a swaggering self-indulgent man to come prancing into the room with his hat.

Richard was much more of a producer than I've ever had before. He really was a hundred percent there, and even though I had to fight with him about a lot of tunes, he is the strongest producer I've ever known, and his personality goes right into all of his records. It's indisputably there.

James, what is the relationship between you and Peter Asher on your albums?

James: Peter produces or directs differently from Richard Perry. He's there more to help the artist get his thing out on tape. Peter's not an accomplished musician. He is a musician from a certain point of view. He's a vocalist, certainly, and he's produced a lot of albums. He's written songs before, but there's a difference between Carly's working with the producer and my working with one. I've never been produced by

253

anyone but Peter. He's very helpful, and he's a fantastic organizer.

When Peter is there as a producer, it's not only in his capacity that he contributes to what's being done in the studio. Aside from the music that is made, Peter is responsible for the environment in which I record.

The word producer can mean many different things. It can mean someone the company hires to time the tracks. It's too vague a term.

Carly: I like working with different influences. I feel best, in a way, when I'm unsafe. I felt unsafe with Richard, and therefore more adrenalin was flowing.

James: Well, you like the security of turning to someone and saying, "What do we do now," too. Do you think you'd be settling for more or less than you do when you settle for your producer's point of view?

Carly: I feel as if I need another point of view. I feel as if I can't be as objective as a producer can be about my songs. And I like to have new people introduce new ideas for my songs.

BOTH OF YOU WERE INVOLVED *with the McGovern benefit concerts.*

Carly: Warren Beatty, who is a friend of mine, called and said he needed our support very badly. He called me; he didn't know James, and he said he thought that if a few performers got behind him and enough young people were encouraged to become interested in politics, they would naturally be interested in McGovern. Warren was preparing a big concert in Los Angeles. This was in April. And he wanted me to talk James into getting involved, so I telephoned James on the Cape, and Warren got in touch with James, and he wanted to do the concert. That was about the main thing that I had to do with McGovern, other than some private parties that I sang at.

You did the last concert for McGovern, when the polls said it was hopeless.

James: It was hopeless that he would win the election. McGovern was an enigma. I think in ordinary good times, no one like him would be allowed to come anywhere near being President. I thought that perhaps things were just bad enough in this country so that they might elect him. But the main reason why Nixon got such a landslide victory was that he offered the American people a lie, a fairy tale of what life is really like, that Americans could continue living the way they have been, that our society is valid, that

for all practical purposes the point of view of the average American citizen is true when just the opposite is the case.

Some fantastic shifts have to happen, some incredible reversals, not only American society but human nature itself. The idea of the importance of the individual, of the importance of intellect, people's ways of viewing death, the concept of self—an awful lot of things have to change. And McGovern represented change to the people of the United States. After a while he began to represent the unknown—an unsure and not a very pleasant future.

Carly: I don't think that Western civilization as it is now is going to survive for an eternity—I don't believe that—but I believe that Ben and Sarah will be part of perhaps another civilization. . . .

James: We've got hypothetical children . . .

Carly: . . . which will be growing up, whether it's a civilization on another planet or whether it's a civilization in Egypt which will start flourishing in twenty years. Western civilization is in grave danger at the moment.

James: But it's in a state of transition, too, from a positive point of view. Look at all the spiritual upheaval that's going up in this country. People are shifting values. . . . It's never stayed the same. But I mean, we're at the end of a line of . . . we've run out, that's all covered ground.

Do you have views on the changing of traditional sex roles?

Carly: It is something that I've been thinking about a lot and struggling with, because it's hard to remember that I'm any different from my male counterpart and that there are any differences in role. The biological-physical differences have caused a great many role differences which I'm not sure are presently valid. I think if little boys and girls were raised thinking that their physical differences didn't imply role differences such as male "dominance" and female "subservience," women would develop tools to deal with their aggressiveness which they are otherwise taught to suppress, and men would be allowed to be passive and not fear for their masculine ego every time a woman took the reins.

James: There are some realistic differences between men and women, and there are some culturally imposed jive differences. There are evolutionary differences between men and women in their physical forms and their functions and their outlook. . . . Pyschologists say that they dream differently and stuff like that.

I think men and women can understand and

appreciate the differences and equally appreciate the overlap in powers. Men can be emotional. Men can be practical, and women can be bread-winners. It's more and more overlapping. Everything is becoming more homogenized.

It's been a man's world. It's been a world controlled by the male outlook. That's changed a lot, too.

Carly: My own conditioning is that one voice says to me, "Carly, you mustn't try to dominate the situation; you mustn't tell everybody what to play; you mustn't expect James to do the dishes." And the other voice is saying, "I want my musicians to play in a slower tempo, and it's James' turn to do the dishes tonight."

You said that you're more influenced by male singers than female singers.

Carly: When I realized that I wanted to have my own career, I didn't want to sound like any other female vocalists. I began to listen to male vocalists for sounds and phrasings. I listened to James a lot, and Cat Stevens, too. I also admired Jagger's performances.

I feel more competitive toward women, and I'm not as comfortable in such a competitive situation. I don't like to set myself up for it, even though I know there's plenty of room for female talent and a lot of great female talent around. But I listen to male artists more because I feel it's unfair of me to criticize female singers. This is derived from historic feelings of female rivalry. When I was in high school, it was important for me to feel pretty, and I had a hard time saying anyone else was pretty.

You've become close with a lot of the male artists that you respected. Did you seek them out?

Carly: It's more like we were thrown together, doing double bills. I had a number of relationships that were publicized beyond what they really were.

Cat Stevens, for instance.

Carly: Cat and I worked together many times; I always respected him. As with other men I worked with, I always had a hard time figuring out whether I admired them more as musicians than as people. I found myself talent-struck, and usually it would turn out that I had the feeling I was more involved with the person than I really was. I had a distorted way of looking at them through rose-colored glasses and tone-deaf ears.

I never really got to know a lot of the people that I was supposed to be involved with. But Rona Barrett jumps on everything. Interviewers always seemed more interested in my love life than my music, which I suppose is an extension of male chauvinist pigism.

*P*ERFORMERS USUALLY RELATE *sensually to the audience, and both of you have that quality of being attractive and being attracted to the audience. Can you relate to the audience and be attractive and yet at the same time not let it turn into burlesque?*

James: I think perhaps my act is the most unburlesque imaginable. I sit in a chair and don't move for two hours.

Carly: But you have a very strong sexual appeal. Do you mean you relate to an audience on a completely asexual level?

James: Yes.

It probably relates to Carly more. . . .

James: She's a piece of ass. It bothers me. If she looks at another man, I'll kill her.

Carly's appeal in the beginning was to a female audience, and now there's a large male audience.

James: Mae West in the flesh.

Do you feel that's something desirable to your act?

Carly: I don't necessarily underplay my sexual appeal or attractiveness, whatever it may be. I think it's an asset to a performer to be sexually attractive. And I think James is a nice piece of ass.

You wear long dresses instead of hot pants?

James: She wears short dresses onstage sometimes. Sure. Why not? As long as you're asking that, it carries over farther than that. If two people are married and take vows to be true to each other, how far does that carry over? Obviously, I don't want Carly to sleep in another man's bed, or another man sleeping in my bed, for that matter. Not on this couch, either. And forget about the back seat of the car. It's obviously important that between two people, man and woman, there'd be a certain amount of sexual overtones in the conversation. In other words, if she's at a party and she meets someone she likes, she likes to feel as though they're attracted to her sexually, and when I meet a woman, I like to feel as though there's a certain amount of rapport. I guess marriage vows sort of pertain to a certain amount of closeness. It really depends on what she would consider my betraying her.

Carly: What's safe.

James: Or, what I would consider her betraying me. And I think, interestingly enough, or boringly enough, depending upon how drunk you are, what it really comes down to is that when I feel threatened or when I feel somebody else is taking my place, that's when she shouldn't do it.

A lot of Joni Mitchell's new album seems directed towards her feelings about James. What are your reactions?

255

James: I think I heard a track of it on the radio; I haven't picked it up. I'd be very interested to hear it because I really love Joni's music.

There are references to a man in suspenders—I guess you'd have to hear it.

James: Joni's music is much more specifically autobiographical than a lot of other people. Everyone who writes songs writes autobiographical songs and hers are sometimes really disarmingly specific.

How much of what you do are you doing for yourself? How much because it's expected of you?

Carly: I think, as far as the songs that I'm writing now, they're much more what's expected of me rather than for myself. If I was writing songs just for myself now, I could be a lot more satisfied with the process of writing them.

You don't need the money, so why do you continue to do it?

Carly: For the same reason that I wanted to be popular in high school, because I still don't have enough of the internal Carly Simon saying, "You're all right." I still need the applause. I still need people from the outside saying, "Carly Simon, you're all right."

James: Carly and I agree that the best thing for us to do would be to really get into our own selves in terms of writing music for ourselves to try to screen out the public point of view of doing things for an audience, for record sales, thinking in terms of singles, that sort of thing.

We seem to agree that if we are ready to do good work it has to be for us. One of the inevitable disadvantages of success in this culture of this time is that the more successful you get, the more your point of view swings around towards feeding that whole mechanism of being appreciated or being acknowledged. But that's a degenerate process. It's not totally degenerate. It can stimulate you to doing more work, but still, the experience has to be a private one, I believe.

What steps are you taking to do this?

James: We plan to spend more time for ourselves. We plan to live, instead of perform.

Carly: Sometimes I see the key word as being relaxation. If we'd learn to relax with ourselves . . .

James: Throw ourselves away.

Carly: Throw ourselves away.

James: Carly and I are in love with each other, but love is not a thing that you can find. Love is something that is an accumulated emotion, in any one person, and love always has strings attached. When I love someone, I remember that love has hurt me, and passed. When Carly loves me, she remembers that in order to get love she has had to do things that she resented having to do.

We really appreciate having an audience, we appreciate being acknowledged, we like to think that people like our music and we like to give it to them. We love to shine, but, on the other hand, we don't like it so much that we want to sacrifice everything to it, including our private lives. It's important that people be informed if we're going to be public figures, and I suppose we're going to continue to be. And it's better that people know the truth and make up their own minds.

You have this very sincere idea of what you want to do, yet you end up doing things you don't want to do.

Carly: I can imagine getting to a frame of mind where the audience won't make any difference to me. Just that I'm into what I'm doing, and it doesn't matter if there's two people, doesn't matter if there are a million people, but that my performance will be the same, and I'll feel secure enough within myself to be the same under any circumstance. Now, because I'm a scared performer, because their opinion is so important to me, I like to make contact with each individual person. I want them to really see me. . . .

James: If I know what I want, if I know those things in life that are important to me, my wife, my music, my home, my family, if I know what those are and where those are and I know where they come into play . . . then what I seek in life . . . is to react honestly to circumstances as they come along.

I don't want to be frightened by someone because they remind me of an old circumstance which no longer exists.

I don't like any more than anyone else being overwhelmed by feelings, and like the song "Carolina in My Mind" says, I don't like being hit from behind. I don't like being snuck up on from somewhere in my subconscious and captured by some old set of circumstances which no longer should be bothering me. I want to know what's important to me.

Do you think that circumstances are under your control now?

James: No human being is ever under control, although control is one of the most important things to man. Control is the human dilemma, wanting to be in control. But we're more in control now than we were before. The fact that we have each other helps us a lot, too, because the thing that we have between each other is a large amount of what we want out of life. The fact that we have each other is very important, and it makes a lot of other things less important. It makes some things that were crucial a year ago, less crucial for me, and for Carly, too, I suppose, if I can speak for her, which I guess I do too often.

But the fact that things are getting better for me doesn't cancel out the fact that I write songs. Sometimes I worry about the fact that music comes from a painful place in me, often, and often I write a song because I have the blues.

Carly: Every time I go onstage I go back to that feeling of it being a primal fact of life and death whether my parents loved me or not. In order to get my parents' love at a certain point, I felt that it was necessary that I perform for them. Their love meant survival, so sometimes I transfer that to an audience, and if they don't love me, it's my death.

James: If you're afraid they're not going to love you, it just becomes so crucial a thing . . .

Carly: It becomes much more than it is in reality. Sometimes an audience is imbued with that kind of importance. Of course, they don't realize they've got it, and, of course, they shouldn't have. It's terribly out of focus. They don't realize that the performers up there onstage are making a demand of them for the performer's life.

James: They can't realize that. When you get successful, sometimes an audience can be as bad as when you're unknown, and they just ignore you. Sometimes they don't ignore you, but what they're focusing upon is somewhere other than where you are, and that's uncomfortable, too, but I find that mostly it's positive. Being successful is good. I'm usually wrong when I think it's bad. For the most part, I love it. But one negative thing about it is that before I ever played in front of an audience, I used to sit down with the guitar and sing and play just so I could say to myself, "See, I can really sing and play the guitar. It sounds great, and I love to do it." Or I could do it at a party or something like that. I can't do that anymore. I very seldom do it. Sometimes I sit down and sing and play to myself, but mostly I do it from the audience's point of view or from the point of view of doing it for an audience. In other words, your value focus shifts. It starts off being a vital, personal sort of endeavor, kind of an aspiration, and it ends up being focused on a specific thing, and that's a limiting quality to the problem of success. I'm reminded of Dylan when he went electric. The people yelled at him for it. They didn't want to see it. It reminds me of Ricky Nelson's writing his present hit, his Garden experience. He's doing something new. They don't want to hear. I mean, that's a fucking drag. He should know to expect it, and he does. That's what the song's about. You really have to please yourself. It's the most important thing, and it's also best in the long run for what kind of music you come up with.

21

INTERVIEWED BY BEN FONG-TORRES (1973)

In 1972 Ray Charles had just celebrated his twenty-fifth anniversary in the music business, but, it seemed, he was doing more music than business. His old classics were getting some airplay on the FM "progressive" stations, and a couple of new songs were getting some attention.

His concerts drew well, as always, but he wasn't getting the respect that, say, Aretha Franklin was. He hadn't received the "hip" acclaim that Otis Redding had.

But his history was undeniable. At age forty-three, he had a lot to look back on, and, as far as he was concerned, a lot more to look forward to. He jumped at the chance to talk with ROLLING STONE and made himself available for two days of observation—and a few questions—in his recording studio in Los Angeles while he did overdubs, then for the interview in a Washington D.C. hotel room, all within a week in September 1972.

A year later, the interview won the ASCAP-Deems Taylor Award for magazine writing; Ray Charles himself would return to Atlantic in 1977 with the album, *True to Life,* and tell his own story in book form with *Brother Ray.*

—BF-T

RAY CHARLES IS ONE OF THE GREAT ones, a genius, as he's been called for some thirteen years, or, as Sinatra put it, "the only genius in the business." He is the major influence on dozens of blues, jazz, R&B, pop and rock & roll musicians. Joe Cocker idolized him, from faraway England, to the point of imitation. So did Billy Preston, who would show up at Ray's doorstep in L.A. to audition. Aretha Franklin called him "the Right Reverend," and Georgia legislator Julian Bond picked up the beat, in a poem called "The Bishop of Atlanta: Ray Charles."

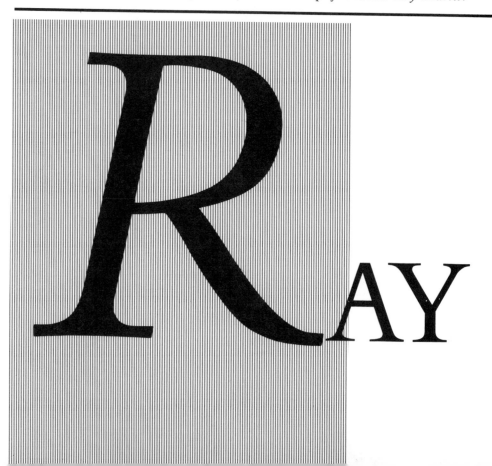

CHARLES

THE ROLLING STONE INTERVIEWS

Ray Charles' twenty-six years in the business are represented by some forty albums. He got his first gold record with "What'd I Say" for Atlantic Records in the summer of 1959, seven years after he'd joined that label. Charles then switched to ABC and began a streak with "Georgia on My Mind," "Ruby," and "Hit the Road Jack." He topped them all with a country & western album that gave him a three-million-selling single, "I Can't Stop Loving You," along with criticism from fans who didn't want to hear the Genius kicking shit. Others, like Gladys Knight, listened: "Ray Charles," she said, "hipped a lot of the black people to country & western bands . . . we was kind of listening before, but he made it even more down-to-earth where you could dig it." And Quincy Jones, longtime friend and arranger with Charles, appreciated his pioneer sense of eclecticism: "Ray Charles was responsible," he said, "for us opening our ears to all kinds of music."

Born September 23rd, 1930, in Albany, Georgia, Ray first jumped onto a piano bench, for fun, at age five in Greensville, Florida, where his parents had moved into what he remembered as a "shotgun house"—"If you stood on the porch and shot a gun you'd go right through it." Over the next two years, he lost his sight (he had been stricken with glaucoma, doctors determined years later); his parents, Bailey and Araetha, were laborers who couldn't afford medical help. "When I woke up in the mornings," Charles recalled, "I'd have to pry my eyes open." Blinded, he learned to work to help out, washing clothes, scrubbing floors, even chopping wood, until he went to a school for the blind in Orlando, Florida. He studied music there—he'd begun to pick out tunes on a neighbor's piano by age seven—and by fifteen was writing arrangements for big bands he heard in his imagination. Then his mother died, following his father by five years, and Charles left school to play in combos around Georgia and Florida. He was "crawling," he said, until he split to Seattle and got a record contract from Swing Time, a small label. He cut "Confession Blues," and then had his first success, "Baby, Let Me Hold Your Hand," done in the style of one of his main influences—or, as Johnny Otis put it, "It was a wonderful thing, but he definitely was aping Charles Brown." Ray would soon develop his own fusion of blues, jazz and gospel, touring with Lowell Fulsom, then forming a backup group for Ruth Brown in New York. He returned to Seattle and formed the Maxim Trio, worked at the Rocking Chair club and on local TV, and found himself signed to Atlantic Records when Swing Time sold his contract. First sessions were done with studio musicians (and, one time, with a pickup band including a Mexican-dominated horn section at a radio studio in New Orleans). At Atlantic, Ray began to write arrangements and compose his own great songs, blended gospel with a rocking R&B sound, formed a septet, cut "I've Got a Woman" and moved onto the first of many heights.

And all the time, he was on junk. He'd been using heroin since 1948, when he was eighteen, and he'd been busted before, around 1956, but it had all been kept hushed. Then, in 1965, Charles was arrested in Boston, reportedly in possession of a planeload of heroin, and entered a hospital in Lynwood, California. According to published stories, he spent three months undergoing medical and psychiatric help, followed by a year off. He saw a Viennese psychoanalyst regularly.

Charles has his own version of his involvement with drugs, but over the years, he has refused to discuss it. When Playboy asked him, in 1970, how he started, he begged off the question. Asked if he might not be an influence to stop potential drug users, he replied: "Bullshit. Everybody's aware that cigarettes probably cause cancer, but how many people do you think would give them up just because Ray Charles stopped smoking?" And, he continued, "I'm fed up with talking about that aspect of my life. Jesus Christ couldn't get me to say another word on the subject to anybody."

So when we got the conversation around to dope, to his nineteen-year addiction to heroin, it was a surprise to hear Ray plunge into his hooking and kicking, and it was no surprise that the stories sometimes seemed, in at least two definitions of that word, fantastic. Example: Ray says he took that year off the road, after his bust in '65, to make the courts happy (he continued to produce records, including "Crying Time" and "Let's Go Get Stoned"). He'd kicked even before the bust, he hinted in our talk. But Ron Granger, who was director of Tangerine for three years and knew Charles from long ago, told us: "He took that year off to kick it. It took a year."

But the man is clean, a nonstop worker, a perfectionist/taskmaster devoted to his music. He moves around his office building with ease, with no cane, still missing a stairstep now and then as he moves between control room and main studio, instructing musicians, running the console, re-doing his vocals. He is a gentleman as I toss in questions over an eleven-hour mixing session. Sometimes, ego challenged, there's volcanic action, as he stands up, all dressed in black, and shouts a reply, punctuating it with a "Hel-lo!" before he sits again. In his hotel room, with milk in the refrigerator and coffee and toast on the table, he writhes on the couch, sits forward pensively, falls almost onto his knee to find another restful position.

We accentuated the positive for a bit, talked about how he plays chess with a specially carved set, how he admired Bobby Fischer for insisting on championship playing conditions, how he "saw" baseball games by *going to the stadium with a transistor at his ear, how he chose the songs for the new album, 'Through the Eyes of Love.'*

We began by asking him to recall himself as a five-year-old, when his eyes began to run, to hurt.

I T DIDN'T HAPPEN LIKE ONE DAY I could see a hundred miles and the next day I couldn't see an inch. Each day for two years my sight was less and less. My mother was always real with me, and bein' poor, you got to pretty much be honest with your children. We couldn't afford no specialists. I was lucky I could get a doctor—that's a *specialist.*

When you were losing your sight, did you try to take in as much as possible, to remember things?

I guess I was too small to really care that much. I knew there were things I liked to watch. I used to love to look at the sun. That's a bad thing for my eyes, but I liked that. I used to love to look at the moon at night. I would go out in the backyard and stare at it. It just fascinated the hell out of me. And another thing that fascinated me that would scare most people is lightnin'. When I was a kid, I thought that was pretty. Anything like brightness, any kind of lights. I probably would've been a firebug or somethin'.

And there were colors. I was crazy about red. Always thought it was a beautiful color. I remember the basic colors. I don't know nothin' about chartreuse and all—I don't know what the *hell* that is. But I know the black, green, yellow, brown and stuff like that. And naturally I remember my mother, who was pretty. God, she was pretty. She was a little woman. She must have been about four feet eleven, I guess, and when I was twelve or thirteen, I was taller and bigger than my mother, and she had this long pretty black hair, used to come way down her back. Pretty good-lookin' chick, man {laughter}.

A lot of people have asked you to define soul. I'd like to get a definition of beauty.

If you're talkin' about physical beauty, I would have to say that to me beauty is probably about the same thing that it means to most people. You look at them and the structure of their face, the way their skin is, and say like, a woman, the contour of her body, you know what I mean? The same way as I would walk out and feel the car. Put my hands on the lines of a car, and I'd know whether I'd like it or not from the way the designs of the lines are. As I said, I was

fortunate enough to see until I was about seven, and I remember the things that I heard people calling beautiful.

How about beauty in music?

I guess you could call me a sentimentalist, man, really. I like Chopin or Sibelius. People who write softness, you know, and although Beethoven to me was quite heavy, he wrote some really touching songs, and I think that *Moonlight Sonata*—in spite of the fact that it wound up being very popular—it's somethin' about that, man, you could just feel the pain that this man was goin' through. Somethin' had to be happenin' in that man. You know, he was very, very lonesome when he wrote that. From a technical point of view, I think Bach, if you really want to learn technique, that was the cat, 'cause he had all them fugues and things, your hands doin' all kinda different things. Personally, outside of technique, I didn't care for Bach.

Did you try to catch up with high school or college after you left school?

No. When I left school, I had to get out and really tough it, as you know, because my mother passed away when I was fifteen. I didn't have no brothers or sisters. But my mama always taught me, "Look, you got to learn how to get along by yourself," and she's always tellin' me, "Son, one of these days I'm gonna be dead, and you're gonna need to know how to survive, because even your best friends, although they may want to do things for you; after all, they will have their own lives." So at that point I started tryin' to help myself. So what do I do to help myself? The thing I can do best, or figure I can do best, anyway. And that is sing or play the piano or both.

What else did they teach you in school that could have been applied to a career?

Well, I don't know where I would have used it, but I can probably type as fast as any secretary. Well, not *any.* I can type about sixty to sixty-five words a minute, somethin' like that, when I wanna. Then I can make all kinds of things with my hands. I can make chairs and brooms and mops and rugs and pocketbooks and belts and all kinds of things like that. So guess if I had to, I would go and buy me some leather. I love to work with my hands, and I'm sure that's what I would do had I not played music, you see, because it's the kind of a thing that you can use plenty of imagination in it, you know what I mean? And so I know how to do various kinds of stitchin'. Mexican stitchin' and regular stitchin' overlappin' it and stuff. So I guess I would have—although it would have been a very meek

261

livin', I suppose. You can't turn out a lot by hand.

Music was a meek living for a long time, too.

Yeah, it was really crawlin'. I became very ill a couple times. I suffered from malnutrition, you know. I was really messed up because I wasn't eatin' nothin', and I wouldn't beg. Two things you don't do, you don't beg and you don't steal. That's right.

What kind of music education did you have in Florida?

They taught you how to read the music, and I had to play Chopin, Beethoven, you know, the normal thing. Just music lessons. Not really theory. I don't know what that *is*. It's just, they taught me how to read music, and naturally how to use correct fingerin', and once you've learned that you go from the exercises into little compositions into things like Chopin. That's the way it went, although I was tryin' to play boogie-woogie, man, 'cause I could always just about play anything I heard. My ear was always pretty good, but I did have a few music teachers, and so I do know music quite well, if you don't mind my saying so. I was never taught to write music, but when I was twelve years old I was writing arrangements for a big band. Hell, if you can read music, you can write it, and I think certainly what helped me is that I'm a piano player, so I know chords. Naturally, I can hear chords, and I could always play just about anything I could hear. It was just a question of learning how to put it down on paper. I just studied how to write for horns on my own. Like, understanding that the saxophone is in different keys, and also, when I was goin' to school I took up clarinet. See, I was a great fan of Artie Shaw. I used to think, "Man, ooh, he had the prettiest sound," and he had so much feelin' in his playin', I always felt that, still feel it today.

Where were you hearing this boogie-woogie?

We lived next door for some years to a little general store in Greensville, Florida, where the kids could come in and buy soda pop and candy and the people could buy kerosene for their lamps, you know. And they had a jukebox in there. And the guy who owned it also had a piano. Wylie Pittman is the guy. Even when I was three and four years old, if I was out in the yard playin', and if he started playin' that piano, I would stop playin' and run in there and jump on the stool. Normally, you figure a kid run in there like that and jump on the stool and start bangin' on the piano, the guy would throw him off. "Say, get away from here, don't you see me" . . . but he didn't do that, I always loved that

man for that. I was about five years old, and on my birthday he had some people there. He said, "RC"—this is what they called me then—"look, I want you to get up on the stool, and I want you to play for these people." Now, let's face it. I was five years old. They know damn well I wasn't playin'. I'm just bangin' on the keys, you understand. But that was encouragement that got me like that, and I think that the man felt that anytime a child is willin' to stop playin', you know, out in the yard and havin' fun, to come in and hear somebody play the piano, evidently this child has music in his bones, you know. And he didn't discourage me, which he could have, you know what I mean? Maybe I wouldn't have been a musician at all, because I didn't have a musical family, now remember that.

You were also able to hear 'The Grand Ole Opry' when you were a kid?

Yep, yeah, I always—every Saturday night, I never did miss it. I don't know why I liked the music. I really thought that it was somethin' about country music, even as a youngster—I couldn't figure out what it was then, but I know what it is now. But then I don't know why I liked it and I used to just love to hear Minnie Pearl, because I thought she was so funny.

How old were you then?

Oh, I guess I was about seven, eight, and I remember Roy Acuff and Gene Austin. Although I was bred in and around the blues, I always did have interest in other music, and I felt it was the closest music, really, to the blues—they'd make them steel guitars cry and whine, and it really attracted me. I don't know what it is. Gospel and the blues are really, if you break it down, almost the same thing. It's just a question of whether you're talkin' about a woman or God. I come out of the Baptist church, and naturally whatever happened to me in that church is gonna spill over. So I think the blues and gospel music is quite synonymous to each other.

Big Bill Broonzy once said that "Ray Charles has got the blues he's cryin' sanctified. He's mixin' the blues with the spirituals. . . . He should be singin' in a church."

I personally feel that it was not a question of mixing gospel with the blues. It was a question of singin' the only way I knew how to sing. This was not a thing where I was tryin' to take the church music and make the blues out of it or vice versa. All I was tryin' to do was sing the only way I knew how, period. I was raised in the church. I went to the Sunday school. I went to the morning service, and that's where they had the young people doin' their performin', and I went to night service, and I went to all the revival meetings. My parents said, "You *will* go to *church.*" I mean they ain't no *if* about *that.* So singin' in the church and hearin' this good singin' in the church and also hearin' the blues, I guess this was the only way I *could* sing, outside of loving Nat Cole so well, and I tried to imitate him very much. When I was starting out, I loved the man so much that's why I can understand a lot of other artists who come up and try to imitate me. You know, when you love somebody so much and you feel what they're doin' is close to what you feel, some of that rubs off on you— so *I* did that.

But, say, Joe Cocker is a white man, and British; you were emulating a fellow black.

I'm not the kind of a guy that wants to generalize and say that you can't do this if you're black or you can't do that if you're white. I think that if a man has had the kicking around and the abuse and the scorn, I think that if he has talent, he can put that some way or another so that the people can hear him. I remember one time a guy asked me, hey, man, do you think a white cat could ever sing the blues? Which is a legitimate question. It didn't hurt my feelings. I feel that *anybody,* if you ever have the blues *bad* enough, with the *back*ground that dictates to the horror and the sufferin' of the blues, I don't give a damn if he's *green, purple*—he can give it to ya.

I don't have time to be bitter. What I have time for is to try to see what I can do to help the guy that's comin' up and maybe he can make it better if I can help him. You see? I done seen all this, man. I know all about the places where I couldn't drink outta the fountain. I know all about the places I couldn't go to the bathroom when I had to pee—somethin' that's natural for every human bein'. You understand me? See, I know all about that, but I don't want to let that get into what I'm doin'. I figure that, okay, I'm in this business because I love music. So I can't afford to let bitterness get into me, but if when you ask me what's really happenin', if you get people and sit them down and say, hey, man, let's cut all the fat outta this. Get down to the real thing. What is it? This is the real thing I'm tellin' you now. That's without bitterness and I ain't mad. I can afford to tell you that for one reason; you see, thank the Lord, I'm fairly cool about it. My kids ain't gonna starve unless they bomb the country or somethin' with nuclear weapons or somethin'.

Naturally you have, what is it?—fifteen to twenty percent black, you got eighty to eighty-five percent white. Fine. So, as a result of that, if you're not careful, you can become very bitter, because you'll say, well, why in the world—here *I* am, and here's a guy who'll spend millions of dollars to find a white cat just to imitate me, and he'll do far better than me. Well, the only thing that I can say that sort of helps me a little bit, that keeps me goin'—I say two things. First of all, in order for that guy to copy me, he gotta wait 'til I do it first. Now {*laughter*}, the second thing I feel, well, if this is the case, if you take this guy over me and he's just an imitation of me, then that says to me that I must be pretty damn good. Because I don't know nobody that you wanna copy that ain't worth a damn. All right, hello {*laughter*}.

That says it?

That says it all, man. I mean, that's your salvation, 'cause if you don't think like that, you'll be bitter. You really would be bitter.

Other critics have said that when Aretha moved from Columbia to Atlantic, she enjoyed immense success, while you moved to ABC and in the mid-Sixties, you were on kind of a downhill critical slide with records.

Yeah?

Now, how did you feel about that?

Oh, I don't know. I guess that's probably some cat who didn't see my financial sheet. I don't really worry about that, you know. Fortunately for me, throughout my career—now it's true, I haven't had a million seller every time I put out a record, but what has happened with me has been a very simple thing. I've had those 400,000, 700,000, 300,000, 800,000, and that's been constantly goin' on all through my career. I'll tell you what my answer is: When I can walk into an airport and you get little kids sayin' {*whispering*}, "Mama that's Ray Charles," I'm raisin' them. That's where I'm at, man. As long as the people keep doin' that, as long as I can walk anywhere and as I'm walkin' all I can hear is {*whispering*}, "That's Ray Charles!" I don't figure I need to worry too much.

Now, you say this is in the mid-Sixties, right? I just wanna ask you a dumb question. Tell me, what was wrong with "Crying Time"? That was in the mid-Sixties. "Let's Go Get Stoned." I didn't find nothin' wrong with these songs. I mean, they seemed to sell all right.

First of all, I don't tell myself what some people say: "Well, Ray, the genius." I never called myself a genius. I'm not the one to do that, brother. I think that's up to the people to decide, and if they give me the impression, well, Ray, you been out here a long time now, but we want to turn you out to pasture now, you know,

263

that would be all right with me, because, hell, I figure whatever I ain't got in twenty-seven years, I don't deserve to have it. Because I've had every opportunity to do what I need.

We were talking about when you started out. You played what was called "cocktail music," playing piano and singing songs like "If I Give You My Love." But were you always looking to form your own big band?

Well, when I was doing what you're talkin' about right now, my only thing, my goal was, "Wow, if I could only just get to make records, too." That's why, in 1948, when they had the union ban on musicians so they weren't allowed to record, I recorded anyway—first of all, I didn't know about the ban, and, of course, later I had to pay a fine for it—I didn't care. I was only about seventeen or somethin' like that. I was workin' in Seattle, then, and a fellow came up from Los Angeles, Jack Lauderdale, and he had a little record company [Swing Time], and I was workin' at the Rockin' Chair. He came and one night he was in there and heard me playing and he said to me, "Listen, I have a record company. I would like to record you." Man, I was so glad, I didn't ask him how much money I was gonna get. I didn't *care.* I would have done it for nothin'. So he said, "Look, I'm gonna take you down to Los Angeles." And wow, Los Angeles, you know. Ooh, yeah, yeah. And I'm gonna be *recorded,* man. You know, *wow,* my own voice on a record *{laughter}.*

I went down there and we made a song called "Confession Blues." That was my first record. Sold *pretty* good. Then, about a year later, 1949, we made a song called "Baby Let Me Hold Your Hand." Now that really was a big hit. "Confession Blues" sold mediocre—it sold well enough to suit me, because I was hearing it where I went. But when I was out on the road workin' with Lowell Fulsom, he had a big record called "Every Day I Have the Blues." We were on the same label. I had "Baby Let Me Hold Your Hand," and he was singin' "Every Day I Have the Blues," and we were packin' 'em in. This is really where I started touring the country.

When you left Florida, why did you choose to go to the other corner of the country?

It was just—New York I was frightful of, 'cause I just couldn't imagine myself goin' to New York or Chicago or even Los Angeles. They sounded so big, man. I guess I always felt that I was pretty good, but I wasn't sure of myself to want to jump out into a big city like New York. I was too scared for that. So what I wanted to do

was pick a town that was far away from Florida, but not huge, and Seattle really was about as far away as I could get. All across the U.S., and, of course, it wasn't a huge town, half a million people or somethin' like that.

How long did you stay with Swing Time?

I was there until Atlantic bought the contract. I think it was '51 or so. About three or four years.

That was Ahmet [Ertegun] and Herb Abramson, I think, at that time. I don't know how that was done. I met with the people at Atlantic, and they said, "Well, we'd like to record you," so I said, "Well, I'm under contract to somebody." They said, "Well, look, we'll buy the contract." So I said, "Fine, buy it." And that's it. Finished.

Why did you leave Atlantic? Jerry Wexler told me it was a "shock" to him.

Well, you know the people at Atlantic—Jerry, Ahmet, Nesuhi . . . I love *all* the people over there. It was the kind of thing where ABC came up with a contract. I think they were trying to lure somebody there, and I hate to say this, because it makes me sound like I'm blowin' my own horn, but you know, I was with Atlantic and we had this big hit "What'd I Say" and a couple other things, so they came up with a contract and I let Jerry and them know about it. The contract was so unreal. I mean, the thing was that, well, if ABC was really seriously going to do it, Atlantic just couldn't match it, based on the original contract I had with them. But I let them know, because, you know that Jerry and I are the best of friends because I didn't do anything sneaky, in the dark, or nothin' like that. They knew the whole bit, and my thing was, look, I'm not asking you to *better* ABC's deal, I'm just saying if you can *match* it, I'll stay with you. And it was the kind of thing where they said, "Look, Ray, it's *awfully* heavy for us."

You gotta understand the position of each party, and, of course, ABC at the time was offering me the kind of a contract that, believe me, in those days, in 1959, was unheard of. Now, as a result of that, I tell you, I don't even think that they *figured* that I would do as *well,* because, like I say, I've been out there for a while. So what they were basically after was the *name* and to stimulate *other* names.

To sign with ABC.

Right. And so I was like a pawn, but as it turned out we were so lucky, because right after I went with ABC, we came up with "Georgia," and then the country-western stuff, see? But I did a country-western song with Atlantic before I went to ABC, but the other side of it sold, the song "I Believe to My Soul." Well, on the back of that was a song called "I'm Movin' On."

Hank Snow.

That's right. There's where I first get the idea. But it just turned out that once I changed contracts, I followed that idea. Now, with ABC we had people saying, "Hey, man, gee whiz, Ray, you got all these fans, you can't do no country-western things. Your fans—you gonna lose all your fans." Well, I said, "For Christ's sake, I'll do it anyway." Not to be—don't misunderstand me—I didn't want to be a Charlie Pride, now. I'm not saying there's anything wrong with that. I'm just saying that was not my intent. I didn't want to be a country-western singer. I just wanted to take country-western songs. When I sing "I Can't Stop Loving You," I'm not singin' it *country-western.* I'm singin' it like *me.* But I think the words to country songs are very earthy like the blues, see, very *down.* They're not as dressed up, and the people are very honest and say, "Look, I miss you, darlin', so I went out and I got drunk in this bar." That's the way you say it. Wherein Tin Pan Alley will say, "Oh, I missed you, darling, so I went to this restaurant and I sat down and I had dinner for one." That's cleaned up now, you see? But country songs and the blues is like it is.

I did two albums of country-western, you gotta remember I did Volume I, and hell, if you get an album to sell well over a million, you almost gotta do—that's almost forcing you to do one more. But that's all I did with country-western was two albums.

Atlantic gave you musical independence and built a reputation for R&B and jazz. ABC, on the other hand, wasn't known for a sound. Did you have a feeling of trepidation about moving from one to the other?

No, 'cause my thing was that it was a record company, and I thought I could sell records for ABC as well as I could sell records for Atlantic or anybody else. Plus, after all, you gotta understand, man, I had been workin' a long time, strugglin' a mighty long time with nothin', and this was a helluva chance for me to really better myself; if I really had any kind of luck, I really was gonna wind up bein' all right. I made an awful lot of money fast, real fast.

What was the production deal?

I was producin' myself, you see? In other words, it was a contract within a contract. I got paid the regular top artist scale as an artist, but also the producin' end of it was where the extra money came from. That was where, out of every dime I got seven and a half cents, and that's pretty damn good, man. That's besides the artist contract, you know.

After Swing Time, when you began searching around for your own voice, did you find it naturally or did you get help from Ahmet or Jerry?

I gotta tell you the truth, man, about Ahmet and Nesuhi and Herb Abramson and Jerry when he came in, these people never at any time told me what to sing or how to sing it. Okay? I have to be honest with you. I think if they had told me that, I woulda told them where to take the contract. I figured that whatever I'm doin', I'm gonna do it to the best of my ability. Now, you have a right to say you don't want it, but you can't tell me how to do it. I won't allow that. I guess I've always been very firm about that. I didn't have that with Atlantic. I didn't have it with ABC.

All I did, and Jerry can tell you—he never put any pressure on me. I would call him up and say, "Hey, Jerry, I'm ready to record." That's how we did "I've Got a Woman." I was on the road, workin' every day. I called him up in New York and said, hey, I'm ready to record. So he said, where are you, where are you gonna be? I said I'd be in Atlanta in a few days. He flew down to Atlanta, Georgia. That's where we made "I've Got a Woman." Little studio. Just a little bit—I think it was WGST or somethin'. Little bitty, and they weren't equipped for recording. But we went in there and we struggled and we managed it. That's the way we did it. I mean, I didn't have no pressure on me about doing anything, and I didn't have no pressure on me at ABC neither.

The gospel, call-and-responses in your songs—"Drown in My Own Tears," "What'd I Say" and "Hit the Road Jack"—I'd say, were tremendous influences on Motown's sound. How did that develop?

Well, I don't know how anything . . . I just hear things in my head. That's the simplest answer I can give you, man. What I hear is what comes out, and I'm very instantaneous, I guess. I feel somethin', get an idea how I want to do it, and I just do it. I don't have no special ways about it. Anything I do, good or bad, it's very, very natural. That's it.

Sometimes you cry onstage.

That's true, that's true. I'm not embarrassed about that. It's just that some nights, man, I guess my mood, you know. And I don't know what happens in my soul, but I can be singin' a song, and for some reason it'll get to me, you know. I'll feel sorry, feel sad. It'll just hurt me or somethin', I don't know. So I cry. Can't help it.

Do you listen to a lot of today's artists? Marvin Gaye, Sly Stone . . .

Oh, yeah, well, I like these people's music. I like Marvin Gaye. I like some of the things that Sly's done. I like, you know I'm a great fan of Aretha Franklin. I like Stevie Wonder. I like Sinatra. I like Ella Fitzgerald. I like many people, just like I like many varieties of music. On the other hand, say, like here's a guy like—many times, I may go and get out my old Art Tatum records, 'cause I still think that he's the greatest piano player ever lived, bar none. I'm speakin' about playin' jazz music, as we call it. I've never heard nobody before or since this man that could do to a piano what he could do.

How about Aretha? Do you find that she's been consistent in her music the past five years?

I think so. I think basically Aretha in a great sense is very much like myself. She's right outta the church and she can't help what she sounds like. No more than I can help what I sound like. We both, really, were very devoted to the church, and this is just *us.* I think there may be some records come out that you may not necessarily care for, but it's still Aretha, and just like the records that come out of me that you might not care for, it's still me.

Where did you first meet Quincy Jones?

In Seattle. Quincy was wantin' to learn how to write, and he used to come over to my apartment and get me up early in the mornin', you know, and I'd show him how to voice and put the chord structure for a band together. He'll be the first cat to tell you, man, that in comin' up—*he* feels, I don't, but he feels he owes an awful lot to me for that. You know, I'm not a teacher, but if I find somebody who really wants to learn, and if they have the basic idea of what they want to learn, I will help them do it. I can't start a kid off from scratch, 'cause I don't have that kind of patience.

Why don't you write anymore?

I just don't have the time . . . I'm sorry, but . . .

Did you used to have to find time to write?

Well, I *had,* I didn't have to *find.* I had a lot of time, because I wasn't workin', and I didn't have the obligations then. Shit, I was starvin'. So what happens with a thing like that is you got plenty of time, so you utilize it. As Jerry can tell you, they used to send me many, many dubs, and I'd play all of them, and if I didn't like anything, I'd say, "Okay, well, I know I gotta do

a session," so I'd sit down and write one. It's just that I was lucky at it. That's why . . .

More than that.

{Laughter} No, it's the truth.

Were there times back then when songs would just come to you anyway, whether you were looking for them or not?

Well, you know, you might hear somebody say something that would give you an idea.

And that doesn't happen anymore.

Well, it not so much doesn't happen, like I said, I don't have time to really—it's a question of how your life is, man, really. There are other things—I think it's a thing of a man spreadin' himself out too thin. Now, I love writing. But I am not a writer. I think it's fair for you to understand that. I am not a true writer. I wrote because maybe I heard an idea or somebody said something or I needed some material and I couldn't find none that suited me, so I sat down and wrote my own. It took weeks.

Writing your songs, you were in the mainstream of blues and jazz, but in picking music, I find you doing kind of a schmaltzy song like "Breathless," comparing a person to a bird or an angel. You've always done Broadway show tunes along with blues, jazz and country, so you've never allowed yourself to get categorized.

I heard somebody one time say that all black people got rhythm. Bullshit. Ain't no such thing as that. You cannot generalize with people. You can say if you want that maybe the bulk of the people go a certain way. You understand?

Was Tangerine Records part of the ABC deal? That you would have your own company?

Yeah, you could say that. First, when I started out with ABC as an artist, I also was a producer there, and when it was time for renewing my contract, I said, "Well, look, you'll have to come up with somethin' more to my liking." You know, it's not always a question of money, it's a question of the things that I want done, and so this was integrated in the contract.

Has Tangerine generally done well?

We lost quite a bit of money in the beginning of it, and so naturally, when you open up shop, you lose money, you stay in the red for quite a while, and here lately we're not makin' a lot of money. We have gotten out of the red. So that is progress.

Are you a really difficult person to work with?

Well, that depends on how you look at it. I would say no, and then there are people who would say yes. You have to ask someone who works for me. I'm not a difficult person, I don't think, but I do insist that since we are pros, we oughtta act like it. I don't like to play. I love to have fun in my work, but if it's somethin' wrong, let's clean that up and get that right. Let's not play about that, 'cause it ain't funny when it's wrong. It's funny and beautiful and lovable and everything when it's right, you know what I mean. And I'll go along with you.

What is the "fine" system with the band?

We always gonna have that, man. I don't *mean* to have it, but unfortunately, you can't just fire a man all the time. My fine system works this way: I may fine a guy once. Never over twice. After that he's fired, period. Because I figure, if I gotta be finin' you, then we don't need each other. I don't need the fine money; I don't even want it. What I do, I take the fine and maybe later in the year give a party or somethin' for the musicians. So they really get it back.

It's not finin', it's a dock in pay. The union says that I can't fine a person, but I can dock them. For the man who's not getting the money, it's the same thing. Twenty-five dollars is twenty-five dollars or fifty dollars is fifty dollars.

L EONARD FEATHER ONCE CALLED *you "a nervous, restless millionaire."*
Well, I guess if you were talkin' about my, you know, with the assets and so forth—I guess if you wanted to you could call me a millionaire. I wouldn't say that. I figure I got everything it takes me to live. I got a home that's paid for, hell, and my kids are straight for the rest of their life. I got a little studio here I can do my work in. Well, you know, I got a car, a couple of airplanes. What the hell more you want? Shit, you can sleep in but one bed at a time. And according to the law, you ain't supposed to have but one woman at a time or at least under the same conditions {*laughter*}. So I got everything I need.

Have you heard much about the new black movies?

No, not really. I haven't really delved into it.

Some people have charged that movies like 'Super Fly' romanticize those things in the black culture that are romanticized by, say, 'Godfather' or by cowboy movies.

I would have to say that I think if I was gonna make a movie of that kind, I would do it in a different way and still say the same thing. I don't think it's so much of what you're saying, it's the way it was being said to make it seem like it's

quite glamorous, and I don't think I would have went that far. You see, you should also show in that movie, yeah, you can go out and be a coke dealer, too, but you gotta remember you're gonna wind up killin' a few of your brothers, too, dealin' in that kinda stuff, and you're gonna wind up sendin' quite a few people to jail, and you're gonna wind up breakin' a lotta people's hearts, too, when you're doin' that. 'Cause believe me, man, there's nothin' worse than seein' a twelve-year-old kid hooked. I mean, you know when you got coke, you got some heroin around. C'mon now.

Did your own involvement in drugs almost knock you out in music?

No. No. No. Nope. I can't say that.

Heights in music were reached during that stage?

Exactly. So I mean, obviously, I couldn't say that, could I? You know, like I say, I ain't never gonna lie to you. It didn't knock me out or wasn't about to knock me out. My thing was that when my kids started growin' up—I remember one day my oldest son, he was one of the baseball players, they were havin' a little reception Thursday night and they were giving out these little trophies, and I was supposed to go, and what happened, I had a recordin' session that night. I was doing the sound track for *The Cincinnati Kid*, and I did the singin' on that, as you remember, but what I did, I went by there with him to this banquet, and I had to leave before the thing was over, and he cried. And that hurt me. I started thinkin', here's a child. It means so much to him for his father to be at this banquet. And I started thinkin' that suppose that somethin' happened, I get put in jail and somebody comes along and says, "Oh, your daddy's a jailbird." Remember now, he's gettin' up there in age, now. He's a little man, you know, and he gonna cry about that. I figure the next thing he'll do is haul up and knock hell out of 'em, and now he's gonna be in trouble all over me, when you break it down. That was my decision then. I said, look, I mean, that ain't it for me. And I said, okay, I've had enough—it's a risky business, it's a dangerous business, anybody knockin' on your door, you gotta double-check to see who it is.

When was this?

This was like in '64 or '65 or somethin', give or take. I don't know, back in there, anyhow.

That all came to a head right around '65?

That's right. Right then. I just felt that it was a bad scene, and really it just was a bad scene. I got involved in it—my situation is, I was young. I was about maybe seventeen, eighteen years old

267

or somethin' like that, and it always, you know, like, it was a thing where I wanted to be among the big fellas, like cats in the band, and these guys would always go and leave the kid "till we come back," you know. And I wanted to be a part, so I begged and pleaded until somebody said, "Okay, man, goddamn it, come on, all right." And they took me, and there I was, so they were doin' it and I wanted to belong, you know. I mean, this is really how it started, and once it started, there it was, you know. But I never got so involved in it to the point where I was out of my mind or didn't know what the hell I was doin', you know. Like, I heard of people havin' habits of sixty dollars a day or one hundred dollars a day. I never had nothin' like that.

How much did you take per day?

Oh, I probably spent about twenty dollars. Never got above that.

What did you learn through the Viennese psychoanalyst?

Who?

The psychoanalyst that you were supposed to have seen for a couple of years?

What did we talk about? Nothin'. Like, and he's not a psychoanalyst. I mean, what he was, was a psychiatrist. He had no influence, say, as far as my doing or not doing anything. As a matter of fact, we didn't even get into—I told him one thing. I went there and said, "First of all we're gonna get one thing straight. You don't have to convince me not to do anything. I've already made up my mind, I ain't gonna do it, and it's finished. Fine. That's it." And so, when we saw each other we just talked in general about just whatever popped up, and hell, I think I probably talked to him more about his practice, what the hell he was doin', than about myself.

Was that year off hard for you?

I'm basically a lazy person. It's never hard for me to relax. But I do enjoy doin' things. The work I'm doin' is not work to me. It's fun. See, it's like a hobby that I'm gettin' paid for and truly is part of my relaxation. This is really it for me.

Then why did you take a year off?

Well, I felt that I should do it just because I wanted to. Now, it was necessary, of course. I hired a psychiatrist so that when we went into court, I thought it might be beneficial. You tell a judge somethin' like a cat been usin' somethin' for fifteen years, and he all of a sudden the man say he ain't gonna do it no more, and the cat gonna say, "Sure, come on now, let's get down to the facts." But if a psychiatrist says it, for some reason, at least the judge will kinda lean towards believin' the cat. So that was the whole purpose of the whole thing. Because, let's face it, man, if a guy doesn't want to stop doin' somethin', the judge, the psychiatrist, the jailer, ain't nobody gonna—the people stay in jail five years and come out on the street one day right back at it.

You can make yourself stop if you see somethin' happenin' to your children or somethin' happenin' to your life or whatever. You just tell yourself, look, okay, that's a bad scene. I'm gonna quit. Just stop, you know. And once your mind is made up, that's it. That's all it is, man. I know I'm oversimplifying it, but I swear to you, this is the truth.

I believe—I'll tell you somethin', now, I had the psychiatrist, and the man had a legal right to what you call trim me down a little less each day until I got down to nothin'. I didn't do that. Okay? Now, that's somethin'. The doctor didn't believe this himself, that I have never in all my years, I've never seen nothin' like this in my life. They even tested me, man. They thought somebody must be slippin' me somethin'. Then, so they cut my visitation off, just to make sure, and I still was the same way, so they said, no, it can't be that. And then, another thing surprised him. Not only was I not doing anything, but they try to say do you want anything to help you sleep? You want any sleepin' pills? I said, well, I ain't been takin' sleepin' pills. I don't figure I need to take 'em now. So and that was kind of a shocker. Because the hospital didn't believe it, the doctor didn't believe it. And man, they sent me in—they tested me two or three times, the usual testin' that they do on you. They sent me up here to McLean Hospital in Boston, because this was ordered by the court. Like, they called me up one day and I'm workin' like hell, you know? Doin' my concerts, and they called me up one day and said, "Hey, we want you to go to McLean's Hospital and check in tomorrow." Now that meant one thing. If I was doin' it, they ain't no way in the world I could get it outta my system in a day. So they sent me up there. Not only did they send me there, but what they did, they waited until the weather got kinda cool. Now, they know if you usin' any kinda drugs, you can't stand that cold. You just can't take it. So, man, they cut off the heat on me. Made me mad as hell. I went up and told the nurse I'm gonna sue the goddamn hospital if I catch cold. I know what y'all been doin'. I want some heat put back in my room. I mean, I'm not stupid. But, I'm literally freezin'. So you put the heat back in there. I'll be damned if I—once I leave here, I got to go back to work, and I refuse to have

268

pneumonia behind some bull. I guess the woman must have said they can't be nothin' wrong with this man, after all the testin' we done and everything else, and all he can do is get mad, you know. So after a while they got to believe me, but it took an awful lot of doin', because it was unusual, quite unusual.

This came after your stay at St. Francis Hospital in Lynwood, California?

Yeah, well, this was somethin' ordered by the court. This was part of my thing. They didn't tell me I couldn't work or nothin', they just said, look, any day we might call you, you know, and say this to you. What they did, they watched my schedule and knew I was workin', so they knew of a day when I wasn't workin'. They knew my schedule better than me, and all of a sudden they just, bam—you just got to go, man. So they did test me a couple of times just to make sure.

I didn't have a wind-down program. I just *stopped,* period. You hear about people who bite the sheets and eat up the pillow, and I didn't do none of that. So that worried people. They took all my clothes. They searched them. And they came in my room one day, they looked under the mattress, shit. I said, "I don't know what the hell you all lookin' for, but they ain't any way in the world I can get anything. Nobody's comin' here, and I don't know where I could find it." And you know, they watched me like a hawk.

You were once asked about the messages in your songs; or, rather, the lack of messages. Only last year, in fact, did you devote an album, 'Message from the People,' to anything but love songs. Was there a particular moment that you thought was right for such an album?

No, it was a matter of getting material I could handle. Believe it or not, it is very difficult to make an album like that, unless you're just tryin' to throw somethin' together. Remember, I got to first feel the music, do somethin' with the song. And that's why in that album you have a song like "America." I wasn't tryin' to just say the country is all bad, because it ain't all bad. I love this country, man. And I wouldn't live in no place else. You understand. My family was born here. My great-grandparents were born here. I think I got as much roots in this country as anybody else. So I think when somethin's wrong, it's up to me to try to change it. I was sayin' that America is a beautiful country. It's just some of our policies that people don't dig. That's what "Hey Mister" is all about. How can you live in the richest country in the world—I can see havin' po' people, don't misunderstand me, you always gonna have the po'. But ain't no need to have no

hungry people, because if you got a million dollars, and I ain't got say $30,000, I'm po' compared to you. But the difference is that in a country with so much, where we *pay* people not to *grow* food, ain't no reason for us to have hungry people.

You said onstage that "I Gotta Do Wrong" is "the story of my life," that "I gotta do wrong before they notice me."

Well, I kind of think that what I meant was is that it seems that out of all the pleading that a people can do, all the crying out and all the conversations, you know, we've had that for years and years and years, and nothin' really happened. They said, well, those people are happy, and they're smiling and dancing, and so they must be cool. And nobody paid them the mind, until the people began to do wrong things. And, of course, what I was really saying is not that this was anything to be proud about. I was saying that it's something to be ashamed of, that you got to do wrong before a country as rich as we are—we're the richest country in the world. We got more money and we got more of everything. I don't care what any other country's got for the most part, we got that, and the chances are, nine times out of ten, we got more of it on top of it. And it's a shame that in order for our leaders to really pay us some attention, we gotta go and burn this down, and we gotta go and break into this, and we gotta go and picket this, and we gotta go and stand on this lawn—that's pitiful.

On the other hand, you take the Indian. What has he got? We found him here when we got here. But I guarantee you—well, hopefully this doesn't happen. This may be bad for me to say this, because I don't wanna start anything, but you know, the chances are the Indian's never gonna get a damn thing until he go out and scalp a few people, you understand, and do a little wrong. And then, he'll have the same questions we used to have. "Well, what's wrong with him? I can't understand. What's he asking for? What does he want?" Everybody knows what is needed or what is desired, what it is to help a man lead a decent life. Everybody who's in power—the leaders know this, but they're not—unfortunately, it doesn't seem like they want to do anything unless they're *forced* to it, unless they are made to feel *shame* about it. And when I sing this song—I gotta do wrong before people notice me—I'm not braggin' about that. I'm saying that that's a pity. It is, it's sad, man. So when the Indian goes out and he kills off or scalps a couple of people, and they go and burn down a couple of buildings, or whatever it is that's necessary, and when our officials begin to notice, then *he'll* get a little more, too. I feel bad to have to say that. Now he's gotta go and destroy somethin'. Get out the National Guard and the federal troops and everything else, you know, to quiet the people down. There's a man, I understand, who was asking for something that we wanted to throw away. This was Alcatraz or somethin'. We said we don't want the place out there no more, and the man said, "Okay, this belongs to us anyway, let us have it." We wouldn't even give him that, somethin' we don't want, we wouldn't give it to 'im. That's sick. *Sick!* I'm gonna get mad now.

22

INTERVIEWED BY ROBERT HILBURN (1973)

As interviewer Robert Hilburn recounts in his introduction, Johnny Cash, 40, was flattered to be featured in ROLLING STONE in 1973 and had long wondered whether the magazine was interested in "someone like me."

But ROLLING STONE had been interested a long time. Cash was pictured on page one of issue number eleven, five years before; and, in an article about renewed connections between Cash and Bob Dylan, and between country and rock, Jann Wenner wrote: "Johnny Cash, more than any other country performer, is meaningful in a rock & roll context." Later, we'd cover Cash's TV show when Dylan was a guest; Cash performing at San Quentin Prison; Cash playing for Nixon at the White House; and the release of his *Original Golden Hits Volumes I and II,* including "I Walk the Line," the classic "Ballad of a Teen-Age Queen" and the original "Folsom Prison Blues."

So when Hilburn, who'd covered Cash for a number of years for the Los Angeles *Times,* suggested an extended interview of Johnny Cash on the occasion of his breakthrough Las Vegas engagement, he got a quick OK.

—BF-T

WHEN YOU SPEAK OF THE GREATS IN country music, three names naturally come to mind: Jimmie Rodgers, Hank Williams and Johnny Cash. Together, they helped shape the content/direction of country music and helped spread its popularity to a vast, new audience. Besides similarities in music and background (each was born to a poor family in the rural South), they also became something in life of the tragic figure that country music, with its songs about honky-tonks and troubled times, so often speaks.

Rodgers, who died in New York City in 1933, was the victim of tuberculosis at a time when cures for the illness were still rare. He was thirty-five. Williams' problems were more directly related to the

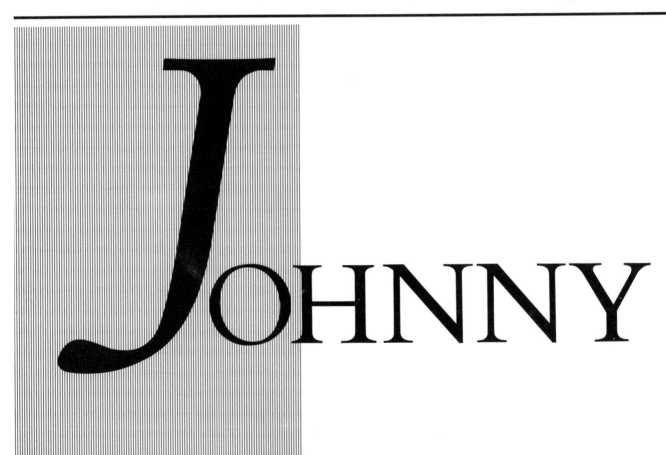

CASH

pressures of success. His behavior became so troublesome and unpredictable that he was eventually thrown off the Grand Ole Opry, country music's most important outlet. Williams was twenty-nine when he died—some said of "too much livin'"—in the back seat of a car that was taking him to a New Year's Day concert in 1953.

Cash, too, some feared, was going to succumb to the pressures of success. It's the Hank Williams story all over again, many in the country music business began whispering in the early Sixties as Cash—generally viewed as the field's most dynamic figure since Williams—began missing shows, taking pills and living recklessly. But Cash caught himself in time. Some speak of his experience in terms of a reprieve. If so, he's been making the most of it. In 1968, Cash went to Folsom Prison in California to record a live album that revitalized his career. It brought him back the recognition that had seemed, in some quarters, to be slipping away. And he used that recognition to good advantage, helping expose his friends—the singers and songwriters he so respects—to wider audiences.

When ABC gave him a television show, he brought on guests who were far above the quality television viewers had ever seen on a weekly series. Some of them were already major figures, others on the way: Bob Dylan, Gordon Lightfoot, James Taylor, Kris Kristofferson, Mickey Newbury, Waylon Jennings, Joni Mitchell.

This spring Cash played Las Vegas for the first time in a decade, and he did it on his own terms. He brought what was essentially the same show he offers in auditoriums and concert halls around the world, ignoring the traditional Vegas ingredients. He didn't use a comedian to open the show (something even Elvis Presley does), and he didn't use the house orchestra (something everybody else does). Instead, he brought his own musicians (the Tennessee Three, Carl Perkins, the Carter Family and the Statler Brothers), and he not only packed the town's biggest showroom (Las Vegas Hilton) nightly but drew standing ovations nightly.

We talked first after one of his midnight shows in the thirtieth-floor penthouse the hotel supplies for its entertainers, and again over breakfast. He was pleased that this paper, which he'd considered essentially a rock music publication, would be interested in a country artist. "I've often read those interviews and wondered if they'd be interested in someone like me," he said. I was only sorry it was too late to catch Jimmie Rodgers and Hank Williams.

MUSIC SEEMS TO HAVE BEEN *an important part of your life from the beginning. What was the first time you remember listening to music?*

The first I remember was my mother playing the guitar. Before I started school. I was four or five years old, but I remember singing with her. Carter Family songs, a lot of them. I don't remember any of them in particular, but I know they were gospel songs, church songs.

Besides listening to music you had to work on the farm when you were a kid. Was that an important part of your character building?

Hard work? I don't know. Chopping cotton and picking cotton is drudgery. I don't know how much good it ever did me. I don't know how much good drudgery does anybody.

But I get the feeling, though, that you have empathy with people who work hard, that you want to reassure them in your music that their life has meaning.

Yeah. I got a lot of respect for a man that's not afraid to work. I don't think a man can be happy unless he's working. And I work hard on my music. I put in a lot of thought. I lose a lot of sleep, a lot of nights, because I'm laying awake thinking about my songs and about what's right and wrong with my music. I worry about whether that last record was worth releasing, whether I could have done it better. Sometimes I feel that the last record was exactly like the one I released fourteen years ago. I wonder if I'm just spinning my wheels sometimes. I wonder if I'm progressing, if I'm growing musically, artistically. I guess I've quoted Bob Dylan a million times, his line, "He who is not busy being born is busy dying." I've always believed that. And I believe it is certainly true in my case.

Even though I'm forty years old and I'm getting a little gray hair on my head, I'm still growing. You're being born a little bit every day. And I love performing. It's my first love. I love performing even more than writing. And something you love you try to do well.

Going back to your childhood, what was the next step—musically?

I started writing songs myself when I was about twelve. I started writing some poems and then made some music up to go along with them. They were love songs, sad songs. I think the death of my brother Jack, when I was twelve, had a lot to do with it. My poems were awfully sad at the time. My brother and I were very, very close.

Did you sing the songs to your family? What was the reaction?

Oh well, you know how families are. My dad would pat me on the head and say that was pretty good, but you'd better think about something that will buy you something to eat someday. My mother was a hundred percent for my music. When I was sixteen she wanted me to take piano, and voice lessons. She even took in washing to get the money. I think I had one voice lesson. The teacher told me not to take any more because it might affect my delivery.

What was the first time you sang in public?

I guess it was at high-school commencement. I sang Joyce Kilmer's "Trees." I had a high voice, a tenor when I was a teenager. I had just piano accompaniment. I was pretty scared. I didn't do anything else until after I got out of the Air Force.

Did you have a feeling at that time, when you went into the Air Force, that you were ever going to really get into music?

Yeah, I always knew. I really did. I always knew. I remember writing my brother when I was in the Air Force telling him that I'd be recording within a year after I was discharged. I wrote "Folsom Prison Blues" while I was in the Air Force in Germany. I wrote it one night after seeing a movie called *Inside the Walls of Folsom.* I also wrote "Belshazzar" and "Hey Porter" in the Air Force.

When you got back to Memphis, how did you get into the music business?

I found out about Sun Records in Memphis. They were getting pretty hot with Elvis about that time, so I called about an audition. I remember how scared I was the first time I walked into Sun. It was Sam Phillips and his secretary, Miss McGinnis. They didn't even remember I had an appointment to record. I got the first of seven "come back laters." I told Phillips that I wrote gospel songs. I thought "Belshazzar" was the best song I had to show him. He said, "Well, the market is not too good for gospel songs. Come back sometime when you feel like you've got something else."

But we eventually got together, and I believe we recorded "Hey Porter" the same day. The first session was really something. Luther Perkins had a little secondhand Sears amplifier with a six-inch speaker. Marshall Grant had a bass that was held together with masking tape. I had a $4.80 guitar that I had brought back from Germany. Phillips had to be a genius to get anything out of that conglomeration.

Not long after "Hey Porter" was released, I was back in the studio recording everything I had written and some songs that I hadn't written. It

was exciting, things were happening so fast. I remember one day going into the studio and Elvis and Jerry Lee Lewis were both there. Carl Perkins came in a few minutes later, and the four of us stood around the piano singing hymns.

I think we sang for a couple of hours, and I understand Sam had the recorder on and there is something like ten hymns recorded by that "quartet."

Do you remember any of the songs?

I think we sang "Old Rugged Cross," "Vacation in Heaven" and "Will the Circle Be Unbroken." I don't remember the others. Elvis played piano on some of them. Jerry Lee played piano on some others. I don't know what will ever be done with that tape. I suppose Sam has the right to release it, but I think it is probably too bad to be released.

How did you get together with Luther Perkins and Marshall Grant?

We met at a garage where my brother worked. They were mechanics. They had just been fooling around with music. Roy told me they were both guitar players. Marshall had never touched a bass at that time. So, here we were: three guitar players. We tried to get Marshall to start playing the bass, and Luther agreed to try the electric guitar. We felt we needed the instruments to round out the sound.

How did you work out the arrangements?

I just had it all in my head. I'd show Luther the notes on the guitar, and he'd play it over and over until he learned it.

How did the Johnny Cash sound come about?

That boom-chick-a-boom sound? Luther took the metal plate off the Fender guitar and muted the strings because he said he played it so ragged that he was ashamed of it and he was trying to cover up the sound.

What did Phillips say when he heard the sound?

He thought it was really commercial. He just flipped over it.

How did you feel when you had the first record in your hand? It must have been a big day for you.

It was the most fantastic feeling I ever had in my life. I remember signing the recording contract the day the record was released. I had both the contract and "Hey Porter" in my hand when I left Sun that day. And I had fifteen cents in my pocket. I remember coming out of the studio and there was a bum on the street. I gave him the fifteen cents. That's true. Then I took the record to the radio station, holding it like it was an old master painting. And the disc jockey *dropped it* and *it broke.* By accident. It was the next day till I could get another one. That was

275

really heartbreaking. But the record went on to get a lot of airplay, especially in the South. Presley's first manager, Bob Neal, called me and wanted me to do some concerts with Elvis. The first place I played was Overton Park in Memphis. I did "Hey Porter" and "Cry, Cry, Cry" and the reaction was good, very good.

"I Walk the Line" was the big record for you. Did you have a special feeling about it when you finished it?

I thought it was a very good song, but I wasn't sure about the record. I was in Florida when I first heard it on the radio, and I called Phillips and begged him not to send any more copies out. I thought it was so bad. I thought it was a horrible record. And he said let's give it a chance and see. But I didn't want to. I wanted it stopped right then. I got upset with him over it. I thought it sounded so bad. Still sounds bad.

Your voice or the arrangement?

The arrangement. And I didn't like the sound, the modulation and all. But that's what turned out to be the most commercial part of it. Sam was right about it.

What made you eventually leave Sun?

There were also some business matters that we didn't see eye to eye on. He had me on a beginner's rate after three years, and I didn't feel right about it. But, mainly I knew that I could do different kinds of things with a larger label. I could record an album of hymns for Columbia, for instance, and that was important to me at the time.

What was it like returning home to Arkansas after you had become famous?

Well, I was still the country boy to those people. I mean I wasn't anything special to them. A lot of places I'd go in those days made you feel like the big radio star that I had wanted to be, and it felt good. I really ate it up. But at home all the old people would come up and say, "Boy, I remember when you used to bring me buttermilk every other Thursday" or something.

Was there a point that you ever lost touch with those people? During the bad years? Was there a point where you really didn't think of them as friends anymore?

Yes, right. I felt like I didn't belong, and for about seven years I didn't go back. I didn't go back around those people. I didn't want any of them to see me.

That was the bad time for you, the pills and all.

Yeah, not too long after I moved to California. I still don't know why I ever moved to California. I liked it there, had worked out there quite a bit and thought I'd love living there. But I didn't really belong out there. I never really felt at home there. I tried to, but I just didn't. I got into the habit of amphetamines. I took them for seven years. I just liked the feel of them.

Was it the lift?

Yes, it lifts you, and under certain conditions it intensifies all your senses—makes you think you're the greatest writer in the world. You just write songs all night long and just really groove on what you're doing, digging yourself, and keep on taking the pills. Then, when you sober up later, you realize it wasn't so good. When I run across some of the stuff I wrote, it always makes me sick . . . wild, impossible, ridiculous ramblings you wouldn't believe.

You took more pills to cover up the guilt feelings. And I got to playing one against the other, the uppers against the downers, and it got to be a vicious, vicious circle. And they got to pulling me down. On top of that, I thought I was made of steel and nothing could hurt me. I wrecked every car, every truck, every jeep I ever drove during that seven years. I counted the broken bones in my body once. I think I have seventeen. It's the grace of God that one of those bones wasn't my neck.

Over a period of time, though, you get to realizing that amphetamines are slowly burning you up, and burning you up is the truth—because they are hot after a while. Then you get paranoid, you think everybody is out to do you in. You don't trust anybody—even the ones who love you the most. It's like a bad dream now.

Weren't there times you missed the shows regularly during those years?

I got to where I had chronic laryngitis because I kept myself so dried out. And my voice would go and stay gone. I'd feel sorry for myself, and I'd go off and hide somewhere. I'd go up into the mountains or the woods and hide. And the more I'd go, the worse I'd get.

Was there a point in your life that you think you hit bottom? Like the time in Georgia when you woke up in jail?

Yeah, that was in '67. That's when things started turning. But that was just one of the many awakenings I had. You know, that one has been written up in a lot of books and magazines, but that was just one of dozens or hundreds of times that I started reawakening and realizing that there was something good that was going to happen to me, that I had to pull myself out, that life was going to take a turn for the better.

I'd had seven years of roughing it and I felt I

had seven years of good times and good life coming. I really felt in 1967 that there were seven big years ahead.

How did you start pulling out of those bad times?

Well, it really started about the time June and I got married. The growth of love in my life and the spiritual strengthening came at about the same time. Religion's got a lot to do with it. Religion, love, it's all one and the same as far as I'm concerned, because that's what religion means to me. It's love. About the time I married June, we started growing in spiritual strength together. And it shows up onstage.

You can't fool the audience. You can't fool yourself. If you're not yourself onstage, it shows. I'm really happy now. But that's not the same as being content. I still want to grow more as a performer, as an artist, as a person. So, I'm still working hard at it. I never go on that stage when I'm not scared. There's always that fear that somebody's going to throw eggs at you or something.

How would you get yourself up physically and emotionally for a recording session during those troubled years?

I missed a lot of sessions. I'd come into the studio with a fog over my head, not really caring what condition I was in. Just go in on sheer guts and give it a try. It showed up on a lot of my recordings.

But you were still able to come up with a quality product.

I managed somehow. Something like the *Bitter Tears* album was so important that I managed to get enough sleep to do that one. Peter LaFarge and Ed McCurdy and I spent about three days together, talking and deciding that I needed some rest before I did the album. And I got the rest. I think *Bitter Tears* was one of my best works.

I've read that you once listed LaFarge and Dylan as two of the biggest influences on your outlook and style as a songwriter. Is that true?

Well, there was a time I guess they influenced me quite a bit. Of course, Dylan is going to influence anybody that is close to him, I think, as a writer, some way or another. He's a powerful talent. But the influences in my life come and go and there's always something fresh coming along. There's always a change taking place. I don't know what the influences might be right now.

There's a lot to be said for music and friends. We were talking about the bad times earlier—the pills and things. And why I took them. I know why I took them now. It was to try and get

a high like I naturally do now. I knew it was there and I thought I could get it on pills. But you can get it without pills because the greatest times I remember were with my friends at my house—Dylan, Joni Mitchell, Kris Kristofferson, Mickey Newbury were all at the house one night, all those great songs.

What was it about Dylan that attracted you?

I thought he was one of the best country singers I had ever heard. I really did. I dug the way he did the things with such a country flavor and the country sounds. "World War III Talkin' Blues" and all those things in the *Freewheelin'* album. I didn't think you could get much more country than that. Of course, his lyrics knocked me out, and we started writing each other. We wrote each other letters for about a year before we ever met.

I was playing here in Las Vegas the first time I heard one of his albums. I played it backstage, in the dressing room, and I wrote him a letter from here telling him how much I liked his songs, and he answered it and in so many words told me the same thing. He had remembered me from the days of "I Walk the Line" when he was living in Hibbing, Minnesota. I invited him to come see me in California, but when he came to California later he couldn't find my house.

I got another letter that was written in Carmel and by the time I answered it, he'd already gone back to New York. When I was in New York not long after that John Hammond told me that Bob was in town. So he came up and we met at Columbia Records. We spent a few hours together, talking about songs, swappin' songs and he invited me up to his house in Woodstock. After the Newport Folk Festival, he invited me to his house again.

Some people say that Dylan is aloof or withdrawn, that he is hard to talk to. Did you find him that way?

We never did really talk all that much. There's a mutual understanding between us. I never did try to dig into his personal life and he didn't try to dig into mine. If he's aloof and hard to get to, I can understand why. I don't blame him. So many people have taken advantage of him, tried to do him in when they did get to him, that I wouldn't blame him for being aloof and hard to get to. Everybody tells him what he should write, how to think, what to sing. But that's really his business.

Is he the one you have most admired among songwriters?

Well, he's one of the top three or four . . . of course, he is one of the top . . . in the last decade. He's probably the most important in the last decade, but there are others I admire very much. Kris Kristofferson. Mickey Newbury. There's a new writer named Dick Feller. Just watch for him. He's going to be great someday.

How did you first meet Kris?

He was working at the Columbia Records studio in Nashville. He had a pocketful of songs but no place to stay so he got a job as a janitor in the recording studio. And for two or three years, he was at all my sessions. I used to see him there working as a backup engineer or cleaning up or something. And he had his songs back then, and they always just knocked me out. I still don't know why I didn't record any of them sooner. I really don't. I could have helped him along before I did.

Did people take his music seriously in those days?

June always loved his songs, his approach. He was so humble. He'd slip her the tapes to give to me—so the people around the studio wouldn't see him do it. He was still trying to eat, so he didn't want to get fired. I'd take the tapes home and lay 'em somewhere and forget them.

Then we started inviting him to our home, and we had him sing every time he came out. And I guess I heard him sing so many times that it got through my thick head that I should try to do something with some of his songs. And then we took him to the Newport Folk Festival and he took the show away from me completely. It was one of the happiest days of my life. He really deserves it.

Let's talk about your own songs. Do you have any special memories about them?

Sure, most of my songs bring back memories. Things like how I happened to write them, where I was when they were released and so forth.

"Train of Love"—I remember writing that in 1955 when I was on the *Louisiana Hayride* show in Shreveport. Sam Phillips happened to be there. And I called him into the dressing room and asked him what he thought about the song. He really liked it. We recorded it on the next session.

"Home of the Blues"—that was the name of a record shop in Memphis and I always liked the name. Thought it was a great name for a song, so Glen Douglas and I wrote a song about it.

I wrote "Give My Love to Rose" about ten blocks from San Quentin prison. I was playing a club there one night in '56, the first time I came to California. And an ole boy came backstage, an ex-con, to talk to me about Shreveport. He was from there. And I'm not sure his wife was named Rose, but his wife was in Shreveport and he said something about "giving my love to my wife if you get back to Shreveport before I do." He had just gotten out of prison. I wrote the song that night.

"Big River"—I wrote it as a real slow bluesy thing. I remember sitting in the back seat of the car going through White Plains, New York, singing . . . "I ta—ught the wee—ping wil—low how to cry." Real slow and bluesy.

I wrote "Hey Porter" when I was overseas. That was my homesick song for the South. "So Doggone Lonesome" was written with Ernest Tubb in mind. A lot of times I'd write songs with some singer in mind, never really intending to even let them hear it, but with them in mind. After I recorded "So Doggone Lonesome," Tubb heard it and did record it.

I wrote "Get Rhythm" for Elvis. But I never did let him hear it before I recorded it. "Come in Stranger" was just my life-on-the-road song.

Didn't you give Carl Perkins the idea for "Blue Suede Shoes"?

I remember the guys in the Air Force saying, "Don't step on my blue suede shoes." I thought it was a good line and told Carl he should put it into a song. But he wrote it all. It's his song.

During the early days of rock, the time of "Blue Suede Shoes" and so forth, did Sam Phillips try to push you toward rock? Did he want you to be a rock singer rather than a country singer?

No, Sam didn't push me. I think I always knew where my place was in music. I did a few things like "Get Rhythm," but that was all. That song got a lot of requests in my performances, but I never really tried to get into rock & roll. But I always had a feel for it. I wrote songs like "Rock 'n' Roll Ruby" that Warren Smith recorded. And I wrote a song called "All Mama's Children" with Carl Perkins. I always liked it.

Are there certain rock groups you've particularly enjoyed?

Yes, very much. Creedence Clearwater. Eric Clapton. A bunch of them. Mainly, though, people like Carl Perkins, Chuck Berry.

When you went to Columbia, you started recording in Nashville rather than Memphis. That's when you got into the concept albums like 'Ride This Train.'

Yeah. *Ride This Train* was something I really worked on. I think I must have had a country opera in mind without knowing it at the time. It was a kind of travelogue about the country. That was my pride. I'm still proud of that album.

What's something else you're proud of from those days?

One of the things I was really proud of was an EP called *The Rebel.* It contained "The Big Battle," "Remember the Alamo," "Lorena" and "The Rebel." I think that was some of my best work. "The Big Battle" was one of the first social-comment things I wrote. It was about the needless killing in war. That was in 1961. I thought it was a good record, and I still think it is. The idea being that the big battle comes after the killing . . . in the conscience, in the hearts and grief of people that suffer the loss.

"Ira Hayes" was another controversial record.

Right. I really got some feedback from country disc jockeys on that song. And I remember—in one of my wilder moments—putting an ad in the trade magazines telling off the jockeys for not playing it.

Which of the two prison albums— 'Folsom' or 'San Quentin'—is closer to you?

Folsom. That's where I met Glenn Sherley. That's where things really started for me again. The *San Quentin* album was something I put a lot of heart into, a lot of feeling, and I'm very proud of it, but they had the television cameras going, and I was under a lot of pressure because I was right in the middle of a concert tour. I wasn't as relaxed at San Quentin. And the place is tighter anyway. There's a lot more tension at San Quentin.

What about the 'Holy Land' album?

Israel is just like home to June and me. I've sung about the Holy Land and Jesus all my life. The first time I got there was in '65 or '66 and we only had a week. But we decided to go back with a tape recorder and do a kind of travelogue album of songs about the people and the land. We went back in '68 and made the album. And at that time I got the idea to do a film about it.

That's what we did last November. We're editing it now. It's the life of Jesus. Birth through death and resurrection. His teaching. It's directed by Robert Elfstrom who has a couple of Academy Award nominations. We financed it.

With the television show gone, you'll have more time to concentrate on your records. Do you think your records suffered because of the time devoted to the series?

During the whole time I was on television, about two years, I didn't spend one good session in the studio and your records have to suffer when you don't spend time working at them. I've just built my own studio in Nashville. It started as a dubbing studio to record some of the writers I have signed. And then I decided to expand it and make it big enough for me to do my sessions in. We had the room so I put in sixteen tracks. It winds up as the biggest studio in Nashville. Now, I'll have all the time I want to record. I'll be able to just go in and play around with sounds and songs and work with musicians until we get it all together.

Do you think about the future much?

I just feel it as it goes. I do whatever I feel is right for me at the time. I don't try to get the jump on anybody or anything.

Are you an optimistic person?

Oh, yeah. I sure am. I've had seventeen years of nothing but good times as far as my music has gone. It's all been good for me. All the years have been good for me. And I see nothing but growth as far as the music business is concerned. I'm really optimistic about that, the fact that the best talents will be making it. Good talent will always be heard. There's nothing going to take the place of the human being. They can get all the Moog synthesizers that they want but nothing will take the place of the human heart.

279

23

INTERVIEWED BY BEN FONG-TORRES (1973)

Stevie Wonder, at age twenty-two in 1972, had recorded *Talking Book,* an enormous artistic breakthrough with songs like "Superstition" and "You Are the Sunshine of My Life." And he was becoming impatient with people and record companies who kept treating him like he was still the twelve-year-old "blind genius, 'Little Stevie Wonder'"!

He was a splendidly maturing musician, sending off surprising shocks and sparks with each successive, progressive album, and he was threatening to bolt from his mother label, Motown, if they wouldn't treat (read "pay") him right.

As he was growing, he was also reaching back, years before Alex Haley's epic, to his roots. So it was, for Wonder, a time of discovery, a time to be itchy, fitful, full of new ideas and music.

I talked with him in a Holiday Inn near Chinatown, San Francisco, after a concert at Winterland Auditorium.

—BF-T

"I REMEMBER ONE TIME WE WERE IN Puerto Rico, and it was a sunshiny day," said Ira Tucker. "And Stevie was saying it was gonna rain. He said he could smell the moisture in the air, and we were all laughing at him. Three hours later, sure enough, it came. A hailstorm!"

What Tucker—an assistant to Stevie Wonder for five years now—was saying was that Wonder wasn't handicapped. Born blind, yes. Hampered, no.

"He can hear," Ira continued, here in his Holiday Inn room across a concrete bridge from Chinatown, San Francisco. "Like when I get stoned and listen to the radio, and then I can pick up things. He's there all the time." Tucker sat back in a yellow T-shirt named after Wonder's latest single, "You Are the Sunshine of My Life."

WONDER

"He even turns the lights on and off when he goes to the bathroom," said Ira. "What for? I don't know. He said it's 'cause he hears everybody else do it. Click, you go in, click, you're out. So he does it, too. But he goes to the movies, runs from place to place, going out to airports by himself. And on planes people think he's a junkie 'cause he sits there with these glasses on, and his head goes back and forth, side to side when he feels good. . . ."

STEVIE WONDER ENTERED THE SYN-agogue for a post-concert party Motown was throwing for him. Half a year after the tour with the Stones, he was completing his show of new strength. He had conquered New York a month ago; here, he was headlining two shows, at Winterland and at the Berkeley Community Theater. He sold out both shows and won over both audiences. For the wider, whiter crowds he now draws, Wonder mixes together an Afro consciousness, a jazz/soul/rock/synthesized-up music, medleys of old hits and bits of other people's hits and, in one quick exercise in excess, a shot of one-man-band razzmatazz, as he moves from drums to electric piano to ARP-wired clavinet to guitar to harmonica. What he cannot achieve through eye contact is reached by output of energy, by a music that is by turns loving and lusty, that tells how Stevie Wonder cherishes freedom and how he uses it.

And the music, sure enough, reflects the man.

For the party, Wonder put aside his Afro gown and shark's-tooth necklace and dressed up in a champagne-gold suit, matched by a plaid bow tie and metallic-copper platforms stacked four inches high. He plopped down onto the floor to talk with people; he played the harmonica; with Coco, his most constant companion since his divorce last year from Syreeta Wright, he explored the building. Upstairs is the old synagogue, complete with balconies and pews enough to hold 1000 worshippers, fixed up with red carpeting, showboat lighting and stained-glass windows all shaped into colored Stars of David. Stevie and Coco and their entourage sat in a pew, feeling the airiness of the room, listening to the music coming off the speakers on the stage where the altar used to be. Suddenly, the synagogue was filled with "Superstition." The disc jockey at KSAN had been alerted, and she was putting together a string of Wonder hits. Stevie's head snapped up, started to go from side to side. . . . You would've thought he was a junkie. . . .

Stevie was born Steveland Morris on May 13th, 1950, in Saginaw, Michigan; he was the third oldest in a not particularly musical family of six children. They moved to Detroit in the early Fifties, where they lived a lower-middle-class life. Despite his blindness, Stevie was never treated special by his family; in fact,

he claims, he hung out more than his four brothers did. He listened to a radio show in Detroit called Sundown and got filled with blues and jazz. He began playing the piano, and by age eleven, he was also playing drums, "harmonica, bongos and hookey." He would play with a cousin, a friend of the brother of Ronnie White of the Miracles. White auditioned Stevie and took him to Motown, where staff producer Brian Holland listened. Motown signed him and advertised him as a twelve-year-old genius.

Now in his eleventh year in show business, formerly Little Stevie Wonder is finally in absolute control.

"He feels he's back to making music again," said Ira Tucker. "There was a lull for a time, from the time he was seventeen to 'Music of My Mind' (which followed 'Where I'm Coming From' in Wonder's post-'Signed Sealed and Delivered' progression in music). After two five-year contracts with Motown, Stevie was looking around, stalled six months, finally negotiated six weeks over a 120-page contract and made a deal. He got his own publishing—an unprece-dented achievement for any Motown artist—and a substantially higher royalty rate (guessed at fifty percent by one close associate; Stevie would say only that he felt "secure").

"It was a very important contract for Motown," said Wonder's attorney, Johannan Vigoda (who negotiated contracts for Jimi Hendrix and Richie Havens, among others), "and a very important contract for Stevie, representing the artists of Motown. He broke tradition with the deal, legally, profession-ally—in terms of how he could cut his records and where he could cut—and in breaking tradition he opened up the future for Motown. That's what they understood. They had never had an artist in thirteen years; they had singles records, they managed to create a name in certain areas, but they never came through with a major, major artist. It turned out they did a beautiful job."

For Stevie Wonder—too young in the days of "The Sound of Young America" to be so integral a part of the family—the price for staying at Motown was security and freedom. Now he writes and produces for himself; he books his own concerts; he manages himself and he can free-lance at will. He is producing an album by his group, Wonderlove, a second LP for Syreeta and one for the Supremes. He has worked in sessions with Eric Clapton, Graham Nash and Jeff Beck; on tour, he jammed with the Stones.

On the road and off the stage, Stevie spends his time in his hotel room, composing on a clavinet wired up to an ARP synthesizer, writing two or three tunes a day. He also explores, walking through Chinatown in gold lamé, head swaying from side to side as he passes the stores and smells the fish, the ducks, the pickled greens. And he loves to talk. He establishes rapport on the *basis of astrological signs and otherwise talks in black-hippie fashion, zigzagging, sometimes from Pollyan-nish to apocalyptic. He sees the earth zigging towards a destructive end; he can see himself dying soon, and he hopes by his music, to be able to leave something for the rest of us—even if we ain't that far behind him.*

———————————

I T'S AMAZING, I BEEN IN THE BUSI-ness ten years, going on eleven now, and I look back and see so many things, changes; it's almost like I'm an old person sometimes. . . . The musical changes, how different eras have come and gone, a lot of people that I thought would be major people have died. Otis, Jimi Hendrix . . . you know, Michael Jeffrey was killed recently, goin' from Spain to London. Two planes collided, one exploded, the other landed safely. I heard there were some bitter things that went down, that Hendrix was ripped off fantastically by Jeffrey, but I don't know how true those stories are. . . .

It's heavy, and I guess you could say if he did the things that I heard he did, then that's his karma, but again, what about the other people on the plane? That's the question I always ask.

It's been really amazing . . . like when certain things I felt were gonna happen, I'd have dreams. I had a dream about Benny Benjamin [Motown's first studio drummer, who died of a stroke in 1969]. I talked to him a few days before he died; he was in the hospital. But in my dream I talked to him; he said, "Look, man, I'm . . . I'm not gonna make it." "What, you kiddin'!" The image . . . he was sitting on my knee, which means like he was very weak. And he said, "So, like I'm leavin' it up to you." That was like a Wednesday, and that following Sunday I went to church and then to the studio to do a session; we were gonna record "You Can't Judge a Book by Its Cover," and they said, "Hey, man, we're not gonna do it today, Benny just died."

He died without notice. I mean, nobody really knew who he was.

Man, he was one of the major forces in the Motown sound. Benny could've very well been the baddest—like [Bernard] Purdie. He was the Purdie of the Sixties. But unknown.

Why unknown?

Well, because for the most part these cats'd be in the studios all day, and as musicians they weren't getting that recognition then, you know. People weren't really that interested in the musicians.

Couldn't they also have had jobs with performing groups?

They'd do clubs; but Benny would be late for sessions, Benny'd be drunk sometimes. I mean, he was a beautiful cat, but . . . Benny would come up with these stories, like *{in an excited, fearful voice}:* "Man, you'd never believe it, man, but like a goddamn *elephant,* man, in the middle of the road, stopped me from comin' to the session so that's why I'm late, baby, so *{clap of hands}* it's cool!" But he was *ready,* man. He could play drums, you wouldn't even need a bass, that's how bad he was. Just listen to all that Motown shit, like "Can't Help Myself" and "My World Is Empty without You Babe" and "This Old Heart of Mine" and "Don't Mess with Bill." "Girl's All Right with Me," the drums would just *pop!*

Did Benny teach you a lot about drumming?

Yeah, you can hear it, you know. I learned from just listening to him.

Is it true that you put out a drum album once?

Well, I put out an album that I played drums on, called *The Jazz Soul of Little Stevie.* I did another album which was called *Eivets Rednow* about '68, an instrumental with "Alfie" and a few other things . . . "Eivets Rednow" being "Stevie Wonder" spelled backwards.

Everybody knew who it was right away. . . .

Some people did, some didn't. As a matter of fact, there was a cat in the airport that came up and said, "Hey, man" *{laughs},* he said, "Man, these whites takin' over everything," he says. "Look, I heard a kid today, man, played 'Alfie' just *like* you, man!" "Oh, yeah, this cat named Rednow?" "Yeah, that's it!" I said, "Ooooh, man, that cat is—well, don't worry about *him"* *{laughs}.*

You've said that the first song that you ever wrote was "Uptight," but the credits were given to Sylvia Moy, Henry Cosby and an "S. Judkins." Was that you?

Well, Judkins is my father's name. But it's crazy to explain it. Morris was on my birth certificate and everything, but Judkins was the father. I took his name when I was in school. We just signed the song contract like that.

Why didn't you sign, Stevie Wonder?

I don't know.

You signed "Wonder" on songs like "I'm Wonder-ing" and "I Was Made to Love Her."

Well, that was later; I decided I wanted people to know that I wrote those songs.

How did you get the name Wonder?

It was given to me by Berry Gordy. They didn't like "Steve Morris," so they changed it.

Were there some alternatives?

"Little Wonder" . . . "Wonder Steve." I

283

think we should change it to Steveland Morris {laughs}. That would put a whole different light on everything.

You weren't an immediate hit, were you? You put out a record called, "I Call It Pretty Music."

It was a thing that Clarence Paul wrote . . . an old blues thing. . . . The first thing I recorded was a thing called "Mother Thank You." Originally it was called "You Made a Vow," but they thought that was too lovey for me, too adult.

How did the first records do?

They started after we did "Contract on Love." That made a little noise. "Fingertips" was after that. That was a biggie.

The first production credit you were given was on the 'Signed Sealed and Delivered' album, but that wasn't the first producing you did.

Well, that was the first that was *released*. I also did a thing with the Spinners, "It's a Shame," and the followup, "We'll Have It Made." I wanted that tune to be big. I was so hurt when it didn't do it.

You also produced Martha {Reeves} once?

Yeah, they never released it. Called {sings, snapping fingers}, "Hey, look at me, girl, can't you see . . ."

And one on David Ruffin.

Yeah {sings}, "Lovin' you's been so wonderful. . . ." In the midst of all that, I was in the process of gettin' my thing together and decidin' what I was gonna do with my life. This was like I was twenty, goin' on twenty-one, and so a lot of things were left somewhat un-followed up by me. I would get the product there, and nobody would listen, and I'd say, "Fuckit" . . . I wouldn't worry about it.

This was around 'Signed Sealed and Delivered' . . .

It was a little after that. *Signed Sealed and Delivered* was like the biggest thing I'd had.

Then you went into a lull.

Yeah, we did *Where I'm Coming From*—that was kinda premature to some extent, but I wanted to express myself. A lot of it now I'd probably remix. But "Never Dreamed You'd Leave in Summer" came from that album, and "If You Really Love Me" . . . but it's nothing like the things I write now. I love gettin' into just as much weird shit as possible. I'll tell you what's happening. Syreeta's album is better than my last two albums, man, shit {laughs}! No, but it's cool. . . .

How about Syreeta's first album?

For some reason it wasn't accepted. I don't know if it was lack of promotion. . . . I told them I didn't want to be associated so much with the album, the wife/husband thing, which I think was not an asset.

What are the difficulties, if any, in producing your ex-wife?

It's still going through things . . . but I'm always a friend. It's kinda hard for friends to understand it; women think, "I know you guys are here, so I know you're gonna get back together." But if your head is really cool . . . like I used to always worry about when I used to go with someone, about them doing something with somebody else. . . .

You were always the jealous type. . . .

Well, not really. I wouldn't even show it—but I was. . . . This is like one thing that I've tried to do, and I think successfully, that when you realize that nothing really belongs to you, you begin to appreciate having an understanding of just where your head is at, and you feel so much better.

That's easy to say.

I know, but I'm telling you, I'm doing it, man!

How long did your marriage last?

A year and a half.

MY LADY FRIEND, ONE thing we have that's good is she can feel people like I do; when you meet all the phony bullshit people, she's able to sense that, so I feel there is someone that is there with me.

I've never dealt with a woman on the "Stevie Wonder" level. When you meet someone and begin to like them, then you do let them know you even more personally than the public knows. There's not really a difference between me and "Stevie Wonder"—only thing is I'm not singing "Fingertips" or "Big Brother" or "Superstition" all the time. There's other things, listening to other people, and going to the park or seeing a movie or going bowling.

But the public Stevie Wonder is a lot of ideas and images that people have of you, regardless of what you actually are.

I know there are thousands of images of me. There was a guy one time, I heard: "Hey, uh, Stevie Wonder told me to come and get this grass from you, so where is it?" He said, "Stevie Wonder told you? He didn't, man, 'cause I'm his guitar player, and he doesn't even smoke grass. He doesn't even get high." I guess people expect or figure me to be a lot of different things.

You never got into drugs?

No.

Never?

I smoked grass one time, and it scared me to death.

Put images into your head?

Well, things just got larger. It was something new and different, but I found I'm so busy checking things out all the time anyway that I don't really need it.

Are there times when you wish you could see?

No. Sometimes I wish I could drive a car, but I'm gonna drive a car one day, so I don't worry about that.

And fly, too?

I've flown a plane before. A Cessna or something, from Chicago to New York. Scared the hell out of everybody.

Who was your copilot—God?

No {laughs}, this pilot was there, and he just let me handle this one thing, and I say, "What's this?" and we went *whish, whoop*. . . .

You've actually said that you considered your blindness to be a gift from God.

Being blind, you don't judge books by their covers; you go through things that are relatively insignificant, and you pick out things that are more important.

When did you discover that there was something missing, at least according to other people's standards?

I never really knew it. The only thing that was said in school, and this was my early part of school, was something that made me feel like because I was black I could never be or would never be.

So being black was considered to be more a weight . . .

I guess so {laughs}. This cat said in an article one time, it was funny: "Damn! He's black! He's blind! What else?!" I said, "Bull*shit*, I don't wanna *hear* that shit, you know."

So you wouldn't even bother having people describe things to you. Colors and . . .

Well, I have an idea of what colors are. I associate them with the ideas that've been told to me about those certain colors. I get a certain feeling in my head when a person says "red" or "blue," "green," "black," "white," "yellow," "orange," "purple"—purple is a *crazy* color to me. . . .

Probably the sound of the word . . .

Yeah, yeah. To me, brown is a little duller than green, isn't it?

Yes, you got it. . . . What about sex?

What about it {laughs}? It's the same *thing*, Jack! As a matter of fact, it's probably even more exciting to the dude. Ask my woman what it's like. . . . No, no {laughs}! I mean, you just have to get in there and *do* that shit, you know. That shit is just fantasticness!

I used to live on a street called Breckinridge. They just tore my house down. I wish I could've gotten a few pictures of it, too . . . but . . .

So you didn't miss a thing.

We listened to Redd Foxx and did all that stuff! We tried to sneak and do it to little girls. I used to get into a lot of shit, Jack! I got caught trying to mess with this girl. I was about eight years old. It was the playhouse trip. And I really was like taking the girl's clothes off and everything, I don't understand how I did that stuff, you know. I mean, I was *in* it! I had her in my room with my clothes off. And she gave it away 'cause she started laughin' and giggling 'cause I was touching her.

I used to hop barns with all the other dudes. You know those small sheds they used to have in back of houses; in the ghetto where I lived, we'd hop atop them from one to the other. I remember one time my aunt came and said, "Okay, Steve, Mama said don't be doin' that," and I said, "Aw, fuck you," and there're some neighbors out and they said, "Aw, child, you oughta be ashamed of yourself; I thought you was a child of the Lawd, you out there cussin' 'n' everything." That was like back of our house in the alley, you know, so I just kept on, just hopping the barns, jumping around and everything, till all at once I jumped and fell right into my mother's arms. The ironing cord, the whipping. The Magic Ironing Cord Whipping.

Y OU'VE MENTIONED IN VARIOUS *interviews that you feel like you haven't paid a lot of dues. You were talking about Ray Charles, how you can sense the pathos in that man's voice.*

I heard a lot of things, you know, the way people really did him in, but I think he's doing a lot better now.

People did him in?

Well, they knew like when he was on drugs. A lot of people would like bust him, just to get money, or they would put him in jail in some of the southern places just to get some bread.

In school, what subjects did you like best?

History, world history, but it got kind of boring. And science. The history of this country was relatively boring—I guess because of the way it was put to us in books. The most interesting to me was about civilizations before ours, how

285

advanced people really were, how high they had brought themselves, only to bring themselves down because of the missing links, the weak foundations. So the whole thing crumbled. And that's kind of sad. And it relates to today and what could possibly happen here, very soon. That's basically what "Big Brother" is all about.

I speak of the history, the heritage of the violence, or the negativeness of being able to see what's going on with minority people. Seemingly it's going to continue to be this way. Sometimes, unfortunately, violence is a way things get accomplished. "Big Brother" was something to make people aware of the fact that after all is said and done, that I don't have to do nothing to you, meaning the people are not power players. We don't have to do anything to them 'cause they're gonna cause their own country to fall.

"My name is Secluded; we live in a house the size of a matchbox." A person who lives there, really, his name *is* Secluded, and you never even know the person, and they can have so many things to say to help make it better, but it's like the voice that speaks is forever silenced.

I understand that when you don't hear anything and you hear this very high frequency, that's the sound of the universe.

Or a burglar alarm, which takes some of the mystery out of it. . . . Tell me about your experiments with electronic effects and music. First, have you listened to Beaver and Krause, or Pink Floyd, Emerson, Lake and Palmer, or Walter Carlos?

Walter Carlos, yes, but for the most part I've listened to just what's in my head, plus Bob Margoloff and Malcolm Cecil—they just built a new synthesizer you should see—they have their own company, Centaur, and they did an album, *Tonto's Expanding Headband.* They are responsible for programming, and I just tell them the kind of sound I want.

I hadn't got tired of strings or horns or anything, it's just another dimension. I'd like to get into doing just acoustic things, drums, bass, no electronic things at all except for recording them.

How about the Bag {a throat-sound amplifier made by Kustom}? What does that do for communication?

It creates an emotion in that the voice is low. And it frightens you a little. We used it on Syreeta's album, "She's Leaving Home," I was just playing the ARP, not really singing, but playing the note and moving my mouth.

What else are you checking out these days?

There's this string instrument made in Japan. You tune it like a harp to a certain chord scale. It

takes you somewhere else that's sort of earthy and in the direction where my head is slanting—like going to Africa. Maybe I'll take a tape recorder over there and just sit out and write some stuff.

In concert, your opening number includes African scatting.

I got that from this thing called *The Monkey Chant* that we used in different rhythms, and we came up with {chop-chants in speedtime} ja-ja-ja-jajajajajaja . . .

And there are three pairs of drumsticks going.

It's like fighting. I'd love to go to Ghana, go to the different countries and see how I'd like to live there.

Do you know Sly Stone?

I've seen him a couple of times. I haven't heard too much about him lately, just rumors.

He influenced you to a degree.

. . . Ah . . . I think there's an influence in some of the things I've done, like "Maybe Your Baby." But I can hear some of the old Little Stevie Wonder in a lot of his early things {Stevie sings a bit of "Sing a Simple Song"}. It used to tickle me. . . .

You've said that your writing was influenced by the Beatles.

I just dug more the effects they got, like echoes and the voice things, the writing, like "For the Benefit of Mr. Kite.."

Did it make you feel that you could be more loose yourself?

Yeah. I just said, "Why can't I?" I wanted to do something else, go other places. Same thing about keys. I don't want to stay in one key all the time.

"Blowin' in the Wind" and "Alfie" were unusual songs for a Motown artist to be doing back when you did them.

Most of them came about from doing gigs and wanting certain kinds of tunes. Clarence Paul, who was my arranger and conductor when we had the big group—we would work out doing tunes, ridin' in cars like in England around '65. We'd think of different songs like "Funny How Time Slips Away" or "Blowin' in the Wind."

Writers are so important. I think a lot of our artists could have been more successful if they had other writers, besides Holland-Dozier-Holland, because then they would have found their identity—and that's what everybody needs.

So you can understand why groups like Gladys and the Pips, Martha and the Vandellas, the Tops, the Spinners left.

I do; when you become just one of the others, it's difficult to be a sustaining power for a long period of time. It's like a person comes out with a beat, and you keep on doing it and doing it and driving it to the ground.

Did you hang out around Studio A at Motown?

I did when I was younger, but like when I was twelve or thirteen, I couldn't 'cause I was in school. I used to play on a lot of gospel sessions.

Did you play in sessions outside of Motown?

No, but I have now, recently.

You were working with Jeff Beck last year; then he got angry at you because you put out "Superstition" as a single before he did.

Well, I'd written a thing for them—they wanted "Maybe Your Baby," and I said no, do this, this is even better, and I wrote "Superstition" that same night. And they wanted the track, which I couldn't give them 'cause of Motown, so I said, "I'll give you a seven [a 7½ ips tape], and you all work on it and I'll play on the session, 'cause he said he'd play on a thing of mine. And I wrote another thing for them which was even more like Jeff Beck, a thing called "Thelonius" which they haven't done anything with, it's really bad *{Stevie sings, scatting with triple-timed knee slaps}* . . . but I told him I was using "Superstition" for my album. The tune I wanted to release as a single was "Big Brother,' but that was done too late to come out as a single. Motown decided they wanted to release "Superstition." I said Jeff wanted it, and they told me I needed a strong single in order for the album to be successful. My understanding was that Jeff would be releasing "Superstition" long before I was going to finish my album; I was late giving them *Talking Book.* Jeff recorded "Superstition" in July, so I thought it would be out. But I did promise him the song, and I'm sorry it happened and that he came out with some of the arrogant statements he came out with. I will get another tune to him that I think is as exciting, and if he wants to do it, cool.

After the Stones tour, there was a story in a magazine where the Stones—Keith Richards—was yelling about you, calling you a "cunt" when you couldn't make a gig because of your drummer. There were claims that you'd been partying instead of working.

If Keith did say that, it's just childish, because I love people too much to just want to fuck up and miss a show. And it's crazy, the things he said, if they were said—and if he did not say them, he should clarify them because I will always hold this against him; I can't really face him, I'd feel funny in his presence.

Was Keith pretty friendly throughout the tour?

I had mixed emotions about where he was comin' from, you know, so I wouldn't be surprised if he said it, but I'm really not too surprised about anybody saying anything about anything. What really bugged me about the whole thing was that our drummer was in a very bad situation, mentally and spiritually, and that's why he left. What climaxed the whole thing was, we got into an argument. I told him he was rushing the tempo—this was in Fort Worth, Texas—and he said, "I'll tell you what: You know how to play harmonica; you take the mike, you sing and play drums and all that shit at the same time, 'cause I quit," and he split. I called up the Stones and said, "Look, man, our drummer left, and we might not be able to make the gig, so we'll try to make the second one, but we won't be able to make the first show." And they said, "Okay, that'll be cool." The next thing, I saw the Stones, and they heard the new drummer and said, "Oh, out of sight!" Then the next thing was I read all this shit.

Were you treated fairly, financially, for the tour?

It wasn't a money-making thing, that wasn't the idea—exposure was the thing.

I want to reach the people. I feel there is so much through music that can be said, and there's so many people you can reach by listening to another kind of music besides what is considered your only kind of music. That's why I hate labels where they say, *This Is Stevie Wonder and for the Rest of His Life He Will Sing 'Fingertips'*. . . . Maybe because I'm a Taurean, and people say Taureans don't dig change too much. I say as long as it's change to widen your horizons, it's cool.

24

INTERVIEWED BY PAUL GAMBACCINI (1973)

Paul Gambaccini, an American in England since 1970, was thumbing through a music trade paper, as he's wont to do, one day in 1973 when he realized that Elton John had become "the best-selling pop artist in the world." He was riding high with "Crocodile Rock"; "Daniel" was in the wings, and *Don't Shoot Me I'm Only the Piano Player* had followed *Honky Chateau* into the Number One album slot.

Gambaccini decided that his revelation called for a ROLLING STONE interview.

Elton, then twenty-six, would go on to score seven straight Number One albums and become the decade's most popular pop star, even if only by the numbers. But he was more than that, and, as Gambaccini says, "I don't know if his career would have dipped if he didn't let it. I saw him in March 1976, and he said he was gonna give it all up." Elton was upset, Paul says, by a visit from a washed-up Sixties rock singer "who crawled up to his house, drunk" and by the drug-related death of guitarist Paul Kossoff. "He thought the rock life was sordid, and the pace was crazy." Also, John got seriously interested in the operations of a soccer team he owned.

"He stopped for a year," says Gambaccini, "and that killed the momentum. He lost his band and his producer."

In 1979, Elton returned to the Top Ten, he regained the services of his band members and his old lyricist Bernie Taupin, and Gambaccini reported in 1981: "He's happy with his pace now."

—BF-T

ELTON JOHN WANTED TO DO THE ROLLING STONE Interview when we first suggested it to him in February. A grueling British tour kept him occupied for over a month. It was only when Bernie Taupin got enthusiastic for a joint interview that

ELTON

JOHN

prospects really brightened. Three days after the tour ended and four days before an Italian jaunt began, the talk took place at Elton's home in the London suburb of Virginia Water.

Bernie drove down from his cottage in Lincolnshire, where he lives with his wife, Maxine. We met Elton in the London offices of Rocket Records, his new label for promising artists.

As we walked to the chauffeured Rolls outside Rocket, Elton gazed in the direction of Oxford Street. "You know," he remembered, "when we were doing 'Empty Sky' {the first U.K. LP} we would get out onto Oxford Street at four in the morning and we'd be so excited we couldn't sleep, so we'd just sit in the Wimpy Bar and talk about the album. There was so much excitement in those days. We'd keep track of what albums would be coming into the import shops; when and if they were a day late we'd be crushed, our day ruined. But then if we were the first to get the new Jefferson Airplane, we'd feel on top of the world. Now we just get the American trades, tick off the new releases we want and get them shipped over. So much magic has been lost."

When we reached the homestead, 'Hercules,' Bernie had already been there for fifty minutes, talking to the photographer about growing cabbages and sowing seeds. They hadn't discussed the recent U.S. and U.K. Number One album, 'Don't Shoot Me, I'm Only the Piano Player,' so it seemed logical to start there.

T**HE GENERAL CRITICAL RE-** *sponse to 'Don't Shoot Me' was that it represented the end of the three-year critical rise and fall and rise of Elton John. Do you think that's fair?*

Elton: Everyone's got this myth about the fall. The fall is probably because of *Madman Across the Water*. It didn't get into the Top Ten or Top 20 in England but it still sold 65,000 albums, which isn't bad. I think because we didn't have a single out for a year and a half people thought we were dead, but the album still did very well everywhere else in the world. So that was the "fall," as it were.

Bernie: I think there's a lull in everybody's career. You can rise with tremendous popularity, and then everybody sort of jumps on your back. They're writing everything about you, and you get to a stage where people want to see if you can maintain that popularity, and the press coverage goes down slightly during a phase when you're trying to change your system of doing things, and you have to come back. It's like crossing a bridge. You either cross it or you fall off it. I

think Bowie will go through the thing as well.

Elton: We got through spates where for six months you're acclaimed and then for six months you're not, and we've learned to ride with it now. We're very, very popular at the moment; we've got the press on our side with *Don't Shoot Me*. I'm surprised. I thought *Don't Shoot Me* would get ripped apart—

Why?

Elton: Because I think it's a very happy album, very ultrapop; if you look at any of our other albums it's very poppy, just very straight pop. I don't think there'll be another *Don't Shoot Me* album from me. The reason it came out like this was we'd done *Honky Chateau* and were really knocked out with it, and everyone was so happy that the songs came out that way. It was just done with a tremendous amount of energy. Don't you agree it's a very sort of poppy album? I always think of it as Elton John's disposable album.

Bernie: Well, as you've said before, a lot of times it's good to write disposable songs anyway. You can write one or two "classics" that will last and be covered again in a few years' time, but I think a majority of good pop songs nowadays are disposable. They're songs for the time they're in the charts, and three months later they're just completely forgotten and nobody bothers with them again. I think that's healthy in a way. You should always have fresh material coming along.

The reason we've survived and will continue to survive for a good long time is because we've got the upper hand on everybody else and can turn our ideas into anything, any sort of music. We can do things like just playing rock & roll, twelve bars, to country material, blues . . . I mean, we've done every type of music. You could compile an album taking tracks from all the things we've done and come across with the most amazing cross section of material.

Elton: We're influenced by so many things. You could say I'm the Ray Coniff of the pop world.

Bernie: But other people who are sort of on the same level of popularity tend to have the same feel on all their albums.

Elton: A Neil Young or a Carole King or a James Taylor album all have the same sort of thing. They do it for three or four albums, getting away with having the same sound. We've never had an album that had the same sound.

Bernie: It's amazing that the Moody Blues can release an album every six months and bang, straight to Number One. It's like listening to the same album again. It amazed me a while ago when people said our things sounded the same and that we should get out of a rut. That's really strange. Why pick on us? Why not pick on somebody like Jethro Tull, where it's always the same sort of line-up, the same sort of construction of the song, the same feel—not that that's bad, I like Jethro Tull.

Elton: With all due respect to Carole King, *Tapestry* was a great album, but the other two albums after that sounded like they were recorded at the same sessions but that *Tapestry* was the first ten tracks done and the next twenty were done when everyone was getting increasingly more tired. She should worry, though, having written some of the world's great songs, but I couldn't work with that same line-up on every album.

Bernie: I think that's important to get across, because some people . . .

Elton: I get fucking pissed off at people saying, "Their songs always sound the same." How can you say "Have Mercy on the Criminal" sounds like "Daniel" or "Daniel" sounds like "High Flying Bird"?

Bernie: Somebody once said that "Burn Down the Mission" sounded like "Friends" *{laughter}*. That's true, that's an actual quote from a paper.

Elton: Someone said I sounded like Joe Cocker, which I thought was rather amusing. I can see José Feliciano, but not Joe Cocker.

Bernie: That José Feliciano thing has sort of leveled out now, it was just around . . .

Elton: Well, they were saying Elton John sounds like José Feliciano, now José Feliciano sounds like Elton John. I mean, isn't that stupid?

DURING THE CONVERSATION, *Elton has been examining the cover of* ROLLING STONE *No. 84, which showed him in boots. Finally he breaks out laughing.*

Elton: I used to think those were really high heels. I thought those boots were really hip because they had high heels. Shit!

Bernie: I remember when you got those. They were so outrageous because they had stars on them, and they were silver.

Now you say you won't wear anything except the heels you're wearing now.

Elton: I feel so short, I never wear really short shoes. I rarely wear tennis shoes. I'm five feet eight, I hate being short. I'm sure I *will* wear

something that's flatter. Then, in a couple of years' time I'll probably look at a picture of me in platforms and say, "What the hell was I doing?" Those are, again, disposable. Everything's becoming disposable. Disposable Me, disposable . . . *{makes shriveling-up noise}.*

What have you got ready for the next American tour, or have you started thinking about that yet?

Elton: I've got a couple of ideas. I think a couple of dates on the next American tour are going to be very bizarre. Not bizarre weirdo, like the Cockettes or anything, but bizarre show biz. We got a nice idea for Hollywood Bowl if we get the date.

Bernie: We're gonna blow the audience up.

Elton: Steinway has offered to build me a special piano; I would like to get a special piano made. I think visuals are very important to me, not in the sense of an act like Alice Cooper who's got it down to a fine art, but in the sense of high camp and just very, very tongue-in-cheek. We did "Singin' in the Rain" as a tongue-in-cheek thing on the last American tour, "Legs" Larry Smith and I; it was his suggestion, and I said, "You must be mad, they'll wonder what the fuck's going on," but they loved it! They'd sing along with it, and I thought, well, there you go.

The act is going to become a little more Liberaceized, not in a clothes sense, or Busby Berkeleyized—I'd like to have nine pianos onstage, a cascade of pianos, and make my entrance like that. Just give the audience a really nice sort of show. I don't like to look at groups who come out standing looking like they've just been drowning at Big Sur for five years. I could never go onstage in denims.

Of the pianists, you've mentioned Liberace, and many people have said there's a lot of Jerry Lee Lewis influence in your jumping about, but you said in the car you're not really a big Lewis admirer.

Elton: Well, I used to be until I saw him, and then I went off him a bit. I still think his rock & roll records are amazing, but I'm more a Little Richard stylist than a Jerry Lee Lewis, I think. Jerry Lee is a very intricate piano player and very skillful, whereas I think Little Richard is more of a pounder. I think his rock & roll records are the best rock & roll records ever made, as far as just the genuine sound on them goes. Apart from "Hound Dog" which is amazing.

Bernie: The stuff Jerry Lee Lewis is into at the moment—

Elton: It's just taking the country road, which so many people do, and he treated his audience like shit, which I've never ever done.

Bernie: He treats everybody like that, smoking

291

his big fucking cigars and pretending he's such a heavy.

Elton: And calling himself "The Killer." I could kill more people with one fucking finger than he did when I saw him. I always find rock & roll acts like that now pathetic. I mean, I've seen them all, and I feel it's sad. Chuck Berry is God, but what the fuck has he written? I mean, people say he wrote all those great rock & roll songs and we never wrote any, but at least we're still writing things. He hasn't written anything decent for fifteen years. It amazes me why everybody exults him. Why, Muddy Waters can grow old gracefully; you can still go see Muddy Waters and enjoy him. He'll still play "Got My Mojo Working," but he'll throw something new in. I think it's about time all this Chuck Berry idolizing came to a halt. I can dig the nostalgia trip, and I dig his old records, but I find that side of the business very irritating. I feel sorry for them. I wouldn't like in fifteen years' time to still be playing "Crocodile Rock."

Elton, basically your musical career started with Bluesology, didn't it?

Elton: Actually, it all started when I became old enough to listen to records, because my mother and father collected records, and the first records I ever heard were Kay Starr and Billy May and Tennessee Ernie Ford and Les Paul and Mary Ford and Guy Mitchell. I grew up in that era. I was three or four when I first started listening to records like that. I obviously took great interest in them, and then I went through the skiffle thing with Lonnie Donegan. The first records my mom brought home that I was really knocked out by were "Hound Dog" and Haley's "ABC Boogie."

They changed my life. I couldn't believe it. I heard Little Richard and Jerry Lee Lewis, and that was it. I didn't ever want to be anything else. I just started banging away and semistudied classical music at the Royal Academy of Music but sort of half-heartedly. I was never really interested in it.

Bluesology got together when I was about fourteen, playing in scout huts and youth-club dances. Just one ten-watt amplifier with the piano unamplified. We started off by playing . . . we started off by playing . . . *{annoyed}* I can *never* remember what we started off by playing . . . gradually we got into playing Jimmy Witherspoon numbers. We were always playing the wrong stuff. Bluesology were always two months too late, or three years too early. Never playing the right thing at the right time. They were always appealing to minority tastes.

We always thought we were hip because we were playing Jimmy Witherspoon songs and Mose Allison numbers. It sounds ludicrous, but they were sort of the hip figures of that era. It was the time of Georgie Fame and the Blue Flames. What was that classic Ray Charles thing *{sings piano part}* . . . "Let the Good Times Roll," things like that. Then we started to add brass, because brass was the thing.

Then we went for an audition at the State Cinema at Kilburn on a Saturday morning. There were thousands of groups, and you had to play two or three numbers. The guy there from the agency, the Roy Tempest agency, I don't know where he ever disappeared to, asked if we would be interested in turning professional and backing all these American people. Backing Major Lance was probably the biggest thing that ever happened to me. So we said yes; originally it was going to be Wilson Pickett, but his guitarist didn't like the band. The first person I ever played for really as a professional was Major Lance, although when we turned professional I was working at a music publisher's, taking tea around and packing the parcels. While I was in school I was playing in a pub every Friday, Saturday and Sunday night for a year. This was all to earn money to buy electric pianos and mikes and amplifiers and things. I used to make a quid a night, but then I'd take my box around and people would put donations in it. For my age, I was making a fortune, getting about thirty-five quid a week, I think.

But it was Major Lance who was the first person in our lives, and from then on it was a succession of people. Patti LaBelle twice. Looking back on it, it was the most miserable existence, but at the time it was quite happy. We backed . . . let's see . . . Patti LaBelle twice, the original Drifters for two gigs; we did a whole tour with Doris Troy and a whole tour with the Ink Spots *{laughter}* and Billy Stewart. In between not working, by that I mean not backing people, we did the traditional months in Hamburg. That was another thing that changed my life and made me grow up. Then we went to Sweden and then the South of France for a month. We just did mediocre things

I used to make records, you know, those cheap cover versions. I did backup vocals for those: Stevie Wonder's "Signed Sealed and Delivered," a cover of "United We Stand," "My Baby Loves Loving." I used to do the "oooohs" and "ahhhhhs." The lead singer of Uriah Heep, David Byron, used to sing all the lead vocals. Musically, they were very, very good, but the songs were awful. "I'll be your Jack-in-the-Box," and I used to go, "whoop-doop-doop."

Bernie: And Robin Gibb.

Elton: Oh, I did a cover for a Dutch record company of "Saved by the Bell," and I *literally* did it like that *{sings his Robin Gibb imitation}*. They did five takes, and by the end, my neck was really red, sort of hanging down there like a chicken.

Then when John Baldry came along and said, would you like to join up, I said, well, at least it's a step in the right direction. So we backed John for a year, starting off with a soul package, really. It was our singer, who was Stuart A. Brown, Marsha Hunt, another singer called Alan Walker and Baldry. Baldry had just finished with the Brian Auger thing, and Julie Driscoll, the Steampacket, with Rod Stewart, and he wanted to start another similar thing. It really didn't ever get off the ground, we were never a success, so Baldry decided to make a commercial record and made a hit record with "Let the Heartaches Begin." That changed his life for two or three years and began to change mine, because it meant instead of playing in clubs you played in cabaret, which really drove me around the bend. I think that's the graveyard of musicians, playing cabaret. I think I'd rather be dead than work in cabaret. It's just so depressing.

So I was always getting depressed, and it was in Newcastle that I saw the advert in the New Musical Express saying, "Liberty leaving EMI, going independent, need singers and talent." I didn't know what I was going to do, I just knew I wanted to come off the road. So I went up for an appointment. I was still with the band. I said I can't write lyrics and I can't really sing well because I wasn't singing with Bluesology, but I think I can write songs. So they gave me this audition; it was in a recording studio; they said, "Sing us five songs." I didn't know five songs; all I knew were the songs Baldry was singing and the Jim Reeves records I used to sing with at home. So I sang five Jim Reeves songs, and they turned me down flat. I don't really blame them. They put me in touch with Bernie, only through letter or by phone, because Liberty didn't want us.

But some guy at Liberty told me to go to Dick James Music and do some demos. I was receiving Bernie's lyrics and writing the songs and doing demos before I even met Bernie. One day I was doing a demo session and noticed him in the corner. I said, oh, are you the lyrics writer, and he said, yeah, and we went around the corner for a cup of coffee, and that was it, really.

We'd made millions and millions of songs up before anybody discovered we were making demos at Dick James. Dick James had a purge because he discovered that people were using his studios just to make endless demos. So he heard our stuff, liked it and signed us up. As soon as he signed us up at ten quid a week advance royalties I left the group. That was the best day in my life, when I quit the group.

Was it then he suggested the name change?

Elton: Oh, no, I was coming back from Scotland, or somewhere, after doing a gig with John and Caleb Quayle, who was engineer at the Dick James studio at the time, and had a lot to do with my early encouragement and played the guitar for Baldry some of the time, with Bluesology, and I said, I've got to think of a name. I'm fed up with Reg Dwight. I can't be Reg Dwight if I'm going to be a singer, so I've got to think of a name. So Elton Dean's name I pinched {Elton Dean was in Bluesology and later the Soft Machine] and John Baldry's name and I said, oh, Elton John, there you go.

One report in the national press awhile back said you'd once almost gotten married to a millionairess.

Elton: Me?

And called it off three weeks before?

Elton: Oh, that's true. I wouldn't say she was a millionairess, that's the national press boosting their headlines—"One-Armed Man Swims Channel" or something like that, you know what I mean. It was a girl I met when I was in Sheffield one miserable Christmas doing cabaret with John Baldry. She was six foot tall and going out with a midget in Sheffield who drove around in a Mini with special pedals on. He used to beat her up! I felt so sorry for her, and she followed me up the next week to South Shields—this gets even more romantic, folks—and I fell desperately in love and said, come down to London and we'll find a flat. Eventually we got a nice flat in this dismal area. It was a very stormy six months, after which I was on the verge of a nervous breakdown. I attempted suicide and various other things, during which Bernie and I wrote nil, absolutely nothing.

Bernie: Don't forget the gas.

Elton: I tried to commit suicide one day. It was a very Woody Allen-type suicide. I turned on the gas and left all the windows open {laughter}.

Bernie: I remember when I told Linda and said, "My God, he's tried to commit suicide," and she said, "Why, he's wasted all the gas!"

Elton: It was just like six months in hell. I got the flat, I bought all the furniture, the cake was made, it was three weeks away, Baldry was going to be best man, and in the end Baldry, we were out in the Speakeasy . . . no, it was the Bag of Nails . . . no . . .

Bernie: It was the Bag of Nails.

Elton: Baldry was there, and one of the Supremes—one of the Supremes used to go out with the singer of Bluesology, how about *that* for a piece of gossip—Cindy Birdsong used to go out with our singer. Anyway, we're there at the Bag of Nails and Baldry is saying, "You're mad, man, you're mad, you don't love her," and I was saying, "I do, I do," and he was saying, "She beats you up, she smashes you on the face," and we got more and more depressed sitting there until four in the morning, setting off burglar alarms when we staggered out, and I shouted, "It's over, it's finished!" and then came a couple of days in hell. In the end my dad came with his Ford Cortina, and how he managed to cram all that stuff in there I don't know, and my mother said, "If you marry her I'll never speak to you again"—oh, it was just amazing. So she sued me for breach of promise and all that shit. She got away with quite a lot of money in shares.

Bernie: It was so outrageous . . .

Elton: It was outrageous because she was six foot and she used to beat me up and *she* used to be beaten up by a midget, so how about that? It was so weird. You know, I have always expected her to show up one of these days.

Of course, the worst thing in the papers about you was the Observer's *comment about you and Liberace.*

Elton: I didn't see that.

Do you want to hear it?

Elton: Yes, yes!

It said that at the Royal Variety Performance, Liberace made you look like the musical dwarf you were.

Elton: Well, I think he did, I think he was the only decent thing on the Royal Variety show. I don't mind, I don't find that offensive at all.

I had two numbers to do, which was really great; everybody was saying, do "Your Song" and "Rocket Man," you better be nice, Elton John, and do "Your Song." Boring! So we brought "Legs" Larry Smith to tap-dance to "I Think I'm Gonna Kill Myself," and the whole effect was lost on television, but he released balloons that actually made farting noises. Of course, the audience was full of the most dreadful people imaginable, and all these balloons were going pfft, pfft, pfft, all over the audience, and they were all sitting there in their tiaras going, "Ooooh! Oooooh!" *{Bernie convulsed with laughter.}*

Larry had all these flowers because he came on

dressed as a wedding man, and I thought it was great—it sounds abysmal—we thought we had problems; the poor Jackson Five singing, trying to sing without much amplification in the Palladium—and they were trying to get me to take Larry out of the show, and I was in a panic because I had to fly back to Tulsa to do another show. Liberace was great; he just kept wheeling trunks of clothes in. I just sat there watching him; he kept calm through the whole thing. All these people were badgering him all the time for autographs, and he does the most ornate autographs, he draws a grand piano, and he was great.

You mentioned one of the reasons you did it was to plug "Crocodile Rock." A lot of the critics, especially in America, have had fun trying to identify the songs that influenced you for that song.

Bernie: We got sued by the people who wrote "Speedy Gonzales."

Elton: Yeah, but they dropped that. I mean, that's so stupid. But there are the obvious ones, "Oh Carol"—we wrote one song, "Rock and Roll Madonna." I always wanted to write one song, a nostalgic song, a rock & roll song which captured the right sounds. "Crocodile Rock" is just a combination of so many songs, really. "Little Darling," "Oh, Carol," some Beach Boys influences, they're in there as well, I suppose. Eddie Cochran. I mean, it's just a combination of songs. People say it's like Freddie Cannon. We've written a new one, "Your Sister Can't Twist," and everyone's gonna go, "You've pinched it from Loggins and Messina!"

Bernie: Loggins and Messina? *What?*

Elton: "Your Mama Don't Dance." Oh, well,. It all comes from the subconscious. And there's Del Shannon in there, that high stuff. And I love Bobby Vee.

WERE YOU SURPRISED 'ELTON *John' really broke first in America?*

Elton: Well, it had come out in England and died. It had come out in May of 1970, got into the BBC chart at forty-five, and straight out again. [The BBC LP chart contains fifty albums.] We thought it would get into the charts 'cause it was a special-type album with orchestra and all kinds of things. We had a crisis meeting to say, "Why isn't it on the charts?" "Why isn't it selling?" and I didn't want to go on the road, I just didn't want to know. They said, you're just going to have to go out on the road and promote it. We went to the States primarily because the record company said, "You come over here, we'll break this." I didn't believe them. I really went to the States to have a look at some record stores. And also it was either join Jeff Beck or go to the States, or Jeff Beck was going to join us. But it turned out we would have had to join Jeff Beck, it was one of those ego things. So we went to the States, and it broke. I wasn't surprised because there was so much hype going on I could have believed anything that was going on when I was over there.

Bernie: It was all just one night, that one night at the Troubadour.

Elton: It really was just that first night, like you said, like *The Eddie Duchin Story* or "dis boy is a genius." One of those old films, "Look, the boy is conducting the orchestra, he's fourteen years old and he's blind and he's got one leg and everybody's going 'hooray!'"

Bernie: The next morning, like, wham, bam, there on the front of all the papers . . . it's just . . . *{sighs}*.

Elton: People were flocking to us. I couldn't believe it. Second night I played, Leon Russell was in the front row, but I didn't see him until the last number. Thank God I didn't, because at that time I slept and drank Leon Russell. I mean, I still really like him, but at that time I regarded him as some kind of a god. And I saw him and I just stopped. He said, "Keep on," and he shouted something, and I said, oh fuck, and he said, "Come up to the house tomorrow." I figured, this was it, he's going to tie me up in a chair and whip me and say, "Listen here, you bastard, *this* is how you play the piano," but he was really nice instead. It was like schoolboy's fantasies coming true. Really strange. Quincy Jones . . .

Bernie: All the pop stars . . .

Elton: Quincy Jones, he must have brought his whole family, he has 900 children, Quincy Jones, and I kept shaking hands coming through the door. The whole week at the Troubadour should have been called The Million Handshakes. David Ackles was on the bill. I mean, *that* was the first thing I couldn't believe, that we were playing *above* David Ackles. In England he had much more prestige than he apparently had in America.

It was very, very weird. I loved it, though. I went to Disneyland and sang "Your Song" onstage in shorts and Mickey Mouse ears. Looking back on it I think it's horrific. I mean, when we went back the second time and I was big

enough to play Santa Monica Civic on my own for one night and Ry Cooder was first on the bill and then Odetta and then us. I had four suits of clothing on.

I had this cape on, and this hat. I took that off and had a jump suit on. Took that off and I had another sort of jump suit on. Then I took that off and had a long Fillmore West sweater. Maxine had gone out and said *{imitating Maxine}*, "Oooh, I've found these mauve tights, I bet you wouldn't wear them onstage," and I said I would, and this was all filmed, it was on the Henry Mancini show *{Bernie in hysterics}*. Oh, weird! And we had this big feller (he does the Sonny and Cher show now), better not call him a big mincing queen, who kept saying, "Oh, my God, oh, my God, what's he doing, what's he doing?" He's one of those intolerable people who were going, "It's a disaster, it's a disaster, what's he doing?"

I mean, I look back and say, fuck me, did they actually happen, all those things?

Of course, one thing that had to do with the initial American success was "Your Song."

Elton: Yeah, well, I think when people think of Elton John they think of either "Your Song" or "Crocodile Rock." You know what I mean?

Bernie: I can't even remember writing that song.

Elton: I remember the girl you were going out with, the girl you wrote it about.

Bernie: I didn't write it about anybody, really.

Elton: I thought you wrote . . .

Bernie: Well, that wasn't . . .

Elton: Still, you were quite steep. When you did have your little affairs and things, you got very steeped in them.

Bernie: Yes, but I've never aimed that song at anybody, really.

Elton: But "First Episode at Heinton" was . . .

Bernie: Oh, yes, that was. I forgot about that. See, I forget about songs, I have to be reminded.

Elton: Somebody says to me, play the songs off *Tumbleweed,* I can't even remember the songs on the album.

Bernie: The biggest confidence trick as far as a song is concerned to me is "Take Me to the Pilot." It's great that so many people have covered that and sort of put their all into it, and that song means fuck-all, it doesn't mean *anything.*

Elton: We're doing a documentary, and I said it's probably the most unlikely song of all time to be covered, because of the words.

Bernie: They don't mean anything.

Elton: It's had so many covers, Ben E. King . . .

Bernie: That song proves what you can get away with.

Has anybody ever asked you about any religious insights?

Elton: Oh, I was just going to say that.

Bernie: That was a great one.

Elton: People thought we were anti-Semitic; we were everything—

Bernie: Do you remember "I Need You to Turn To"? The guy who came in, that college guy, and thought it was about the Crucifixion? We said, "How on earth can you say it's about the Crucifixion?" and he proceeded to condense it and to change all the meanings. One line was great. He said about being "nailed to your love in many lonely nights," thinking that being "nailed to your love" was being nailed to the cross. That's amazing.

Elton says "Tiny Dancer" is about Maxine. Is that true?

Bernie: That's true, yes.

Elton: What about "Daniel," who is obviously a homosexual. Somebody said it's obviously a homosexual song, Daniel, my brother, I love you—

Bernie: Who said that?

Elton: Some skinhead in Manchester. He said, "That 'Crocodile Rock' is rubbish, and 'Daniel' is a homosexual song."

Bernie: NO! Did he?

Elton: So many people have said they can't understand what "Daniel" means. It's because I left the last verse out. I still think it's quite self-explanatory. {Daniel is a one-eyed war veteran who can only find peace in Spain.}

Bernie: People get their knickers completely in a twist just because Levon called his son Jesus, and he was a balloon salesman. Just because he didn't call his child "George," and he wasn't a mechanic or something. I don't know, the story's completely simple; it's just about a guy who wants to get away from his father's hold over him. Strange.

Elton: Then there was the whole Jewish thing.

Bernie: Oh, the anti-Semitic period, where everybody thought "Border Song" was anti-Semitic. Don't ask me why, I don't know. Most of my friends are Jewish. I married one {laughter}.

Elton: It's never been disclosed, but lyrically I wrote the last verse of "Border Song" because it was only two verses long and we thought it really needed another verse. That's why the last verse is very mundane. That's never been disclosed before. . . .

Is that the only verse of a song you've written?

Elton: Oh, yes.

You were quoted recently as saying you'd one day like to do an album of your own stuff but inevitably it would turn out gloomy.

Elton: I think it would. I like writing songs like "First Episode at Heinton," which really doesn't have any shape or form, it just meandered with a general feel of wistfulness. I'd love to eventually, I feel I could write lyrics someday; I might want to, but I just can't see it happening imminently.

"Talking Old Soldiers" was rather unusual in being almost a narrative.

Elton: That was a very David Ackles-influenced song. If you notice, *Tumbleweed Connection* is dedicated "with love to David." That's David Ackles. It is sort of a narrative.

There has been critical controversy concerning Paul Buckmaster's correct role in your recordings. In the suggestion of a little instrumental overkill on 'Madman,' for example.

Elton: That was an album of frustrations for everybody; we were all going through heavy stages. Paul was getting . . . well, he's very strange, Paul, he can't work under pressure. We were *all* under pressure because we had to get that fucking album going. I don't know how that album ever got out. When we were doing the actual track, "Madman Across the Water," for example, Paul arrived with no score! There were sixty string musicians sitting there, and we had to scrap it. There were all those sort of disasters.

But overall I don't think Paul has gotten the credit he deserves. He's influenced so many string writers, especially the *Elton John* album; everybody pinches off Paul Buckmaster. Like Lennon on *Imagine*, I'm not saying he pinched it, but he used a lot of strings on "How Do You Sleep?" I think nobody really used strings until Buckmaster came along and showed them you can use strings without having them being sugary and awful. I think Jack Nitzsche's arrangement on the Neil Young is very Buckmasterish.

Bernie: What, on *Harvest?* I thought they were disgusting, those arrangements, they just crucified those songs. They were like, yeccch.

Which current artists do you like?

Elton: I like Stealers Wheel.

Bernie: I was just going to say that; I like that a lot. And Joni Mitchell, the longer she's been around, the more she's grown on me. I was playing that album today again in the car, *For the Roses.* I just find myself playing that all the time. Fucking incredible album. She sees so brilliantly. She's a genius. There are a lot of different standards as far as lyricists are concerned; I wouldn't say I'm the same kind as Joni Mitchell is, but on her level there is nobody who can touch her. The more I listen to her, the more phenomenal she gets. Some of the lines she writes. I could go on for hours just thinking of lines of hers.

Elton: I like Stevie Wonder. I usually wind up playing the same old tapes in the car.

Bernie: There are four things I can think of offhand that I play all the time. Joni Mitchell, Stealers Wheel, the Johnny Nash, which is my favorite album, and the Beach Boys album I play a lot. I still like Jesse Winchester. I wish somebody would do something for him. He's got a great voice.

Bernie, you've said you generally start with a first line or two and grow from there. Do you do this mostly at home, and do you use a musical instrument?

Bernie: It varies. I could never define to anybody the way I write a song because it varies so much. Sometimes I'll just come up with a title, and I'll try to write a song around that title. Other times I'll come up with a first line or a first two lines. With "Rocket Man" the first two lines came to me when I was driving along. I just thought . . . hmmm, can't remember what the first two lines are . . . hmmm . . . well, whatever they were, they came to me as I was driving along, and by the time I'd gotten home I'd written the song in my head. I got inside and had to rush and write it all down before I'd forgotten it. Seldom do I think I'd like to write a song about a particular subject or person and sit down from scratch. Usually it's either a first line, a line somewhere in it or a title; then the song comes alive.

Basically it takes me very little time to write a song. If I find myself taking more than an hour to do it, I usually forget it and try something else. I like to work quickly; I never like to waste any time. I never write half a song and come back to it later at all. It all has to be done at once. I lose interest if it doesn't.

It took two weeks to write twenty songs, and I only have to write two albums' worth a year, so that's on the whole about twenty-four songs. It takes me a month to write twenty-four songs.

WHAT ABOUT YOUR NEW LAbel, Rocket? What exactly is your plan with it? When did you first think about it, and whose idea was it?

Elton: It was conceived when we were doing *Don't Shoot Me,* right?

Bernie: In France, the idea came about, because Davey Johnstone [Elton's new guitarist] was going to make an album, and he hadn't got a label to go out on.

Elton: We went to a lot of companies, but nobody would give us a reasonable deal. So we were sitting around the table saying, what are we going to do, and I think it was me, actually, who said, "Start our own fucking label!" Because we'd all been drinking wine. We all said, "Yeah!" Then we went to bed and we all got up the next morning and said, "Was everybody serious?" We all decided we were, so it all started as a result of Davey Johnstone and nothing else. After hearing Davey's album, which has taken a year to get together, not for lack of work but because he hasn't had much studio time, those people are really going to kick themselves, because it's a fucking masterful album. That's how it started.

I mean, I've always dreamed of having my own record company. As a kid I used to watch the 78s when the labels were beautiful to look at; I'd watch them go round. I'm fascinated by records. Anything on London was boring, or EMI, because of those plain labels. Now, what used to have good labels? *[Thinks for a few seconds.]* Polydor was quite interesting. . . .

Bernie: There's a picture of James Brown now on his own records.

Elton: The five of us involved sat down—Bernie and I, Steven Brown, who handles the A&R side, John Reid [Elton's manager] and Gus Dudgeon, who does production, although Bernie and I will be doing production as well, Steve and John will basically handle the business side—and we just set out to cultivate new talent. MCA gave us a good advance, but that's more or less gone in finding offices, staff and decorating the offices. We can't go out and pay $50,000 in advance, and therefore we can't sign any name acts. We didn't particularly want to, anyway. It's very odd, we're just trying to find people from scratch. We're going to give a fair deal and a better royalty rate than they could get from WEA. I know it's very idyllic and the Moody Blues have done it and the Beatles did it, but I really think Rocket will be something different. The good thing about it is I'm not on it. It

297

would be hopeless from the start. It would dampen everybody else. It's like the Moody Blues are on Threshold, and so are Trapeze. It would be Elton John is on Rocket, and so are Longdancer and Davey Johnstone. Longdancer are not mind-shattering yet, but most of them are only eighteen. They've got a long way to go. It's hard to find mind-shattering talent.

And Bernie and I are producing Kiki Dee, who's been around for a long time, living in the wake of Dusty Springfield, really, gradually fading into the background, and she could sing the balls off Rita Coolidge any day. We're trying to write a special song for her. We've never done that for anybody else, to try to get her off the ground, to try to get her publicity and everything. Bernie's task is really hard because he's got to write one as a girl. So he slips into Maxine's dresses every morning. . . .

When we were in France, Jean-Luc Ponty [the French violinist] played on *Honky Chateau,* and we're desperately trying to get him because he's so fantastic.

In interviews over the past couple of years you've dwelled on retiring early. In one you predicted you'd retire in mid-'72.

Elton: And I'm still here! It's like Gracie Fields . . . no . . .

Bernie: Dorothy Squires.

Elton: Right. I couldn't stand the pace; if you've noticed I'm cutting down the live dates. I really do want to retire doing gigs eventually, that's what I meant.

Does Bernie follow radio play of singles as closely as Elton?

Bernie: No way. I'm always amused when he phones me up and such-and-such did a three-trillion advance or some such figure, and I'll just say, "Is that good?"

Elton: "Daniel" came into one of the charts at 65 the first week and he said, "Oh, is that good?" He's really a dampener for the enthusiasm, Bernie is, because you'll say, "Fucking hell,

the album went up to 91 from 176!" And he'll say, "Is that good?"

Bernie: He follows the playlists and who went how many places and who's got a bullet—that all confuses me. I look at the charts just to see if it's still on top.

Elton: I love the way the American trade magazines never give anybody a bad review because they're afraid the advertising will be taken out. It's so hysterical. They say albums will be hits, and they've got no fucking chance. "Noddy and the Jerk-Offs on the Shit label, this is a cross between Creedence Clearwater and"—and I *believe* them and order the record and I can't wait, and the fucking thing turns out to be dreadful. I *always* get hooked by those ecstatic reviews.

Bernie: You're very gullible.

Elton: Totally. Adverts, too.

Bernie: I bought Bruce Springsteen just on the basis of the advert.

Elton: I quite like that. It grows on me like the Dory Previn.

Bernie: The worst thing about me is that I'll buy albums and put them away on the shelf and forget that I've got them.

Elton: That's why I keep those down on the floor [points to huge piles of LPs] so I can flick through them.

Bernie: The last three Jefferson Airplane albums suck, fucking horrible. I can't get into people like that anymore.

Anything you'd like to do you haven't done yet?

Bernie: I'd like to make it with Princess Anne.

Elton: Oh dear, oh dear, there go my connections with the Royal Family, up in flames. Actually, I'd like to make a movie and show people there's more to me than meets the eye. It's got to be hilariously funny if I'm going to do it. But that's boring. Pop stars always want to make movies. What else would I like to do? I don't know. My ambitions go from day to day. All my childhood ambitions have been fulfilled.

25

INTERVIEWED BY PAUL GAMBACCINI (1974)

"Lennon had been done, and it just seemed a natural to do." That's how Paul Gambaccini explains the first ROLLING STONE Interview with Paul McCartney, and that says it all. Almost. Lennon had, indeed, been "done," and he'd disemboweled the Beatles myth, putting Beatle Paul in his place in the process. Now it was McCartney's turn.

But it was late 1973; the Lennon interview came out in early 1971. Why the wait?

Gambaccini offered an answer in his introduction; now he adds, "He wanted to promote *Band on the Run.*" After the critical failure of the *Red Rose Speedway* album, and the departure of two members of his band, Wings, McCartney had recharged himself in Nigeria. Backed only by his wife Linda and loyalist guitarist Denny Laine, Paul came up with his best effort in five years of solo work. Now he had to get the word out.

"And maybe," Gambaccini adds, "it was a case where something has been so major in your life"—in this case, the Lennon interview—"and you haven't had a chance to talk about it."

McCartney, then 31, first met with Gambaccini for a BBC show promoting the album. "The publicist told me if Paul liked me, we could keep going." As it turned out, "Linda liked me—we're both American, and I'd gone to Dartmouth, and she'd been a Westchester girl—and that was the way in."

—BF-T

THIS JANUARY MARKS THE TENTH AN-niversary of the Beatles' appearance on the American charts. Last month ROLLING STONE conducted its first full-scale interview with Paul McCartney, in six sessions starting in a London recording studio and ending on a New York street. The New York sessions took place the day after McCartney had entered the U.S. for the first time in two years, visa problems

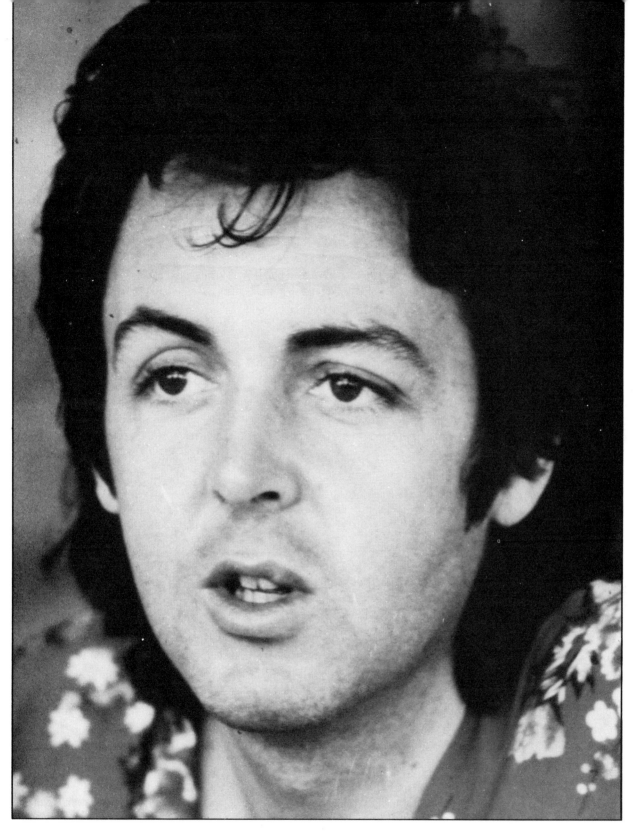

McCARTNEY

stemming from two marijuana violations now finally resolved.

McCartney was cautious in his responses during the first two sessions. He and Linda remembered being on vacation in Scotland when they were first shown John Lennon's lengthy interview (ROLLING STONE, January 21st and February 4th, 1971), and having been deeply hurt by it. At first he seemed to want to avoid the kind of controversy Lennon's interview had generated, but in later conversations he became freer with his answers.

Our interviews were delayed some months, first by a Wings tour and later by a series of recording sessions in Nigeria. Even after that wait, the McCartneys seemed surprised at how much we wanted to know. In the end they were interviewed in a London recording studio, Paul's Soho office, Lee Eastman's offices and apartment in New York (where baby Stella McCartney wore the interviewer's watch on her foot) and the studio of photographer Francesco Scavullo. As the interview begins, Paul is telling how he wrote one of the songs he recorded in Nigeria.

W E WERE IN JAMAICA ON holiday and we were staying in a Little house outside Montego Bay, and we read in the local newspaper, *The Daily Gleaner,* that Dustin Hoffman and Steve McQueen were in town filming *Papillon.* They were just along the coast from us. We were saying it would be great to meet him, have dinner with him, so Linda rang up. She's good at that; I'm always a bit embarrassed.

We got friendly and were chatting away. We'd been talking about songwriting, and Dustin was saying he thought it was an incredible gift to be able to write a song about something. People think that, but I always maintain it's the same as any gift. It probably is more magical because it's music, and I think it is more magical. But take his acting talent. It's great. I was saying, "It's the same as you and acting; when the man says, 'Action!' you just pull it out of the bag, don't you? You don't know where it comes from, you just do it! How do you get all of your characterizations? It's just in you."

So he says, "You mean you can just do it, like that?" He was lovely, Dustin. *{Does Dustin Hoffman impersonation.}* "You can just do it?" We went back a couple of days later, and he said, "I've been thinking about this, I've seen a little thing in *Time* magazine about Picasso, and it

struck me as being very poetic. I think this would be really great set to music." It was one of those Passed On bits, you know, Transition or whatever they call it. . . . So he says there's a little story here. In the article he supposedly said, "Drink to me, drink to my health, you know I can't drink anymore." He went to paint a bit, and then he went to bed at three in the morning. He didn't wake up the next morning, and they found him, dead.

I happened to have my guitar with me; I'd brought it around, and I said, yeah, sure. I strummed a couple of chords I knew I couldn't go wrong on and started singing, "Drink to me, drink to my health," and he leaps out of his chair and says, "Annie! Annie!" That's his wife. He says, "Annie! Annie! The most incredible thing! He's doing it! He's writing it! It's coming out!" He's leaping up and down, just like in the films, you know. And I'm knocked out because he's so appreciative. I was writing the tune there, and he was well-chuffed [pleased].

Then we went to Nigeria, and we were working in Ginger's studio—Ginger Baker/ARC Studio in Lagos, nice studio down there. We thought we'd do this Picasso number, and we started off doing it straight. Then we thought, Picasso was kind of far out in his pictures, he'd done all these different kinds of things, fragmented. Cubism and the whole bit. I thought it would be nice to get a track a bit like that, put it through different moods, cut it up, edit it, mess around with it—like he used to do with his pictures. You see the old films of him painting; he paints it once and if he doesn't like it he paints it again, right on top of it, and by about twenty-five times he's got his picture. So we tried to use this kind of idea. I don't know much about it, to tell you the truth, but what we did know we tried to get in the song, sort of a Cubist thing.

Then there was the trouble in Nigeria with Fela Ransome Kuti, who had been in Ginger Baker's Air Force.

You heard about that? All it was, was we were recording in Lagos. Lately we've gone to two different places to record, just for the fun of it. We've been to Lagos and to Paris, and in both of the places they say, "Why did you come here? You've got much better studios in England or America, you must be daft!" And we say, "Well, it's just for the fun, it's just to come somewhere different for a different type of turn-on, that's all." They never really seem to be able to understand it. I think old Fela, when he found us in Lagos, thought, "Hello, why have they come to Lagos?" And the only reason he could think of was that we must be stealing black music, black African music, the Lagos sound; we'd come down there to pick it up. So I said, "Do us a favor, we do okay as it is; we're not pinching your music."

They felt that they have their own little ethnic thing going, and these big foreigners are taking all their bit and beating them back to the West with it. Because they have a lot of difficulty getting their sound heard in the West. There's not an awful lot of demand, except for things like, what was it, "Soul Makossa." Except for that kind of thing they don't really get heard.

And they are brilliant; it's incredible music down there. I think it will come to the fore. And I thought my visit would, if anything, help them because it would draw attention to Lagos, and people would say, "Oh, by the way, what's the music down there like?" and I'd say it was unbelievable. It is unbelievable. When I heard Fela Ransome Kuti the first time, it made me cry, it was that good.

IN THE FILM 'A HARD DAY'S Night,' there were the stereotypes—if you remember, John the thinker, Ringo the loner and Paul the happy-go-lucky. Did you object to that?

No. I didn't mind it. No, no; I still don't. I was in a film. I don't care what they picture me as. So far as I'm concerned, I'm just doing a job in a film. If the film calls for me to be a cheerful chap, well, great; I'll be a cheerful chap.

It does seem to have fallen in my role to be kind of a bit more that than others. I was always known in the Beatle thing as being the one who would kind of sit the press down and say, "Hello, how are you? Do you want a drink?" and make them comfortable. I guess that's me. My family loop was like that. So I kind of used to do that, plus a little more polished than I might normally have done, but you're aware you're talking to the press. . . . You want a good article, don't you, so you don't want to go sluggin' the guys off. In the normal day-to-day life a lot of polished talk goes on . . . you don't love everyone you meet, but you try and get on with people, you know, you don't try and put 'em uptight; most people don't, anyway.

So to me that's always been the way. I mean, there's nothin' wrong with that; why should I go around slugging people? I really didn't like all that John did. But I'm sure that *he* doesn't now.

Have you talked to him about that?

No, but I know John, and I know that most of it was just something to tell the newspapers. He was in that mood then, and he wanted all that to be said. I think, now, whilst he probably doesn't *regret* it, he didn't mean every single syllable of it. I mean, he came out with all stuff like I'm like Engelbert Humperdinck. I know he doesn't *really* think that. In the press, they really wanted me to come out and slam John back, and I used to get pissed at the guys coming up to me and saying, "This is the latest thing John said, and what's your answer?" And I'd say, "Well, don't really have much of an answer. He's got a right to say . . ." You know, really limp things, I'd answer. But I believe, keep cool and that sort of thing, and it passes over. I don't believe if someone kind of punches you over you have to go kind of thumping him back to prove you're a man and that kind of thing. I think, actually, you do win that way in the end, you know.

What was your reaction when you read that stuff at the time?

Oh, I hated it. You can imagine. I sat down and pored over every little paragraph, every little sentence. "Does he really think that of me?" I thought. And at the time, I thought, "It's me. I am. That's just what I'm like. He's captured me so well; I'm a turd, you know." I sat down and really thought, I'm just nothin'. But then, well, kind of people who dug me, like Linda, said, "Now, you know that's not true, you're joking. He's got a grudge, man; the guy's trying to polish you off." Gradually I started to think, great, that's not true. I'm not really like Engelbert; I don't just write ballads. And that kept me kind of hanging on; but at the time, I tell you, it hurt me. Whew. Deep.

Could you write a song or songs with John again?

I could. It's totally fresh ground, right now, 'cause I just got my visa, too. About two or three days ago, and until then, I couldn't physically write a song with John; he was in America. He couldn't get out. I couldn't get in. But now that's changed, so whole new possibilities are opening up. Anything could happen. I like to write with John. I like to write with anyone who's good.

HOW DID YOU MEET LINDA? Linda and I met in a club in London called the Bag of Nails, which was right about the time that the club scene was going strong in London. She was down there with some friends. I think she was down there with Chas Chandler and some other people, and I was down there with some friends, including a guy who used to work at the office. I was in my little booth and she was in her little booth, and we were giving each other the eye, you know. Georgie Fame was playing that night, and we were both right into Georgie Fame.

When did you first realize you wanted to marry her?

About a year later. We both thought it a bit crazy at the time, and we also thought it would be a gas. Linda was a bit dubious, because she had been married before and wasn't too set on settling. In a way, she thought it tends to blow things, marrying ruins it. But we both fancied each other enough to do it. And now we're glad we did it, you know. It's great. I love it.

Some of the critical notices on her debut performances seemed to ask where she had come from.

Yeah. Well, the answer is, nowhere, really.

Mick Jagger had that quote. He wouldn't let . . .

. . . his old lady in the band, yeah. That was all very understandable at the time because she did kind of appear out of nowhere. To most people, she was just some chick. I just figure she was the main help for me on the albums around that time. She was there every day, helping on harmonies and all of that stuff.

How did you feel people would react to Linda's presence?

She was on *Let It Be* doing backup vocals. That was her first appearance, and nobody said much about that. The time we did *McCartney*, as it was largely recorded in the back room, she was always there. That was how she came to be on the album as much as she was.

You did have the release date close to 'Let It Be.'

There was some hassle at the time. We were arguing over who had mentioned a release date first. It was all a bit petty. I'd pegged a release date, and then *Let It Be* was scheduled near it. I saw it as victimization, but now I'm sure it wasn't.

Seeing that 'Let It Be' was released basically after the fact, do you wish it had not been released?

Oh, no. I don't wish that about anything. Everything seems to take its place in history after it's happened, and it's fine to let it stay there.

It was the first album to have the little bits on, like the type that also appeared on 'McCartney.'

I rather fancied having just the plain tapes and nothing done to them at all. We had thought of doing something looser before, but the albums always turned out to be well produced. That was the idea of the whole album. All the normal

things that you record that are great and have all this atmosphere but aren't brilliant recordings or production jobs normally are left out and wind up on, say, Pete Townshend's cutting floor. It ends up with the rest of his demos.

But all that stuff is often stuff I love. It's got the door opening, the banging of the tape recorder, a couple of people giggling in the background. When you've got friends around, those are the kinds of tracks you play them. You don't play them the big, finished, produced version.

Like "Hey Jude," I think I've got that tape somewhere, where I'm going on and on with all these funny words. I remember I played it to John and Yoko, and I was saying, "These words won't be on the finished version." Some of the words were, "The movement you need is on your shoulder," and John was saying, "It's great! 'The movement you need is on your shoulder.'" I'm saying, "It's crazy, it doesn't make any sense at all." He's saying, "Sure, it does, it's great." I'm always saying that, by the way, that's me, I'm always never sure if it's good enough. That's me, you know.

With "Hey Jude," everyone was trying to figure out who Jude was.

I happened to be driving out to see Cynthia Lennon. I think it was just after John and she had broken up, and I was quite mates with Julian [their son]. He's a nice kid, Julian. And I was going out in me car just vaguely singing this song, and it was like "Hey Jules." I don't know why, "Hey Jules." It was just this thing, you know, "Don't make it bad/ Take a sad song- . . ." And then I just thought a better name was Jude. A bit more country & western for me.

Once you get analyzing something and looking into it, things *do* begin to appear and things *do* begin to tie in. Because *everything* ties in, and what you get depends on your approach to it. You look at everything with a black attitude and it's all black.

This other idea of Paul Is Dead. That was on for a while. I had just turned up at a photo session, and it was at the time when Linda and I were just beginning to knock around with each other steadily. It was a hot day in London, a really nice hot day, and I think I wore sandals. I only had to walk around the corner to the crossing because I lived pretty nearby. I had me sandals on and for the photo session I thought, I'll take my sandals off.

Linda: No, you *were* barefoot.

Paul: Oh, I was barefoot. Yeah, that's it. You know, so what? Barefoot, nice warm day, I didn't feel like wearing shoes. So I went around to the photo session and showed me bare feet. Of course, when that comes out and people start looking at it, they say, "Why has he got no shoes on? He's never done *that* before." Okay, you've never seen me do it before, but, in actual fact, it's just me with my shoes off. Turns out to be some old Mafia sign of death or something.

Then the this-little-bit-if-you-play-it-backwards stuff. As I say, nine times out of ten it's really nothing. Take the end of *Sgt. Pepper,* that backward thing, "We'll fuck you like Supermen." Some fans came around to my door giggling. I said, "Hello, what do you want?" They said, "Is it true, that bit at the end? Is it true? It says, 'We'll fuck you like Supermen.'" I said, "No, you're kidding. I haven't heard it, but I'll play it." It was just some piece of conversation that was recorded and turned backwards. But I went inside after I'd seen them and played it studiously, turned it backwards with my thumb against the motor, turned the motor off and did it backwards. And there it was, sure as anything. "We'll fuck you like Supermen." I thought, Jesus, what can you do?

And then there was "I buried Paul."

That wasn't "I buried Paul" at all; that was John saying "cranberry sauce." It was the end of "Strawberry Fields." That's John's humor. John would say something totally out of synch, like "cranberry sauce." If you don't realize that John's apt to say "cranberry sauce" when he feels like it, then you start to hear a funny little word there, and you think, "Aha!"

When you were alive and presumed dead, what did you think?

Someone from the office rang me up and said, "Look, Paul, you're dead." And I said, "Oh, I don't agree with that." And they said, "Look, what are you going to do about it? It's a big thing breaking in America. You're dead." And so I said, leave it, just let them say it. It'll probably be the best publicity we've ever had, and I won't have to do a thing except stay alive. So I managed to stay alive through it.

A couple of people came up and said, "Can I photograph you to prove you're not dead?" Coincidentally, around that time, I was playing down a lot of the old Beatle image and getting a bit more to what I felt was me, letting me beard grow and not being so hung up on keeping fresh and clean. I *looked* different, more laid back, and so I had people coming up and saying, "You're not him!" And I was beginning to think, "I am, you know, but I know what you mean. I don't *look* like him, but believe me."

You were supposedly Billy Shears, according to one of the theories.

Ringo's Billy Shears. Definitely. That was just in the production of *Sgt. Pepper.* It just happened to turn out that we dreamed up Billy Shears. It was a rhyme for "years" . . . "band you've known for all these years . . . and here he is, the one and only Billy Shears." We thought, that's a great little name, it's an Eleanor-Rigby-type name, a nice atmospheric name, and it was leading into Ringo's track. So as far as we were concerned, it was purely and simply a device to get the next song in.

LINDA MENTIONED YOU "BOUNCE off" people. After you left George Martin and the other three, was Linda the only person to bounce your ideas off of?

For a while, yes. Oh, yes.

Did you miss not having more people? Is there anyone you ask now outside of people in the band?

Sometimes now I mainly bounce off myself. I do that more now, call it what you will—maturity? Sometimes if a friend is in the studio, I'll ask for their opinion, and that will make it easier on me. The laugh of all this is I say all this rubbish, and it all changes the next day.

I still read the notices and stuff, and they're usually bum ones when you're expecting them to be great. Like after *Ram,* there were a lot of bum notices after *Ram.* But I keep meetin' people wherever I go, like I met someone skiing. As he skiied past me he said, "I loved *Ram,* Paul." So that's really what I go by. Just the kind of people who flash by me in life. Just ordinary people, and they said they loved it. That's why I go a lot by sales, not just for the commercial thing. Like if a thing sells well, it means a lot of people bought it and liked it.

"Hi, Hi, Hi" was the one that brought you back to the Top Ten, after "Give Ireland Back to the Irish" and "Mary Had a Little Lamb," although in Britain they played "C Moon" because "Hi, Hi, Hi" was banned by the BBC.

I thought the "Hi, Hi, Hi" thing could easily be taken as a natural high, could be taken as booze high and everything. It doesn't have to be drugs, you know, so I'd kind of get away with it. Well, the first thing they saw was drugs, so I didn't get away with that, and then I just had some line, "Lie on the bed and get ready for my polygon."

The daft thing about all of that was our publishing company, Northern Songs, owned by

305

Lew Grade, got the lyrics wrong and sent them round to the radio station and it said, "Get ready for my body gun," which is far more suggestive than anything I put. "Get ready for my polygon," watch out, baby, I mean, it was suggestive, but abstract suggestive, which I thought I'd get away with. Bloody company goes round and makes it much more specific by putting "body gun." Better words, almost.

It made it, anyway, in the States.

Yeah, well, the great laugh is when we go live, it makes a great announcement. You can say, "This one was banned!" and everyone goes, "Hooray!" The audience love it, you know. "This next one was banned," and then you get raving, because everyone likes to. Everyone's a bit anti-all-that-banning, all that censorship. Our crew, our generation, really doesn't dig that stuff, as I'm sure you know.

"Helen Wheels" has done better in America than England, as have many of your records past, back to the old days. Have you ever thought of a reason why?

The only thing I can think of is the foreigner syndrome. We're British, and that means something to an American. It's like some Americans who do better over here, like Cassidy and the Osmonds, even Elvis.

It's been suggested that the Beatles provided something for Americans they had lost with the death of Kennedy—youth, happiness, freedom from inhibitions. Does that make much sense to you?

No, none at all.

In songwriting technique, how did you compose with John? How did you compose yourself, and then with Linda?

Well, first, I started off on my own. Very early on I met John, and we then gradually, started to write stuff together. Which didn't mean we wrote everything together. We'd kind of write eighty percent together, and the other twenty percent for me were things like "Yesterday" and for John things like "Strawberry Fields" that he'd mainly write on his own. And I did certain stuff on my own. So I've *done* stuff on my own.

When I said how do you compose, I meant actually sitting down and doing it. Did you use guitar, or did you use piano?

When I first started writing songs I started using a guitar. The first one I ever wrote was one called "My Little Girl" which is a funny little song, a nice little song, a corny little song based on three chords—G, G7 and C. A little later we had a piano, and I used to bang around on that. I wrote "When I'm Sixty-Four" when I was about sixteen. I wrote the tune for that, and I was vaguely thinking then it might come in handy in a musical comedy or something. I didn't know what kind of career I was going to take.

So I wrote that on piano, and from there it's really been a mixture of the both. I just do either, now. Sometimes I've got a guitar in my hands; sometimes I'm sittin' at a piano. It depends whatever instrument I'm at—I'll compose on it, you know.

Do you start with a title or a line, or what?

Oh, different ways. Every time it's different. "All My Loving"—an old Beatle song, remember that one, folks?—I wrote that one like a bit of poetry, and then I put a song to it later. Something like "Yesterday," I did the tune first and wrote words to that later. I called that "Scrambled Egg" for a long time. I didn't have any words to it. {*Paul sings the melody with the words "scrambled egg . . . da da da da . . . scrambled egg . . ."*} So then I got words to that; so I say, every time is different, really. I like to keep it that way, too; I don't get any set formula. So that each time, I'm pullin' it out of the air.

When did you get the idea you were going to bring in a string quartet on "Scrambled Egg"?

First of all, I was just playing it through for everyone—saying, how do you like this song? I played it just me on acoustic, and sang it. And the rest of the Beatles said, "That's it. Love it." So George Martin and I got together and sort of cooked up this idea. I wanted just a small string arrangement. And he said, "Well, how about your actual string quartet?" I said great, it sounds great. We sat down at a piano and cooked that one up.

How would you see George Martin's contributions in those songs in those days?

George's contribution was quite a big one, actually. The first time he really ever showed that he could see beyond what we were offering him was "Please Please Me." It was originally conceived as a Roy Orbison-type thing, you know. George Martin said, "Well, we'll put the tempo up." He lifted the tempo, and we all thought that was much better, and that was a big hit. George was in there quite heavily from the beginning.

The time we got offended, I'll tell you, was one of the reviews, I think about *Sgt. Pepper*—one of the reviews said, "This is George Martin's finest album." We got shook; I mean, "We don't mind him helping us, it's great, it's a great help, but it's not his album, folks, you know." And there got to be a little bitterness over that. A bit of help, but Christ, if he's goin' to get all the credit . . . for the whole album . . . {*Paul plays with his children.*}

THE WINGS TOUR IN 1972 WAS the first time you had toured in six years, Wasn't it?

Yes.

Had you intended to keep it that long?

Oh, no, no, no. With the Beatles we did a big American tour, and I think the feeling, mainly from George and John was, "Oh, this is getting a little bit *uhhh . . .*" but I thought, "No, you can't give up live playing, we'd be crazy to." But then we did a concert tour I really hated, and I came off stormy and saying, "Bloody hell, I really agree with you now."

Where was that?

In America, somewhere, I can't remember exactly. It was raining and we were playing under some sort of big canopy, and everybody felt they were going to get electric shocks and stuff. We were driven off in a big truck afterwards, and I remember sitting in the back of the truck, saying, bloody hell, they're right, this is stupid.

So we knew we were going to give up playing, but we didn't want to go make some big announcement that we were giving it all up or anything, so we just kind of cooled it and didn't go out. When anyone asked we'd say, "Oh, we'll be going out again," but we really didn't think we would. So we recorded a lot and stuff, and nobody felt the need to go out and play.

After six years I just thought it would be good to get out, because live shows are a lot of what it's about. If nothing else, you get out there and see what people want. I remember at the end of the Beatles thinking that it would be good if I just went out with some country & western group. To have a sing every day surely must improve my voice a bit.

When did you first think you wanted to be in a band?

I didn't think I wanted to be in one; I wanted to do something in music, and my dad gave me a trumpet for my birthday. I went through trying to learn that. But my mouth used to get too sore. You know, you have to go through a period of gettin' your lip hard. I suddenly realized I wouldn't be able to sing if I played trumpet. So I figured guitar would be better. It was about the time that guitar was beginning to be *the* instrument. So I went and swapped my trumpet for a guitar, and I got that home and couldn't figure out what was wrong, and I suddenly decided to turn the strings around and that made a difference, and I realized I was left-handed. I started from there, really; that was my first kind

of thing, and then once you had a guitar you were then kind of eligible for bands and stuff. But I never thought of myself being in a band.

One day I went with this friend of mine. His name was Ivan [Vaughn]. And I went up to Woolton, in Liverpool, and there was a village fete on, and John and his friends were playing for the thing. My friend Ivan knew John, who was a neighbor of his. And we met there, and John was onstage singing, "Come little darlin', come and go with me . . ."

The Dell-Vikings' "Come Go with Me"?

But he never knew the words because he didn't know the record, so he made up his own words, like "down, down, down, down, to the penitentiary." I remember I was impressed. I thought, wow, he's good. That's a good band there. So backstage, in the church hall later, I was singing a couple of songs I'd known.

I used to know all the words to "Twenty Flight Rock" and a few others, and it was pretty much in those days to know the words to that. John didn't know the words to many songs. So I was valuable. I wrote up a few words and showed him how to play "Twenty Flight Rock" and another one, I think. He played all this stuff, and I remember thinking he smelled a bit drunk. Quite a nice chap, but he was still a bit drunk. Anyway, that was my first introduction, and I sang a couple of old things.

I liked their band, and then one of their friends who was in the band, a guy called Pete Shotton who was a friend of John's, saw me cycling up in Woolton one day and said, "Hey, they said they'd quite like to have you in the band, if you'd like to join." I said, "Oh, yeah, it'd be great." We then met up somewhere, and I was in the band.

I was originally on guitar. The first thing we had was at a Conservative Club somewhere in Broadway, which is an area of Liverpool, as well as New York. There was a Conservative Club there and I had a big solo, a guitar boogie. I had this big solo, and it came to my bit and I blew it. I blew it. Sticky fingers, you know. I couldn't play at all, and I got terribly embarrassed. So I goofed that one terribly, so from then on I was on rhythm guitar. Blown out on lead!

We went to Hamburg, and I had a real cheap guitar, an electric guitar. It finally blew up on me, it finally fell apart in Hamburg. It just wasn't used to being used like that. Then I was on piano for a little while. So I went from bass to lead guitar to rhythm guitar to piano. I used to do a few numbers like Ray Charles' "Don't Let the Sun Catch You Cryin'" and a couple of Jerry

Lee Lewis' like "High School Confidential."

Then Stuart [Sutcliffe] left the group. He was the bass player. He lent me his bass, and I played bass for a few weeks. I used to play it upside down. And he used to have piano strings on it, because you couldn't get bass strings. They were a bit rare, you know, and they cost a lot, too, about two pounds for one string. So he could cut these big lengths of piano strings from the piano and wind them on this guitar. So I played that upside down for a while. I'm pretty versatile, I'll give that to myself. I wasn't very good, but I was versatile.

I'm in Hamburg, and I have a little bit of money together and finally saved enough money to buy myself a Hoffman violin bass. It was my bass, then, that was the one. And I became known for that bass, a lot of kids got them. That was my big pride and joy, because it sounded great.

And that was it, basically. The rest you know.

---

*I*N AMERICA, THE ANTHOLOGY AL-bum ['Beatles 1967–70'] and 'Red Rose Speedway' were back-to-back Number Ones. You were replacing yourself. Did that strike you as odd?

I thought it was good, rather than odd, because obviously the big hang-up after the Beatles broke up was, and really still is, can any of them be as good as the unit? The answer in most people's minds, I think, is, "No. They can't." Because the unit was *so* good.

Were you glad those anthology albums were released for the historical record or to combat the bootleggers?

The bootlegging thing was one of the reasons. I didn't take an awful lot of interest in them, actually. I still haven't heard them. I know what's on them because I've heard it all before, you know. I haven't really taken much interest in Beatles stuff of late just because there has been this hangover of Apple and Klein. The whole scene has gone so bloody sick. The four ex-Beatles are totally up to here with it. Everyone wants it solved so everyone can get on with being a bit peaceful with each other.

There was a lawsuit recently, the three others against Klein.

Of course, I loved that. My God, I hope they win that one. That's great. You see, apart from everything that went down, all the little personal conflicts, the reason why I felt I had to do what I had to do, which ended up specifically as being I had to sue the other three, was that there was no

way I could sue Klein on his own, which is what I wanted to do. It took me months to get over the fact. I kept saying, I can't sue the other three, just because it's very hard news to go suing someone you like, and no matter what kind of personal things were going down and John writing songs about me and all that stuff, I still didn't feel like the coolest thing in the world was to go and sue them. But it actually turned out to be the only way to stop Klein, so I had to go and do it.

If Klein was the big reason for the breakup of Apple, do you think there would have been difficulties anyway without him?

I think there would have been difficulties. Had the Eastmans come in like I wanted, the others would have feared I was trying to screw everyone for the Eastmans. It would have been a bit hard for the others to swallow, I'm afraid, since the Eastmans were so close to me. But they didn't want to screw anybody, and the way it's turning out they're settling up most of it anyway. Some people say, "People are all the same in business," but they're not.

I think the Apple thing was great. As it turned out, the one thing about business is that it does have to be looked after. If you have paperwork and bills and royalties and accounts and stuff, they all have to be handled very well, or else things get lost and then accountants have great difficulty in making up the final picture for taxes.

Apple was together in a lot of other ways. Although he didn't get treated brilliantly at Apple, it was right for James Taylor to make his first record then. I think it was shameful of them to sue him afterwards, but I think that was largely Klein's imagination because of the way he works. He's kind of, "Okay, git the bastard. He's left us and he's a success, let's sue him. We got him, we got his contract."

But I still think all the records that came out of it, Billy Preston and James Taylor, Badfinger, Mary Hopkin, all the people we did take on all had very good records. George, even with the Radha Krishna Temple, I think that's great stuff. I don't think you can fault any of the artistic decisions. Looking back on it, I think it was really a very successful thing.

The main downfall is that we were less businessmen and more heads, which was very pleasant and very enjoyable, except there should have been the man in there who would tell us to sign bits of paper. We got a man in who started to say, come on, sign it all over to me, which was the fatal mistake.

Now that you're in New York, I suppose the Beatles reunion rumors will start again.

Well, I must say, like as far as getting together as we were, as the Beatles were, I don't think that'll ever happen again. I think now everyone's kind of interested in their little personal things. I kind of like the way we did *Band on the Run,* the way we did it. Something we've never done before, and it's very interesting. But I do think that I for one am very proud—although I don't like the word proud, it tends to be—ex-servicemen have used the word . . . if you know what I mean . . . "proud of my country" . . . but I will use the word—I am proud of the Beatle thing. It was great, and I can go along with all the people you meet on the street who say you gave so much happiness to many people. I don't think that's corny. At the time, obviously, it just passes over; you don't really think they mean it. Oh, yeah, sure, and you shake their hand or whatever.

But I dig all that like mad now, and I believe that we did bring a real lot of happiness to the times. So I'm very proud of that kind of stuff, and consequently I wouldn't like to see my past slagged off. So I would like to see more cooperation. . . . If things go right, if things keep cool, I'd like to maybe do some work with them; I've got a lot of ideas in my head what I'd like, but I wouldn't like to tell you before I tell them. We couldn't be the Beatles-back-together again, but there might be things, little good ventures we could get together on, mutually helpful to all of us and things people would like to see, anyway.

I wouldn't rule everything out; it's one of those questions I really have to hedge on. But, I mean, I'm ready. Once we settle our business crap—there was an awfully lot of money made, of course, and none of it came to us, really, in the end. Virtually, that's the story. So I'd kind of like to salvage some of that and see that not everything's ripped off.

Through all that kind of bitterness I tended to think like John a bit, "Oh, the Beatles . . . naww . . . crap." But it really wasn't. I think it was great. So I'd like to see that cooled out and restored to its kind of former greatness, agree that it was a good thing and continue in some kind of way. I don't see gettin' the Beatles back together—there's certain things we could do quietly and still produce some kind of ongoing thing. I don't think you'll ever get anyone to give up all their individual stuff now; everyone's got it going too well now.

Would you consider the Ringo album an example of that type of cooperation?

Yeah, but I think more than that. . . . I think that's a beginning; that shows what someone can do just if he asks. That's all he did. He just asked us all. So that's what I like, that no one says, "Naw, you go on and make your own album." So if it's that easy, then lots of things could be done in the future. And I'd like to see some great things done.

26

INTERVIEWED BY CAMERON CROWE (1975)

Guitarist Jimmy Page, 31, and singer Robert Plant, 27, were the spokesmen for Led Zeppelin, in 1975 probably the most popular heavy-metal rock act in the world. Only they weren't talking—at least not to ROLLING STONE. The band and the magazine never hit it off, and from the beginning of Led Zep—in 1969—Page took negative reviews as personal attacks.

Now Cameron Crowe decided to take a shot at landing the Zep. As a freelancer, he'd written about the band, and he knew their publicist, who arranged for Crowe to go on the road with them. "Plant OK'd doing an interview," says Crowe, "but Page refused. So I began his psychological breakdown. I talked to Plant. We were going to do a Led Zep cover, and it was going to be just Plant. The others followed Page, but then John Paul Jones [the bassist] decided he'd talk, too. Then John Bonham [their late drummer]. They didn't want it to be just Plant. So I had everybody except Jimmy. One day he said to me, 'Man, I just don't want to be exploited by a magazine that never helped us . . . but if you want to get together and talk . . .'"

The interview went well, and Page even sat for a follow-up session. Crowe then "combined the Page and Plant interviews," and "they loved it. Then ROLLING STONE gave them some more bad reviews and pissed them off again."

—BF-T

JOHN PAUL JONES, LED ZEPPELIN'S bassist and keyboard player, was quietly playing backgammon and half listening to a phone-in radio talk show on New York FM.

"I was in a club last night when someone asked me if I wanted to meet Jimmy Page," the show's host suddenly offered between calls. "You know, when I

ROBERT PLANT

think about it, there's no one I'd rather meet less than someone as disgusting as Jimmy Page."

Jones bolted up from his game. "Let me just say that Led Slime can't play their way out of a paper bag, and if you plan on seeing them tomorrow night at the Garden, those goons are ripping you off. Now don't start wasting my time defending Led Slime. If you're thinking about calling up to do that, stick your head in the toilet and flush."

Jones, normally a man of quiet reserve, strode furiously across the room. He snapped up a phone and dialed the station. After a short wait, the talk-show host picked up the phone.

"What would you like to talk about?"

"Led Zeppelin," Jones answered coolly in his clipped British accent. The line went dead. Victim of an eight-second delay button, the exchange was never given air time.

It was a familiar battle, as Jones saw it. Although Led Zeppelin has managed to sell more than a million units apiece on all five of its albums and is currently working a U.S. tour that is expected to be the largest-grossing undertaking in rock history, the band has been continually kicked, shoved, pummeled and kneed in the groin by critics of all stripes. "I know it's unnecessary to fight back," Jones said. True enough: The Zep's overwhelming popularity speaks for itself. "I just thought I'd defend myself one last time."

The night after that aborted defense, in the first of three concerts at Madison Square Garden, Led Zeppelin brought a standing-room-only audience to its feet with one of the finest shows of its six-year career. On Page's unexpected midset impulse, the band launched unrehearsed into a stunning twenty-minute version of his tour de force, "Dazed and Confused." The tension of uncertain success was an evident and electric element in Zeppelin's performance that evening. "No question about it," lead singer Robert Plant enthused before returning to the stage for a second encore of "Communication Breakdown," "the tour has begun."

It has been a long time since Zeppelin last rock & rolled. After eighteen months spent laboring over their new double album, 'Physical Graffiti,' the band has some warming up to do. "It's unfortunate there's got to be anybody there," Plant said. "But we've got to feel our way. There's a lot of energy here this tour. Much more than the last one." The tour's official opening night, January 18th at the Minneapolis Sports Center, went surprisingly well considering the circumstances. Only a week before, Jimmy Page broke the tip of his left ring finger when it was caught in a slamming train door. With only one rehearsal to perfect what Page calls his "three-and-a-half-finger technique," the classic Zeppelin live pieces, "Dazed and Confused" and "Since I've Been Loving You," were indefinitely retired. Codeine tablets and Jack

Daniel's deadened the pain enough for Page to struggle through the band's demanding three-hour set.

Peter Grant, Led Zeppelin's manager and president of Swan Song, the group's record company, found those first few dates strange: "A Led Zeppelin concert without 'Dazed and Confused' is something I'll have to get used to. In a lot of ways that number is the band at its very best. There's one point in the song where Pagey can take off and do whatever he wants to. There is always the uncertainty of whether it will be five or thirty-five minutes long."

Page reacted to his injury with quiet desperation. "I have no doubt the tour is going to be good; it's just, dammit, I'm disappointed that I can't do all I can do." He began beating a fist quietly into the palm of his crippled hand. "I always want to do my very best, and it's frustrating to have something hold me back. You can bet that 'Dazed and Confused' will be back in the set the very second I'm able to play it. We may not be brilliant for a few nights, but we'll always be good."

The tour progressed satisfactorily through three nights at the Chicago Stadium and visits to Cleveland and Indianapolis until Plant came down with the flu. A show in St. Louis was postponed until mid-February, and while Plant stayed behind to convalesce, the band flew to Los Angeles for a day off.

The rest sparked a shift into second gear, and subsequent concerts in Greensboro, Detroit and Pittsburgh progressively improved, leading up to Led Zeppelin's tumultuous New York victory and the first version of "Dazed and Confused" on the tour. In the meantime, there was little of the savage hotel-room-splintering road fever Zeppelin is known for. "There hasn't been much room," said drummer John (Bonzo) Bonham a little sadly. "The music has taken up most of our concerns."

It was in late 1968 that Jimmy Page first put together the band that was to become Led Zeppelin. The name was suggested by Who drummer Keith Moon and embodies an irony that hardly needs to be commented upon. Page first approached Robert Plant, then the lead singer for a raucous Birmingham group called the Band of Joy. "His voice," said Page, "was too great to be undiscovered. All I had to do from there was find a bassist and a drummer."

The latter came easily. Plant suggested Bonham, the drummer from the Band of Joy. Bassist John Paul Jones was the last to join. "I answered a classified ad in 'Melody Maker,'" he said. "My wife made me." Jones had a sessionman's background. He had arranged some of the Stones' 'Their Satanic Majesties Request' album. He also arranged albums for producer Mickey Most's stable. "I arranged albums by Jeff Beck, Lulu, Donovan and Herman's Hermits."

All four members used the word "magic" when recalling Zeppelin's first rehearsal. "I've never been so turned on in my life," says Plant. "Although we were all steeped in blues and R&B, we found out in the first hour and a half that we had our own identity."

ROBERT PLANT, TWENTY-SIX, GREW up in the Black Country, where the English industrial revolution began. He says he lived "a sheltered childhood" and that he began picking up on Buddy Guy, Blind Lemon Jefferson and Woody Guthrie almost as soon as he entered school. Drifting in and out of groups like the Delta Blues Band, the Crawling King Snakes and the Band of Joy, Plant became known locally as "the wild man of blues from the Black Country." He met Page in 1968, just before the formation of Led Zeppelin.

"Pagey and I are closer than ever on this tour," Plant said after the New York concert. "We've almost jelled into one person in a lot of ways."

Jimmy Page, thirty-one, grew up in Felton, a dreary community near London's Heathrow Airport. An only child, he had no playmates until he began school at the age of five. "That early isolation," says Page, "it probably had a lot to do with the way I turned out. A loner. A lot of people can't be on their own. They get frightened. Isolation doesn't bother me at all. It gives me a sense of security."

Page started playing the guitar when he was twelve. "Somebody had laid a Spanish guitar on us . . . a very old one. I probably couldn't play it now if I tried. It was sitting around our living room for weeks and weeks. I wasn't interested. Then I heard a couple of records that really turned me on, the main one being Elvis's "Baby, Let's Play House," and I wanted to play it. I wanted to know what it was all about. This other guy at school showed me a few chords, and I just went on from there."

After a stint of several years as one of England's leading session guitarists (he played on the Kinks' "You Really Got Me," Van Morrison and Them's "Here Comes the Night" and "Gloria," the Who's "I Can't Explain" and several Burt Bacharach hits, among others), Page joined the Yardbirds as a second lead guitarist to Jeff Beck. Beck was soon to leave the band, and Page was left alone in the spotlight for a time. When the Yardbirds finally crumbled, Page was free to form Led Zeppelin.

The following conversations with Page and Plant took place over a period of two weeks. We began over tea in Plant's suite at Chicago's Ambassador Hotel. The talk continued three days later in Page's darkened room. "It's still morning," he shivered, sitting underneath a blanket on his sofa. "We may have to talk for three hours before I make any sense." The resulting interview, from which most of this material is taken, stretched into late afternoon. Page, a soft-spoken man, apparently preferred candles to electric light.

A visit to Plant several days later provided more material, and one final visit with Page on the plane flight to New York supplied the remaining details.

IT WASN'T UNTIL LED ZEPPELIN'S American tour in '73 that the media fully acknowledged the band's popularity.

Plant: We decided to hire our first publicity firm after we toured here in the summer of '72. That was the same summer that the Stones toured, and we knew full well that we were doing more business than them. We were getting better gates in comparison to a lot of people who were constantly glorified in the press. So without getting too egocentric, we thought it was time that people heard something about us other than that we were eating women and throwing the bones out the window. That whole lunacy thing was all people knew about us, and it was all word-of-mouth. All those times of lunacy were okay, but we aren't and never were monsters. Just good-time boys, loved by their fans and hated by their critics.

Do you feel any competition with the Stones?

Page: Naw. I don't think of it that way. I don't feel any competition at all. The Stones are great and always have been. Jagger's lyrics are just amazing. Right on the ball every time. I mean, I know all about how we're supposed to be the biggest group in the world and all, but I don't ever think about it. I don't feel that competition enters into it. It's who makes good music and who doesn't . . . and who's managed to sustain themselves.

What motivates you at this point?

Page: I love playing. If it was down to just that, it would be utopia. But it's not. It's airplanes, hotel rooms, limousines and armed guards standing outside rooms. I don't get off on that part of it at all. But it's the price I'm willing to pay to get out and play. I was very restless over the last eighteen months where we laid off and worked on the album.

Plant: There's a constant conflict, really, within me. As much as I really enjoy what I do at home . . . I play on my own little soccer team and I've been taking part in the community and living the life of any ordinary guy, I always find myself wistful and enveloped in a feeling I can't really get out of my system. I miss this band when we aren't playing. I have to call Jimmy up or something to appease that restlessness. The

313

other night when we played for the first time again I found the biggest smile on my mouth.

You've managed to continue undaunted in the midst of criticism—especially in the early days of Zeppelin. How much do you believe in yourself?

Page: I may not believe in myself, but I believe in what I'm doing. I know where I'm going musically. I can see my pattern, and I'm going much slower than I thought I'd be going. I can tell how far I ought to be going, I know how to get there; all I've got to do is keep playing. That might sound a bit weird because of all the John McLaughlins who sound like they're in outer space or something. Maybe it's the tortoise and the hare.

I'm not a guitarist as far as a technique goes. I just pick it up and play it. Technique doesn't come into it. I deal in emotions. It's the harmonic side that's important. That's the side I expected to be much further along on than I am now. That just means to say that I've got to keep at it.

There's such a wealth of arts and styles within the instrument . . . flamenco, jazz, rock, blues . . . you name it, it's there. In the early days my dream was to fuse all those styles. Now composing has become just as important. Hand in hand with that, I think it's time to travel, start gathering some real right-in-there experiences with street musicians around the world. Moroccan musicians, Indian musicians . . . it could be a good time to travel around now. This year. I don't know how everyone else is gonna take that, but that's the direction I'm heading in right now. This week I'm a gypsy. Maybe next week it'll be glitter rock.

What would you gain from your travels?

Page: Are you kidding? God, *you* know what you can gain when you sit down with the Moroccans. As a person and as a musician. That's how you grow. Not by living like this. Ordering up room service in hotels. It's got to be the opposite end of the scale. The balance has got to swing exactly the opposite. To the point where maybe I'll have an instrument and nothing else. I used to travel like that a long while ago. There's no reason I can't do it again. There's always this time thing. You can't buy time. Everything, for me, seems to be a race against time. Especially musically. I know what I want to get down, and I haven't got much time to do it in. I had another idea of getting a traveling medicine wagon with a dropdown side and traveling around England. That might sound crazy to you, but over there it's so rural you can do it. Just drop down the side and play through big battery

amps and mixers, and it can all be as temporary or as permanent as I want it to be. I like change and I like contrast. I don't like being stuck in one situation, day to day. Domesticity and all that isn't really for me. Sitting in this hotel for a week is no picnic. That's when the road fever starts and that's when the breakages start, but I haven't gotten to that stage yet. I've been pretty mellow so far. Mind you, we're only into the tour a week.

How well do you remember your first American tour?

Plant: Nineteen years old and never been kissed. I remember it well. It's been a long time. Nowadays we're more into staying in our rooms and reading Nietzsche. There was good fun to be had, you know; it's just that in those days there were more people to have good fun with than there are now. The States were much more fun. L.A. was L.A. It's not L.A. now. L.A. infested with jaded twelve-year-olds is not the L.A. that I really dug.

It was the first place I ever landed in America: the first time I ever saw a cop with a gun, the first time I ever saw a twenty-foot-long car. There were a lot of fun-loving people to crash into. People were genuinely welcoming us to the country, and we started out on a path of positive enjoyment. Throwing eggs from floor to floor and really silly water battles and all the good fun that a nineteen-year-old boy should have. It was just the first steps of learning how to be crazy. We met a lot of people who we still know and a lot of people who have faded away. Some ODed. Some of them just grew up. I don't see the point in growing up.

You seem sincerely depressed over the matter.

Plant: Well, I am. I haven't lost my innocence particularly. I'm always ready to pretend I haven't. Yeah, it is a shame in a way. And it's a shame to see these young chicks bungle their lives away in a flurry and rush to compete with what was in the old days the good-time relationships we had with the GTOs and people like that. When it came to looning, they could give us as much of a looning as we could give them. It's a shame, really. If you listen to "Sick Again," a track from *Physical Graffiti,* the words show I feel a bit sorry for them. "Clutching pages from your teenage dream in the lobby of the Hotel Paradise/Through the circus of the L.A. queen how fast you learn the downhill slide." One minute she's twelve, and the next minute she's thirteen and over the top. Such a shame. They haven't got the style that they had in the old days . . . way back in '68.

The last time I was in L.A. I got very bored. Boredom is a horrible thing. Boredom is the beginning of all destruction and everything that is negative. Every place is determined by the characters who are there. It's just that the character rating at the moment has zeroed right out.

Of course, I enjoy it all, but as a total giggle. It's funny. I miss it. All the clamor. The whole lot. It's all a big rush. From the shit holes to the classiest hotels, it's all been fun. From the Shadowbox Motel where the walls crumbled during the night seven years ago to the Plaza, where the attorney general staying one floor above complained about me playing Little Feat records too loud last night.

Do you feel you have to top yourselves with each album?

Page: No. Otherwise I would have been totally destroyed by the reviews of our last album, wouldn't I? You see, this is the point. I just don't care. I don't care what critics and other people think. So far I've been very, very fortunate because it appears that people like to hear the music I like to play. What more fortunate position can a musician be in? But I will still carry on, changing all the time. You can't expect to be the same person you were three years ago. Some people expect you to be and can't come to terms with the fact that if a year has elapsed between LPs, that means one year's worth of changes. The material consequently is affected by that, the lyrics are affected by that . . . the music, too. I don't feel I have to top myself at all.

H OW DOES IT FEEL TO BE YOUR *own record-company executives?*
Page: I guess we are our own executives now, aren't we? Listen, give us time with Swan Song. You'll be surprised. We've got some pretty good things lined up. I think the Pretty Things LP is brilliant. Absolutely brilliant. We're executives and all that crap, but I'll tell you one thing, the label was never—right from the top—Led Zeppelin records. It's designed to bring in other groups and promote acts that have had raw deals in the past. It's a vehicle for them and not for us to just make a few extra pennies over the top. That's the cynical way of looking at a record company.

Do you feel that the music business is sagging in any way?

Page: People always say that amidst their search for The Next Big Thing. The only real woomph was when the Stones and Beatles came over. But it's always said, "The business is dying! The business is dying!" I don't think so. There's too many good musicians around for the music business to be sagging. There's so many different styles and facets of the 360-degree musical sphere to listen to. From tribal to classical music, it's all there. If the bottom was to sag out of that, for God's sake, help us all.

If there was never another record made, there's enough music recorded and in the vaults everywhere for me to be happy forever. Then again, I can listen to all different sorts of music. I don't really care about The Next Big Thing. It's interesting when something new comes along, a band of dwarfs playing electronic harps or something, but I'm not searching. Look at Bad Company and the Average White Band. Those guys have all been around in one form or another for a very long time. How many of the new ones coming through have really got a lot of substance? In Britain, I'm afraid there's not much at all. We've got to deal with Suzi Quatro and Mud. It's absurd. Top Ten shouldn't be crap, but it is.

How difficult was the first Led Zeppelin album to put together?

Page: It came together really quick. It was cut very shortly after the band was formed. Our only rehearsal was a two-week tour of Scandinavia that we did as the New Yardbirds. For material, we obviously went right down to our blues roots. I still had plenty of Yardbirds riffs left over. By the time Jeff [Beck] did go, it was up to me to come up with a lot of new stuff. It was this thing where Clapton set a heavy precedent in the Yardbirds which Beck had to follow, and then it was even harder for me, in a way, because the second lead guitarist had suddenly become the first. And I was under pressure to come up with my own riffs. On the first LP I was still heavily influenced by the earlier days. I think it tells a bit, too. The album was made in three weeks. It was obvious that somebody had to take the lead, otherwise we'd have all sat around jamming and doing nothing for six months. But after that, on the second LP, you can hear the real group identity coming together.

Plant: That first album was the first time that headphones meant anything to me. What I heard coming back to me over the cans while I was singing was better than the finest chick in all the land. It had so much weight, so much power, it was devastating. I had a long ways to go with my

315

voice then, but at the same time the enthusiasm and spark of working with Jimmy's guitar shows through quite well. It was all very raunchy then. Everything was fitting together into a trademark for us. We were learning what got us off most and what got people off most, and what we knew got more people back to the hotel after the gig.

We made no money on the first tour. Nothing at all. Jimmy put in every penny that he'd gotten from the Yardbirds and that wasn't much. Until Peter Grant took them over, they didn't make the money they should have made. So we made the album and took off on a tour with a road crew of one.

JIMMY, YOU ONCE TOLD ME THAT *you thought life was a gamble. What did you mean?*

Page: So many people are frightened to take a chance in life, and there's so many chances you have to take. You can't just find yourself doing something and not happy doing it. If you're working at the factory and you're cursing every day that you get up, at all costs get out of it. You'll just make yourself ill. That's why I say I'm very fortunate because I love what I'm doing. Seeing people's faces, really getting off on them, makes me incredibly happy. Genuinely.

What gambles have you taken?

Page: I'll give you a gamble. I was in a band, I won't give the name because it's not worth knowing about, but it was the sort of band where we were traveling around all the time in a bus. I did that for two years after I left school, to the point where I was starting to get really good bread. But I was getting ill. So I went back to art college. And that was a total change in direction. That's why I say it's possible to do. As dedicated as I was to playing the guitar, I knew doing it that way was doing me in forever. Every two months I had glandular fever. So for the next eighteen months I was living on ten dollars a week and getting my strength up. But I was still playing.

Plant: Let me tell you a little story behind the song "Ten Years Gone" on our new album. I was working my ass off before joining Zeppelin. A lady I really dearly loved said, "Right. It's me or your fans." Not that I had fans, but I said, "I can't stop, I've got to keep going." She's quite content these days, I imagine. She's got a washing machine that works by itself and a little sportscar. We wouldn't have anything to say

anymore. I could probably relate to her, but she couldn't relate to me. I'd be smiling too much. Ten years gone, I'm afraid. Anyway, there's a gamble for you.

Page: I'll give you another one. I was at art college and started to do session work. Believe me, a lot of guys would consider that to be the apex—studio work. I left that to join the Yardbirds at a third of the bread because I wanted to play again. I didn't feel I was playing enough in the studio. I was doing three studio dates a day, and I was becoming one of those sort of people that I hated.

What was the problem with session work?

Page: Certain sessions were really a pleasure to do, but the problem was that you never knew what you were gonna do. You might have heard that I played on a Burt Bacharach record. It's true. I never knew what I was doing. You just got booked into a particular studio at the hours of two and five-thirty. Sometimes it would be somebody you were happy to see, other times it was, "What am I doing here?"

When I started doing sessions, the guitar was in vogue. I was playing solos every day. Then afterwards, when the Stax thing was going on and you got whole brass sections coming in, I ended up hardly playing anything, just a little riff here and there . . . no solos. And I remember one particular occasion when I hadn't played a solo for, quite literally, a couple of months. And I was asked to play a solo on a rock & roll thing. I played it and felt that what I'd done was absolute crap. I was so disgusted with myself that I made my mind up that I had to get out of it. It was messing me right up.

And how do you look back on your days with the Yardbirds?

Page: I have really good memories. Apart from one tour which nearly killed all of us, it was so intense—apart from that, musically it was a great group to play in. I've never regretted anything I've ever done. Any musician would have jumped at the chance to play in that band. It was particularly good when Jeff and I were both doing lead guitar. It really could have been built into something exceptional at that point, but unfortunately there's precious little on wax of that particular point. There's only "Stroll On" from the *Blow-Up* film—that was quite funny—and "Happenings Ten Years Time Ago" and "Daisy." We just didn't get into the studio too much at that time.

Obviously, there were ups and downs. Everybody wants to know about the feuds and personality conflicts. . . . I don't think that it ever got *really* evil. It never got that bad. If it was presented in the right way, maybe a Yardbirds reunion album would be a good thing to do someday. Somehow I can't see Jeff doing it, though. He's a funny bloke.

You live in Aleister Crowley's home. [Crowley was a poet and magician at the turn of the century and was notorious for his Black Magic rites— Ed.]

Page: Yes, it was owned by Aleister Crowley. But there were two or three owners before Crowley moved into it. It was also a church that was burned to the ground with the congregation in it. And that's the site of the house. Strange things have happened in that house that had nothing to do with Crowley. The bad vibes were already there. A man was beheaded there, and sometimes you can hear his head rolling down. I haven't actually heard it, but a friend of mine, who is extremely straight and doesn't know anything about anything like that at all, heard it. He thought it was the cats bungling about. I wasn't there at the time, but he told the help, "Why don't you let the cats out at night? They make a terrible racket, rolling about in the halls." And they said, "The cats are locked in a room every night." Then they told him the story of the house. So that sort of thing was there before Crowley got there. Of course, after Crowley there have been suicides, people carted off to mental hospitals. . . .

And you have no contact with any of the spirits?

Page: I didn't say that. I just said I didn't hear the head roll.

What's your attraction to the place?

Page: The unknown. I'm attracted by the unknown, but I take precautions. I don't go walking into things blind.

Do you feel safe in the house?

Page: Yeah. Well, all my houses are isolated. Many is the time I just stay home alone. I spend a lot of time near water. Crowley's house is in Loch Ness, Scotland. I have another house in Sussex, where I spend most of my time. It's quite near London. It's moated and terraces off into lakes. I mean, I could tell you things, but it might give people ideas. A few things have happened that would freak some people out, but I was surprised actually at how composed I was. I don't really want to go on about my personal beliefs or my involvement in magic. I'm not trying to do a Harrison or a Townshend. I'm not interested in turning anybody on to anybody that I'm turned on to . . . if people want to find things, they find them themselves. I'm a firm believer in that.

What did you think about your portrayal in 'Rock Dreams'? As a guitar Mafioso along with Alvin Lee, Jeff Beck, Pete Townshend and Eric Clapton?

Page: There's nothing about Zeppelin in there at all. The artist spends his whole time masturbating over the Stones in that book, doesn't he? The Stones in drag and things like that. When I first saw that book, I thought, aw, this is really great. But when I really started to look at it, there were things that I just didn't like. People can laugh at this, but I didn't like to see a picture of Ray Charles driving around in the car with his arm around a chick. It's tasteless. But the guy's *French,* so what can we say? Ray Charles is blind. What kind of humor is that? They may be his rock dreams, but they sure aren't mine.

Out of all the guitarists to come out of the Sixties, though, Beck, Clapton, Lee, Townshend and I are still having a go. That says something. Beck, Clapton and me were sort of the Richmond/Croydon type clan, and Alvin Lee. I don't know where he came from. Leicester, or something like that. So he was never in with it a lot. And Townshend, Townshend was from Middlesex, and he used to go down to the clubs and watch the other guitarists. I didn't meet him, though, until "I Can't Explain." I was doing the session guitar work on that. I haven't seen Townshend in years. But I suppose we've all kept going and tried to do better and better and better. I heard some stuff from Beck's solo LP recently that was fucking brilliant. Really good. But I don't know, it's all instrumental and it's a guitarist's guitar LP, I think. He's very mellow, and Beck at his best can be very tasty.

Have you seen Eric Clapton with his new band?

Page: Oh, Eric. Fucking hell, Eric. Yes, I saw him with his new band and also at his Rainbow concert. At least at the Rainbow he had some people with some balls with him. He had Townshend and Ronnie Wood and Jimmy Karstein and [Jim] Capaldi. "Pearly Queen" was incredible. And I would have thought that after that, he would have said, "Right, I'm gonna get English musicians." Ever since he's been with American musicians, he's laid back further and further.

I went over to see him after he'd done his Rainbow concert, and it wasn't hard to sense his total disappointment that Derek and the Dominoes were never really accepted. It must have been a big thing for him that they didn't get all the acclaim that the Cream did. But the thing is, when a band has a certain chemistry, like the Cream had . . . wow, the chances of re-creating

317

that again are how many billion to one. It's very, very difficult.

The key to Zeppelin's longevity has been change. We put out our first LP; then a second one that was nothing like the first, then a third LP totally different from them, and on it went. I know why we got a lot of bad press on our albums. People couldn't understand, a lot of reviewers couldn't understand why we put out an LP like *Zeppelin II,* then followed it up with *III* with "That's the Way" and acoustic numbers like that on it. They just couldn't understand it. The fact was that Robert and I had gone away to Bron-Y-Aur cottage in Wales and started writing songs. Christ, that was the material we had, so we used it. It was nothing like, "We got to do some heavy rock & roll because that's what our image demands. . . ." Album-wise, it usually takes a year for people to catch up with what we're doing.

W HY DID YOU GO TO BRON-Y-
Aur cottage for the third album?
Plant: It was time to step back, take stock and not get lost in it all. Zeppelin was starting to get very big, and we wanted the rest of our journey to take a pretty level course. Hence, the trip into the mountains and the beginning of the ethereal Page and Plant. I thought we'd be able to get a little peace and quiet and get your actual Californian, Marin County blues, which we managed to do in Wales rather than San Francisco. It was a great place.

"The Golden Breast" is what the name means. The place is in a little valley, and the sun always moves across it. There's even a track on the new album, a little acoustic thing, that Jimmy got together up there. It typifies the days when we used to chug around the countryside in jeeps.

It was a good idea to go there. We had written quite a bit of the second album on the road. It was a real road album, too. No matter what the critics said, the proof in the pudding was that it got a lot of people off. The reviewer for ROLLING STONE, for instance, was just a frustrated musician. Maybe I'm just flying my own little ego ship, but sometimes people resent talent. I don't even remember what the criticism was, but as far as I'm concerned, it was a good, maybe even great, road album. The third album was the album of albums. If anybody had us labeled as a heavy metal group, that destroyed them.

But there were acoustic numbers on the very first album.

Page: That's it! There you go. When the third LP came out and got its reviews, Crosby, Stills and Nash had just formed. That LP had just come out, and because acoustic guitars had come to the forefront, all of a sudden: LED ZEPPELIN GO ACOUSTIC! I thought, Christ, where are their heads and ears? There were three acoustic songs on the first album and two on the second.

You talk of this "race against time," Jimmy. Where do you think you'll be at forty?

Page: I don't, know whether I'll reach forty. I don't know whether I'll reach thirty-five. I can't be sure about that. I am bloody serious. I am very, very serious. I didn't think I'd make thirty.

Why not?

Page: I just had this fear. Not fear of dying, but just . . . wait a minute, let's get this right. I just felt that . . . I wouldn't reach thirty. That's all there was to it. It was something in me, something inbred. I'm over thirty now, but I didn't expect to be here. I wasn't having nightmares about it, but . . . I'm not afraid of death. That is the greatest mystery of all. That'll be it, that one. But it *is* all a race against time. You never know what can happen. Like breaking my finger. I could have broken my whole hand and been out of action for two years.

You've been criticized for writing "dated flower-child gibberish" lyrics. . . .

Plant: How can anybody be a "dated flower-child"? The essence of the whole trip was the desire for peace and tranquillity and an idyllic situation. That's all anybody could ever want, so how could it be "dated flowerchild gibberish"? If it is, then I'll just carry on being a dated flower-child. I put a lot of work into my lyrics. Not all my stuff is meant to be scrutinized, though. Things like "Black Dog" are blatant let's-do-it-in-the-bath-type things, but they make their point just the same. People listen. Otherwise, you might as well sing the menu from the Continental Hyatt House.

How important was "Stairway to Heaven" to you?

Page: To me, I thought "Stairway" crystallized the essence of the band. It had everything there and showed the band at its best . . . as a band, as a unit. Not talking about solos or anything, it had everything there. We were careful never to release it as a single. It was a milestone for us. Every musician wants to do something of lasting quality, something which will hold up for a long time, and I guess we did it with "Stairway." Townshend probably thought that he got it with *Tommy.* I don't know whether I have the ability to come up with more. I have to do a lot of hard work before I can get anywhere near those stages of consistent, total brilliance.

I don't think there are too many people who are capable of it. Maybe one. Joni Mitchell. That's the music that I play at home all the time, Joni Mitchell. *Court and Spark* I love because I'd always hoped that she'd work with a band. But the main thing with Joni is that she's able to look at something that's happened to her, draw back and crystallize the whole situation, then write about it. She brings tears to my eyes, what more can I say? It's bloody eerie. I can relate so much to what she says. "Now old friends are acting strange/They shake their heads/They say I've changed." I'd like to know how many of her original friends she's got. I'd like to know how many of the original friends any well-known musician has got. You'd be surprised. They think—particularly that thing of change—they all assume that you've changed. For the worse. There are very few people I can call real, close friends. They're very, very precious to me.

How about you?

Plant: I live with the people I've always lived with. I'm quite content. It's like the remnants of my old beatnik days. All my old mates, it lends to a lot of good company. There's no unusual reaction to my trip at all because I've known them so long. Now and again there will be the occasional joke about owing someone two dollars from the days in '63 when I was a broke blues singer with a washboard, but it's good. I'm happy.

Do you have any favorite American guitarists?

Page: Well, let's see, we've lost the best guitarist any of us ever had, and that was Hendrix. The other guitarist I started to get into died also, Clarence White. He was absolutely brilliant. Gosh. On a totally different style—the control, the guy who played on the Maria Muldaur single, "Midnight at the Oasis." Amos Garrett. He's Les Paul-oriented, and Les Paul is the one, really. We wouldn't be anywhere if he hadn't invented the electric guitar. Another one is Elliot Randall, the guy who guested on the first Steely Dan album. He's great. Band-wise, Little Feat is my favorite American group.

The only term I won't accept is "genius." The term "genius" gets used far too loosely in rock & roll. When you hear the melodic structures of what classical musicians put together and you compare it to that of a rock & roll record, there's a hell of a long way rock & roll has to go. There's a certain standard in classical music that allows the application of the term "genius," but you're treading on thin ice if you start applying it to rock & rollers. The way I see it, rock & roll is folk music. Street music. It isn't taught in school. It has to be picked up. You don't find geniuses in street musicians, but that doesn't mean to say you can't be really good. You get as much out of rock & roll artistically as you put into it. There's nobody who can teach you. You're on your own, and that's what I find so fascinating about it.

Last question. What did you think about President Ford's children naming Led Zeppelin as their favorite group on national television?

Plant: I think it's really a mean deal that we haven't been invited around there for tea. Perhaps Jerry thought we'd wreck the joint. Now if we'd had a publicist *three* tours back, he might be on the road with us now. I was pleased to hear that they like our music around the White House. It's good to know they've got taste.

Final comments?

Page: Just say that I'm still searching for an angel with a broken wing. It's not very easy to find them these days. Especially when you're staying at the Plaza Hotel.

27

INTERVIEWED BY CAMERON CROWE (1975)

When he got his first story into ROLLING STONE in 1973, Cameron Crowe was a sixteen-year-old from San Diego with a gift for setting his subjects at ease with his humor, then drawing them out with fresh, perceptive and pointed questions.

Crowe was freelancing for ROLLING STONE in 1975 when he landed the Neil Young interview,

and for his coup, he was placed on staff and onto the magazine's masthead. Young had shied away from the press for years; now he had an eccentric album out *{Tonight's the Night}* that he thought he should explain. As things turned out, "Neil was very easy to talk to," Crowe remembers. "I ran out of tapes, and he gave me cassettes which he'd be using to record alternate versions of his songs. So I have these tapes that have the names of songs on them, but it's just him and me talking."

The interviews were done, Cameron says, "while cruising down Sunset Boulevard in a rented red Mercedes, and on the back porch of his Malibu beach house." At the end of the sessions, Young made only one request:

"Just keep one thing in mind: I may remember it all differently tomorrow."

—BF-T

NEIL YOUNG IS THE MOST ENIGMATIC of all the superstars to emerge from Buffalo Springfield and Crosby, Stills, Nash and Young. His often cryptic studies of lonely desperation and shaky-voiced antiheroics have led many to brand him a loner and a recluse. 'Harvest' was the last time that he struck the delicate balance between critical and commercial acceptance, and his subsequent albums have grown increasingly inaccessible to a mass audience.

Young's first comprehensive interview comes at a seeming turning point in his life and career. After an amicable breakup with actress Carrie Snodgress, he's

YOUNG

moved from his Northern California ranch to the relative hustle and bustle of Malibu. In the words of a close friend, he seems "frisky . . . in an incredible mood." Young has unwound to the point where he can approach a story about his career as potentially "a lot of fun."

WHY IS IT THAT YOU'VE FI-*nally decided to talk now? For the past five years journalists requesting Neil Young interviews were told you had nothing to say.*

There's a lot I have to say. I never did interviews because they always got me in trouble. Always. They never came out right. I just don't like them. As a matter of fact, the more I didn't do them the more they wanted them; the more I said by not saying anything. But things change, you know. I feel very free now. I don't have an old lady anymore. I relate it a lot to that. I'm back living in Southern California. I feel more open than I have in a long while. I'm coming out and speaking to a lot of people. I feel like something new is happening in my life.

I'm really turned on by the new music I'm making now, back with Crazy Horse. Today, even as I'm talking, the songs are running through my head. I'm excited. I think everything I've done is valid or else I wouldn't have released it, but I do realize the last three albums have been a certain way. I know I've gotten a lot of bad publicity for them. Somehow I feel like I've surfaced out of some kind of murk. And the proof will be in my next album. *Tonight's the Night,* I would say, is the final chapter of a period I went through.

Why the murky period?

Oh, I don't know. Danny's death probably tripped it off. [Danny Whitten, leader of Crazy Horse and Young's rhythm guitarist/second vocalist.] It happened right before the *Time Fades Away* tour. He was supposed to be in the group. We [Ben Keith, steel guitar; Jack Nitzsche, piano; Tim Drummond, bass; Kenny Buttrey, drums; and Young] were rehearsing with him, and he just couldn't cut it. He couldn't remember anything. He was too out of it. Too far gone. I had to tell him to go back to L.A. "It's not happening, man. You're not together enough." He just said, "I've got nowhere else to go, man. How am I gonna tell my friends?" And he split. That *night* the coroner called me from L.A. and told me he'd ODed. That blew my mind. Fucking blew my mind. I loved Danny. I felt

responsible. And from there, I had to go right out on this huge tour of huge arenas. I was very nervous and . . . insecure.

Why, then, did you release a live album?

I thought it was valid. *Time Fades Away* was a very nervous album. And that's exactly where I was at on the tour. If you ever sat down and listened to all my records, there'd be a place for it in there. Not that you'd go there every time you wanted to enjoy some music, but if you're on the trip it's important. Every one of my records, to me, is like an ongoing autobiography. I can't write the same book every time. There are artists that can. They put out three or four albums every year, and everything fucking sounds the same. That's great. Somebody's trying to communicate to a lot of people and give them the kind of music that they know they want to hear. That isn't my trip. My trip is to express what's on my mind. I don't expect people to listen to my music all the time. Sometimes it's too intense. If you're gonna put a record on at 11:00 in the morning, don't put on *Tonight's the Night.* Put on the Doobie Brothers.

'Time Fades Away,' as the follow-up to 'Harvest,' could have been a huge album. . . .

If it had been commercial.

As it is, it's one of your lowest-selling solo albums. Did you realize what you were sacrificing at the time?

I probably did. I imagine I could have come up with the perfect follow-up album. A real winner. But it would have been something that everybody was expecting. And when it got there they would have thought that they understood what I was all about, and that would have been it for me. I would have painted myself in the corner. The fact is I'm not that lone, laid-back figure with a guitar. I'm just not that way anymore. I don't want to feel like people expect me to be a certain way. Nobody expected *Time Fades Away,* and I'm not sorry I put it out. I didn't need the money, I didn't need the fame. You gotta keep changing. Shirts, old ladies, whatever. I'd rather keep changing and lose a lot of people along the way. If that's the price, I'll pay it. I don't give a shit if my audience is a hundred or a hundred million. It doesn't make any difference to me. I'm convinced that what sells and what I do are two completely different things. If they meet, it's coincidence. I just appreciate the freedom to put out an album like *Tonight's the Night* if I want to.

You sound pretty drunk on that album.

I would have to say that's the most liquid album I've ever made *{laughs}.* You almost need a life preserver to get through that one. We were all leaning on the ol' cactus . . . and, again, I think that it's something people should hear. They should hear what the artist sounds like under all circumstances if they want to get a complete portrait. Everybody gets fucked up, man. Everybody gets fucked up sooner or later. You're just pretending if you don't let your music get just as liquid as you are when you're really high.

Is that the point of the album?

No. No. That's the means to an end. *Tonight's the Night* is like an OD letter. The whole thing is about life, dope and death. When we [Nils Lofgren, guitars and piano; Talbot, Molina and Young] played that music we were all thinking of Danny Whitten and Bruce Berry, two close members of our unit lost to junk overdoses. The *Tonight's the Night* sessions were the first time what was left of Crazy Horse had gotten together since Danny died. It was up to us to get the strength together among us to fill the hole he left. The other OD, Bruce Berry, was CSNY's roadie for a long time. His brother Ken runs Studio Instrument Rentals, where we recorded the album. So we had a lot of vibes going for us. There was a lot of spirit in the music we made. It's funny, I remember the whole experience in black and white. We'd go down to S.I.R. about 5:00 in the afternoon and start getting high, drinking tequila and playing pool. About midnight, we'd start playing. And we played Bruce and Danny on their way all through the night. I'm not a junkie, and I won't even try it out to check out what it's like . . . but we all got high enough, right out there on the edge where we felt wide open to the whole mood. It was spooky. I probably *feel* this album more than anything else I've ever done.

Why did you wait until now to release 'Tonight's the Night'? Isn't it almost two years old?

I never finished it. I only had nine songs, so I set the whole thing aside and did *On the Beach* instead. It took Elliot [manager Elliot Roberts] to finish *Tonight's the Night.* You see, a while back there were some people who were gonna make a Broadway show out of the story of Bruce Berry and everything. They even had a script written. We were putting together a tape for them, and in the process of listening back on the old tracks, Elliot found three even older songs that related to the trip, "Lookout Joe," "Borrowed Tune" and "Come on Baby Let's Go Downtown," a live track from when I played the Fillmore East with Crazy Horse. Danny even sings lead on that one. Elliot added those songs to the original nine and sequenced them all into a cohesive story. But I still had no plans whatsoever to release it. I already had another new album called *Homegrown* in the can. The cover was finished and everything *{laughs}.* Ah, but they'll never hear that one.

Okay. Why not?

I'll tell you the whole story. I had a playback party for *Homegrown* for me and about ten friends. We were out of our minds. We all listened to the album, and *Tonight's the Night* happened to be on the same reel. So we listened to that, too, just for laughs. No comparison.

So you released 'Tonight's the Night.' Just like that?

Not because *Homegrown* wasn't as good. A lot of people would probably say that it's better. I know the first time I listened back on *Tonight's the Night,* it was the most out-of-tune thing I'd ever heard. Everyone's off-key. I couldn't hack it. But by listening to those two albums back to back at the party, I started to see the weaknesses in *Homegrown.* I took *Tonight's the Night* because of its overall strength in performance and feeling. The theme may be a little depressing, but the general feeling is much more elevating than *Homegrown.* Putting this album out is almost an experiment. I fully expect some of the most determinedly worst reviews I've ever had. I mean, if anybody really wanted to let go, they could do it on this one. And undoubtedly a few people will. That's good for them, though. I like to see people make giant breakthroughs for themselves. It's good for their psyche to get it all off their chests *{laughs}.* I've seen *Tonight's the Night* draw a line everywhere it's been played. People who thought they would never dislike anything I did fall on the other side of the line. Others who thought, "I can't listen to that cat. He's just too sad," or whatever . . . "His voice is funny." They listen another way now.

Y OU DIDN'T COME FROM A MUSI- *cal family. . . .*

Well, my father played a little ukulele *{laughs}.* It just happened. I felt it. I couldn't stop thinking about it. All of a sudden I wanted a guitar, and that was it. I started playing around the Winnipeg community clubs, high school dances. I played as much as I could.

With a band?

Oh, yeah, always with a band. I never tried it solo until I was nineteen. Eighteen or nineteen.

Were you writing at the time?

I started off writing instrumentals. Words came much later. My idol at the time was Hank B. Marvin, Cliff Richard's guitar player in the Shadows. He was the hero of all the guitar players around Winnipeg at the time. Randy Bachman, too; he was around then, playing the same circuit. He had a great sound. Used to use a tape repeat.

When did you start singing?

I remember singing Beatles tunes . . . the first song I ever sang in front of people was "It Won't Be Long" and then "Money (That's What I Want)." That was in the Calvin High School cafeteria. My big moment.

How much different from the States was growing up in Canada?

Everybody in Canada wants to get to the States. At least they did then. I couldn't wait to get out of there because I knew my only chance to be heard was in the States. But I couldn't get down there without a working permit, and I didn't have one. So eventually I just came down illegally, and it took until 1970 for me to get a green card. I worked illegally during all of the Buffalo Springfield and some of Crosby, Stills, Nash and Young. I didn't have any papers. I couldn't get a card because I would be replacing an American musician in the union. You had to be real well known and irreplaceable and a separate entity by yourself. So I got the card after I got that kind of stature—which you can't get without fucking being here . . . the whole thing is ridiculous. The only way to get in is to be here. You can't be here unless it's all right for you to be here. So fuck it. It's like "throw the witch in the water, and if it drowns it wasn't a witch. If it comes up, it is a witch, and then you kill it." Same logic. But we finally got it together.

Did you know Joni Mitchell in those days?

I've known Joni since I was eighteen. I met her in one of the coffeehouses. She was beautiful. That was my first impression. She was real frail and wispy-looking. And her cheekbones were so beautifully shaped. She'd always wear light satins and silks. I remember thinking that if you blew hard enough, you could probably knock her over. She could hold up a Martin D18 pretty well, though. What an incredible talent she is. She writes about her relationships so much more vividly than I do. I use . . . I guess I put more of a veil over what I'm talking about. I've written a few songs that were as stark as hers. Songs like "Pardon My Heart," "Home Fires," "Love Art Blues" . . . almost all of *Homegrown*. I've never released any of those. And I probably never will.

I think I'd be too embarrassed to put them out. They're a little *too* real.

How do you look back on the whole Buffalo Springfield experience?

Great experience. Those were really good days. Great people. Everybody in that group was a fucking genius at what they did. That was a great group, man. There'll never be another Buffalo Springfield. Never. Everybody's gone such separate ways now, I don't know. If everybody showed up in one place at one time with all the amps and everything, I'd love it. But I'd sure as hell hate to have to get it together. I'd love to play with that band again, just to see if the buzz was still there.

There's a few stock Springfield myths I should ask you about. How about the old hearse story?

True. Bruce Palmer and I were tooling around L.A. in my hearse. I loved the hearse. Six people could be getting high in the front and back, and nobody would be able to see in because of the curtains. The heater was great. And the tray . . . the tray was dynamite. You open the side door, and the tray whips right out onto the sidewalk. What could be cooler than that? What a way to make your entrance. Pull up to a gig and just wheel out all your stuff on the tray. Anyway, Bruce Palmer and I were taking in California. The Promised Land. We were heading up to San Francisco. Stephen and Richie Furay, who were in town putting together a band, just happened to be driving around, too. Stephen Stills had met me before and remembered I had a hearse. As soon as he saw the Ontario plates, he knew it was me. So they stopped us. I was happy to see fucking *anybody* I knew. And it seemed very logical to us that we form a band. We picked up Dewey Martin for the drums, which was my idea, four or five days later. Stephen was really pulling for Billy Munday at the time. He's say, "Yeah, yeah, yeah. Dewey's good, but *Jesus* . . . he talks too fucking much." I was right, though. Dewey was fucking good.

How much has the friction between you and Stills been beneficial over the years?

I think people really have that friction business out of hand. Stephen and I just play really good together. People can't comprehend that we both can play lead guitar in the band and not fight over it. We have total respect for musicianship, and we both bring out the perfectionist in each other. We're both very intense, but that's part of our relationship. We both enjoy that. It's part of doing what we do. In that respect, being at loggerheads has worked to our advantage. Stephen Stills and I have made some incredible music with each other. Especially in the Springfield. We were young. We had a lot of energy.

Why did you leave the band?

I just couldn't handle it toward the end. My nerves couldn't handle the trip. It wasn't me scheming on a solo career, it wasn't anything but my nerves. Everything started to go too fucking fast, I can tell that now. I was going crazy, you know, joining and quitting, and joining again. I began to feel like I didn't have to answer or obey anyone. I needed more space. That was a big problem in my head. So I'd quit, then I'd come back 'cause it sounded so good. It was a constant problem. I just wasn't mature enough to deal with it. I was very young. We were getting the shaft from every angle, and it seemed like we were trying to make it so bad and were getting nowhere. The following we had in the beginning, and those people know who they are, was a real special thing. It gave all of us, I think, the strength to do what we've done. With the *intensity* that we've been able to do it. Those few people who were there in the very beginning.

Last Springfield question. Are there, in fact, several albums of unreleased material?

I've got all of that. I've got those tapes.

Why have you sat on them for so long? What are you waiting for?

I'll wait until I hear from some of the other guys. See if anybody else has any tapes. I don't know if Richie [Furay] or Dicky Davis [Springfield road manager] has anything. I've got good stuff. Great songs. "My Kind of Love," "My Angel," "Down to the Wire," "Baby Don't Scold Me." We'll see what happens.

What was your life like after the Springfield?

It was all right. I needed to get out to the sticks for a while and just relax. I headed for Topanga Canyon and got myself together. I bought a big house that overlooked the whole canyon. I eventually got out of that house because I couldn't handle all the people who kept coming up all the time. Sure was a comfortable fucking place . . . that was '69, about when I started living with my first wife, Susan. Beautiful woman.

Was your first solo album a love song for her?

No. Very few of my albums are love songs to anyone. Music is so big, man, it just takes up a lot of room. I've dedicated my life to my music so far. And every time I've let it slip and gotten somewhere else, it's showed. Music lasts . . . a lot longer than relationships do. My first album was very much a first album. I wanted to prove to myself that I could do it. And I did, thanks to the wonder of modern machinery. That first

album was overdub city. It's still one of my favorites, though. *Everybody Knows This Is Nowhere* is probably my best. It's my favorite one. I've always loved Crazy Horse from the first time I heard the Rockets album on White Whale. The original band we had in '69 and '70—Molina, Talbot, Whitten and me. That was *wonderful.* And it's back that way again now. Everything I've ever done with Crazy Horse has been incredible. Just for the *feeling,* if nothing else.

Why did you join CSNY, then? You were already working steadily with Crazy Horse.

Stephen. I love playing with the other guys, but playing with Stephen is special. David is an excellent rhythm guitarist, and Graham sings so great . . . shit, I don't have to tell anybody those guys are phenomenal. I knew it would be fun. I didn't have to be out front. I could lay back. It didn't have to be me all the time. They were a big group, and it was easy for me. I could still work double time with Crazy Horse. With CSNY, I was basically just an instrumentalist that sang a couple of songs with them. It was easy. And the music was great. CSNY, I think, has always been a lot bigger thing to everybody else than it is to us. People always refer to me as Neil Young of CSNY, right? It's not my main trip. It's something that I do every once in a while. I've constantly been working on my own trip all along. And now that Crazy Horse is back in shape, I'm even more self-involved.

How much of your own solo success, though, was due to CSNY?

For sure CSNY put my name out there. They gave me a lot of publicity. But, in all modesty, *After the Gold Rush,* which was kind of the turning point, was a strong album. I really think it was. A lot of hard work went into it. Everything was there. The picture it painted was a strong one. *After the Gold Rush* was the spirit of Topanga Canyon. It seemed like I realized that I'd gotten somewhere. I joined CSNY and was still working a lot with Crazy Horse . . . I was playing all the time. And having a great time. Right after that album, I left the house. It was a good coda.

How did you cope with your first real blast of superstardom after that?

The first thing I did was a long tour of small halls. Just me and a guitar. I loved it. It was real personal. Very much a one-on-one thing with the crowd. It was later, after *Harvest,* that I hid myself away. I tried to stay away from it all. I thought the record *[Harvest]* was good, but I also knew that something else was dying. I became very reclusive. I didn't want to come out much.

325

Why? Were you depressed? Scared?

I think I was pretty happy. In spite of everything, I had my old lady and moved to the ranch. A lot of it was my back. I was in and out of hospitals for the two years between *After the Gold Rush* and *Harvest*. I have one weak side, and all the muscles slipped on me. My discs slipped. I couldn't hold my guitar up. That's why I sat down on my whole solo tour. I couldn't move around too well, so I laid low for a long time on the ranch and just didn't have any contact, you know. I wore a brace. Crosby would come up to see how I was; we'd go for a walk, and it took me 45 minutes to get to the studio, which is only 400 yards from the house. I could only stand up four hours a day. I recorded most of *Harvest* in the brace. That's a lot of the reason it's such a mellow album. I couldn't physically play an electric guitar. "Are You Ready for the Country," "Alabama" and "Words" were all done after I had the operation. The doctors were starting to talk about wheelchairs and shit, so I had some discs removed. But for the most part, I spent two years flat on my back. I had a lot of time to think about what had happened to me.

Have you ever been in analysis?

You mean have I ever been to a psychiatrist? No *{laughs}*. They're all real interested in me, though. They always ask a lot of questions when I'm around them.

What do they ask?

Well, I had some seizures. They used to ask me a lot of questions about how I felt, stuff like that. I told them all the thoughts I have and the images I see if I, you know, faint or fall down or something. That's not real important, though.

Do you still have seizures?

Yeah, I still do. I wish I didn't. I thought I had it licked.

Is it a physical or mental . . .

I don't know. Epilepsy is something nobody knows much about. It's just part of me. Part of my head, part of what's happening in there. Sometimes something in my brain triggers it off. Sometimes when I get really high, it's a very psychedelic experience to have a seizure. You slip into some other world. Your body's flapping around and you're biting your tongue and batting your head on the ground, but your mind is off somewhere else. The only scary thing about it is not going or being there; it's realizing you're totally comfortable in this . . . *void.* And that shocks you back into reality. It's a very disorienting experience. It's difficult to get a grip on yourself. The last time it happened, it took about an hour and a half of just walking around the ranch with two of my friends to get it together.

Has it ever happened onstage?

No. Never has. I felt like it was a couple times, and I've always left the stage. I get too high or something. It's just pressure from around, you know. That's why I don't like crowds too much.

What were the sessions like for 'Déjà Vu'? Was it a band effort?

The band sessions on that record were "Helpless," "Woodstock" and "Almost Cut My Hair." That was Crosby, Stills, Nash and Young. All the other ones were combinations, records that were more done by one person using the other people. "Woodstock" was a *great* record at first. It was a great live record, man. Everyone played and sang at once. Stephen sang the shit out of it. The track was magic. Then, later on, they were in the studio for a long time and started nit-picking. Sure enough, Stephen erased the vocal and put another one on that wasn't nearly as incredible. They did a lot of things over again that I thought were more raw and vital-sounding. But that's all personal taste. I'm only saying that because it might be interesting to some people how we put that album together. I'm happy with every one of the things I've recorded for them. They turned out really fine. I certainly don't hold any grudges.

You seem a bit defensive.

Well, everybody always concentrates on this whole thing that we fight all the time among each other. That's a load of shit. They don't know what the fuck they're talking about. It's all rumors. When the four of us are together, it's real intense. When you're dealing with any four totally different people who all have ideas on how to do one thing, it gets steamy. And we love it, man. We're having a great time. People make up so much shit, though. I've read so much gossip in ROLLING STONE alone . . . Ann Landers would blanch. It would surprise you. Somehow we've gotten on this social-register level, and it has nothing to do with what we're trying to put out. The music press writes the weirdest shit about us. They're just wasting their fucking time.

WHY DID YOU MAKE A MOVIE, Journey Through the Past? It was something that I wanted to do. The music, which has been and always will be my primary thing, just seemed to *point* that way. I wanted to express a visual picture of what I was singing about.

One critic wrote that the movie's theme was "life is pointless."

Maybe that's what the guy got out of it. I just made a feeling. It's hard to say what the movie means. I think it's a good film for a first film. I think it's a really good film. I don't think I was trying to say that life is pointless. It does lay a lot of shit on people, though. It wasn't made for entertainment. I'll admit, I made it for myself. Whatever it is, that's the way I felt. I made it for me. I never even had a script.

Did the bad reviews surprise you at all?

Of course not. The film community doesn't want to see me in there. What do they want with *Journey through the Past {laughs}?* It's got no plot. No point. No stars. They don't want to see that. But the next time, man, we'll get them. The next time. I've got all the equipment, all the ideas and motivation to make another picture. I've even been keeping my chops up as a cameraman by being on hire under the name of Bernard Shakey. I filmed a Hyatt House commercial not too long ago. I'm set *{laughs}*. I'm just waiting for the right time.

Why did you leave the ranch?

It just got to be too big of a trip. There was too much going on the last couple of years. None of it had anything to do with music. I just had too many fucking people hanging around who don't really know me. They were parasites, whether they intended to be or not. They lived off me, used my money to buy things, used my telephone to make their calls. General leeching. It hurt my feelings a lot when I reached that realization. I didn't want to believe I was being taken advantage of. I didn't like having to be boss, and I don't like having to say, "Get the fuck out." That's why I have different houses now. When people gather around me, I just split now. I mean, my ranch is more beautiful and lasting than ever. It's strong without me. I just don't feel like it's the only place I can be and be safe anymore. I feel much stronger now.

Have you got a name for the new album?

I think I'll call it *My Old Neighborhood.* Either that or *Ride My Llama.* It's weird, I've got all these songs about Peru, the Aztecs and the Incas. Time travel stuff. We've got one song called "Marlon Brando, John Ehrlichman, Pocahontas and Me." I'm playing a lot of electric guitar, and that's what I like best. Two guitars, bass and drums. And it's really flying off the ground, too. Fucking unbelievable. I've got a bet with Elliot that it'll be out before the end of September. After that we'll probably go out on a fall tour of 3000 seaters. Me and Crazy Horse again. I couldn't be happier. That, combined with the bachelor life . . . I feel magnificent. Now is the first time I can remember coming out of a relationship, definitely not wanting to get into another one. I'm just not looking. I'm so happy with the space I'm in right now. It's like spring *{laughs}*. I'll sell you two bottles of it for $1.50.

28

INTERVIEWED BY JONATHAN COTT (1978)

Ten years after Jonathan Cott's first interview experience, with Mick Jagger the subject, the Rolling Stones went on with the albums *Let It Bleed, Get Yer Ya-Ya's Out* and then, on their own Rolling Stones label beginning in 1971, *Sticky Fingers, Exile on Main Street, Goat's Head Soup, It's Only Rock 'n' Roll, Made in the Shade* and *Black and Blue.*

They'd weathered Altamont and the death of original member Brian Jones; through their tours, their music and their times, they'd been crowned the world's greatest rock & roll band.

But for a while, Cott had stopped listening—he found something missing in their music.

Then, in 1978, quite by coincidence, he heard the initial tapes of the album, *Some Girls.* "I was in Paris," he recalls, "in February, at a friend's apartment. And suddenly Earl McGrath (president of Rolling Stones Records) walked in. My friend knew the Stones people—and it turned out that Jagger was next door—and they had a demo. Jagger said they'd be happy to let me hear it, and it knocked me out. I think we talked right then about doing an interview, and he said OK right away."

—BF-T

A certain prudent man,
when he felt himself to be in love,
hung a little bell round his neck
to caution women that he was danger-
ous. Unfortunately for themselves
they took too much notice of it;
and he suffered accordingly.

—A. R. ORAGE

I'VE BEEN MISSING THE ROLLING STONES for years—ever since they released 'Exile on Main Street,' as a matter of fact. Of course, I've seen them on their occasional concert tours—which have become more

MICK

JAGGER

and more circuslike—and enjoyed a number of their mid-Seventies songs ("Star Star," "If You Really Want to Be My Friend," "Time Waits for No One," "Fool to Cry," "Memory Motel"). But during their post-'Exile' period, the Stones seem to have been around more in body than in spirit.

In their original Sixties incarnation, the Rolling Stones presented an eerie quality that combined the hustling menace of the spiv, the coolness of the dandy and the unpredictable amorality and frivolity of the Greek gods. And in such a guise, they exuberantly took on the role of devil's advocate for what was beginning to be thought of as the Love Generation—ridiculing the vices and hypocrisies of family and social life in songs like "19th Nervous Breakdown" and "Mother's Little Helper" ("Doctor, please/Some more of these/Outside the door/She took four more"). But the Stones didn't stop there. As seemingly unassimilable voices of disengagement, they attacked the vice of the spirit of society itself in such songs as "Sympathy for the Devil" and "2000 Man" ("Oh, daddy, is your brain still flashing/Like it did when you were young?/Or did you come down crashing/Seeing all the things you done?/Oh, it's a big put-on").

As spoken and sung by their shining and narcissistic knight, Mick Jagger, the Rolling Stones—as I once wrote—presented themselves as beings of exalted indifference, innocent malice, careless cruelty. It was these ambiguous mixtures of emotions that one found in such songs as "Play with Fire," "Back Street Girl" and "Star Star"—a mixture revealing the disturbing yet fascinating quality of a child grown up too soon, like a six-year-old dragging on a cigarette. And it was this "child" who dangerously explored the ever-lurking but disapproved world of sex and drugs in such songs as "Under My Thumb," "Sister Morphine" and "Monkey Man."

Yet when the Stones were at their most exploitative, they seemed their most liberating, because we became aware of the reversal of that social and psychological pathology by which the oppressed identify with their oppressors: we sensed that the Stones, from their position of indifferent power, were singing in the voice of the hurt and abused, thereby magically transcending all humiliating barriers ("But it's all right now/In fact it's a gas").

It is exactly this kind of playful yet powerful ambiguity that I have missed in the Stones' work during the recent, musically dispiriting past few years. But now we have 'Some Girls'—an album that draws on, in a remarkably unhackneyed way, the Stones' love for blues, the Motown sound, for country music and Chuck Berry, and that combines and transforms these elements into the group's most energized, focused, outrageous and original record since the days of 'Between the Buttons,' 'Beggar's Banquet,' 'Let It

Bleed' and 'Exile on Main Street.' And it is an album that thematically crystallizes the Stones' perennial obsession with "some girls"—both real and imaginary.

After years of standing in the shadows, the soul survivors are back on their own, with no direction home, sounding just like . . . the Rolling Stones.

The following interview with Mick Jagger took place during two evenings in late April and early May at Rolling Stones Records in New York

---

Y OU'VE BEEN A ROLLING STONE *for about fifteen years. how does it feel?* What a funny question! It's a long time, maybe too long. Maybe it's time to restart a cycle—yeah, restart a five-year cycle.

The Rolling Stones and the Who are two of the last Sixties English rock groups that are still together.

I think both groups are very fragile.

There are rumors that the Rolling Stones will break up very soon.

That's rubbish. They said it in 1969, too. They say it all the time. Both groups are fragile because they've got problems of various kinds. The Who's are different from ours. In our case, if Keith [Richards] gets put into prison, it makes the future of our band a bit shaky. I mean, he goes on trial October 21st, and you know what the charge is: peddling heroin, which is punishable by life imprisonment.

Maybe we can start talking about "Miss You," which you've released in three versions: a 45 disc, an LP track and a twelve-minute version, on which there's a fantastic harmonica solo by a guy named Sugar Blue, who plays like a snake charmer.

Yeah, Sandy Whitelaw discovered him playing in the Paris Métro. He's a blues harpist from America, and he plays not only in the subway but in a club called La Vielle Grille. He's a very strange and talented musician.

The lines in the song about being called up at midnight by friends wanting to drag you out to a party remind me of "Get Off of My Cloud."

I've a limited number of ideas {laughing}.

And I like the line, "You've been the star in all my dreams."

Dreams are like movies, in a way. Or movies are like dreams.

You once sang: "I only get my rocks off while I'm dreaming."

I don't dream more than anybody else. But dreams are a great inspiration for the lowliest rock & roll writer to the greatest playwrights.

Chaucer was a great one for dreams. He was a great one for explaining them and making fun of the astrological explanations. He used to take the piss out of most of them, but some of them he took seriously. Shakespeare, too, knew a lot about early English witchcraft and religion, and Chaucer had some sort of similar knowledge. Today we have psychiatrists to interpret dreams.

Have you ever been to one?

Never, not once. I've read a lot of Jung, and I would have gone to see him because he was interesting, do you know what I mean? . . . Anyway, dreams are very important, and I get good ideas from them. I don't jot them down, I just remember them—the experiences of them—they're so different from everyday experiences. But the line in "Rocks Off" is really a joke.

How about the beautiful line, "I'm hiding sister and I'm dreaming," from "Moonlight Mile"?

Yeah, that's a dream song. Those kinds of songs with kinds of dreamy sounds are fun to do, but not all the time—it's nice to come back to reality.

What about the girl with the faraway eyes on your new album ("Faraway Eyes")? The lines "And if you're downright disgusted and life ain't worth a dime/Get a girl with faraway eyes" make it sound as if this dreamy truck-stop girl from Bakersfield, California, is really real.

Yeah, she's real, she's a real girl.

Is she a girl you know?

Yeah, she's right across the room . . . a little bleary-eyed.

Well, there's no one else here except for that poster of a Japanese girl. Is that whom you mean?

Naw, she's not in a truck stop.

Right, she's standing under a parasol, in fact. . . . Let me have another glass of wine and maybe I'll see her, too {laughing}.

You know, when you drive through Bakersfield on a Sunday morning or Sunday evening—I did that about six months ago—all the country-music radio stations start broadcasting black gospel services live from L.A. And that's what the song refers to. But the song's really about driving alone, listening to the radio.

I sense a bit of a Gram Parsons feeling on "Faraway Eyes"—country music as transformed through his style, via Buck Owens.

I knew Gram quite well, and he was one of the few people who really helped me to sing country music—before that, Keith and I used to just copy it off records. I used to play piano with Gram, and on "Faraway Eyes" I'm playing piano, though Keith is actually playing the top part— we added it on after. But I wouldn't say this song was influenced specifically by Gram. That idea of country music played slightly tongue in cheek— Gram had that in "Drugstore Truck Drivin' Man," and we have that sardonic quality, too.

The title of your new album is the title of one of your most powerful and outrageous songs—"Some Girls"— and I wanted to ask you about some of the girls in your songs. Here are a few lines taken at random from several of your older albums: "Who's that woman on your arm/All dressed up to do you harm?" ("Let It Loose"); "Women think I'm tasty/But they're always trying to waste me" ("Tumbling Dice"); "But there is one thing I will never understand/Some of the sick things a girl does to a man" ("Sittin' on a Fence").

I didn't write all those lines, you know {laughing}.

All right, we'll reduce the charge. But obviously, in your songs of the mid-Sixties, you were at pains to accuse girls of being deceptive, cheating, greedy, vain, affected and stupid. It was a list of sins. Whether you were singing about rejecting the girl ("Out of Time," "Please Go Home") or about the girl rejecting you ("All Sold Out," "Congratulations") or about both ("High and Dry," "Under My Thumb"), almost all the songs from that period . . .

Most of those songs are really silly, they're pretty immature. But as far as the heart of what you're saying, I'd say . . . any bright girl would understand that if I were gay I'd say the same things about guys. Or if I were a girl I might say the same things about guys or other girls. I don't think any of the traits you mentioned are peculiar to girls. It's just about people. Deception, vanity . . . On the other hand sometimes I do say nice things about girls {laughing}.

Some of those other girls—"Ruby Tuesday," "Child of the Moon" or the girls in songs like "She's a Rainbow" and "Memory Motel"—are all very elusive and mystical.

Well, the girl in "Memory Motel" is actually a real, independent American girl. But they are mostly imaginary, you're right. . . . Actually, the girl in "Memory Motel" is a combination. So was the girl in "Faraway Eyes." Nearly all of the girls in my songs are combinations.

What about in "Till the Next Good-bye"?

No, she was real {laughing}, she was real . . . If you really want to know about the girls on the new album: "Some Girls" is all combinations. "Beast of Burden" is a combination. "Miss You" is an emotion, it's not really about *a* girl. To me, the feeling of longing is what the song is—I don't like to interpret my own fucking songs— but that's what it is.

On 'Some Girls,' it seems to me that you've taken all those "immature" feelings from the mid-Sixties and

331

really focused and concentrated them into powerful songs like "Lies," "Respectable" and especially "Some Girls," which is a kind of exorcism of all those girls you used to sing about.

Yeah, well . . . I really don't know why it came out like that {laughing}. There were so many other songs we cut . . . I guess we picked those because they hung together, lyrically and musically. They were all written over a short, recent period of time.

Let's see if I can get back to the question in a different way. You mentioned Jung, and it seems to me that your "dream" girls are like anima figures. Do you ever think in those terms?

My anima is very strong. . . . I think it's very kind. . . . What you're saying, though, is that there are two different types of girls in my songs: there's the beautiful dreamy type and the vicious bitch type. There are also one or two others, but, yeah, you're right—there are two kinds of girls . . . only I never thought about it before.

You don't have too many girls in your songs that share both qualities.

Ah, I see, I'm not integrating them properly. Maybe not. Maybe "Beast of Burden" is integrated slightly: I don't want a beast of burden, I don't want the kind of woman who's going to drudge for me. The song says: I don't need a beast of burden, and I'm not going to be your beast of burden, either. Any woman can see that that's like my saying that I don't want a woman to be on her knees for me. I mean, I get accused of being very antigirl, right?

Right.

But people really don't listen, they get it all wrong; they hear "Beast of Burden" and say, "Argggh!"

They sure heard "Under My Thumb" ("Under my thumb's a squirming dog who's just had her day").

That's going back to my teenage years!

Well, it's both a perverse and brilliant song about power and sex.

At the time there was no feminist criticism because there was no such thing, and one just wrote what one felt. Not that I let it hinder me too much now.

Did you hear about the dinner honoring Ahmet Ertegun [president of Atlantic Records]? Some feminists were giving out leaflets saying what terrible things he'd done {laughing}, saying that the Average White Band's new cover depicts a naked woman standing in a steaming bath of water, which could cause "enormous pain and possible death" {laughing}—things like that.

How about your woman-in-bondage poster for your 'Black and Blue' album? Many people may have a deep masochistic streak, but that poster and some of your songs certainly seem hung up on that.

Yeah, we had a lot of trouble with that particular poster. As far as the songs go, one talks about one's own experience a lot of the time. And you know, a lot of bright girls just take all of this with a pinch of salt. But there are a lot of women who are disgraceful, and if you just have the misfortune to have an affair with one of those . . . it's a personal thing.

And the "squirming dog" image?

Well, that was a joke. I've never felt in that position vis-à-vis a person—I'd never want to really hurt someone.

What about the groupies on the road ready for anything? What about "Star Star"?

Exactly! That's real, and if girls can do that, I can certainly write about it because it's what I see. I'm not saying all women are star fuckers, but I see an awful lot of them, and so I write a song called that. I mean, people show themselves up by their own behavior, and just to describe it doesn't mean you're antifeminist.

That bondage poster, though, was pretty blatant.

Well, there are a lot of girls into that, they dig it, they want to be chained up—and it's a thing that's true for both sexes.

But why use it to advertise a record?

I don't see why not. It's a valid piece of commercial art, just a picture.

Would you show yourself getting whipped and beaten?

Sure, if I thought it was more commercial than a beautiful girl!

People are obviously going to take a few of these songs on the new LP as being about your domestic situation.

Well, I actually mention "my wife" in "Respectable."

"Get out of my life, go take my wife—don't come back." And there's also: "You're a rag trade girl, you're the queen of porn/You're the easiest lay on the White House lawn."

Well, I just thought it was funny. "Respectable" really started off as a song in my head about how "respectable" we as a band were supposed to have become. "We're" so respectable. As I went along with the singing, I just made things up and fit things in. "Now we're respected in society. . . ." I really meant us. My wife's a very honest person, and the song's not "about" her.

But people will probably take this song, as well as the album, to be about you, in the same way they took 'Blood on the Tracks' to be about Dylan or John Lennon's "I don't believe in Beatles" song to be about him.

But it's very rock & roll. It's not like "Sara." "Respectable" is very lighthearted when you *hear* it. That's why I don't like divorcing the lyrics from the music. 'Cause when you actually hear it sung, it's not what is, it's the way we do it.

I'll let the existentialists debate that statement, but "Respectable" certainly does sound a lot like "Miss Amanda Jones."

Yeah, it's not that serious: "Get out of my life, go take my wife—don't come back" . . . it's not supposed to be taken seriously. If it were a ballad, if I sang it like: "Pleeese, taaake my wiiiiife"—you know what I mean?—well, it's not that, it's just a shit-kicking, rock & roll number.

I've heard you sing "Stray Cat Blues" and take those lightly malicious, flippant verses and turn them into a dark elegy—which was really unnerving and just the opposite of what you're saying here.

It's whatever works. "Respectable" is lighthearted. So is "Lies." We don't overemotionalize the way we sing them.

Keith Richards once said something to the effect that rock & roll really is subversive because the rhythms alter your being and perceptions. With your words and your rhythms, your stuff could do, and has done that, don't you think?

Rhythms are very important. But subvert what?

Well, Keith Richards' implication was that words could be used to lie, but that what the Stones did was just to let you see clearly the way things were. And that that vision—or so I inferred—was what was subversive.

Maybe Keith did mean that. Music is one of the things that changes society. That old idea of not letting white children listen to black music is *true*, 'cause if you want white children to remain what they are, they mustn't.

Look at what happened to you {laughing}.

Exactly! You get different attitudes to things . . . even the way you walk. . . .

And the way you talk.

Right, and the way you talk. Remember the Twenties when jazz in Europe changed a lot of things. People got more crazy, girls lifted up their dresses and cut their hair. People started to dance to that music, and it made profound changes in that society. . . . That sounds awfully serious!

To keep on the semiserious keel for a second, the song "Some Girls" seems to be about what happens when hundreds of idealized Twenties girls—like the ones drawn by Guy Peelaert on your 'It's Only Rock 'n' Roll' album—decide to come to life, and, like maenads, try to eat you up, destroy you—taking your

money and clothes and giving you babies you don't want.

Well, it could be a bad dream in a way. I had a dream like that last night, incidentally, but there were dogs as well as girls in it.

Maybe you can call your next album 'Some Dogs.'

{Laughing} I'd get in trouble with the antidog defamation league.

I wonder what the girls and women, of all races, in the audience are going to think of lines like: "Black girls just want to get fucked all night, I just don't have that much jam!" or "Chinese girls, they're so gentle—they're really such a tease."

I think they're all well covered—everyone's represented {laughing}. Most of the girls I've played the song to like "Some Girls." They think it's funny; black girlfriends of mine just laughed. And I think it's very complimentary about Chinese girls, I think they come off better than English girls. I really like girls an awful lot, and I don't think I'd say anything really nasty about any of them.

Are you running for president?

{Laughing} The song's supposed to be funny.

I couldn't help noticing that the way you sing lines like "Some girls they're so pure, some girls so corrupt" are perfect mimicries of Bob Dylan's phrasing and tone of voice during his 'Blonde on Blonde' period.

If that's how you think of it . . . yeah. Dylan's very easy to imitate. Sometimes I imitate Van Morrison, too, for laughs. That song is a kind of joke, too, but you haven't got it yet, so I'm not going to tell you.

The chorus of the song goes: "So give me all your money, give me all your gold/ I'll buy a house back at Zuma Beach and give you half of what I owe." Isn't Zuma Beach up in Malibu, near where Dylan lives?

Is it? . . . "Some Girls" isn't really about me.

"Some girls take my money, some girls take my clothes,/Some girls take the shirt off my back and leave me with a lethal dose." I wonder whom those lines are about?

No reply {laughing}. I made most of it up just off the bat. I made it up as I went along. I had another version of the song, but when it came to the take, I sang a completely different version— it was eleven minutes long—and then edited it down.

I remember that when I wrote it, it was very funny. 'Cause we were laughing, and the phone was ringing, and I was just sitting in the kitchen and it was just coming out . . . and I thought I could go on forever!

The first time I heard it, I started making up my own lyrics: "Green girls get me anxious/Blue girls get me sad/Brown girls get me silly/And red girls make me mad." It's like a kid's song.

{Laughing} That's why I said it wasn't serious, it's just anything that came to my head.

Do you remember the Beach Boys' "California Girls"?

Yeah, I love that song.

Well, it seems to me that instead of all the girls in your song being California girls, they've all turned into a different type of girl, and certainly from another state!

I know what you mean. I never thought of it like that. I never thought that a rock critic of your knowledge and background could ever come out with an observation like that {laughing}.

You mean it's pretentious?

Not at all. It's a great analogy. But like all analogies, it's false {laughing}.

On your 'It's Only Rock 'n' Roll' album you did a great version of the Temptations' "Ain't Too Proud to Beg," and now you're doing a version of "Imagination."

It's like a continuation, and I've always wanted to do that song—originally as a duet with Linda Ronstadt, believe it or not. But instead we just did our version of it—like an English rock & roll band tuning up on "Imagination," which has only two or three chords . . . it's real simple stuff.

I like the lines: "Soon we'll be married and raise a family/Two boys for you, what about two girls for me?" There are those girls in there again.

Yeah, I made that up. In reality the girl in the song doesn't even know me—it's a dream . . . and we're back where we started this conversation.

"Of all the girls in New York she loves me true" is one of the lines from your version of this song. And in fact the entire album is full of New York City settings and energy.

Yeah, I added the New York reference in the song. And the album itself is like that because I was staying in New York part of last year, and when I got to Paris and was writing the words, I was thinking about New York. I wrote the songs in Paris.

It's a real New York record.

Hope they like it in south Jersey {laughing}.

There's the gay garbage collector on Fifty-Third Street in "When the Whip Comes Down," Central Park in "Miss You," the sex and dreams and parties and the schmattas on Seventh Avenue in "Shattered"—and there's a distinct Lou Reed-cum-British vaudeville tone to some of your singing on "Shattered."

Every time I play guitar my engineer, Chris Kimsey, says: "Oh, here comes Lou Reed again." But I think a lot of English singers do that—

there's a kind of tradition, it's natural. In "Shattered," Keith and Woody [Ron Wood] put a riff down, and all we had was the word "shattered." So I just made the rest up and thought it would sound better if it were half-talked.

I'd written some of my verses before I got into the studio, but I don't like to keep singing the same thing over and over, so it changed. And I was noticing that there were a lot of references to New York, so I kept it like that. *Some Girls* isn't a "concept" album, God forbid, but it's nice that some of the songs have connections with each other—they make the album hold together a bit. . . . But then there's Bakersfield {laughing}.

My favorite song on the album is "Beast of Burden," in which your voice and the filigreed interplay of the guitars bring back for me Otis Redding, Wilson Pickett, Smokey Robinson and even the early guitar solos of Peter Tosh.

I quite like it, but I didn't expect anyone to really go for it, certainly not as much as you. It's surprising. But I wonder what other people are going to think of the album. I mean, we've been knocked a lot recently—I don't really know what they expect us to do.

'Exile on Main Street' was probably the last of your albums to have been widely admired.

Yeah, but if you read the reviews, you'll find that they were terrible!

How successful were your last few albums?

It depends on how you measure it. We sell about 2 million albums worldwide. It's nothing compared to Fleetwood Mac, and if we'd been a bit more aggressive, perhaps we could have sold more. But life goes up and down. Some people sell 20,000; we sell 2 million, so that's not bad. I think there are some good songs on our last albums, but they probably lacked direction.

On the new record, the band is much more together; they really played well during the sessions—and not only on what you hear, but also on all the stuff we did. We did so much that we didn't know what to do with all of it. We had four songs with the same uptempo idea, and I originally thought of having every song be a continuation of the other. Ian Stewart, who plays piano with us, said: "Everything seems to be in A." And I said: "Well, Beethoven wrote whole symphonies in one key, what does it fucking matter?" So we decided that the songs that would go on the album would be the ones that we finished first!

I've noticed that you can really hear the words on 'Some Girls,' whereas on other albums, they're mostly buried.

During the mix, I kind of decide—not very

consciously. I just put it up and that's how it comes out. It depends on the song. If the words are good, we bring them up; if they're useless, then . . .

But on 'Exile on Main Street' the words were great, yet it was hard to hear them—"Tumbling Dice," "Rocks Off," "Rip This Joint."

Yeah, a lot of people told me that. Maybe the rest of the band would prefer it if I weren't too loud, and I'm so good *anyway* {*laughing*}. But you know, people often interpret lyrics in ways you never meant. Sometimes I'm aware, when I write something, that a line can be taken in two ways, and I don't really want to say what everything is about. It's a lot more fun for people to interpret them in their own way.

With a song like "Shattered," however, I thought we had to hear the words a bit, so . . . it's not really just a question of loudness, it has to do with clarity of diction—whether I enunciate properly. And if I don't, you have to have it louder, and even then people don't understand what you're saying.

I read somewhere that you bit off the front part of your tongue when you were a kid, and that this was a kind of initiation rite.

{*Laughing*} Bullshit. I just bit a little bit off. That idea sounds as if it came from someplace like *Creem* magazine.

At the risk of being so accused, it sometimes seems that the way girls swallow you up—as some of your songs suggest—is the way you yourself seem to swallow up your words.

Maybe it's just my bad enunciation {*laughing*} running away with me. And it's also because I like the sound of words, the way the *noises* come out. In "Shattered," where you have "*sha-dooby,*" I wanted that to be heard, because it's as much a part of the song as the words. Van Morrison and Dylan do that kind of thing. Everyone does it, actually.

And on "Beast of Burden" you sing: "You're a pretty pretty pretty pretty pretty pretty girl," which seems to me a sexier, more ironical variation on Buddy Holly's "Pretty pretty pretty pretty Peggy Sue."

Yeah, it's true, I never thought of it. It's funny, that. But to me it's just a *sound*—it could be "pretty pretty happy happy" . . . or whatever. I wasn't thinking of Buddy Holly at all; it's a completely unconscious thing.

I heard that you were considering playing Antonin Artaud in a film.

I haven't decided on that yet, but I admire Artaud.

He once took peyote in Mexico, and described the experience as the three happiest days in his life. This is what he said about that time: "Boredom disappeared, I ceased looking for a reason to live, and I no longer had to carry my body. I grasped that I was inventing my life, that this was my function and my raison d'être, and that I got bored when I had no more imagination." To me this quotation suggests you and your public persona quite a bit.

Strange, no? Uh-*huh*. I think it applies to most everybody, surely. But as Artaud said, he only had three happy days in his life. He was an unhappy person, and I'm not. I was just born happy, and he wasn't. But if I had the tiniest bit of the talent Artaud had, I'd be even happier than I am. I find him very interesting as a poet and in terms of his interest in theater and cinema . . . and also interesting as an individual because he was so tortured. But I don't identify with him.

I don't continually question my reason to live—it's just a state of being. I'm just here. The real question is what you're doing with the living you're doing, and what you want to do with that living.

What do you think you've been doing with the living you've been doing in the Seventies?

Wasting my time.

Yet during that time you also wrote "Time Waits for No One," which really is a powerful, ominous, vatic song that no one commented on that much—as if it were a Seventies throwaway.

I liked it a lot. But I don't see things in terms of years—the Sixties, the Seventies—it's just a journalistic convention.

Punk rock, too. I don't want to get into the accusations that the Rolling Stones gave in or up or whatever. It's sort of vaguely true, but it's not really true. To me, rock & roll just goes back to the basic things. It doesn't exist because other people *don't* come across, it exists because kids want to get up and play very simple. The punk-rock movement said things to get a lot of copy. It's just an excuse to say that Rod Stewart lives in Hollywood and spends millions of dollars. It was just a good line. It wasn't the real reason punk rock existed.

What song or songs have you heard in the past few years that really got to you?

Really got to me? Hardly any. I don't listen seriously to rock & roll today. I never really did listen to white English bands. I like Latin music, all kinds of Caribbean music—I prefer that to white rock bands. I recently saw Tuff Darts and the Jam, right? Tuff Darts are pretty good, but the music really didn't swing. It's like white people, you know what I mean? I liked disco music when it was very Latin—two or three years ago—it was all Latin steps.

Now it's Australian.

Right, Australian. I liked John Travolta.

How does his dancing rate with yours?

It's not really difficult to be a better dancer than I am. I think I'm a terrible dancer, and I'd love to have gone to school and learned it properly, but I don't have the time nor the discipline.

I once heard Nureyev on television say that you were a terrific dancer.

That's very kind of him, because he's a *great* dancer. I can't dance a waltz or a quickstep. I can't dance steps. I just leap about, and sometimes it's very ungainly. It's hard dancing while you're singing.

You're also a dynamic singer/actor onstage.

Well, Bob Marley, for instance, is a good example of someone who really acts out a song and dances and plays guitar—it's what singers have always done. Etta James is really fantastic. But I think everyone does it, more or less.

You and Keith call yourselves "The Glimmer Twins" when you credit yourselves as producers. Someone once compared you two to Romulus and Remus.

{Laughing} We're very close, and we always have been. He was born my brother by accident by different parents. . . . That sounds all right to me. Let me ask you this: What did you think of Keith's song on the album, "Before They Make Me Run"?

It sounds like a goodbye song, with those lines: "I'm gonna find my way to Heaven/'Cause I did my time in Hell"—almost as if it were sung by Clarence White and the Byrds.

Keith's got a strong optimistic streak. His last complete song was "Happy." And he wrote nearly all of this one except for one or two "Oh, yeahs" in the middle. It's definitely his song.

People don't know who does what. And it's very difficult for me to remember who wrote what particular verse or song. Rock reviewers say: "That's a typical Keith Richards song." But they don't know. They often get it wrong, and it makes me laugh.

How long have you known Keith?

Twenty-nine years.

How old are you?

Thirty-four. I met him when I was six.

Legend has it that you met him for the first time on a train when you were both grown-up students.

No, we lived on the same block for a while when we were kids. Another guy who lived on the block was the painter Peter Blake . . . it was a pretty awful block, though *{laughing}*. Keith and I went to the same school at one point, and we walked home together.

Sounds like "Hey little girl in the highschool sweater."

{Laughing} Then I met him later on, and we really remembered each other.

When I listen to you on your records, I sometimes get the sense of a ten- to fourteen-year-old singing, as if inside you were a young boy still. What age do you feel close to?

About eleven or twelve. Just prepuberty. I know it sounds immature *{laughing}*, but one day I'll do it properly when I'm a big boy.

You once said that you didn't want to be singing "Satisfaction" when you were forty-two.

No, I certainly won't.

You often convey a feeling that combines the fearlessness and rambunctiousness that young kids have, and it seems to be a feeling that charms and bothers people.

It bothers them because they can't be like that themselves. I consider myself very lucky, and one of the reasons for that is that when I'm singing or acting or playing or anything—even at home—I feel just like a baby—like I'm ten or eleven or twelve. Whether that's my fantasy, whether it's right or wrong—I know that it's something that other people can't do. I mean, I can act like a thirty-four-year-old, too—I've trained myself to act in this manner *{laughing}*—but when I'm playing I can go back in time. I think that's true for many musicians and actors and dancers, and people envy that.

Are you planning on going back to the basics when you tour? The last time I saw you perform in New York, in 1975, you and the group seemed to be involved in fancy stage spectacle, buffoonery and horseplay.

It may have looked like that, but I didn't feel like that. Which means I wasn't acting it properly.

Maybe young kids who had never seen you before thought differently from me.

Exactly. It's easy to say: "Ah well, they're not as good as they were before." It may be your eyes that are jaded, rather than *us*.

I saw you in 1965, and it was pretty basic then.

The only people who did things like that in the old days were us—a little bit—the Who and the MC5. Everyone else stood up there like a bunch of assholes—they were *terrible* . . . with their suits and ties. The Jam is sort of like an English rock group of 1965, but not as good. You can't really return to basics in big gigs.

So what do you plan to do?

It's going to look different. I'd like to play lots of guitar. And I'd like to play the newer songs, but you can't do that in big places because no one wants to know. I'd like to play some smaller halls, but we've got to play some big outdoor ones in order to pay the roadies. It will be a varied tour—with both large and small gigs.

I was thinking of the lines in "As Tears Go By": "It is the evening of the day/I sit and watch the children play/Doing things I used to do/They think are new." It must be amazing to you that there are all these kids who were three years old in 1964–65 and who are seeing you now for the first time.

Sure. When I was already in Los Angeles in my pink Cadillac, they were just three years old, and now I go *out* with them {*laughing*}. It feels all right.

Do you like older women?

No.

And not lying, cheating, vain, affected girls.

It's easy for me to write that kind of song because my talent seems to lie in that direction, and I can only occasionally come up with a really good love song—it's easier to come out with the other side of the coin. So I choose what I do best, that's all.

I remember your old song "Off the Hook": the girl's phone is always busy, you wonder what she's doing and finally you just take your own phone off the hook. She's off the hook, but so are you.

We're all off the hook.

People seem fascinated with whether your phone is on or off the hook—in your personal life, in other words. Why do you think that is?

It's amazing to me that people want to know about my soap opera. Not just mine, of course, but mine's been a very long-running soap opera for a rock & roll singer. I mean, people aren't interested in Roger Daltrey's soap opera. I'm not trying to put people down, I wish I didn't have a soap opera. Bob Dylan they're interested in now only because he's getting a divorce. Before they weren't—they didn't seem to care; he was just married and had a lot of children, and they didn't write about when he went out or whatever. No one was really *that* interested in any of the Beatles' soap operas—not to the extent that I go through it. Of course, John and Yoko did get attention in the late Sixties by making an exhibition of themselves—sitting in bed, etc. But I try to avoid publicity, I'm *running*.

I don't put out wild pictures of me and whomever I'm going out with. I try to avoid going to openings as much as I possibly can. Even before I was married, with girls I was seeing or living with—most of the stories were completely untrue, and it's hopeless trying to tell people that it's not true. They'll print anything you say, anything. And by the time it gets to Hong Kong, it's ridiculous. Before you know it, you've gone out with Mrs. Trudeau, which is rubbish. The only reason I'm known in Turkey is because I'm supposed to have "gone out with Mrs. Trudeau."

I really don't like being a soap opera. It must be some sort of sexual interest. People who've got some kind of sexual attraction—and I hope I'm not being immodest by saying this—but when I was a kid I had it, I didn't have a problem getting girls. I did have a problem, though, until I started singing—I don't mind saying that. I got *nothing*. Maybe I was just shy.

It's that androgynous image that seems to attract both girls and boys.

Yeah, I don't think it did in earlier years, but maybe there was always room for the androgynous type. Anyway, all guys have a feminine side. But most girls don't really fall in love with a completely gay guy, even though they like the feminine side showing. And vice versa with men. They like a woman who combines things, too. They don't want someone who's either butch or totally *helpless*.

But, as we said before, your songs don't always combine things—maybe that's what gives the power to the songs.

Well, there is one song that's a straight gay song—"When the Whip Comes Down"—but I have no idea why I wrote it. It's strange—the Rolling Stones have always attracted a lot of men {*laughing*}. That sounds funny, but they're not all gay. And, of course, I have a lot of gay friends, but I suppose everyone does in New York City, and what's that have to do with the price of eggs? . . . I sure hope the radio stations will play "When the Whip Comes Down."

You can't really make out the words. All you hear is the chantlike chorus. Did you intend it to be a kind of Anvil Chorus?

{*Laughing*} Well, yeah. I know what you're thinking about. I don't know why I wrote it. Maybe I came out of the closet {*laughing*}. It's about an imaginary person who comes from L.A. to New York and becomes a garbage collector. . . . But whatever: I don't like this gossip interest in me today at all. It upsets a lot of people, and it creates a lot of diversions in my life. I can ignore it in America—it's not so bad here—but in Australia and England there are so many competing gossip columns. I don't trust journalists, generally, because they don't write the truth.

'Some Girls' seems to me the first Rolling Stones album in years that presents a dramatic quality—as if each song were an element in a play—and at the same time goes back to the rock & roll energy of 'Between the Buttons.'

I think *Some Girls* is the best album we've done since *Let It Bleed*. I hate to say that because

337

usually I say I love all the albums, or I hate them all, or none of them means anything to me, don't bother me with it, etc. But I do think it's a good album, and I'm not going to be too modest about it. I think it has a continuity in the characterizations—it doesn't have the holes, it's a bit better than the others. Most albums I buy have four out of ten good songs. And this one has, I think, more than that.

It's like in the Sixties when every song was expected to be good.

Yeah, every song should be good . . . and the reason perhaps *why* this album *is* good is that we did forty-two songs *{laughing}*. So we could cut the deadwood away, but there was a lot of good material.

Does it help you to produce your own albums?

No, it takes too long. I'd like someone else to produce them, but I can't find anybody. . . . No one even calls us up and offers! Luckily, we've got Chris Kimsey, who's our engineer, and he made things easier. We didn't have to spend a lot of time in the control room. I knew he'd get a good drum sound, so I didn't have to run in all the time and worry. He was great.

Whatever you did, you certainly put it together right with this album.

Well, I just realized that we had to. People expect a lot more of us than they do everybody else.

29

INTERVIEWED BY PETER HERBST (1978)

Linda Ronstadt had been profiled several times in ROLLING STONE over the course of her career, from its shaky start in 1971 with the Stone Poneys, but she'd never sat for a Q-and-A session. She'd always been bright and perceptive beyond her sex-kitten image, and now, in 1978, on the occasion of her fourth successive million-selling album (*Living in the USA*), the thirty-two-year-old Ronstadt could prove it.

Music editor Peter Herbst, who'd interviewed her four years before for the Boston *Phoenix,* got the assignment and conducted two two-hour sessions with her in New York. "Then I decided I needed more, so I flew to Maryland; she was in Wincopin. When I called her she was just waking up, and we spoke for an hour. I found her to be unusually candid. She was perky, affable, always willing to talk."

Linda was planning at that time to move to New York; instead, she stayed in California and bought a house in Malibu Colony, where she stayed until 1980. She took on a role in the Gilbert and Sullivan light opera, *Pirates of Penzance,* first in Central Park and then on Broadway, and Ronstadt was finally a New Yorker. At least for a while.

—BF-T

EVER SINCE THE ENORMOUS SUCCESS of 'Heart Like a Wheel' four years ago, Linda Ronstadt has been by far America's best-known female rock singer. Before that epochal album, her first with producer manager Peter Asher, she had enjoyed moderate popularity as a country-rocker and a pop-music sex symbol and had had a few hit singles, most notably "Different Drum" and "Long, Long Time." But she was not a household word.

She is now. She's had four platinum albums in the last four years, her newest, 'Living in the U.S.A.,' shipped double platinum and she's had a steady stream

340

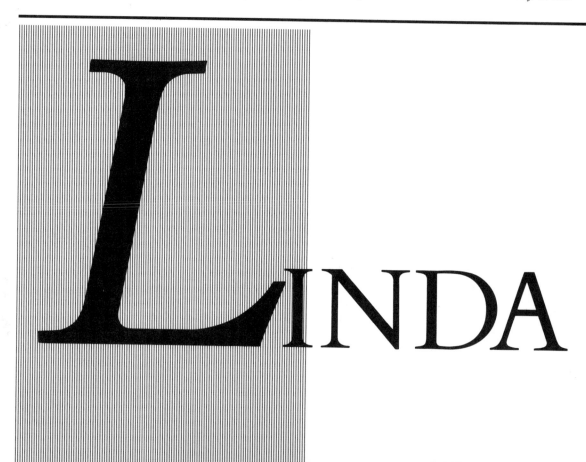

RONSTADT

of hit singles. But with her success has come a raft of problems. When I interviewed Ronstadt two years ago, she was struggling to deal with the terrifying novelty of being a celebrity. She suffered, Ronstadt said at the time, from free-floating anxiety, a serious lack of confidence in her voice and a somewhat scattered personality. And she was quick, perhaps too quick, to discuss the details of her personal life ("I wouldn't say open—I was compulsive," she says).

Now, two years later, she exudes self-confidence and a striking sense of purpose and seems to have gained a firm hand over the affairs of her life. She refuses to be pushed around, either by fans invading her privacy or by causes and candidates asking her to donate her services. She's about to risk a major move, leaving the comforts of L.A., her home for twelve years, for the uncertainty of New York City. She's less willing to discuss her personal life ("It's not anybody's business to air my laundry anymore," she says).

But as we talked, once at a hotel named the Cross Keys Inn in suburban Maryland and twice at the Plaza Hotel in New York, Ronstadt's base of operations while she and her band (guitarist Waddy Wachtel, bass guitarist Kenny Edwards, drummer Russ Kunkel, keyboardist Don Grolnick, pedal steel player Dan Dugmore) toured the Northeast, she revealed a stubborn streak of conservatism, a strong need for privacy, a fear of performing and a longing for a kind of settled life she thinks she might never attain. And she talked about her music, which remains the compelling presence in her life.

W**HAT KIND OF FAMILY DO** *you come from?*
My grandfather was a rancher in Arizona. His father was the first mining engineer in the northern part of Mexico, and he was also in the Mexican army. He was born in Germany. My grandfather also owned a wagon-making shop which was eventually turned into a hardware store in Tucson. My dad grew up on the ranch and in the hardware business.

Ronstadt's Hardware Store?

Right. And he also wanted to sing—he was a wonderful singer. My father had a radio show when he was in his twenties. Oh, he was so dishy, so good-looking, the real dashing type. He rode his horse up the steps of my mother's sorority house. He was a real cowboy. My mom came from Michigan, and my grandfather was a real well-known inventor. He invented things like the grease gun and the electric stove. My mother was not quite East Coast but sort of back-

East, sort of DAR. I'm starting to learn a little bit more about my family history.

I had thought you had Mexican ancestry, or that was just your father?

Yeah, Mexican-German on my father's side, and English also—he's Mexican, German and English. My mother's side is German, English and Dutch.

In my heart I feel Mexican-German. I feel if I were to organize it correctly, I would try to sing like a Mexican and think like a German. You know what I mean? I get it mixed up sometimes anyway. I sing like a Nazi and I think like a Mexican, and I can't get anything right.

You have a sister and a brother or two brothers?

Two brothers and a sister.

Did anybody in your family have an outstanding voice?

Well, my older brother actually had a beautiful soprano voice. My father always had a rich, melodious, lovely slow vibrato. He was a baritone, I guess, but he could get it way up to tenor notes. Beautiful voice, just so thick, it's like honey. His voice has lots of soul and no time. My dad had the worst time in the universe. It comes from not playing with a band a lot—he has got that Creole drag time. I can always harmonize with him because I know exactly what kind of sense of time he's got. But boy, it really rubbed off on me. My older brother was the one I always tried to copy because he was in the Tucson Boys Choir, and he had a glorious soprano. I wanted to sing like that. I can remember sitting at the piano. My sister was playing and my brother was trying out something, and I went, "I want to try that." My sister turned to my brother and said, "Think we got a soprano here." I was about four, and so I remember that real well.

So I was a soprano for a real long time, and then one day, I was fourteen, my sister and brother were singing some folk song that was probably something they learned off of a Peter, Paul and Mary record. It was called "The Stockade Blues." I came walking around the corner, and I just threw in the high harmony. I did it in my chest voice, and I surprised myself. When I started out with my chest voice, I could only sing straight, with no vibrato. As I have gotten older, my voice has turned more like my father's. My older brother really had the most musical talent.

What does he do now?

He's a cop. He's good at that, too. He's a captain now. He always wanted to achieve things like that. He likes to be on the street.

What does your sister do?

She got married and had a million kids.

Does she live in Arizona?

Yeah. She has her hands full with the kids, I think. She does probably more than any of us.

When did you decide that you were real good? That, coming from a family of people who were musical, you were special?

When my sister said, "We have a soprano," I just went, "I'm a singer, that's what I do." And when I went to first grade, as far as I was concerned that's what I was. I remember there'd always be a certain time of the day to get up and sing; you'd have to sing some hymn or the way you sing in churches. Everybody would be real embarrassed and wouldn't want to do it, but I knew I could. It didn't occur to me that I wasn't very good until I started to do it for a living. I realized that it was hard, and I wasn't real great.

W HAT DOES THE INVASION OF *privacy do to your life?*
    What it does is it makes people look like enemies all the time, 'cause you never know what someone's going to do. Somebody will come up and say, "Gee, you and some other singer (who you think is the worst singer in the world) are my favorite singers . . . ." Or you're trying to have dinner with a friend and not have people . . . I mean, it's a distraction and it's an annoyance, and they don't realize it's rude. You see it coming, and you start to wince and you start to get defensive, because as far as I'm concerned that person is going to hurt me. The only thing I can do is look cold, or I can be rude—I can tell them just flat out, "Go away, don't bother me," or I can sit there and put up with it and store a lot of pissed-offness. No matter what, it's a no-win situation . . . . This is one of the major icky side effects of my job, and if I don't want to go completely nuts, I'm going to have to put up with a certain amount of it.

Has it gotten a lot worse in the last couple of years?

A lot worse, yeah. There's been so much press, you know. I went to some beach club on the Fourth of July, and I couldn't believe it. I mean we just got jumped on—literally jumped on!

Do you find it easier in New York than other places?

Sometimes it's easier, but on St. Patrick's Day I got chased by millions of people, literally chased. And I came running up the steps of the Plaza, and there were these four little boys after me. They had locked the doors and they wouldn't let anybody in unless they had a room key, and my room key was in the bottom of my purse. I was sort of going, "But you don't really understand. Those people are chasing me with green faces."

Basically, people are just rude. I mean, they just don't have any manners. They're only thinking of themselves. They'll say, "But this is the only chance I'll ever get to talk to you." That's not my problem, you know. There isn't really any reason for them to talk to me. If they want to hear me sing, they can go buy a record—that's the way I feel about it.

Do you think that, to some degree, the reason you're a star is because of people like that?

But I don't think of myself as a star. I didn't set out to become a star; I set out to become a singer. I would have sung, no matter what. The star part is just something that they made up in Hollywood in 1930.

But you do play along. Your album covers are very sexy, and you're a sex symbol to people. How can you say you're not a star?

I'm not saying I'm not a star, I'm just saying that that's not what I set out to be. I wanted to be a success, and being successful means that I have more freedom with the music, that I can have a bigger budget for my albums, that I can afford to hire better musicians who I really like to play with and that I can become a better singer as a result of playing with really good musicians. And the more successful I am on the road, then the better show we can present. We can get better monitors, we can hear better onstage, you can fly around in Lear jets. All of it makes us more comfortable so we can do a better show. The stardom aspect of it is an unpleasant side effect of success, because a businessman can become an enormous success without having his privacy completely destroyed.

So alluring album covers make it possible to do what you want musically?

Yeah, it's just basically the same. What should I do, put out an ugly picture? People look at it, and they go, "Uuugh." It's incidental, you know what I mean. It's nice to have pretty pictures. It's part of the frosting on the cake for the audience.

Do you feel like you've taken control of your life in the last couple of years?

Yeah, I think I have.

What happened to get that going?

Well, I got a little older. It's wonderful that age gives you this amazing perspective and a couple of extra little facts that you need to know. It really helps a lot. I'm kind of a survivor, and I

343

don't think that I could have gotten this far if I hadn't been. Being a survivor doesn't mean that you have to be made out of steel, and it doesn't mean that you have to be ruthless. It means that you have to basically be on your own side and want to win. The person that's the best at that of anyone that I've ever met is Dolly Parton. She's just amazing at being ambitious without being ruthless and at being so sensitive to other people's needs. She's a great lesson to me.

What happened to the album you were going to make with Dolly and Emmylou Harris?

We're going to make it; it's just going to take a long time. It's not easy for three different managers and three different record companies to come to an agreement.

Say we made a record and Dolly's record company thought that it was something that she shouldn't have out just then. Say she had an album out then and it would be competing with her own album. It's also difficult trying to find a style to record us in when we have three completely different styles.

They called me up when I was on the road and said, "Hey, let's do this," 'cause we've talked about it for so long and wanted to do it for so long. And I just went, "Oh, sure, we'll do it, we'll just go out and sing and we'll make this record and it'll come out and everybody will say, 'Isn't that nice?' and that'll be the end of it." I told Peter about it, and Peter just sort of went, "Ohhh." He didn't stand in my way—he never does if I want to do something—but he knew that it was going to be a hell of a headache, and it was.

You did record some tracks?

We recorded some stuff, but let me tell you, we did it in ten days. Now, I've never made a record in less than three and a half months, and I don't think Dolly has, and I don't think Emmy has either. But we got scared because Emmy had to go on the road, and Dolly had to start writing her album, and I only had a certain amount of time off, and we wanted to do it so badly. I remember Dolly just making these decisions. She said: "We're just going to have to try." And Emmy's got kids—Dolly was such an inspiration to her because she's so well organized. I remember Emmy saying, "Well, I'm just going to do it for Dolly, because it shows me that I'll just have to get things organized; I'll simply have to do it."

I was the most flexible of the three because I have no family, and I had just come off a tour. So we just went, "We'll just hold our breaths and try." Well, it wouldn't have mattered if Jesus Christ and *Buddha* had been producing that album—you can't do something like that in ten days. We thought that somehow we would just break all the rules and we would do it, and we didn't.

We got a couple of things that are just lovely. One particular thing just turned out gorgeous, just the three of us with an acoustic guitar, and God, it just killed us when we heard it. I learned so much, singing with them. There were times when I would have to match Emmy's vibrato and Dolly's intonation in order to blend, finding out that I could make noises with my throat that I did not make. I was able to apply it on this album and really got my voice up another notch, which I probably obliterated with this tour.

I NOTICED THE BREWER'S YEAST. *Are you on a health kick?*

I'm real off and on trying to be healthy. It's just that when I eat so badly and I start to get sick that out of guilt I start pouring brewer's yeast in my orange juice.

Do you jog when you have a chance?

That's the one thing, that's the only panacea that I've ever known of. I'm convinced that it can make up for lack of a good diet, but that a good diet can't make up for lack of exercise. Also, running is the best and I think the only real cure for depression. There have never been any drugs that I could take that would make depression go away. Depression, you know, seems to affect women worse, but it is such an insidious crippler because it starts and you are aware of it the first few days that you feel bad, and then it just kind of settles in and it prevents you from doing things. After a while you get used to it. You don't realize how much it's preventing you from living the way you want to live until something lifts it. I'm just so afraid of it now that it stops me completely cold. If I get depressed, I just go to bed for a week.

What happens on tour?

I run, I run. I have one of these little things, if I can't go outside, that you run on. It's got little springs; it's like a little trampoline. I have ways of tricking myself: I have weights in the room, and then I have weights that go on the truck so they're at the sound check, and I have weights put in the studio, and I have them at home, too, so that no matter what I do, there's never any excuse.

What are your plans for touring this year?

We're just going to do this tour, which is a

month, and then we're going to do another tour which will be a month, and then we'll probably do Australia and New Zealand and Japan, maybe. I'm not really sure if we're going to do the one, that would be another month.

How come?

'Cause it's too rough on me. It's really hard, you know? I mean, just the physical changes, hopping in and out of the plane every day and hopping in and out of the hotel. And endless long empty hours of waiting that are the hardest. And then there's the repetition of the sound check, which makes it hard to get yourself in the frame of mind to really want to do the music. Plus the music is repeating over and over and over, and if you play music and it's not satisfying, it's painful.

That's why you like to do new stuff in your shows?

Yeah, but there's a lot of hits I can't throw out. It would be unfair to charge the kids money to come and see it if they can't see those songs, 'cause they haven't heard 'em every single night for the last nine years. So we really do try hard to find ways to change 'em so that it won't be too weird for the kids but so we'll be able to stand it. You can't always do it.

How do you sing a song that you've sung 200 times? How do you get some feeling into it?

Sometimes something new will happen to make that song come alive again, to give it a little bit of a fresh interpretation. Sometimes I'll go, "I'm just going to sing rhythm." Or sometimes you just sort of try another attitude with it, you know: sometimes it will be sort of cute. I'm sure there are more ways to sing the songs than I often do, but over the years they've changed a lot. One song is "Willin'." That's something I never get tired of.

Last night I was thinking while I was standing onstage that you have to perform to the audience. I have a tendency, 'cause I'm so scared of them, to dismiss them entirely. I try to pretend they're not there, and I just do the show with the band. No wonder I think it's boring. So I was thinking last night that you have to include them, you can't take them for granted, no matter how much they like you. Your attitude should be that they're a bunch of nonbelievers and you're the only person that could convince them.

Do you think sometimes that you don't do enough onstage?

I think that most of the time I don't do enough onstage. It depends on how you look at it: You can say basically I do enough because I get up there and sing and I don't hold back; but in terms of getting to be pals with the audience

every night, I've gone through periods of being able to do it, and then I've gone through periods where I just looked at them and I didn't know what to say to them.

Do you ever watch Mick Jagger or Bruce Springsteen onstage?

Never seen Bruce Springsteen. I've seen Mick Jagger really only once. I went to an Anaheim concert, but I couldn't see any of it 'cause everyone stood up. I never got to see the show and I was real disappointed, so I flew to Tucson just to go. It was a wonderful show. I loved it, and I got so many great ideas; he's a teacher, you know.

What was it like to sing with the Stones?

I loved it. I didn't have a trace of stage fright. I'm scared to death all the way through my own shows. But it was too much fun to get scared. He's so silly onstage, he knocks you over. I mean, you have to be on your toes or you wind up falling on your face. He's amazing. Mick just scolds all the time, you better do right, he's usually right when he scolds.

What do you think when you see people moving around that much?

I like it, but it would be silly for me to do something like that. I'm not naturally that outgoing; it would be very strange. My sister could have done that; she was the oldest, and she was the most outgoing. I was the youngest for six years till my brother was born, so I was sort of trailing around, singing the high harmony.

D O YOU THINK YOU'RE GOING *to cut back touring as the years go by?*
Yeah, I do, and I've actually given some vague thought to something else I could do. There are a couple of avenues open to me, some of them that are completely not involved with show business at all.

Like what?

Well, I don't know; I hate to say it, really, because it steals thunder, you know what I mean? Talking about it sort of takes some of the energy away from it.

Movies?

No, no, no, no, that's show business. See, the reason movies are weird is because you don't have much control, and for me to do a movie would be a gigantic risk. I'm not saying that I wouldn't do it.

Do you think that you might make records but not tour?

345

I don't think that's possible, really. I can't think of anybody that's been successful doing that, and if they have been, it's really been the exception. You pretty much *have* to tour if you want to make records. It's like you do the record, you do the tour. But touring is a way of life, and it's a steady occupation. Some people are . . . that's what they do, that's how they identify themselves. They really see themselves more clearly in a state of flux. And I am in a state of flux. But I'd like to establish something a little more than that. I'm not sure I can. But I'd like to do something else, too.

Do you feel that being in rock & roll touring creates a prolonged adolescence?

Yeah, it sure does.

Well, maybe you're coming out of your adolescence in a way?

I think it's the loneliness. I think that some people are loners by nature. Some people are real afraid of being close. An illusion of intimacy is created by the little family group that travels around the road and by the amount of energy and affection you get off the audience every night. It does not penetrate into my soul. It's valid, but I just can't recognize it.

Is it conceivable that you might not make records at some point?

It's conceivable, yeah, or I may do it, instead of one a year, one every two years. I may go into farming. I mean, I don't know. The most important thing to do is something that's satisfying and something you do well and that you enjoy doing. If you're doing that, it doesn't matter.

Is making albums more rewarding than performing?

It is to me, yeah, because of the teamwork aspect, communication with a bunch of people I really know. I can understand what they're going to do on the records, and Peter and Val [Garay], the engineer, and I have got this team thing down with the band where it's amazing. And I love it when one person says, "Well, I have this idea," and then somebody says, "Oh, yeah, we could take that and add this to it," and then somebody else goes, "Oh, yeah, and this and this and this." That's just like sitting around with a bunch of people that are great to talk to, and you start an idea and the rest of the people begin to illuminate the idea until it gets into this sort of full-blown wonderfulness.

Making albums is physically tough on me. I always wind up looking like I got run over by a cement truck. I get up in the morning, put on my track shoes and shorts and I go down there. We try to keep bankers' hours, bankers' hours

being regular hours. My feeling is that if you're in there for more than seven hours, you've really gone stale. Sometimes you get something that's plain old mechanical work and you've just got to finish it up, and sometimes you hit a hot streak, and sometimes you just think you hit a hot streak and you come back the next day and you sound like old, tired, weird people.

Some of the things we get on the first take. There's a Little Feat tune on the album called "All That You Dream" we'd worked all afternoon on. Things kept breaking, and we got a track and we just knew we could play it better, and so we left it there and we'd worked the arrangement out all very carefully, and the next morning, while they were running it down—before Peter and I even got there—they cut a track. I came in and listened to it, and I went, "That's it. That's it. It's great." I put a vocal on it, and that was the one we used. And then there were some of them like "Back in the U.S.A." where we just walked in and did it on the first take, you know; we just played it once and it was fine.

Do you think 'Living in the U.S.A.' is an improvement?

I think that I've improved on it. There's no way that I can be objective and say one album is better than another one. I never listen to them anyway.

Never?

I listen to them when we're making them, and I listen twice through after they're finally mixed and sequenced, and I never hear them again. Every now and again something comes on the radio, and I'll push it off. It just makes me nervous.

People often assume that Peter Asher picks all your songs, the musicians come in and tell you what to do and you just get up there and sing.

I don't read or anything like that, but I pick the tunes, and I often pick a general setting to them. Peter figures out the best ways to implement that. I also choose the band. I choose them all for their particular style and ability, and I just let them play. And then Peter and I both act as editors when it comes to making arrangements. Choosing the players is like doing the arrangements in a sense, 'cause you know what they're going to play.

Replacing Andrew Gold with Waddy Wachtel seems to have changed your sound.

Well, Waddy is a little bit more rock & roll, where Andrew is more rock. And Andrew's style was beginning to mature so rapidly and turn into Andrew Gold. It wasn't like Andrew quit or was fired, he just wanted to make Andrew Gold records. When we replaced him with Waddy, things got a little more aggressive.

What were you looking for when you found Waddy?

We were looking for a guy that could play real well, and we got the attitude to boot.

Where was he playing?

Kenny [Edwards] knew him. Kenny was responsible for getting Waddy and Dan Dugmore into the band. Dan just comes up with these amazing things. He came up with the iba introduction on a song called "Blowin' Away." The iba is some strange instrument, the Stonehenge of the steel guitar.

How do you pick the songs?

Well, I pick them because something will happen in my life and I want to describe that situation, and it sets off a tape recorder in my head of a song. Peter heard this Elvis Costello record and said, "This is a hit song for somebody." I really loved the song, but I didn't see any way that I could do it. Then I met a girl like Alison who became a real good friend to me. So I changed it around a little bit in the gender—I made it like I heard the girl had run off with some guy. And I was hoping that she would stay away from my particular property. Whereas with him it's kind of a vague love song. I reduce it to friendship, but that described this girl. I had a reason to sing it, so then I *had* to do "Alison."

Do you think about balance in an album?

We try to think of it in terms of packing. We always try not to do oldies and we always wind up doing them, because there is always a song I want to do. "Ooh, Baby, Baby" came about because I just wanted to do a song with David Sanborn so badly. I went to this stupid Hollywood party, and I heard that song and I went into a dream. I loved the song so much that I was just transported by it.

"Back in the U.S.A." is an oldie also.

Yeah, that came about because I was driving around in the car with Glenn Frey. Glenn Frey is the best single source of material for singers. He's got stacks and stacks of cassettes he's made of all these different things. We were driving, and I looked at him and went, "Remember when we used to sit around the Troubadour bar and go, 'Oh, it's so horrible and I can't get a record deal.'" We were so broke and so miserable, and we'd feel sorry for ourselves and we were so precious about it. Then all of a sudden I looked at him, and I went, "Boy, life's really tough. We're going off to ski with all this money in our pockets, we're going to have a good time and

we've got great music on the tape player." "Back in the U.S.A." came on right then, and I just went, "God, that would be a great song to sing. I think I'll do that one."

To me there's a real resurgence of patriotism in this country. We all went through trying to criticize it in the Sixties, but then everybody went, "Well, we're going to go looking around the rest of the world. It must be better over here, and it must be better over there." But everybody's coming here, so I guess it must be best here. I like that line about "Anything you want we got it right here in the U.S.A." or "Looking hard for a drive-in, searching for a corner cafe where hamburgers sizzle on the open grill night and day and the jukebox jumping with records back in the U.S.A.!" I mean, Chuck Berry really knew how to write folk poetry!

"Mohammed's Radio" sounds like a very serious song the way you sing it. Do you take it that way?

Yeah. I think that's an amazingly well-written song. I went through that once with a friend metaphor by metaphor, and I really see it. I always think things are about myself; they have to be about me. When I was little, the radio was like a drug for me. It was my complete escape and my whole life.

Is that what you think that song is about?

Yeah. He uses the metaphor of Mohammed's radio like . . . it's omnipresent and it's powerful, almost godlike. He uses Mohammed instead of Jesus or Buddha. He just happened to pick Mohammed, I guess. God, Warren [Zevon] probably will be throwing up if he reads this and I'm interpreting his song for him.

The first verse deals with problems of living and then, "Don't it make you want to rock & roll?" When it comes right down to it, I'd rather just turn on the radio and crank it up loud and just get off on the music. And the last verse says, "Oh, everybody is desperate trying to make ends meet/ work all day, still can't pay the price of gasoline and meat." And there's one line you just have to yell: "Alas, their lives are incomplete." It's like a double twist. It's curious to me that they're incomplete. I feel compassionate, but at the same time I feel like, boy, those dumb slobs. Isn't that terrible?

And then the last verse, "You've been up all night just listening for his drum/ hoping that the righteous might just come." And I remember when I was little I'd just wait all night long until the moment when something wonderful comes on the radio that's just better than anything else. And you're inspired all over again.

347

YOU'RE MOVING TO NEW YORK. *What attracts you to it?*

I don't think it's an accident that everybody is starting to drift there. Just like it wasn't any accident people started drifting to the West Coast when they did. The business goes in a cycle: New York, L.A., England, London and back to New York. And as long as I've been in the music business, that has never stopped. Every now and again Nashville sticks in an oar, but it's only an oar. When everybody came in—the Eagles, Jackson [Browne], Neil Young and Joni Mitchell, everybody listened to California music. Then it just moved to London, and the punk thing got started.

Do you care for punk music at all?

Well, I like the New Wave stuff, and that couldn't possibly land in L.A. because nobody moves that intensely. So, of course, it would have to come to New York, because New York is in a similar situation economically. I mean, it's a similar sort of sociological greenhouse, so to speak, for developing this style of music. The punk stuff is not very musical nor very multi-faceted. It seemed to me, when I saw the Ramones, for instance, that they had taken one facet of what Mick Jagger does, which is a kind of stance, maybe one move and maybe one little chip off of an emotional statement, and it was sort of limited to that. Mick Jagger has such a tremendous overview that is so many-faceted that it makes it sound so much more. But if you just take a chunk of it, it doesn't glimmer as much.

Are there any punk rock groups that you've thought made it?

Well, I like Television a whole lot, and I love Elvis Costello. Elvis Costello just touches my heart. The first thing that you associate with him is anger. But there's also tenderness and a great deal of humor.

Have you seen him perform?

I've seen him perform, and I was just mesmerized. I saw him at Hollywood High. I was in the back row, and I had to stand on my seat through the whole thing. I mean, I wouldn't stand on my seat for anybody.

So was it mostly the music that brought you back to New York, or is there some excitement in the air?

The thing about New York is that there are so many different top-quality things. One time I was in New York and I went to see Baryshnikov dance, and it put something that I badly needed to have back in perspective—which was what a show looks like from the audience's point of view. Because when I go on the road I have so much stage fright that I tend to ignore the audience completely, and, of course, if I think of them I go ooohhh, they're looking at me.

You can go to New York and see the best ballet, you can see the best jazz and you can see the best everything. You can see an amazing play, you know, and you can see an amazing movie and you can see an amazing idea everywhere you turn. And you don't even have to spend any money to be entertained. I love just seeing beautiful buildings, and there are beautiful little visual jewels everywhere to see. My favorite thing to do is walk around with somebody that can see things like that. Danny Aykroyd is a great example of that. I mean, those guys are like mental photojournalists; Billy Murray is the same way. They're just always gathering data. And I think that the *Saturday Night* show was really enormously responsible for this sort of renaissance thing that's happening in New York. I think that *Saturday Night* brought a lot of different kinds of artists together. And it created a focal point. All those people were really into hanging out so it was something to do. There's a purpose around hanging out.

When you walk around New York, do you get spotted a lot? What's that like?

Annoying.

You've seen 'Annie Hall,' where Woody Allen is standing . . .

Yeah, I loved that, that's perfect. Can you see how uncomfortable and embarrassed that made him? It's exactly what it makes you feel like. It makes you feel uncomfortable and horribly embarrassed because it makes you feel like you're not a human. People are staring at you, and if somebody comes and stares at you, you're going, "What are they seeing? A pimple?" I mean, ooohhh, it's horrible. I don't like it.

I think that people who go to Elaine's {an exclusive N.Y. restaurant} find it very comforting to be around other famous people because they're not treated that way.

There's a reason for that, but there's also a danger. Just because everybody is famous doesn't mean they've got anything to say to each other. Or even that they're the same quality or anything like that. If I hang around exclusively with the musicians, I think that I'm the worst [in terms of musical talent]. And if I hung around with schoolteachers, I would think that I was the greatest. So you have to have a mixture of all those things, and that's why, in the last five or six years, I've made a real attempt to have friendships that were outside of my business.

I never hang around with actors, but if I know

an actor real well and see him on the screen, what I know of him is only a distraction to the character that he's trying to portray. And that's why I feel that with me the more that's known about my personal life, the more people think about that when they hear you do what you're doing. For instance, one of the reasons that I don't think that rock & rollers should do benefits is because if people hear me on the radio, I don't want them to be thinking, "Oh, well, she's for this and she's for that." I don't want them to start thinking about causes. I know that when I see John Wayne in a movie, I think, "Ooohh, he's a right-winger." It's not fair to John Wayne.

But do you think art can exist separately from politics?

No, but I don't think that it has to be public. I did a couple of benefits when my social consciousness was awakened a little bit. I started reading newspapers about four years ago, and I went, "Wait a minute, we should maybe try to do something about this because somebody has to take responsibility." But you take as much responsibility as the next guy.

The other reasons are that I don't think it's fair, because it's still an individual contribution. If, for instance, I were going to do a political benefit for somebody, I couldn't do it while my band was scattered in the wind and my crew wasn't together. So we'd have to add another date to a tour. And all it would mean was that it's money out of my pocket, whether you look at it that way or not. And also I think it is irresponsible because the kids tend to think that because your music is hip, that your choice in political candidates is automatically good. And I know from getting to know people whose work I respect and admire that I don't necessarily agree with their political reasoning, and also we're not experts. I mean, it curls my hair to think about some rock & roll group being able to give a candidate a quarter of a million dollars, when they didn't even read the newspaper. They're not informed and they don't know. I think it's just dreadful.

I did one benefit for Jerry Brown, I did one for Tom Hayden and I did one for Gary Hart. And I've done a couple of things for antinuclear stuff, which are all things that I was behind at that time. But all it taught we was that I really didn't know what I was talking about, even though I consider myself a lot better informed than most people on the street. Who knows who should be president and if anybody should have a big interest in determining those things? Shouldn't Standard Oil? I mean, they have more to gain

and more to lose. If something terrible happens to Standard Oil, a lot of people will be out of jobs. You can say what you want about big multinationals running the country and stuff, but the fact remains that we need that; we need their services, we need jobs from them, and they are in a better position to decide what's going to be good for the economic climate of the country and for the rest of the world. I'm not saying that they should have all the power, but I'm saying that they shouldn't have less power than the Eagles. It's ridiculous.

Standard Oil is going to do what benefits them, not necessarily what benefits . . .

They will, and all you can do is fight. But I would rather fight them as a private citizen.

But if you believe that there's a terrible danger in the fact that there is no way to dispose of nuclear wastes and nuclear energy is a very dangerous thing, you have a chance, by appearing in these benefits, to draw people to that cause. Don't you think that's a hard thing to give up?

I think that one is a little, it's hard to give up. It really is. And when you really are just convinced that a candidate that you really want badly to win is the right guy it's hard to resist that temptation, but so far I've been successful. As far as the nuclear thing was concerned, we gave an antinuclear organization a T-shirt concession, and it goes to all the grass-roots groups, so that doesn't go into one great big giant group.

We got to this through New York, I don't know how but . . .

Well, New York is great. I love it. There are a number of other people who I've heard about who are moving to New York from L.A.

The thing about L.A. is that it doesn't have any cafe society as such. You have to go to somebody's living room, and I have to know somebody pretty well before I let them in my living room, you know. In New York there's always a bar, there's a club or there's just the street. You're always going someplace, and there's always a lot of people.

Do you think this is the end of an era for Los Angeles?

Yeah. And there'll be another one to start up, but I think in a sense it just has moved.

What do you think Los Angeles music had that was so appealing?

Comfort. It reflected the comfort, but also it reflected an empty, sort of disillusioned hollowness of the same kind of hollow friendships that—now I'm not saying this is absolutely true—I mean, I hate it when New York people come out and they go, "Oh, how L.A.!" you

349

know? And they sort of curl their lip. That's stupid, that's just a generalization, and it's silly. It doesn't mean that all Los Angeles friendships and all Los Angeles people are shallow. But the tendency to make very strong friendships, very deep friendships is more pronounced here, simply because there's such a tough environment you have to have those kind of friendships in order to keep body and soul together. L.A. is real comfortable, but on the B side of that is that things tend to get a little bit too laid back and mellow. Then, also, in New York people tend to get very tough and very brittle and very hard and too callous. So, along with the excitement and the stimulation, sometimes your circuits get burned out, and that's the risk you run.

Y OU PUT ABOUT THREE AND A *half months into 'Living in the U.S.A.' and you're going to be touring for a couple of months. Are you feeling that this is too much? Are there a lot of other things you want to do?*

I don't know. I wonder if I've a choice. We were talking about that the other night, you know, about whether we actually have a choice as to what we do. Because I really don't know how to do much of anything else, though I think I could learn. I'm pretty inertia-ridden in this. I would have to make a conscious choice; it would be pretty hard for that to happen; something actually would have to happen in my life. It's like making a snowflake: You have to have the nucleus for the crystal to form around. It just cannot spring out from the head of Zeus full-blown, you know. I just don't know. The answer to that question is that I don't know.

Do you think about what you might be doing in five years?

See, it's hard to say, because who knows? I might decide to fall in love with somebody and stay with them, in which case I wouldn't want to go on the road. Or I might discover that I'm not the kind of person that can stay with anybody.

Do you enjoy the periods of time when you're just off the road and not making an album and just hanging out?

Uuuh, no. I like to work. But, I don't like to be harassed. It's hard to say; maybe I'm not very happy because it seems like I'd do something. I like to go camping, that's what I really like to do.

Do you like to be alone?

It's boring, there's no one to talk to mostly. I

know this is going to sound really corny, but what I like the very best is when there's people over for dinner. I can barely cook but I can bake good bread, and when there are people that are close and my little brother Mike and Marilyn and Lois (Marilyn is my foreman at home; she oversees all the construction and she takes care of all the animals; she used to work for a vet and she's just one of my dearest friends), those people are in the kitchen, and we're all sitting around and Nicky's always got her guitar and we're singing or something like that. I mean, to me that's heaven, that's my favorite thing to do.

Do you think about having children, that your career prevents that?

I think the fact that I haven't met a man that I want to have children with has prevented me from having children. It's interesting that you would bring that up, 'cause I was sitting with two other lady journalists that I know and a guy, and we were talking about that. The thing that I thought the most about was that if I did get married and have children and it was too comfortable for me, it would take away my desire. Right now I *have* to keep going because it's the only way to survive.

So you're saying a family would be a substitute for what you're doing?

It might be, and it's also an excuse. If you have a family, there's always an excuse not to do it. I'll do any excuse I can think of to not go on tour.

I suppose if I did have a family and it were successful as a family that maybe I'd be very happy, and maybe it wouldn't matter whether I went out on the road. The only thing that really matters is whether you're satisfied with the work you're doing. The thing that would be horrible would be that if I had a family and I would, through inertia, sort of give up my singing. If the family wasn't a success and if it were an unhappy family, I can't think of anything worse. It's a big gamble, a big risk, but it's a moot point because it just isn't an issue right now. I don't know anybody that I would like to have a family with.

Well, does it scare you that maybe in five years things will be the same and you will be touring and you'll be making albums and you'll be farther away from . . .

That I'll just pass it by? I think of that sometimes, and I think that again enters whether it's a choice. One thinks that one has a choice. I think that duality is omnipresent. It is both a choice and it is decided for you. It's not that I don't look around every now and again and sort of go, "Uuh, what's around?" you know. But I mostly only meet people in show business, and I'm not really interested in show business. I like 'em in ties and three-piece suits.

Do you think that the fact that you have this very directed career and music is the center of your life is a way for you to avoid finding somebody that you might want to settle down with?

I honestly don't. Freud says sometimes a cigar's a cigar, you know, and I think that this is a cigar. I did have talent for singing; I chose to become a singer. I did just get up and leave home one day when I was eighteen years old and say, I'm going out to L.A. to become a singer. "Goodbye, Mother, goodbye, Daddy." That was my choice, but after that things were just sort of decided for me, and all the little by-products of being a singer make it very difficult to form a relationship that lasts—not only because of the kind of person that it turns me into but because of the kinds of people that I come in contact with, and the kinds of people that I become attracted to.

It's only natural, for instance, all during my twenties that I would be attracted to people that excelled at what I did, people like John David Souther, who I think is brilliant, you know, or Lowell George, whose musicianship is so wonderful. It's only understandable that there would be fatal flaws in our relationship that would make it just very difficult to trust each other or to surrender to each other, so to speak. So there you have it. It's a tough one. I used to think, "It's so terrible and tragic." I don't even think that anymore. I just think that's just one of the cards that I got.

I started to read a book called *Flower in Willow World*. It's about the history of the geisha. I'm very fascinated with the whole concept of the geisha. The forerunners of the geisha were in China, and they were called "singing girls"—they actually were the ones who were responsible for acting as catalysts to high fashion, art, all of the arts, including literature, calligraphy, dancing and music. And they were the ones who associated with the most important men, the people from the government and the people from the military and the most successful merchants. They were highly educated, and they had an enormous impact on the cultural development of China and later on Japan, where the geisha was expected not only to sing and dance and draw and paint and act, but she was also expected to be able to sit at the tea table, for instance, and discuss high finance and politics with the gentlemen who came around. She wasn't just someone that you were supposed to hire to get laid—she was supposed to be that complete aspect to complement a man. She had apparent freedom in that she could have many lovers and had access to all these ideas and could act as an emulsifier to blend all these elements of the military and business and government.

The wife in Japanese society was the head of the household, and because Japan is so family oriented, that really is a position of enormous power. The wife has no apparent freedom, but she has this power, and she also has a stable position forever. Now, if a geisha wanted to be taken as a concubine into someone's household, maybe after her beauty or her ability to charm or seduce began to fade, she would always have to be second to the wife.

The price you pay for security.

Exactly, and that really went straight to my heart. It teaches you not to fool around with somebody else's husband, for one thing. You know you're always second to the wife, and also it's the best lesson of which path to choose, and to me those are still the two paths that are open for women: It's the geisha or the wife.

Do you think that's unfortunate?

I don't think it's unfortunate. I think it is the order of things. I think that is the natural order of things. I think that maybe in that time and civilization, maybe that was a good thing. I mean, women do seem to be by nature more inclined to be monogamous. I'm going to incur the wrath of every women's rights person, but I just think that that's more of a natural inclination.

Not in my experience.

Maybe not, maybe we're starting to get trained out of it. I'm more inclined to be that way. I'm not saying that I've only had one lover—my nose would grow clear to the other side of the wall—but my life is set up for it. A man can have more children, and it's sort of a thing for them to just go around and fertilize every woman. The independent woman that has a career is different, she's the exception to the rule. It's an unnatural situation in a sense.

But wouldn't you say that that's increasing?

It is increasing, and God only knows what the results will be. I don't know. I'm no expert. But a woman that has a family, just because of the fact that she bears children and has to stay home and a certain amount of her duties are taken up in tending to the family, that makes her less inclined to be promiscuous.

So you're saying that instead of taking the role of the wife you took the role of the geisha?

Yeah, most people are single in my business, anyway. It's just that that's the way I see myself. It's just a strange choice. You have apparent freedom but you're not really free, you know, because probably the most, the greatest thing you can aspire to is domestic bliss and tranquility, probably the highest state of being for a human being.

WHAT'S IT LIKE TO KNOW PEOple who you came up with, who you played music with in the beginning, who haven't really made it to your level, or who haven't made it at all? Do you lose friends because of your own accomplishment?

It depends on how strong they are. I love that line in a Joe Walsh song. Something about "I haven't changed. Everybody else has." You know? It's really true! I mean, it really is their attitude and their reaction to you that makes you react to them. It's not that you changed so much. It's just the way everybody else reacts to you that makes you go nuts. Everybody treats me like I'm weird now.

Real close friends treat you like "Linda Ronstadt"?

Some people did. And they didn't stay around. They couldn't. Neither one of us could stand how uncomfortable it was. And then there are people who were so sure of themselves that it didn't matter. And I'm so grateful for those people. I mean, it's the only continuity in my life. You hang onto them forever.

It must be very hard to come to a city like New York and meet a lot of new people.

It's hard to sort them out. It's like going to a place where they speak a foreign language.

How do you sort them out?

I don't know how to, exactly. You try to be real standoffish, because sometimes people worm their way in on the pretext of something. People say to me, "You're getting harder and harder to get to." My relatives say stuff like that. I've had to design it that way because it screens a lot of people, and so you're left with the most aggressive people. And lots of times the most aggressive people want to get at you for the worst reasons. It's a strange way to make friends. You have to sort of erect a fence and say, "Okay, scale this." It's like living on top of a glass mountain.

What can you do to change that?

Nothing. I think it's the only way to do it. Keep moving and keep it vague. I never make plans in advance. They want to know what I'm doing next month; I don't know. But if you shut it all off, then you don't get any input. You gotta stick your neck out, all the time.

Do you feel stronger and more capable of doing that now?

I've always been a risk-taker. I was when I was two. I take so many risks in my daily existence I think that it's made me very conservative in other areas. I don't take risks skiing or driving my car; I don't jump out of airplanes or parachute or things like that, but I think the personal risks I take are enormous. That's why I have to be . . . I try to cut corners on the risks. But gotta take risks.

The album and the tour are specific activities, and after that, everything's unspecific. What happens after that?

Take geisha lessons? I don't know. The trouble with being a latter-day geisha is that those geishas really could do it. They could dance and write and do art, and they could act and they could sing. They could do everything to perfection. I'm only a half-assed geisha. I can only sing.

INTERVIEWED BY JONATHAN COTT (1978)

In late 1977, Jonathan Cott conducted a lengthy interview with Bob Dylan, inspired by and centered on Dylan's film, *Renaldo and Clara*.

Now, in the fall of 1978, Dylan was on the road again, and hurting a little from reviews of his *Street-Legal* album. He'd also done something of a turnaround from his usual diffident/defiant stage manner; now he was trying, it seemed, to communicate with his audiences, with offhanded remarks, introductions of songs and band members, even jokes. For this, he was accused of going Las Vegas. That smarted, too.

So when Cott approached Dylan about an encore, he was hesitant. Once they got going, Cott found Dylan—as ever—"enigmatic, fascinating, witty and alert." Still, "he'd been much more accommodating the first time. On tour, he opened and closed and opened and closed—that kind of thing."

Soon after the 1978 tour, Dylan converted to "born-again" Christianity. "I had no clue that was happening," says Cott.

A final note about Cott: He's been faulted by some readers for questions loaded with obscure literary references. Or, as Cott says, "They say, 'The questions get too scholary, or overly serious.' I say: Maybe they're right. I just like to treat people I admire in a serious way—but playfully, too. To talk with rock artists with the same seriousness with which I'd talk to William Butler Yeats, were he alive. The idea is to get away from the 'What's-your-favorite-color?' and 'What-kind-of-girls-do-you-like?' questions." The idea, in short, of the ideal ROLLING STONE INTERVIEW.

—BF-T

ON THE EVENING OF SEPTEMBER 15TH, the Boston Red Sox were in New York City trying to get back into first place. In New Orleans, just before

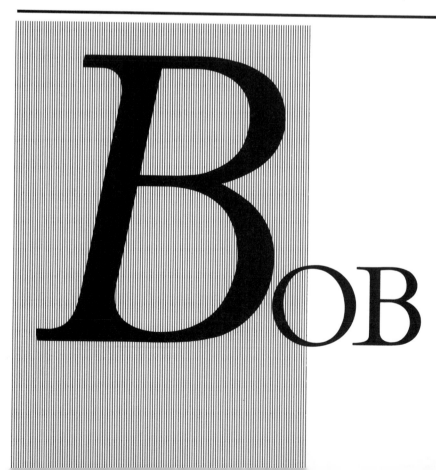

DYLAN

Muhammad Ali made his comeback, TV commentator Howard Cosell introduced the fighter by quoting from the song "Forever Young": "May your hands always be busy/May your feet always be swift/May you have a strong foundation/When the winds of changes shift." And in Augusta, Maine, the composer of that song was inaugurating a three-month tour of the United States and Canada that will include sixty-five concerts in sixty-two cities.

According to an Associated Press review of the opening night, Bob Dylan "drove a packed-house audience of 7200 into shrieks of ecstacy. The thirty-seven-year-old folk-rock singer mixed old songs and new. His audience in the Augusta Civic Center was a mixture of people who first knew Dylan as an angry young poet in the early Sixties and high-school students more accustomed to punk rock. Dylan satisfied both, although his veteran fans seemed the happiest."

After a highly successul series of concerts in Japan, Australia, New Zealand and Western Europe earlier this year, it might seem peculiar to think of Dylan's latest American tour as a kind of comeback. But, at least in this country, Dylan recently has been the recipient of some especially negative reviews, both for his film, 'Renaldo and Clara' (which, incidentally, was warmly greeted at this year's Cannes Film Festival), and his latest album, 'Street-Legal.' This billingsgate, moreover, has come from a number of Dylan's "veteran fans." In the 'Village Voice,' seven reviewers—a kind of firing squad—administered justice to the film with a fusillade of abuse. And ROLLING STONE, in its two August issues, featured a column and review that pilloried the album. Yet 'Street Legal' seems to me one of Dylan's most passionate, questing and questioning records.

I ran into Dylan in the hallway of his Portland motel at noon on September 17th—an hour before the entourage was to take off for New Haven. He was heading to breakfast and wasn't looking forward to it. "I ran into a girl last night," he told me as we walked to the dining room, "whom I knew in the Village in 1964. She figured the food wouldn't be too good up here, so she said she'd bring some with her this morning. But I haven't seen her."

"Maybe her love's in vain," I joked.

"Maybe," Dylan laughed.

But just after we had sat down and were told that breakfast wasn't being served any longer, a lovely woman appeared next to us with the promised feast in a basket. We ate, saved the muffins to give to the band later on and went out to catch the Scenicruiser bus that was to drive us to the local airport for the flight—on a chartered Bac III jet—to New Haven, where the group was to perform that night at the Veterans' Memorial Coliseum.

Dylan and I sat at the back of the bus. The musicians and tour organizers—the most organized and sweet-tempered people I've met in years—listened to a cassette recording of Ray Charles and the Raelettes. As the bus started, I foolhardily tried to interest Dylan in a theory I had about "Changing of the Guards"— namely, that the song could be seen to have a coded subtext revealed by the characters of various Tarot cards—the Moon, the Sun, the High Priestess, the Tower and, obviously, the King and Queen of Swords—the two cards Dylan specifically mentions. My idea was that the attributes associated with these images make up the "plot" of the song.

"I'm not really too acquainted with that, you know," he warded me off. (What was that Tarot card doing on the back of the jacket of 'Desire'? I wondered.) Undaunted, I mentioned that it had been said that Tarot diviners discover the future by intuition, with "prophetic images drawn from the vaults of the subconscious." Didn't Dylan think that a song like "Changing of the Guards" wakens in us the images of our subconscious? Certainly, I continued, such songs as that and "No Time to Think" suggested the idea of spirits manifesting their destiny as the dramatis personae of our dreams.

Dylan wasn't too happy with the drift of the discussion and fell silent. "I guess," I said, "there's no point in asking a magician how he does his tricks."

"Exactly!" Dylan responded cheerfully.

"Okay," I said, "we have to start someplace. What about the first line of 'Changing of the Guards'? Does 'sixteen years' have anything to do with the number of years you've been on the road?"

"No," Dylan replied, "sixteen is two short of eighteen years. Eighteen years is a magical number of years to put in time. I've found that threes and sevens . . . well, things come up in sevens. . . . What am I saying? I mean, what am I saying?"

I started rambling on about the possible mystical significance of numbers (sixteen equals one plus six, which equals seven, love minus zero, etc.), but by this time I realized that only the bus was going anywhere. It was time to get the interview rolling.

The Bus

W HEN I TELL ROLLING STONE what we've been talking about, they won't believe it.

They had the nerve to run the reviews they did on *Street-Legal*— why should I give them an interview, anyway?

Are you going to kick me off the bus?

No, it's your interview. It's okay. But if you were doing it for another magazine, it'd be okay, too.

Think I should go somewhere else with it?

Yeah—'Business Week.'

{The tape of Ray Charles and the Raelettes that has been counterpointing our banter has now given way to Joe Cocker's 'Mad Dogs and Englishmen.'} It's strange, but I noticed in your last two performances that your phrasing and the timbre of your voice at certain points resemble those of Little Anthony, Smokey Robinson and Gene Chandler. Are you aware of this?

No. When your environment changes, you change. You've got to go on, and you find new friends. Turn around one day and you're on a different stage, with a new set of characters.

In your new song, "No Time to Think," you list a series of qualities and concepts like loneliness, humility, nobility, patriotism, etc.

Is pregnancy in there?

It wasn't in there the last time I heard it. But I was thinking that it's these kinds of concepts that both free and imprison a person. What do you think?

I never have any time to think.

I should have known you'd say something like that. Maybe someone else should be up here doing this interview—a different character.

Someone who's not so knowledgeable. You're too knowledgeable.

I had the idea of just asking you the questions from "A Hard Rain's A Gonna Fall": Where have you been? What did you see? What did you hear? Whom did you meet? What'll you do now?

{Laughing} I'd be here the rest of my life talking to you. . . . Just look outside the window at the picket fences and the pine trees. New England falls are so beautiful, aren't they? Look at those two kids playing by the train tracks. They remind me of myself. Both of them.

Did you ever lie down on the tracks?

Not personally. I once knew someone who did.

What happened?

I lost track of him. . . . You should describe in your interview this village we're passing through, Jonathan. It's real special. Go ahead, describe it.

There's a little pond at the edge of the road . . .

. . . and here's the Stroudwater Baptist Church. We just turned the corner and are heading on down . . . I'll tell you in a minute. What do you call this kind of architecture? . . . Look at the ducks over there . . .

. . . and that little waterfall.

This is Garrison Street, we've just passed Garrison Street—probably never will again.

You're never coming back?

Oh, I bet we come back.

Clothes on the line behind that house.

Yeah, clothes on the line. Someone's frying chicken—didn't Kris Kristofferson say something like that? You don't see this in New York City . . . well, maybe at McDonald's. *{The bus pulls into the airport.}* This may be our last chance to talk, Jonathan. I hope we've got it down right this time.

The Plane

LET'S FIND SOMETHING TO talk about.

Maybe I should ask a question that Jann Wenner, the editor of ROLLING STONE, *wanted to ask you.*

Ask me one of his.

Okay, why are you doing this tour?

Well, why did I do the last one? I'm doing this one for the same reason I did the last one.

And what reason was that?

It was for the same reason that I did the one before that. I'm doing this tour for one reason or another, I can't remember what the reason is anymore.

Articles about the tour always mention that you're doing it for the money.

They always say that. There are more important things in the world than money. It means that to the people who write these articles, the most important thing in the world is money. They could be saying I'm doing the tour to meet girls or to see the world. Actually, it's all I know how to do. Ask Muhammad Ali why he fights one more fight. Go ask Marlon Brando why he makes one more movie. Ask Mick Jagger why he goes on the road. See what kind of answers you come up with. Is it so surprising I'm on the road? What else would I be doing in this life—meditating on the mountain? Whatever someone finds fulfilling, whatever his or her purpose is—that's all it is.

You recently said that you do new versions of your older songs because you believe in them—as if to believe in something is to make it real.

They *are* real, and that's why I keep doing them. As I said before, the reason for the new

357

versions is that I've changed. You meet new people in your life, you're involved on different levels with people. Love is a force, so when a force comes in your life—and there's love surrounding you—you can do anything.

Is that what's happening to you now?

Something similar to that, yeah.

When you introduce the singers onstage as your childhood sweethearts, your present girlfriend, your former girlfriend—is that literal?

Oh, of course.

May I list the themes I found on 'Street-Legal'?

Yeah.

Survival, homelessness, trust, betrayal, sacrifice, exile, tyranny and victimization.

All right, those things go through all of my songs because I feel those things. And those feelings touch me, so naturally they're going to appear in the songs.

I've got twenty-two or twenty-three albums out on Columbia alone and about seventy-five bootleg records floating around, so it gets to a point where it doesn't matter anymore. You want each new record to be your best, but you know you're going to write more songs and make another album anyway. People who get hit with the new album for the first time . . . it surprises them, it's coming at them from someplace and maybe they haven't thought about things that way. But that's not for me to say. That's my life, and if they can find identity in that, okay—and if they can't, that's okay, too.

A song like "No Time to Think" sounds like it comes from a very deep dream.

Maybe, because we're all dreaming, and these songs come close to getting inside that dream. It's all a dream anyway.

As in a dream, lines from one song seem to connect with lines from another. For example: "I couldn't tell her what my private thoughts were/But she had some way of finding them out" in "Where Are You Tonight?" and "The captain waits above the celebration/Sending his thoughts to a beloved maid" in "Changing of the Guards."

I'm the first person who'll put it to you and the last person who'll explain it to you. Those questions can be answered dozens of different ways, and I'm sure they're all legitimate. Everybody sees in the mirror what he sees—no two people see the same thing.

Usually you don't specify things or people in your songs. We don't know who Marcel and St. John are in "Where Are You Tonight?" or who the "partner in crime" is in that same song. . . .

Who *isn't* your partner in crime?

But in a song like "Sara" you seem fairly literal.

I've heard it said that Dylan was never as truthful as when he wrote *Blood on the Tracks*, but that wasn't necessarily *truth*, it was just *perceptive*. Or when people say "Sara" was written for "his wife Sara"—it doesn't necessarily have to be about her just because my wife's name happened to be Sara. Anyway, was it the real Sara or the Sara in the dream? I still don't know.

Is "Is Your Love in Vain?" to be taken literally? You've been accused of being chauvinistic in that song, especially in the line, "Can you cook and sew, make flowers grow?"

That criticism comes from people who think that women should be karate instructors or airplane pilots. I'm not knocking that—everyone should achieve what she wants to achieve—but when a man's looking for a woman, he ain't looking for a woman who's an airplane pilot. He's looking for a woman to help him out and support him, to hold up one end while he holds up another.

Is that the kind of woman you're looking for?

What makes you think I'm looking for any woman?

You could say that th. song isn't necessarily about you, yet some people think that you're singing about yourself and your needs.

Yeah, well, I'm everybody anyway.

There's a lot of talk about magic in 'Street-Legal': "I wish I was a magician/I would wave a wand and tie back the bond/That we've both gone beyond" in "We Better Talk This Over"; "But the magician is quicker and his game/Is much thicker than blood" in "No Time to Think."

These are things I'm really interested in, and it's taken me a while to get back to it. Right through the time of *Blonde on Blonde* I was doing it unconsciously. Then one day I was half-stepping, and the lights went out. And since that point, I more or less had amnesia. Now, you can take that statement as literally or metaphysically as you need to, but that's what happened to me. It took me a long time to get to do consciously what I used to be able to do unconsciously.

It happens to everybody. Think about the periods when people don't do anything, or they lose it and have to regain it, or lose it and gain something else. So it's taken me all this time, and the records I made along the way were like openers—trying to figure out whether it was this way or that way, just what *is* it, what's the simplest way I can tell the story and make this feeling real.

So now I'm connected back, and I don't know how long I'll be there because I don't know how long I'm going to live. But what comes now is for real and from a place that's . . . I don't know, I don't care who else cares about it.

John Wesley Harding was a fearful album—just dealing with fear *{laughing}*, but dealing with the devil in a fearful way, almost. All I wanted to do was to get the words right. It was courageous to do it because I could have *not* done it, too. Anyway, on *Nashville Skyline* you had to read between the lines. I was trying to grasp something that would lead me on to where I thought I should be, and it didn't go nowhere—it just went down, down, down. I couldn't be anybody but myself, and at that point I didn't know it or want to know it.

I was convinced I wasn't going to do anything else, and I had the good fortune to meet a man in New York City who taught me how to see. He put my mind and my hand and my eye together in a way that allowed me to do consciously what I unconsciously felt. And I didn't know how to pull it off. I wasn't sure it could be done in songs because I'd never written a song like that. But when I started doing it, the first album I made was *Blood on the Tracks*. Everybody agrees that that was pretty different, and what's different about it is that there's a code in the lyrics and also there's no sense of time. There's no respect for it: you've got yesterday, today and tomorrow all in the same room, and there's very little that you can't imagine not happening.

In 'Tarantula' you write about a woman named Justine who tells you that "only God can be everywhere at the same Time and Space."

That's right, but that was unconscious. And that drilled me down—doing it unconsciously was doing it like a primitive, and it took everything out of me. Everything was gone; I was drained. I found out later that it was much wiser to do it consciously, and it could let things be much stronger, too. Actually, you might even live longer, but I'm not sure about that.

From that point I went on to *Desire*, which I wrote with Jacques Levy. And I don't remember who wrote that. And then I disappeared for a while. Went on the Rolling Thunder tour, made *Renaldo and Clara*—in which I also used that quality of no-time. And I believe that that concept of creation is more real and true than that which *does* have time.

When you feel in your gut what you are and then dynamically pursue it—don't back down and don't give up—then you're going to mystify a lot of folks. Some people say, "I don't like him anymore." But other people do, and my crowd gets bigger and bigger. But who cares, really *{laughing}*? If you fall down and you're hurting, you care about that immediate situation—if you have the energy to care. Who *really* cares? It's like that line—how does it go?—"Propaganda, who really cares? . . ."

I wanted to ask you about love.

Go ahead, but I'm not too qualified on that subject. Love comes from the Lord—it keeps all of us going. If you want it, you got it.

You've described and communicated the idea of two aspects of love—the love that longs for commitment and the love that longs to be free. Which is the most real to you?

All of it. It's all love that needs to be love.

You often sing about having a twin, a sister/wife, a dream/lover for one's life.

Everyone feels these feelings. People don't like to admit that that's the way things are because it's too confusing.

A famous short poem by William Blake goes: "He who binds to himself a joy/Doth the winged life destroy/But he who kisses the joy as it flies/Lives in Eternity's sun rise."

Allen Ginsberg quoted that to me all the time. Blake's been a big influence on Kristofferson, too.

What about soul mates?

What about them?

Do they exist?

Sure, they do, but sometimes you never meet them. A soul mate . . . what do they mean by soul mate? There's a male and a female in everyone, don't they say that? So I guess the soul mate would be the physical mate of the soul. But that would mean we're supposed to be with just one other person. Is a soul mate a romantic notion or is there real truth in that, señor?

That's what I was asking you.

How would I know?

Well, a lot of your songs are concerned with that . . . Someone once said that one's real feelings come out when one's separated from somebody one loves.

Who said that?

Nietzsche.

Well, I guess he's right. Your real feelings do come out when you're free to be alone. Most people draw a line that they don't want you to cross—that's what happens in most petty relationships.

In a song such as "Like a Rolling Stone," and now "Where Are You Tonight?" and "No Time to Think," you seem to tear away and remove the layers of social identity—burn away the "rinds" of received reality—and bring us back to the zero state.

That's right. "Stripped of all virtue as you crawl through the dirt/You can give but you cannot receive." Well, I said it.

{At this point the pilot announces that we'll be landing in five minutes.} Just a few quick questions before we land. Coming back to "Changing of the Guards" . . .

It means something different every time I sing it.

The lines, "She's smelling sweet like the meadows where she was born/On Midsummer's eve, near the tower," are so quiet and pure.

Oh, yeah?

Those lines seem to go back a thousand years into the past.

They do. "Changing of the Guards" is a thousand years old. Woody Guthrie said he just picked songs out of the air. That meant that they were already there and that he was tuned into them. "Changing of the Guards" might be a song that might have been there for thousands of years, sailing around in the mist, and one day I just tuned into it. Just like "Tupelo Honey" was floating around and Van Morrison came by.

It's been said that the Stones' song, "Some Girls," hints at being about you a bit.

I've never lived at Zuma Beach.

Jagger imitates your phrasing, though.

He always does. . . . He imitates Otis Redding, too, and Riley Puckett and Slim Harpo.

In "One More Cup of Coffee" you sing about a sister who sees the future, and in "Changing of the Guards" you sing about "treacherous young witches."

I meet witchy women. Somehow I attract them. I wish they'd leave me alone.

Well, there are some good witches, too, though that voodoo girl in "New Pony" was giving you some trouble.

That's right. By the way, the Miss X in that song is Miss X, not ex-.

In "We Better Talk This Over," is the line, "I'm exiled, you can't covert me," in some way about being Jewish?

Listen, I don't know how Jewish I am because I've got blue eyes. My grandparents were from Russia, and going back that far, which one of those women didn't get raped by the Cossacks? So there's plenty of Russian in me, I'm sure. Otherwise, I wouldn't be the way I am.

Do you agree with Octavio Paz' idea that "all of us are alone, because all of us are two"?

I can't disagree, but I've got to think there's more than two. Didn't Leonard Cohen sing something like, "I'm the one who goes from nothing to two"? I don't remember.

We're back to numbers.

Leonard Cohen was really interested in numbers: "I'm the one who goes from nothing to one."

You're a Gemini, and the Gemini twins have been seen by one writer, Marius Schneider, as symbols of the "harmonious ambiguity of paradise and inferno, love and hate, peace and war, birth and death, praise and insult, clarity and obscurity, scorching rocks and swamps surrounding the fountains and waters of salvation." That sounds like a good description of some of your new songs.

Right, but you can't choose the month of the year you're born in.

"Sacrifice is the code of the road" is what you sing in "Where Are You Tonight?" To die before dying, shedding your skin, making new songs out of old ones.

That's my mission in life. . . . "He not busy being born is busy dying." Did you bring your parachute?

The interview was that bad, huh?

{Talking to a friend} Bring a parachute for Jonathan.

I'd prefer the pathway that leads up to the stars.

The Dressing Room

I RAN INTO DYLAN BACKSTAGE half an hour before a sound check at the Veterans' Memorial Coliseum in New Haven. He invited me into his room, where we concluded our talk.

When I was waiting to pick up my ticket for your Portland concert last night, I happened to ask the woman behind the desk where all these kids were coming from. And she said: "For Bobby Dylan, from heaven—for Black Sabbath, who knows?"

Well, I believe it, don't you? Where else could my particular audience come from?

I've already met two angelic types—one in your dressing room here in New Haven, the other the girl whom you knew fifteen years ago who brought you a breakfast in Portland.

They're all angels. . . . But I wanted to ask you about something Paul Wasserman [who's in charge of Dylan's publicity] said that you said to him, and that is: "A genius can't be a genius on instinct alone."

I said that? Maybe, but really late at night.

Well, I disagree. I believe that instinct *is* what makes a genius a genius.

What do you think of all the criticisms of 'Street-Legal'?

I read some of them. In fact, I didn't understand them. I don't think these people have had the experiences I've had to write those songs. The reviews didn't strike me as being particularly interesting one way or another, or as compelling to my particular scene. I don't know who these people are. They don't travel in the same crowd, anyway. So it would be like me criticizing Pancho Villa.

The reviews in this country of 'Renaldo and Clara' weren't good, either. The writers went out of their way to call you presumptuous, pretentious and egocentric.

These people probably don't like to eat what I like to eat, they probably don't like the same things I like, or the same people. Look, just one time I'd like to see any one of those assholes try and do what I do. Just once let one of them write a song to show how they feel and sing it in front of 10, let alone 10,000 or 100,000 people. I'd like to see them just try that one time.

Some of these critics have suggested that you need more sophisticated record production.

I probably do. The truth of it is that I can hear the same sounds that other people like to hear, too. But I don't like to spend the time trying to get those sounds in the studio.

So you're really not a producer type?

I'm not. Some musicians like to spend a lot of time in the studio. But a lot of people try to make something out of nothing. If you don't have a good song, you can go into the studio and make it appear to be good, but that stuff don't last.

You've had producers—Tom Wilson, Bob Johnson, Don De Vito. . . .

But that wasn't all that sophisticated. I mean, John Hammond produced my first record, and it was a matter of singing into a microphone. He'd say, "It sounded good to me," and you'd go on to the next song. That's still the way I do it.

Nowadays, you start out with anything *but* the song—the drum track, for instance—and you take a week getting the instruments all sounding the way they should. They put down the rhythm track or whatever sound they want to hear in the ghost tracks. If you have a good song, it doesn't matter how well or badly it's produced. Okay, my records aren't produced that well, I admit it.

Personally, I love the "primitive" sound of Buddy Holly demo tapes or the original Chuck Berry discs.

But in those days they recorded on different equipment, and the records were thicker. If you buy one of my early records—and you can't today—they weren't like Saran Wrap, as they are now. There was quality to them . . . and the machinery was different and the boards were different. The Beach Boys did stuff on two-track in the garage.

But you do need a producer now?

I think so. You see, in the recent past my method, when I had the songs, was to go in, record them and put them out. Now I'm writing songs on the run again—they're dear to me, the songs I'm doing now—and I can't perfect them. So if I can just block time out, here and there, I can work on an album the way the Eagles do. I've got so many records out that it doesn't matter when I put out a new one. I could release one a year from now—start working on it in January and have it produced right.

What's the longest it's taken you to record a song?

About six or seven hours. It took us a week to make *Street-Legal*—we mixed it the following week and put it out the week after. If we hadn't done it that fast we wouldn't have made an album at all, because we were ready to go back on the road.

You've got a bigger sound now—on record and onstage—than you've ever had before.

I do—and I might hire two more girls and an elephant—but it doesn't matter how big the sound gets as long as it's behind me emphasizing the song. It's still pretty simple. There's nothing like it in Vegas—no matter what you've heard—and it's anything but disco. It's not rock & roll—my roots go back to the Thirties, not the Fifties.

On this tour, you've again been changing some of the radically new versions of songs that I heard you perform in Europe this past summer.

Yeah, we've changed them around some—it's a different tour and a different show. The band has to relearn the songs, but they're fast and the best at that.

Do you write songs now with them in mind?

I've had this sound ever since I was a kid—what grabs my heart. I had to play alone for a long time, and that was good because by playing alone I had to write songs. That's what I didn't do when I first started out, just playing available songs with a three-piece honky-tonk band in my hometown. But when I was first living in New York City—do you remember the old Madison Square Garden? Well, they used to have gospel shows there every Sunday, and you could see everyone from the Five Blind Boys, the Soul Stirrers and the Swan Silvertones to Clara Ward and the Mighty Clouds of Joy. I went up there every Sunday. I'd listen to that and Big Bill Broonzy. Then I heard the Clancy Brothers and hung out with them—all of their drinking songs, their revolutionary and damsel-in-distress songs. And I listened to Jean Ritchie, Woody Guthrie, Leadbelly.

What about the doo-wop groups?

They played at shows, and those artists didn't have to be onstage for more than twenty minutes. They just got on and got off, and that was never what I wanted to do. I used to go to the Brooklyn Fox a lot, but the band I liked the best at that time was Bobby Blue Bland's, and I heard them at the Apollo. But the people whose floors I was sleeping on were all into the Country Gentlemen, Uncle Dave Macon, the Stanley Brothers, Bill Monroe. So I heard all that, too.

You seem to like music that's real and uncorrupted, no matter what its tradition. But some of your folk-music followers didn't care much for your own musical changes.

But don't forget that when I played "Maggie's Farm" electric at Newport, that was something I would have done years before. They thought I didn't know what I was doing and that I'd slipped over the edge, but the truth is . . . Kooper and Michael Bloomfield remember that scene very well. And what the newspapers say happened didn't actually happen that way. There wasn't a whole lot of resistance in the crowd. Don't forget they weren't equipped for what we were doing with the sound. But I had a legitimate right to do that.

The Beatles and the Rolling Stones were already popular in this country at that time, though.

I remember hanging out with Brian Jones in 1964. Brian could play the blues. He was an excellent guitar player—he seemed afraid to sing for some reason—but he could play note for note what Robert Johnson or Son House played.

In songs like "Buckets of Rain" or "New Pony," you seem just to go in and out of musical traditions, pick up what you want and need, and transform them as you please.

That's basically what I do, but so do the Stones. Mick and Keith knew all that music. America's filled with all kinds of different music.

When you sang "Baby Stop Crying" the other night in Portland, I remember thinking that your voice sounded as if it combined the following qualities: tenderness, sarcasm, outraged innocence, indignation, insouciant malice and wariness.

The man in that song has his hand out and is not afraid of getting it bit.

He sounds stronger than the woman he's singing to and about.

Not necessarily. The roles could be reversed at any time—don't you remember "To Ramona"? "And someday maybe, who knows baby, I'll come and be cryin' to you."

In the song "Baby Stop Crying," it sounds as if the singer is getting rejected—that the woman's in love with someone else.

She probably is.

There's also a "bad man" in the song. It's almost as if three or four different movies were taking place in one song, all held together by the chorus. And the same thing seems to be happening in "Changing of the Guards" and some of your other new songs. What's that all about?

Lord knows.

How come you write in that way?

I wouldn't be doing it unless some power higher than myself were guiding me on. I wouldn't be here this long. Let me put it another way. . . . What was the question?

There are all these different levels in many of your recent songs.

That's right, and that's because my mind and my heart work on all those levels. Shit, I don't want to be chained down to the same old level all the time.

I've seen you tell people who don't know you that some other person standing nearby is you.

Well sure, if some old fluff ball comes wandering in looking for the real Bob Dylan, I'll direct him down the line, but I can't be held accountable for that.

A poet and critic named Elizabeth Sewell once wrote, "Discovery, in science and poetry, is a mythological situation in which the mind unites with a figure of its own devising as a means toward understanding the world." And it seems as if you have created a figure named Bob Dylan. . . .

I didn't create Bob Dylan. Bob Dylan has always been here . . . always was. When I was a child, there was Bob Dylan. And before I was born, there was Bob Dylan.

Why did you have to play that role?

I'm not sure. Maybe I was best equipped to do it.

The composer Arnold Schönberg once said the same thing: Someone had to be Arnold Schönberg.

Sometimes your parents don't even know who you are. No one knows but you. Lord, if your own parents don't know who you are, who else in the world is there who would know except you?

Then why do children keep on wanting things from their parents they can't give them?

Misunderstanding.

In contradistinction to the idea of being true to oneself, there's an idea of the personality—suggested by Yeats—which states that "man is nothing till he is united to an image." You seem to have your foot in both camps.

I don't know about that. Sometimes I think I'm a ghost. Don't you have to have some poetic sense to be involved in what we're talking about? It's like what you were saying about people putting my record down. I couldn't care less if they're doing that, but, I mean, who are these people, what qualifications do they have? Are they poets, are they musicians? You find me some musician or poet, and then maybe we'll talk. Maybe that person will know something I don't know, and I'll see it that way. That could happen. I'm not almighty. But my feelings come from the gut, and I'm not too concerned with someone whose feelings come from his head. That don't bother me none.

This criticism has been going on for a long time. It's like a lover: you like somebody, and then you don't want to like them anymore because you're afraid to admit to yourself that you like them so much. . . . I don't know, you've just got to try, try to do some good for somebody. The world is full of nonsupporters and backbiters—people who chew on wet rags. But it's also filled with people who love you.

There are lines in your new songs about the one you love being so hard to recognize, or about feeling displaced and in exile. It seems as if the tyranny of love makes people unhappy.

That's the tyranny of man-woman love. That ain't too much love.

What's your idea of love?

{Pause} Love like a driving wheel. That's my idea of love.

What about Cupid with his bow and arrows aimed toward your heart?

Naw, Cupid comes in a beard and a mustache, you know. Cupid has dark hair.

31

INTERVIEWED BY PAUL GAMBACCINI (1979)

Between the first long Paul McCartney interview and this one, London correspondent Paul Gambaccini filed what seemed to him like hundreds of stories and random notes about McCartney and Wings.

"I began to feel embarrassed by the number of McCartney pieces I'd done," he says. "But it was simple. Paul doesn't like schedules. So you couldn't plan weeks ahead, from America, and nail him down on a specific date. And if he wanted to do something, he'd ring up two or three days in advance."

In spring 1979, a McCartney aide rang up Gambaccini. Paul had just finished the album *Back to the Egg,* "and they knew ROLLING STONE was interested—the magazine had sent a writer over a couple of years before, and he could never pin McCartney down, so this was the interview that was supposed to have been done in 1977."

Back to the Egg turned out to be "McCartney's major disappointment," says Gambaccini. But he would bounce back, in 1980, with the hit, "Coming Up," reunite with Beatles producer George Martin and release *Cold Cuts.*

—BF-T

FIFTEEN YEARS AGO THE BEATLES' first film, 'A Hard Day's Night,' opened around the world. The mere fact that it was a black-and-white film tells us how much time has passed. During the intervening decade and a half, millions of lives were affected, some profoundly, by the Beatles. It sounds heretical and contradictory, but one person who seems relatively unchanged is Paul McCartney. He is definitely a richer man, but his wealth has merely brought him the freedom to do what he wants, and that is simply, to make music and be with his family. He makes few concessions to his celebrity and attends few public functions, unintentionally ensuring that each appearance is an event. The Buddy Holly tributes he

McCARTNEY

has been involved with have drawn the most star-studded assemblies the London musical fraternity has seen during the last three years. At home on his estate south of London, Paul watches a good deal of television with Linda and the kids. He listens to BBC radio going to and from his London studio, preferring to drive himself rather than be chauffeured. Anyone searching for a departure in his behavior from that of the people who buy his records would be disappointed.

Whereas 'Please Please Me,' the Beatles' first British album, was recorded in one day, McCartney now works for weeks on a Wings LP. He records where fancy strikes: in Nigeria ('Band on the Run'), New Orleans ('Venus and Mars'), on a boat afloat in the Caribbean ('London Town') or, in the case of the new LP, 'Back to the Egg,' in a castle overlooking the English Channel.

'Back to the Egg' does not include his recent disco-influenced hit single, "Goodnight Tonight," simply because McCartney felt it would not fit musically. While the LP makes few obvious concessions to disco or New Wave, it rocks more than 'London Town'; "Old Siam, Sir," the new single in Britain, sounds more like Tina Turner or a manic bluesman than Paul McCartney.

Paul is frightened of critical rejection, but this is nothing new: He remembers when a top BBC disc jockey predicted "She Loves You" would not be a hit. Time and public acclaim of his work have given him the confidence to plan activities that critics may not consider rock & roll. He is also relieved to have put behind him the financial mismanagement the Beatles suffered and to be in the skilled hands of his father-in-law, Lee Eastman, who with his son John has succeeded both in negotiating the most preferential recording contracts in history and in investing the McCartney profits in publishing catalogs that have already earned many times their purchase prices. John also represents Paul in the seemingly never-ending negotiations to allocate the funds of the Beatles' now-defunct record company, Apple.

I have known Paul McCartney for over five years, since just before the release of 'Band on the Run.' When I first met him, he was struggling to establish Wings. After an inauspicious start with "Wild Life," "Mary Had a Little Lamb" and "Give Ireland Back to the Irish," the group had rallied for three hits: "Hi, Hi, Hi," "My Love" and "Live and Let Die." Not surprisingly, McCartney at that time was desperate to avoid talking about the Beatles, especially about the never-ending reunion rumors. He regarded me with the suspicion he had for any inquisitive young reporter and dismissed mention of the Beatles' early days as "ancient history."

In the years since 'Band on the Run,' Paul has let down his defenses. Anecdotes about the Beatles now flow, in addition to reminiscences of pre-Beatles days. He seems pleased with his past. This is a product of being happy with his present.

This interview was conducted in two installments in late March 1979. We began in EMI Studios, Abbey Road, where McCartney worked with the Beatles and where he works with Wings whenever they are not flying around the world. "Silly Love Songs" and "My Love," Wings' biggest American hits, as well as "Goodnight Tonight," their latest hit single, were cut here.

The second phase of the interview was held in a photography studio above Belsize Park subway station in north London. While the cover picture of the new album was being set up, a long and exhausting process, we chatted in a third-story room discussing the new album, the two-song supersession that Paul calls the Rockestra and McCartney's hope that Wings can tour later this year and turn up unannounced at small clubs. We also talked about his opinion of the British New Wave; the time Paul and the original Beatles drummer, Pete Best, were deported from Germany; how McCartney considered counseling Sid Vicious; the Beatles' fear that Gerry and the Pacemakers would be more popular—things like that.

I REMEMBER READING A QUOTE from journalist-broadcaster Tony Palmer, I believe, who said at one point in the Sixties, "It must be the hardest thing in the world to be Paul McCartney." Have you ever thought it was hard to be you?

No, I think it would be harder to be Idi Amin and one or two others. To go from being a kid living on a street on some council estate [public-housing project] to becoming very famous is a big change. Living with all the trappings of that isn't an easy adjustment; your privacy has to go a bit. It is a bit humiliating sometimes if you have a hangover or you really just feel rough, and you've got to do an autograph or stand while someone takes a picture. But you reach a point where you realize you can't turn back.

I wonder if live television would be too nerveracking now for groups, considering that the audiences would just multiply a millionfold by international broadcast. Do you think that would be a bit nerveracking?

I don't think any group minds an audience of millions. I think they thrive on that.

That's interesting, because when those silly offers to reunite the Beatles were being made a couple of years ago, I thought the most terrifying aspect of it would *have been so many people watching, but that wasn't scaring you?*

No, I don't think that had anything to do with it. The whole Beatles reunion thing was always a nonstarter, because we had all just broken up. It is like getting divorced: After you've made the big decision you don't want someone coming up and saying, "Hey, listen, I think it would be a great idea if you all got married again." Things like money and TV exposure are not relevant. If we'd wanted to get together, instead of the opposite, then I'm sure no one would have minded. They would have wanted all that TV exposure. In fact, I remember when the Beatles were breaking up, my thought was that what we needed to do was get back on the road and do what I want to do now, which is sort of turn up at small clubs. And I remember John saying, "No way. We want to play to 200,000, don't we?"

Well, do you think you will be turning up unadvertised with Wings?

Me? Yes, I think so. I like just turning up on a bunch of people. There is a different kind of electricity when they didn't expect you. *You* get something and *they* get something, which was my original idea for the Beatles [in the late Sixties]. As far as a Beatles reunion is concerned, I don't think that would ever happen. . . . I don't think it would really be a good thing if it did.

By now it has taken on such a mythic quality. . . .

Yeah . . . it gets a bit that, doesn't it? A bit legendary, and the mists of time roll back to reveal . . . I mean, you know, there's no use. You can't say, "Look, you know we're all humans, and we were in this fun group together and we had a great time, but it ended for various reasons." I don't need to go into them for you; it was bad enough going into them for me. So you don't really need people expecting all that sort of stuff to happen, but people still do.

There are still little legal hassles to this day, aren't there?

Not legal hassles. What happened is that when we were the Beatles, instead of setting us all up legally as individuals, everyone set us up as a partnership. So when we wanted to split up I just naively thought, "Well, I'll take my ball and go. I'll just have my bit, and we'll call it a day." But we found that you couldn't just take your little ball and go because of millions of legal reasons. So it's now ten years since we started the whole thing, and you wouldn't believe what we've been through. You just wouldn't.

How much of this is because of being young and naive when you originally signed your contracts, and how much of it is because of disagreements within the group?

Well, I think I *was* young and naive about all of that until the Beatles broke up. It was just, "Well, we all know nobody will screw each other. We all pretty much know each other. We'll all do it okay." It's just disagreements within the group because, as I say, all the contracts that were signed could have been broken up quite easily. I would be happy to do a deal that's going now. Just so that we don't have that hanging over our heads and can just say hello again without having to say, "Hello, and by the way, Apple requires you to sign this."

Have you been following the trial of Allen Klein? [The Beatles' short-term mentor after the death of Brian Epstein, Klein was convicted this year on one count of income-tax evasion for failing to declare a "substantial" amount of cash obtained in 1970 by selling promotional copies of Beatles albums. He was to be sentenced June 18th and faced up to three years in prison and a maximum fine of $5000.]

No, I just started reading about it the other day. I feel sorry for him now. I was caught in his net once, and that panicked me. I really wanted to do everything to get him. I was contemplating going to where he lives and walking outside his house with placards, doing all that. I was really that crazy at the time. I would have done anything to get out of it, but it all turned out okay.

Do you now regret selling the publishing rights to some of the Beatles songs?

I don't now because I own some of my new stuff totally, and my company is into publishing. So I don't mind, but it is funny to think that somebody owns, "Yesterday" and that it's only to do with me as far as the royalties are concerned. It's funny to think of some of the things that went down. In fact, it's more than funny, it's crazy, because companies were sold behind our backs, and we always had a tiny share of everything. And all the big businessmen always advised us to sell everything. They never said, "Hold onto your paintings because one day they might be valuable." So we were persuaded to sell all the bits and pieces of our rights, which is about the worst advice you can get. Lord Goodman, who shall not be nameless, was one of the people advising us at that time. I don't think it was good advice, and he ended up advising the Labour government. So he told us the wrong things; he probably told them the wrong things.

367

Were you really on one percent royalty at the beginning?

To tell you the truth, I don't remember. I don't really know what percent. Those days I just signed the contract. It was too long and boring to really read. It would have taken way too much time, plus I couldn't understand it.

You said something very revealing when I was changing the tapes, which is that you are still a bit shy to say you own "Stormy Weather."

You've got to do something with money. You've got to invest it in something. I love songs, and the opportunity came up to do all that, and so I'm now a publisher and a businessman, which to me is something I don't like to talk about too much. Maybe I'm not grown up enough.

What originally happened was, Lee Eastman . . . asked me, "If you were to invest in stuff, what kind of stuff do you like?" And I said, "Music." And he said, "Well, what kind of people in music do you like?" I told him a few. I said, "Buddy Holly, but if you're talking about more up-to-date people, Harry Nilsson, Randy Newman."

I love Buddy Holly, I've been crazy about him since I was a kid. And Lee rang up one day and said, "Buddy Holly's publishing is up for sale." I said, "Fantastic, I don't believe it." And he said, "We got it, for the company, we got it." So, I just thought, well, either we just get it and leave it, which would be possible, or we try and make a bit of noise about it and get some bit of activity going. So I said, "Let's have Buddy Holly Week; let's have it on his birthday instead of his death day and just try to get people to play his music, 'cause there are kids who've never even heard him." It's a pretty haphazard thing, but last year we had Buddy's film [*The Buddy Holly Story*], which worked out great; the year before we had the Crickets [Holly's band]; and the year before we had Norman Petty [Holly's producer]. It awakened a lot of interest. You suddenly started to find Teds pouring out of the cracks in the floorboards 'cause there was incredible interest there that I hadn't even realized, really. Finding these fourteen- and fifteen-year-old kids coming in—all the hairdos—saying, "Yeah, man, Buddy Holly, he's my favorite, him and Eddie Cochran." And Eddie Cochran was dead before they were born. But they still got this big feeling for him. And Buddy is now like the big hero. Not that he wasn't always, but there is new interest in him, which I think is great.

It must have been a relief when you realized that all of these protracted Apple negotiations really don't matter that much anymore, because your current fiscal structure means that, while it may not be a drop in the bucket, nonetheless you don't need it.

Indeed. That was it. For a while it wasn't so much that I needed it; it was just that the whole thing was like a headache, an emotional headache. This is getting like a psychiatrist's interview, isn't it? It wasn't particularly all the money. It was just that it was a drag to be arguing with these three people whom I'd come all this way with, and it just wasn't possible to wink and say, "Come on, let's sit down at the table and just talk about it."

How much were you involved in the decision to switch labels in America from Capitol to Columbia?

I stay along with the trip on top of it all, and I'm very involved in the decisions. But I don't do the deals, and I don't go to the meetings and sit down and make demands. We're really lucky to have . . . some honest people whom you feel you can trust. I think most people have slight suspicions about their managements or their lawyers.

Would you feel comfortable advising some of the younger musicians, like the Sex Pistols? They obviously went wrong financially from your point of view.

It would be very easy; I'd know exactly what to tell them, having come through it, but there would be certain conditions. One is, find yourself an honest person to do that bit for you. Did you mean it on the level of, would I as an elder feel like the kids would say, "Aw, piss off, you old fart . . . what do you know?" [*Gambaccini nods.*] Yeah, because I know that they've got to be just like what we were. So for that reason it isn't easy to approach people like that. I certainly thought of going to see Sid Vicious and trying to say something to him that would cool him out and make it all okay, 'cause I feel I can really understand people who get into things like that.

And then Sid Vicious dies, and what do you think?

Well, exactly. You don't know. You didn't know what to think before he died. I don't know [*shrugs*]. Lord Lucan is missing. [A young British lord, who is suspected of murder and has disappeared.]

I was thinking this when you were talking about the Apple hassles. Do you have days now when you never once think of the Beatles?

Oh, yeah. Most days. When the Beatles broke up it was painful to talk about. It was just hard. So you found yourself thinking about it. Now, having come all this way, I can remember only the good stuff. I know one or two spicy stories and I have my bitch now and again, but generally I always did dig it; I always did think that what we were doing was great. Even when we broke up, I never thought like John did. Who knows why he thought that? John's pretty complex. He possibly didn't even mean it. All the stuff about how we were "bastards." . . . He brought out the worst side, as if to exorcise it. But I really didn't agree. It was pretty good, you know. But there are days when I don't think about it because I'm doing all sorts of other stuff.

Actually, it's fifteen years ago. . .

That "Can't Buy Me Love" was out? No!

Well, that the Top Five in the States were all yours.

Oh, was it? *Great!* So what shall we do about that?

Well, I think that whenever that week comes along, you should just have a little toast.

You'll have to play them one by one [on the radio].

You must have taken so many plane rides. Do you feel safe flying? Have you ever had any close shaves?

Oh, yes, too many, but for me, flying has been sort of like a long story. It started off when me and Pete Best, who used to be the drummer with the Beatles in bygone ages, got deported from Hamburg, and the first time I'd flown was on that plane back.

Why?

We got deported because we'd been changing clubs. We used to play this place called the Indra, and we got an offer to work another club for higher pay. So we were going to move to this other club called the Top Ten. And we'd been stuck in the back of a cinema by our employer, a really dirty old place right next to a bog [toilet]. It was all concrete walls. No sort of paper on the walls—really damp and everything. We used to sleep there in our leather jackets—camp beds, two in a room.

Pretty punk?

Pretty punk, man! The jeans and leather jackets, next to the bog—pretty New Wave at the time. Anyway, we always thought our employer had never done well by us. So I seem to remember that Pete Best had a contraceptive in his luggage, so when we were moving, just as a joke, we pinned it up and set it up in smoke, which left a kind of black mark about two feet long on this wall.

We packed up and went to the other club. As we were walking down the street, same evening, the German police pulled up [*imitates a siren and the police voices saying, "Come on, step inside please, hello!"*]. And they slung us in the jail, and we were in there for about three or four hours with one of those little peepholes and we couldn't see anything, and we didn't know what we were in for. Eventually it transpired that this guy had said we tried to burn down his cinema. He was kidding; he should have known better. But I think it was basically because he was sore at us for leaving him. He tried to nail us for breaking contracts. And the fellow from the other club came down with a bottle of scotch for the police—or whatever, I don't really know—and he eventually got us out and we went and played at the Top Ten.

So anyway, we got woken up one morning—me and Pete. I think it was because we'd set the little fire, that's why. And the cops just said, "You come with us." And we got in the back of the car, went down to a place called the Rathaus, which is like some government building—it means something in German. It doesn't mean rat house, it just felt like one. And they had these lifts with no fronts on them, you know, these things like big boxes that keep coming at you. You just gotta jump on one. It was all a bit surreal. And we had to wait outside this passport office for hours and hours before the guy eventually said to come in. We tried our best to persuade him it was nothing, and he said, "Okay, fine, well, you go with these men." And that was the last we knew of it. We just headed out to the airport with these couple of coppers. And we were getting a bit—"Oh, dear, this could be the concentration camps"—you never know, you know; it hasn't been that long.

I READ AN INTERVIEW WITH BILLY Joel in 'Melody Maker,' in which he said that he wouldn't know what to do if he met you because he admired you so much.

Yeah, I saw that, too. It's weird. I'd be the same. Dave Bowie came 'round when we were in the basement of our office. We had a studio down there called Replica, which is a replica of Abbey Road Studio Number Two. He came down, and we just had a laugh. I reminded him of the day when he brought round a demo to me when he was still Davy Jones. It was all just chat.

Whom could you meet now and feel a great deal of respect for?

You mean that I'd be tongue-tied with?

Yeah.

Probably Dylan. I'm exaggerating, really, because I do like him. There's no point going round and just not being able to say anything.

369

But, you know, I don't want them to read this. People know enough of my insecurities and my weaknesses, and they blast me left, right and center with it. I don't want to give them any more.

You mentioned to me once, jokingly, that you remembered when the Bee Gees came in and applied for work, as it were, at Brian Epstein's while Robert Stigwood was there. Can you actually recall any of their earlier days?

One night in 1967 I turned up at Robert Stigwood's place, and he said, "What do you think of this record?" And he played some young songwriters that he was thinking of signing. It was a couple of their early songs. I liked them, and he said, "Oh, great, 'cause I'm thinking of signing them." And that was really the start of them for me.

Your disco single, "Goodnight Tonight," has made a tremendous entry in the American charts. It's actually something that you recorded a while ago, isn't it?

Yes, about a year ago.

It seems to be out at the right moment because of the popularity of disco material, but had you foreseen this would be the right time?

No, I didn't plan the timing at all. We had a meeting and decided it would be nice to have a single while the TV show [*Wings over America*, which aired March 16th, 1979] was out, because it had been something like seven months since we'd put a record out. "Goodnight Tonight" was going to be the B side and "Daytime Nightime Suffering" was going to be the A side. So we sat around for years—well, it seemed like years—discussing it; you know, the normal soul-searching you go through. And we decided, "No, it *isn't* all right; we won't put it out." So we scrapped the whole thing. And about a week later, I played the record again. I thought, "That's crazy, we've made it; it's stupid, why not put it out? Just because people are going to pan it." I liked it, and other people had taken it home and played it to people at parties. So we decided to do it.

It's a bit of a shame, isn't it, if as an artist you are inhibited by what you feel people's reactions might be to something that is an expression of what you want to do?

Yes, but you can't help it; you've just got to put it out and hope for the best.

Obviously you're not a hungry artist in the sense that, "We've gotta maximize our profit, so let's put the hit single on the LP."

I think that's the record company's view, you know. It's understandable that kids who don't want to buy singles will be waiting for the album, and when it's not on the album, they might feel a little bit cheated.

Have you gotten some word from the company saying, "Please Paul. . . ."

Yes, the companies here and in America, worldwide, would like a single on the album. It makes more sense merchandisingwise. But sometimes, I just have to remember that this isn't a record retail store I'm running; this is supposed to be some kind of art. And if it doesn't fit in, it doesn't fit in. They're not really strict on it. We've got a lot of artistic control, thank goodness. But I can see the wisdom of what they're asking.

I remember Al Coury. We weren't gonna put "Helen Wheels" on the American *Band on the Run* [1973], and he rang up and said, "I can give you quarter of a million more sales if you put it on." And I said, "We don't want it, we really don't want it." I was being kind of reticent, and in the end he persuaded me anyway. He said, "Just do it, just in America or something." I suppose he was right: *Grease* and *Saturday Night Fever* and the way they have been selling albums recently, having four hit singles and then making it all come out as an album. So you've gotta have an album with that many hits on it. . . .

'Wings Greatest' didn't do very well in the States, and I think I know why, but . . .

Why? Tell me. . . .

Did it have something to do with the fact that it was your last album for Capitol? You're kind of a lame-duck artist for them, so they might as well promote somebody else whom they have a long-term contract with. . . .

I see, well, yes. I supposed that's a possibility, but I really don't know the ins and outs of stuff like that. I'd really be up to my neck in it if I got involved in all those little side issues. I don't know, to tell you the truth. Lord Lucan is missing.

Do you feel any degree of panic that it wasn't a big album?

No, no. I don't really feel the need for everything to be incredible and great. I'd probably get quite annoyed if I had a big string of albums that didn't do it, but I'm more interested in the new thing. To me it was just a repackage. I'm not into Beatles repackages or anything myself because it seems like a second-class item to me.

DID YOU EVER CARE WHEN *Capitol in the States would repackage the Beatles albums?*

Yeah, I really didn't like it. The worst one, I think, was *Help*. We didn't have a very good communications system then; it was like ringing up the moon. When we brought *Magical Mystery Tour* over, it was an EP, and they said, "We don't do EPs in America." We said, "You're gonna have to, because we made one." He said, "No, no, you're gonna have to make it an LP because rack jobbers won't take it," and all that technical stuff. But the worst was when we did *Help*. We arranged for the album over in Britain not to include any film music by Ken Thorne, who did the incidental music in the score. But in America they put on bits and pieces of his music. We turned up in California one day, and we played *Help* and found all this funny music on it that we couldn't believe. So those things used to happen.

And we had covers and stuff that they'd veto. Like *Yesterday and Today*. They wanted a repackage album, they wanted a cover, so we gave them [a photo of] butchers in white coats and babies—not real babies, but dolls—and meat and stuff. . . . It's a bit sick, isn't it? But yeah, it's a laugh. So we did it, and of course, Capitol said, "No way are we gonna do this." So we just sent them some more photos.

By the way, did you do 'Please Please Me' (the first British Beatles album) in one day?

I think it was probably done in a day or two. We never used to take much longer than a day. We did the first album in a day, fourteen hours, I think it was. "Please Please Me" was originally to be a slow song. It was more like Roy Orbison: "Come on . . . come on [*he sings the words*] please please. . . ." Yeah, Roy Orbison stuff. And when we took it in, George Martin said, "Can we uptempo it a bit?" And we said, "Are you crazy?" And we tried it through like that.

So many of the old song credits said "Lennon and McCartney," even when they were written by one of you. Did you ever wish or do you wish now that the McCartney ones had said McCartney and the Lennon ones had said Lennon?

No. Okay, rephrase that answer. Yes. Because you asked me if I ever think that. Yeah, I do, and not just out of a personal thing for me; I sometimes feel it for John, things getting called Lennon and McCartney, things like "Strawberry Fields," "Norwegian Wood," certain ones John wrote and I just helped a little bit. And there are certain ones that I wrote. There's probably only about, say, twenty that are really our own. On the rest there's quite a lot of collaboration. I suppose you do get a little niggled; you wish people knew that was mine. But, hell, how much credit do you want in a lifetime?

Do you ever hope that John records again? Do you think he should?

I hope that if he would like to record again, he will record again, but I hope that if he doesn't want to, he doesn't. This is something totally down to his own personal feeling. Whatever gets you through the night.

Do you happen to know what his personal feeling is? Because nobody else seems to.

Not particularly. I would imagine he's just getting on with his own life. He has a son by his previous marriage whom he didn't get to spend a lot of time with, and possibly he felt that having a new son by Yoko, with Yoko—it sounds a bit like a racehorse, out of Yoko—that he would want to spend time with his son and see him grow up. I suspect that's what he's doing. But I don't really want to go talking for him. I would imagine he's just getting on with his life and being cool, and I hope he's digging it.

Do you feel that you are maintaining a proper balance between your family life and your work?

What's proper? Proper would be, possibly, to be with them all the time because they are my kids and it's my family, so it would be really great just to be totally with them and give them any support they need. But I work. I come in to do music, and I'm not there all the time. But yeah, I do think I've a good balance, myself. It feels good, but if anything, I wouldn't mind being with them even more. I just like them.

It seems to me that you have an excellent working arrangement here at Abbey Road; maybe some people don't realize how close you are to home.

Well, actually, *you* don't, because I'm not living there now! Which is crazy: I've got a house right around the corner, but we live in the country, which is two hours away. So I drive in—would you believe? Having a house around the corner and driving in every day, two hours. And that is mainly just because the family is living there.

Do you drive yourself?

Yeah, I don't like to be driven. Except wild.

And this is down south?

Yeah.

So if you drive home, it takes two hours. How long do you spend in the studio?

A long time. I kind of just drive in, make music all day, drive back, go to sleep, get up, drive in, make music all day.

Linda's the cook of the house?

371

Yeah, she's great.

I remember her telling me that you and she had agreed that if things ever went wrong, there would be no big alimony settlement and everything.

Well, you know, it depends if you think that money would be a compensation for a breakup like that. I don't think it would be. I can't imagine her ever ringing up and saying, "Oh, by the way, I'm having half of the mantelpiece, and you can have the Volkswagen."

HAVE YOU TALKED TO AL Coury about the RSO 'Sgt. Pepper'?

No, I haven't seen Al since he went to RSO. He used to be with Capitol, so I used to talk with him a lot there. Ah . . . he's very good, obviously he's gotta be good, he's sold a lot of records for people, he's what you want behind you. A sort of vital force. Yeah, yeah, sell sell sell . . .

Did you see the film?

No, I haven't seen it yet, so I can't talk about it. I thought at the time of *Sgt. Pepper* that they couldn't make a film of it. We used to be stoned all the time and talk about things like that and say, "Hey, what a great film this would make." But we used to say that the trouble is that people are all freaking out on acid with this album. You're never gonna be able to get those big elephants that are coming through their heads. And we just thought, you just can't capture it: Once it gets to be a film, it's always going to be a bit plodding compared to the album. Those days it was a fantasy thing; it all took place in your mind, and it would really be harder than anything to capture that feeling. And I think from what I've heard of the Stigwood thing, it doesn't seem to have captured it.

Did you have any particular images in mind?

No there were too many . . . I couldn't tell you . . . they were silly things: tigers leaping and herds of horses, you know, and good morning [*he sings*], good morning, good morning. Well, I mean, there's a hunt that comes through there and galloping horses come through, a fox and some hounds come through. I mean, in your mind, you see the band and you can see all the horses. Your mind is a great thing—especially when you're hallucinating [*laughter*].

You mentioned the other day that Paul Simon had dropped by and that he is interested in doing a lot of film work, which is one of the reasons he went to Warner Bros. Do you have any desire to do more film

work? Do you ever think, "My God . . . before my life is through, I want to have this done."

Yeah. We're doing a couple of film projects with the group. But there's one thing I haven't really got together yet. One of the big ambitions is to do a thing called *Rupert*. He's a white bear, a cartoon from a newspaper strip, and he's got a bunch of mates. He's very England in the Forties. We've recorded a demo album, and I've written a story. That, I suppose, is my big ambition before my life is over. I wouldn't mind making that into, like, a Disney film, only I'd even like to get it better. Yuk, yuk.

Of course, there will be somebody who says, "'Rupert the Bear' is not rock & roll. Why are you doing this?"

Oh, well. It doesn't matter, I'm not just rock & roll; I don't live my life by that kind of limitation, you know. I like stuff that isn't necessarily rock & roll.

I know you were thinking about doing a Christmas show last year and didn't. But of course in the Beatles days you did have a Christmas show. People in the States don't really know what a Christmas show is like in England and the kind of people you used to have on it.

It would be a residency thing for a couple of weeks at a big theater like Finsbury Park [now the Rainbow] or something. What Brian Epstein did was get a producer who was used to putting on shows like that. You know, it was more of a variety show in a way. But based on the groups and after Billy J. Kramer and the Fourmost, maybe Gerry [and the Pacemakers]. They didn't take too much out of you. And with the residency thing, you got this great feeling of going into the same place; it got very easy to do. We'd stand behind the big screen while they did an introduction on film. Then they'd turn it off and we'd appear, and everyone would go, "Yeahhhhh!" And then we'd run off; there'd be a blackout and we'd run off. We did various things. Like old music-hall things, where we'd all dress up and John would be the wicked Sir Jasper. I'd be the hero and knock him out at the end; George would be the wanton woman who is saved from being tied on railway lines. It was all daft stuff, but it worked. It was just . . . the audience just wanted to see us; they didn't mind what we did. And we had a bit of a laugh with it.

Do you think rock has gotten too big to do anything like that?

No, it's just that the style has changed. I still feel it would go down as well. But stars have changed. For instance, everyone used to go on all the plug shows. Anything that would have a song, we went on: local shows, network things, interviews here, people and places, regional news, you'd just go on anything. And that's something people don't do half as much these days. I think it maybe didn't please everyone, but the nice thing was that you had a very varied day.

How did you assemble your "Rockestra"?

A lot of people in music have been thinking about using a rock & roll lineup instead of an orchestra. So I wrote a tune, and finally I just asked the people who would like to be in a Rockestra. Keith Moon was going to turn up, but unfortunately he died a week before. So he couldn't make it. It's a bit sick, but he would have laughed along with all that stuff.

But Jeff Beck was gonna come. And Eric Clapton. And they actually didn't turn up. Beck was worried about what would happen if he didn't like the track. He wanted to be able to say, "Well, I don't like it so it can't go out." So there were a few of those little political things. So he just didn't turn up in the end. Eric didn't feel like it. There was some kind of reason; he had the flu or something. But he didn't come. Most of the people did turn up: Pete Townshend, Dave Gilmour, Lawrence Juber of our group and Denny Laine. And Hank Marvin. That was the guitar lineup. On drums we had Kenney Jones, John Bonham and Steve Holly [also of Wings]. And then on bass we had me and Bruce Thomas of the Attractions and Ronnie Lane. And then we had John Paul Jones, who did some bass and some piano. And then we had Gary Brooker, who played piano. We had Speedy Acquaye. We had Tony Carr and Ray Cooper on percussion. We had our brass section from the American tour. Linda played keyboards, and we had Tony Ashton, also on keyboards. Oh, and we had Morris Pert on percussion, and that is the full lineup, I think.

Where you happy with the turnout?

It was great, actually, 'cause we filmed it. You saw how we actually built the whole thing. So that's being put together at the moment as a film by Barry Chattington. It shows certain people in the music scene today trying to get together. For instance, Pete, of course, got roped into ending everything with one of his big jumps. So he got that.

DO YOU WORRY ABOUT YOUR *image?*

I try not to these days, 'cause it's stupid to; I mean, we're all gonna be dead soon, so there's not an awful lot of point, you know. The main thing is to be able to enjoy it in some form or another. So worrying about your image and your reviews stops you from enjoying it. Takes away what there used to be in music, which is just trying to avoid doing the job and just getting out and doing it just for a laugh. So I'm all right, actually, recently . . . even . . . I don't know, just not even bothering if we get bad reviews and stuff. Which really used to; I used to go off in the corner and I'd go, "My God, the critic is right; I'm terrible; he's got it; we're useless." But then you'd go out and you'd play to somebody, you'd play live. You start to see critics being wrong, so generally everyone should be able to ignore them and just get on with the work that he does. Basically, I'm not too careful about image. If I were careful, I would try to avoid that "family man" and "he lives on a farm." 'Cause you know that kids and the farm are ammo, and they say, "Here's old family man Paulie, back with the sheep, what a yawn." I give them all the ammo with that. If I were really concerned with it, I'd live in London. And always be down in the clubs and always be buying them drinks and always be popping pills just to show them how hip I am. But you reach a point where it just doesn't work; you can't live for all of that. You reach a point where it all becomes real and you become all that. And if you don't like it, then you suddenly . . . wait a minute. So, I'm down trying not to bother with all that stuff now.

On this new album, which I haven't heard yet, have you been able to investigate—this sounds really corny, but—new areas?

Slightly, yeah. You start off really wanting to do something very new, but eventually you come back to what is you. So it always gets an imprint of what is you, and you always do what you do. You know what I mean. The sort of magnetic forces, or whatever it is around you, make a certain mold, I think. I think you must listen to the music because I can't really talk about it. I think so many different things about it. So if anyone asks me what it is, I can't tell you. "It now is a ballad of the Sixties" [*McCartney proclaims in a strong voice*]. You know, until about after ten years, then, oh, yes, it was a ballad of the Sixties.

Do you have any particular current favorites?

373

In records just knocking around, I like "The Logical Song" [by Supertramp]; I like a few of the young bands, a few of the British ones—it wouldn't mean that much in America—I like Squeeze, Jam and a few people. I'm not into it but I like some of the good stuff that's going on. I like some of Elvis Costello's stuff; I like a lot of that stuff anyway—the newer stuff. And I still think Stevie Wonder is amazing. I like Elvis Presley a lot. I like the Gene Chandler record. I like "Lord Lucan Is Missing." Who does that one, do you know? [Peter and the Test Tube Babies.] John Peel keeps playing it, has played it a few times.

You met a couple of the Boomtown Rats, I hear.

Yeah, They're great, because they're exactly what we were; they are doing the same thing we were doing. And it's crazy that anyone should ever forget that. They're all lads just let off the leash from school or college or home, and they are just having a ball. Some of the music is really good; I really like some of the directions because it's brought a lot of rock back into rock. A lot of what it was all about back into it. But so is the revival of the Fifties stuff. It's all brought back a kind of feel that was missing for a while there or was underplayed.

D**ID THE BEATLES EVER GET** *bad reviews?*
Yeah, sure we did, sure. I remember before 'Sgt. Pepper,' we were coming in for a lot of flak. People were saying. "The Beatles are finished: they're rubbish." Because we weren't doing anything, we were just hiding away in the studios, out of our skulls making this album— we were having a great time. And then it came out and they changed their tune and they said, "They're all right, they are okay."

Did you ever personally feel part of the "Merseybeat" movement?

No, that was just something the journalists called us. We just laughed about it. God, what did they call us: the Merseybeats, the Mop Tops, the Fab Four. God. Couldn't they think of anything better? It just used to be a joke, all that stuff. We never used to take it seriously. But the *Merseybeat* was quite a good little paper. The most fun we used to have out of it. And then we won a poll. They had a poll for who was the best group, and that was a tense moment because we thought Gerry and the Pacemakers were defi-

nitely gonna take it off of us. So we bought a few copies and filled them in.

Did you really?

Yeah, of course, doesn't everyone?

Actually, yes.

I'm sure Gerry bought just as many copies as we did.

Have you ever wondered why someone like him hasn't really survived in terms of the charts?

Not really. I mean, Gerry's thing was great, he was very good, but he didn't have as natural of a thing going as we did. We had at least two writers, and George turned out to be a writer, and even Ringo. So we potentially had four writers, and they had just Gerry, who wasn't as prolific as John and I. He wrote a couple that were good, but he had to rely mainly on other writers for his big hits. We were very keen on getting our own stuff in. Because . . . we sort of arrived at the end of an era; most of the groups around about then were just doing impressions of Roy Orbison or the Shadows or Cliff Richard. And we liked Bo Diddley more and Chuck Berry and things like that. So we'd do stuff that was slightly more obscure. "If You Gotta Make a Fool of Somebody," by James Ray. And we'd do covers of those kinds of things. And we were writing a couple of not very good tunes. We had one we used to do called "Like Dreamers Do," which was pretty bad. But it used to go down quite well, so we latched onto this idea—it gave us a special identity. Because you wouldn't hear these songs anywhere else, just when you came to see us. So it started to work, so we went a bit more in that direction of trying to get our own thing going rather than have it laid on us by a producer. So George wasn't too happy in the beginning, and "Love Me Do," wasn't a very big hit, but it was our first one. The second one was a Number One. So it worked out.

Gerry did have three Number Ones in a row with his first three records. Were you ever afraid that they might beat you to the brass ring?

Oh, yeah. And Dave Clark was the other big threat. There were a couple of moments when we were worried, but our philosophy then was that something would happen.

Since so few British artists had made the American charts in a big way, did you think that you might do it, or any of those groups might do it?

We thought of this; we said, "We're only going to America." It was a bit of a big statement, but we did decide among ourselves that we'd only go to America if we had a Number One. We'd walk in a bit cocky. We were playing in Paris when the news came through—telegram—"I Want to Hold Your Hand" was Number One in the States. Wow! So we were able to go to the States without begging.

When we arrived, there was this big thing at the airport, all the millions of DJs; it was on all the stations, and we'd arrived. So it worked out. It was a great way to do it. And then there was a terrifying interview. I never used to think I was good at press conferences because I'm one of those people who—I don't think I'm good at it; I'm probably all right. But John was always much better with a snappy remark. Then, Ringo was good at that, too. It turned out we all managed to get a quick remark in there, and we did well at that press conference. And because we were just so keen on America and R&B and all the great New York stations, we used to just ring them up all the time. "Hello Murray. . . .

Yeah, why don't you come around and interview us?" We were in it totally; it was magic for us; we'd just arrived in America, Land of Promise. We had a great time with it all—meeting the Ronettes and Phil Spector and people like that. What more could you ask?

Last question for today. You've had many chances to leave England, and yet you choose to remain here. Is there a reason, other than that it's your home, why you enjoy living here?

No, there isn't any other reason; I just live here. There are all sorts of reasons, really. I've been a lot of places on tours and I enjoy them all for visits, but after a while I don't feel at home. England's not the greatest of places all the time. But I don't want money to dictate where and how I live. I live here and try to pay the taxes and avoid as much as possible going to buy guns and sandbags and vaguely try and keep it all straight and be reasonable about it all.

INTERVIEWED
BY
CAMERON
CROWE (1979)

"With ROLLING STONE, I had my own little territory," says Cameron Crowe, who in 1979 lived in Los Angeles. "I became identified with Southern California musicians: The Eagles; Joe Walsh; Crosby, Stills, Nash and Young . . . and I'd run across Joni Mitchell in various situations for seven years. And I pestered her for an interview for seven years. I even wrote her a letter

when *Don Juan's Reckless Daughter* came out (in early 1978), saying, this was the time for her to talk. She was not interested."

Especially in ROLLING STONE, which she had not forgiven for calling her a "groupie" in a year-end awards issue. She hadn't spoken to the magazine in eight years.

But shortly after Mitchell finished *Mingus,* her collaboration with the jazz bassist Charles Mingus, Crowe got a call from her manager. "He said she wanted to talk and wanted to talk to me and she didn't care who for." Crowe called ROLLING STONE. And although Mitchell had hit her commercial peak with the 1974 album, *Court and Spark,* and had been moving for several years into jazz—that is, away from her mass audience—there was no question. We wanted to hear from her.

—BF-T

SEVERAL DAYS BEFORE BEGINNING these interviews, I overheard two teenagers looking for a good party album in a record store. "How about this one," said one, holding up Joni Mitchell's 'Miles of Aisles.'" "Naaaaaah," said the other. "It's got good songs on it, but it's kind of like jazz." They bought a Cheap Trick album.

When I told this story to Joni Mitchell later, I could see the disappointment flicker across her face for an instant. Then she laughed and took a long drag from her cigarette. "Here's the thing," she said

376

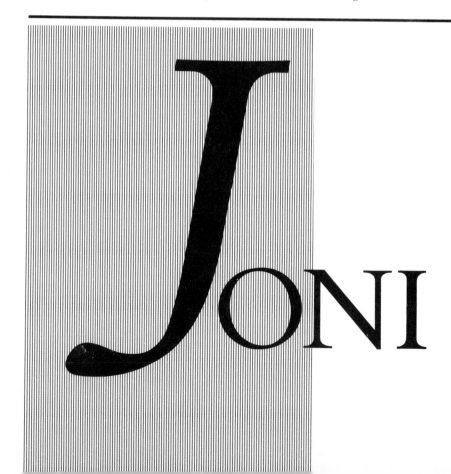

MITCHELL

forcefully. "*You have two options. You can stay the same and protect the formula that gave you your initial success. They're going to crucify you for staying the same. If you change, they're going to crucify you for changing. But staying the same is boring. And change is interesting. So of the two options,*" she concluded cheerfully, "*I'd rather be crucified for changing.*"

Joni Mitchell, thirty-six, has been living in exile from a mainstream audience for the last three years. Her last resoundingly successful album of new material was 'Court and Spark,' a landmark in poetic songwriting, performing and in the growth of an artist we had all watched mature. From folk ballads through Woodstock-era anthems to jazz-inflected experimentalism, Joni Mitchell had influenced a generation of musicians.

Then, in 1975, she released 'The Hissing of Summer Lawns,' her ambitious follow-up to 'Court and Spark.' She introduced jazz overtones, veered away from confessional songwriting and received a nearly unanimous critical drubbing. Mitchell reacted to the criticism by keeping an even lower personal profile. She spent most of her time traveling (the road album, 'Hejira,' was released in 1976), associating with progressive jazz artists and asking questions. With 'Don Juan's Reckless Daughter,' a double album released in the winter of 1977, she and pop music had nearly parted ways. In a time when the record-buying public was rewarding craftsmen, Mitchell seemed to be steadfastly carrying the torch for art. Her sales suffered, but this direction was leading to a historic juncture in her career.

Word first reached her in early 1978 that Charles Mingus was trying to get in touch with her. The legendary bassist-bandleader had been battling Lou Gehrig's disease out of the public eye. She contacted him, and they began a long-distance friendship. Mingus had noticed her ambitions and wondered if she would assist him by condensing T. S. Eliot's 'Four Quartets,' recite it and play guitar behind it for a composition he had been working on. She read the book and called him back. "I'd rather condense the Bible," she told him, and Mingus said he could dig it. They didn't speak for a time. Then, another phone call.

Mingus had written what would later become his last six melodies ("Joni I-VI," he called them), and he wanted Mitchell to write and sing the lyrics for them. She spent the last year and a half working on the project, her first collaboration, working mostly in her apartment in New York's Regency Hotel.

When Mingus died on January 5th this year, Mitchell continued writing and recording and finally finished in late spring. Inlcuding tape recordings of Mingus' voice as segues between tracks, she eventually chose to title the album simply 'Mingus.'

About marketing an all-jazz Joni Mitchell album,

Elektra/Asylum Chairman of the Board Joe Smith says this: "She has taken a chunk out of her career and accomplished something truly monumental. When we received this album, I got on a conference call and talked with all our promotion men. If any radio station calls itself a trend setter, it must recognize this album and Charles Mingus. I'm also having a contest for my promotion men," he laughed; "first prize is they get to keep their jobs."

Had Smith, in the course of running the company, ever discussed commercial direction with Mitchell?

"You don't tell Joni Mitchell what to do," he said.

It was Joni's idea to do this, her first in-depth interview in over ten years. She entered the office of her manager, Elliot Roberts, one afternoon and sat down on a sofa. She wore no makeup, a tan blouse and slacks.

"Let's turn the tape on," she said, addressing my recorder. "I'm ready to go."

An enthusiastic conversationalist, Joni Mitchell speaks quickly and purposefully, structuring her thoughts like a writer's third draft. The sessions continued at various locations over the next three days.

"If I'm censoring for anyone," she warned, "it's for my parents. They are very old-fashioned and moral people. They still don't understand me that well. I keep saying, "Mama, Amy Vanderbilt killed herself. That should have been a tip-off that we're into a new era. . . ."

WOULD YOU LIKE TO SHATTER any preconceptions?

I do have this reputation for being a *serious* person. I'm a very analytical person, a somewhat introspective person; that's the nature of the work I do. But this is only one side of the coin, you know. I love to dance. I'm a rowdy. I'm a good-timer. Mind you, I haven't seen too many good parties since I left my hometown. People go to parties here mostly to conduct business.

There's a private club in Hollywood that usually is very empty, but on one crowded evening, I stumbled in there to this all-star cast. Linda Ronstadt was running through the parking lot being pursued by photographers, Jerry Brown was upstairs, Bob Dylan was full of his new Christian enthusiasm—"Hey, Jerry, you ever thought of running this state with Christian government?" Lauren Hutton was there, Rod Stewart. . . . There were a lot of people and this little postage stamp of a dance floor, and nobody was dancing on it. These are all people who dance, in one way or another, in their acts.

So the *renowned introvert* comes in, and I just wanted to dance. I didn't want to dance alone, so I asked a couple of people to dance with me, and nobody would. They were all incredibly shy. So I went to the bathroom, and a girl came in and hollered to me from the sink over the wall, "Is that you? I'll dance with you." I said, "Great." It was just like the Fifties, when none of the guys would dance. And it was at this moment that the girl confided to me, "You know, they all think of you as this very sad person." That was the first time that it occurred to me that even among my peer group I had developed this reputation. I figured, these guys have been reading my press or something *{laughs}*. But as far as shattering preconceptions, forget it. I feel that the art is there for people to bring to it whatever they choose.

I wonder if you feel like you've beaten the odds at this point? Even the biggest pop performers usually become the victims of a fickle audience.

It's typical in this society that is so conscious of being number one and winning; the most you can really get out of it is a four-year run, just the same as in the political arena. The first year, there's the courtship prior to the election—prior to, say, the first platinum album. Then suddenly you become the king or queen of rock & roll. You have, possibly, one favorable year of office, and then they start to tear you down. So if your goals end at a platinum album or being king or queen of your idiom, when you inevitably come down from that office, you're going to be heartbroken. Nobody likes to have less than what he had before.

My goals have been to constantly remain interested in music. I see myself as a musical student. That's why this project with Charles [Mingus] was such a great opportunity. Here was a chance to learn, from a legitimately great artist, about a brand-new idiom that I had only been flirting with before.

How did you decide to make this commitment?

Every year, when I've completed a project, I ask myself, "What am I going to do now?" In the process of asking myself that question, a lot of possibilities come up. I heard on the street that Charles was trying to contact me. He tried through normal channels and never made it. People thought it was too far-out to be true. They had all sorts of reasons for thinking it was an impossible or ridiculous combination. To me, it was fascinating. I was honored. I was curious.

Mingus was a man who generally was difficult to get close to. When did you know that you had really made the connection with him?

Oh, immediately. Immediately I felt this kind of sweet giddiness when I met him. Like I was in for some fun. He teased me a lot. He called me hillbilly; it was charming. We went through some of the old songs. "Goodbye Pork Pie Hat" was the one we decided on immediately. So there was this search for another one, and he played me a lot of material. Charles put on this one record, and just before he played it, he said, "Now this song has *five* melodies going all at once." I said, "Yeah, I bet you want me to write *five* different sets of words for each one of the melodies, right?" And he grinned and said, *"Right."* He put on the record, and it was the *fastest*, smokingest thing you ever heard, with all these melodies going on together.

Did you find yourself cast in the role of easing Mingus from his fear of dying?

No, that was up to him. You can't do too much to assuage someone of their fears. I wasn't in that personal a role that I was his comforter. It was a professional partnership with a lot of affection. But one day I called him up and I said, "How are you, Charles?" I never really asked him too much about his illness, but that day I did. And he said, "Oh, I'm *dying*. I thought I knew how to do it, but now I'm not sure." At that point I had three songs to finish, and I thought, "Oh, boy, I want him to be in the studio when I start to cut them. I want his approval on this. I want him to like my direction."

This was a unique position. I've never worked for somebody else before. Although in the treatment of the music, it was much more *my* version of jazz. As far as the music was finally recorded. He's more traditional in a way—antielectronics and anti-avant-garde. I'm looking to make modern American music. So I just *hoped* that he would like what I was doing. I was taking it someplace where I would be true to myself. It was never meant as a commemorative album while we were making it. I never really believed completely that he was going to die. His spirit was so strong.

Did he hear all the songs before his death?

He heard everything but "God Must Be a Boogie Man," which he would have liked, since it is his point of view about himself. It's based on the first four pages of his book {*Beneath the Underdog.*}

How did you go about writing lyrics to "Goodbye Pork Pie Hat?" This is a classic piece of music that has . . .

. . . been around. That was a very difficult one. I had to find my own phrasing for the notes. The real difficulty for me was that the only thing

379

I can believe is what has happened to me firsthand, what I see and feel with my own eyes. I had a block for three months. It's hard for me to take someone else's story and tell only *his* story in a song.

Charlie assailed me with historial information about Lester Young [in whose memory "Goodbye Pork Pie Hat" was written] and his family background, concerning his early playing days. He used to tap-dance in his family band with his father and mother. He was married to a white woman, traveling through the South in a time when that was just taboo. A lot of the great black musicians were forced into cellars or the chitlin' circuit. So I had all these details, but I still couldn't, with any conscience, simply write a historical song.

Then something very magical happened. One night Don Alias and I—he plays congas on the album, and he and I have been very close for the period of the last two years—were on the subway, and we got off, I don't know why, two stops early. We came up into this *cloud of steam* coming out of a New York manhole. Two blocks ahead of us, under these orangeish New York lights, we see a crowd gathered. So we head toward the crowd. When we get up on it, it's a group of black men surrounding two small black boys. It's about midnight, and the two boys are dancing this very robotlike mime dance. One of the guys in the crowd slaps his leg and says, "Isn't that something, I thought *tap dancing* was gone forever." Immediately I'm thinking about Lester Young. They were dancing under one of those cloth awnings that goes out to the curb of a bar. I look up—and the name of the bar is the Pork Pie Hat. The music they were dancing to was jazz coming off the jukebox inside. There were big blown-up pictures of Lester Young all around the place. It was wild.

So that became the last verse of the song. In my mind, that filled in a piece of the puzzle. I had the past and the present, and the two boys represented the future, the next generation. To me, the song then had a life of its own.

LOOKING BACK, HOW WELL DID *you prepare for your own success?*
I never thought that far ahead. I never expected to have this degree of success.
Never? Not even practicing in front of your mirror?
No. It was a hobby that mushroomed. I was grateful to make one record. All I knew was, whatever it was that I felt was the weak link in my previous project gave me inspiration for the next one. I wrote poetry and I painted all my life. I always wanted to play music and dabbled with it, but I never thought of putting them all together. It never occurred to me. It wasn't until Dylan began to write poetic songs that it occured to me you could actually *sing* those poems.

Is that when you started to sing?
I guess I really started singing when I had polio. Neil [Young] and I both got polio in the same Canadian epidemic. I was nine, and they put me in a polio ward over Christmas. They said I might not walk again and that I would not be able to go home for Christmas. I wouldn't go for it. So I started to sing Christmas carols, and I used to sing them real loud. When the nurse came into the room I would sing *louder*. The boy in the bed next to me, you know, used to complain. And I discovered I was a ham. That was the first time I started to sing for people.

Do you remember the first record you bought?
The first record I bought was a piece of classical music. I saw a movie called *The Story of Three Loves,* and the theme was {*she hums the entire melody*} by Rachmaninoff, I think. Everytime it used to come on the radio it would drive me *crazy*. It was a 78. I mean, I had *Alice in Wonderland* and *Tubby the Tuba,* but the first one that I *loved* and had to buy? "The Story of Three Loves."

How about pop music?
You see, pop music was something else in that time. We're talking about the Fifties now. When I was thirteen, *The Hit Parade* was one hour a day—four o'clock to five o'clock. On the weekends they'd do the Top Twenty. But the rest of the radio was Mantovani, country & western, a lot of radio journalism. Mostly country & western, which I wasn't crazy about. To me it was simplistic. Even as a child I liked more complex melody.

In my teens I loved to dance. That was my thing. I instigated a Wednesday night dance 'cause I could hardly make it to the weekends. For dancing, I loved Chuck Berry. Ray Charles. 'What I'd Say.' I liked Elvis Presley. I liked the Everly Brothers. But then this thing happened. Rock & roll went through a really *dumb* vanilla period. And during that period, folk music came in to fill the hole. At that point I had friends who'd have parties and sit around and sing Kingston Trio songs. That's when I started to sing again. That's why I bought an instrument.

To sing at those parties. It was no more ambitious than that. I was planning all the time to go to art school.

What kind of student were you?

I was a bad student. I finally flunked out in the twelfth grade. I went back later and picked up the subjects that I lost. I do have my high-school diploma—I figured I needed that much, just in case. College was not too interesting to me. The way I saw the educational system from an early age was that it taught you what to think, not how to think. There was no liberty, really, for free thinking. You were being trained to fit into a society where free thinking was a nuisance. I liked some of my teachers very much, but I had no interest in their subjects. So I would appease them—I think they perceived that I was not a dummy, although my report card didn't look like it. I would line the math room with ink drawings and portraits of the mathematicians. I did a tree of life for my biology teacher. I was always staying late at the school, down on my knees painting something.

How do you think other students viewed you?

I'm not sure I have a clear picture of myself. My identity, since it wasn't through the grade system, was that I was a good dancer and an artist. And also, I was very well dressed. I made a lot of my own clothes. I worked in ladies' wear and I modeled. I had access to sample clothes that were too fashionable for our community, and I could buy them cheaply. I would go hang out on the streets dressed to the T, even in hat and gloves. I hung out downtown with the Ukrainians and the Indians; they were more emotionally honest, and they were better dancers.

When I went back to my own neighborhood, I found that I had a provocative image. They thought I was loose because I always liked rowdies. I thought the way the kids danced at my school was kind of, you know, *funny*. I remember a recurring statement on my report card—"Joan does not relate well." I know that I was aloof. Perhaps some people thought that I was a snob.

There came a split when I rejected sororities and that whole thing. I didn't go for that. But there also came a stage when my friends who were juvenile delinquents suddenly became criminals. They could go into very dull jobs or they could go into *crime*. Crime is very romantic in your youth. I suddenly thought, "Here's where the romance ends. I don't see myself in jail. . . ."

So you went to art school and at the end of your first year you decided to go to Toronto to become a folk singer.

I was only a folk singer for about two years, and that was several years before I ever made a record. By that time, it wasn't really folk music anymore. It was some new American phenomenon. Later, they called it singer/songwriters. Or art songs, which I liked best. Some people get nervous about that word. Art. They think it's a pretentious word from the giddyap. To me, words are only symbols, and the word *art* has never lost its vitality. It still has meaning to me. Love lost its meaning to me. God lost its meaning to me. But art never lost its meaning. I always knew what I meant by art. Now I've got all three of them back *{laughs}*.

Did your folk-singing period include the time you spent in Detroit working with Chuck Mitchell?

Yes. We never really were a full-fledged duo. I'm a bad learner, see. I bypass the educational system. I learn by a process more like osmosis. It's by inspiration and desire. So when we would try to work up songs together, we would bang into differences of opinion. Some people say, "Oh, Joan, that's just because you're lazy." But in a way, more than laziness, it's a kind of block that runs all through my rebellious personality. If someone tries to teach me a part that I don't find particularly interesting, it won't stick. I'll end up doing what I wanted to do in the first place, and then they're annoyed.

We had a difference of opinion in material. It was more like two people onstage at the same time, sometimes singing together. We had a difficult time.

When your marriage broke up, you moved to New York City, and artists like Tom Rush began covering your songs. You became totally self-sufficient—booking your own tours and handling all your financial affairs. Was that your nature, or was it a reaction to the end of the marriage?

Both. At that point, I didn't know how far it was going to carry me. I had a little circuit of clubs that I could go in and say, "Okay, your capacity is such and such. I've got you up to full capacity now. Last time I made *this* much; this time, why don't you pay me *this* much more, and you can still make a profit. Let's be fair." People were starting to record my songs; I drew {audiences] even though I didn't have a record out. I really felt self-sufficient. I was working constantly, every night, and I was trying to build up a bank account because I didn't think it was going to last too long. I thought I was going to have to go back into what I knew, which was

381

women's wear. Become a buyer for a department store. But I was going to go on with it as long as I could. Or maybe into commercial art. Whatever.

So you were less sure then that the songs would keep coming?

In some ways I had *more* confidence. I was outspoken. I *enjoyed* performing. I loved the compliments I received when I came offstage. Everything seemed to be proportionate to me. I had $400 in the bank. I thought I was *filthy rich*. I liked the liberty of it all. I liked the idea that I was going to North Carolina, visiting all these mysterious states. I used to tell long, rambling tales onstage. It was very casual.

I remember the first time I played the Newport Folk Festival. It was the first glimmering of what was to come. We went to a party—it was held at a fraternity house, and it was guarded. Only people who were supposed to be there were there. I was with a road manager at that point, a girlfriend who was helping me out. They said, "You can't come in." My girlfriend said, "Do you *know* who this is?" She said my name, and these people standing by the door let out this *gasp*. My eyes bugged out of my head. I had the strangest reaction: I turned on my heel and I ran for ten blocks in the other direction. It pumped me so full of adrenalin, I bolted like a deer. I came back to Janie and said, "I'm *so* embarrassed, man, why did I *do* that? It's a mystery to me." Well, she had lived with . . .*{laughs}* retarded children, right. And a retard is smart in a lot of ways. They're simplified down to a kind of intelligence that a more complex mind is not hip to. Janie said, "I think that's one of the sanest things I have ever seen, you know."

Then it began to get really disproportionate. I couldn't really enjoy it after that. I know it was *good*, but the adoration seemed out of line. The next thing was going through the primary adjustments, where more people are attracted to you because you smell of success. And they're simultaneously saying to you, "Don't change." But as soon as you have so many hangers-on, you have to change, and then you go through the pains of hearing that you *"changed*, man." It goes to your head. There's a whole lot of levels of adjustment. There are no books written on it; nobody tells you what to expect. Some people get all puffed up and say, "I deserved it." I thought it was too much to live up to. I thought, "You don't even know who I am. You want to *worship* me?"

That's why I became a confessional poet. I thought, "You better know who you're applaud-ing up here." It was a compulsion to be honest with my audience.

You and Neil Young have always been close. How did you first meet?

I was married to Chuck Mitchell at the time. We came to Winnipeg, playing this Fourth Dimension [folk] circuit. We were there over Christmas. I remember putting up this Christmas tree in our hotel room. Neil, you know, was this rock & roller who was coming around to folk music through Bob Dylan. Of course. Anyway, Neil came out to the club, and we liked him immediately. He was the same way he is now—this offhanded, dry wit. And you know what his ambition was at the time? He wanted a *hearse*, and a chicken farm. And when you think of it, what he's done with his dream is not that far off. He just added a few buffalo. And a fleet of antique cars. He's always been pretty true to his vision.

But none of us had any grandiose ideas about the kind of success that we received. In those days it was *really* a long shot. Especially for a Canadian. I remember my mother talking to a neighbor who asked, "Where is Joan living?" And she said, "In New York; she's a musician." And they went, "Ohhh, you poor woman." It was hard for them to relate.

Later, you know, Neil abandoned his rock & roll band and came out to Toronto. I didn't know him very well at the time we were there. I was just leaving for Detroit. We didn't connect then. It was years later, when I got to California—Elliot [Roberts] and I came out as strangers in a strange land—and we went to a Buffalo Springfield session to see Neil. He was the only other person I knew. That's where I met everybody else. And the scene started to come together.

By this time, David Crosby had "discovered" you singing in a club in Coconut Grove, Florida. What was he like back then?

He was tanned. He was straight. He was clearing out his boat, and it was going to be the beginning of a new life for him. He was paranoid about his hair, I remember. Having long hair in a short-hair society. He had a wonderful sense of humor. Crosby has enthusiasm like no one else. He can make you feel like a million bucks. Or he can bring you down with the same force. Crosby, in producing that first album, did me an incredible service, which I will never forget. He used his success and name to make sure my songs weren't tampered with to suit the folk-rock trend.

I had just come back from London. That was during the Twiggy-Viva era, and I remember I wore a lot of makeup. I think I even had on false eyelashes at the time. And Crosby was from his scrub-faced California culture, so one of his first projects in our relationship was to encourage me to let go of all this elaborate war paint {laughs}. It was a great liberation to get up in the morning and wash your face . . . and not have to do anything else.

Is there a moment you can look back on when you realized that you were no longer a child, that you had grown up?

There's a moment I can think of—although I'm still a child. Sometimes I feel seven years old. I'll be standing in the kitchen and all of a sudden my body wants to jump around. For no reason at all. You've seen kids that suddenly just get a burst of energy? That part of my child is still alive. I don't repress those urges, except in certain company.

My artwork, at the time I made the first album, was still very concerned with childhood. It was full of the remnants of fairy tales and fantasia. My songs still make references to fairy tales. They referred to kings and queens. Mind you, that was also part of the times, and I pay colonial allegiance to Queen Lizzy. But suddenly I realized that I was preoccupied with the things of my girlhood and I was twenty-four years old. I remember being at the Philadelphia Folk Festival and having this *sensation*. It was like falling to earth. It was about the time of my second album. It felt almost as if I'd had my head in the clouds long enough. And then there was a plummeting into the earth, tinged with a little bit of apprehension and fear. Shortly after that, everything began to change. There were fewer adjectives to my poetry. Fewer curlicues to my drawing. Everything began to get more bold. And solid, in a way.

By the time of my fourth album {*Blue*, 1971}, I came to another turning point—the terrible opportunity that people are given in their lives. The day that they discover to the tips of their toes that they're *assholes* {*solemn moment, then a gale of laughter*}. And you have to work on from there. And decide what your values are. Which parts of you are no longer really necessary. They belong to childhood's end. *Blue* really was a turning point in a lot of ways. As *Court and Spark* was a turning point later on. In the state that I was at in my inquiry about life and direction and relationships, I perceived a lot of hate in my heart. You know, "I hate you some, I love you some, I hate you some, I love you some, I love you when I forget about me" ["All I Want"]. I perceived my inability to love at that point. And

it horrified me some. It's still something that I . . . I hate to say I'm *working* on, because the idea of work implies effort, and effort implies you'll never get there. But it's something I'm *noticing*.

Having laid so much of your life out for public ears, do you now look back on some things and wince?

The things that I look back on and sort of shrug off, maybe in a weak moment *grimace* over {*smiles*}, are the parts when I see myself imitating something else. Affectations as opposed to style. It's very hard to be true to yourself. For instance, I don't care too much for the second album I made {*Clouds*}. I like the first one; the first one's honest. *Blue* is an honest album. *Clouds* has some honest moments on it, but at the time, I was singing a lot with Crosby, Stills, Nash and Young, and *they* had a style, out of necessity, to blend with one another. They had a way of affecting vowel sounds so that when they sang together, they would sing like a unit. I picked up on that, and there's a lot of that on the album. I find it now kind of irritating to listen to, in the same way that I find a lot of black affectations irritating. White singers sounding like they come from deep Georgia, you know? It always seems ridiculous to me. It always seemed to me that a *great* singer—now we're talking about excellence, not popularity—but a *great* singer would sing closer to his or her own speaking voice.

I think Billie Holiday was a very natural singer. In the context of opera, Maria Callas was an excellent singer. I think the lead singer from the Doobie Brothers [Mike McDonald] is a very natural singer.

TEN YEARS AGO, YOU HAD *begun to represent the Woodstock ethic. Someone could say, "there is a Joni Mitchell type," and you would know exactly what he meant. Was that a concern of yours?*

Very much so. I remember showing up at a Carole King concert in Central Park in a pair of Yves St. Laurent pants. And a good shirt. They were simple clothes, but they were of a good quality. And I felt . . . really *uncomfortable*. I felt there were certain things that I liked, that were a part of me, that were outside the hippie guard. Things that were a part of me from before this delicious period in the Sixties when we were fresh and were thinking fresh things. . . . It was a good time period. It was a healthy idea that we were working toward, but there came a time when it had become a ritual, a flat-out style.

I began to make this transition, under a lot of peer pressure. I remember seeing, even when I went to *The Last Waltz,* "Miss Mitchell showed up looking like a Beverly Hills housewife." I was outside the uniform of rock & roll, and it was annoying to some people. And as a reply to this prejudice, I wrote that song, "The Boho Dance": "Nothing is capsulized in me/In either side of town." As a demand for liberty.

There was a time when you and Laura Nyro were considered to be the two purveyors of female singer/ songwriting. Now it's all but taken for granted that Laura Nyro wasn't "tough enough" to survive in the business. Do you think that your own survival has meant a certain toughness?

Gee, I don't know if that's the case. Inspiration can run out, you know. Laura Nyro made a choice that has tempted me on *many* occasions. And that was to lead an ordinary life. She married a carpenter, as I understand, and turned her back on it all. Which is brave and tough in its own way. Many, many times as a writer, I've come to a day where I say, "None of this has any meaning." If you maintain that point of view, if you hold onto it and possess it, that's *it* for you. There's a possibility that you can come firmly to that conclusion, as Rimbaud did, and give it up. I've always managed to move out of those pockets.

At a certain point, I actually tried to move back to Canada, into the bush. My idea was to follow my advice and get back to nature. I built a house that I thought would function with or without electricity. I was going to grow gardens and everything. But I found that I was too spoiled already. I had too much choice. I could take the more difficult, old-fashioned way for a short period of time, but the idea of doing it *forever* would not work. I have reclusive fits, though, all the time. Not that it isn't rewarding, you know. It is. I mean, I do it for myself first, but I don't want to do it for myself only. I feel I can still share my work with people, and they appreciate it. I guess it is my calling.

Around 1971, after 'Blue,' it was reported that you had retired from the road. You returned a year and a half later with 'For the Roses.' Was that material that you had written up in Canada?

Yes. Most of *For the Roses* was written there.

What did your parents think of the inside shot?

I remember my mother putting on glasses to scrutinize it more closely. Then my father said, "Myrtle, people *do* things like this these days." Which was a great attitude. It was the most

innocent of nudes, kind of like a Botticelli pose. It was meant to express that line: "I'm looking way out at the ocean, love to see that green water in motion, there's this reef around me ["Lesson in Survival"]. Joel Bernstein is the only photographer I would feel comfortable enough to take off my clothes for. It was part of our concept for the cover when we were going to call the album *Judgment of the Moon and Stars.* We were originally going to set that photograph in a circle and replace the daylight sky with the starry, starry night, so it would be like a Magritte. At that time, no one was paying homage to Magritte. Then Elliot said, "Joan, how would you like to see $5.98 plastered across your ass?" {*Laughs*} So it became the inside.

How aware were you that your songs were being scrutinized for the relationships they could be about? Even ROLLING STONE drew a diagram of your supposed brokenhearted lovers and also called you "Old Lady of the Year."

I never saw it. The people that were involved in it called up to console me. My victims called first {*laughs*}. That took some of the sting out of it. It was ludicrous. I mean, even when they were drawing all these brokenhearted lines out of my life and my ability to love well, I wasn't so unique. There was a lot of affection in those relationships. The fact that I couldn't stay in them for one reason or another was *painful* to me. The men involved are good people. I'm fond of them to this day. We have a mutual affection, even though we've gone on to new relationships. Certainly there are pockets of hurt that come. You come a little battered out of a relationship that doesn't go on forever. I don't live in bitterness.

I'm a confronter by nature. I have a tendency to confront my relationships much more often than people would care. I'm always being told that I talk too much. It's not that I like to, but I habitually confront before I escape. Rather than go out and try to drown my sorrows or something, I'll wallow and muddle through them. My friends thought for a long time that this was done out of masochism. I began to believe it myself. But at this time in my life, I would say that it has paid some dividend. By confronting those things and thinking them through as deeply as my limited intelligence would allow, there's a certain richness that comes in time. Even psychiatrists, mind whores for the most part, don't have a healthy attitude toward depression. They get bored with it. I think their problem is they need to be *deeply* depressed.

My relationship with Graham [Nash] is a

great, enduring one. We lived together for some time—we were married, you might say. The time Graham and I were together was a highly productive period for me as an artist. I painted a great deal, and the bulk of my best drawings were done in '69 and '70 when we were together. To contend with this hypercreative woman, Graham tried his hand at several things. Painting. Stained glass. And finally he came to the camera. I feel he's not just a good photographer, he's a great one. His work is so lyrical. Some of his pictures *are* worth a thousand words. Even after we broke up, Graham made a gift of a very fine camera and a book of Cartier-Bresson photographs. I became an avid photographer myself. He gave the gift back to me. Even though the romance ended, the creative aspect of our relationship has continued to branch out.

This is the thing that ROLLING STONE, when it made a diagram of broken hearts, was being very simplistic about. It was an easy target to slam me for my romantic alliances. That's human nature. That hurt, but not nearly so much as when they began to tear apart *The Hissing of Summer Lawns*. Ignorantly. I couldn't get together, in any way; it being human nature to take the attacks that were given certain projects. I got very frustrated at the turning point, when the press began to turn against me.

WHEN DID YOU FIRST MEET *Bob Dylan?*
The first official meeting was the *Johnny Cash Show* in 1969. We played that together. Afterward Johnny had a party at his house. So we met briefly there.

Over the years there were a series of brief encounters. Tests. Little art games. I always had an affection for him. At one point we were at a concert—whose concert was that? *{Shrugs}* How soon we forget. Anyway, we're backstage at this concert. Bobby and [Dylan's friend] Louie Kemp were holding up the wall. I went over there and opened up the conversation with painting. I knew he was discovering painting. At that point I had an idea for a canvas that I wanted to do. I'd just come from New Mexico, and the color of the land there was still very much with me. I'd seen color combinations that had never occured to me before. Lavender and wheat, like old-fashioned licorice, you know, when you bite into it and there's this peculiar, rich green and brown color? The soil was like that, and the foliage coming

out of it was *vivid* in the context of this color of earth. Anyway, I was describing something like that, really getting carried away with all of the colors. And Bobby says to me *{an inspired imitation}:* "When you paint, do you use *white?*" And I said, "Of course." He said, "'Cause if you don't use white, your paint gets muddy." I thought, "Aha, the boy's been taking art lessons."

The next time we had a brief conversation was when Paul McCartney had a party on the *Queen Mary,* and everybody left the table and Bobby and I were sitting there. After a long silence he said, "If you were gonna paint this room, what would you paint?" I said, "Well, let me think. I'd paint the mirrored ball spinning, I'd paint the women in the washroom, the band. . . ." Later all the stuff came back to me as part of a dream that became the song "Paprika Plains." I said, "What would *you* paint?" He said, "I'd paint this coffee cup." Later, he wrote "One More Cup of Coffee."

Is it true that you once played Dylan a just-finished tape of 'Court and Spark' and he fell asleep?

This is true.

What does this do to your confidence when Bob Dylan falls asleep in the middle of your album?

Let me see, there was Louie Kemp and a girlfriend of his and David Geffen [then president of Elektra/Asylum Records] and Dylan. There was all this fussing over Bobby's project, 'cause he was new to the label, and *Court and Spark,* which was a big breakthrough for me, was being entirely and almost rudely dismissed. Geffen's excuse was, since I was living in a room in his house at the time, that he had heard it through all of its stages, and it was no longer any surprise to him. Dylan played his album *{Planet Waves},* and everybody went, "Oh, *wow.*" I played mine, and everybody talked and Bobby fell asleep. *{Laughs}* I said, "Wait a minute, you guys, this is some different kind of music for me, check it out." I knew it was good. I think Bobby was just being cute *{laughs}.*

PRIOR TO 'COURT AND SPARK,' *your albums were mostly kept to sparse interpretations. Had you always heard arrangements like that in your head?*
Not really. I had attempted to play my music with rock & roll players, but they couldn't grasp the subtlety of the form. I've never studied music, so I'd always be talking in abstractions. And they'd laugh, "Aww, isn't that

385

cute? She's trying to tell us how to play." Never negatively, but *appeasingly*, you know. And finally it was Russ Kunkel who said, "Joni, you better get yourself a jazz drummer."

One night I went down to the Baked Potato [an L.A. jazz club] to hear the L.A. Express play. I knew Tom Scott; I'd done some work on *For the Roses* with him. When I heard the band, I was very enthusiastic, and I asked them to play on my next session.

When they got in the studio, it was the same problem. They didn't really know how heavy to play, and I was used to being the whole orchestra. Many nights I would be very discouraged. But one night we suddenly overcame the obstacles. The next thing we knew, we were all aware we were making something quite unique.

A commonly asked question among your long-term fans right now is, what happened to the melodies?

The album with Charles is incredibly melodic. What it is, is *more* melody. Granted, "Coyote" is not a melodic tune. It's rhythmic; it's almost chantlike. A lot of it is spoken: "No regrets, Coyote." But I've always been a lover of melody. I don't think that I've ever lost that. It's just that at a certain point, my poetry began to spill out of the form and into something more relative to a jazz sense of melody, which was restating the melody in variation. If you have four verses, maybe it'll be slightly different every time it comes around. But that's just different. It doesn't always have to be melodic. So what, you know? You take a painter, and maybe he's been painting multicolored canvases. All of a sudden he decides to paint two-tone compositions. I figure anything Picasso could do {*laughs*}. . . .

Don't you believe in compromise?

I don't believe so much in compromise as I don't believe in art that has become so elitist that only fourteen people in the world can appreciate it. For instance, on this project there was a possibility that people would have this prejudice—"Oh, it sounds like cocktail lounge music." Or, "That sounds like Johnny Carson show music." I wanted somehow or other to make something that transcended that prejudice. I feel that I solved that problem. It remains to be seen, but I feel that the music, while being very modern, still contains an almost folk-music simplicity. I don't think that it's intimidating. Some people get intimidated by jazz. It's like higher mathematics to them.

Was 'The Hissing of Summer Lawns' more of an L.A. album for you than 'Court and Spark'?

Yes, because *Court and Spark* still contains a lot of songs written up in Canada. The song "Court and Spark" itself was written up on my land there. It deals with a story based on Vancouver and the Sunshine Coast.

The Hissing of Summer Lawns is a suburban album. About the time that album came around I thought, "I'm not going to be your sin eater any longer." So I began to write social description as opposed to personal confession. I met with a tremendous amount of resentment. People thought suddenly that I was secure in my success, that I was being a snot and was attacking *them*. The basic theme of the album, which everybody thought was so abstract, was just any summer day in any neighborhood when people turn their sprinklers on all up and down the block. It's just that *hiss* of suburbia.

People thought it was very narcissistic of me to be swimming around in a pool, which I thought was an odd observation. It was an act of *activity*. As opposed to sexual posturing, which runs through the business—nobody ever pointed a finger at narcissism *there*. I had stopped being confessional. I think they were ready to nail me, anyway. They would have said, "More morose, scathing introspection." They were ready to get me; that's the way I figure it. It was my second year in office. The cartoonists had their fun. There weren't enough good jokes left, so it was time to throw me out of office and get a new president. It's politics.

It sounds like it surprised you when it actually happened.

It really surprised me. In retrospect, it doesn't surprise me at all. I listened to that album recently, 'cause I was going to rework "Edith and the Kingpin." I was surprised. I feel that the times have caught up with it. At that time, I was beginning to introduce—for lack of a better word—jazz overtones. Nobody was really doing that. In the two years that followed, it became more acceptable, and when Steely Dan finally made *Aja*, with some of the same sidemen, it was applauded as a great, if somewhat eccentric, work. I fail even to see the eccentricity of it, myself. Perhaps there was a weary tone in my voice that irritated people, but there was so much of it that was accessible.

I REMEMBER HAVING A CONVERSA-*tion with you about a year ago. Months had gone by, and you were still smarting over the criticism you'd received for your last album, 'Don Juan's Reckless Daughter.' What exactly was your frustration?*

If I experience any frustration, it's the frustration of being misunderstood. But that's what stardom is—a glamorous misunderstanding. All the way along, I *know* that some of these projects are eccentric. I *know* that there are parts that are experimental, and some of them are half-baked. I certainly have not been pushing the limits and—even for myself—not all of my experiments are completely successful. But they lay the groundwork for further developments. Sooner or later, some of those experiments will come to fruition. So I have to lay out a certain amount of my growing pains in public. I like the idea that annually there is a place where I can distribute the art that I have collected for the year. That's the only thing that I feel I want to protect, really. And that means having a certain amount of commercial success.

It's a credit to the people that have supported me in spite of the bad publicity of the last four years—the out-and-out panning of a lot of fine and unusual projects—that at least they felt this work had some moments of accessible beauty. If a reviewer sits down and he plays [one of these albums] two or three times, it's just going to sound freaky to him. There are moods I'm in when I can't *stand* to listen to some of my own music. I don't expect it to always be appropriate. But come the right moment, where we're on the same wavelength, it might slip in on you.

I feel frustrated sometimes. I feel bitterness, but I'm not embittered. Feelings pass. A lot of the humor in the music is missed. They insist on painting me as this tragic . . . well, not even a tragic, because in this town people don't understand tragedy. All they understand is drama. You have to be *moral* to understand tragedy *{laughs}*.

Elliot Roberts, your manager, realized not too long ago that he had canceled more shows than you'd actually played. Was there an instance when you walked offstage after two songs?

There was one time that I was onstage for one song. And I left. I felt very bad for the audience. It was impossible for me to continue. There's that old show-business axiom that the show must go on. But if I listed for you the strikes that were against me that night, I think that you could dig it. It's not easy to leave an audience sitting there. I was still in bad health from going out on Rolling Thunder, which was *mad*. Heavy drama, no sleep—a circus. I'd requested before the show went on to get out of it. But it was too late. I had bronchitis. A bone in my spine was out of place and was pinching like crazy. So I was in physical pain. I was in emotional pain. I was going with someone in the band, and we were in the process of splitting up. We were in a

Quonset hut, and the sound was just ricocheting. And I just made the decision.

That can get to be costly.

The money is not the motivation, anyway. I use one of two analogies all the time with Elliot. One that I was his racehorse. Or if I really wanted out of something I would say to him, "Be a good pimp, Elliot, don't put me out *{laughs}*."

I stopped touring for a while for a couple of reasons. One of them was that I felt it threatened my writing, that it limited my experience to that of a traveling rock & roll singer. I didn't want only to be a scribe to that particular facet of life, a minority experience. There were so many people documenting that already. That's rock & roll calling itself rock & roll simply by talking about rock & roll.

You may tour this summer with a band including Pat Metheny and Jaco Pastorious, presumably to play material from the Mingus album. What kind of set would you do?

With these players, we're talking about young musicians who have no real musical or categorical preferences. We all love rock & roll. We all love folk music. And we all love jazz. If anything, we want to be considered a musical event. We're going to do some traditional African ceremonial drum pieces. I would like to get loose enough to dance. Jaco, you know, is a bass player, but he's also a fantastic keyboard player. In this band, we're going to try to switch instruments. It should be very creative.

What were the origins of 'Hejira'? That album seems to have a sound all of its own. . . .

Well, after the end of my last tour, it was a case of waiting again. I had an idea; I knew I wanted to travel. I was sitting out at the beach at Neil's [Young] place, and I was thinking, "I want to travel, I don't know where and I don't know who with." Two friends of mine came to the door and said, "We're driving across country." I said, "I've been waiting for you; I'm *gone*." So we drove across country; then we parted ways. It was my car, so I drove back alone. The *Hejira* album was written mostly while I was traveling in the car. That's why there were no piano songs, if you remember.

Hejira was an obscure word, but it said *exactly* what I wanted. Running away, honorably. It dealt with the leaving of a relationship, but without the sense of failure that accompanied the breakup of my previous relationships. I felt that it was not necessarily anybody's fault. It was a new attitude.

YOU WERE NOWHERE TO BE found in the Dylan film from Rolling Thunder—'Renaldo and Clara.'
Yes. I asked not to be in it.
Why?

I joined Rolling Thunder as a spectator. I would have been content to follow it for three cities just as an observer, but since I was there I was asked to participate. Then, for mystical reasons of my own, I made a pact with myself that I would stay on the thing until it was over. It was a trial of sorts for me. I went out in a foot soldier position. I made up songs onstage. I sang in French, *badly*. I did a lot of things to prevent myself from getting in the way. What was in it for me hadn't anything to do with applause or the performing aspect. It was simply to be allowed to remain an observer and a witness to an incredible spectacle. As a result, the parts of the film that I was in . . . for all I know, it was powerful and interesting footage. But I preferred to be invisible {laughs nervously}. I've got my own reasons why.

Do you make it a point to check out some of the newer female songwriters—like the Wilson sisters from Heart or Rickie Lee Jones?

I'll tell you, the last three years I have been very narrow. In a way, I turned my back on pop music and rock & roll. I was concentrating mostly on jazz, modern classical music, Stravinsky, polyphonic music. During that time I developed a lack of appreciation for pop music.

Out of cynicism?

No no. It was part of an artistic process. It seemed to me, in the context of what I was exploring, there was no reason in the world you should be comparing Stravinsky to Heart. But if you're given Heart or Stravinsky, I was more interested in Stravinsky. Or *In a Silent Way*.

Now, I don't even listen to the jazz station in my car. The jazz station is full of mediocrity, too. I listen to AM, and I like what I hear. There's only a certain amount of fine work in *any* idiom. The rest of it is just copyists. Regurgitation. Obvious rip-offs. Mingus has a song, "If Charlie Parker Was a Gunslinger, There'd Be a Whole Lot of Dead Copycats." Sometimes I find myself sharing this point of view. He figured you don't settle for anything else but uniqueness. The name of the game to him—and to me—is to become a full individual. I remember a time when I was very flattered if somebody told me that I was as good as Peter, Paul and Mary. Or that I sounded like Judy Collins. Then one day I discovered I didn't want to be a second-rate *anything*. I have to remember to be compassion-

ate. Otherwise it really *pisses* me off to hear somebody getting a whole lot of public roar and, "Oh, this is the newest and the greatest," when it's really the newest and greatest *copy*. There are bands coming now that are really good. They're interesting; they've got some vitality and some fire, but—say they're Englishmen who sound like Bob Dylan. I listen to it and it's pleasant on the radio, but as an artist I say to myself, "If you're that good, how come you can't be yourself?"

Has anyone played you Elvis Costello? Any New Wave music?

I don't know enough to talk about it. It's ignorance speaking a bit, but one of the things I like that's coming out in rock & roll now is the Archie and Betty and Veronica aspect of the characters. I like the way [Rick Nielsen] wears a high-school sweater and bow tie and beanie. [Bun E. Carlos] will have an accountant's short-sleeved shirt and short haircut and wire-rimmed glasses. I love the look of Cheap Trick.

I understand the punk movement. It reminds me of a very exciting time in my own life. It's nothing new—I was a punk in the Fifties. Devo, I think, is great. I love them. They are like Dadaists to me. Everything that they express is a complete reaction against everything that we stood for. But they do it so well, theatrically speaking. And with a great sense of humor. I love it. Now, as far as putting on a Devo album? It wouldn't be something I would do. It's the visuals that make them fresh and fascinating to me.

Do you think you've achieved greatness?

{Long pause} Greatness is a point of view. There is great rock & roll. But great rock & roll within the context of music, historically, is slight. I think that I am growing as a painter. I'm growing as a musician. I'm growing as a communicator, a poet, all the time. But growth implies that if you look back, there was improvement. I don't see necessarily that this album is any, to use your word, *greater* than the *Blue* album. This has a lot more *sophistication,* but it's very difficult to define what greatness is. Honesty? Genius? The *Blue* album, there's hardly a dishonest note in the vocals. At that period of my life, I had no personal defenses. I felt like a cellophane wrapper on a pack of cigarettes. I felt like I had absolutely no secrets from the world, and I couldn't pretend in my life to be strong. Or to be happy. But the advantage of it in the music was that there were no defenses there either.

The vocals are real on this *Mingus* album. The interplay between the musicians is spontaneous and real. I can put my dukes up now if I have to in life, but out of appreciation for honesty. I won't settle for anything less in the studio. So much of music is politics. It's going for the big vote. It amounts to a lot of baby kissing.

Do you listen to Fleetwood Mac?

I enjoy them. To make a whole album like that, I think, would leave me wanting something more. For my own self. Not to put them down in any way. I'm still obsessed with pushing the perimeters of what entails a pop song. I can't really let go of that impulse yet. I don't know where I'm going. I never really do. My songs could come out any shape at this point. I *am* thinking now of keeping it simpler. Quite naturally, my experimentation has led me to a conclusion, and I feel myself returning more to basics and to my roots in folk music. But I don't even know what that simplicity might turn out like.

Do you still feel a comradeship with the Eagles, Jackson Browne and Linda Ronstadt?

The Eagles have really stretched out thematically. Jackson writes fine songs. Linda is very special. I'm a great appreciator of all those people. But at a certain point, I don't know if it was to protect me from getting a swelled head or what, I was denied any kind of positive feedback from a lot of sources. Like I go to a party and everybody shows up. I figure everybody must have a tape of their album on 'em. I figure, "Let's sit down and play these things." *Right?* A lot of times it would end up where I would be the only one who would end up being that pushy.

I always had this childhood idea that artists in a scene, you know, compared and discussed and disagreed with each other. But it was all done openly, perhaps in a shadowy cafe over wine. But because of this pressure for commercial success, maybe in a way we're deprived of this interchange.

HAVE YOU MOVED TO NEW York City?

I consider myself spread across this continent in a very disorganized manner. I have three residences. One is wild and natural. One is New York, which needs no description. California, to me, represents old friends, and health. I love to swim. If there's anything that I love about this place here it's the luxury of being able to swim, which is like *flying* to me. I could get in the pool, float around for about two hours and never touch

the sides. That's better than any psychiatrist to me. I'm working out my body, working out my lungs—the poor things are blackened with cigarette smoke—and looking at nature. I don't have that in New York.

New York gives me an opportunity to flex a muscle that I don't really get to use; for instance, out there, there is directness. I find that it makes me stronger. You don't have so many anonymous encounters out here. In New York, constantly, the street is challenging you to relate to it.

What do you think of the theory that great art comes from hunger and pain? You seem now to be living a very comfortable life.

Pain has very little to do with environment. You can be sitting at the most beautiful place in the world, which doesn't necessarily have to be private property, and not be able to *see* it for pain. So, no. Misery knows no rent bracket *{laughs}*. At this time in my life, I've confronted a lot of my devils. A lot of them were pretty silly, but they were incredibly real at the time.

I don't feel guilty for my success or my lifestyle. I feel that sometimes having a lot of acquisitions leads to a responsibility that is more time-consuming than the art. That's probably one of the reasons why people feel the artist should remain in poverty. My most important possession is my pool—it's one luxury I don't really question.

Do you have many close women friends?

I have a few good women friends. I like them and I trust them. But generally speaking, I'm a little afraid of women. I don't know, it's a funny time for women. We demand a certain sensitivity. We've made our outward attacks at machoism, right, in favor of the new sensitive male. But we're just at the fledgling state of our liberty where we can't handle it. I think we ask men to be sensitive and equal but deep down think it's unnatural. And we really want them to be stronger than us. So you get into this paradoxical thing.

I believe in equality. I believe that I am male and I am female. Not that I'm saying I'm bisexual—I believe in heterosexuality. I think ultimately it's the most difficult and nourishing of them all. But I do understand homosexuality in these times. It seems to be a peculiar, in many cases, necessary alternative to this *mess* that's happening between the men and the women. I know a lot of women now who have come through the whole gamut, and they're at the position where they almost don't want to *deal* with it anymore. They want to be celibate. Men are not at this place at all. The new woman is embracing this as a possibility. If there wasn't always this intense sexual competition between women, it *might* provide a climate for them to develop a camaraderie. In my observation, what passes for feminine camaraderie is conspiracy. I would *love* to make new women friends, but I hardly have time to do justice to the ones I have.

Did it change your concept of dying to spend the last year and a half with Charles Mingus?

Not completely. See, in my lifetime, I've had so many brushes with death myself, not that I'm saying that I'm not afraid to die—of course, I still am. *Afraid* of it. 'Cause it's so *final,* you know. As far as a ceremony, of how I would like it to be treated, I'm not really sure. I mean, it's an inevitable thing. I feel I'll live a long time. I'm confident that I'll live to be in my eighties. So I have a more immediate problem than confronting death.

Filling those years?

Aging gracefully. Which is easier in some societies than in this one. Especially in this very glamour-conscious town where women become neurotic at a certain age and go for surgery and any number of things to disguise that fact.

I had an interesting experience concerning aging in Hollywood. A friend of mine and I went to this Beverly Hills restaurant. It happened to be Fernando Lamas' birthday. So, sitting at the table next to us was this long supper of the old Hollywood. They were drinking toasts to Marilyn Monroe, and there were lots of stories flying around about celebrities and people who they had known. There was a tremendous amount of glamour represented. *Well-tended* glamour. The fourth face-lift. Maintaining the youthful silhouette. I looked around and thought, "Is this the way that we must go in this town?" Is our hippie philosophy going to surrender to *this?*

I think if you're healthy, aging can be quite a beautiful process, and I think we've created an artificial problem for ourselves. Generally speaking, men are very generous. But I think that's the main problem, you know, at thirty-six, I'm examining.

You hold Georgia O'Keeffe as an ideal. Yet there she is in her nineties, living in the middle of the desert with only her art. She has no children. It seems like it could be a very lonely life. . . .

That's the part about it. I don't know, really, what your choices are. Obviously, that's a constant battle with me. Is my maternity to amount to a lot of black plastic? Am I going to annually bear this litter of songs and send them out into the marketplace and have them crucified for this reason or that. . . .

Or praised.

Or praised. Let me not get lopsided about that. I certainly get my fair share of appreciation. You know, in a few years, I'll be past a safe childbearing age. I don't see many women raising children successfully alone, and as yet I haven't been able to bond with a man who I could see myself with in constant company for the twenty years that're necessary to do a good job of that. I would take that job seriously. I wouldn't just frivolously get pregnant and bring a child into this world, especially a world that has such a difficult future as the one we're facing. Also, the children of celebrities have been notoriously troubled. But when it comes to the business of raising children, I *finally* feel emotionally stable enough to deal with it. It's taken me this long, but it may be something that's denied me. It may be one of my little regrets in my old age. I still leave the future open, and given the right relationship, even if I thought the relationship had a potential longevity of, say, *six* years, I might do it.

David Crosby once said this about you, with all affection: "Joni Mitchell is about as modest as Mussolini." [She smiles, shakes head.] And while it's been my observation that you have a much better sense of humor than Mussolini, it's also true that you have no apologies to offer for anything in your career.

I like to work myself up to a state of enthusiasm about anything I do; otherwise, what's the point? I see a lot of people and say, "Hey, you got an album coming out, what's it like?" They say, "Oh, it's *okay.*" I say, "Gee, you're putting an album out and you think it's *okay?* Where is your enthusiasm, man?" They don't like to hear that. I'm not talking about arrogance, but I believe in real enthusiasm. That's probably where Crosby's quote comes from.

There is also a deeper point to be made. In looking back over all that we've talked about, it seems that everything about you is geared to your creative muse, and it is to that muse that you have remained true. At any expense.

I'll tell you, any acts of frustration or concern or anxiety in my life are all peripheral to a very solid core. A very strong, continuing course I've been following. All this other stuff is just the flak that you get for engaging in the analytical process in the first place. Even Freud knew that; to me it was the hippest thing he ever said: "Dissection of the personality is no way to self-knowledge." All you get out of that is literature, not necessarily peace of mind. It's a satisfying, but dangerous, way to learn about yourself.

Ever find yourself the only one speaking out on certain subjects?

All the time. On many nights I go home and say, "Mitch, you know, you're gonna have to start going only to comedies now. And only reading Kurt Vonnegut. Put those Nietzsche books away."

Last question. What would you have listed, as Woody Allen did at the end of 'Manhattan,' as your reasons why life is worth living?

It would be very similar to his. I would name different musicians, but it might finally be a beautiful face that would make me put the microphone down. I would just be thinking fondly of someone who I love, you know. And just dreaming of . . . Basically if you want to say it in one word? Happiness?

It's a funny thing about happiness. You can strive and strive and *strive* to be happy, but happiness will sneak up on you in the most peculiar ways. I feel happy suddenly. I don't know why. Some days, the way the light strikes things. Or for some beautifully immature reason like finding myself running to the kitchen to make myself some *toast*. Happiness comes to me even on a bad day. In very, very strange ways. I'm very happy in my life right now.

33

INTERVIEWED
BY
PETER
HERBST (1979)

Six years after his duet-interview with Carly Simon, James Taylor was no more interested in talking to the press than before. But in 1979, the sales on his album, *Flag,* were . . . well, flagging.

Peter Herbst happened to live in the same building in New York as Taylor, and they'd say "hi" from time to time. Now, with some encouragement from his record company, Taylor was willing to say significantly more.

In Detroit, Herbst found Taylor, 31, in excellent musical shape and, thanks to an exercise program, in terrific physical shape as well. But the singer, so quick and affable onstage, clammed up during the first interview after a concert. "He doesn't like doing them," Herbst recalls. "He feels burned. He was very nervous, inhibited, not relaxed. It was like pulling teeth. The next day, at their hotel, it was still rough."

A few nights later, back in New York, Herbst got a knock on his door. It was his neighbor James Taylor; he'd been locked out of his apartment and needed to use the phone. "I told him he owed me one," says Herbst, "and he came back to my apartment. We played some records and talked about musicians we both liked—Sinatra and Ry Cooder. And finally, he opened up."

—BF-T

BEFORE JAMES TAYLOR WENT OUT ON his recent tour, he had doubts about how much longer he could rock & roll in public. At thirty-one, with a wife (Carly Simon) and two children (Sarah, 5, and Ben, 2), he began to think of performing his music as being "a bit adolescent." His new album, 'Flag,' had not sold nearly so well as his last, 'JT,' and the photograph of Taylor tucked inside his LP showed an artist who seemed to want to make everyone understand that he was aging.

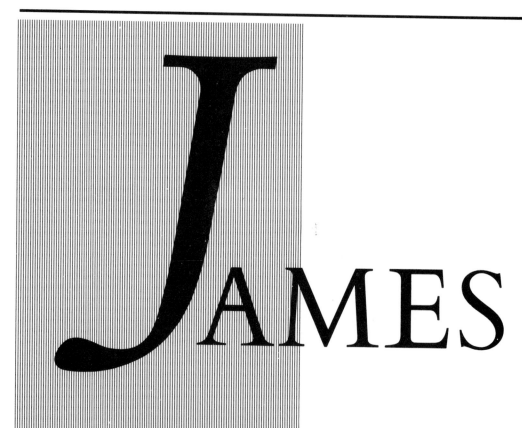

JAMES

TAYLOR

But when I got on the bus with Taylor and his band on the way to Pine Knob, a beautiful, acoustically superior open-air theater outside Detroit, I sensed that I hadn't been getting the complete picture. Unlike most tours, the musicians didn't seem to be dragging themselves around, trying to fight road stupor. Taylor's tour manager had hired on a karate instructor, to give the band workouts. And they looked it.

The tour was drawing well. At Pine Knob, Taylor was about to play for his third of four successive sellout crowds (12,000 per night) that were wildly enthusiastic. Honest-to-goodness rock & roll made up a healthy portion of the performance. And Taylor, who more than any other singer has been branded with the term "mellow," belted out the songs with fire and closed each hard number with flying leaps that brought the audience to its feet.

Taylor almost never grants interviews. He trusts only these things: playing music in front of an audience that asks only that he be himself; working with musicians he admires; writing his songs; and, most of all, being with his family.

W**HEN DID YOU DISCOVER** *that you could write songs?*
I started when I went to McLean, a psychiatric hospital, in 1965. It was where I started writing seriously. I wrote two songs in McLean, and after that, I went down to New York with the Flying Machine in 1966 and wrote most of the music on my first Apple album [*James Taylor,* 1969]. That was a hot time; a lot of stuff was getting written, and I thought it was good stuff, too.

I've written a hundred songs since then, and I think that's a lot of songs. A lot of them are repetitive and a number of them are lightweight. But I think I'm pretty prolific.

Do any of your old songs embarrass you now?
I was gonna open this tour with "Blossom," but "Blossom" sort of bothers me. It seems so floral, it seems so cute. Actually, there are so many songs that came after it in that mode that are really a drag.

Did the confessional nature of those songs bother you at the time?
When you write a song, it may come from a personal space, but it very seldom actually represents you. It comes out of a sort of mood of melancholy, somehow. It's almost theatrical.

Where did you pick up the folk guitar?
Well, probably on Martha's Vineyard; I used

to go there in the summertime, heard some music there. Someone must've taught me what used to be called Travis picking; I suppose Elizabeth Cotten is probably more to be credited.

When did you first start playing guitar?
I think I was twelve or so. I played the cello from when I was ten, and then I bought a guitar from the father of some friends of mine and played that for a while. And then when I was fourteen or so, I bought a guitar—a real nice one—in Durham, North Carolina, that I worked with up until I was about twenty-five. Then Mark Whitebook built me the guitar I use now.

When did you start playing rock & roll?
Gee, I suppose I started playing rock & roll when I was thirteen. Kooch [Danny Kortchmar] started to show me a few loose changes and played me some Lightnin' Hopkins and Muddy Waters and John Lee Hooker and stuff like that. I suppose that was the start of it. But my brother Alex had a pretty educated ear. He went out and listened to as much as he could, and I think he probably got me started as much as Kooch did. And then Kooch and I played blues for a while—or we attempted to play blues. And then I had a band with my brother Alex down South, and we just played whatever hits were around there, played on weekends and whatever gigs we could get.

When did you hook up with Flying Machine?
Well, let's see, I went down to New York in 1966 and saw Kooch, and he said, "Why don't we try this?" I was with my friend Zach Weisner, who is a bass player, and we decided to do some rehearsing. Kooch had been with Joel O'Brien, who drummed in the King Bees. And Joel also showed me a lot of stuff—I had never known much jazz before.

How did you meet your producer, Peter Asher?
Kooch had worked with Peter and Gordon on an American tour as a member of the backup band, and I was in London to do some traveling and to take it easy, and I'd hoped to be able to sing some small clubs here and there and just make my way through Europe. But it wasn't as easy as I thought it might be. You had to have papers and had to worry about immigration, and I got more and more interested in making a record, a solo album. I went to a little two-track studio in Soho and made an album for eight pounds. I bought forty-five minutes of time and made forty-five minutes of music. And then I doubled-tracked a lot.

A lot of this was on the first album, 'James Taylor'?
Yeah, pretty much the first album. And I

started taking that around to a lot of people, but I couldn't seem to get any reaction. I'd heard from someone that Peter Asher was A&R for Apple and was listening to everything that came in. So I got his number from Kooch and went back to the States. I took the tape by: Peter liked it; Paul McCartney liked it, too. And they signed me.

What did you want to get out of it?

To emote and really get as much attention and satisfaction and gratification as I could. I wanted to perform, I wanted to write songs and I wanted to get a lot of chicks.

Did you have a hard time before that? Were you shy?

I was shy. I went to a boarding school that was all male, and I think that was an absurd thing. But I don't blame anybody for sending me there or anything. I had a rigorously academic direction that gratified me not even in the slightest. I didn't think I could break out of it. That was mainly why I went to McLean, because I saw no way out of it.

You went to Warner Bros. in 1970 and made your second album, 'Sweet Baby James.' I guess "Fire and Rain" was the first big hit you had—you were thrust into the limelight. Was it unsettling?

No, it was very gratifying to have a hit. I think there were some things about it that I wasn't really ready for—perhaps there are some aspects of being a star that I'm not very strong in. Some people can really handle an awful lot of it. And other people just continue to do their work and continue to do it well and have a good attitude toward what they're doing and know how to enjoy themselves and disregard things that are gonna mess with their heads.

When you were going through that period of time, there was a 'Time' cover story that had a lot to do with your family and your heroin addiction. Was that very upsetting?

The press want something that'll sell copy. They pick up on the mental hospital, family stuff, try to invent some category of rock that I belong to, or perhaps they pick up on my drug problem. But it gets to the point sooner or later when you start to think about your kids: "What does your daddy do for a living?" "He plays the guitar and he talks about his drug problems." It's embarrassing to read the drivel that comes out of your mouth sometimes. So I guess maybe the question is, why am I doing this in the first place? And honestly, I suppose I'm doing it because I'd like to promote my record.

I know you don't have very positive feelings about the rock press.

A review can really do a number on you.

One of the last reviews I read was in your paper. And it was by a guy named Kit Rachlis. The review came out, "Carly's Best, James' Worst," I think was what it was. That was for *In the Pocket.* It really changed my opinion of the album. My opinion was that it was a good record. Anyway, it sunk me, and I've decided two things about critics since then. I've decided that it's not worth my while to read them until somebody tells me it's okay to read them. And the other thing is that it's okay for people to not like what you do. It's okay to put out an album that nobody likes at all. 'Cause the alternative is demographic radio.

WERE YOU FEELING, OVER *the last few months, a little shaky about performing again?*

Just prior to going out on the road there was all this business about these gigs we've been playing that are about thirty miles away from any city. I didn't know what the gas shortage was going to mean in terms of attendance. It's been two years since I've been out. There are the psychological effects of losing about two years of confidence off my guitar style because of an accident to my hand.

What happened to your hand?

Well, I was in Tortola in February of last year with Carly and the kids—in the British Virgins. I was taking the meat out of a coconut. I had a knife—kind of like a butcher knife. I was just holding half of the coconut in my left hand and the knife in my right, and I put the knife underneath a section of the white meat of the coconut and flicked it out of that hard shell. A pelican landed in the water while I was about to flick, and I looked off and flicked it, and the coconut shell slipped out of my palm and the knife just grazed my palm. It was a minor cut, but I knew immediately that I'd severed a nerve 'cause I had no sensation, and it's the thumb-side edge of my left index finger. I cut through that. It was really a minor cut, but a major injury if you play the guitar.

Did you think that you might never be able to play the guitar again?

Well, I may never be able to play as well as I could two years ago. I can't play "Secret o' Life." There was a lot of buzz in that. I hope I'll be able to play it again.

But anyway, it's been a couple of years since I've been out, and it's good to be back again. The

395

thing with this business is, it's so abstract. You go in the studio, you make an album. You can't tell whether that's your best performance of it or not. But if you spend as much time as I have, and as I intend to, on the road, *that* really is playing music for me—performing in front of an audience. And that really gives you a sense of where things are at. Before this tour started, I thought to myself, well, perhaps this is a bit adolescent; maybe I shouldn't be out here trying to rock & roll for the people anymore. You know, I've got a wife, I've got a couple of kids, I'm getting older. I'm not a country artist. Maybe I can't do this forever.

I used to think of the age of thirty-five as being the cutoff point. But I don't know if that makes sense or not.

Do you have any fear of performing?

Well, it makes me nervous, but it's a combination of anxiety and excitement—there's a lot that's pleasurable about it, too. I think, generally, you have to be on top of it; you have to really be able to give yourself some distance from the performance. You have to try to diffuse some of the urgency that can gather around it. Not worry about it too much. Like, first of all, I try to be physically strong and clean and in good shape when I go out. I like to make sure that my guitar's in good shape, that my fingernail's not going to break, my voice is in good shape and stuff like that. Then when you feel yourself really warming to the music, or softening because of some phrase or because of the way things are going or something like that, you can let your heart melt and sort of go down into it.

I have a few things I think about when I need to get distance again. I think about a surface of a pool, you know, like a tidal pool, or a very still pond with ripples on it, and I try to imagine that. And sometimes I think of a glacial plain, a sort of blue-ice color. Sometimes I try to think of my heart or my center becoming hard, cold and hard.

Have you gone out on tours where it's just not there, where you're not enjoying playing?

Not for a long time. I think the last time was probably in '73, maybe in '74. I think '73. I had an awful tour, but I think it was because I was wasted. I was just totally abusing myself all the time. I was taking a lot of drugs. I went on methadone maintenance immediately after the tour. I also met Carly about the same time. Since then I've been careful to make it work for me.

How long have you been off methadone maintenance?

That tour I was talking about must have been '71 or '72. 'Cause I went on methadone in '72 and got off in '74.

Is there more camaraderie on this tour, an especially good feeling? Riding the bus was like being with a winning football team.

Yeah, you feel very high after a successful show, one that you feel went well. It's been two years since we went out. Everybody is glad to be back at it. I love being out.

You seem to really enjoy doing the rock & roll numbers on this tour.

They're a lot easier to bring off than something that requires a more subtle kind of punch. If I'm singing a song like "Long Ago and Far Away" or "Secret o' Life" or something that really requires that I get into the lyric and the performance in kind of a subtle way, I'm a lot more intimidated by the presence of 20,000 people in a huge place than I am when Russell goes into "Summertime Blues" and people start to clap their hands.

Do you think that part of the reason you include more rock & roll numbers is to deal with an audience of that size?

They seem to really like it. They come up off their feet for that stuff. The show is paced a little bit differently this time. It starts off with the usual thing of me playing by myself, and then it builds up pretty quickly with "Brother Trucker" and "Johnnie Comes Back" in the early part of the first set. Then it comes down again to "Rainy Day Man," "Secret o' Life" and "Anywhere like Heaven," and then "Your Smiling Face," "Up on the Roof" and then closes with "Company Man." The second set starts with "Steamroller" and "Day Tripper" and then comes down to "Don't Let Me Be Lonely Tonight" and "Long Ago and Far Away." We used to start quiet and get loud with both sets. And now, I think it breathes a little bit more. Also, it doesn't wear you out as much as singing four rockers in a row.

Did you make any preparations for your voice for the tour?

Nothing in particular except no smoke, no coke and no—you can't overdo it. There are things you do to loosen up your voice; some of those are built right into the set, just because it starts soft. I never had any formal training, but I think that my voice has come a long way over fifteen years or so.

I know you like Sinatra. Have you ever studied his way of singing?

I don't phrase anything like Sinatra at all except the way he ritards things. But no, the people I like are Ray Charles, George Jones, Hank Williams, the Beatles, Stevie Wonder. I love Mike McDonald. I love the way Randy Newman sings. And I love Ry Cooder's attitude, too; it's great. I like Nat King Cole. Sam Cooke was so terrific.

Your voice is more similar to Sam Cooke's than Ray Charles'. Smooth and under control. Have you ever aspired to sing more like Ray Charles—do you wish that you could really belt it out?

I consciously have tried to steal a couple of Ray Charles' phrases. If we listened to a show, I could point out a couple of points where it was like that. I could point out what I consider to be a Jackson Browne phrase without consciously trying to steal. . . . Yeah, sure, I try to; I consciously try to take a lot of things that I really admire.

You like the way Jackson Browne sings?

Yeah.

It's funny because I'm sure you influenced him when he was starting out.

I don't mean to lump people together. I have more respect for the individuals than this. Jackson and the Eagles and the Beach Boys have that West Coast *r* thing; they really bear down on that *r.* I spent a lot of time listening to the Beatles and Stones and playing music in England, so my *r*'s got real soft. But when I listen to George Jones or the boys from out on the Coast, I really fall in love with those Beach Boys *r*'s: the East Coast girls, surfing safari.

WHY ARE YOU LIVING IN *Martha's Vineyard rather than in New York? Does that have a lot to do with kids?*

We have a real nice place up there, and my family lives up there, too. And I find it a lot healthier for me to be someplace where I can go outside in my bare feet.

What's an average day like there?

It's very laid back. It starts at about five o'clock when Ben gets up. And Sarah gets up at eight. If it's my morning with Ben, I'll go downstairs and cook him some scrambled eggs, and he and I will talk about a couple of things, and maybe we'll go in and watch a videotape about animals or some such thing. We might go outside, or I might take him for a ride into town to look at the boats in the harbor. All of this is around seven o'clock when no one's up. I used to have a seat on the back of my bicycle, and we'd go into town on the bicycle. Then I'll come back around the time that Sarah gets up, and she'll get Carly up, too. Or vice versa, if it's Carly's day.

This is what happened last fall. Since the beginning of the year, I've spent about half my time away from home, recording in L.A. and being on the road. Then phone calls will start and stuff like that. I'll hear from a friend or a relative or something. Maybe I'll have a little time to write. I've got a little studio there with an eight-track.

I have a small boat in the harbor that I row, and it makes me feel good to pull around the harbor a couple of times. Martha's Vineyard people aren't employed in the same way they're employed in other places. In ways, it reminds me a little bit of a certain kind of atmosphere that was in the mental hospital I spent time in. It's a little bit protective.

How has having kids changed your life?

It has totally changed it, 180 degrees. People say you don't change that much. It's taken my horizon from two months from now to twenty years from now. Not only am I thinking about what kind of role model I am for my kids; the first two years of their lives, what you're doing is trying to keep them alive. I want to spend time with them, and I feel bad if I don't. It also kicks you upstairs. You can't be a kid anymore, in a sense. You can; it's sort of like a little of both. It reacquaints you with what that frame of mind is. Musically, all I listen to is kids' records and Walt Disney and *Grease,* so it's been devastating.

Do you think it's a healthy thing to have a framework, certain responsibilities and certain times that you have to deal with your kids?

Yeah, but at the same time, it takes away freedom. And a certain overview that I require, too.

What kind of freedom does it take away?

You spend most of your time maintaining this environment for these kids to live in. Carly will probably laugh when she hears this, because I've been on the road for half of the past six months. And she's been the one who's had to maintain the environment for the kids. But doing that eats up your time. For instance, if I wanted to stay out until three o'clock and get down and get crazy and make some music, I've got to think about what's going to go on two hours later. And if I wanted to get really drunk and all fucked up, I'd have to worry about whether or not I would hear the baby crying if it fell out of the crib. You've got to worry about driving in the automobile; it's just a big dose of straight. It's what they need, you know. And it's not necessarily what you need, but what they need seems to take precedence in a lot of different instances. It really changes. It's helpful in as much as I'm less likely

397

to die of an overdose, I believe. In a way, it sort of takes you down to earth.

Does it hold you back from getting wild, partying?

I'm not that much into partying. I think I'm more of a depressed type of personality. I'm not saying that I'm depressed, because I've learned to deal with that largely. My tendency is to crawl into a hole and poison myself, intoxicate myself. That was my danger, you know. And so I don't miss going out too much.

Do you think that having kids has helped you deal with your depressions?

My family—not only the children, but Carly—has moved me away from the way I used to deal with it, which was my completely over-touted drug problem. But the way that I deal with it now is physical activity. I think that it's becoming more and more apparent that that's the way I want to deal with it now. I'm not saying that I'm free of all my problems because there's always that temptation, and some people say that it may even be hereditary. People tend to want to be drunk or high or up or down. But I find that really pumping your body out—in other words, exhausting yourself, doing some exercise regularly—must bring all of your system into some kind of alignment. I think that a jump rope can be as helpful to a depression as two years on methadone maintenance or five years in psychotherapy. I think that buying a jump rope for $8.50 can do a whole lot.

Obviously you have to worry about your kids growing into a world with a lot of serious problems. Have you gotten involved in things that you think can help make it a safer world?

I haven't gotten into many causes. I've supported a number of political candidates but not really with too much conviction.

What about the antinuclear thing?

That's something else again. As far as the energy problem is concerned, I feel that the sane course is to ration and cut back. Somehow I'm asking this of a government that doesn't seem to be willing to do anything, to take any initiative whatsoever. I think nuclear energy is very dangerous, but I think the real danger is not necessarily that there may have to be a couple of nuclear plants. The main thing that I worry about with nuclear power is that we will continue at the same wasteful level, that we will start to substitute more and more nuclear for our other, more difficult-to-attain fuels, and then we'll be back into the corner where we have to depend on it. We need to accept living with less and living smaller.

Doesn't that make you want to get more politically involved? Especially since you have kids who are going to grow up in that world?

My reaction is a selfish one. My initial reaction is to try to become self-sufficient in some way, although that's like people in the Second World War believing that there's such a thing as being in isolation. It just doesn't exist.

So do you feel guilty that you're not more politically active?

It's difficult for me to find a movement or a group that is . . . I'm into the nuclear thing because it's so clearly insane. The problem for me is to become politically active: I'm not a scientist and I'm not a politician and I'm not an economist; I'm not a student of social trends. My credentials are only as a musician who entertains people.

Given your more stable life, your songs no longer reflect the pain you were feeling and dealing with before; what do you think they reflect?

Just different things I get interested in.

On 'Flag,' most of the songs are about people or occupations: "Millworker," "Brother Trucker," "Company Man" and "Johnnie Comes Back." It seems like you're branching out into more of a storytelling direction.

Yes, well, it's a nice direction to go in.

Why are you going in that direction?

It's hard to say. I guess it started when [director] Stephen Schwartz asked me to write a few tunes for the show *Working*, and so I just sort of did that. I liked it; it seemed to work.

Since you've never been a truck driver or a millworker, how do you feel you can put yourself in their place?

I'm not sure I can put myself in their place. I don't know whether or not I've accurately gotten into being a truck driver. I'm sure there's a millworker somewhere who's closely approximated by that song. They are just little imaginings of different people. I know what it's like to be a prisoner because I spent a lot of time behind walls and used to spend twenty hours a day sleeping. I know what it's like to spend an awful lot of time rolling around on the road, you know.

How did "Johnnie Comes Back" come about?

It started with a musical line and something on the guitar. The line just came into my head: "All last week and half of today/Johnnie has been a good little girl." And that sat for about six months. I played it for Peter, I played it for Danny. Danny said, "That's good, why don't you work on that song?" I sat down and worked on it, and it came out, you know. It's about

398

some guy who gets a little girl off the street strung out so she'll keep coming back. The line is, "She only shows up for meals/My medicine chest and my automobiles." But it's just a kind of interest in a seedy little love story; that's what it is. Not a love story, necessarily, just a seedy little relationship.

Are you tired of writing about yourself?

Yeah, I think perhaps I am.

Do you think there's less to write about in your personal life now?

I think I probably just about covered it. Either I've covered it or else I filled whatever need I had to write that kind of stuff.

Are you a much happier person than you were, say, seven or eight years ago?

Well, I think I'm probably better adjusted. I see a certain continuity, and I know better how to deal with those times of insecurity or those feelings of trepidation.

Do you still go through the same kind of depressions you used to experience?

That still happens, but it's okay now somehow.

Do you know why it happens?

I'm not sure. Some of it may be physical. I did a lot of psychoanalysis or psychotherapy, you know. And everybody has the blues—that's what it comes down to.

Do you find anything out in psychotherapy?

No, I never did seem to get too close to solving anything. I have a few personal ideas having to do with my family situation and things like that. But, in fact, I can't really explain it away very well. I'm still subject to it from time to time. Sort of like unexplainable onsets of black moods. But I've grown used to it and know how to deal with them.

When you say black mood, what is that like?

It starts with just not feeling terribly well. But there's a type of despair that I experience as being very deep.

So what do you do about it now when it happens?

Talk to Carly about it. Ask her to please answer the phone for me. Ask her for some sort of reassurance. And she's good at that; she's very supportive. She's also subject to phobias and anxiety attacks, and I'm sure everyone is. But we can be relatively supportive of each other.

Would you say that the beginning of your relationship with her was a real turning point in being able to deal with a lot of those problems?

I would say so, yeah. Our relationship and my family is the focus of my life. And the other thing that's important to me is my working relationship with the people I'm touring with.

Do you ever want to go back to an intensity like that of "Fire and Rain"? Something that would knock people on the seat of their pants?

Again, it wasn't any kind of premeditated attempt at knocking down an audience. I was just writing down a song for myself. The song came in three different portions. The first verse came in a basement apartment in London. The second verse, in a hospital room in Manhattan where I was recovering from what made me leave England—some hard times and stuff—and the third verse was written in Austin Riggs hospital in Stockbridge, Massachusetts. So it's a three-month period of time in 1968. It's like three samplings of what I went through then.

You have a beautiful apartment in New York and a house in Martha's Vineyard, and you've got a stable family and enough money so you don't have to worry about that. Do you think that your lifestyle breeds a kind of complacency?

More than complacency, it occupies my time more and more. To get up early in the morning with the children and to be part of the running of the house. I still play and try to write and stuff. I write an album a year; I probably write ten to twelve songs a year, which is okay. Carly is always writing, too. When I'm not working, she is. Although we're quite comfortable, our schedule is really very hectic. We have times when there's very little going on: For writing, it's very necessary to have some time like that. But complacent, I don't know if that's so much the word. I want to write great songs, but I don't want to suffer, you know. I'm not going to wear a couple of shoe sizes too small just because I might write a better song.

I think that *Gorilla* [1975] and *In the Pocket* [1976] had some of my best material, although neither of those sold terribly well. I much prefer my later material, as a matter of fact. I don't consider any of it great art, but I much prefer my later material. I think "Sleep Come Free Me" is as good a song as I've written in a long time. And I think "Millworker" is, too. It may not affect a large cross section of a generation the same way that "Fire and Rain" did, but you never have that in mind when you write a song.

Why do you think your work is not great art?

Well, I think "great art" is a pompous phrase. To me, that's a little tough to swallow, and it's tough to spit out, too. I think Sam Cooke singing "I Taught My Baby How to Cha Cha Cha" is a terrific song, but you'd have a hard time calling it great art.

399

So you think that "great art" is an illusory phrase?

I don't think it necessarily applies to what I consider to be folk music. I think the best I'm hoping for is just a real good song.

What kind of music do you like to listen to?

I like light classical music, and I have a few tapes that from time to time are popular with me. There's no kind of music that I really go for. Sometimes I get tapes from friends of mine that I like to listen to. There's a record called *The Pygmies of the Ituri Forest,* which is real good. I like to listen to some Copland and Debussy. It's all pretty run-of-the-mill stuff. I like to listen to David Sanborn and Charlie Parker. I like the Brazilians an awful lot. For a while I listened to reggae a bunch. And then there will be a period when I'll get hooked on a record, like the Spinners, one of their records that I've been playing a lot. And I hear a lot of Carly's and my music just because we're making it all the time.

"B.S.U.R." on the new album seems to relate to you and Carly.

The chorus came first, since it's all in initials, and I wanted to write the whole tune that way, just a sort of—exercise. You find people who write lyrics spend a lot of time making spooner-isms. It's one of those relationship songs. The lyric didn't seem to be about me and Carly at all, but she finds some correlations. I suppose it may be—I mean, after all, I wrote it. It's probably not about Haldeman and Erlichman.

Do you think, as the song suggests, that you fall down in her estimation?

I think that sometimes my behavior threatens her, 'cause she feels I might really harm myself. And it's hard to commit yourself emotionally to someone who could do damage to you through your commitment to them. It's this business of whether or not you can afford to really put your life in the hands of someone who may not be in enough control of themselves to keep themselves alive. And I think there have been times when Carly worried about that with me. It's not that she was trying to control me; she was just trying to decide whether or not she was gonna be able to stand to love me if she might have to lose me. And there were years and there have been instances when that was possible.

You mean when you were back on drugs?

Yeah, on drugs, you know, drunk driving, anything.

So, you never feel the drug problem is totally past, even if, as now, you're feeling good?

I like to think that this is the point at which I finally get off the cycle. It's not that I've been wasted for the past two years; I've been in pretty good shape. I'm subject to binges, which frightens me. And I want to put that behind me.

---

*I*S THERE A LOT OF COMPETITION *between you and Carly?*

There's a predictable amount, but it seems to be something we can handle. It makes things hectic. If both of us try to make an album a year, it's really tough. If we stagger them one year and then the next year, that may work. I think that may make some sense.

Well, this year you both came out with albums at the exact same time.

That was because I had intended to record a year ago, in June, but I opened my hand up in February, and it was pretty much unusable at that point. And Carly had already booked time [in the studio]. It was really my accident that landed my recording in the middle of Carly's. It was tough. It was hard for us to do it. When one of us is recording, the other one should be around to help with the family and to be supportive musically.

Do you go through periods when you're really blocked as far as songwriting goes, and Carly is whipping out a bunch of songs? Do you sit there and resent her?

Well, sometimes she comes and shows me something that's she just come up with. I say, "That's beautiful," but at the same time I say, "Jesus, I should write something." Her melodies are so strong. That's the main thing that I envy about her songwriting. Her lyrics are good, too. And God knows her instrument's terrific. She writes songs that you can sing without having any kind of accompaniment, and that's a good melody. But it's like there's a trade-off. As difficult as it is for us both to be in the same business, there's the benefit of our really understanding and being able to support each other. 'Cause we really know about it. When I find her being worried about something that's really bullshit, I can, with real authority, tell her that she's worrying about something that doesn't deserve her attention. And she's the same way, too.

Are there times when you feel like your career's going great, her career's not going great? Does that cause tension?

Yeah, I think it does. She's, generally speaking, bigger about it than I am. She's more generous than I am. She feels she can get more satisfaction from the fact that I'm doing well than I can from the fact that she's doing well. What I'm thinking of specifically is when she did *No Secrets* and I did *One Man Dog* [late 1972]. *One Man Dog* sold less than anything I ever put out. And hers sold a whole lot. There were different success levels going on, and, yeah, it got to me.

So, it did affect your relationship at the time?

Well, yeah, I guess it did a little bit. More than affecting our relationship, it affected the way I felt, and that affected our relationship. It's more of a positive factor than a negative one to be in the same business. But it's true that sometimes she gets involved—it's almost like there's never a respite from dealing with show business. Because when I'm not worrying about it, she is. And if we try to give ourselves a break by both releasing [albums] at the same time, then neither of us is there to support the other one (a) when we're making the album, and (b) about how the album's doing.

So this is that kind of time, I guess?

This is that kind of time. Carly's having a rough time now. She feels hurt and disillusioned, and I don't blame her. There's an attitude to adopt about this thing. It has to do with realizing where things are really at. It's harder for her to do it without many other outlets, and also feeling—as she does—much more restricted by family life and raising children than I appear to be.

Well, are you gonna bring her out on tour with you; is that gonna work out?

Well, she's gonna come out and sing a song in the show with me. It's not gonna be the same as it would be if she were working from her own material and she were billed herself and the audiences were coming to see her. She's a surprise guest, and it's great. And I think it's also very gratifying. But at the same time it's part of my trip, and I think it'll be frustrating for her, too.

None of this stuff can shape us, you know. But it can certainly get in the way of our feelings about making music, and that's where the media and the business can be a little bit poisonous.

But the key thing is you enjoy making music.

I want to concentrate and do that on the road. And you may be able to say to yourself, "I'm not going to make an album for commercial consumption, I'm going to make an album that I want to make; I'm willing to write this one off." I'd like to make an album like that. I probably won't.

You were involved with Joni Mitchell in the early

Seventies, *and it drew a lot of publicity, which must have really changed the relationship.*

I wasn't really very aware of it, but, yes, it must have changed the relationship. The relationship was what it was. Carly and I also were very public.

What does it do when you see stories about you and Carly? Do you ignore them?

I don't know anything else. I think it's necessary for Carly and me both to have identities. I don't think I could be with a woman who didn't. She and I are in many ways complementary. Often she fills an area that I am lacking in.

It's hard for me to talk about Joni because I still feel very strongly about her. I saw her recently, and she and I spent a little time talking. Not to get into what our personal relationship was like, but I've never seen anyone create the way that she does. An aspect of that leaves another side of her life lacking. She, more than I, I think, has a need for creativity, for her art. More of a need to relieve herself, to satisfy herself, than almost anyone else I've ever met.

Do you think that that happens at the sacrifice of an enduring relationship?

Perhaps it's because of the difficulty of an enduring relationship. I don't know which comes first.

D O YOU THINK THAT, TALKING *about yourself in terms of creativity, you're inspired less frequently now, that your most inspired songs are behind you?*

No, I don't. I think that it's just changing to a different type of work. It was a much more personal and urgent need, and now it's a power that I can . . . if I can get some kind of spiritual . . . spiritual sounds a little bit too magical. If I could get some kind of a hold on myself, I could be able to direct this capacity I have to share my point of view with other people. A song can do incredible things incredibly fast.

Where would you say that comes out in your recent songs?

I think "Secret o' Life" is a spiritual song. The reason I call it "Secret o' Life," sounding like an *o*, is because it sounded like such a preposterous title. So presumptuous. So I wanted to make it sound like a Lifesaver flavor, you know. I think that song is about the decaying universe, about entropy, about being in the Now. I can't wait to

401

imagine what Randy Newman will say if he reads that. He's so caustic. Jesus, he's amazing.

Do you consider yourself more of a craftsman than before?

Well, I want to think that I am. "Johnnie Comes Back" or "I Was Only Telling a Lie" or "Secret o' Life"—songs on the past couple of albums—I have to believe that they're as good as the few songs on my first album. They don't have the same direct connection with the audience. My energy was channeled directly into those things because of an urgency, because of a buildup; there was a flow that happened when I got access to be able to communicate that way. And now I'm much more spread out, but I'm no less capable of feeling strongly, and—aside from not wanting to believe that it's all behind me—it may be possible that my best work is behind me now. But it certainly isn't a very productive frame of mind.

I feel very strongly, and Carly also has recently—because of some real disappointments in her career, and also because of some disillusionment with the record business, which she has been less cynical about and more willing to participate in, in the past, than I have been—that the main thing that gets in the way of our music and our growth is the industry itself.

How so?

Just because something that's successful tends to get held onto. I mean, they want to keep that coming.

So you think that a record company inhibits . . .

Well, no, they also say you gotta change, you gotta change. Also, if you start being dissatisfied, if you get anything less than a gold record, if you start going nuts about every reviewer who wants to detract from what you're trying to become and if you listen to every person who tries to put you in a bag, it will just drive you absolutely nuts. What you have to do is somehow deemphasize and take away the urgency of that. Of that whole industry frame of mind and media slant on things. For me to be able to go

out and work helps, you see. All of a sudden I'm valid in that context. Carly doesn't have that access. So she puts out a record every two years, and when all of a sudden it doesn't get the promotion she thinks it should and when it gets reviewed just totally off the wall, if that's all she gets, that can be devastating. I got a review in *Billboard* that showed a picture of my last album *[JT]*. They said I was using Jackson Browne's band and that my vocals were bland, and it drove me nuts. So I did read a review; I just totally confirmed my worst fears.

In other words, I put out this album now; the cover is two colors on one side and two on another and it's called *Flag*, which is a little bit obscure.

Why is it called 'Flag'?

An album is a flag. Two years' work, a personal statement. It's a standard in the sense that a standard is a flag. It represents you; you put it out there; you express; let's run it up the flagpole. The flag on the cover means "man overboard," too. I didn't know that that was the case at the time. Anyway, and there's a picture on the inside of me looking skeptical. The photo session lasted for half an hour. We said, okay, we'll take this home. We made the front pink and yellow. We'll make the back turquoise and dark blue. Let's put the thing out. I spent very little time agonizing over what the cover would be. And it's all fast on one side, or mostly all fast on one side, and on the other side it's all slow; it's hot and cold and stuff. And I've gotten a lot of feedback that people don't want to see a picture of me looking like a guy not being able to move his bowels. They don't want to see an album cover without my face on it, the record company says. They want *Sweet Baby James*. And the audiences may want *Sweet Baby James*, too. So I thought, the next cover I make, I'll get someone with an airbrush; I'll get a tan on my ass, and I'll get someone to photograph it with one of those lights that makes a halo around you, and I'll call it *James Taylor—Like You Like Him.*

34

INTERVIEWED BY GREIL MARCUS (1980)

In the spring of 1980, the Who were sixteen years old, older than all their fellow British rock bands of the Sixties except for the Stones and the Kinks.

The Who had suffered, but survived, the death of drummer Keith Moon. But now there was another shadow: the Cincinnati disaster of 1979.

The band was on its first tour since Cincinnati when associate editor Greil Marcus met with Pete Townshend, now 35, in a Berkeley hotel room for this interview

Marcus, best known as a critic and essayist, was new to the Q-and-A form and, despite the remarkable job he did, said he found the session "unsatisfying." Townshend, he says, "was defensive. It was cut-and-dried. I showed up; we shook hands; two hours later we shook hands again."

—BF-T

THE INTERVIEW THAT FOLLOWS TOOK place on April 17th, just a few days into the Who's eighteen-date spring tour of the United States and Canada: their second new-world tour since drummer Keith Moon died at thirty-one on September 7th, 1978, and their first since eleven people died in the crush of fans trying to force their way into the Who's concert at Cincinnati's Riverfront Coliseum on December 3rd, 1979.

That event made headlines all over the world, most often as a condemnation of rock & roll (as on CBS news), or simply of America (as in Europe). Sixteen years as a unique and seminal rock & roll band aside, what happened in Cincinnati has probably made the Who more famous than they have ever been. Millions who had never heard of Keith Moon now think they know who the Who are.

In the world of rock & roll, the Who's status has also changed. People have rallied around the band.

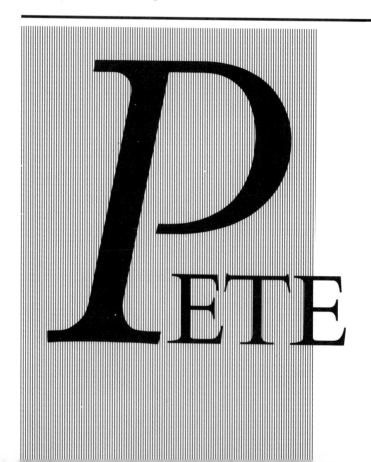

PETE

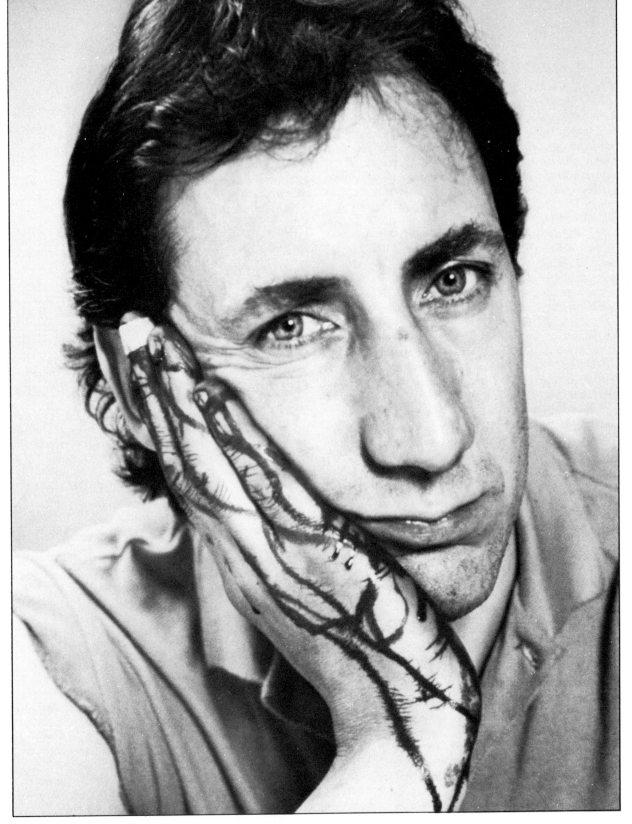

TOWNSHEND

Though the Who have never placed a Number One album or single on the 'Billboard' charts, they have represented the very spirit of rock & roll to a growing mass of fans; the Who's confrontation with disaster has made the group even more important as a standard bearer and raised the possibility that, having only just returned to live performances after two and a half years off the road, the band might be forced off the stage for good. The T-shirts fans are wearing tell the story: I SURVIVED THE WHO, on the backs of a few; THE WHO CARES, on the backs of a lot more.

In the San Francisco Bay Area, where Townshend and I talked, excitement, at least in the media, was pervasive. For days preceding the Who's three sold-out concerts at the 14,000-seat Oakland Coliseum Arena, the drums were beating with a message that could not be missed. Along with the usual ticket giveaways, radio stations programmed "all-Who" weekends, "the Who A-to-Z" weekends (and they have a Z, too: "Zoot Suit," the B side of their first record, cut in 1964 as the High Numbers), ran long, pretaped interviews with Pete Townshend and fondly recalled the Who's "American debut" at Monterey in 1967 (it wasn't; it was in New York in 1966). Smaller cinemas put on double bills of the band's two 1979 films, the fictional 'Quadrophenia' and the career-documentary 'The Kids Are Alright,' both of which had died early at local first-run houses. The day the Who left town, the radio jumped on 'Empty Glass,' Pete Townshend's new solo album—with vocals, guitar and synthesizer by Townshend, piano and organ by John "Rabbit" Bundrick and bass by Tony Butler of On the Air, a band led by Simon Townshend, Pete's brother.

Such a buildup (and follow-through—two weeks after the Who left town, the airwaves were still full of their music) was common in the late Sixties, but nothing like it had been heard since: not for the Stones, not for Dylan, not for anyone.

The Who are, in some ways, a new band: along with Kenney Jones (who replaced Moon on drums), they have added Rabbit on piano, organ and synthesizer. After the end of the spring tour the Who returned to England to complete an album, tentatively set for release in the fall {'Face Dreams,' as it appeared, was not released until April 1981}. They hit the U.S. in June for another tour, this time touching down in Los Angeles and heading for the South.

At the same time, the band is caught in its past. It's not the immediate past, of Keith Moon's death and the disaster in Cincinnati. ("We can do fourteen dead here," said a woman outside the Oakland coliseum, handing out fliers for the forthcoming concert by John Lydon's PiL. "We can beat Cincinnati." The Bay Area has always had the world's stupidest punks.)

When we talked—before the show I saw—Pete Townshend spoke of the Who's history as, among other things, a burden: "A great knapsack—you carry it around, and nobody ever empties it. You've got the old stale sandwiches in it, as well as the new ones." But that history—and the Who's history may be more vivid, more coherent, than that of any other band with a tenure even approaching theirs—can also be a crutch.

As their show opened—with "Substitute" (1966), "I Can't Explain" (the band's first record as the Who, 1965) and "Baba O'Riley" (1971)—it was impossible to think of the songs as oldies, or even as classics. With the volume loud enough to be totally satisfying—and loud enough to leave me with a partially paralyzed lower lip and a sore wrist for three days—the songs were undeniable: rock & roll facts, preexistent entities waiting for the Who to discover them. The Who didn't sound like they were referring to what had gone before: they sounded as if they were starting all over again, from the necessary beginning.

But as the show moved on—and into the more abstract and less social material from 'Tommy,' or 1978's 'Who Are You'—the performance, at least for me, settled down. Other fans—the teenage junkie behind me, the college students in front—grew ever more excited, but in a way they also settled down: They were waiting for their favorites, and the shape of the concert insured that they would get them. If the show was not quite the Who's Greatest Hits, it was the History of the Who. Aside from a couple of numbers from 'Quadrophenia,' and "Dancing in the Street" as part of a three-song encore, there were no surprises: no unrecorded material, nothing from the unfinished album, no obscurities, be they "I Don't Even Know Myself" or "Pictures of Lily" or "The Seeker." The band gave the audience what it wanted, but they didn't entice the audience to want more than it had thought of wanting—which is what the Who, like all great rock & roll bands in their great days, have been all about.

Technically, the show was superb: shot through with fun and movement. Roger Daltrey seemed to run in place for two solid hours. Townshend's crouched leaps were thrilling—spectacular but not gaudy, aggressive but not cruel. No one in the Who ever seemed bored by the material. The band changed the show over the next two nights. They cut it down, stretched it out, shuffled the songs, varied the encores—and, according to one fan who saw all three concerts, Townshend never played the same solo twice. The band sounded as compact and uncompromised as it ever has. Rabbit and a horn section added a kind of subliminal fullness. But it was a show based on the "stature" Pete Townshend talks about below, not a show intended to subvert it.

To a man, the Who looked terrific. Roger Daltrey and Kenney Jones were dressed in T-shirts and denims, and worked like athletes. John Entwistle, as always, stood stock still and this time wore a neat white suit, which set him off perfectly. As for Townshend, he appeared onstage in an impressive navy-blue jacket: He looked like a world-beater. When, after a few numbers, he took it off, revealing a Clash T-shirt with the sleeves rolled up, his pants suddenly seemed baggy—and he struck me as just another rock & roll anomaly. Just another Buddy Holly: the kid you laugh at, if you bother to do that, the kid who one day comes out of his shell and changes your life.

As that Clash T-shirt was no doubt meant to show, Townshend remains a fan. Since "I Can't Explain" he has been one of rock & roll's first-rank creators, definers; but since a memorable interview appeared in these pages in 1968, he has also been its premier participant-philosopher—or, if you like, player-coach. What follows below is merely the latest installment of that career.

I *T SEEMS TO ME THAT THE LOVE songs on 'Empty Glass' are much more personal than they've been for the past few years—not confessional, but clearly directed to a person. There's a passion in "A Little Is Enough" that seems very new.*

I think probably because I've had a harder time, lately. Before Keith died, I decided that practically all the personal problems I had—whatever they were, whether it was boozing, or difficulty at home with my family—was because of the Who on the road. When we came off the road, I spent two and a half years not touring—under great pressure from the band to tour, but I resisted, and said, "No, I want to try it and see what happens." I got to the end of that period, and all my problems were still there. Some of them were worse. But what was strange about that time was that it somehow opened me up: I was able to put a slightly different slant on the qualities that I look for, or that other people look for, in life.

With a song like "A Little Is Enough," what was interesting to me was that I was able to very easily put into words something that had actually happened to me when I was a thirty-four-year-old. It wasn't self-conscious; it wasn't a song written from a *stance*. It wasn't objective. It was *purely* personal: instant, and purely transparent. It's very emotional, but it's also very straightforward and clear. Just the fact that you can't *fucking have the world*. If you're lucky enough to get a tiny piece of it, then—fine. When that's applied to something as *immense* and *intangible* as

love—whether it's spiritual love or human love . . .

I suppose I wrote the song about a mixture of things: I wrote it a little bit about God's love. But mainly about the feeling that I had for *my wife*—and the fact that I don't see enough of her, and that when we are together there's lots of times when things aren't good, because of the period of adjustment you require after a long tour: stuff like that. She would always want a deeper, more sustained relationship than I would—but in the end I suppose we're lucky that we do love one another *at all*. Because love, by its very nature, is an infinite quality, an infinite emotion—just to experience it *once* in a lifetime is enough. Because a lot of people don't—don't *ever* experience it.

A lot of the songs on the album—well, "Let My Love Open the Door" is just a *ditty*—but particularly "A Little Is Enough" and a couple of the others—"I Am an Animal," I think—are getting *close* to what I feel I want to be writing: in terms of somebody who's thirty-five writing a rock song, but one which isn't in the George Jones-Willie Nelson tradition—"I'm a smashed-up fucker standing at the bar. . . ." "Empty Glass" is a direct jump from Persian Sufi poetry. Hafiz—he was a poet in the fourteenth century—used to talk about God's love being wine, and that we learn to be intoxicated and that the heart is like an empty cup. You hold up the heart and hope that God's grace will fill your cup with his wine. You stand in the tavern, a useless soul waiting for the barman to give you a drink—the barman being God. It's also Meher Baba talking about the fact that the heart is like a glass, and that God can't fill it up with his love—if it's already filled with love for yourself. I used those images deliberately. It was quite weird going to Germany and talking to people over there about it: "This 'Empty Glass'—is that about you becoming an alcoholic?"

That George Jones tradition—which is apparently where the person in Germany plugged in "Empty Glass"—can be just as stultifying as if you felt it always necessary to write in the voice of a seventeen-year-old: as if that were the only way a song you wrote could have any validity as rock & roll.

I think what's always been my problem, though, is that I've always been *fascinated* by the period of adolescence—and by the fact that rock's most *frenetic* attachments, most long-lasting attachments, the deepest connections, seem to happen during adolescence, or just postadolescence. Rock does evolve, and it does change and it does go through various machinations, but to

407

you, as a listener, someone who needs both the music *and* the exchange of ideas—you always tend to listen in the same way. You expect—and you feel happiest when you get—an album that does for you what your first few albums did. You're always looking for that: You're always looking for that *first fuck.* Of course, you can never have that first fuck, but you're always looking for it. Occasionally, you get very close. Always chasing the same feeling, the same magic.

I think the strangest thing for me—and I think perhaps the Who are unique in this respect—is that we *seem* to be able to continue, even though I think my writing is clumsier than it was in the early days. It's less easy for me to completely open up, because I'm not *alone* anymore. When I wrote the first five or six hit songs for the Who, I was *completely and totally alone.* I had no girlfriend, no friends, no nothing—it was me addressing the world. That's where the power of that early stuff comes from. But despite the fact that the later material is less transparent, less wholesome to some extent, we still appeal to a very young audience. Sometimes preadolescents. But always, *always,* there is a very, very strong *grab*—a deep, instant grab—which lasts . . . forever. It's not like a fad. People who get into the Who when they're thirteen, fourteen, fifteen, sixteen, never stop being fans. The Who don't necessarily captivate the whole teenage generation—as each batch comes up ever year—but we certainly hit a percentage of them, and we *hold* them.

Just after Cincinnati, just after the news hit that eleven people had been killed trying to get into your show, there were statements on the radio from you and from Roger Daltrey, and my wife was very disturbed by something Roger said: simply a reference to the people who had died as "the kids." She said, "But they weren't all kids—one of those people was a mother with two kids of her own." What that expression meant to her was that the audience was no longer real to the band: The audience had become faceless, physically present but also somehow invisible. Whoever was in the audience, they were "the kids." It was as if there were an enormous gulf separating the band from its audience—as if there were no way to feel the kind of identification she and I felt when we first saw the band in 1967, when it became obvious that the band and its audience were part of the same reality, a reality we were both creating, or a story we were both telling. Do you think there is that kind of gulf?

Yes. I think there is. When I think back to the days at the Marquee—we got a regular Tuesday night residency, which was a big coup for us because we didn't even have a record out. The first night, there were maybe fifty people, the next night, two hundred, and after that we were packing it. We were a cult within a cult—our whole audience was nineteen years old, as we were—and there's a great feeling of affirmation when the audience knows they're sharing in the success; they're making the success happen as well. So you become *incredibly* close. The two or three thousand people who regularly attended the Marquee residency—I think I know them all by their first names.

One of the problems, today, is not an obvious one. Roger—who, dare I say it—tends occasionally to jump to conclusions about what's going on and maybe sticks to them until someone can talk him out of them, jumps to a *wrong* conclusion when he feels that the gulf is created by a difference in age. I think it's more to do with a difference in *stature.* The Who are an enormous business machine, surrounded by all kinds of controversy—and I suppose a great amount of media power. A lot of that comes from the success of things that are happening *around* the band. The *Tommy* film is a case in point: an average, entertaining film, blown all out of proportion—the *David Frost Show,* Allan Carr with his famous parties, Oscar presentations. It's really got very little to do with *front-line* rock & roll, but it does affect the way people see the band.

But there is also the fact that the band's history starts to accumulate. To be in existence for fifteen years and still be working, still be appearing on a stage . . . People can actually pay money and go and see this band who have got—not so much a wonderful backlog of material behind them, but who have actually got a history.

It's like discovering a new author. You run out of books to read, and suddenly you discover that you like F. Scott Fitzgerald. You start, and you read all his books, and you're really pissed off the day you come to the end of them. Then you go on to your next author—you might discover Salinger. And you go through that lot. And you get pissed off when you run out. This often happens to you when you're quite young—and what's a big kick for a lot of young kids who get into the Who is the discovery that there's so *much* to get into. We do exist now, we are putting out product, but there's a lot more they can find. So although there is a gulf, I think there is also a fascination in the fact that people might feel that gulf to start with but also feel there's an opportunity, by a kind of investigative listening and studying and reading books about the band or going to see the films—there's a chance they can *get* closer.

All I can tell you is that I meet kids on the road—and they are kids, sixteen to twenty—and they treat me just like the guy next door. They've got *no* deep respect for me; there's no fanaticism. It's an absolute, one-to-one relationship. There's a familiarity, a sense of naturalness. I think that could only come about if they felt close to me. It doesn't happen with everybody—but it happens with quite a few people.

Of course, it's going to be different if you're fucking eighteen- or nineteen-year-olds—I don't think *I'd* go and watch the Who, even if I lived in America. I mean, I'd sit and wait until the Clash came: I'd go and see them. And hope I'd get one of their good nights!

Is there any point to the Who carrying on, as a touring band, any point beyond pandering to an audience that has become so conservative, so fearful of new experiences, that latching onto a rock legend—and whatever else the Who is, it is that—can become a reactionary, defensive way of resisting new and challenging music? That isn't to say—or to deny—that your music today is unimaginative, old-fashioned, or whatever—that's irrelevant. I've been struck, over the last few years, by the fact that the great bulk of the American rock & roll audience will do almost anything to avoid having to deal with something that's radically new.

Me too—I think you're absolutely right. It's very, very strange: In Britain, at the moment, we've got 2-Tone, we've still got punk, we've got mod bands, we've got heavy-metal bands, we've got established supergroups, we've got all kinds of different *families* of music—*each* of which takes an enormous amount of adjustment. They're intense and very socially . . . jagged. They don't fit neatly into existing society: They challenge it. And yet in America, kids seem to be quite happy. Rock, to them, is enough: Establishment rock *is enough*. That seems very peculiar to me. There are obviously lots of subdivisions of music in America, but I think that's something record companies dream up. In reality, whether it's black music or white rock music, I think the truth of the matter is exactly as you've said. It's not necessarily something as big as fear—it's fucking *uncomfortableness*, listening to a Sex Pistols record. It worries you, because somebody is speaking the truth.

People in the States don't necessarily refuse to admit that problems exist but it's a country that believes in *success*—that ultimate success lies in the hands of man. Whereas, *rock* doesn't. Newer rock, particularly, actually affirms the *futility* of man, in all respects but one. It says, in a word, in a sentence, what Meher Baba said: "Don't worry—you're not *big enough* to deal with it." It's just gone *too crazy.* Do your best and leave the results to God.

When you listen to the Sex Pistols, to "Anarchy in the U.K." and "Bodies" and tracks like that, what immediately strikes you is that *this is actually happening.* This is a bloke, with a brain on his shoulders, who is actually saying something he *sincerely* believes is happening in the world, saying it with real venom, and real passion.

It touches you, and it scares you—it makes you feel uncomfortable. It's like somebody saying, "The Germans are coming! And there's no way we're gonna stop 'em!" That's one of the reasons a lot of new music is harder to listen to. So you get a band like the Clash, and they come out with a nifty little song like "Clampdown," and you can't hear the words, and they'll play it on the radio in L.A. You read the fucking words, they scare the shit out of you. Or the Pretenders—Chrissie Hynde's got a sweet voice, but she writes in double-speak: She's talking about getting laid by Hell's Angels on her latest record! And *raped*. The words are full of the most *brutal*, head-on feminism that has ever come out of any band, anywhere!

And yet it's only because it's disguised that it's getting played, and getting appreciated. To some extent, both the Clash and the Pretenders are getting played because their music is slightly more palatable, slightly closer to the old form. I saw so many new bands go *down* in England, so many great bands, because unless you were in exactly the right frame of mind, felt the same way, felt as abandoned, felt as anarchistic and felt as I-don't-give-a-shit as they did, you just couldn't enjoy it. And in fact—to answer the question you asked at the beginning of all this—for the Who, at the moment, to go out as an established band requires a lot of that don't-give-a-shit attitude. We *don't give a shit* whether the audience has a problem or not. All we know is that *for us,* to go on a stage, get instant communication, know that people have done their homework, have an instant connection with the audience, *go* backstage afterward into a dressing room full of the most beautiful women you can ever hope to lay your eyes on, never have *anybody* say anything nasty to you, everybody's friendly, everybody's *wonderful,* people don't throw us out of hotels anymore—.

I mean, life revolves quite nicely—you know **409**

what I'm saying? I'm getting paid a lot of money for the privilege. The first ten years in the Who were fucking *awful*; miserable, violent, unhappy times. It's nice to now sit back and enjoy it. It might be brief; for the sake of rock music in some ways I hope it is brief. For me, maybe I don't hope it's brief.

We've very much dropped our idealistic stance in terms of *our* weight of responsibility to rock's evolution. We haven't stopped caring about where it's going to go; I think we've realized that we're not capable of doing *that much*, in terms of actually pushing it forward. If we have got a chance of pushing it forward, I think we've got a better chance of doing it on the road than we do on record, to be quite honest.

So can the band still make history? Obviously, it has made rock & roll history, and it's certainly affected social history as such. You seem to be saying that can't continue.

Maybe only history in terms of *statistics*, now—how many years we've been together; how many disasters we can survive.

Which is not what I meant. I meant exactly what you meant: pushing the music forward.

Well, I don't know. Who's that down to? Is it down to me? As a writer? I don't know. I think if it's down to me as a writer there might be a chance, but I don't know how much stamina I've got left.

Let me put it another way. What strikes me most about what happened in Cincinnati is that it seems, now, not to have happened at all. It has not become part of the rock & roll frame of reference, as Altamont instantly and permanently did. It seems to me that it was an event that should have signified something new about the relationship between bands and their audiences, or about rock & roll as mass culture, was taking place. It ought to have forced people to reexamine a lot of assumptions, a lot of what they took for granted. That hasn't happened.

Will that event have an effect on the Who's music? I don't mean in terms of the Who putting out a nice little commentary about it, as the Grateful Dead did after Altamont with "New Speedway Boogie"; I mean over the years, in a more profound way.

I think what's not apparent to the outside world, in the Who, is our—bloody-minded brutality. Our—determination. Our stamina, and our *strength*. It's not apparent because we seem to brood so incessantly on our weaknesses, we seem to have so many phobias; like everybody who really cares about rock, we spend so much time worrying how many more years . . . But the amazing thing, for us, is the fact that—when we were *told*, told about what happened at that gig, that eleven kids had died—for a *second*, our guard dropped. Just for a second. Then it was back up again.

It was, fuck it! We're not gonna let a *little thing* like this stop us. That was the way we *had* to think. We had to reduce it. We had to reduce it, because if we'd actually *admitted* to ourselves the *true* significance of the event, the *true* tragedy of the event—not just in terms of "rock," but the fact that it happened at one of our concerts—the tragedy to us, in particular, if we'd admitted to that, we could not have gone on and worked. And we had a tour to do. We're a rock & roll band. You know, *we don't fuck around*, worrying about eleven people dying. We *care* about it, but there is a particular attitude I call the "tour armor": When you go on the road you throw up an armor around yourself, you almost go into a trance. I don't think you lose your humanity, but think: For ten, maybe fifteen years, the Who smashed up hotel rooms—why? Where's the pleasure in it? We actually quite relished general violence. I don't understand why it happened. It doesn't happen now, but it did happen, for a long time. I think that, for me, tours were like a dream.

I was literally wearing armor. The only thing that would ever crack it, for me, at a show would be if my wife and kids were there. Or my brother—he'd be, what? Eleven or twelve years old. Simon: He's got a band of his own now, On the Air. I used to really worry about him. He'd like to be right up front, and if I saw trouble happening—that would be my link. That would pierce my armor.

In a way, I think you're wrong about what you were saying about a gulf. When I say armor, I mean armor that actually *allows* you to be more abandoned, and freer, that allows you to be tougher, harder—*genuinely* tougher and harder. I'm not trying to glamorize it, and it's not something that I'm necessarily proud of. The Who's macho tendencies, in some ways, weaken our audience; our audience is about eighty percent male.

You say that if you had allowed yourself to really think about, to really face the true tragedy of what happened in Cincinnati, you would have had to stop—but you couldn't stop, you didn't want to stop, there was no point to stopping. But once the tour was over—or maybe a year after, or two years—isn't it important, if the band is going to continue to make sense of where it's been and where it's going to somehow integrate that event, to absorb it: to allow it to affect you, in terms of the music you make and the way you perform it?

I don't know, because so far we've had a series of quite unfortunate reactions.

How do you mean?

I think the way festival seating was blamed, wholesale, for practically all the problems was quite a nasty, negative overreaction—because I *like* festival seating. When I go to a concert I don't want to have to fucking sit in a numbered seat and get clobbered over the head every time I stand up. I like to be able to move about; I like to be able to *dance* if I want to, or go and buy a Coke if I want to, or push my way to the front if I want to or hide in the back if I want to! I also know, from the stage, that you get the best atmosphere with festival seating.

Yesterday was a case in point: the second date we did in Seattle. I saw five or six punch-outs because of people just not wanting to stand up at the same time as the person in front of them. You see one guy punching some guy out 'cause he's standing up, and fifteen minutes later *he's* standing up and the guy behind *him* is punching him out. Everybody's got a different reaction time—a different moment when they feel they want to get up and jump. One person thinks that the time to get up and jump is the guitar solo in "My Wife," and somebody else thinks it's when Roger goes, "See-ee meeee, fee-eel me—" I mean, who knows? You don't get that kind of conflict at general-admission shows.

That's one reason. Another is that immediately after the Cincinnati gig, to protect ourselves partly from *legal* recriminations, we doubled, trebled and quadrupled external security at halls. The *problem* with Cincinnati was external security, external control: external people control. People in large numbers *need controlling.* They're—they're like cattle. But a lot of kids complained; everywhere they'd look there was a cop. It spoiled their evening for them. They felt, okay, it happened in Cincinnati, but *we don't need that.* There was an article in the paper in Seattle, complaining about the fact that there was *too much security.* It said, "This isn't Germany. The kids in Seattle *don't* rampage. There's never been even a slight *injury* at a concert. . . ." Et cetera, et cetera, et cetera.

All of which is quite meaningless: "It can't happen here." That's just what I meant about the event seeming not to have happened, to have been deflected.

Probably—but at the same time, it was interesting that the first serious problems they had at Seattle Coliseum were at our two gigs [this tour]: the first two gigs they've done with reserved seating on the floor. It's the first time they've actually had audience-inflicted injuries.

The other side of it is worth mentioning: the fact that the Who don't just get their strength from wearing armor. We did go home, and we did think about it, and we talked about it with our families and our friends. I went home to about ten letters, from the families of the kids who'd died: letters full of deep, deep affection and support and encouragement. It wasn't like these people were being recriminatory. The father of the girl who died who had two children was writing to say that it would hurt *him,* the family, the friends of the family and friends of the girl, if they knew that because of what happened, because of her death, we changed our feelings about rock. They understood her feelings about the band, and about the music—you know what I'm saying?

We actually left the States—I know Roger and I had a long conversation about it—with an *incredible* feeling of, without being mordant about it, of *love* for the American people. Everybody had been so positive and so supportive and *understanding*—even to the point where people would come up to me and say, "We know it wasn't your fault." And to some extent it *was* our fault. It's not exactly the way the Cronkite report made it look, but there was a great share of responsibility there, and people were so willing to—not so much to *forgive,* but firstly to get us back into shape, so that perhaps it was possible for us to behave in a truly realistic, responsive way about the whole thing.

I think only time will tell. If I could dare say it, I'd say that Cincinnati was a very, very positive event for the Who. I think it changed the way we feel about people. It's changed the way we feel about our audience.

In terms of affection?

In terms of affection, and also remembering constantly that they are human beings—and not just people in rows. And I hope the reverse: that people who come to see the band will know that we're human beings too, and not this *myth* you were talking about earlier.

I mean, I watched Roger Daltrey cry his eyes out after that show. I didn't, but he did. But now, whenever a fucking journalist—sorry—asks you about Cincinnati, they expect you to come up with a fucking theatrical tear in your eye! You know: "Have you got anything to say about Cincinnati?" "Oh, we were *deeply* moved, terrible tragedy, the horror, loss of life, *arrrrghh*—" What do you do? We did all the things we thought were right to do at the time: sent flowers to the fucking funerals. All . . . *wasted.* I think when people are dead they're dead.

411

When I was in England a couple of months ago, there was constant talk of youth-culture violence, particularly from skinheads, and there seemed to be a general feeling that the violence was increasing. Geoff Travis of Rough Trade {a record shop and label in the Notting Hill Gate area of London} spoke of the violence, in his store and on the street, as a day-to-day fact. I asked him why he thought this was happening, and he gave me various explanations having to do with the economic and political situation in Britain—but he also said that he thought 'Quadrophenia,' the movie, had had an effect. He thought that the movie glamorized violence between youth movements, and also very much exaggerated the mod-rocker violence that did take place in the early to mid-Sixties, when the movie is set—that the violence was nowhere near so intense as the movie shows it to be. What do you think about that?

Well—I'm sorry to say that I suppose in a way I think he's right. It's very difficult when you make a film—when you *produce* a film—because in the last analysis you have to hand it over to the director. I wrote the script, originally—the first draft screenplay I wrote with Chris Stamp—and there was no riot scene at all. Not at all. For me, Quadrophenia was about the fights and the riots, happening in the kid's *head*. The *threat:* "I'll do anything, I'll go anywhere"—and what you're dealing with is a little wimp. Who's fucking *useless.* Who couldn't fight anybody. He had his few pills and his bottle of gin, and he *felt* like he could.

It was a study in spiritual desperation: the fact that all that desperation and frustration leads somebody to the point where for the first time in their life they realize that the only important thing is to open their heart. It wasn't about blood and guts and thunder—in the way that the film turned out to be.

It wasn't about the clash of youth cultures.

No. I suppose the director, Franc Roddam, thought it would make good cinema. And I think to some extent it's possible [the film] has sharpened [the violence] up, but I think it runs a bit deeper. A lot of skins would naturally go and see *Quadrophenia,* but the thing that makes sinkheads violent is that—well fundamentally they're fascists. They despise *everybody*—who isn't like them. It's a kind of *toy* fascism, fed by organized fascism: fed by Martin Webster and the National Front.

You know, I'm not afraid to say that I think fascism *stinks,* and I think a lot of skins stink. But I suppose I think any violence stinks, and if you pin down any of these kids, you could actually get it across to them that neither their

violence nor their outfits nor their stance is going to *change* anything in British society. But most of all, they're wrong anyway: There's nothing wrong with our society. It's perfectly all right as it is. The way all societies are is that some people get, and some people *don't.* And if you don't fucking *get,* you don't go around slashing people on the face because you've not got enough money to buy a car. You bear it with dignity. The problem to some extent—when you've got a film like *Quadrophenia*—is that it's *exploited* something that's already there; the violence was already there. I don't know quite where the responsibility lies—maybe you could use the same terms I used for Cincinnati: I suppose the responsibility lies in direct proportion to everybody who makes money out of it.

Earlier, we were talking about the different strains of music that exist in Britain now, and you said each was jagged, challenging, didn't fit easily into the social order—and that things didn't seem to be that way in America. In America, when a problem becomes evident, it's common to hear, "Oh, it's just a problem in communications"—as if there couldn't really be anything that truly divides people. Whereas in Britain, the class system is recognizably the basis of the way the country works—it's part of the way this country works, too, but not recognizably—and, in Britain, there is an understanding that real things can divide people: that, inevitably, they do. That, to me, is one of the reasons you can have intensely different audiences and musics, each "jagged," not because one form of music simplistically represents a given class, but because the idea of clashing, of being separated, is part of the society itself: It's not the slightly unreal concept it often is in America. Such conflict implies change, and yet you're saying society as it is right now is just fine—perfect. I'm quite taken aback to hear you say that. It seems to me you're saying a lot more than that it's pointless to try and change society.

I'm saying it's pointless to try and change it through violence. And it's pointless to try and change it through *complaint.* Probably anarchy . . . Anarchy in organized society means standing up and saying, "Listen, I don't fit in, and I refuse to fit in"—and, presumably, you end up in jail. But you don't necessarily have to hurt anyone by being an anarchist; the old image of the anarchist walking around with a bomb, about to blow up the British Museum, is *dated.*

No—I don't think society's perfect at all. What I'm saying is that a lot of the problems that lead to violence, that occur within separatist youth movements in Britain, come from resentment that somebody is better off than they are, and they can't understand the reason why. And they then feel that if this person is better off than they—if there's a Rolls-Royce to be had, and it happens to be driven by a Pakistani, then he doesn't deserve it; it belongs to *me*. Charlie Wilkins from Camden Town. With his Dr. Marten boots with steel-toe caps and his hair shaved off. He probably works for the GPO—and has probably got an IQ of four. And deserves a Rolls-Royce as much as a kick in the head. I mean, he deserves *nothing*, is what I'm saying.

Why do British rock movements last so long? There are still Teds, or the Tedrockabilly subculture; there are mods again; there are still skinheads, after more than a decade. London and towns outside it are full of very young kids in pure 1977 Sid Vicious regalia. Why do these movements last so long, and without developing?

I don't know. There is that deeply ingrained sense of class, and it shatters down now into separatism—but it goes a little bit deeper. There's a need for uniforms; and to some extent it doesn't matter which uniform you choose, just so long as you choose a uniform.

A lot of skins are just kids that like the look. They like football, they like to go and jostle at football matches, get involved in a few punch-outs, but not *kill* people. Not slash people. It's something like getting involved in a fight, and going down to the pub the next day as the hero, with a black eye.

What's important about the uniforms is that they're so *extreme*. You adopt the heavy-metal uniform: You wear a denim jacket, you cover it with badges of this band and that band—UFO—you take your cardboard guitar, and you go down to the Roundhouse, and you wave your long, greasy hair—

Cardboard guitars? To mime playing along?

Right. Then rockabilly: bright pink jackets, with velvet collars; drapes that go halfway down your legs; great big brothel creepers—

Brothel creepers?

Shoes with great, thick crepe soles. And drainpipe trousers, pink socks. Punk: people with beehive, pointed hair, their legs chained together, girls going to clubs with no skirts on. Mod: short, clean haircuts; military clothes—

They're all so fucking extreme: I think it *invites* a them-and-us situation, *wherever it occurs*. The way Franc Roddam tried to *justify* the sensationalist violence in *Quadrophenia* was by analyzing the relationship between the two friends: Kevin, who was the rocker; and Jimmy, who was the mod. Despite the fact that they were friends, and had a hell of a lot in common, and could have gone on to become closer, Jimmy ends up finding himself beating his own friend up, simply because he's wearing the wrong clothes.

It's so *clear* who are "they" and who are "us"—animosity comes quite naturally. Quite why there is the need for uniforms, I don't know. I'm still trying to work that out.

35

INTERVIEWED BY TIMOTHY WHITE (1980)

By the spring of 1980, Billy Joel, the "Piano Man" turned platinum star, deserved a cover. But it was another deadline rush that forced the story into a Q & A format. As interviewer Timothy White recalls, another cover story had fallen through, and his editors decided he should do the Joel story he'd previously been assigned. White knew Joel from an earlier article and quickly arranged a meeting. When he met Joel in Long Island, however, Billy backed out, pleading personal difficulties. But with the deadline only a week away, White pursued Joel to Detroit where the singer finally relented.

After the show—the last one on a tour to promote the *Glass Houses* album—White walked into Joel's hotel room.

"He was there with two bottles of Johnnie Walker Red, two glasses and ice. I said, 'Billy, I never drink liquor, and I *never* drink scotch.' He looked at me and said, 'Yeah? You don't drink scotch? Well, I don't do interviews.' He dropped ice into a glass, filled it to the brim and said, 'Let's get started.' I'll never forget him holding out that glass with a big shit-eating grin on his face. We finished both bottles with a little help. The sun was up when we finished the interview."

Back in New York, White met the press just in time. As for Joel: "He went into seclusion after the tour," says White. "He knew he was a big success. He had achieved it." Joel ironed out his personal problem and, as White concludes: "The story has a happy ending all around."

—BF-T

HIS NOSE WAS LYING ON ITS SIDE, bleeding on his swollen cheek. Billy Joel studied himself in the mirror; his thoughts darted back to the solid punch that had numbed his face for the rest of the bout, held as usual at a boys' club gym in the Hicksville, Long Island, shopping center.

BILLY

JOEL

Before the amateur welterweight had another minute to dwell on his disfigurement, a buddy ambled by, sized up his mushed mug and calmly said, "It's just cartilage; it'll be okay." Then this guy pushed Joel's nose back into what seemed like its former position. Later, a little surgical tape and gauze held the damage in place.

"My nose was never the same after that," says Joel, who won twenty-three of his twenty-six bouts during a three-year period in his midteens. "I've got one nostril smaller than the other. See, my nose is kind of bent. I thought about having an operation, but I wondered if it would change my voice. Now I kinda like it," he says of his altered appearance. "I don't know if I'd want to look like I did when I was a kid. As my mother would say, 'It gives you character.'"

In other words: Hey, no big deal, okay?

Billy Joel, 31, has been defensive most of his life—often with good reason. His father, a Jew born in Nuremberg and raised in Nazi Germany, divorced his wife during Billy's adolescence and left for Vienna, reducing the family's economic standing from lower middle class to scrambling-for-rent status.

"My father never abandoned us," Joel insists. "He sent a check every month." But when pressed, the cautious, ever-sparring pop star adds, "Well, my mother took any gig she could get: bookkeeper, secretary. We went hungry a lot. Sometimes it was scary, not eating. We were in the suburbs, in Levittown, but we were the antithesis of the suburban situation. Do you know what it's like to be the poor people on the poor people's block?!"

To shield himself against a Long Island suburban ethos that ridiculed his threadbare circumstances, Joel fell into a neighborhood gang, wore a leather jacket, sniffed glue, dabbled in petty theft and drank a lot of Tango wine (easily the toughest belly-wash for a macho young pug to keep down).

H E WAS ALWAYS ANGRY, yeah, but the anger fed his hunger, and his hunger found its focus in music. His mother dragged him to piano lessons at the age of four, hoping he would emulate his father, a classical pianist whose love of music and life helped him survive a stretch in Dachau during World War II. Howard Joel escaped to New York via Cuba and became an engineer for General Electric. Billy Joel quit Hicksville High and escaped into rock & roll.

Or so he thought. What initially seemed like a release soon proved to be a snake pit, and Joel was bitten badly as he stumbled from group to group, label to label, viper to viper. Even after he landed a deal

with a reputable label (Columbia), the financial returns were paltry. Desperate, he turned to wife Elizabeth (who had previously been married to the drummer in one of Joel's early bands, the Hassles) and begged her to use the know-how she'd acquired at UCLA's Graduate School of Management to pull him out of his predicament. She maintains that as late as the summer of 1978, Joel's debut platinum album for CBS, 'Piano Man,' had netted him only $7763.

Reputed to be a tough businesswoman, Elizabeth, 32, initiated a flurry of lawsuits, took charge of Joel's books and fought to get her hapless husband his fair share of the profits by setting up their own corporation, Home Run Systems. "This is a business," she has stated. "People never expected me to be as smart as I was, and they would be totally frank because they didn't realize I was building my empire. Money is the bottom line of everything."

Secure in the knowledge that he is finally in good hands monetarily, Joel now pays attention only to his music. After a decade of bar bands, indecent record deals and disdainful press, he presented Columbia Records with the biggest album in its history—1977–1978's 'The Stranger,' which has sold more than 5 million copies to date.

Onstage, during a three-encore performance at Detroit's Joe Louis Arena in late July, Joel was raucous and riveting as he raced from keyboard to keyboard on his multiramped set, pressing his fine band (Russell Javors, rhythm guitar; David Brown, lead guitar; Doug Stegmeyer, bass; Richie Cannata, horns and organ; and drummer Liberty DeVitto, a veteran of Mitch Ryder's early groups) to its limits. Billy seemed as pugnacious as his face-off stance suggested when he spit out "It's Still Rock and Roll to Me," openly taunting the critics who dismiss him as a mere pop phenomenon. But it's important to look past the pose, to read between his lyric lines and recognize his urgency—and boyish fear of rejection.

"All the digs he gets in the press really hurt him," says producer Phil Ramone, who Joel willingly admits turned his career around with his studio expertise on 'The Stranger,' '52nd Street' and 'Glass Houses,' the last three of his seven albums.

"He's very disciplined," says Ramone. "We—he, the band and I—generally get a song done in just two or three takes. And it's all part of his tough, seasoned exterior, born out of years of double crosses. But behind his hard facade is a great, great tenderness. I think, for example, that I took some of the rigid perfectionism out of his classical training and made 'Just the Way You Are' less like a stiff nightclub ballad and more like a powerful, deliberate love statement."

This interview with Billy Joel took place in his room at the Hotel Pontchartrain following his Detroit performance. Dressed in a droopy red T-shirt, sneakers *and jeans, he lounged on a couch and we talked nonstop from one a.m. until dawn. At first, he came off randy and offhanded. But as he grew more tranquil, I thought back on a story he'd told me three years earlier about his maternal grandfather, who became his surrogate father after Billy's dad left the family.*

"He was an English gentleman," Joel had said, "a brilliant man who inspired me to read, and he was a music lover. We would go to the Brooklyn Academy of Music to see these great classical performances. And because he knew the guy at the door, he'd slip him a pack of Camels to get us good seats.

"He was," Joel assured me then, his voice cracking, "a real gentleman."

I reminded Joel of that recollection and asked him how he saw his current stage of personal development. "Part of me is an adult," he said quietly, rubbing his crooked nose, "and part of me is a kid. I want to hold onto both. Very much."

YOU ONCE TOLD ME THAT THE *image on the cover of 'The Stranger'—you sitting on a bed in a suit and tie, staring at a mask, boxing gloves hanging nearby—came to you in a dream. There's something surreal about the cover of 'Glass Houses,' too. What's the story behind it?*

The mask actually had nothing to do with the song, "The Stranger," where I talk about faces, the sides of ourselves that we hide from one another. The *Glass Houses* jacket was the same kind of thing. I kept thinking *{exasperated}*, "Well, I suppose people think of me as a pop star," and right up to this second, I remain uncomfortable with that tag. That rock-star thing, that was not the purpose of making this latest record. I'm going to do whatever I feel like doing, and whatever I do, I know I'm going to get rocks thrown at me, so I figured, what the hell, I'm just gonna throw a rock through my window, at myself—meaning the whole narrow image people have of me!

{Smiling} And that *is* my house, by the way. People think I've got this multimillion-dollar mansion. I paid $300,000 for it, and that wasn't even money up front; I've got a mortgage. I'm not a *multi*millionaire. Frankly, I'm not really sure what I'm worth. It's safe to say I'm a millionaire—that's a possibility. I honestly don't know and don't ask.

Does having a mortgage mean you couldn't buy the house outright?

Yes, I couldn't do that.

Even though you're one of the largest sellers of records in recent years? It sounds as if you should renegotiate your contract with Columbia Records.

Well, I can't turn around now and renegotiate something I've already agreed to. That's my concept of good business, and I admit I did sign a lot of lousy papers over the years.

Are you content, overall, with this situation?

It was more fun when there were a lot less dollars involved and a lot less greed. And there was a lot less pressure to make megabucks. And I had fewer responsibilities to people. I tend to get pissed off about money, and that's why I have lawyers and managers to keep it fairly distant from me. It used to be fun to just to go out and play rock & roll.

What was the first record that really turned your head around, influenced you?

"You've Lost That Lovin' Feelin'" by the Righteous Brothers. And almost every record the Ronettes did—their sound was bigger than the radio. To me, Phil Spector was like composer Richard Wagner. Any song by Otis Redding, Sam and Dave, Wilson Pickett—early Motown.

See, when I was twelve or thirteen, I didn't have any money. My sister had a little record case for 45s that said I LOVE YOU, ELVIS on the side, and I'd sneak into it and borrow what she had. The singles had no photos on them, so you didn't know whether the groups were white or black.

You speak of your reverence for black R&B, but I think it's fair to say that your sound is a lot closer to white pop.

That's probably because I'm white *{laughing}*. The closest I can get to sounding black might be something near Stevie Winwood. You know, I really wanted Ray Charles to record "New York State of Mind," and I approached Al Green with some stuff.

I loved Streisand doing "New York State of Mind," and Sinatra just did "Just the Way You Are," but the *biggest* kick was when Ronnie Spector cut 'Say Goodbye to Hollywood,' 'cause I heard Ronnie in my head as I wrote the lyrics! It was wild! And then to have Miami Steve Van Zandt and the E Street Band back her up was the best. God, that made me truly happy. That's jukebox music, man, good car-radio music! And I helped make it happen!

In my teens, I was in bands with names like the Emerald Lords and the Lost Souls. We wore matching jackets with velvet collars. I didn't know from extended guitar solos, or that you were supposed to drop *this* drug while listening to *that* record and then read the album cover upside down as the record played. I tried being a

417

hippie for a year—it was a total loss; I was a *lousy* hippie. I became the keyboard player for this band called the Hassles. We put out two albums, *The Hassles* and *The Hour of the Wolf*. It was real psych-e-whatever.

This was about the time Hendrix was out. His music really got to me, and the Hassles drummer and I decided we were gonna do a power duo. It was the loudest thing you ever heard. We made one album for Epic, called *Attila*. It had this weird cover. The art director had us in a meat locker, with carcasses hanging around us, and we were dressed up as Huns. I got talked into it.

So how'd you become a solo singer/songwriter hiding out in L.A. under the pseudonym Bill Martin and playing Buddy Greco songs in the Executive Cocktail Lounge?

I started writing songs on my own, taking odd jobs in New York in the meantime. I thought, "Okay, I'm gonna be a songwriter and write for other people." I had gotten the whole rock & roll thing out of my system, or so I thought. But everybody in the business told me, "If you want other artists to hear your material, why don't you make a record?" Once I made the record, they wanted me to go on tour to promote it, so one thing led to the other. The first album was called *Cold Spring Harbor,* on Paramount Records. That was a *weird* deal. ["The strangest thing happened," says producer Artie Ripp. "The sixteen-track machine ran slow, and when we mixed the final master, Billy sounded like a chipmunk. I said, 'Billy, it doesn't matter if it's fast or slow. We'll remix it sometime later in our lives.'"] I went on tour, and nobody got paid. I signed away everything; I just didn't know. This was right before *Piano Man*. I went to the West Coast. I just disappeared. I really didn't want to leave, but I had to get out of these contracts [with Ripp and Paramount], and I didn't want these people to know what I was doing. So I used the name Bill Martin, and I got a gig working in a piano bar for about six months.

It was all right. I got free drinks and union scale, which was the first steady money I'd made in a long time. I took on this whole alter identity, totally make-believe; I *was* like Buddy Greco, collar turned up and shirt unbuttoned halfway down. The characters that Steve Martin and Bill Murray do as a goof, I was doing, too, only people didn't know I was kidding. They thought, "Wow, this guy is really hip!"

Eventually, the people who had me under contract—and couldn't find me—realized they were either going to have to renegotiate and compromise, or they weren't going to get anything out of me.

It was 1972. I was about twenty-three. I still had no idea what a mess this whole business is.

I notice that Family Productions, the company run by Artie Ripp that signed you to Paramount Records, still has Ripp's logo, Romulus and Remus being suckled by that she-wolf, on the label of every one of your albums. Do you think that someday you'll ever be free of Ripp?

{*Shaking his head in disgust*} I don't know. I get a dollar from each album I sell. Ripp gets twenty-eight cents out of that for "discovering me." Once in a while I get pissed off about it, but until the situation changes, it's not really healthy to dwell on it. I deserve that money a lot more than Ripp does, but I signed the papers, so what can I do? It was the only way I could get free of his Family Productions, although he wouldn't let me go entirely. And he seems willing to continue to take the money.

Do you own your publishing?

I have a deal with CBS' April-Blackwood Publishing; I do not own my publishing, but I do own my copyrights now—meaning that I own, like, fifty percent {*sighs*}. Live and learn, eh?

Incidently, I read recently in Random Notes about this guy [John Powers of Reno] who said that I stole his song, that he wrote "My Life." Now, my initial instinct is to just go beat the hell out of the guy, but my lawyers say I can't do that. I've had more leeches and sharks preying on me over the years, and it hasn't been dramatized in the press much because, until recently, Billy Joel wasn't very interesting to people.

But I never stole anybody's song. People send me tapes through Columbia all the time, and I *do not* and *will not* listen to them. As it is, I'm getting sued; I've got lawsuits up the gazool, which is something that disillusions me a lot about writing. I don't want to steal from anyone, because I know the feeling—my stuff's been getting ripped off all my life.

How have things with "My Life" ended up?

Lawyers {*whistles whimsically*} . . . It was a settlement. I said, "How much am I going to pay you if we go to court?" And the lawyers said X. "How much?! The guy is wrong. I never heard his song. He wants to take me to court, I'll go to court. I'll kill him. I want to kill him. I'll kill anybody who says I stole his material."

Maybe he did have a melody that was copyrighted. But don't tell people I'm a thief. When they question my intentions, that bugs me. Enough about that. I never stole nobody's song.

I should clear up the Dakota thing. You know it?

No.

During the Madison Square Garden gig [in July], it came out in the *New York Post* and the *New York Times* that I had applied for an apartment in the Dakota [an exclusive Manhattan apartment building] and had been turned down because I admitted to being a drug user and because I had groupies! Number one: I did not want an apartment at the Dakota; my wife did. Elizabeth no longer manages me. She is involved with me: fundraising, movie production, film editing. But she's got twenty other things going. I said, "Enough of the strain of being wife and manager; let's just be man and wife."

There was a rumor that all these things put a strain on your personal relationship.

Yeah, I've heard rumors, too: "Are you and Elizabeth gettin' divorced?" or, "You separated?" It's like, what? Give me a break. Everything's *fine.*

Now, tell me more about the Dakota incident.

It wasn't enough for Elizabeth to apply; I had to appear. This is typical. . . . It's typical of the Equal Rights Amendment not being passed. A wife is considered chattel to the husband. They were worried about me. I showed up in my suit, I went to the interview, I did the Dakota. The man, the heavy guy who was the deciding guy, had the nerve to have me sign albums for his daughter. There had been an interview in *Us* magazine right before we went to this Dakota interview. So because I had said, "Once I did this and once I did that. . . ." it was picked up in the *Times* as, "He has admitted that he is a drug user." I got a family, you know. I got a mother. I got a sister. I got a father. And now the press is calling me a known drug user because I happened to say that once I went onstage stoned.

It's like Gloria Vanderbilt getting turned down at the River House. "Ha, ha, isn't it great that this multimillionaire got turned down?" I'm *not* a multimillionaire. People think I have much more money than I have. I pay high salaries. I am in no way set for the rest of my life. I make a nice living, okay? But I go into the red on the road. The salaries and the costs and the production. It's a recession, man. I'm like everybody else. I don't make any money at a gig. I go on the road because I like to play. I'm not bitching about it, but I'm constantly behind.

Even with full arenas of people paying $12.50 a seat?

If you look at the marketplace, $12.50 is *not* in line with ticket prices, which tend to run as high as fifteen dollars or more. It's a pretty low price, and I do it that way because I want the kids to be able to afford to see the shows.

So where do you make your money?

Well, for the last three years the revenues have mainly come from record sales.

There are several charities you contribute to on a steady basis. Which are they?

The Rehabilitation Institute in Mineola, New York, which handles a lot of causes, and the Little Flower school in Suffolk, for orphans and kids who are emotionally troubled. There are several others.

Incidentally, have you heard the new rumor? It was on the radio today that I'm retiring. They even had a tribute to me! Unbelievable. Anyhow, go ahead.

You've talked before about sharing your wealth and growing up with socialism. Your parents were socialists?

No, their parents were. I don't think they were in the party, but that was their philosophy. My grandfather fought in the Abraham Lincoln Brigade in the Spanish Civil War. My mom and dad were registered as Democrats, but they were never less than liberal in their politics.

When was the first time you met your dad after he divorced your mother?

I was living in a rented house in the Malibu mountains in 1972. Soon as he got off the plane, I knew who he was. He's got the same bug eyes. It's very strange. I mean, we look a lot alike in a way, and he's lookin' at me like, "Is that what I used to look like?" and I'm lookin' at him like, "Is that what I'm gonna look like?" He's a great piano player in the classic sense. Trained by a Prussian.

Have you ever been in a working situation together?

He's been in recording sessions. He was there for "My Life," and he said, "You're making the piano sound out of tune." And I said, "That's the *idea,* Pop." You can't explain Elvis Presley to my father.

What do you get musically from your old man?

I get the feeling that he don't know rock & roll. "Just the Way You Are" was a big hit. He called me and said, "You've written better songs than that."

What do you get from your father as a dad?

As a dad, it's too late. I'm thirty-one. I met him again when I was twenty-three. What can I tell you? I was already me. I knew a lot of kids when I was growing up who were afraid of their

419

fathers; their fathers beat them up, were bastards, creeps. . . . I was brought up by women. I happen to have had a nice upbringing. The worst my mother did was grab hangers off the rack and whip me over the shoulders. Your mother, your father, it doesn't matter—that hanger hurts. But I never grew up in fear of men.

My mother . . . she's loving, she's people-oriented, a fucking blast. She is not awed by stardom. She's not a stage mother. Her whole thing was just *be happy.*

Are you happy? Is anything plaguing you?

A lot of people who are attracted to me haven't been exposed to black music; they think right off the bat that all black music is disco, so they think that my ballads are something to be played only on Adult Contemporary Dentist's-Office Easy-Listening stations. I'm just trying to be accepted for doing a diversity of things.

'Glass Houses' was recently the Number One album in the country; "It's Still Rock and Roll to Me" was the top single. You can't expect to please everybody.

Right. But when the Beatles did "Yesterday," did that mean that they became an Adult Contemporary group suitable only for dentists' offices? No, that didn't stop them from doing any of the trashy rock & roll stuff they did. Same thing with the Stones. They did "Angie" and "Ruby Tuesday," but it didn't mean they weren't the Stones anymore or had deserted their audience.

You know, there's been an evolution in my music. For instance, *52nd Street* was a much different album than *The Stranger.* It had a harder edge, although there was still orchestration on it. But I think people thought we were going into a jazz vein in, say, a Steely Dan sense. I was getting hung up on public reaction to my work.

But, hell, I've got a lot of good friends and success, so what am I complaining about?

Well, you've gotten praised and panned for your studio output. Are you going to attempt a live LP?

Actually, we've been taping everything from club dates at the Paradise in Boston to the Spectrum in Philly, dates in Milwaukee and St. Paul, and the Madison Square Garden shows, too. Thus far, we're doing it simply to document what we do on the road, but it could possibly wind up a live LP.

What you do is too eclectic to be called rock & roll— it is, well, energetic pop. That seems to rile rock critics, and they give you a hard time. Does that bother you?

What bothers me is the untruths, the lies, the slander and libel. Bad reviews don't bother me. But a lot of these critics are looking for *art.* I run into this all the time. Robert Hilburn [music critic for the *Los Angeles Times}* does this all the time, saying, in so many words, that "Billy Joel is not an *artist* but a *pop star."* The thing that got me about that was, people who are looking for art in rock & roll or pop are looking for something that either doesn't or shouldn't exist there.

An artist is a guy with a beret who sits in a park and paints pictures, and he starves in a garret somewhere.

Why must an artist do that to earn the title?

Because he's *only* after art.

And art is—

His special, elitist, intellectual view of how life should be represented on canvas or in music. Now, when you do that consciously, I believe you're really shutting yourself off from what's going on. I do what I do because of *radio.* Consider Devo: my, how *artistic,* what a great *concept;* deevolution and industrial rock for the Eighties. Intellectually, the whole *image* of it is very well put together, but it doesn't make it on the radio. If I'm driving in my car, I'd rather hear Donna Summer—*that's* where it's at.

But rock & roll, pop, funk, they can all be so many things—both reflective and reactive.

But let's remember the essence of popular music. A song comes on. What do you hear first? Words? *Nah,* you hear a beat, then a melody. Take "My Sharona." If you really liked the song, then you took the time to dig out the words, and they're pubescent, dumbo words, but they fit the song.

Journalists, for the most part, always tend to tune into a lyric. I've never wanted to print my lyrics on my LPs because lyrics are not poetry; they're part of songwriting; they're coloring, and they have to be heard at the same time as the music.

If they wrote out the lyrics to all these incredible Motown records, it would be rotten poetry. It's really stupid stuff. The O'Jays can go, "I love you/Yes I do." But if they sing it in a particular harmony and do a particular hand-jive, it's okay, see? But if Warren Zevon or Neil Young wrote it, it would be, "What a dumb lyric."

I think it's racism.

You're damn straight it's racism. Now, has a great lyric ever defined a great song? *Never.* I write what I write because I wanna hear something else on the radio. I can't stand the Grateful Dead jamming for an hour. I like what I hear on the jukebox. I like Frank Sinatra—whatever that makes me.

I wasn't crazy about the Four Seasons and the

Belmonts, or what they call "ethnic New York." Now me and Springsteen are defined this way, like we got a gang war going. Bruce is from New Jersey. I'm from Levittown. Like we have any kind of claim to New York?!

I have no pretensions to Bruce's throne. I have no arguments with Bruce, but we get pitted against each other, right? I know if I sat down with Bruce and talked to him head to head, it would be like, "Yeah, let's go have a hot dog."

So what is important to you?

I like to play music. We're not in the studio to make important records. We go into the studio, the song gets mixed and it's eventually heard through tiny car-radio speakers. We also like being together onstage. You should never lose sight of the fact that you're there to entertain. People don't pay money to see art. They don't pay money for you to sit there and be "Billy Joel."

Onstage, "It's Still Rock and Roll to Me" is probably your most intense, even angry, song. Explain what it is you're getting at.

New Wave songs, it seems, can only be about two and a half minutes long. That's about it. Only a certain number of instruments can be played on the record—usually a very few. Only a certain amount of production is allowed or can be heard. The sound has to be limited to what you can hear in a garage. A return to that sound is all that's going on now, so don't give me any of this New Wave—using a Farfisa organ because it's so hip. It's just a reaction to a rediscovered past, and a rejection of Emerson, Lake and Palmer using multideck synthesizers.

You feel pretty strongly about all this, don't you?

I grew up on jukebox music, and everybody in the band has played this music all their lives, and they range in age from twenty-eight to thirty-one. We played the Top Forty singles in bars. Then, when *Sgt. Pepper's Lonely Hearts Club Band* came out, everybody started smoking pot and tripping and listening to the 13th Floor Elevator. Suddenly, everything changed—all the formats for playing and recording and listening to music. You could hear twenty-five minutes of music on the air with no commercial break.

Which also raises the point that no black artist, not the Spinners or the O'Jays, has been played consistently on FM radio in proportion to the way Hendrix was in his heyday. Elitism is rampant. FM radio cut out black music at the peak of the Al Green era.

New Wave has the same problem, but the Sex Pistols' "God Save the Queen" bored the hell out of me. If I go to a disco and hear one *boom-sup-*

boom tempo all night, I get a headache and split. If I go to a New Wave club and all I hear is, "Fuck you!" and the guy spits on me all night, I'm sorry, I don't like it. If I go to a folk club and all I hear is some girl strumming a guitar, singing, "Give me some wine and cheese, *please,*" I don't want it. I would rather go and hear a good Top Forty bar band—which is what *we* still are, basically.

Now, if I'm considered part of that overhyped, overproduced, overindulgent supergroup style, then I'm bummed. But I do admit that some of my earlier albums had that quality. What I'm saying in "It's Still Rock and Roll" is that I happen to like Donna Summer's hits. I'd never listen to them from the perspective of a Van Halen or Rush freak, who'd blow Donna's brains out with a shotgun simply for being herself musically. That's *sick.*

As for New Wave, I think it's good and necessary. Kick out the Emerson, Lake and Palmer shit and all that overindulgence. Give the whole damned industry an enema, jam that plastic tube right up its rear end.

In a song like "The Stranger," you hint that there are sides to you, deep secrets, little things that even those closest to you aren't aware of.

Big things, man. We all have a face, we all have another side. I'm still learning. It never stops. We're all under this pressure.

When were you most frightened of yourself?

Right now.

What about back in your early twenties, when you voluntarily checked yourself into the psychiatric ward of a Long Island hospital because you broke up with your girlfriend and felt lost, alone?

No. Now.

Why now?

Because these things I don't know about my image scare the hell out of me. But I just don't have the time to sit around and think about *me* anymore.

I'll go to bed, and my wife and I will try to say to each other, "What are ya thinkin' about?" and I think {sings}, "I am the knight in shining armor and I want to go slay dragons." You get to a point in your life when there aren't any obvious dragons.

When you were in the hospital, were you scared about different things?

I was into a real self-pity trip. "Oh, gee, I have to face all this shit. Isn't it easier to just cut your throat or slit your wrist?" I think everybody goes through that at one time or another. Facing adulthood. So I checked into a place where they wouldn't let me kill myself. It was the best thing

421

I ever did. There were all these really sick people, really screwed up. Like in *One Flew Over the Cuckoo's Nest.* I said, "Hey, I'm really okay, *these* people are really sick."

At the end of every concert you say, "Don't take any shit from anybody!" When did you start doing that?

I don't know, around the same time I started wearing a jacket and tie onstage, about 1977. If you're really good at what you do, you really don't have to take any shit from anybody. But you have to be in a privileged position. It also means not giving any shit *to* anybody. I really believe it. I love swimming upstream.

Well, if you're swimming upstream, there's only one way to do that, and that's by not taking . . .

. . . any shit . . .

. . . *from* . . .

. . . anybody.

CONTRIBUTORS BIOGRAPHIES

JOHN CARPENTER (1941–1976) was ROLLING STONE's first Los Angeles correspondent. He went on to become editor of the Los Angeles *Free Press* and Los Angeles radio station KPFK's first rock jock.

JONATHAN COTT is the author of *He Dreams What Is Going On in His Head—Ten Years of Writing* (Straight Arrow), *City of Earthly Love* (Stonehill), *Stockhausen: Conversations with the Composer* (Simon & Schuster) and *Beyond the Looking Glass* (Stonehill/Bowker). His most recent book is *Wonders* (Rolling Stone Press/Summit). He has been an editor and contributor to ROLLING STONE since 1967 and has contributed to the New York *Times, American Review, Ramparts* and *American Poetry Review.*

CAMERON CROWE, an associate editor of ROLLING STONE for many years, is the author of *Stairway to Heaven: A Year in High School* (Simon & Schuster).

DAVID DALTON was an associate editor at ROLLING STONE from 1968 to 1971. He is the author of *James Dean: The Mutant King* (Straight Arrow/Simon & Schuster); and *Janis* (Touchstone/Simon & Schuster). His forthcoming book, *The Rolling Stones Record Book,* will be published by Stonehill Press.

BEN FONG-TORRES is a former senior editor of ROLLING STONE, joining the magazine in 1969. He has edited several anthologies, including *What's That Sound? Readings in Contemporary Music* (Rolling Stone Press/Anchor).

PAUL GAMBACCINI has been a regular contributor to ROLLING STONE since the early Seventies. He currently lives in London and broadcasts regularly on the BBC, and is the co-author of *The Guinness Book of British Hit Singles* (Guinness) and the forthcoming *Guinness Book of the American Top 40* (Guinness).

RALPH J. GLEASON (1917–1975) was a co-founder of and steady contributor to ROLLING STONE. He was a columnist for the San Francisco *Chronicle* for twenty-five years, and wrote *The Jefferson Airplane and the San Francisco Sound* (Ballantine) and *Celebrating the Duke* (Atlantic Monthly Press) among other books. He also produced a series of two dozen television shows entitled *"Jazz Casual,"* including one on B. B. King.

ROBERT GREENFIELD, a former associate editor in the London bureau of ROLLING STONE, is the editor of two books of nonfiction, *S.T.P.: A Journey Through America with the Rolling Stones* (Saturday Review Press/Dutton) and *The Spiritual Supermarket* (Saturday Review Press/Dutton), and a novel, *Haymon's Crowd* (Summit).

PETER HERBST was an editor of the Boston *Phoenix* and music editor of ROLLING STONE from 1977 to 1980. He is currently an editor of the New York *Daily News.*

ROBERT HILBURN is the pop music critic for the Los Angeles *Times.*

JERRY HOPKINS has been a contributing editor to ROLLING STONE since issue number five. He is the author of two books, *Elvis* (Simon & Schuster) and *Elvis: The Final Years* (St. Martin's Press), and is co-author of the best-selling biography of Jim Morrison, *No One Here Gets Out Alive* (Warner). He is currently writing a book on the history of the hula.

424

JON LANDAU is the author of *It's Too Late to Stop Now* (Straight Arrow). He has written extensively about rock in the Boston *Phoenix, Crawdaddy* and ROLLING STONE, where he was an associate editor for many years. Currently he is managing Bruce Springsteen and he produced "The Pretender" for Jackson Browne.

GREIL MARCUS is the author of *Mystery Train: Images of America in Rock 'n' Roll Music* (Dutton) and editor of *Stranded* (Knopf). His articles have appeared in the *Village Voice, The New Yorker,* the San Francisco *Express-Times* and many other publications, He is an associate editor of ROLLING STONE and is currently working on a new book.

JOHN MORTHLAND was an associate editor of ROLLING STONE, and contributed to *Creem, Country Music* and Boston's *Real Paper.* He is currently a free-lance writer based in New York.

PATRICK WILLIAM SALVO is a West Coast free-lance writer.

HAPPY TRAUM is a singer/instrumentalist/songwriter specializing in folk, blues and country music. He is also the author of over a dozen best-selling guitar instruction books and is a frequent contributor to *Sing Out!, Frets, Guitar Player,* ROLLING STONE and other publications. His latest album is *Bright Morning Stars* for Greenhays/Flying Fish Records.

JANN WENNER is the editor and publisher of ROLLING STONE, which he founded in 1967. Two of his ROLLING STONE interviews have been published in book form: *Garcia: A Signpost to New Space* (Straight Arrow) and *Lennon Remembers* (Straight Arrow/Popular Library.)

STUART WERBIN has been a frequent contributor to the Boston *Phoenix, New Times* and ROLLING STONE.

TIMOTHY WHITE, a former senior editor at ROLLING STONE, is now a contributing editor. He was formerly the managing editor of *Crawdaddy* and a reporter for the New York bureau office of the Associated Press.

PHOTO CREDITS

SONG LYRIC CREDITS